# Greek Waters Pilot

# Contents

# Greek Waters Pilot

## *A yachtsman's guide to the coasts and islands of Greece*

## ROD HEIKELL

**Imray Laurie Norie & Wilson Ltd**

ISTANBUL

URKEY

29°

# Rod Heikell

Rod Heikell has spent more than twenty years cruising the coasts and islands of the Mediterranean.

In the 1970s he took time off from academic life and sailed *Roulette*, a 1950s JOG plywood hard chine sloop all of 20ft LOA and 6ft beam, from England to Greece. He fell in love with the life and stayed in the Mediterranean. For a number of years he worked in the yacht charter business, delivered yachts and was a freelance photographer.

In 1979 he bought *Fiddlers Green*, a 28ft Cobra 850, and sailed it down to the Mediterranean in the winter months. Three years later he acquired *Tetra (Tetranora)*, a 31ft Cheverton New Campaigner built in 1962. In *Tetra* he travelled extensively around the Mediterranean researching his pilots and recently sailed her to Southeast Asia and back. In 1987 he sailed down the Danube and on to the Aegean in a 19ft Mirror Offshore, *Rozinante*. His latest yacht, *seven tenths*, a Cheoy Lee Pedrick 36, is his fifth and is now in the Mediterranean from the Caribbean.

Rod Heikell is the acknowledged expert on sailing in the Mediterranean. His pilots have become the model for others and are often referred to as 'the bible'! Since the publication of his first book, *Greek Waters Pilot*, in 1982 and now in its eighth edition, he has written over a dozen others on related matters and also edits the Imray-Tetra chart series.

He is currently working on several new books including one on cruising strategies and at the same time updating his back list of pilots. He prefers gunk-holing to long passages, frequently sailing alone with only rock and roll, a lot of books and the BBC World Service for company.

**Imray Mediterranean Almanac** (editor)
**Mediterranean Cruising Handbook**
**Mediterranean France & Corsica Pilot**
**Mediterranean Sailing**
**Italian Waters Pilot**
**Greek Waters Pilot**
**Ionian**
**Saronic**
**Turkish Waters & Cyprus Pilot**
**The Turquoise Coast of Turkey**
**The Danube – A river guide**
**Yacht Charter Handbook**
**Indian Ocean Cruising Guide**

## Author's note

Photocopies and downloaded information from my books circulate around the Mediterranean. For those of you sitting and reading a photocopy or information downloaded off internet sites, I suggest you reflect on the fact that you forfeit your own moral basis for objecting to any theft from yourself or your boat. You have after all stolen something from me and my publishers, both in a moral and legal sense, so when you have something stolen, think about how it feels.

Published by
Imray Laurie Norie & Wilson Ltd
Wych House The Broadway St Ives Cambridgeshire PE27 5BT
England
☎ +44(0)1480 462114 *Fax* +44(0)1480 496109
*E-mail* ilnw@imray.com
2001

1st edition 1982, Revised reprint 1983
2nd edition 1985
3rd edition 1987
4th edition 1990
5th edition 1992
6th edition 1994
7th edition 1998
8th edition 2001

A catalogue record for this book is available from the British Library.

ISBN 0 85288 534 2

## CAUTION

Every effort has been made to ensure the accuracy of this book. It contains selected information and thus is not definitive and does not include all known information on the subject in hand; this is particularly relevant to the plans, which should not be used for navigation. The author believes that his selection is a useful aid to prudent navigation, but the safety of a vessel depends ultimately on the judgement of the navigator, who should assess all information, published or unpublished.

## PLANS

The plans in this guide are not to be used for navigation. They are designed to support the text and should at all times be used with navigational charts.

## CORRECTIONAL SUPPLEMENTS

This pilot book will be amended at intervals by the issue of correctional supplements. These are published on the internet at our web site www.imray.com and may be downloaded free of charge. Printed copies are also available on request from the publishers at the above address.

This work has been corrected to August 2001.

Printed in Great Britain at
Bath Press Colour Books, Blantyre, Scotland

# Preface

Membership of the EU has changed Greece in all sorts of ways. New roads criss-cross the coast and islands. A huge suspension bridge is under construction across the Strait of Rion and Andirrion in the Gulf of Patras to join the Peloponnese and the western edge of mainland Greece. The new airport outside Athens is open and the city is no longer blighted by aircraft using Ellinikon. You can get a good cappuccino in most places and the brand names of well-known fashion labels dot the boutiques.

For those on the water things are also changing. Around the coast new marinas are under construction and the infrastructure has improved. You can get most yacht spares and a new engine will likely cost you the same or less than in other EU countries. Yacht service companies are now more common and the standards of workmanship and reliability are better.

Despite these massive changes, the land and the people remain the same. The coast and islands still bathe in that light, both soft and harsh, that no photo and no landscape painter can quite capture. The sea still has that steep decline from darkest cobalt to sandy turquoise as you nose into an anchorage. The spirit of the place washes over you and that relentless adulation of the great god economy, work, long hours and secure loans that northern Europe has adopted, that mindless devotion to mortgages and pension funds, somehow appears less important and pressing than it once did.

For this edition I pottered around the Ionian for a bit, savouring the slow gentle sailing and seeing old friends, before setting off around the Peloponnese to the Saronic. Through the late summer and autumn I picked my way across the Cyclades to the Dodecanese and by early winter was on my way back through the southern Cyclades to the Corinth Canal. After the Gulf of Corinth and Gulf of Patras I steered *seven tenths* across the Ionian in November, alone on the sea after the busy summer months. If one thing is changing it is the weather. From what I see and from conversations with others, it seems that either global warming or some micro-climatic cycle is affecting the weather. In general the normal patterns seem to be shifting by a month or two to later in the year. The settled summer weather starts later in the year, including the *meltemi* in the Aegean, and stays on into the autumn. Autumn has nudged into early winter. On *seven tenths* in October the Aegean had a few gales, but overall the weather was warm and settled. In November I sailed back through the Ionian in shorts and a T-shirt.

For this edition much of the text has been re-worked and the big difference is that the book is now in colour. All plans have been re-drawn to a new specification and I have added many new ones. While working on it through the long grey winter in London I longed to be out on *seven tenths* and away from the incessant telephone calls and hurried footsteps of my fellow Londoners. The gods listened and I write this on board in the Ionian.

## Acknowledgements

My thanks to Nigel Patten who provided many photos and much valuable information. Nigel is a shining example of getting lots of miles per foot or pound of boat. In *Mercury*, a Mirage 28, he sailed around Greece and Turkey clocking up a lot of miles. He spends the winters teaching drama and the summers sailing, now in his latest boat *Magellan*. Lucy Michell assiduously recorded waypoints, climbed hills for photos and helped proof the book, as well as helping to recover the genoa from the water while the seas from a Force 7 tried to wash us overboard. Yes, I'll remember to insist on harnesses next time.

My thanks also to Nikitas Kiriakoulis at Kalamata Marina, Dimitris Koutsodontos at Gouvia Marina, to Robin & Di Brown on *Solveig of Lorn*, to Joe and Robin in Levkas, Nicki and Via and the boys at CYS including 'St Pip of the Engine', Laurie Campbell, the boys at Nielson in Porto Kheli, to Conrad Jenkin and the RCC, to the CA for information, particularly Tom Geddes, Andrew Smyth and the other members out there on the water, to Julian Blatchley on *Dark Star*, to Richard in Póros, to Stephen Davies and Elaine Morgan on *Fiddlers Green II* for updates on Crete, to Duncan Gilchrist, C. Hinge, Mary Neate, Adonis in Levkas, Bill Keating, Paul Braddock, S. Lewis, Steve Goulden on *Small Consolation* and Constantinos Livadiotis at Porto Carras. As always, a lot of people helped with information for this edition and it is impossible to mention you all.

My thanks to Julia Knight, Chris Holley, Debbie Stapleford and Jill Eaton at Imrays who produced the book you hold in your hands. Willie Wilson was, as ever, at the helm to steer it through and to him my thanks for all the care and industry that has gone into producing this book. As ever the mistakes are mine and despite the care taken to eliminate them, the little typos still creep in.

Rod Heikell
Levkas 2001

# KEY TO SYMBOLS USED ON PLANS

**3 2** depths in METRES

**<1** shallow water with a depth of 1m or less

**+ +** rocks with less than 2 metres' depth over them

**(*)** rock just below or on the surface

**(2)** a shoal or reef with the least depth shown

wreck partially above water

**© ©** eddies

wreck

**(4)Wk** dangerous wreck with depth over it

rock ballasting on a mole or breakwater

above-water rocks

cliffs

anchorage

prohibited anchorage

church

mosque

windmill

chimney

castle

airport

ruins

houses

port police

fish farm

customs

travel-hoist

yacht club

water

fuel

post office

**O.T.E** telecommunications

**i** tourist information

electricity

pine

trees other than pine

port of entry

**V** visitors' berths

waypoint

yacht berth

local boats (usually shallow or reserved)

beacon

port hand buoy

starboard hand buoy

mooring buoy

### Characteristics

light

lighthouse

E  fixed

Fl.  flash

Fl(2)  group flash

Oc.  occulting

R  red

G  green

W  white

m  miles

s  sand

m  mud

w  weed

r  rock

---

# KEY TO QUICK REFERENCE GUIDES

**Shelter**
A Excellent
B Good with prevailing winds
C Reasonable shelter but uncomfortable and sometimes dangerous
O In calm weather only

**Mooring**
A Stern-to or bows-to
B Alongside
C Anchored off

**Fuel**
A On the quay
B In the town
O None or limited

**Water**
A On the quay
B In the town
O None or limited

**Provisioning**
A Excellent
B Most supplies can be obtained
C Meagre supplies
O None

**Eating out**
A Excellent
B Average
C Poor
O None
(*Note* These ratings are nothing to do with the quality of food served in restaurants, but relate only to the numbers of restaurants.)

**Plan**
• Harbour plan illustrates text

**Charges**
Charges are for the daily high season rate for a 12-metre yacht, at the exchange rates current when this volume went to press. Prices are in GBP sterling. For smaller or larger yachts make an approximate guesstimate.
1. No charge
2. Low cost (under £15)
3. Medium cost (£16–£25)
4. High cost (£26–£35)
5. Very high cost (over £36)

# Introduction

## Yacht and equipment

### Engines

A reliable engine is necessary for motoring through the inevitable calms a yacht will encounter. On other occasions a powerful engine will be required to motor against the strong winds and short steep seas of the Mediterranean to get into harbour. A petrol engine, whether inboard or outboard, can be dangerous in the Mediterranean where the high temperatures cause petrol to vaporize easily and the risk of an explosion and fire is a constant risk. This risk applies equally to outboards, whether for the tender or as back-up on small motorboats, and it pays to think carefully about ventilation and petrol stowage. I have witnessed several explosions fuelled by petrol and the results have not been pretty.

If you are installing a new engine try to purchase one for which it will be easy to find spares in the Mediterranean. A less well known make may be cheaper for the initial purchase, but can lead to trouble if you have to continually get spares sent out to wherever you are in the Mediterranean and if the local mechanics have little or no knowledge of your engine. It is all very well getting a marinised diesel block that is common, but it is usually the marinised add-ons that cause the trouble and they may be made only in the country of origin. Getting hold of a service and spares manual is also worth the effort. Although not exhaustive, spares for the following list of common marques can usually be found without too much bother: Volvo Penta, marinised Fords, Perkins, Yanmar, Mercedes, Caterpillar, MAN, and marinised GM diesels.

### Electricity

In all marinas and some other harbours it is possible to plug into mains electricity on the pontoon or quay. Most marinas include electricity in the berthing charge so it is worthwhile being equipped to take advantage of it. Unfortunately this will mean a variety of connectors to plug into whatever socket a marina is using and it is really a matter of adapting what you have in the best way possible. Most connections are 220V 50Hz, but some marinas also have 380V. In some of the municipal harbours where electricity and water 'boxes' have been installed the connections can be potentially dangerous and the supply is prone to surges. Turn off any sensitive equipment on board or it may be damaged by the irregular nature of the supply.

When you are away from all singing and dancing marinas then you will have to rely on generating the stuff yourself. Around the gulfs and in any of the anchorages and in some harbours you must be pretty well self sufficient for electricity on board and that means totting up your consumption and fitting batteries with sufficient capacity and the means to charge them. Most yachts opt for solar panels or wind generators to top up the charging from the engine alternator. In addition it is worthwhile fitting a 'smart' regulator to the alternator in place of the standard regulators supplied by the manufacturer. It may also be possible to fit two alternators to an engine depending on the relative size of the engine to the boat.

If at all possible don't rely on running a generator to top up batteries and run equipment. There is nothing more irritating than to be near a boat with its generator running in what would be an otherwise tranquil anchorage. If you really need to pollute the air with engine and exhaust noise and pollute the water with exhaust emissions please go to a noisy harbour, preferably one that is already suffering from a diesel slick, and stay there to run your generator.

### Ventilation

Most yachts from northern waters have inadequate ventilation for the hot Mediterranean. Extra skylights and vents and additional insulation can help solve the problem. An air scoop to funnel air down the front hatch is an excellent investment and will repay its modest cost tenfold. Make your own or buy one of the commercially produced scoops on the market.

### Refrigerator

A refrigerator is considered by many to be a necessity in the Mediterranean. If it is going to draw power from your batteries it may be necessary to install an additional battery and revise your charging methods – a refrigerator is estimated to use around 50–60% of the total power consumption on yachts. Smaller yachts without auxiliary generators usually fit a solar panel or wind generator to supply the much needed amps to avoid that dull 'thunk' in the morning when you go to start the engine on flat batteries.

The heat absorption and thermoelectric types do not work well in the high ambient temperatures in the Mediterranean. The type having a compressor working off the batteries (high current drain) or off the engine (expensive to purchase and install) with a holding plate work the best. As a general rule most refrigerators do not have adequate insulation – 10 cm/4 inches should be the minimum. Get the top opening type so the cold air does not fall out every time the refrigerator is opened (a good illustration of the principle underlying a katabatic wind, as it happens).

### Ice

Large blocks of ice or ice cubes can be bought in many places. Many fishing boats use ice either to supplement their own refrigeration systems or as the sole means of keeping the catch cold on smaller boats. In most harbours there is an ice factory which supplies the fishing boats and it is usually a simple matter to locate the 'ice-man' or the local supplier. Some of the ice contains chemicals to keep it solid longer and is unsuitable for consumption in drinks. In some of the larger harbours used regularly by yachts, ice cubes suitable for those all-important cold drinks, can be found.

Using ice, whether in blocks or in cubes, is the cheapest way of keeping food cool and at the height of summer helps out refrigeration systems which are usually struggling to keep things cold. As a friend put it: 'ice is nice and freon is for peons'.

### Shower

A shower is useful inside a yacht, but in the Mediterranean it is perhaps more useful if it can be used outside on deck or in the cockpit to wash off after swimming in the sea. Modern yachts with a sugar scoop transom can install a shower unit there so swimmers can wash the salt off immediately after emerging from the sea. Larger water tanks or even a separate water tank may be required.

A cheap alternative is a pressurised garden spray unit. Replace the spray head with a shower rose, pump it up, and you have a portable and economical shower unit. The sun-shower, basically a black plastic bag with a shower rose attached that you haul up on a halyard, works well – but beware of the water getting too hot.

At the height of summer it can get very hot and you don't always want to go for a swim or deplete the water tanks having a full blown shower. A useful way of cooling off is to buy a spray bottle, the sort used for indoor plants will do, and spray a fine mist of water over the face, neck, arms and legs, indeed any exposed bit of the anatomy. This will cool you off surprisingly well with a minimum of water consumption. Sounds silly I know, but try it and you will be pleasantly cooled.

### Holding tanks

Holding tanks are not yet required by law for private yachts visiting Greek waters. They are required on charter boats. Despite the fact they are not required, you can be fined a substantial amount for pumping out a toilet in harbour or in an enclosed bay. Prosecutions have gone ahead with fines up to £400 levied for pumping out a toilet or holding tank in harbour. It is likely that a requirement for holding tanks on private (non-charter) yachts will be made law at some time in the future.

Any holding tank installation must be able to pump out at sea (the requirement is theoretically 3 miles offshore) as few marinas and no harbours have pump-out facilities ashore. In practice the requirement is something of a nonsense when in some places sewage is emptying into the harbour around your boat. Despite the anomalies every yacht should endeavour to do its bit to keep harbours and anchorages free of faeces and either use toilets ashore or utilise the holding tank on board. If you are not going 3 miles offshore then I would suggest that 2 miles offshore is better than in the anchorage.

The installation must be installed with odour-free hose, a good sized vent/breather and preferably a vent filter of which there are several available on the market. The combination of these three ingredients will keep holding tank smells at bay assuming the rest of the installation is professionally fitted and a stainless steel or preferably a polypropylene tank is used. The holding tank on my boat is installed in the heads and the toilet pumps through it all the time. To use the holding tank the toilet outlet seacock is closed. To empty the holding tank the outlet is opened and gravity and a bit of pumping do the rest.

### Anchors

Preference for different anchors varies with the individual, but the following information may be useful for coping with the different types of bottom found near Greek coasts. Often the bottom will be hard sand covered with thick weed and some anchors have difficulty penetrating the weed and digging in. It is common practice to go astern once the anchor is down to ensure it bites. Otherwise the anchor could be caught on weed or just be sitting on the bottom until a puff of wind blows you astern and the anchor drags. It is also worthwhile snorkelling over the anchor to check it is holding and if possible dive down to bury it properly if it is not dug in. Commonly the CQR and Bruce will lie on their side without turning over to dig in.

*Bruce* A good main anchor. It holds well, even on a short scope, and is good over a range of different holding ground. Some people have reported difficulties getting the Bruce to dig through thick weed. It will sometimes collect a clump of weed and must be raised to clear it.

*CQR* A good main anchor. Holds well in mud and sand though it will sometimes pull through soft mud. In weed it will often pick up a clump on the point and must be raised to clear it.

*Delta* A new anchor similar to the CQR, but with no moving parts. Its one-piece construction makes it strong and it has been designed to turn itself over to a holding position however it lands.

*Bugeleisen* A German anchor with a single pointed plough and a heavy semi-circle ring on the top which is designed to roll it over so the point digs in. Reported to be good at penetrating hard sand or thick weed bottoms.

*Danforth* Good for getting through weed, but like the CQR picks up weed easily. My favourite for a kedge.

*Fortress* A new Danforth lookalike, but

Going stern-to can be a bit of a tricky business until you get used to it. Just have everything ready and take it easy

constructed of aluminium and therefore very light. This anchor defies the long-held notion that an anchor must be heavy to hold and in my experience works well with the advantage that it is easy to lay from a dinghy.

*Fisherman* Excellent for getting through weed but doesn't have the holding power of the plough types. However it will hold on rocky bottoms, in thick weed, and on very soft bottoms where other anchors don't get through. A good alternative to the Danforth for a kedge.

*Grapnel types* The folding grapnel anchors are useless except on a rocky bottom. A few yachtsmen swear by the large grapnels used by the Greeks, but I have never found them to be very good.

### Berthing Mediterranean-style

For the most part berthing is stern or bows-to in the Mediterranean. In some harbours yachts berth alongside, mostly commercial or fishing harbours little frequented by yachts, where an anchor line would obstruct passage in the harbour, or where a current makes going stern or bows-to difficult. There are advantages to going stern or bows-to:

1. A yacht can leave comparatively easily from a berth. When alongside there may be three or four yachts outside making it a difficult process to leave.
2. Privacy. When alongside there will always be people walking over the decks if you are on the inside of any boats. When bows-to there is increased privacy from the gaze of onlookers on the quay.
3. Safety. If there is a surge in a harbour a yacht will not be squashed and scratched on the quay and yachts on the inside will not have unfair loads put on their hulls and mooring lines from boats on the outside. When stern or bows-to it is possible to ease off on the lines ashore and pull yourself off the quay a short distance if there is a surge in a harbour.

4. Vermin. Going stern or bows-to makes it less likely that cockroaches and rats, and other animals, can get on board.

It takes some skill to go stern-to, especially if there is a strong crosswind and a narrow gap to fit into between other yachts. Always have plenty of fenders out and when close to the quay warp the yacht into place rather than using the engine. For yachts up to 10–13m long it is easier to go bows-to as a yacht can more easily be manoeuvred into a berth when going forward. If ballasting extends a short distance underwater (as it often does) then damage to the rudder is avoided by going bows-to. Moreover there is a gain in privacy as people on the quay cannot see into the cockpit or into the cabin.

There are few laid moorings in Greece and where there are, these will nearly always be a line tailed from the mooring to the quay or a small buoy. However fishermen often have laid moorings with a line tailed to the quay and this will almost always be a floating line which can easily get caught around the rudder and propeller of a yacht berthing amongst or near to fishing boat berths.

### Berthing lines

It is useful to have two stout lines made up for the stern lines when mooring stern or bows-to. A short loop of chain on the end of the line which can be dropped over a bollard (or unfastened with a carbine clip or shackle to go through a mooring loop) will reduce chafe on the line. Care is needed not to brain bystanders or anyone helping you to berth when throwing the lines ashore. The line should be fairly heavy as the surges which can develop in some harbours with gale force winds can be greater than those encountered in many other cruising grounds.

### Gas

In most of the larger towns *Camping Gaz* can be obtained, but it may be difficult to find in the islands where stocks of full canisters can run down and may

Berthing bows-to may be necessary in some places where ballasting extends underwater from the quay

not be replenished for weeks. If a yacht is fitted with Calor Gas type bottles an adaptor can be bought in Greece to take Greek gas bottles. As elsewhere the common practice is to change the old empty bottle for a full new one.

If staying for an extended period and if a lot of gas is used for a refrigerator, hot water, heating and cooking, then it is worth changing over to Greek gas which is comparatively cheap. There are gas filling stations at Gouvía, Kalamata, Piraeus, Kalimnos, Rhodes and Iraklion.

### Paraffin

It is getting more and more difficult to find paraffin as the ubiquitous bottled gas takes over. It is normally sold by one dealer in a village or town and his shop can be anything from a general grocery shop to a bulk wine dealer. Ask for *petroleon katharon*. Methylated spirit is easily obtained in grocery shops.

### Yacht spares

Much yacht equipment is now available in Greece or can be ordered now that Greece is part of the EU. On the whole the cost of equipment, including major items like marine engines, is cheaper than many other EU countries. At worst it will be only marginally more expensive and it is hardly worth going to the trouble of bringing most items in.

Any equipment shipped or mailed to Greece is subject to Greek VAT.

Locally produced goods can often be used instead of imported goods – especially paint, adhesives, sealants, bronze and stainless steel gear like cleats and fairleads, batteries and cordage.

Small engineering works are good at making boat bits and pieces for more ancient bits of equipment for which spares are not readily available.

### Antifouling

A yacht bottom fouls more quickly in the warm waters of the Mediterranean than it would in more northerly waters. Consequently a more potent antifouling must be used. Eroding antifoulings such as International *Micron*, Blake's *SeaTech*, and Hempel's *Mille* work well as long as your boat is moving and not sitting still at anchor or berthed for long periods, when the build-up of weed and coral worm overcomes the antifouling's ability to erode itself and rubbing down just takes the antifouling off. Hard scrubbable antifoulings like Blake's tin-free *Tiger*, International *Cruiser*, and Veneziani *Rafaello 3* work well and although they tend to foul more quickly than eroding antifoulings, they can be satisfactorily rubbed down without removing all the antifouling. Brands like *Yotun* and an Israeli paint called *Tammarin* that a friend of mine swears by can also be found.

Local antifouling of the soft type (*TransOcean* is popular and works well) is widely available, cheap, and effective. You cannot of course rub it down through the season, but generally for an eight-month sailing season and four months on the hard I find it copes well, with fouling just beginning in the eighth month. If you haul every winter then in terms of cost effectiveness the local soft antifouling is difficult to beat – working out at around one third the cost or less of more sophisticated antifoulings.

### Gang planks (passerelles)

They can be an elaborate affair or simply a plank. Make sure the halyard supporting the end is beefy enough and comes off a substantial mast – I've seen a few mizzens with an unnatural curve to them. Some yachts which always berth bows-to have had stainless steel boarding ladders made up that hang over the pulpit and make getting on and off that much easier.

### Awnings

A good sun awning is a necessary piece of boat equipment in the Mediterranean. Much of your time will be spent in the cockpit and the awning should be designed to be a comfortable height above the cockpit seats and ideally should have side curtains for when the sun is low in the evening. Make the awning from dark coloured canvas, as light coloured materials cause an uncomfortable glare and nylon or Terylene materials flap and crack in the slightest breeze.

A permanent awning rigged over the cockpit along the lines of the Bimini common in the Caribbean keeps you cool not only in harbour, but when sailing or motoring as well. Some skippers worry about the bimini being up in strong winds, but most people, myself included, have only found it necessary to fold them away when the wind gets above 35 knots or so. In fact on *Tetra* the bimini stayed up for the entirety of the trip to SE Asia and back and on *seven tenths* the only time the bimini was removed was when Hurricane George threatened in Miami. Otherwise it stayed up for some 8000 miles around the Caribbean and back to the Mediterranean.

# Navigation

A yacht will require no more navigation equipment than would be used around other areas and in all probability will use less in practice.

A depth-sounder is useful, although after a while when you have become adept at judging depths in the clear water (it is not uncommon to see the bottom at 7–10m) it will be redundant except in murky water or at night. However, remember it takes a little time to become adept at judging the depth visually. As a general rule deep blue is 15m plus, turquoise is 10m, green is 5m, and brown is rock just below the water. Colours vary with the type of bottom and in places fine silt in the water reduces visibility.

### Electronic navigation aids

The new breed of electronic navigation equipment has revolutionized position finding, but some care is needed if you are using it in Greece.

***GPS (Global Positioning System)*** The original acronym NAVSTAR more properly describes how it works. NAVSTAR is **Nav**igation **S**ystem by **T**ime **a**nd **R**anging. GPS simply means **G**lobal **P**ositioning **S**ystem, which tells us little. In fact the way GPS works is simple and familiar to anyone who has done some coastal navigation. If we know the position and distance of an object then our own position can be plotted on a line from that known object. Plot three known objects and distances and we have a relatively accurate position fix. In practice three satellites' distances and positions are plotted because of the inaccuracy of receiver clocks and degrading effects from the signals passing through the ionosphere. The resulting cocked hat gives a consistent accuracy of ±20 metres for 95% of the time.

Modern GPS receivers are all multi-channel and can receive from three to twelve signals at any one time and decode them to determine a position. The speed at which a GPS receiver can do a cold start and produce a position is now around 30 seconds. The ease with which we retrieve data has been simplified by software that enables us to scroll through pages and pick out how we want to view the data. From the stream of position data we get speed over the ground, course heading in true and magnetic, distance off course from a waypoint, and a graphic display of our course.

GPS is the cheapest form of position finding around, with a handheld set costing less than a good hand-bearing compass. Now that US has turned off selective availability most modern multi-channel receivers are accurate to around 20 metres in practice, an accuracy greater than the yachtsman needs to establish a position.

The very accuracy of GPS can be misleading and seeing a position to two or three decimal points can induce a false sense of confidence in the user. The problem is simply that we do not have charts accurate enough to make full use of such precise positions. Read over the caution carefully at the end of this section.

Although satellites are turned off for maintenance every now and again and in places coverage by the satellites is not enough to give an accurate position, in my experience these gaps in coverage have never exceeded an hour. Nonetheless it is worthwhile thinking carefully before linking the GPS to the autopilot so that the autopilot is steering a true course relative to currents, tide, etc.; or you may end up like the yacht in the Caribbean which hit a reef because the inattentive owner missed the error warning on his GPS. Without coverage the GPS kept a course using the last data that had arrived from the satellite and without any new data to correct for currents and other errors steered straight towards a reef.

**DGPS** There are currently no DGPS stations in Greece and in any case now that selective availability has been turned off there is little point in using DGPS add-ons.

**SDGPS** (Satellite Differential GPS) Works by a network of ground reference stations receiving GPS signals and then correcting them for known errors: GPS satellite orbit, clock errors, and transmission errors caused by the atmosphere and ionosphere. A GPS correction signal is then transmitted to geostationary satellites on the same frequency as GPS signals. An accuracy of 2–3 metres is claimed.

In the USA the WAAS (**W**ide **A**rea **A**ugmentation **S**ystem) has been approved for some uses. In Europe the EGNOSS satellite system will be used in conjunction with ground stations in Europe. SDGPS does not operate in Europe at the time of writing despite the fact that SDGPS is being sold in Europe with a claimed accuracy of 3 metres. In any case this increased accuracy is of no practical use for yachtsmen in Greece. See the caution below.

***Gallileo*** The EU alternative to GPS is at present being approved for start-up costs and operational uses. When the satellites necessary are launched and the system is operational (around 2006–2007) it is envisaged users will pay a licensing fee to some authority. Since GPS is free this is hardly likely to catch on too quickly.

***Loran C*** Loran C is the official EU backup to GPS for position finding. Although all EU countries have signed up for this, little has been done in the way of funding the manning and maintenance of Loran transmitters, which were formerly maintained by the US. At the time of writing Loran C is effectively useless because the Turkish transmitters are out of action. At some time in the future these transmitters maybe reinstated to restore coverage in the eastern Mediterranean. Although the technology is dated compared to satellite position-finding systems, nonetheless good accuracy can be obtained throughout most of the Mediterranean with a little care. In the SE Mediterranean you are on the limits of signal reception and around the SE Aegean there is a hole in the coverage covering the sea area around Kós, Rhodes, and the E tip of Crete.

Accuracy varies, but is normally within 0·1 mile to 0·5 mile when the relevant offsets are included. The latitude is usually within 0·1 mile with the longitude giving the maximum error. Like RDF or any radio signals, care is needed at dawn and dusk when the signals can be refracted and inaccurate fixes result.

***Chart plotters*** A number of yachts are fitting dedicated chart plotters which, when interfaced to an electronic position-finding system, show a yacht's position on a chart. Dedicated chart plotters are a useful adjunct to the navigation table or cockpit and I use one on *seven tenths*. Despite the usefulness of a plotter it does not replace the usefulness of a chart in the cockpit for me. With that old-fashioned paper chart I can put it anywhere, hold it up while looking at a feature or danger to navigation and quickly pan from one side of the chart to the other. You can get irritated with the *please wait, chart loading* message on chart plotters as you either zoom in or out or pan from one part to another. If the chart plotter is located at the chart table then you must constantly run up and down to check the map against the view above and this can make it difficult to mentally fit the 3D real view to the 2D chart view. A chart in the cockpit lets you constantly scan from one to the other and fit the chart to the real world. In addition the problems outlined below are exacerbated on electronic charts where an electronically derived 'real' position is displayed on a cartographically inaccurate chart.

***Laptop computers*** A number of yachts now have laptop computers on board. There are a number of software packages which reproduce charts and if GPS, Loran, and radar are interfaced this can be a useful navigation tool. One of the problems with most systems is that the laptop is not fitted into the navigation area and so is difficult to use when conditions are rough. Most people don't want to risk their laptop slithering all over the place when things get a bit bumpy. If you are contemplating a laptop-based navigation system incorporating charts and instrumentation, then some thought needs to go into securing the laptop on the navigation table or as a modular unit with the screen on a bulkhead and the keyboard secured on the chart table. There are also a number of remote waterproof screens available which can be installed in the cockpit to reproduce the charts, GPS position and other data where it is easy to see when sailing. The following points should be kept in mind when looking at plotting software.

1. You will need to choose between raster and vector charts. Basically raster charts are scanned originals. Vector charts are redrawn digitally from the original. In practice the best choice is to go for vector charts. They occupy less space on the hard disk, load more quickly and, importantly, can be read when you zoom in or out. Raster charts are scanned at one resolution so when you zoom in or out you lose definition and get a fuzzy pixellated image. That is intensely irritating and the only answer is to buy a large folio of charts, although that means the laptop grinding away to load a chart on a smaller or larger scale. Raster charts also take longer to reload, which is annoying when you are trying to get from one side of the chart to the other on a 14 inch laptop screen.

2. Don't go for a chart plotter that has all the bells and whistles. Even a basic plotter has more than enough for practical navigation and the more you squeeze onto a toolbar the more confusing it gets when conditions are a bit bumpy at sea. Even a basic plotter will insert waypoints, construct routes, let you keep an automatic log off the GPS input and an annotated log as well. Just as most of us never use half of the functions on a word processor, so you will never need to use a lot of the functions on some chart plotters.

3. Ease of use and large icons are important when it's blowing half a gale and the boat is bucketing to windward. You don't want to have to work out how to construct a route when the rest of the crew are sick and you are not feeling too bright yourself. And get a mouse for your laptop instead of using the touchpad or that little joystick stuck

in the middle of the keys, or every time the boat hits a wave the mouse pointer will shoot across the screen as you twiddle with the touchpad or the miniature joystick.

Laptops are also commonly used for weatherfax systems using a HF receiver and the appropriate software.

***Radar*** Now radar is more compact and more economical with your amps, it can be used as a useful navigation tool. Its great value is in reproducing a map of what is there, rather than a latitude and longitude that you then plot on an (inaccurate) chart.

***RDF*** Few yachts these days are still equipped with Radio Direction Finding equipment, but nonetheless marine and aero beacons still transmit along the Greek coast and on some of the islands. Details are given on page 36.

***A caution*** Most of the charts for Greece were surveyed in the 19th century using celestial fixes and basic triangulation techniques. Subsequent observations have shown considerable errors, in some cases up to 1 minute of longitude. While you may know your latitude and longitude to within 20 metres, the chart you are plotting it on may contain errors of up to 1 mile, though normally less. The practice of including the datum point for a chart and an offset to be used with electronic position-finding equipment only confuses a very complicated picture because the old charts have varying inaccuracies over the area they cover. For instance, one cape may be in position and another half a mile out of position. For the most part errors have been corrected, but there are still discrepancies and you should not be lulled into a false confidence because everything appears to be turning up in the right place. The next time it may not happen and the situation may be more critical.

The solution to the problem lies in the hands of the relevant hydrographic authorities who could use satellite-derived photographs to resurvey the areas and produce new charts – however this seems unlikely to happen in the near future and so we are left with what amounts to basically 19th-century charts patched up here and there as best the hydrographic departments are able. The problem is further complicated because the old 19th-century 'fathoms' charts are being metricated and so look like new surveys – even when the attribution is to a recent Greek survey, this will be for only a part, often a small part of the chart, while the basis for the chart will still have been the original Admiralty 19th-century survey.

It hardly needs to be stated that you should exercise great caution in the vicinity of land or hazards to navigation – eyeball navigation rules OK.

## Fuel

Where fuel is shown in the pilotage notes as being close to or on the quay I am referring in most cases to diesel fuel. In some cases petrol will also be available, but often you will have to go to a petrol station in the town to obtain it. There are a number of dedicated fuel quays for yachts in Greece, but in most places fuel is delivered by mini-tanker, usually a pick-up with a tank on the back and a petrol powered delivery pump. In many places the telephone number for the fuel truck is on a notice-board at the yacht quay. If not, enquire locally and someone will usually give you a phone number or will ring up the fuel supplier for you.

Duty-free fuel is no longer available to EU registered yachts. Theoretically non-EU registered yachts can obtain duty-free fuel, although in practice it is difficult to find anyone prepared to do so. If you are going to the trouble of trying to get duty-free fuel it is only worth doing so for large amounts. Briefly it works like this:

1. Get a form from the bank showing you have changed foreign currency to drachmas.
2. Get a pink slip from customs.
3. Locate the supplier and customs will annotate the pink slip.

### Water

The English quarrel about the respective merits of different beers, the French about wines, and the Greeks about water. Water is important above all else in Greece and to abuse it is to insult it. In many of the islands and some mainland areas water is in short supply. Towards the end of the summer is the most critical period and at this time some places which normally have water will turn off public supply points.

In most harbours a local is appointed as the 'water-man' who controls the water and charges for it. The charges for water are normally fixed by the local council, but usually vary according to what the 'water-man' thinks he can get. Ask beforehand and if the charge seems excessive, haggle a bit. In some harbours a local entrepreneur will truck water in and in this case there is no fixed charge and the cost will inevitably be higher because of the costs of operating a tanker service. A length of hosepipe (about 25m) with a selection of connectors is useful for refilling the water tanks.

The water is nearly always safe to drink except where a sign states otherwise or in a few places I have mentioned. To any water of doubtful quality add the requisite number of proprietary water-purifying tablets (such as *Puritabs*) or a little bleach solution (around 3%) or potassium permanganate.

It is now possible to buy bottled water all over Greece, though I don't encourage it. It is an affectation encouraged by the bottling companies that does not reflect upon the quality of most of the tap water available. Enough thoroughly obnoxious plastic mineral water bottles already litter the seas and shores of Greece and as far as I am concerned the practice of drinking bottled mineral water should be actively discouraged.

The recent mild and dry winters in Europe have meant that summer water supplies in the Mediterranean have been steadily eroded. For several summers water has been in short supply in Athens and water rationing was imposed. Though many optimistically pin their hopes on a mini-climatic aberration that will right itself in a few years, evidence for the 'greenhouse effect' continues to accumulate and if this is so then water poverty in the Mediterranean will become a fact of life.

Already I see yachtsmen, both local and foreign, surreptitiously washing their boats down when there is a ban on this activity, and they have only themselves to blame if they are denied water altogether. In recent years small communities have denied yachtsmen water because the precious stuff is in short supply and yachtsmen have abused it. It is an insult to wash your boat down when the supplies in a small village may not last the summer and just because you are paying for it, don't assume you can abuse it. I can see the day when water-makers become a common piece of equipment on board cruising yachts.

### Hauling and boatyards

The following list gives the current location of yards with travel-hoists in Greece. There are also a number of yards which have hydraulic trailers or slipways using the old fashioned sledge on wooden runners or a modern variant on the slipway method. Yachts are also hauled by crane in a number of places, but I only include yards here which are well organised and not places where yachts are craned onto any old bit of hardstanding that is around. It is important to remember that whether hauling by travel-hoist, slipway or crane, there may be constraints on draught, beam and LOA that limit the size of yacht that can be hauled even though the dead weight of the boat is within the tonnage limit.

**Gouvía** 75-ton travel-hoist
**Préveza** Three yards. 50-ton travel-hoists and 50-ton hydraulic trailer. Also sledge and runners in the N bay.
**Levkas** Sledge and runners.
**Nidri/Vlikho** Sledge and runners.
**Katakólon** Crane and trailer.
**Kalamata** 50-ton travel-hoist to be installed.
**Patras** Yachts craned ashore.
**Isthmia** Yachts craned ashore.
**Salamís** Sledge and runners.
**Ambelákia** 100-ton travel-hoist.
**Pérama** Slipways to 1000-tons. 250-ton travel-hoist.
**Kalamáki Marina** Yachts craned ashore.
**Aigina** 60-ton travel-hoist and sledge and runners.
**Póros** 20-ton crane.
**Porto Kheli** 40-ton crane.
**Koiládhia** 50-ton crane to be installed.
**Síros** 65-ton hydraulic lift. Sledge and slipway.
**Olympic Boatyard** 50/200-ton travel-hoists.
**Angistri (S Gulf of Evia)** To 55ft on hydraulic trailer.
**Volos** Yachts craned ashore.
**Vathoudhi** Sledge and runners.
**Aretsou (Thessaloníki)** Yachts craned ashore.
**Porto Carras** 50-ton travel-hoist to be installed.
**Khíos Marina** Travel-hoist planned.
**Pithagorion Marina (Samos)** Travel-hoist planned.
**Lakkí (Léros)** 50-ton travel-hoist.
**Partheni (Léros)** 70-ton travel-hoist
**Kós Marina** Travel-hoist to be installed.
**Rhodes** 60-ton travel-hoist. 200-ton travel-hoist planned.
**Iraklion** Yachts craned out. Also sledge and runners.
**Áy Nikólaos (Crete)** Travel-hoist to be installed.

There are plans to install more travel-hoists around parts of Greece, but it is best to adopt a 'wait and see' policy in case the hoist fails to materialise. There are also a lot of smaller yards that haul a few yachts using either a sledge and runners or a crane with strops.

## Fast ferries

The advent of new fast ferries running between Greece and Italy and in some places through the Aegean islands has brought with it the problem of massive ferry wash. At speed these ferries push a massive wall of water that crashes into what were otherwise protected anchorages and harbours causing damage to yachts and other small craft. When the ferries first began running they caused a lot of damage and there were hundreds of claims against the ferry companies involved. This has caused the ferries to slow down in coastal waters, but some of them still push a lot of water even at slower speeds.

The main problem area is in the northern Ionian, particularly around Corfu, Cephalonia and Ithaca. In a few places in the Aegean such as Ios and Siros there can also be a problem. The only solution is to anchor off with a long line ashore rather than go on jetties exposed to the wash but otherwise sheltered from the wind, and in harbour, to pull yourself well off the quay.

If you do experience damage from one of these ferries document the time, damage, etc. and make a claim. If possible take photographs and if you get no satisfaction, get in touch with the Greek Tourist Board. Eventually the ferry operators will get the message that speeding in coastal waters is not only environmentally damaging, but it is also going to cost them.

## Macho man

In recent years there has been an increase in small craft based in Greece and, sad to say, many of these are driven by souls with the money to acquire a boat but none of the wit to learn seamanship and care for others using the sea. Most of these newly acquired craft are motorboats and while some are skippered in a sensible and seamanlike way, others are driven by macho man and all the baggage he carries with him. While I am quite happy for these sad souls to crash around where they affect no one else, not surprisingly they seem to frequent those places where others are quietly enjoying themselves. Dangerous situations have developed with craft entering and leaving harbour at high speed, creating large amounts of wash that damage craft berthed in the harbour as well as posing a danger to any craft manoeuvring within the harbour. Dangerous situations have also arisen with boats navigating around an anchorage at speed where people are swimming or pottering around in dinghies. Often RIBs or waterbikes navigate carelessly and at speed in bays where people are swimming and it should be made plain to anyone doing so that not only is their sport antisocial in such situations, but it is also dangerous should they hit anyone swimming in the water.

## Sails

Under the hot Mediterranean sun a yacht's sails suffer from ultra-violet degradation faster than in more northerly climes. All sails should be covered when not in use. Roller reefing headsails should have a sacrificial strip on the leech and foot and must be rolled up so that the sacrificial strip covers the sailcloth. I see a lot of roller reefing headsails rolled up with a barber pole effect where some sailcloth is left exposed to UV degradation. Likewise roller-reefing mains should have a sacrificial patch on the tack where it protrudes from the mast slot.

If you have a conventional main then it is worthwhile investing in a cover permanently attached to the boom and held in place with lazyjacks which will guide the main down into it. These self-stowing affairs go under different names ('easy-stow', 'pack-away', etc) and can be ordered from a sailmaker for retro-fitting if necessary. Apart from letting you drop the main quickly and easily, the fact that the cover is permanently in place and easy to use encourages laid-back crew and skippers to cover the mainsail up and prevent UV damage.

## Garbage

The steady increase in man-made disposables found in the oceans and seas of the world is saddening. Around the seas of Greece the amount of rubbish, particularly plastic, has steadily increased. Locals are partly to blame for this – in many Greek villages you will see garbage thrown into the sea – but shore-based tourists and sadly some yachtsmen are also to blame. No one on a yacht has any excuse for polluting somebody else's waters and anybody who does so should not be there. In most harbours there are containers for garbage and it is here and not in the sea that it belongs.

## Rescue services

Many of the larger harbours and some smaller harbours now have lifeboats. These range from all-weather lifeboats to large RIBs. In addition many harbours have fast coastguard patrol boats ranging from large offshore craft to what are effectively fast speedboats.

Hellas Radio monitors Ch 16 and 2182MHz. Some coastguard stations are equipped with VHF and MF DSC facilities. The SAR co-ordinating centre for all rescues is in Piraeus. In a number of recent situations the coastguard has responded reasonably quickly to distress calls and dispatched a craft to the scene.

Piraeus JRCC MMSI 237670000
VHF DSC HF DSC
☎ 01 411 2500 *Fax* 01 411 5798

At the beginning of each chapter the relevant coastguard stations are shown on the introductory map with all radio frequencies including DSC capability if applicable.

## GMDSS (Global Maritime Distress and Safety System)

GMDSS consists of several integrated systems which are now required on all ships with the exception of the following:

Ships other than passenger vessels of less than 300 gross-tonnage.
Passenger ships carrying less than 6 passengers.
Ships of war.
Ships not propelled by engines.
Pleasure yachts not engaged in charter.
Fishing vessels.
The integrated system is composed of the following components:
*COPAS-SARSAT* The international satellite-based search and rescue system which receives the 406MHz signal from EPIRBs.
*NAVTEX* See section under *Weather* on NAVTEX functions.
*Inmarsat* Data transmission by satellite and also broadcasts all NAVTEX functions for areas not within NAVTEX coverage.
*SART* Search and rescue transponders.
*Digital Selective Calling* VHF, MF and HF will utilise DSC for ship-to-ship, ship-to-shore, shore-to-ship and will also generate a pre-formatted distress signal giving a location position if connected to GPS or any other position-finding receiver.
Of all these it is really DSC which most affects pleasure yachts. All GMDSS equipment had to be fitted to ships by 1 February 1999. Ships are no longer required to keep a listening watch on 2182MHz and will not have to keep a listening watch on VHF Ch 16 after 1 February 2005. It is uncertain yet whether shore stations will likewise stop listening on VHF Ch 16. Ch 70 is now banned for voice transmission and is the DSC distress frequency.

DSC stations have been introduced in Greece and details are given on the area maps for specific chapters.

### Insurance

A comprehensive insurance policy for the eastern Mediterranean is not excessively expensive, but shop around the various companies to get the best deal. Most policies do not cover you after 34°E, but since this covers all Greek waters there is no problem here. In 1999 new insurance requirements for all yachts (regardless of flag) in Greek waters were introduced. The details of the requirements, mostly to do with third party liability, are outlined below, but most reputable insurance policies will already provide the amounts required by the new Greek law. What you may not have is a certificate stating the amounts for which you are covered and this is now required to be carried on board the yacht. Contact your insurance company and they will be able to provide the necessary documentation. It may also be worth checking that you are covered for liability for pollution.

Greek insurance requirements:

1. All yachts must have insurance for liability for death or injury for those on board and any third party for a minimum of 100 million drachma (approx. £182,000).
2. Insurance for liability for damage of at least 50 million drachma (approx. £91,000).
3. Liability for pollution resulting from an incident of 30 million drachma (approx. £54,500).

### Documents

Passports are required for all the crew including EU nationals. Even though EU nationals can freely pass between EU countries, they are still required to carry either a passport or identity card. Non-EU nationals must have a passport although for most countries no visa is required. Check with the relevant authorities if you have an 'unusual' passport. You must also have yacht registration papers, either full Part 1 registration papers or SSR papers for UK yachts. You may be asked for proof of competence to handle a yacht such as the RYA Helmsman's certificate or Yachtmaster's certificate, insurance documents, and a radio licence.

## General information

### Tourist offices
In the cities and larger towns there are tourist offices which can often provide useful maps and pamphlets relevant to the local area.

### Banks
Major credit cards (*Visa, MasterCard* and *American Express*) and travellers' cheques are accepted in the cities, larger towns and popular tourist spots. Many places have ATMs (Automatic Teller Machines or 'hole in the wall machines' to you and me), which work well with the major credit cards and a PIN number. In general there are few places of any size where you cannot change money either at an ATM, in a bank, post office, or at a tourist agent who will usually have a sideline changing money. Banks are open from 0800–1300 Monday–Friday.

Getting money sent to Greece from outside the country is a tedious and prolonged affair – expect it to take literally weeks longer than you anticipate.

### Public holidays
January 1 New Year's Day
January 6 Epiphany
March 25 Independence Day
May 1 Labour Day
August 15 Assumption Day
October 16 St Dimitrius' Day (Salonika)
October 28 *Ochi* ('no') Day
December 25 Christmas Day
December 26 St Stephen's Day
*Moveable*
First day of Lent
Good Friday
Easter Monday
Ascension

### Laundry
In most places there will be someone who takes in laundry. Often a laundry will be associated with a dry-cleaner. The charge is usually per item so it doesn't pay to have your 'smalls' laundered this way. There are few self-service laundromats in Greece. Prices vary considerably, and are usually comparatively high, so ascertain the cost first.

## Security

By and large Greece is an honest country, but in the cities and larger resorts crime is on the increase. Take all sensible precautions. In general the harbours around Athens have a bad reputation for theft.

In recent years the deteriorating situation in Albania has leaked over the border to Corfu and the sea area around the North Corfu Channel. There have been numerous reports of theft from yachts in Corfu by Albanians coming over in fast speedboats and recently a British couple on a charter yacht were forced into an isolated cove by armed Albanians and stripped of their valuables before being released. More disturbing still is the case of the yachtsman in Gouvía who was shot dead by armed Albanians when he attempted to stop them stealing his dinghy. Yachts on passage through the North Corfu Channel must keep close to the Greek side and at the present time it would be wise to avoid the mainland anchorages close to the Albanian border.

## Drugs

There are very strict penalties for the importation of drugs (hashish, cocaine, etc.) in Greece and severe sentences are handed out for possession of even small amounts of 'soft' drugs such as marijuana. Your yacht can be confiscated if drugs are found on board so play it safe and avoid them and anyone associated with them. A momentary 'high' is hardly worth the loss of your yacht and a stiff jail sentence.

## Health

All cities and large towns have a hospital and for the most part treatment is good. Smaller towns and tourist areas will often have a health centre which can attend to more minor injuries and assess whether the patient should be taken to a hospital for further treatment.

In most cases treatment for EU nationals is free of charge with Form E111. In some cases you may have to pay part of the cost of treatment. It is worthwhile taking out comprehensive medical insurance which includes the costs of repatriation if necessary.

Dental treatment is good in the cities and large towns with well equipped practices and dentists who have often trained abroad.

## Medicines

Specially-prescribed drugs should be bought in sufficient quantities in England before departure. Most drugs and medical requisites are freely available over the counter in Greece (including contraceptive pills, wide-spectrum antibiotics, antibiotic powder etc.) although they may be under unfamiliar brand names.

## Mail

The postal system is reliable and efficient for letters, but packages take a long time to be distributed. A private address is preferable to *Poste Restante*. Most marinas and boatyards will hold mail for you.

## Telecommunications

### Telephone

Most of Greece is served by a good telecommunication network, much of which has been upgraded in recent years.

All towns and most villages have an overseas telephone exchange (OTE) where international calls can be made. Even the smallest village will have a metered telephone in a hotel, shop, taverna, or commonly in a *periptero* (the kiosks that sell everything from cigarettes to sweets), though charges will be slightly more (in hotels considerably more) than in the OTE.

Telephone cards are now widely available in Greece and can be purchased from grocery and other shops, even from the *periptero* that have metered telephones.

IDD is now possible from all phones except for a few ancient exchanges on the smallest islands. Now new equipment has been installed the communication services in Greece are considerably improved and direct dialling to other countries is normally fairly quick, although delays occur at peak periods when a lot of business calls are made.

**Fax** Many travel agents and stationery shops operate a fax service, although charges vary enormously.

**Mobile phones** Digital cellular phones with GSM (Global System for Mobile Communications) capacity can be used in Greece. Your own service provider will need to have an agreement with the main service providers in Greece (*Panafon*, *Telestet*, and *OTEnet*). In practice the system is seamless and your phone will register with a provider in Greece when you turn it on. Most phones will automatically register although at times it is worth manually changing provider where your phone 'sticks' on one provider even though the signal is weaker than a rival's signal.

With your own phone it is worth remembering that you pay for the cost of the signal into and out of your service provider's country. For a UK service provider you pay the cost of the call both to and from the UK plus around 20% on top. The person you are calling or who calls you will only pay for the point-to-point call in the UK. This means that using say, a UK phone, in Greece costs a lot of money whatever your provider tells you – usually not a lot because the person selling you the phone either doesn't understand the tariffs or only tells you half the story. If you are going to spend some time in Greece it is worth either getting a Greek chip for your phone or, as I do, getting another pay-as-you-go phone with a Greek number. You can then ask people to phone you on the Greek number rather than your home country mobile where the call is costing YOU a lot of money. I use my UK mobile for collecting e-mail and making short calls out.

Hand-held sets are limited to around 2 watts so you will not be able to transmit when too far away from any particular station. Portables (around 5 watts) or proper marine installations have a greater range. Portable phones, like VHF sets, are limited by the distance from the receiving and transmitting station and are also shut out by high land. Enclosed bays or high islands and mountains will cast a transmitting shadow over the phone. Having said all that, I find that at times I can get enough of a signal 30 miles and more offshore to use the phone. In general you should not rely on too much over 15–20 miles offshore.

Fax connections from digital phones are available with dedicated PC cards for your specific cellular phone. You will need a PC, a fax PC card or modem, some sort of software to run it, and an interface between the portable phone and fax PC card or stand-alone modem.

**E-mail** There are a number of ways of sending and receiving e-mail while cruising. The following is a brief round-up of ways and means of doing so.

1. Using a GSM phone and dedicated connection cord and appropriate modem you can connect at 9600 baud wherever you can get a signal. This is the system I most commonly use as it allows you to connect in the comfort of your boat. 9600 baud is not a very fast speed these days but it is sufficient for e-mail. Transmission charges vary not only with your local provider in Greece, but also with your provider in the UK or wherever your phone is registered. It is worthwhile doing a comparison of costs on providers to see who is giving the best deal.

    The new second generation phones (G2) only offer 14400 baud which hardly makes it worthwhile investing in a new (expensive) phone and invariably a new cable and perhaps a PC card modem for it. But in 2002–2003 the third generation phones (G3) using the Unified Mobile Telephone Service (UMTS) will come into being and that should offer a whacking 2Mbps, faster than anything you can get on a landline at present. In the interim the so-called 2·5G transmission technologies are underway which offer up to 57·6–115kbps utilising the present GSM networks, and one of these technologies may be the way to go. Invariably the different providers are using different transmission technologies and so compatibility with an overseas provider will be a problem. Why oh why do they not agree on one technology and roll it out across the board? For information on 2·5G (utilising HSCSD, GPRS, or EDGE) contact your service provider or change to another.

2. Using a satellite system such as INMARSAT you can send and receive e-mail just about anywhere in the world. INMARSAT transmissions vary depending on the system used. INMARSAT C (the most common system used on yachts) is painfully slow at around 2400 baud although better transmission rates are planned. Inmarsat mini M is also slow although higher transmission speeds (64kbps) are to be implemented soon. INMARSAT B (replacing INMARSAT A) offers fast enough speeds for video conferencing, but is also the most expensive and biggest of the range.

INMARSAT D+ is for brief messages (max 128 characters per message). The costs of the systems are expensive and transmission charges are expensive, typically $4–8 a minute.

3. Cyber-cafés. Many quite small places have a cyber-café these days and if you have an internet e-mail provider such as *Hotmail* or *Yahoo!* then it takes little time to download and send mail using a floppy disk. If you do not have a laptop to compile mail on and download it from the desktop in the café then most cyber-cafés will let you print out the mail for a small fee. Costs are low and of course connection rates are high at typically 56K. I use this method of connecting when I cannot get a connection via GSM or when I feel like a coffee with my mail.

4. Acoustic couplers. This sort of connection whereby you use an acoustic coupler onto the mouthpiece of a public phone used to be popular but connection rates are slow and errors can creep in. Despite claims to the contrary, it is unusual to get connection rates much over 2400 baud.

5. HF Radio. There are a number of companies who will transmit data via HF radio including Pinoak, GlobeE-mail and the Ham Radio Network. Data rates are slow, typically less than 2400 baud, and costs for the service are relatively expensive for the commercial concerns (the Ham network is a co-operative group and you must be a licensed ham operator to use it). In addition you must make a substantial investment in a HF modem and the appropriate software. For the Mediterranean the system is probably too expensive in investment and running costs but does have the advantage of operating in many parts of the world.

6. Magellan GSC 100. This is a combined GPS and e-mail device. The e-mail is sent and received via the ORBCOMM satellite network. Because of the cost of the service it is really only suitable for short messages and besides the small keypad interface would make it tedious to send long messages. Like the HF radio services it does offer near global coverage.

7. Other satellite phone services. A number of new satellite phone services are beginning operation using either high (GEO), medium (MEO) or low (LEO) earth orbiting satellites.

    *Iridium* The failed Iridium system formerly run by Motorola has been bought by a consortium and should be operational by the end of 2001. Data transmission rates should be 9600 baud. Coverage is worldwide using LEO satellites.

    *Globalstar* Coverage over most land areas and the Mediterranean using LEO satellites, but patchy or non-existent (as yet) for offshore waters. Data transmission at 9600 baud.

    *Thuraya* Using one GEO satellite, covers mid-Atlantic to India except for low latitudes. Another GEO satellite planned. Data transmission and the phone incorporates a GPS receiver.

*Emsat* Uses one GEO satellite, giving coverage of northern Europe and the Mediterranean.

*ICO* Uses MEO satellites and should be operational by 2002.

8. Plugging in to a conventional socket. If you can find somewhere to plug into a conventional telephone socket ashore with (usually) a meter on the time used, then this is a quick and easy way to send and receive e-mail using your own laptop. There are certain things to be borne in mind. If you connect to an ISP in the country you are in then the cost is that of a local or at most a national call. Large companies like CompuServe and AOL will most likely have a server in the country you are in, but unless your home ISP has a reciprocal agreement in other countries (and some do), you will have to dial up to the country your home ISP is in and this obviously will be an overseas call. I use CompuServe and mostly find I can connect to a server in the country I am in when I use this method. Many marinas, service companies and a whole host of other places will let you plug in to a metered telephone line. Remember you will need an adapter for the Greek telephone jack, although sometimes you will be able to connect simply through a normal US jack plug commonly found on many fax machines.

### Internet

There are numerous internet providers in Greece including the big-name suppliers like CompuServe and AOL. Transmission rates are generally good, but for some reason connection speeds do not always seem to match those in other parts of Europe. This may be a telecommunications problem with slow data transmission rates or it may be to do with the servers used by the ISPs in Greece. In general you will just have to be a bit more patient and in the end you should have no problem downloading information from the internet.

### Provisioning

In all but the smallest villages you will have few problems obtaining the basic provisions. In the larger towns and popular tourist resorts there is now a wide range of imported goods available and even in small villages you will find the ubiquitous fare that some tourists feel they cannot do without. Why some people should feel an overwhelming need for Heinz baked beans or spaghetti hoops in Greece is beyond me, but they are there.

Fresh fruit and vegetables are seasonal, although now Greece is an EU member there is a better selection over a longer period and, of course, prices have gone up.

Shopping hours are 0800–1300 and 1630–2000, although shopkeepers will stay open through the siesta period or later at night if there are enough customers to warrant it. Shops often close on Monday afternoon and sometimes on Wednesday afternoon as well.

*Meat* Is usually not hung for long, if at all, and is invariably butchered in a peculiarly eastern Mediterranean fashion so that none of the normal cuts of meat can be recognised. Lamb and beef are the most expensive and pork and chicken the cheapest. Meat is reasonably priced though of inferior quality and cut compared to that in some other European countries.

*Fish* Is expensive. Large fish such as red snapper and grouper are very expensive and the prices of prawns and lobsters are considerable – certainly comparable to or higher than in Italy and France. Fish from fish farms is a lot cheaper than the wild variety and farmed shellfish, predominantly mussels, are also available

*Fruit and vegetables* Are reasonably priced and usually fresh. Outdoor native tomatoes, the knobbly ones, taste better than any of the ubiquitous greenhouse tomatoes now distributed throughout the EU. In the smaller centres fruit and vegetables are seasonal. All fresh produce should be washed.

*Staples* Can be obtained in even the smaller villages. Many items (sugar, rice, legumes, beans etc.) are often sold loose. Both loose and packaged items may contain weevils.

*Cheese* Imported cheeses such as Dutch Edam and Gruyere are widely available and not too costly. Local hard cheeses such as *Kaseri* are good and *Feta*, a soft sheep's cheese, is available everywhere and is good value. Much of the 'Greek' *Feta* is now imported from Denmark.

*Canned foods* Local canned goods are excellent and cheap, but there is not a wide variety. Canned tomatoes and fruit are good value. Canned meat is usually imported and is expensive.

*Bread* Bakers are a growth industry in Greece and even small villages often have a good bakers with all sorts of bread from white through all shades of brown. They will also often have mini-pizzas, cheese or spinach pies, bacon and egg pies, stuffed croissant, in fact whatever the baker reckons he can sell.

*Coffee and tea* Most popular brands of instant coffee are commonly available although it costs more than in some of the other European countries. Good filter coffee is also widely available and is not too expensive. Some of the specialist coffee shops and larger supermarkets do freshly ground coffee. Local teabags make an insipid cup of tea and if you want something akin to English tea then you will have to pay for imported tea bags. I usually take a couple of boxes of Earl Grey with me. Some of the loose tea packed locally is cheap and good.

*Wines, beers and spirits* Bottled wines are numerous and vary from excellent to terrible. Local wine can often be bought cheaply from the barrel, but taste it first. The ubiquitous retsina is an acquired taste. Wine is on the whole cheap. Local beer is quite palatable and cheap. Local spirits, ouzo (akin to Pernod) and brandy (sweetish) are excellent value, especially when bought in bulk. Imported spirits are expensive.

# Formalities

Greece as part of the European Union (EU) comes under EU legislation regarding the implementation of the Single Market Agreement. From 1 January 1993 the Single Market Agreement for the EU states that customs borders between member countries were removed and goods could be imported from one EU country to another free of hindrance. This agreement effectively removed temporary importation agreements previously in operation for pleasure craft. Prior to this date it was possible to purchase a yacht without paying VAT and keep it in another EU country under the temporary importation agreements. The new agreement which came into force in 1993 exempted pleasure craft on which VAT had not been paid and which were built before the 1 January 1985 (or on which the VAT was negligible) and which were in an EU country at midnight on the 31 December 1992, from VAT payment. Which means that if you have a boat built after 1.1.85 and on which VAT has not been paid and were in an EU country on the 1.1.93 then you are liable for VAT payment.

The following points will hopefully clarify what is a murky area despite the terms of the EU Single Market Agreement.

1. The following countries come under the Single Market Agreement: United Kingdom, Ireland, Denmark, Sweden, Finland, Holland, Germany, Austria, Luxembourg, Belgium, France, Spain, Portugal, Italy, and Greece.

   The Channel Islands, Gibraltar, Malta and Cyprus do not come under the agreement. Any future additions to the EU will automatically come under the Single Market Agreement.

2. Under the Single Market Agreement it should be possible to move a yacht on which VAT has been paid or which is VAT exempt without involving customs in import and export regulations. However you are still subject to other customs regulations in force in a country (e.g. carrying banned drugs or unauthorised firearms on board is illegal in most countries) and all countries will carry out random customs enquiries.

3. VAT can be paid in the EU country in which a boat is based or in the EU country of registration. In practice boats have moved from one country to another to pay VAT, usually to take advantage of a lower VAT rate or valuation by customs.

4. Evidence of VAT payment or exemption from VAT must be obtained unless you want to be liable for VAT payment. In the UK customs introduced a simple method of paying VAT or acquiring proof of exemption with the SAD (Single Administrative Document) form. In Greece customs have been slow to implement the rule on VAT.

*Practical note* Very little notice has been taken of the requirement to pay VAT on yachts built after 1985 and yachts subsequently brought into Greece. Until recently there was no paperwork in place to obtain a certificate to show exemption from VAT and it was extremely rare for the authorities to ask for any relevant paperwork. There have been a few cases of customs requesting a certificate from foreign flag yachts but all in all the situation remains fairly fluid over the VAT situation. If you are contemplating paying VAT the rates are:

18% on new craft.

18% on non-Greek-flagged second-hand craft.

3·6% on Greek-flagged second-hand craft.

### Customs *(Telenion)*

Greece as part of the EU comes under EU legislation regarding the payment of VAT. Proof of payment or exemption from payment should be carried. Yachts from other EU countries which have paid VAT can keep their boats in Greece without any further restrictions. Non-EU boats should report to customs at the first Port of Entry. Here you will be issued with a Transit Log which is valid for 6 months renewable for another 6 months before you must leave Greece for a non-EU country.

### Cruising permit

On 14 January 2000 Law 2743/1999 Article 11 was activated. It didn't take long for all hell to break loose and for e-mails, snailmail and faxes to zoom back and forth with some facts, some rumour and a lot of misinterpretation of the law. At the time of writing there is no certain way of knowing whether the law will continue as is, be revoked, or as has happened in the past, just be quietly left to fade away.

The basics of Law 2743 are as follows.

1. Any yacht (EU and non-EU flags) entering Greek waters must obtain a cruising permit. The cost of this permit is 2000Dx per metre per month.

2. This tax is valid for 30 days and can be renewed after 30 days at the same rate of 2000Dx per metre.

3. Yachts which leave Greece and re-enter within a 30 day period will be fined 15000Dx per metre and will be allowed to cruise for a 30-day period.

The following should be borne in mind.

1. The tax applies to yachts not permanently based in Greece. If a yacht is permanently based in Greece, that is if it has an annual contract with a marina, a recognised boatyard or other accredited agency, then the tax is applicable once only and the yacht can remain in Greece for 3 years without paying further tax.

2. The tax appears to contravene EU regulations for free travel within EU countries and it is possible the law will be repealed or changed to conform with EU regulations. It also contravenes EU legislation for equal treatment for all as Greek-flagged boats are exempt from this law.

3. The fact that yachts permanently in Greece can make a one-off payment points to a change of culture in Greece whereby yachts must take annual contracts with marinas or boatyards as is common in other EU countries. There may also

be the matter of tax regulation going on whereby the Greek tax authorities can better control the assets owned by Greek nationals.

4. It is also thought that the tax may be an attempt to regulate yacht charter in Greece when the requirement to have Greek-flagged charter yachts (cabotage) is waived under EU regulations for free trade within the EU. This is now stated to be for 2002–2003.

5. For the time being I suggest a 'wait and see' policy as it may be that the tax is dropped, officially or unofficially, as has happened in the past for similar ill-conceived laws. There are already reports that the tax has been dropped in a number of places, but as yet I do not have concrete substantiation. A lot of Greeks involved in the marine trade including marina managers, boatyard owners, suppliers and local traders are worried that the law will cause an exodus of yachts from Greece and are furious that they were not consulted. As ever it seems that a small band of civil servants with no knowledge or interest in yachting in Greece have produced this ill-conceived law and the horrendous amount of paperwork that accompanies it. Write to your local MEP as I have.

At the time of publication the latest I have had from Brussels is as follows:

From Fritz Bolkestein, the Commissioner responsible for this area, in reply to my questions through my MEP Richard Balfe. He says:

'Following a preliminary analysis, the Commission services believe that this permit is a tax, which is not compatible with articles 23, 25 and 133 of the Treaty. These articles prohibit taxes that have an equivalent effect to customs duties on imports from other Member States or third countries. On this basis, the Commission sent on 12 September (2000) a letter of formal notice to the Greek authorities, inviting them to submit their observations on this matter in compliance with article 226 of the Treaty.

An answer to this letter has been received by the Commission. It is being translated, so as to be studied.'

How long the process of examining the legality of the Permit will take is difficult to know. Add to that some time for port police on small islands in Greece to be notified of any changes and I think you have to be looking at 2002 or later before this silly bit of bureaucracy is removed.

### Entry formalities
EU yachts on which VAT has been paid or which are exempt can enter Greece from another EU country without formalities, except for the regulations pertaining to the Cruising Permit described above. If you are entering Greece from a non-EU country (Turkey, Croatia, Malta etc.) then in theory you should fly a 'Q' flag and enter at a Port of Entry. In practice it depends on the attitude of the officials in a port as to whether you need to do so, but along the Turkish-Greek border it would be wise to do things by the book.

A Greek courtesy ensign should be flown.

Non-EU yachts should fly a 'Q' flag and a Greek courtesy ensign and make their first port of call at one of the designated Ports of Entry. Here a Transit Log will be issued on which is listed an inventory of dutiable goods and crew members. A Transit Log is issued for 6 months renewable for another 6 months.

### Other EU laws for yachts
***Small craft licences*** At the time of publication there was no clear EU directive on small craft licenses and it appeared to be up to individual countries to determine agreement on what license or certificate corresponded with what. At the present time the RYA Helmsman's Certificate of Competence or Yachtmaster's Certificate are accepted in Greece. In practice a small craft licence is rarely asked for, in fact I can't remember the last time I was asked. In the future it is to be expected that there will be some harmonisation of small craft licences for EU countries.

### *Recreational craft directive*
On 15 June 1998 the Recreational Craft Directive came into existence. There is still a lot of wrangling about the exact interpretation of the directive, but effectively the following applies.

1. All recreational craft between 2·5 and 24 metres and constructed (partly or wholly) in the EU must display a CE mark which guarantees certain standards of construction.
2. All recreational craft between 2·5 and 24 metres imported into the EU must also have a CE mark.
3. All these craft should be accompanied by the Manufacturers Declaration of Conformity, usually in the owner's handbook.
4. Craft built before 15 June 1998 and in the EU at that date are exempt.
5. Craft built before 15 June 1998, but imported into the EU after that date, must have a CE mark. (This is a nonsensical requirement because the mark did not exist and therefore no one would have been able to get one anyway. It remains to be seen whether this interpretation will be revised.)
6. Craft built before 15 June 1998 in the EU and exported out of the EU must have a CE mark if imported back into the EU. (Also nonsensical, as for 5.)
7. Craft built outside the EU after 15 June 1998 must have a CE mark to be imported into the EU.
8. Home built boats may be exempt if not resold for 5 years after construction. There is some doubt over whether this is in fact the case and the strict interpretation may be that home built boats must have a CE mark.
9. Historical replicas of pre-1950s designs are exempt.

It appears that the original brief, to have certain common standards of construction for the EU market so that trade within the EU could be facilitated by one kitemark, have been extended in an irrational and protectionist manner to exclude a large number of craft from being sold on in the EU market. I suggest you petition your local Euro MP to introduce some sanity into this directive which in its simpler form was no bad thing.

In practice most EU countries are ignoring the daft requirements of the RCD for the simple reason it is just not enforceable. If a boat built prior to 15 June 1998 is brought into the EU, how can the officials possibly work out whether it should be awarded a CE mark. Are they going to tell you your boat will be impounded or that you must leave EU waters? No. We will just have to wait and see what happens and like many nonsensical rules applied from Brussels, the RCD will most likely just be ignored by officials in the Mediterranean.

### Harbour dues

Harbour dues are levied in Greek harbours where there are port police or someone else appointed to collect the dues. The charge is administered by the *Limeniko Tameio* (harbour financial committee) and not the *Limenario* (port police) although in practice it is usually collected by the port police. The charges are as follows on entering harbour each time:

Gross-tonnage x 100Dx one off for the first time in harbour

Per day berthed alongside: LOA in metres x 100 Dx

Per day berthed stern or bows-to: LOA in metres x 33·33 Dx

VAT at 18% is payable on the total

Charter boats pay 50% of the above

Non-EU flag boats pay 150% of the above.

Craft under 5GRT pay a flat rate of 3300Dx a month, a move calculated to appease all the small *caïque* owners in harbour.

For an average 12-metre yacht the charge amounts to around 1000Dx one-off tonnage charge, 400Dx stern or bows-to, with VAT a total of 1650Dx (around £3.00 or $4.20 US at the time of writing).

This is not an unreasonable charge for sheltering within a harbour and those who go around moaning that there are no facilities for the money they pay should try heading for shores where there is a marina and somewhat higher berthing charges, though no doubt they will moan about that as well.

These are the charges made when the port police (or *Limeniko Tameio* collector) bothers to charge you. In the last season in Greece I was charged in around 20% of the harbours I visited. The collection of the charge is neither dedicated nor consistent, but I strongly suggest that you are polite and civil towards those port policemen forced to make out the receipts for your boat. They did not devise the charges and really have more than enough other paperwork they wish they did not have to do already. You will come across the odd 'little Hitler' amongst the port police, but they are the exception and it is generally best just to grin and bear it even if it galls you. (Mind you, I can think of one port policeman in Kos last year who by his oafish and rude behaviour can sour all the good images you have of other port police.)

### Port police

The port police offices are generally on the waterfront. They can be easily recognised by the crossed anchors next to the sign saying port police (*Limenario*) and the very large Greek flag flying from the building. The port police handle most of your papers and you can also have your mail sent to them. They will sometimes be able to supply you with a weather forecast.

An interesting point is that the port police can keep yachts in harbour if the weather forecast predicts winds of over Force 6. Often they will not bother. Should they make such a ruling the skipper of a yacht can sign a form which states in effect that he has been warned and any misfortune due to bad weather is entirely his own fault.

In my dealings with the port police I have invariably found them to be courteous and helpful, although business may be conducted with that typical Greek disdain for time that the Anglo-Saxons find so infuriating. Occasionally the yachtsman will come across an official who is rude and difficult, but this does not characterise officialdom in Greece – that, after all, is a disease to be found wherever officialdom exists.

### PORTS OF ENTRY

| | |
|---|---|
| Ayios Nikólaos | (Crete) |
| Alexandroupolis | (Northern Greece) |
| Argostoli | (Cephalonia) |
| Ermoúpolis | (Síros) |
| Gaios (Paxoí) | (Ionian) |
| Iraklion | (Crete) |
| Itéa | (Korinthiakós Kólpos) |
| Kalamata | (Peloponnisos) |
| Katakólon | (Peloponnisos) |
| Kavala | (Northern Greece) |
| Kérkira (Corfu) | (Ionian) |
| Khania | (Crete) |
| Khíos | (Eastern Sporades) |
| Kós | (Dodecanese) |
| Lavrion | (Saronic Gulf) |
| Levkas | (Ionian) |
| Mirina | (Limnos) |
| Mitilíni | (Lésvos) |
| Navplion | (Argolikós Kólpos) |
| Patras | (Patraikos Kólpos) |
| Pílos | (Western Peloponnisos) |
| Pithagorion | (Sámos) |
| Preveza | (Ionian) |
| Rhodes | (Rhodes) |
| Sími | (Dodecanese) |
| Thessaloniki | (Northern Greece) |
| Volos | (Northern Greece) |
| Vouliagméni Marina | (Saronikos Kólpos) |
| Zákinthos | (Ionian) |
| Zéa Marina | (Saronikos Kólpos) |

# Other laws relevant to the yachtsman

There are a number of laws which while not specifically maritime law, nonetheless are of special relevance to the yachtsman.

*Immigration* The first of these is to do with extended stays in Greece. Normally when entering Greece non-EU passport holders are allowed to stay three months without a visa (two months for some passport holders including the USA) and after that period is up, an extension for a further three months' stay must be applied for. However, when you enter on a yacht you can stay indefinitely provided you remain with the yacht. A problem arises if you enter on a yacht and depart by some other means. It is worthwhile obtaining a photocopy of the transit log to present to immigration when departing other than by yacht.

***Antiquities*** The second law of interest concerns the acquisition and export of antiquities. Greece loses valuable and irreplaceable antiquities every year and some of these are smuggled out of the country on yachts. Any antiquities found in Greece must be surrendered to the state. Any yacht with antiquities on board is liable to be impounded and confiscated and I know of several instances when this has occurred. This law also applies to antiquities and works of art which have been sold to you so it would pay to find out if an article can be exported before you exchange any money.

***Diving regulations*** The last law of relevance is that forbidding the use of compressed air tanks for underwater fishing. You may use a spear gun with a snorkel and mask but not with compressed air tanks. Such apparatus may be used for pleasure or filming except in areas where there may be antiquities on the seabed. These prohibited areas are so extensive that the National Tourist Board of Greece finds it easier to list those areas where compressed air tanks can be used for pleasure and filming. These are:

*Kassandra promontory (Khalkidhiki peninsula)*
All along a 500-metre belt of sea stretching out from the eastern shore of the promontory from the village of Polihrono to Ák Glarokavos.

*Sinthonia promontory (Khalkidhiki peninsula)*
All along a similar belt of the eastern shore of the promontory from Ák Armenistís to Ák Dhrépanon.

*Athos promontory (Khalkidhiki peninsula)*
a. Along a 500-metre belt from the shore in Órmos Provlaka from Pirgos Oranoupolis to Xerxes Canal.
b. Along the northern shore of Nisís Ammouliani from Ák Trigona to Ák Kókkino, within a 300-metre belt running parallel with the shore.

*Míkonos*
Within a 500-metre belt around the island's shores, save for the stretch from Ák Ayios Yeóryios to Ák Alogomandra.

*Kérkira (Corfu)*
a. Within a 500-metre belt around the island's shores from Ák Rodha to Ák Dhrastis.
b. Within a similar belt of sea from Palaiokastrita to Ák Arkoudila, with the exception of the waters surrounding Nisídhes Langoudhia.
c. Within a similar 500-metre belt of sea from Ák Koundhouri to Ák Agni, with the exception of the waters surrounding the islands of Vidho and Lazaretto.

*Paxoí*
Within a 500-metre belt of sea round the island's shores except for the area of Voutsi.

*Levkas*
a. Within the usual 500-metre belt along the island's western shores from Yiropetra to Ák Dhoukaton.
b. Within a similar 500-metre belt along the island's eastern shore from the point on the beach in line with the village of Katouna as far as the eastern entrance to Órmos Rouda, but not within the bay itself nor around the island of Madhouri.
c. Within a 500-metre belt of sea all round the island of Meganísi.

*Cephalonia*
a. Within a 500-metre belt along the island's shores, except for Dhíavlos Ithaca from the level of Fiskárdho to Órmos Andísami and Órmos Samí to Áy Eufimia.
b. Also excluded are the stretches of coast from Ák Kapri to Ák Mounda, the waters round the Variani islets and the coast from Ák Ortholithia to Ák Atheras.

*Zákinthos*
All around the island's shore, along a 500-metre belt.

Obviously it would pay to check with the local port police since any of these areas can be designated 'out of bounds' if the Archaeological Service suspect there are antiquities on the seabed.

In most areas you go to there will be a commercial operation that organises diving courses and holidays. It makes sense to talk to the operators in an area to find out exactly what restrictions there are and what local conditions are like. There have been a number of accidents over the years where divers have got into trouble with currents which although not always strong, can be tricky in tight situations.

Divers caught diving in prohibited areas face large fines, confiscation of their equipment and in some cases confiscation of the dive vessel if it is thought that the diving activities have been carried out to retrieve antiquities from the sea bottom.

# Chartering

Sometimes when I am talking about sailing in Greece, particularly to newcomers, I realise it sounds as if I have spent a lifetime sailing here. I suppose more than 20 years is a lifetime for some of you. Yet in that time there have been quite substantial changes for the yachtsman. Just prior to my arrival in *Roulette*, Law 438 was passed by the Legislature and this law effectively stopped foreign-registered yachts from chartering. Many charter boats left Greece. Their place has largely been filled by bareboat and flotilla charter, all under the Greek flag, but most owned and organised by English and German companies.

Flotilla chartering involves a group of boats, usually ten to twelve, sailing in company around a more or less planned route. In this way someone with only a little experience can skipper his own boat, but remain confident that help is at hand should anything go wrong. If anything does go wrong there is a lead boat constantly with the group and on board are a skipper, a hostess and an engineer who can sort out any problems you have.

Bareboat charter has grown rapidly in recent years and now accounts for the majority of charter boats in Greece. Bareboat basically means you charter a boat and sail independently in a given area. Most companies require you to return the boat to the home base but many now offer a one-way cruise from one base to another. Bareboats are not bare, but come with everything you need except the provisions. In fact many companies can arrange to provision your boat should you desire it.

If you are going bareboat it is important that you take some time over choosing a charter company, pick your fellow companions carefully, and put some thought into planning the cruise. When choosing a charter company check on what is included in the inventory. What safety equipment is there? What anchors, chain and warp is supplied? What navigation equipment is supplied and what charts and local pilots? Pretty soon you will get an idea of how well equipped a yacht is and some idea of how well it has been maintained. Ask about backup should any problems occur. There is nothing worse on a bareboat charter than being stuck in a harbour for five days with a ripped sail or a blown gasket on the engine because the charter base couldn't get anyone out to you and didn't have any contacts on the island to effect repairs.

It seems to be a commonplace dream among impoverished yachtsmen arriving in Greece that they will quickly replenish their coffers by chartering – until they learn of the regulations governing charter. It's Law 438 again. If your yacht is to be chartered in Greek waters then it must be registered in Greece. To obtain a Greek flag you will need to acquire the services of a Greek agent to whom you will sign away 51 per cent of your yacht or yachts. After being measured, checked for safety equipment and entered on the maritime register you will be issued with a wad of certificates and you can then raise your Greek flag. You still have not finished with the paperwork. For every charter party you must fill out a charter agreement detailing the duration of the charter, the number and nationality of the charterers, the cost of the charter and so on. The cost of the charter is detailed because you are required to have a certain proportion of the charter fee paid in Greece. The amount of paperwork is prodigious and the charter agreement may be checked at any port.

In 2002–2003 the laws on cabotage and Law 438 are expected to be rescinded so that Greece falls in line with the other EU countries. This will mean any EU-flagged boat can charter in Greece as long as it complies with Greek safety regulations for charter boats.

If your yacht exceeds a certain length (about 15m I believe) then you must employ a Greek captain and crew. This was the reason for so many foreign-registered yachts leaving Greece when Law 438 was passed. A couple or a family using their yacht and home to make a living by chartering it in the summer months could not afford to have it Greek registered or to engage a Greek captain and crew to do their job. To charter outside these regulations is to run the risk of having your yacht impounded.

Despite the entry of Greece into the EU, law 438 remains in place for charter yachts. The deadline given by Brussels for cabotage (the restriction of operating under Greek flag only) to be dropped was to be 2004. After the recent spate of ferry accidents that date has been brought forward by the present Greek government to 2002, although we need to see what happens in practice on that date and whether other restrictive practices are introduced. Some in Greece believe that part of the intention of the new cruising permit is to deter charter yachts crossing back and forth between Greece and other countries.

For more detailed information on the whys and wherefores of chartering I suggest you get in touch with the National Tourist Board of Greece. On a more practical level you would do better to talk to someone in the charter game in Greece. A number of English and German companies will put your boat under the Greek flag and charter it, paying you a percentage of the returns as well as allowing you the use of your boat in the off-season and for a limited period (usually two weeks) in the season. Just be sure you choose a reputable company or your beautiful new yacht may be a wreck by the end of a season of bareboat charter.

# Food and wine

Compiled by Bridgit Marsh

Greece is not a country for the gourmet. Eating out is as much a part of life in Greece as in other Mediterranean countries, but the food is not the sophisticated fare found in Italy or France or the carefully prepared food of the Levant. Not that the Greeks don't eat well – they do. The food is invariably fresh, simply cooked, and appetizing, but the choice will often be limited, the food sometimes served cold or lukewarm, and the garnishing meagre. In the larger towns and cities a wider choice will be found on the menu than in the smaller islands and villages.

In some areas, especially the more touristy areas, you get the kidnap and hustle tavernas. Waiters stand outside the taverna and actively and often physically attempt to hustle you inside. Some of these will proffer enticements like a free drink or free entertainment. Generally these tavernas have to resort to hustling because their food is mediocre and the prices high. Those offering a freeby of some sort will make sure it is recovered by charging more for other items. My advice is you pass them by and resist being kidnapped until you have inspected the other tavernas nearby. You can always go back if you decide the taverna-with-hustle was worth visiting anyway.

One of the things which will be most noticeable is the seasonality of the food. Although most fruits and

Greece is not a gourmet destination but the location of the tavernas is as good as you get

vegetables are available in Greece they may only be available during the ripening season. Apricots for instance ripen in early June and will only be in the shops for two to three weeks. This can be quite surprising to the visitor who is used to being able to buy fruit over an extended season. The seasonality of ingredients leads to a variation in the dishes served in the tavernas. This of course applies with special significance to the small village tavernas where only those foods in season will be served, whereas places with access to better markets will be able to serve such things as *moussaka* (normally only served when aubergines are in season) most of the year round.

Now that increasing numbers of tourists arrive in the summer the bigger tourist areas have to import considerable amounts of foodstuffs for the bulging taverna tables. Often your *kalamari* will come frozen from Californian waters, your lamb will come frozen from New Zealand, your *feta* was probably manufactured in Denmark, and even the aubergines in your *moussaka* may have come from Spain. Only in the smaller, more out-of-the-way places will you get locally grown produce tossed into the salad or grilled over the charcoal.

A taverna generally prepares its dishes for the day in the morning and these will be cooked in time for the midday meal when they will be served hot. These oven dishes will stand on a hot plate or by the oven for the rest of the day and by evening will be luke-warm at best. You will find that it is better in Greece to eat the baked dishes such as *moussaka*, stuffed vegetables, or *pastitsio*, at midday and in the evening order something grilled or fried which will be served hot. In recent years the introduction of the convenient microwave has meant food can now be warmed quickly for the evening meal, but this is really stale midday food warmed over and not that appetizing.

Do not expect food to be rushed steaming hot to your table as the Greeks are not used to eating their food piping hot and do not always understand our continued repetition of the word *zeste* (hot) whenever we are ordering in a taverna. In the more touristy spots food arrives hotter than it used to, but this is the exception rather than the rule. On the other hand do expect most food to be served dressed with olive oil. Everything from salads to roast beef will be seasoned with oil before being brought to the table. Unless you decide you like this method of serving you will need to learn to ask for your food without oil – *ochi lathi*.

When you first go into a taverna do not be confused by the menu. It will probably (if there is one, that is) have printed on it a large variety of food and drink. Some of the items will have prices beside them. These are the ones available that day and the menu should be dated at the top. There will be two prices on the menu, the one on the right proportionately more than the one on the left. The first is the price without service and the second the price with service, but as food always comes with service, you pay the higher price on the right. This means a service charge is included in your bill and consequently a tip is not required.

A word of advice: do not order your food all at once or your main course, side orders and starters will arrive at the table at the same time. Eating is done slowly and leisurely in Greece and it is quite alright to occupy a table all night.

**The menu**

You can start with appetizers. Common appetizers are: *tzatziki* (yoghurt flavoured with grated cucumber and garlic); *taramasalata* (cod roe ground into a paste); aubergine salad; *merithes*, small fried fishes (eaten whole, head and all); *kalamaris* (fried baby squid); peas or green beans in a tomato sauce; and invariably a Greek salad consisting of some or

Butcher with good home-made sausages in Ermoúpolis on Síros

Sign language. Fish and chicken and chips on the menu

following: grilled chops (beef, pork or lamb); grilled fish depending on what the local fishermen have caught; *souvlaki* (pieces of pork or beef on a skewer grilled over charcoal); kebabs which are a bigger version of *souvlaki*, usually with pieces of tomato and onion between the meat; lamb baked in a pastry case; a beef stew (*stifado*) or beef cooked in a garlic sauce (*sofrito*); *moussaka* (Greek shepherd's pie); *pastitsio* (lamb or beef in pasta); barbecued chicken, lamb or beef; spaghetti with a variety of sauces ranging from terrible to passable; meatballs; and probably a variety of leftover baked dishes from the midday meal.

In the larger towns choice will be good and there may be specialities depending on the skill and whims of the cook, but in the smaller islands and villages you must get used to a more limited choice. Chips are served with everything and although delicious when hot (they are usually home-made and not the instant packaged 'French fries'), are not at all appealing when cold.

It is usual to finish a meal with fresh fruit, but occasionally some form of sweet may be offered such as *créme caramel* or ice cream. Cakes, pastries and sweets are more often eaten in a 'cake shop'. Here you will find *baklava* (pastry filled with walnuts and steeped in honey); *loukamathes* (fritters coated in honey); *kadaifi* (nuts and honey in shredded pastry); and the best yoghurt in the world which can be eaten plain or mixed with honey and fruit.

## Wines

Wine has been made and drunk in Greece for centuries and in ancient times was carried to most parts of the known world. It is thought the wine was stored in amphoras and pine resin poured on top to seal them – from this ancient practice it is believed we get the retsina wines which are artificially produced today.

You either like or hate retsina. Do not be put off by the bottled varieties which are much inferior to retsina from the barrel. Retsina is made locally all over Greece and often a café or taverna will be famous not only for its food or company, but also for its retsina.

Locally produced wines, resinated and unresinated, are available in bulk in some places and are served in tavernas by the litre or half litre. They vary a great deal, can be quite palatable, and if awful at least have the merit of being cheap. Do not try to carry them for any distance as they do not usually travel or keep.

At *The Real Greek* restaurant in London the owner has put together a fine list of bottled wines that are reproduced here and would be hard to better. The cooking is good too, with the normally robust Greek cuisine refined and fused into one of the best Greek menus in London (book ahead for a table).

Beer is also brewed in Greece and the common *Heninger*, *Mythos*, and *Amstel* beers are cheap and palatable.

all of the following – tomatoes, onions, green peppers, olives, cucumber, *feta* (sheep's cheese) dressed in oil and oregano.

This can be followed with soup or a vegetable dish: fish, tripe or bean soups are common; vegetables are often stuffed and you will find tomatoes, green peppers and aubergines stuffed with a rice and cheese mixture as well as *dolmades* (stuffed vine leaves often cooked in a tomato sauce mixture). Garlic is a favourite seasoning and is used frequently and liberally. Lemon is probably the second most popular seasoning and you will find it by the side of most of your dishes and in the cooking of everything from egg and lemon soup to the flavouring of rice pudding.

The main course will probably be a choice of the

Besides wine and beer there are several other drinks deserving a mention. Firstly, ouzo which qualifies as the national tipple of Greece. It is similar to French *pastis* and may be drunk with or without water. Greek cognac or brandy is another popular drink and makes a refreshing long drink mixed with Coca-Cola and ice. *Metaxa* and *Botrys* are two of the better known brands. Ouzo and brandy can be bought in bulk from the barrel and are very cheap and not at all inferior when purchased like this. Take along a bottle to a *cava* or wine shop (or in the smaller villages the local grocer or café) and you will be able to get a litre or more of either ouzo or brandy for very little.

### Miscellaneous

There are a few sundry items not often found on the menu but nonetheless an important part of Greek life. First, in the *galaktopolia* or dairies, you will find fresh yoghurt made from cow or sheep milk. The dairy will also probably stock the variety made in Athens and strained so that you believe you are eating not yoghurt, but tasty whipped cream. These shops also have *feta* (a soft cheese made from sheep's milk), local honey and eggs.

In some of the cafés you will see a long homemade sausage cooking on the spit. Made from lamb's offal and cooked with garlic and herbs, it is called *kokoretsi* and is delicious. Technically it is illegal under EU law to make and sell *kokoretsi* as it includes offal not prepared and cooked in the required EU manner, but like some other EU laws, it is disregarded by many.

At every bus station or ferry terminal you will find a kiosk where pork or beef *souvlaki* are soused in lemon juice and herbs and cooked on the spot as a snack. You may also find the Greek hamburger which is pitta bread (unleavened) filled with a *souvlaki*, tomato, onion and a dollop of yoghurt. The kiosk will probably also have cheese pies (*tiropitta*) or spinach pies (*spinakopitta*).

*Kali oretsi – bon appetit!*

# Marine life

The marine life in the Mediterranean is at first disappointing to the yachtsman used to life around the English coast. It is not as prolific or as diverse as you might imagine; there are fewer seabirds, good eating fish are scarce and difficult to catch and in places the sea bottom can be quite bereft of interest compared with, say, the Red Sea or the west coast of France.

There are a number of reasons for the relative paucity of marine life. The first is the non-tidal nature of the sea which means there is not the inter-tidal zone in which a varied and rich amount of life can live and contribute to the whole marine ecosystem and nor are there the bottom currents to stir up the waters of the eastern Mediterranean basin and provide the nutrients that plankton need to feed on. Add to that the fact that the Mediterranean has been fished for longer and more intensively than any other region and you do not have the ideal conditions for marine life to flourish. Historically this is nothing new. The Mediterranean is the watery equivalent of marginal land like the prairies or steppes and has never been rich in sea life. The Romans used to complain about poor fish stocks and bad catches and you can hardly say that their fishing methods and craft were raping the sea. Oddly enough the fabled clarity of the Mediterranean, all that transparent blue and turquoise water, comes from the relative absence of plankton.

In Greece fishing methods like the use of dynamite which began after the First World War have decimated the local ecosystems. Despite the fact that the practice carries heavy penalties and some considerable risk, it still goes on in isolated areas. In many coastal villages you will see a man without a hand or an arm, lost when he miscalculated on the fuse.

Although the marine life is initially disappointing, the yachtsman is in a unique position to discover and explore the life in the eastern Mediterranean. Dolphins, whales, turtles, flying fish, tuna, swordfish and sunfish will be seen in many places and, with a mask and a snorkel, the warm waters invite exploration.

### Whales and dolphins (cetaceans)

Dolphins, sadly, are becoming less common in Greek waters than they were even a few years ago. You will still see dolphins and occasionally a school of dolphins will come up to a yacht and play around it. At night the phosphorescence created by dolphins around a yacht is something marvellous to behold. The numbers of dolphins have decreased for several reasons. Food stocks, normally mackerel and tuna, have decreased. Drift netting, common in Italy and unfortunately recently resumed there, catches dolphins as well as swordfish and tuna. Estimates of the numbers killed in this manner vary, but are thought to be in the thousands rather than hundreds. Lastly pollution in the form of heavy metals, PCBs and other carcinogenic compounds, and spills of toxic chemicals, have caused a form of 'flu' similar to that which killed many seals around British coasts. I can only suggest you support any of those groups fighting for the continued survival of this magnificent mammal which has never harmed humans and, anecdotal trivia aside, is known actively to have aided humans in distress in the water. Renew your subscription to Greenpeace, Friends of the Earth, or the Environmental Investigation Agency.

In antiquity the dolphin was mentioned and often depicted in mosaics. Aristotle and Pliny mentioned it as a friend of man and Herodotus tells of the poet Arion of Lésvos who was thrown overboard by mutinous sailors and rescued by a music-loving dolphin. The modern Greek fisherman is not so fond of the dolphin as his ancestors were, believing it to rob him of fish and there are stories (though I cannot vouch for any of them) that the friendly animals have been killed by fishermen.

Cetaceans are divided into toothed and non-toothed whales. In the eastern Mediterranean most of the cetaceans seen belong to the toothed whales, which are fish-eaters and so possess teeth to grip their prey. To this class belong the porpoise, dolphin, pilot whale and killer whale. The common dolphin (*Delphinus delphis*) will often be seen. Less common are the larger bottle-nosed dolphin (*Tursiops truncatus*) and the common porpoise (*Phocoena phocoena*). The pilot whale (*Globicephala melaena*) is fairly common and grows up to 8·5m long. The bottle-nosed whale (*Hyperoodon ampullatus*), Risso's dolphin (*Grampus griseus*) and the killer whale (*Orcinus orca*) have been reported in the eastern Mediterranean.

### Monk seals

The Mediterranean monk seal, *Monachus monachus*, is numbered amongst the twelve most endangered animals in the world and is the rarest species of seal left. It is specific to the warm waters of the Mediterranean, although small numbers are found on the Atlantic coast of Morocco. There are estimated to be only 500 to 800 of these animals left, with approximately half the population in Greece.

One of the big problems is the encroachment of tourism into the habitat occupied by the seals. Illegal spear-fishing using subaqua equipment is eroding the food supply – visitors have been cited as the chief culprits and there have been several convictions, but the blame does not lie solely here. Small powerboats and inflatables with powerful outboards exploit quiet places and the coastal caves where these retiring animals live. Those on the water and the land can help by keeping away from coastal caves and rocky coastlines and at all times should avoid making too much noise – the seals are easily frightened. Any illegal fishing whether by subaqua divers or dynamiting should be reported to the port police or any other authority.

## Good eating fish

Although Greece is fished out to some extent, there are still sufficient good eating fish remaining. If you despair of catching any then treat yourself in a taverna. The fish is mostly grilled and arrives without a sauce or other trimmings. Particularly good eating are the following:

*Tuna (Tonnos)* Frequents northern waters in the summer and travels south to the Mediterranean in winter. The white flesh is a little oily but delicious.

*Swordfish (Xsifia)* As above and just as delicious. In years past the swordfish was not considered a good fish to eat and local lore reckoned if you ate swordfish you went mad. Times have changed and now Greeks consider it one of the best eating fish.

*Grouper (Sfiritha)* Prefers sandy or rocky bottoms and you may be lucky enough to get one in the less populated areas. Pleasant white flesh.

*Red mullet (Barbouni)* Tasty white flesh but full of small bones.

*Bream (Fagri, Sinagritha)* Tasty and not too bony.

*Whitebait (Merithes)* Often served as a starter, the little fish are cooked and eaten whole.

*Octopus (Octopothi)* Sometimes a bit tough but always tasty. Pickled octopus is delicious.

*Squid (Kalamari)* Normally deep-fried. Delicious.

*Prawns (Garides)* Often expensive and not always fresh. Buy them off a fishing boat and cook them yourself for the best results.

*Crayfish (Astakós)* Just as delicious as lobster. Normally boiled or grilled.

## Greek fishing methods

When a fishing boat is sighted a good look-out must be kept for floats and lines in the water. Some of the fishing methods could be dangerous to a yacht if it is not understood what is going on. The following methods are used:

1. Trawling either singly or in pairs.
2. Purse seine netting, in Greek *grigia*, in which a large caïque, a smaller net-*caïque* and two to four small *caïques* or light-floats are used. The smaller *caïques* and/or light floats are set adrift with powerful gas or arc lamps to attract fish to the surface. The large *caïque* and its helper then lay the net in a semicircle around the fish and haul them in. Large catches of mackerel and sardines are made. The gas lamps are conspicuous from a long distance off.
3. Netting off the land. A long rope is run out to a net and then to a *caïque* which circles to enclose any fish. Particularly dangerous to a yacht as the rope is generally just under the water between the *caïque* and the shore.
4. A set net in a bay or near the shore. Usually weighted to be below the surface although sometimes a surface net is laid.
5. *Lampera*. A gas lamp on a *caïque* is used to attract fish which are speared or hooked. Often used for

octopus. The *lampera* method can be confusing at night as the light bobbing up and down on the swell can easily be mistaken for a navigation light and, human beings being what they, the longer you look at it, the more convinced will you become that it is the Fl.2s you have been searching for.

6. Long-lining from a *caïque*: the lines are attached to a float which is allowed to drift.

## Fish farms

With Greece's entry into the EU grants were made available for all sorts of enterprises. One of these was for the establishment of fish farms and in recent years they have proliferated everywhere. Unfortunately for the yachtsman the requirements for a fish farm are much the same as those for a good anchorage – shelter from strong winds and reasonable depths to anchor the farm in. Consequently a number of coves and bays formerly frequented only by yachtsmen and fishing boats have now sprouted fish farms which may obstruct much of the cove or bay.

In most places the operators of the fish farm are content to allow yachts to use the anchorage if there is room, but in some places the operators have expressed disapproval and actively chased yachts out of anchorages. The legality of this is somewhat dubious since it is impossible to own anything below the high-water mark. Even the late Onassis and Niarchos did not own that section of the beach or the sea bed below the high-water mark on their private islands (much to their consternation), so unless legislation has been passed exempting fish farms, it may be illegal. Certainly town councils in the vicinity of some fish farms have had them removed and others have denied operators permission to set up.

I appreciate that fish farms are a possible solution to the natural poverty in fish in the eastern Mediterranean, but such a programme needs to be carefully administered and the operators properly trained. I am sceptical of the ability of many of the operators to safely handle the restricted chemicals necessary to eliminate disease amongst the intensively farmed fish. I suggest that you enquire where the fish in a restaurant has come from before ordering it, especially if it has a muddy taste.

*Note* Fish farms must be moved at regular intervals because of the build-up of detritus under the farm. Consequently the location of fish farms on the plans may vary from that shown and should be interpreted as a general guide to the vicinity of a fish farm, not a precise position.

## Pollution

Being a closed sea it was inevitable that as the population around the shores grew, so pollution in the Mediterranean increased. The less densely-populated eastern Mediterranean is comparatively less polluted than the western half, but around the heavily-populated Saronic Gulf and Thessaloniki Gulf there is some pollution. Around Athens it has been estimated there is more than 50% of Greece's industry and the air and water quality suffers badly because of this. Down by the Ionian Islands there is also some hydrocarbon pollution from the numerous oil-tankers cleaning out their tanks after leaving the Adriatic.

Up until recently nothing was being done about the increasing pollution in the Mediterranean, but in 1975 the United Nations Environment Programme decided to get together the culturally and politically diverse countries around the Mediterranean and work out a programme to clean up the sea. In 1980 all the countries (except Albania) agreed to a ten billion dollar plan to go ahead. Some progress has been made since then, but much remains to be done and it may be that the political will to do something has weakened and that it is up to environmental pressure groups to force the pace of the clean-up programme.

Part of the antipollution plan will probably affect yachtsmen in the future. No thinking yachtsman should ever dump garbage in the sea – especially plastic. In harbour, regulations already exist by which a yachtsman can be fined up to 10,000Dx for pumping out a toilet or dumping waste oil overboard, although these regulations are not rigidly enforced. All charter boats must now be fitted with holding tanks and these should be used when in harbour and pumped out only when well out to sea. It is likely that in the future antipollution measures affecting the yachtsman will be introduced and this is only right. The yachtsman may curse the extra cost, but must acknowledge the necessity of such regulations when so much of the Mediterranean, and for that matter the other seas and oceans of the world, is threatened by pollution of one sort or another.

**Amended Port Authority extract on pollution**

The protection of the environment and particularly of the marine environment is a basic obligation of all concerned due to the known consequences to public health and to the economy of this country.

Garbage, including all non-biodegradable products, when put into the sea, may pose a serious threat to marine life and degrade the aesthetic view of the beaches in the areas affected. In order to reduce pollution by garbage generated on board vessels a new international law came into effect on 31.12.88.

These regulations, MARPOL 73/78 convention annex Y, are applied to all vessels concerning the dumping of garbage overboard. The provisions govern the following:

*Plastics* Any disposal is prohibited.
*Floating* Disposal is prohibited in a distance of less than 25NM offshore.
*Paper, rags, glass, metal* Disposal is prohibited in a distance of less than 12NM offshore.
*Food waste not ground* As above.
*Food waste ground and in solution* Disposal is prohibited in a distance of less than 3NM offshore.

Following the above-mentioned legal requirement please make sure that on-board handling of garbage is carried out in the proper manner. The port authority is sensitive to the protection of the marine environment and in cases where discharges of garbage at sea are substantiated severe penalties will be imposed.

**Note** MARPOL requirements can be applied to pleasure craft and some yachts have been fined substantial amounts for indiscriminate disposal of garbage around the coast.

## Dangerous marine animals

In the Mediterranean there are no more dangerous marine animals than you would encounter off the English coast, but the warm sea temperatures mean that you are in the water more often and therefore more likely to encounter these animals.

**Sharks** Probably the greatest fear of a swimmer, yet in all probability the least to be feared. Films such as *Jaws* and *Blue Water, White Death* have produced a phobia amongst swimmers that is out of all proportion to the menace. After many years of sailing around the eastern Mediterranean I have positively identified a shark in the water on only three occasions. Fishermen occasionally bring in sharks from the deep water – usually the mackerel shark or sand shark. I have not been able to establish one fatality from a shark attack in Greece and so far as I know the total recorded number of fatalities for the Mediterranean is six.

By-the-wind-sailor
*Velella velella*

*Rhizostoma pulmo*

Portuguese man-o'-war
*Physalia physalis*

Compass jellyfish
*Chryassaora hysoscella*

*Pelagia noctiluca*

**Moray eels** Of the family *Muraenidae*, these eels are quite common in the eastern Mediterranean and are often caught by fishermen. They inhabit holes and crevices in rocks and can bite and tear if molested. Usually they will retire and are not aggressive unless wounded or sorely provoked.

**Octopus** Are very shy and do not attack. They have much more to fear from man than man from them.

**Stingrays** The European stingray (*Dasytatis pastinaca*) is common in the Mediterranean. It inhabits shallow waters, partially burying itself in the sand. If it is trodden on accidentally it will lash out with its tail and bury a spine in the offending foot. Venom is injected which produces severe local pain, sweating, vomiting and rapid heart beat, but rarely death. Soak the foot in very hot water and seek medical help.

**Weeverfish** Members of the family *Trachinidae*. The two most common are the great weever (*Trachinus draco*) and lesser weever (*Trachinus vipera*). The dorsal and opercular fins contain venom spines. When disturbed or annoyed the Weever will erect its dorsal fin and attack. The venom injected produces instant pain which spreads to other parts of the body and is very painful. The victim may lose consciousness and death sometimes occurs. There are no known antidotes. Bathe the wound in hot water and seek medical help as soon as possible.

*Note* When walking in the water where stingrays or weevers are thought to be, wear sand-shoes and shuffle the feet along the bottom. Do not handle dead weevers or stingrays.

**Jellyfish** Of all the animals described, the ones you are most likely to encounter are jellyfish. At certain times of the year and in certain places there will be considerable numbers of jellyfish in the water. All jellyfish sting, for this is the way they immobilize their prey, but some species have more powerful stings than others and consequently deserve greater respect.

*Aurelia aurita* The common jellyfish. It is a transparent dome-shaped body with four purple-violet crescents grouped around the centre. Transparent or light violet mouth arms hang below. Up to 25cm in diameter. A light contact with the stings is something like a nettle, but prolonged contact can hurt.

*Pelagia noctiluca* A mushroom-shaped jellyfish up to 10cm in diameter. It is easily identified, being light brown-yellow in colour and covered in 'warts'. It has long trailing tentacles and can inflict severe and painful stings.

*Cyanea lamarckii* A blue-violet saucer-shaped jellyfish up to 30cm across. It can be identified by the frilly mass of mouth arms underneath. It has long tentacles which can inflict severe and painful stings. There is a brown variety (*Cyanea capillata*) which can grow up to 50cm in diameter.

*Charybdea marsupialis* Mediterranean sea-wasp. A transparent, yellow-red box-shaped 'umbrella' up to 6cm high. Rarely seen but can inflict severe and painful stings.

*Physalia physalis* Portuguese man-o'-war. Has a large conspicuous float (pneumatophore) above water growing to 30cm long and 10cm wide. Below it streams very long tentacles. Rarely seen but can inflict dangerous stings.

*Chryssaora hysoscella* Compass jellyfish. Common browny-biscuity coloured 'umbrella' up to 30 cm in diameter with brown patches and radiating 'stripes' from the centre. Frilly lobes and tentacles. Can inflict stings although these are usually not severe.

*Velella velella* By-the-wind-sailor. Flattened oval disc with a gas-filled central float. Silvery float with blue and purple disc and tentacles underneath. In places you can see quite a few of these and they can inflict a severe and painful sting. I've always quite liked their evolutionary stance of having a curved float so that they sail on a beam reach rather than being blown downwind with all the other jellyfish.

*Rhizostoma pulmo* Dome-shaped blue-white jellyfish up to 90cm in diameter. Its mouth arms are fused in a grey-green 'cauliflower' mass below the body. It has no long tentacles and is not known as a vicious stinger.

There are no known antidotes to jellyfish stings, but there are a number of ways of obtaining relief. Diluted ammonium hydroxide, sodium bicarbonate, olive oil, sugar and ethyl alcohol have been used. A tip which I have not tried but which sounds promising is to use a meat tenderizer, which apparently breaks down the protein base of the venom. Gloves should be worn when hauling up an anchor in jellyfish-infested water as the tentacles, especially those of *Pelagia*, can stick to the anchor chain.

**Bristleworms** In some locations numbers of bristleworms, probably of the family *Nereidae*, will be found. They are black and may grow up to 25cm long. The *setae* can produce a mild irritation similar to a stinging nettle if touched.

**Sea urchins** In some places on rocky coasts large colonies of sea urchins (*Paracentrotus lividus* and *Arbacia lixula*) will be found. While they do not have a venom apparatus, the spines penetrate and break off when the urchin is trodden on and are very painful. Care must be taken not to get an infection.

# History

## Sailing in Greece

When you think of Greece you think of the sea and the islands. The bowl of the Aegean Sea is dotted with islands, hundreds of islands with comparatively small distances between them, so that navigation is a matter of looking for the next island and heading in that direction. In this way it is possible to island-hop from one side of the Aegean to the other. Add to this seascape a regular summer wind blowing steadily from a northerly direction and you have the ideal climate for the evolution of sailing craft and associated skills. For this reason the development of sailing craft occurred relatively early on in this part of the world and until the introduction of petrol and diesel motors, sail was the principal method of moving people and goods.

In this setting it would be surprising if the indigenous folklore and mythology were not concerned with the sea and ships. Homer wrote the first great epic of sailors and shipwrecks in the *Odyssey*. The saga of Jason and the Argonauts in pursuit of the Golden Fleece added another classic to bedtime reading. In this atmosphere of sailing craft and adventure it is surprising that there are so few records of sailing for pleasure. Pausanias records that in Ermioni during the festival of Dionysus 'they hold a musical contest in his honour and offer prizes for a diving competition and boat race.' There is some difficulty with the translation of the word for boat race and it may mean a swimming race, so even this brief mention of boating for pleasure is suspect.

Not until the Roman occupation of Greece do we find a concrete reference to sailing for pleasure in the poems of Catullus. Catullus is little known today, but in his time instigated something of a revolution in poetic style. A contemporary of Cicero, he moved in high government circles and is

### The voyage of the Heroes

In 1984 author Tim Severin set out from Volos (ancient Iolcos) to trace the path sailed by Jason and the Argonauts in their search for the Golden Fleece. The craft sailed by Tim Severin and his crew was a twenty-oared scouting galley, a replica of the sort of craft that would have been around in Homeric times. The galley crossed the northern Aegean in May and passed through the Dardanelles to arrive in Istanbul in June. From here it passed through the Bosphorus to the Black Sea and voyaged along its north coast to the mouth of the Rhion in Soviet Georgia, the Land of the Golden Fleece.

In 1985 the same craft investigated the wanderings of Odysseus in the Mediterranean on his way home from the Trojan War. This is the first time a practical experiment to trace the routes of these two early voyages has been carried out and Severin came to some unorthodox conclusions about the voyage of Odysseus. Formerly it was assumed Odysseus was blown around the Mediterranean to such diverse places as Libya, Tunisia, Gibraltar, Malta and Italy, but according to Severin Odysseus took the prudent and logical route home to Ithaca, and all of the places mentioned in Homer's *Odyssey* can be identified in Greece. For instance the one-eyed Cyclops historians assumed to have lived in Sicily can be identified with tales of triamates in Crete. It is a startling hypothesis that anyone sailing in Greek waters will find fascinating. I leave it up to you to determine which holds up best: Severin's hypothesis or the more conventional interpretation of the voyage of Odysseus.

The vessel for the voyage of the heroes, a replica of a Homeric scouting galley, was built in Spétsai according to ancient techniques using mortice and tenon joints to join the planks of Sámos pine. The galley is 16m (54ft) LOA, 2.85m (9ft 4ins) beam, and 0.30m (1ft) draught. It carries a square sail of approximately 300 sq. ft. and is steered with twin steering oars over the stern. The crew was a polyglot bunch that at one time or other contained Greeks, Turks, Russians, a Bulgarian, a Syrian, an Australian, Americans and Norwegians as well as English and Irish members.

believed to have entertained Caesar several times. In addition to his literary credits, Catullus had a small sailing boat constructed for his own pleasure, and in this craft he achieved some notable passages. After visiting his brother in the Troad he sailed across the Aegean and up the Adriatic to the river Po. He sailed up the Po as far as he could and then hauled the boat out and transported it overland to Lake Garda. Catullus retired to a villa on the shores of Lake Garda, spending his last years writing poetry and sailing with friends around the lake.

Not until the 19th and 20th centuries do we know that pleasure craft again sailed around the Greek islands, although during the interim there must have been such craft around. In the late 19th and early 20th centuries gentlemen and their yachts cruised around the Mediterranean, often combining their sailing with shooting expeditions or amateur archaeology. In those days a yacht meant a small ship by today's standards. Some of them still survive – marvellous creations of the boatbuilder's art which would cost a small fortune to duplicate today and must cost the same to maintain. Some are available for charter, but not by the impecunious.

Until thirty years ago Greece was relatively unknown to the cruising yachtsman. A few yachts cruised around the islands simply for the fun of it and a few took charter parties around the islands. To read an account of sailing in Greek waters written then is much like reading an account today of sailing in the Pacific – it all seemed a long way away and somehow exotic. Today, the improved design of small yachts has made the long passages possible and it is now commonplace to see yachtsmen in all manner and size of craft sailing in Greece.

## General

Most people, like myself, arrive in Greece without the benefit of a classical education. We may have heard of Homer, Herodotus, Thucydides, Plato, Aristotle, Pausanias, Livy, Pliny and Catullus and we may even have read some of their works, but we do not know them in the way that schoolboys of old did. The glories of Greece, the might of Rome, the splendour of Byzantium, the atrocities of the Saracens and Turks, the romantic passions of Byron and other Philhellenes we may know of only superficially. In Greece my outstanding difficulty was to put the places inhabited by the ancients, the monuments, castles and forts, into some sort of historical order. The following brief history will sort out some of that chaos, but for more detail and for scholarly wrangling over precise dates and alternative explanations the reader must turn elsewhere.

### Pre-Cycladic times

Little is known of early Neolithic life in the Aegean. A number of Aegean islands were inhabited, and people must somehow have travelled between them to get there in the first place. Mílos was of considerable importance because of the obsidian

The lonely hermitage on Cape Malea

(volcanic glass) found there which was used to make knives, razors, spears and so on.

### Cycladic civilisation

By about 4000BC Neolithic colonists were living on Crete and the Cyclades. It flourished mostly as a farming and fishing community, and artwork in stone, clay, obsidian and later metal has been discovered. The civilisation produced a distinctive form of geometric sculpture which has been found on the Greek mainland and in Asia Minor as well as in graves in the Cyclades. Some of the statuettes are of harp players and the civilisation has been nicknamed 'harpist' after these. From widespread distribution of the geometric statuettes it is believed that sailing craft regularly plied across the Aegean and even as far as France and Spain.

### Minoan civilisation (2000BC–1450BC)

Around 2000BC new peoples bringing with them the advances of the Bronze Age filtered into the Aegean from the Balkans and Turkey. They brought not only the art of working in bronze, but also the Mesopotamian pottery wheel and the eastern Mother Goddess. The Minoan empire based on Crete and Thíra expanded and flourished until it was the dominant civilisation in the eastern Mediterranean.

It was a remarkably advanced and peaceful culture. Knossos on Crete was not a fort but a palace which was both beautiful and functional; the Minoan art form worked into frescoes, pottery, and jewellery was both intricate and graceful and compares with any modern pottery and jewellery; and the Minoan fleet traded all round the Mediterranean and established order and peace under the aegis of the Mother Goddess. The civilisation ended abruptly, probably with the cataclysmic eruption of Thíra round 1450BC – one of the biggest eruptions known to have occurred on the Earth. The tidal waves, earthquakes and ash destroyed the Minoan civilisation overnight.

## Mycenaeans, Dorians and Phoenicians (1500BC–1100BC)

With the demise of the Minoans, the Mycenaeans based at Mycenae on the Peloponnisos became the power to be reckoned with in the Aegean. These are the Achaeans of Homeric fame and were dominant from 1300BC–1100BC. The Mycenaeans were supplanted by the Dorians who invaded from the north and brought with them the Iron Age. For some two centuries between 1100BC and 900BC Greece lay in the grip of an era which is known now as the Greek 'Dark Age'. In this period writing and painting disappeared. The Dorians settled around the eastern Sporades and Dodecanese, while the Phoenicians from the southern shores of the Mediterranean took control of the sea-routes. By 800BC a distinct language was emerging from the chaos of the 'Dark Age'.

## Greek civilisation (800BC–27BC)

What we know as the Classical and Hellenic periods began about 800BC and lasted until the Romans arrived. This era saw the birth of the city-state (*polis*) and for this period there was never a united Greece, more a collection of city-states – some of which were more powerful and existed in alliance with others. Colonies were established all around the Mediterranean and Black Sea.

Homer, Sappho, Alcaeus, and Archilochus belong to the early Greek period. Around 500BC the first threat to the Greeks came from the east when the Persians invaded and captured Naxos. Nine years later they were back and the famous battles of Marathon and Salamís were fought. The latter destroyed the Persian fleet and removed the Persian threat. Athens, the most powerful city-state, formed the Delian league based around the island of Delos to which all other city-states contributed and so Athens, through the league, controlled Greece.

At various times some of the city-states fell out with Athens, but not until the Peloponnesian War (431–404BC) was Athens really threatened. Sparta was the eventual winner, though its influence was not as great as Athens' had been. The islands on the eastern seaboard, Rhodes, Kós, Khíos and Lésvos, became powers unto themselves. In 330BC, Philip II of Macedon conquered most of Greece and later his remarkable son, Alexander the Great, completed the job. Greece continued to prosper, but the country was gradually coming under Roman domination.

## The Romans (27BC–AD330)

By 27BC Greece was part of the Roman Empire. For nearly four centuries Rome controlled Greece, but for the most part had little cultural influence on it. Greek remained the official language and most cities were allowed to remain autonomous. Little by little Christianity filtered into Greece and merged with the ancient rituals and beliefs. The greatest change came with the conversion of the Emperor Constantine to Christianity and the beginning of the Byzantine period.

On many of the islands the main settlement, the *chora*, was built on the highest part of the island so that you could see the pirates coming and at least have some time to get out of the way with your daughters and valuables. This is Skála on Astipálaia

## Byzantium (330–1204)

The foundation of Constantinople and the rise of Christianity marks the rise of the first Christian Empire. In 6AD numerous tribes from the north, the Slavs, Avars, Huns and Bulgars, raided Greece, although the forces of Byzantium afforded protection to many cities. Nonetheless many islands were depopulated and towns contracted in size. Later the Saracens were active in the Aegean and some islands were to become completely deserted. The Saracens completely occupied Crete for some time (810–961). The Emperor Nicephorus regained control of some of the islands, but the power of the Byzantine Empire was waning. The churches, particularly the mosaics and frescoes within, are the most enduring monument of Byzantium.

## The Franks and Venetians (1204–1550)

In 1204 the Fourth Crusade sacked Constantinople and the Byzantine Empire was divided up between Venice and numerous other Italian adventurers. In the eastern Sporades the Gattelusis and Giustianinis, on Naxos Marco Sanudo, and in the Peloponnisos Villehardouin, were the most notable duchies established. On Rhodes, the Knights of St. John established a castle stronghold which they lost to the Turks in 1522. During this period the Venetians established castles and forts at the principal ports along the Aegean trade routes. Many of these strongholds were held well into the Turkish occupation of Greece.

## The Turkish occupation (1460–1830)

In 1453 the Turks took Constantinople and ended the rule of Byzantium. By the end of the 16th century most of Greece was under Turkish rule. The Turkish occupation was partly one of oppression and neglect, although the horrors of Turkish rule have often been exaggerated. In the 17th century the Venetians regained some possessions in the west and English adventurers travelled around Greece collecting the antiquities which can now be seen in British museums. Few remains of the Turkish occupation are to be seen today as after the War of Independence most of the minarets and mosques were torn down, except in Crete and the eastern Sporades.

### The war of independence (1822–1830)

In 1822 the Turks massacred 25,000 people on Khíos and so aroused Greek passions that many parts of Greece revolted against their Turkish masters. Hydra and Spétsai greatly aided the war effort by committing their fleets to the cause, and the war was won when the combined English, Russian and French fleets bottled up the Turkish fleet in Navarino and destroyed it.

### The twentieth century

The newly born republic got off to a shaky start and after a series of assassinations the West put a Bavarian prince on the throne. He was unpopular and was replaced by George I from Denmark who proved to be acceptable. Greece gradually acquired more territory, Thessaly and the Epirus in 1881 and the northern Aegean islands after the Balkan Wars in 1913. The Greeks fought on the allied side in the First World War and with the defeat of the Turks on the Axis side embarked on a disastrous campaign to acquire territory in Asia Minor. When the Greeks were finally driven out the Turkish population remaining in Greece was exchanged for Greeks in Turkey.

Greece fought with the Allies in the Second World War and obtained the Dodecanese at the end of the war. Greece had attempted to remain neutral at the onset of the war, but when Mussolini proposed a coalition with the then Prime Minister of Greece, Metaxa, he declined it with a curt telegram which simply read *Ochi* (No). British, New Zealand and Australian troops fought in Greece, but the Germans overwhelmed them and occupied it until 1944.

After the war a bloody civil war split the country until 1947, when a series of conservative governments ruled until the notorious junta of the Colonels in 1967 which ushered in seven years of autocratic and repressive rule. Democracy returned in 1974 with Karamanlis. The first socialist government, PASOK, under Papandreou, was elected in 1981. In 1986 Greece joined the European Union.

# Technical information

## Climate and weather

I will make only some general comments here as there is a detailed description of the weather patterns for a particular area at the beginning of each chapter.

### Wind strength

All wind strengths are described as a force on the Beaufort Scale.

### Winds

In the summer months the winds in the Ionian and Aegean are predominantly from the north. In the Aegean the constancy of the northerly winds in the summer has been noted from ancient times when they were called the *etesians* from *etos* (annual). Today they are commonly called by the Turkish name – the *meltemi*. This wind begins blowing in June and early July, reaches full strength in July and August, and dies off at the end of September and early October. In the northern Aegean the *meltemi* blows from the NE, in the middle Aegean from the north, and in the southern Aegean from the NW–WNW: in effect the wind describes an arc from the NE through to NW from the northern Aegean to the southern Aegean. In strength it varies from Force 4 to Force 7–8. The *meltemi* blows less strongly in the north and south than it does in the central Aegean.

The *meltemi* is a consequence of a pressure gradient between a low-pressure area over Pakistan (the Asian monsoon low) which extends its influence as far as the eastern Mediterranean, and the high-pressure area over the Azores which affects the western Mediterranean. The pressure gradient between these two stable pressure areas produces the constant northerlies in the summer.

Where the *meltemi* is not found or when it is not blowing a sea breeze predominates, though the direction is much affected by the local topography. For the most part the sea breeze is from the SW/S/SE.

In the spring and autumn the *sirocco* may blow strongly from the S. Sometimes it may blow up to gale force and exceptionally to more. In May 2001 a *sirocco* blew through the Aegean reaching Force 10 at Paros and blowing several yachts ashore. A *sirocco* will often kick in with little advance warning from weather forecasts.

In the winter the pressure gradients over the eastern Mediterranean are not pronounced at all and the winds are not from any constant direction. An almost equal proportion of northerly and southerly winds can be expected. Gales in the winter result from small depressions moving in an easterly direction, either southeastward towards Cyprus or northeastward to the Black Sea. Although these depressions are usually of small dimensions they can give rise to violent winds. In the winter of 1979–80 one such storm was recorded at Force 10–11 and in Corfu a yacht was blown off its cradle in an exposed yard. The depressions can develop rapidly and are often difficult to track as they move rapidly and then stop before moving off rapidly again. Depressions often linger in the Ionian Sea and the southern Aegean.

### Fog

Fog is very rare. It has been reported in the winter and spring, with the highest incidence recorded in January at the entrance to the Dardanelles (3·8 per cent) and in Saronikos Kólpos (2·6 per cent). In all my years of sailing around Greek waters in every

**LOCAL NAMES FOR THE WINDS:**
Vorias, Boreas, Tramonata: *North winds*
Vorias Anatolikos, Gregorio, Grego: *NE winds*
Anatolikos, Levante, Ageliotes: *East winds*
Notios Anatolikos, Sirocco, Souroko, Euros: *SE winds*
Notios Ostra: *South winds*
Notios Ditikos, Garbis: *SW winds*
Pounente, Ditikos, Zephyros: *West winds*
Vorias Ditikos, Maistro, Schiron: *NW winds*
Etesians, Meltemi: *Northerly winds*

PREVAILING SUMMER WINDS
PRINCIPAL SURFACE CURRENTS

### WINDS AND CURRENTS

month of the year, I have encountered fog only rarely.

### Radiation fog

In some areas, especially the northern Ionian and northern Greece, there can be radiation fog in the early morning when conditions are right. This fog will usually be coastal and rarely reaches more than a mile to seaward. The fog has normally burned off by early morning, but in exceptional circumstances may linger to midday.

### Visibility

In the summer, dust particles suspended in the air may reduce visibility to as little as 2 miles, but rarely to less.

### Thunderstorms

These occur most frequently in the spring and autumn and are often accompanied by a squall. They are usually of short duration and are over in one to three hours. The distribution of thunderstorms is reported to vary over the mainland and the islands: thunderstorms are more frequent over the mainland in the spring and autumn and over the islands in the winter.

### Waterspouts

Waterspouts have been reported in some areas in the winter and the spring. Reliable reports of waterspouts have come mostly from the northern Ionian and Saronic. Areas known to be affected are the entrance to Patraikos Kólpos, the channel between Cephalonia and Zákinthos, the northern and eastern side of Corfu and the area around Ídhra and Spetsai. There are certainly other areas prone to waterspouts, but there is a dearth of reliable reports. One story I recently heard was of a yacht knocked down and partially flooded in the sea area between Ídhra and the mainland. It would have been interesting to know if the water was fresh, as waterspouts typically release large amounts of fresh water at the base of the column.

### Humidity

The relative humidity is low in the eastern Mediterranean. At 1400 local time the average value in winter is 50–75% and in summer 35–55%.

### Sea temperature

The monthly average values vary considerably. In the winter (February) it is 10°C in the north and 16°C in the south. In the summer (August) it is 23°C in the north and 25°C in the south.

### Cloud

In the summer cloud is rare. Over the land typical fairweather cauliflower cumulus will form as the day progresses, but unless any weather systems are

## WIND DIRECTION AND FREQUENCY

*Note* For 0800 and 1400 the two most common directions are given with the relevant frequencies.

**At Corfu**

| | frequency 0800 | | frequency 1400 | | Calms |
|------|-----------|------|-----------|------|-------|
| Jan | E-SE/30% | N-NE/17% | E-SE/38% | N-NE/16% | 27% |
| Feb | E-SE/26% | var | E-SE/38% | NW/13% | 21% |
| Mar | SE/19% | var | E-SE/40% | NW/11% | 15% |
| Apr | SE/12% | var | E-SE/37% | NW/15% | 17% |
| May | SE/10% | var | E-SE/29% | NW/13% | 17% |
| Jun | NW/12% | var | NW/29% | SE/20% | 15% |
| Jul | NW/14% | var | NW/32% | NE/21% | 10% |
| Aug | NW/12% | var | NW/36% | NW/16% | 14% |
| Sep | SE/13% | var | SE/25% | NW/23% | 15% |
| Oct | SE/18% | var | SE/26% | NW/14% | 26% |
| Nov | SE/25% | var | SE/32% | var | 26% |
| Dec | SE/25% | var | SE/33% | var | 23% |

**At Athens**

| | frequency 0800 | | frequency 1400 | | Calms |
|------|-----------|------|-----------|------|-------|
| Jan | NE/29% | N/16% | N-NE/37% | S-SW/35% | 9% |
| Feb | NE/24% | N/20% | N-NE/40% | S-SW/38% | 8% |
| Mar | NE/20% | N/14% | S-SW/43% | N-NE/27% | 5% |
| Apr | N-NE/18% | S-SW/18% | S/35% | SW/26% | 5% |
| May | S-SW/27% | N-NE/17% | S-SW/58% | NE/17% | 5% |
| Jun | N-NE/29% | S-SW/12% | S-SW/51% | NE/23% | 2% |
| Jul | N-NE/33% | SW/7% | N-NE/43% | S-SW/39% | 1% |
| Aug | N-NE/35% | SW/6% | N-NE/36% | S-SW/32% | 3% |
| Sep | N-NE/36% | var | N-NE/42% | S-SW/37% | 5% |
| Oct | N-NE/28% | var | S-SW/51% | N-NE/27% | 3% |
| Nov | N-NE/39% | var | N-NE/34% | S-SW/28% | 20% |
| Dec | N-NE/34% | var | S-SW/37% | N-NE/36% | 11% |

**At Rhodes**

| | frequency 0800 | | frequency 1400 | | Calms |
|------|-----------|------|-----------|------|-------|
| Jan | N-NW/32% | SE/24% | N-NW/37% | S-SE/32% | 6% |
| Feb | N-NW/37% | S-SE/24% | N-NW/38% | SE/19% | 4% |
| Mar | W-NW/39% | SE/15% | W-NW/44% | S-SE/29% | 6% |
| Apr | W-NW/50% | SE/14% | W-NW/53% | SE/16% | 4% |
| May | W-NW/65% | SE/10% | W-NW/67% | SE/13% | 6% |
| Jun | W-NW/81% | SW/10% | W-NW/81% | SW/12% | 2% |
| Jul | W-NW/73% | SW/14% | W-NW/71% | SW/23% | 3% |
| Aug | W-NW/84% | SW/12% | W-NW/83% | SW/12% | 1% |
| Sep | W-NW/75% | var | W-NW/78% | var | 3% |
| Oct | W-NW/58% | var | W-NW/55% | SE/16% | 7% |
| Nov | W-NW/36% | SE/14% | W-NW/45% | SE/20% | 9% |
| Dec | S-SE/40% | W-NW/25% | S-SE/50% | W-NW/28% | 9% |

## TEMPERATURE AND PRECIPITATION (AT ATHENS)

| | Av max °C | Av min °C | Highest recorded | Relative humidity | Days 0·1mm rain | Sea temp °C |
|------|-----------|-----------|------------------|-------------------|-----------------|-------------|
| Jan | 13 | 6 | 21 | 62% | 16 | 13 |
| Feb | 14 | 7 | 23 | 57% | 11 | 12 |
| Mar | 16 | 8 | 28 | 54% | 11 | 13 |
| Apr | 20 | 11 | 32 | 48% | 9 | 14 |
| May | 25 | 16 | 36 | 47% | 8 | 15 |
| Jun | 30 | 20 | 42 | 39% | 4 | 18 |
| Jul | 33 | 23 | 42 | 34% | 2 | 22 |
| Aug | 33 | 23 | 43 | 34% | 3 | 24-25 |
| Sep | 29 | 19 | 38 | 42% | 4 | 24 |
| Oct | 24 | 15 | 37 | 52% | 8 | 23 |
| Nov | 19 | 12 | 28 | 56% | 12 | 20 |
| Dec | 15 | 8 | 22 | 63% | 15 | 16 |

around there is seldom any other cloud. In the winter there is more cloud in the northerly regions and the Ionian than in the more southerly regions.

### Swell

Although there is never the large swell encountered in the Atlantic, at times winds from the west and south can build up a large swell. The seas in the Mediterranean with any winds are much shorter, steeper and more powerful than seas around, for instance, the English Channel. Going to windward in a Force 5–6 is a very wet and uncomfortable process.

### Currents

In the eastern Mediterranean there is roughly an anticlockwise current: this flows towards the north up the coast of Asia Minor and then turns to flow towards the west and southwest in the north and middle Aegean before turning to flow towards the northwest in the Ionian close to the Greek coast. The many islands and channels in Greek waters means that this flow can be diverted, so that in places the current flows in a completely opposite direction to the direction of the general flow. Wherever possible I mention particular currents with the description of a specific channel or sea area.

### Sea levels

In most of the eastern Mediterranean the sea level is more influenced by the wind than the tide. The barometric pressure also influences the sea level. With a high barometric pressure and an offshore wind the sea level is lowered, and conversely with a low barometric pressure and an onshore wind the sea level is raised.

### Tides

The spring rise of tides varies from 10 centimetres to 0·8m (2·5ft). The greatest spring rise is in Pagasitikós Kólpos (Gulf of Volos) and Evvoïkós Kólpos (Evia Gulf). Tidal streams are weak in Greece except in the narrow channel between Evia and the Greek mainland where at springs it may reach 7 knots at Khalkís.

For those interested there are a number of software programmes that include data for some Greek ports. These programmes all use standard port offsets and the reliability for Greek waters is dubious to say the least. If you want to see what is available there is a free software package called *WXTide32* which has port offsets for Greece. I suggest doing a general search on the internet as it is can be downloaded from a number of sources.

### Routes

The constancy of the summer wind from the north makes the planning routes quite straightforward. In the spring a yacht should keep to the north and plan to go south and east with the summer northerlies. It can then return to the north and west in the autumn.

At the beginning of each chapter there is a brief section on routes for that area and routes to and from other areas. Because Greece has so many islands and a much indented coastline, there are really any number of routes to and from one place to another. Whatever the weather, there are so many places to shelter within short distances of one another that you can make up your own itinerary, covering as much or as little ground as you want.

At the beginning of each chapter there is also a list of useful waypoints to facilitate route planning. See the section on waypoints under *About the plans and pilotage*.

### Buoyage

IALA Maritime Buoyage System 'A' was introduced in 1983–84. Around large and medium-sized ports which handle commercial traffic and in waters used

## The Tower of Winds

If you wander around Pláka, the old quarter of Athens, you will come across the Tower of Winds standing just outside the site of the Roman market place. Built in the first century BC by the Macedonian astronomer, Andronikos of Kyrrhos, the octagonal tower is remarkable for a number of reasons. On each of the eight marble sides there is a relief of a winged figure representing the wind that blows from that direction. Originally the tower was capped by a revolving bronze Triton holding a wand which pointed to the prevailing wind. It was also a clock-tower. Beneath the figures of the winds are eight sundials. Within the tower a water clock registered the hours, fed by a reservoir on the south side of the roof.

But what is most remarkable is that each of the eight sides of the tower faces the cardinal and half-cardinal points of the compass, although the compass in its most rudimentary form was not introduced from the east until over a thousand years later. Moreover, the figures depicting the wind fly around the tower in an anticlockwise direction, which is the direction in which any cyclonic system entering the Mediterranean also revolves, with the winds of a depression following the same pattern and sequence as that shown on the tower.

### The figures

North: *Boreas*, the violent and cold north wind, represented by a bearded old man wrapped in a thick mantle with the folds being plucked by the wind.
Northeast: *Kaikias*, a cold bitter wind represented by a man holding a vessel from which olives are being scattered, representing the valuable olive crop being destroyed by this wind.
East: *Apeliotes*, a handsome young man, carries flowers and fruit, depicting the mild and kindly nature of the wind.
Southeast: *Euros*, represented by an old man with his right arm muffled in his mantle, heralds the stormy southeast wind.
South: *Notios*, a sour-looking figure, empties an urn, implying rain and sultry weather.
Southwest: *Lips*, represented by a figure pushing the prow of a ship, signifies the wind that is unfavourable for ships leaving Athens.
West: *Zephyros*, the mild west wind, is represented by a handsome youth showering a lapful of flowers into the air.
Northwest: *Skiron*, represented by a bearded man with a vessel in his hands, is interpreted in various ways. Either he is carrying a vase denoting occasional rain showers, or a charcoal vessel with which he dries up rivers.

for navigation by commercial traffic the system is in place and well maintained. In small harbours and areas not frequented by commercial traffic IALA 'A' buoyage is not always used and maintenance of the buoyage system is not always consistent.

### Lights

The coast and islands are surprisingly well lit given the extent of coastline which must be covered. Many of the lights have been converted to solar power with automatic photo-sensitive switches to turn them on when light levels drop below a pre-determined level. In a few places lights are not always maintained as well as they should be although NAVTEX will usually carry a notice advising that a particular light is not working.

# Weather forecasts

Because of the high and large landmasses close to all sea areas in Greece it is extremely difficult to predict what local winds and wind strength will be. The Greek Meteorological Service does its best, but nonetheless cannot give really accurate forecasts for many areas. Warnings of approaching depressions will be given, but again the erratic progress of these makes forecasting difficult.

**VHF frequencies**

A forecast for all Greek waters in Greek and English is given at 0600, 1000, 1600, 2200 UTC. For local time add 2 hours in the winter and 3 hours in the summer. The forecast covers all Greek waters for Z+12 hours. Gale warnings are given at the beginning of the broadcast.

A *sécurité* warning on Ch 16 gives all the VHF channels for the different shore stations and you will need to choose whichever shore station is closest to you. In practice the advice notice on shore stations is often mumbled and at such a speed that it can be difficult to hear, but is worth listening to in case VHF frequencies for the different shore stations are changed, as occurred recently.

At the beginning of each chapter the relevant VHF channels and times for the weather forecasts are annotated onto the introduction map for that chapter.

### Shore station list

| | |
|---|---|
| Corfu (Kérkira) | Ch 02 |
| Cephalonia | Ch 27 |
| Petalidhi (Kalamata) | Ch 83 |
| Kithera | Ch 85 |
| Pérama (Piraeus) | Ch 86 |
| Saronic | Ch 25 |
| Salamis | Ch 23 |
| Siros | Ch 04 |
| Parnis (Khalkhi) | Ch 25 |
| Pilio (Volos) | Ch 60 |
| Sfendarni (Thessaloniki) | Ch 23 |
| Thasos | Ch 85 |
| Limnos | Ch 82 |
| Lesvos | Ch 01 |
| Khíos | Ch 85 |
| Rodhos | Ch 63 |
| Knossos (Kriti) | Ch 83 |
| Sitia (Kriti) | Ch 85 |

The Ch 86 continuous weather forecast broadcast for the Saronic is stated still to be in operation, but I was not able to pick it up in 2000.

A weather forecast from Italy is transmitted continuously on VHF Ch 68. It can be picked up in the Ionian and in fact all the way across to Minorca in the Balearics. It is transmitted using a synthesised voice similar to some US forecasts and gives a forecast for the whole of the Mediterranean, first in Italian and then in English. The format is identical to that for Italian forecasts (see *Italian Waters Pilot*).

**HF Radio**

A forecast in Greek and English is broadcast on the following frequencies for SSB radios. (Receivers only will need a BFO switch).

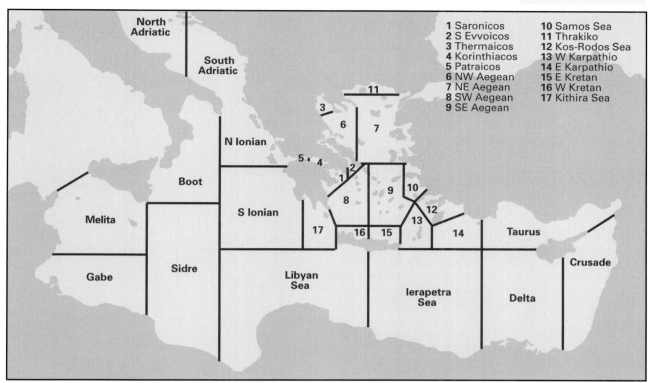

| | | |
|---|---|---|
| **1** Saronicos | **10** Samos Sea | |
| **2** S Evvoicos | **11** Thrakiko | |
| **3** Thermaicos | **12** Kos-Rodos Sea | |
| **4** Korinthiacos | **13** W Karpathio | |
| **5** Patraicos | **14** E Karpathio | |
| **6** NW Aegean | **15** E Kretan | |
| **7** NE Aegean | **16** W Kretan | |
| **8** SW Aegean | **17** Kithira Sea | |
| **9** SE Aegean | | |

**GREEK WEATHER FORECAST AREAS**

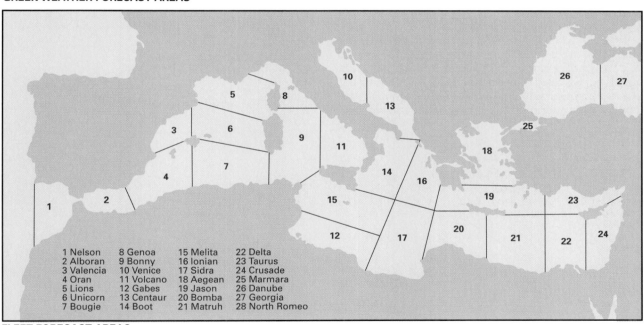

| 1 Nelson | 8 Genoa | 15 Melita | 22 Delta |
|---|---|---|---|
| 2 Alboran | 9 Bonny | 16 Ionian | 23 Taurus |
| 3 Valencia | 10 Venice | 17 Sidra | 24 Crusade |
| 4 Oran | 11 Volcano | 18 Aegean | 25 Marmara |
| 5 Lions | 12 Gabes | 19 Jason | 26 Danube |
| 6 Unicorn | 13 Centaur | 20 Bomba | 27 Georgia |
| 7 Bougie | 14 Boot | 21 Matruh | 28 North Romeo |

**FLEET FORECAST AREAS**

| | | |
|---|---|---|
| Athens | 2590kHz | 0703, 0933, 1503, 2103 UT |
| Limnos | 2730kHz | 0703, 0903, 1533, 2133 UT |
| Iraklion | 2799kHz | 0703, 0903, 1533, 2133 UT |
| Rhodes | 2830kHz | 0703, 0903, 1533, 2133 UT |

| | |
|---|---|
| Rhodes | 1494kHz (200m) |
| Khania | 1511kHz (198m) |
| Patras | 1485kHz (202m) |
| Volos | 1485kHz (202m) |

### Broadcast Radio

Weather forecasts are transmitted on the National Programme in Greek only. The forecasts are at 0630 (0650 winter), 1310 (1350 winter), 2145 (2200 winter), 2400 local time.

| | |
|---|---|
| Athens | 729kHz (412m) |
| Thessaloniki | 1044kHz (288m) |
| Corfu | 1008kHz (298m) |

Around Athens ERA radio 91·6FM is reported to have a forecast in English at 0630–0700 local time. For the eastern Mediterranean a marine weather forecast is given by the Austrian short wave service (in German only) on 6150MHz/49m at 0945 and 1400 local time (from 1 May to 1 October only).

## Television

On several of the television channels a weather forecast in Greek with satellite photos and wind forces and directions shown on the map is given after the news around 2100 local time. Many cafés and bars will have a television somewhere and you should ask for *o kairos parakalo*.

## Port police and marinas

The port police get a weather forecast faxed to them several times a day. Depending on the inclination of the port police it may be worthwhile asking them for a forecast. Most of the few marinas in Greece post a forecast, often taken off the internet.

## Navtex

The data for Navtex stations in Greece and adjacent waters is shown in the accompanying table.

There has been some discussion in the past over message errors and non-recording of messages. In 2000 I experienced no problems with any of the stations listed below and received messages at the times given.

The mounting of the aerial for Navtex reception is often mentioned as critical. My aerial is mounted on the pushpit clear of other aerials and I have had no problems. Others who have experienced problems have connected the aerial to a shroud for better reception. I've also met one boat where the aerial is inside the aft cabin where it gets a clear signal.

In areas where there is high ground surrounding the harbour or anchorage some problems can be experienced getting a clear signal, though less than might be expected. I use a Navtex Pro Plus with the Navtex active aerial. The set is earthed, though I'm uncertain of how good the earth connection really is.

## RADIOBEACONS

*Aero*

**Kérkira** 39°35'·20N 19°54'·63E
*KEK* (−·−/·/−··) 403kHz 25M
**Prevéza** 38°55'·00N 20°46'·00E
*PRV* (·−−·/·−·/···−) 353kHz 50M
**Korinthos** 37°55'·77N 22°56'·18E
*KOR* (−·−/−−−/·−·) 392kHz 50M
**Andravida, Amalias** 37°46'·50N 21°20'·83E
*AML* (·−/−−/·−··) 367kHz 100M
**Kalamáta** 37°04'·17N 22°01'·17E
*KTA* (−·−/−/·−) 348kHz 45M
**Khaniá, Soúdha, Kríti** 35°31'·39N 24°09'·62E
*SUD* (···/··−/−··) 409kHz 200M
**Kárpathos** 35°25'·25N 27°09'·03E
*KRC* (−·−/·−·/−·−·) 314kHz 25M
**Kastellorízon** 36°08'·06N 29°34'·60E
*KZO* (−·−/··−/−−−) 416kHz 25M
**Ródhos, Paradisi** 36°25'·17N 28°07'·12E
*ROS* (·−·/−−−/···) 339kHz 150M
**Kos** 36°47'·70N 27°05'·50E
*KOS* (−·−/−−−/···) 311kHz 25M
**Thíra, Santorini** 36°24'·07N 25°28'·85E
*THR* (−/····/·−·) 307kHz 80M
**Milos** 36°41'·90N 24°28'·37E
*MLO* (−−/·−··/−−−) 378kHz 25M
**Aíyina** 37°46'·02N 23°25'·60E
*EGN* (·/−−·/−·) 382kHz 50M
**Kavoúri** 37°48'·92N 23°45'·60E
*KVR* (−·−/···−/·−·) 357kHz 200M
**Soúnion** 37°40'·27N 24°02'·89E
*SUN* (···/··−/−·) 319kHz 50M
**Karistos** 38°00'·86N 24°24'·83E
*KRS* (−·−/·−·/···) 285kHz 50M
**Sámos** 37°41'·18N 26°55'·02E
*SMO* (···/−−/−−−) 375kHz 80M
**Skiathos** 39°10'·50N 23°30'·07E
*SKC* (···/−·−/−·−·) 326kHz 0·025kW
**Limnos** 39°55'·48N 25°14'·93E
*LIO* (·−··/·/−−−) 429kHz 150M
**Alexandroúpolis** 40°51'·45N 25°56'·65E
*ALP* (·−/·−··/·−−·) 351kHz 25M

## NAVTEX (N4) transmitters

| Country | Transmitter identification character | Freq kHz | Times | Language used | Range NM | Status of implementation character |
|---|---|---|---|---|---|---|
| **Malta** | | | | | | |
| Malta | O | 518 | 0220, 0620, 1020, 1420, 1820, 2220 | English | 400 | Operational |
| **Greece** | | | | | | |
| Limnos | L | 518 | 0150, 0550, 0950, 1350, 1750, 2150 | English | 280 | Operational |
| Iraklion | H | 518 | 0110, 0510, 0910, 1310, 1710, 2110 | English | 280 | Operational |
| Kérkira | K | 518 | 0140, 0540, 0940, 1340, 1740, 2140 | English | 280 | Operational |
| **Turkey** | | | | | | |
| İzmir | I | 518 | On receipt. 0120, 0520, 0920, 1320, 1720, 2120 | English | 300 | Operational |
| Samsun | E | 518 | On receipt. 0040, 0440, 0840, 1240, 1640, 2040 | English | 300 | Operational |
| İstanbul | D | 518 | On receipt. 0030, 0430, 0830, 1230, 1630, 2030 | English | 300 | Operational |
| Antalya | F | 518 | On receipt. 0050, 0450, 0850, 1250, 1650, 2050 | English | 300 | Operational |
| **Cyprus** | | | | | | |
| Troodos | M | 518 | On receipt. 0200, 0600, 1000, 1400, 1800, 2200 | English | 200 | Operational |
| **Israel** | | | | | | |
| Haifa | P | 518 | On receipt. 0020, 0420, 0820, 1220, 1620, 2020 | English | 200 | Operational |
| **Egypt** | | | | | | |
| Alexandria | N | 518 | 0018, 0248, 0448, 0648, 0848, 1048, 1218, 1448, 1648, 1848, 2048, 2248 | English | 350 | Operational |

## NAVTEX AND WEATHERFAX SERVICES

Navtex has three message priorities:

*Vital*      For immediate broadcast

*Important*  For broadcast at the next available period

*Routine*    For broadcast at the next scheduled transmission period

The following subject indication characters are used:

A    Navigational warnings
B    Meteorological warnings
C    Ice reports
D    Search and rescue information
E    Meteorological forecasts
F    Pilot service messages
G    Decca messages
H    Loran messages
I    Omega messages
J    Satnav messages
K    Other electronic navaid messages
L    Navigational warnings
Z    No messages on hand

### Weatherfax (WX)

Weatherfax transmissions in Greece are as follows.

**Roma (IMB)**

| | | | |
|---|---|---|---|
| (IMB 51) | 4777·5kHz | 5·0 | H24 |
| (IMB 55) | 8148·5kHz | 5·0 | H24 |
| (IMB 56) | 13597·3kHz | 5·0 | H24 |

**Map Areas**

A    1:20 000 000(c)
48°N 145°W 32°N 68°E
24°N 69°W 15°N 10°E

B    1:20 000 000(c)
52°N 31°W 45°N 61°E
24°N 10°W 21°N 37°E

B1   1:15 000 000(c)
52°N 31°W 45°N 61°E
24°N 10°W 21°N 37°E

D    1:15 000 000(c)
49°N 25°W 49°N 45°E
28°N 10°W 28°N 30°E

E    1:40 000 000(c)
54°N 90°W 54°N 90°E
17°N 27°W 17°N 27°E

I    1:2 500 000(a)
48°N 05°E 48°N 19°E
35°N 05°E 35°N 19°E

I1   1:4 000 000(a)
50°N 05°E 50°N 20°E
35°N 05°E 35°N 20°E

M    1:15 000 000(c)
51°N 46°W 56°N 60°E
25°N 17°W 27°N 33°E

S    1:10 000 000(c)

45°N 06°W 41°N 39°E
29°N 01°W 26°N 31°E

**Schedule**

| | | | | |
|---|---|---|---|---|
| M | 24h FL390 and 300 wind/Temp Prog.[1] | 0055(12) | 1255(00) | 120/576 |
| | 24h FL340 wind/ Temp Prog.[1] | 0117(12) | 1317(00) | 120/576 |
| | 24h FL240 and 180 wind/Temp Prog.[1] | 0129(12) | 1329(00) | 120/576 |
| | 24h FL100 and 50 wind/Temp Prog.[1] | 0151(12) | 1351(00) | 120/576 |
| | 24h FL100–450 Tropopause/Max wind Prog.[1] | 0248(12) | 1448(00) | 120/576 |
| B1 | 24h Significant Wx Prog.[2] | 0345(12) | 1555(00) | 120/576 |
| D | 3h Pressure change chart followed by: | 0400(00) | 1700(12) | 120/576 |
| B | 500 hPa Anal. | | | |
| B1 | Surface Anal. (Summer only) | 0415(00) | | 120/576 |
| D | Freezing level Anal. followed by: | 0425(00) | 1810(12) | 120/576 |
| B | 850 hPa Anal | | | |
| I | Surface Anal. for Italy | 0437(03) | 1146(09) | 120/576 |
| | | 1610(15) | 2252(21) | 120/576 |
| B1 | Surface Anal. (Replaces 0415 at the end of the Summer) | 0457(00) | | 120/576 |
| B | 700 hPa and 300 hPa Anal. | 0510(00) | 1715(12) | 120/576 |
| | 200 hPa and Tropopause/Max wind Prog. | 0522(00) | 1730(12) | 120/576 |
| I1 | 12h Significant Wx at low level Prog. for Italy | 0535(00) | | 120/576 |
| M | 18h FL390 and 300 wind/Temp Prog.[1] | 0655(18) | 1855(06) | 120/576 |
| | 18h FL340 wind/ Temp Prog.[1] | 0717(18) | 1917(06) | 120/576 |
| | 18h FL240 and 180 wind/Temp Prog.[1] | 0729(18) | 1926(06) | 120/576 |
| | 18h FL100 and 50 wind/Temp Prog.[1] | 0751(18) | 1951(06) | 120/576 |
| | Test chart/Fax Schedule | 0813 | | 120/576 |
| A | 24h 500 hPa Prog.[3] | 0823(00) | 2200(12) | 120/576 |
| M | 18h Significant Wx Prog.[1] | 0848(18) | 2048(06) | 120/576 |

## Weather on the Internet

There are a number of services on the Internet which provide up-to-date surface forecasts, text forecasts and satellite pictures. Access to the internet from a boat can be obtained in a number of ways.

1. Using a GSM phone and dedicated connection cord and appropriate modem. Connection speed is 9600 baud at present which is slow but sufficient to access the internet.
2. Using a satellite system such as INMARSAT. INMARSAT B has adequate speeds and when transmission rates for INMARSAT mini-M are improved it will also have adequate speed to access the internet. INMARSAT provide synoptic charts as part of the service.
3. Cyber-cafés. If you know the sites you are looking for then half an hour will be more than sufficient to get weather data. Most cyber-cafés will let you print out surface charts for a small fee.
4. Plugging into a conventional socket. This is a quick and easy way to access the internet using your own laptop and a modem, preferably a PC card modem.

### Internet sites

#### Mediterranean sailing
http://www.medsail.nildram.co.uk
Rod Heikell's site for sailing in the Mediterranean, with a weather page and links to those sites he considers most useful in terms of content and download time. Includes 36 hour surface charts from NEMOC, satellite loops, wind and sea forecasts from a number of sources. Benefits from actually being used on board in the Mediterranean. Includes forecasts for Greece.

#### Nemoc (Naval European Meteorology and Oceanography Center
http://www.nemoc.navy.mil/about1.htm
This is the US navy site based in Rota which has the best unclassified forecasts and maps for the Mediterranean. Many other private sites use the forecasts and maps from NEMOC (often without a source signature) so this is a good place to go first. Here you can get excellent text forecasts, surface analysis maps showing lows, highs and wind strength for next 36 hours, surface maps showing wave height and surface currents for next 36 hours, Meteosat photos updated hourly, satellite loop mpegs, wind and sea warnings, and much more. Excellent site which is quick to load.

#### Poseidon weather for Greece
http://www.poseidon.ncmr.gr/weather-forecast.html
Up to 72 hour surface wind forecasts for Greece. The best source of weather for Greek waters and adjacent Turkish waters. The chart gives wind direction with colour coding for the wind force in Beaufort (the colour bar is on the right hand side of the chart) On the left hand side is a table for current and up to 72 hour forecast. Choose the one you want and press DISPLAY

#### University of Athens
http://weather.noaa.gov/weather/GR-cc.html
Weather observations at Greek airports.

#### DWD Mediterranean Forecast
http://www.dwd.de/forecasts/seemm.htm
3-day text forecasts for a number of Mediterranean areas including the eastern Mediterranean. In German only but easily read in table form. Forecast areas on a clickable map come up for: Alboran; Golfe de Lion; Balearics; Ligurian; West Corsica; Tyrrhenian; N Adriatic; S Adriatic; Ionian; N Aegean; S Aegean; Rhodes/Cyprus; Biscay
The tables are arranged by column for day (MO=Monday/DI=Tuesday/MI=Wednesday/DO=Thursday/FR=Friday/SA=Saturday/So=Sunday)
Time (UTC+)/Wind direction/Wind force (Beaufort)/Gusts (Beaufort)/Wave height (m)

#### Mediterranean Sea Weather Page
http://www.sto-p.com/atol/
Bracknell surface analysis map, surface analysis maps from NEMOC and wind charts from the University of Athens.

#### Weather Online
http://www.nbn.com/people/lovejoy4/weather.html
Current satellite and radar imagery and text forecasts

#### CompuServe and Yahoo!
The weather data available from CompuServe and Yahoo! includes satellite maps and aviation forecasts.

| | | | | | |
|---|---|---|---|---|---|
| E | 48h 500 hPa Prog. | 0859(00) | 120/576 | 23°N 07°W 21°N 25°E | 33°N 3°W 25°N 31°E |
| | 72h 500 hPa Prog. | 0906(00) | 120/576 | C (c) | |
| | 96h 500 hPa Prog. | 0913(00) | 120/576 | 42°N 23°E 38°N 32°E | |
| | 120h 500 hPa Prog. | 0920(00) | 120/576 | 36°N 20°E 32°N 28°E | |
| | 144h 500 hPa Prog. | 0927(00) | 120/576 | **Schedule** | |
| B1 | 18h Significant Wx Prog.[2] | 1000(18) 2335(06) | 120/576 | A  Surface Anal. | 0845(06) | 120/576 |
| B | 24h Surface Prog. followed by: | 1030(06) 1700(12) 1233(18) | 120/576 | 24h & 48h Surface Prog. | 0857(06) | 120/576 |
| D | 3h Pressure change chart | | | B  30h 36h 42h & 48h Wave Height Prog. | 0921(12) | 120/576 |
| B1 | Surface Anal. for Europe | 1045(06) | 120/576 | C  30h 36h 42h & 48h Wave Height Prog. | 1009(12) | 120/576 |
| I1 | 18h Significant Wx at low level Prog. for Italy | 1100(00) 2240(12) | 120/576 | | |
| S | 18h Med. Sea State Prog. | 1140(00) 2230(12) | 120/576 | **Turkey** | |
| I1 | 24h Significant Wx at low level Prog. for Italy | 1630(00) | 120/576 | **Ankara (YMA20)** | |
| B | Surface Anal. for Europe | 1645(12) 2312(18) | 120/576 | 3377kHz | 1610–0500 |
| | | | | 6970kHz | 0500–1610 |

1. Rebroadcast of Offenbach (Main)/Pinneberg (station 0220) transmissions
2. Transmitted only if the Offenbach (Main)/Pinneberg charts are not available
3. Rebroadcast of Bracknell (station 0035) transmissions

### Greece
**Athinái (SVJ4)**

| | | |
|---|---|---|
| | 4481kHz | 0845–0945 |
| | 8105kHz | 0845–0945 |

**Map Areas**

| | | |
|---|---|---|
| A | 1:15 000 000(c) | B  (c) |
| | 49°N 23°W 45°N 42°E | 54°N 3°W 40°N 44°E |

**Map Areas**

| | | | |
|---|---|---|---|
| A | 1:10 000 000(b) | | |
| | 54°N 13°W | 53°N 76°E | |
| | 18°N 7°E | 17°N 55°E | |

**Schedule**

| | | | |
|---|---|---|---|
| A | 24h and 36h 500hPa Anal. | 0330(12) | 90/576 |
| A | Surface Anal. | 0430(00) 0610(03) 0940(06) 1240(09) 1610(12) 1840(15) 2152(18) | 90/576 |
| | Test chart | 0500 | 90/576 |
| A | 500hPa Anal. | 0640(00) 1910(12) | 90/576 |
| A | 300hPa Anal. | 0710(00) 2015(12) | 90/576 |
| A | 24h significant Wx | 0740(00) 1710(12) | 90/576 |
| A | 24h 700hPa Anal. | 0810(00) | 90/576 |

A  24h 300hPa Anal.    0840(00)
A  48h and 72h
   500hPa Anal        0910(12)              90/576
A  Significant Wx     1010(00)              90/576
A  Maximum wind
   Anal.              1040(00)              90/576
A  200hPa Anal.       1940(12)              90/576

**Egypt**
**Al Qahirah (Cairo) Meteo (SUU)**
   4526·5kHz          1900–0700
   10123kHz           0700–1900
*Note* Bcsts are intended to be received throughout Africa,
Europe and West Asia.
*Map Area*
A  1:20 000 000 (a)
   60°N 20°W 60°N 80°E
   10°S 20°W 10°S 80°E
*Schedule*
*Note* The transmission time for each product extends
approx 20 mins from the time given.
A  Surface Prog.        0000(06) 0600(12)   120/576
                        0640(00) 1200(18)
                        1800(00) 1840(12)
   Surface Anal         0020(18) 1220(06)   120/576
   Upper air 300mb Anal 0040(12) 1300(00)   120/576
   Upper air 500mb Prog. 0340(12) 0940(18)
                        1540(00) 2140(06)    120/576
   Upper air 300mb Prog. 0400(12) 1000(18)
                        1600(00) 2200(06)    120/576
   Upper air 200mb Prog. 0420(12) 1020(18)
                        1620(00) 2220(06)    120/576
   Significant Wx Prog  0440(12) 1040(18)
                        1640(00) 2240(06)    120/576
   Tropopause Max wind
   Prog.                0500(12) 1120(18)
                        1700(00) 2300(06)    120/576
   Upper air 700mb Prog. 0520(12) 1120(18)
                        1720(00) 2320(06)    120/576

Upper air 250mb Prog.   0540(12) 1140(18)
                        1740(00) 2340(06)    120/576
Upper air 850mb Anal.   0700(00) 1900(12)   120/576
Upper air 700mb Anal.   0720(00) 1920(12)   120/576
Upper air 500mb Anal.   0740(00) 1940(12)   120/576
Upper air 300mb Anal.   0800(00) 2000(12)   120/576
Upper air 250mb Anal.   0820(00) 2020(12)   120/576
Upper air 200mb Anal.   0840(00) 2040(12)   120/576
Tropopause Max wind
Anal.                   0900(00) 2100(12)   120/576
Upper air 100mb Anal.   0920(00) 2120(12)   120/576
Satellite Imagery – Wind
Anal.                   1240(00)            120/576

**Bulgaria**
**Sofia (LZJ)**
(LZJ2)              5093kHz      5·0        H24
*Map Areas*
A  1:10 000 000        B 1:3 000 000
   64°N 45°W 60°N 63°E    47°N 13°E 47°N 33°E
   30°N 20°W 28°N 34°E    36°N 14°E 36°N 31°E
*Schedule*
A  Surface Anal        0415(00) 0950(06)
B  Surface Anal        0435(03)¹ 0735(06)   120/576
                       1030(09) 1330(12)
   Test chart          0800

1. Broadcast at 0150 26/9 to 5/4

*Note 1* The following stations no longer transmit
weatherfax signals:
Madrid
Rota (AOK US Navy)
Beograd (Belgrade).

*Note 2* It seems as if weatherfax transmissions are
gradually being phased out as more and more large
ships use INMARSAT or internet weather maps. (I
should stress this is my opinion and not the official
line.)

| BEAUFORT SCALE OF WIND STRENGTH | | | | | | | |
|---|---|---|---|---|---|---|---|
| *Sea State* | *Beaufort No.* | *Description* | *Velocity in knots* | *Velocity in km/h* | *Term* | *Code* | *Wave height in metres* |
| Like a mirror | 0 | Calm, glassy | <1 | <1 | Calm | 0 | 0 |
| Ripples | 1 | Light airs Rippled | 1–3 | 1–5 | Calm | 1 | 0–0·1 |
| Small wavelets | 2 | Light breeze Wavelets | 4–6 | 6–11 | Smooth | 2 | 0·1–0·5 |
| Large wavelets | 3 | Gentle breeze | 7–10 | 12–19 | Slight | 3 | 0·5–1·25 |
| Small waves, breaking | 4 | Moderate breeze | 11–16 | 20–28 | Moderate | 4 | 1·25–2·5 |
| Moderate waves, foam | 5 | Fresh breeze | 17–21 | 29–38 | Rough | 5 | 2·5–4 |
| Large waves, foam and spray | 6 | Strong breeze | 22–27 | 39–49 | | | |
| Sea heads up, foam in streaks | 7 | Near gale | 28–33 | 50–61 | Very rough | 6 | 4–6 |
| Higher long waves, foam in streaks | 8 | Gale | 34–40 | 62–74 | | | |
| High waves, dense foam, spray impairs visibility | 9 | Strong gale | 41–47 | 75–88 | High | 7 | 6–9 |
| Very high tumbling waves, surface white with foam, visibility affected | 10 | Storm | 48–55 | 89–102 | Very high | 8 | 9–14 |
| Exceptionally high waves, sea covered in foam, visibility affected | 11 | Violent storm | 56–62 | 103–117 | Phenomenal | 9 | Over 14 |
| Air filled with spray and foam, visibility severely impaired | 12 | Hurricane | >63 | >118 | | | |

**Local weather lore**

The following is a collection of local weather lore gathered at various times in various places. I vouch for none of it, but it may come in useful when planning passages or deciding where you are going.

1. A warning sign of the *meltemi* is a long white cigar-shaped cloud over an island (particularly in the Cyclades). The cloud will normally form before the wind arrives and will remain in place when the wind is blowing. In the Ionian, low dense cloud hugging the summit of the islands warns of a strong *maistro*.

2. In the summer, dry decks in the early morning forecast wind while dewy decks mean there will be little or no wind.

3. The formation of the stages of the new moon forecast whether there will be strong winds or not in the month. If the phases of the new moon form vertically or sideways (the moon 'can't hold water') then there will not be strong winds. If the phases of the moon form horizontally or from the bottom up (the moon 'can hold water') then strong winds will blow in the month.

4. In the eastern Aegean and Crete the Coptic calendar (reproduced in *Turkish Waters and Cyprus Pilot* and *Mediterranean Cruising Handbook*) showing the dates of gales and their direction and duration could prove useful.

# Coastal radio stations

**Kerkyra (SVK)** 39°45'N 19°52'E
*RT (MF)* Transmits on 2792, 2182, 2607, 2830, 3613kHz. Receives on 2182kHz. Traffic lists on 2830kHz at every H+10
**Iraklion (Kríti) (SVH)** 35°20'N 25°07'E
RT (MF) Transmits on 2182, 1741·4, 2799, 3640kHz. Receives on 2182, 2085·4kHz. Traffic lists on 2799kHz every even H+05
**Rodos (SVR)** 36°27'N 28°15'E
*RT (MF)* Transmits on 2182, 2624, 3630kHz. Receives on 2182kHz. Traffic lists on 2624kHz at every H+03
**Piraeus (SXE2) (Hellenic Coastguard)** 37°58'N 23°40'E
*Note* This station does not accept public correspondence; accepting distress, safety and urgent traffic, port operations and pollution reports. Meteorological bulletins available on request.
*RT (MF)* Transmits on 1698, 1904, 2182kHz. Receives on 2182kHz
*VHF* Transmits and receives on Ch 07, 18, 19, 20, 21
**Aspropyrgos Attikis (SXE) (JRCC)** 38°03'N 23°35'E
*Note* This station does not accept public correspondence; accepting distress, safety and urgent traffic, port operations and pollution reports. Meteorological bulletins available on request.
*RT (MF)* Transmits on1734, 2182kHz. Receives on 2182kHz
**Athínai (1780)** 38°00'N 23°53'E
*RT (MF)* Transmits on 2182, 1695, 2590, 1767kHz. Receives on 2182kHz. Traffic lists on 2590 every even H+05
**Limnos (SVL)** 39°52'N 25°04'E
*RT (MF)* Transmits on 2182, 2730kHz. Receives on 2182kHz. Traffic lists on 2730kHz at every H+05

The call sign to Greek coastal radio stations on VHF and on 2182kHz is HELLAS RADIO. The best policy to elicit a reply is to use a callsign rather than the yacht's name.

All port police stations have a VHF and listen out on Channels 8, 12, 16 and 19. The following stations are the major HELLAS RADIO installations:

**Hellas radio**
Call *Hellas Radio*
The following stations are remotely controlled by Athinai and are available both manually and using 'Autolink'.

| | | |
|---|---|---|
| Kerkyra | 02, 03, 16, 64 | 39°45'N 19°52'E |
| Kefallinía | 16, 26, 27, 28 | 38°08'N 20°40'E |
| Patra | 16, 85 | 38°14'N 21°47'E |
| Koryfi | 16, 87 | 37°46'N 21°26'E |
| Petalidi | 16, 23, 83, 84 | 36°56'N 21°52'E |
| Kythira | 16, 85, 86 | 36°09'N 22°59'E |
| Moystakos | 04, 16 | 35°18'N 23°37'E |
| Knossos | 16, 83, 84 | 35°17'N 24°53'E |
| Faistos | 16, 26, 27 | 35°00'N 25°12'E |
| Sitía | 16, 85, 86 | 35°12'N 26°06'E |
| Kárpathos | 03, 16 | 35°28'N 27°10'E |
| Rodos | 01, 16, 63 | 36°16'N 27°56'E |
| Astypalea | 16, 23 | 36°36'N 26°20'E |
| Pátmos | 16, 84 | 37°18'N 26°32'E |
| Thíra | 16, 26, 87 | 36°25'N 25°26'E |
| Mílos | 16, 82 | 36°41'N 24°24'E |
| Póros | 16, 27, 28, 88 | 37°30'N 23°27'E |
| Gerania | 02, 16, 64 | 38°00'N 23°20'E |
| Pérama | 25, 26, 86, 87 | 37°58'N 23°35'E |
| Andros | 16, 24 | 37°51'N 24°56'E |
| Syros | 03, 04, 16 | 37°27'N 24°56'E |
| Chios | 16, 85 | 33°23'N 26°03'E |
| Mytilíni | 01, 02, 16 | 39°04'N 26°21'E |
| Parnis | 16, 25, 61, 62 | 38°10'N 23°44'E |
| Lichada | 01, 16 | 38°52'N 22°53'E |
| Pilio | 03, 16, 60 | 39°22'N 22°57'E |
| Sfendami | 16, 23, 24 | 40°25'N 22°31'E |
| Tsoukalas | 16, 26, 27 | 40°23'N 23°28'E |
| Limnos | 16, 82, 83 | 39°52'N 25°04'E |
| Thásos | 16, 25, 85 | 40°47'N 24°43'E |

All stations H24

# About the plans and pilotage notes

**Nomenclature**
The spelling of Greek names presents many problems, not the least of which is the difficulty of transforming demotic Greek accurately into English. For instance, the island of Evia (my spelling) may be Euboea, Evvoia, or Evoia. Even if you get the modern Greek nearly right you may find the place is normally talked of in the diminutive, so Levkas, for example, becomes Levkadha. To add to the confusion an alternative name from the Venetian, Turkish, French, Italian or English occupation may be the name by which a place is commonly called. For example, Thíra is commonly called by its Italian name of Santorini.

In this edition I have adopted the convention, in common with all hydrographic departments, of calling a place by the Greek name translated into the Latin alphabet. One interesting point here is that if the rules for transliteration are followed inflexibly, the result can at times be nonsense. Consequently I have modified the rules where I think the end result is truer to the name in Greek. For several places I have used the name commonly used and familiar to English-speaking readers, so Crete is not called Kriti, Corfu is not Kérkira and Piraeus is not Pireefs. After the familiar name I have added the alternative names and any confusing variations so readers can sort through the different names themselves.

## Abbreviations

In the pilotage notes for a harbour or anchorage all compass directions are abbreviated to the first or first and second letters in capitals as is common practice: e.g. N is north, SE is southeast, etc.

## Harbour plans

The harbour plans and charts are designed to illustrate the accompanying notes which are set out in a standard format.

Some smaller places and many anchorages will have just a simple description with an abbreviated form of the above or just a straight description.

It is stressed that many of these plans are based on the author's sketches and therefore should only be used in conjunction with the official charts. They are not to be used for navigation.

## Photographs

Most of the photographs were taken by the author. Many were taken under difficult conditions – when navigating short-handed or single-handed or under poor light conditions – and consequently the quality is not all that might be desired. Because of the sheer number of anchorages and harbours in Greece it is not possible to include shots of all the harbours and anchorages mentioned. Some areas are also out of bounds for military reasons.

## Bearings

All bearings are in 360° notation and are true.

## Magnetic variation

The magnetic variation in Greece is very small and for the normally quite short voyages made, the variation can be ignored. It varies from half a degree to two degrees, but is mostly just over one degree east.

## Soundings

All soundings are in metres and are based on mean low-water springs. In the case of my own soundings there will sometimes be up to half a metre more water than the depth shown when the sea bottom is uneven, but in most cases there is the depth shown.

For those used to working in fathoms and feet the use of metres may prove difficult at first and there is the danger of reading the depths in metres as the depths in fathoms. For all practical purposes one metre can be read as approximately three feet and two metres is approximately equal to one fathom. Therefore as an instant check on the depths in fathoms without reference to the conversion tables in the appendix, it is possible simply to divide the depth in metres by two and that will be approximately equal to the depth in fathoms: e.g. 3 metres = 1½ fathoms (whereas accurately 3 metres = 1 fathom 3·8ft).

## Waypoints

Waypoints are given for all harbours and anchorages. The origins of the waypoints vary and in a large number of cases the datum source of the waypoint is not known. Where I have taken waypoints for a harbour or anchorage it has a note after it reading WGS84. All these waypoints are to World Geodetic Survey 1984 datum which it is intended will be the datum source used throughout the world. Most GPS receivers automatically default to WGS84.

It is important to note that plotting a waypoint onto a chart will not necessarily put it in the position shown. There are a number of reasons for this.

1. The chart may have been drawn using another datum source. Many of the Imray-Tetra charts use European Datum 1950 (Europe 50). There are many other datum sources that have been used to draw charts.

2. All charts, including those using WGS84, have errors of various types. Most were drawn in the 19th century and have been fudged to conform to WGS84 (the term 'fuzzy logic' could aptly be used).

3. Even when a harbour plan is drawn there is still a significant human element at work and mistakes easily creep in.

The upshot of all this is that it is important to eyeball your way into an anchorage or harbour and not just sit back and assume that all those digits on the GPS display will look after you. In the case of waypoints I have taken and which are appended WGS84, the waypoint is indeed in the place shown. Other waypoints may be derived from the light position, from reports in my files, or from other sources.

In this edition I have also included useful waypoints which are listed at the beginning of the relevant chapter and included on the location maps. As above, any that are appended WGS84 are from my own observations, using the radar for distance off and a compass bearing for the direction. Given that some radar distance off readouts can be a bit of a guestimate, these should be used with every caution. In most cases I have endeavoured to keep a reasonable distance off so that an error of, say, 50 metres, should be unimportant when the waypoint is 0·5M from the land. There are other occasions when I have shaved a cape or islet and the distance off is considerably less.

All waypoints are given in the notation:

*degrees        minutes        decimal place of a minute*

It is important not to confuse the decimal place of a minute with the older 60 second notation.

## Quick reference guide

At the beginning of each chapter there is a summary of the important information: Ports of Entry, Prohibited Areas, and Major Lights. Following this there is a list of all the harbours and anchorages described in the chapter with a classification of the shelter offered, mooring, and whether fuel, water, provisions and tavernas are available. Compressing information about a harbour or anchorage into such a framework is difficult and not a little clumsy, but the list can be useful for route planning and as an instant memory aid to a harbour.

See page vi for details.

# I. The Northern Ionian
## Corfu (Kérkira) to Zákinthos

From the heel of Italy most yachts cross the Otranto Strait to Corfu only 70 miles away. Corfu is the first of the Heptanesoi, the seven islands of the Ionian. Proceeding south from Corfu you come to the islands of Paxoí and Andípaxoi, Levkas, Ithaca, Cephalonia and Zákinthos, and the island of Kíthera. Along the eastern shores of the Ionian are Albania, mainland Greece and the Peloponnisos. Some yachts cross direct from Sicily or Malta to Preveza on the mainland, Levkas, Argostoli on Cephalonia or to Zákinthos.

The Ionian derives its name from the goddess Io. Io was a priestess of Hera and for a short time a mistress to Zeus. Inevitably there was conflict when Hera discovered Zeus was deceiving her and, fearing what Hera in her wrath might do, he changed Io into a white cow. Not to be outdone, Hera sent a gadfly to torment the unfortunate Io, who plunged into the sea to rid herself of the stinging pest – hence the Ionian Sea.

Historically the importance of the Ionian was as a stepping-stone route from the Aegean to Italy and Sicily. Corfu has always been identified as the Homeric island home of the Phaeacians, those mythical ancient sailors who ferried Odysseus home to Ithaca. On a more substantive level Corfu was the ancient Corcyra, a colony of Corinth and the stepping-stone to another important Corinthian colony – Siracusa in Sicily.

The seven islands were not united as a historical group until the 14th century when the islands appealed to Venice for protection from their tyrannical Norman and Genoese overlords. Venice seized the chance to consolidate her trade route from Venice around the Peloponnisos to the Aegean and thus the seven islands became one political unit. It was this long occupation by the Venetians that gave the Ionian its Italianate qualities. Many of the old gnarled olive trees seen today were planted during the Venetian occupation so the local population could pay its taxes in olive oil. Later the French and English added their own flavour to the islands until, in 1864, the seven islands reverted to Greece.

To those of you who visualize a Greece of sun-baked rock dotted with dazzling whitewashed houses, the Ionian comes as a gentle surprise. This is not the Greece of the popular travel brochure but a shaded green country, sheltering red-tiled Latin houses – an eccentric collection of Italian and French architecture and English tastes (in Corfu the locals play cricket and you can buy currant buns and ginger beer) welded together into a whole that is indubitably Greek. Evergreen cypress, pine, elm, green fields, flowers even in the height of summer, and everywhere the dull dark sheen of the olive, characterise the lower land, while higher up the slopes are covered in pine and the tenacious Mediterranean *maquis*. If the wind is in the right direction you can smell the pungent herby aroma a mile out to sea.

The green luxuriance of the islands is in direct contrast to the high eroded mountains of Albania and mainland Greece that form the eastern boundary to the Ionian. Here there is a barren backdrop to the islands that gives a taste of the topography to come. In between there are protected waters where the wind seldom blows too strongly, and a multitude of little anchorages accessible only by yacht. From the inland sea bordered by Levkas, Ithaca and Cephalonia you leave the rolling, almost English, landscape of Zákinthos to confront the rocky slopes of the Peloponnisos.

## Weather patterns in the North Ionian

Winds are consistent in the summer. From June to the end of September the normal wind in the northern Ionian is from the NW to WNW. Generally it arrives around noon, blows between Force 2 and 5 and dies at sunset. In the morning there may be a light E or SE wind, but it rarely reaches Force 1–2. After October until April/May winds can be from the N or S, though gales tend to be more from the S–SE.

In July and August a wind known as the *maistro* may blow from the N–NW with a little more strength than the normal NW wind. Care needs to be taken at this time of gusts off the lee side of high islands, especially in the inland sea, where there can be strong gusts off Levkas, Ithaca, Cephalonia and Zákinthos. Usually when the wind is going to be strong, dense white cigar-shaped clouds hug the tops of the mountains on the islands. In the evening there may be a katabatic wind off the high mainland mountains for several hours. It generally blows from a NE direction and can get up to Force 5–6.

In summer the climate in the northern Ionian is sunny with little rain. The temperature can reach 32°C plus in July and August. In the spring and autumn there are often thunderstorms and associated squalls but these seldom last for very long. In the winter Corfu has one of the highest rainfalls in Greece. As you proceed further south and east the rainfall decreases dramatically. So too does the prolific greenery that goes with a high winter rainfall.

## Routes

The geography determines that routes are generally northerly or southerly ones. The prevailing NW winds in the summer mean that going S is pretty much a matter of plotting which harbours and anchorages on the islands and mainland you want to visit and then coasting down to them. You may encounter a few problems coming into bays or entrances which face the prevailing wind such as Palaiokastrita, the northern entrance to the Levkas Canal or the approaches to Argostoli, but generally you will have few problems getting to where you are going.

In places the prevailing NW wind tends to curve around the top and bottom of the high islands and sometimes it is accelerated when it is channelled or where it gusts down valleys. Areas where the wind tends to blow around the land are on the northern side of Corfu where it blows from the WNW and then is channelled down the North Corfu Channel, around the southern end of Corfu and Paxos, around the southern end of Levkas where it blows from the WNW and then the W closer to the Meganísi Channel, down the Ithaca Channel between Cephalonia and Ithaca, around the southern end of Cephalonia, and around the northern and southern sides of Zákinthos. Gusts will be experienced on the lee sides of some islands, especially Paxos and Antipaxos, the E and S sides of Levkas, the E side of Ithaca especially in Kólpos Aetou, around the Kólpos Argostoliou, and on the E side of Zákinthos.

Going N in the summer is usually a matter of bashing up against the prevailing NW wind. If you want to make up ground then the NW wind will not normally get up until around midday, so if you leave early in the morning you can generally motor to destinations in the N. The trip from Levkas going N can often be a bit of a bash and many yachts choose to leave Levkas early and motor at least part of the way to Paxos or Parga.

In the winter there are more southerlies and route planning becomes more of a lottery. Really the only thing you can do here is get a forecast and make your plans from there. Remember that many of the harbours which are safe in the prevailing summer northerlies can be less comfortable and even untenable in strong southerlies.

From the Ionian you can reach the Aegean by one of two routes: around the capes of the Peloponnisos following the old trade route, or through the Gulf of Patras and the Gulf of Corinth to the Corinth Canal that severs mainland Greece from the Peloponnisos.

## Data

### PORTS OF ENTRY
Kérkira (Corfu)
Igoumenítsa
Préveza
Gaios (Paxos)
Levkas
Argostoli
Zákinthos

### PROHIBITED AREAS
The NE coast of Corfu and mainland coast 1M offshore from the Albanian border to Nisís Prasoúdhi. Limín Vathi immediately N of Préveza.

Theoretically permission must be obtained from the navy before entering the prohibited areas around Corfu and the adjacent mainland coast, but in practice this is not normally necessary and no problems have arisen from not obtaining formal permission. Likewise Vathi near Préveza is used by yachts without permission. However it should be remembered that these areas are still classified as prohibited areas on the latest Greek charts.

### Note
There have been a number of incidents of piracy off the Albanian coast, the nearby Greek mainland coast and in Corfu. The present state of anarchy in Albania means that yachts should keep well off the coast and when approaching the North Corfu Channel keep as close as practicable to the Greek coast. Yachts on passage from Italy can head around the south end of Corfu and then up to Gouvía if there is a real need to get there or alternatively it makes more sense to head for Paxos, Préveza or Levkas. Given that the prevailing winds are NW in the summer this presents few problems. At present there is a strong Greek naval presence and this should ensure the safety of craft in the area. However it would pay to keep an eye on developments and act accordingly.

One thing that is for sure is that predicting the political path of a newly emerging country such as Albania is next to impossible. After the demise of communism in Albania it was thought the country would soon open up to yachts and tourism to help out the ailing economy. How wrong we were.

### MAJOR LIGHTS
**Nisís Othoní NE Point (Ákra Kastrí)**
Fl.10s21M
**Nisís Othoní SW Point** Fl(2)6s6M
**Nisís Erikoússa Ákra Potamópoulo**
Fl(3)15s6M

**Kérkira (Corfu)**
**Ákra Aikateríni** Fl.10s6M
**Ákra Sidhero (Citadel/Corfu town)**
Fl(2)6s13M
**Ákra Levkímmis** Fl.6s7M
**Vrákhoi Lagoúdhia** Fl(3)14s7M
**Nisís Prasoúdhi (Igoumenítsa)**
Fl(2)9s8M
**Nisís Sívota** Fl(3)20s12M

**Nísos Paxoí**
**Lákka** Fl(3)24s20M
**Nisís Panayía** Fl.WR.5s10/8M
**Nísos Andípaxoi** Fl.WR.6s12/9M

**Ákra Mítikas (Préveza)**
Fl.WR.3s7/5M

**Nísos Levkas**
**Fort Santa Maura (Levkas Canal N Entrance)**
Fl(2)WR.12s8/5M
**Nisídha Sésoula** Fl.4·5s8M
**Ákra Dhoukaton** Fl.10s24M

**Nísos Kefallinia (Cephalonia)**
**Ákra Yero-Gómbos** LFl(2)15s24M
**Nisís Vardhiánoi** Fl.WR.7·5s6/4M
**Nisís Kalóyeros** Fl.4s8M
**Nisís Pondikos** Fl.3s8M
**Ákra Kateliós** Fl(2)WR.15s11/8M
**Ákra Kapri** Fl(3)WR.9s6/4M
**Ákra Fiskárdho** Fl.3s6M

**Itháki (Ithaka)**
**Ákra Áy Nikoláou** Fl(3)15s7M
**Ákra Áy Ioánnis** Fl.10s10M
**Ákra Pisaitós** Fl.5s6M
**Ákra Oxiá** Fl(2)15s17M

**Zákinthos (Zante)**
**Ákra Skinári** Fl.5s20M
**Nisidhia Áy Nikólaos** Fl.2s7M
**Ákra Krionéri** Fl(2)16s6M
**Ákra Kerí** Fl(3+1)15s17M

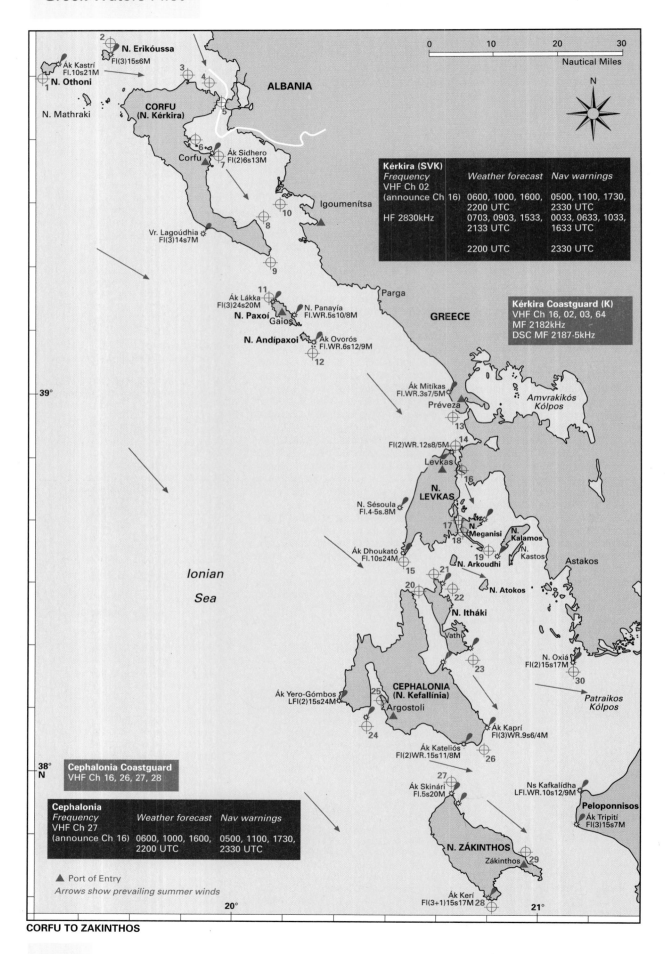

2 &#9775; **N. Erikóussa**
Fl.(3)15s6M

&#9775; Ák Kastrí
Fl.10s21M
1 &#9775; **N. Othoni**

N. Mathraki

3 &#9775;

4 &#9775;

**ALBANIA**

**CORFU
(N. Kérkira)**

5

6 &#9775;

Corfu

Ák Sidhero
7 Fl.(2)6s13M

10 &#9775;

Igoumenítsa

8 &#9775;

Vr. Lagoúdhia
Fl.(3)14s7M

9 &#9775;

Parga

| **Kérkira (SVK)** | | |
|---|---|---|
| *Frequency* | *Weather forecast* | *Nav warnings* |
| VHF Ch 02 | | |
| (announce Ch 16) | 0600, 1000, 1600, | 0500, 1100, 1730, |
| | 2200 UTC | 2330 UTC |
| HF 2830kHz | 0703, 0903, 1533, | 0033, 0633, 1033, |
| | 2133 UTC | 1633 UTC |
| | 2200 UTC | 2330 UTC |

11 &#9775;
Ák Lákka
Fl.(3)24s20M
**N. Paxoí**
Gaios
N. Panayía
Fl.WR.5s10/8M

**N. Andípaxoi**
Ák Ovorós
Fl.WR.6s12/9M
12 &#9775;

**GREECE**

| **Kérkira Coastguard (K)** |
|---|
| VHF Ch 16, 02, 03, 64 |
| MF 2182kHz |
| DSC MF 2187·5kHz |

Ák Mitíkas
Fl.WR.3s7/5M
Préveza
13 &#9775;

*Amvrakikós
Kólpos*

14 &#9775;
Fl.(2)WR.12s8/5M
Levkas

16

**N.
LEVKAS**

N. Sésoula
Fl.4·5s.8M

17 **N.
Meganisi**
18
N.
Kalamos
19 N.
Kastos
N. Arkoudhi

Astakos

Ák Dhoukató
Fl.10s24M
15 &#9775;

21 &#9775;
20
22 &#9775;
**N. Atokos**

**N. Ithák&#305;**

*Ionian
Sea*

Vathí

N. Oxiá
Fl.(2)15s17M
23 &#9775;
30 &#9775;

*Patraikos
Kólpos*

**CEPHALONIA
(N. Kefallínia)**

Ák Yero-Gómbos
LFl.(2)15s24M
25 &#9775;
Argostoli
24 &#9775;

Ák Kaprí
Fl.(3)WR.9s6/4M

Ák Kateliós
Fl.(2)WR.15s11/8M
26 &#9775;

27 &#9775;
Ák Skinári
Fl.5s20M

Ns Kafkalídha
LFl.WR.10s12/9M

**Peloponnisos**
Ák Tripití
Fl.(3)15s7M

| **Cephalonia Coastguard** |
|---|
| VHF Ch 16, 26, 27, 28 |

| **Cephalonia** | | |
|---|---|---|
| *Frequency* | *Weather forecast* | *Nav warnings* |
| VHF Ch 27 | | |
| (announce Ch 16) | 0600, 1000, 1600, | 0500, 1100, 1730, |
| | 2200 UTC | 2330 UTC |

**N. ZÁKINTHOS**
Zákinthos
29 &#9775;

Ák Kerí
Fl.(3+1)15s17M 28 &#9775;

&#9650; Port of Entry
*Arrows show prevailing summer winds*

**CORFU TO ZAKINTHOS**

## USEFUL WAYPOINTS

⊕1  ½M S of Othoní SW point
    light
    39°49'·7N 19°23'·2E

⊕2  ½M N Erikoússa Ák Skotini
    39°54'·5N 19°34'·8E

⊕3  0·35M N of Ák Aikateríni
    (Corfu N)
    39°49'·70N 19°51'·05E
    WGS84

⊕4  Mid-channel between Nisís
    Peristeraí and Ák Psaromíta
    39°47'·29N 19°57'·19E
    WGS84

⊕5  ¼M E of Ifalos Sérpa (Corfu
    N Channel)
    39°46'·24N 19°57'·86E
    WGS84

⊕6  ½M E of Ák Kommeno
    (Gouvía)
    39°39'·9N 19°52'·5E

⊕7  ½M E of Ák Sidhero (Corfu E
    side)
    39°37'·36N 19°56'·61E
    WGS84

⊕8  1M E of Ák Levkímmis light
    (Corfu E side)
    39°27'·7N 20°05'·4E

⊕9  1M S of Ák Asprokavos
    (Corfu S end)
    39°20'·6N 20°06'·8E

⊕10  ½M S of Prasoúdhi
     (Igoumenítsa) light
     39°30'·1N 20°09'·3E

⊕11  ½M N of Lákka entrance
     (Paxos)
     39°15'·2N 20°07'·7E

⊕12  1M S of Ák Ovoros
     (AntiPaxos)
     39°06'·8N 20°15'·6E

⊕13  Entrance to Préveza channel
     (outer buoys)
     38°55'·90N 20°43'·66E
     WGS84

⊕14  N Entrance to Levkas Canal
     38°50'·79N 20°43'·27E
     WGS84

⊕15  ½M S of Ák Dhoukató
     (Levkas SW end)
     38°33'·4N 20°32'·5E

⊕16  S end of Levkas Canal
     38°47'·54N 20°43'·58E
     WGS84

⊕17  N end Meganísi Channel
     38°40'·10N 20°43'·72E
     WGS84

⊕18  S end Meganísi Channel
     38°37'·88N 20°43'·88E
     WGS84

⊕19  1M SE of Ák Kefáli (Meganísi
     S end)
     38°34'·8N 20°49'·8E

⊕20  N end Ithaca Channel
     38°28'·47N 20°35'·73E
     WGS84

⊕21  ¼M N of Ák Marmara (Ithaca
     N end)
     38°30'·47N 20°38'·93E
     WGS84

⊕22  0·10M E of Ák Áy Nikoláou
     (Ithaca NE end)
     38°29'·29N 20°40'·83E
     WGS84

⊕23  1M S of Ák Áy Íoannis light
     (Ithaca SE end)
     38°18'·3N 20°46'·0E

⊕24  1M S of N. Vardhiánoi light
     (Cephalonia SW side)
     38°07'·1N 20°25'·7E

⊕25  ½M W of Ák Áy Theodhoroi
     (Kólpos Argostoliou)
     38°11'·6N 20°27'·6E

⊕26  2M SE of Ák Mounda
     (Cephalonia SE end)
     38°02'·2N 20°49'·15E

⊕27  1M N of Ák Skinari light
     (Zákinthos N end)
     37°56'·9N 20°42'·2E

⊕28  1M S of Ák Marathia
     (Zákinthos SW end)
     37°37'·9N 20°50'·0E

⊕29  Limín Zákinthos entrance
     37°46'·86N 20°54'·41E
     WGS84

⊕30  ½M S of Ák Oxiá
     38°16'·60N 21°05'95E WGS84

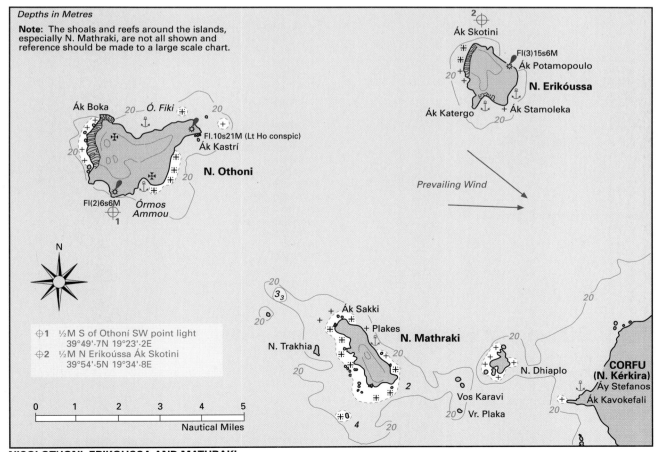

**Depths in Metres**

**Note:** The shoals and reefs around the islands, especially N. Mathraki, are not all shown and reference should be made to a large scale chart.

⊕1  ½M S of Othoní SW point light
    39°49'·7N 19°23'·2E
⊕2  ½M N Erikoússa Ák Skotini
    39°54'·5N 19°34'·8E

**NISOI OTHONI, ERIKOUSSA AND MATHRAKI**

## Quick reference guide

| | Shelter | Mooring | Fuel | Water | Provisioning | Tavernas | Plan |
|---|---|---|---|---|---|---|---|
| **Corfu and outlying islands** | | | | | | | |
| Nisís Othoní | | | | | | | |
| Órmos Fiki (N Bay) | C | C | O | O | O | O | |
| Órmos Ammou (S Bay) | B | C | O | B | C | C | • |
| Erikoússa (S Bay) | B | AC | O | B | C | C | • |
| Plakes | B | AB | O | B | C | C | |
| **Nísos Kérkira (Corfu I)** | | | | | | | |
| 'Kassiopi | B | A | B | B | B | A | • |
| 'Ayios Stefanos | B | C | O | B | C | B | • |
| 'Kouloura | C | C | O | O | O | C | • |
| Kalami | C | C | O | O | O | C | • |
| Agni | C | C | O | O | O | C | • |
| Limín Gouvíon | A | A | A | B | A | A | • |
| Limín Kérkira (Corfu) | A | AB | A | A | A | A | • |
| Mandraki | B | A | O | A | A | A | |
| Naok | B | A | O | A | A | A | • |
| Benitses | O | C | O | O | C | B | |
| Petriti | B | AC | O | A | C | B | • |
| Kávos | C | A | O | O | O | O | • |
| Áy Stefanos (Avliotes) | B | AC | B | B | C | C | • |
| Áy Yeoryiou | O | C | O | O | O | C | |
| Palaíokastrita | B | AC | B | B | B | A | • |
| **Nísos Paxoí** | | | | | | | |
| Lákka | B | AC | B | B | C | B | • |
| Longos | C | C | O | O | C | C | |
| Gaios | A | A | B | B | B | B | • |
| Mongonisi | A | AC | O | O | O | C | |
| **Mainland coast adjacent to Corfu** | | | | | | | |
| 'Pagania | A | C | O | O | O | O | • |
| 'Sayiadha | B | A | O | A | B | B | • |
| Ormiskos Valtou (Igoumenítsa Creek) | A | C | O | O | O | O | • |
| Igoumenítsa | C | AB | B | B | B | B | • |
| Nisís Sívota and Moúrtos | B | AC | B | B | B | B | • |
| Parga | B | AC | B | B | B | A | • |
| Áy Ioannou | C | C | O | O | O | O | |
| Ligia | B | A | O | O | C | C | • |
| Préveza | B | AB | B | A | A | B | • |
| **Amvrakikós Kólpos (Gulf of Amvrakia)** | | | | | | | |
| Vónitsa | B | AC | B | B | B | C | • |
| Loutráki | C | C | O | B | C | C | |
| Amfilokhia | C | BC | B | B | B | C | |
| Menidhion | B | AC | O | B | C | C | • |
| Koronisía | B | AB | O | B | C | C | |
| **Nísos Levkas and adjacent islands** | | | | | | | |
| **Levkas** | | | | | | | |
| Levkas Town | A | AB | A | A | A | A | • |
| Ligia | C | C | B | B | C | B | |
| Nikiana | B | A | B | A | C | C | • |
| Nidri | B | AC | B | A | B | A | • |
| Tranquil Bay | A | C | O | O | O | O | • |
| **Órmos Vlikho** | A | AC | B | B | C | C | • |
| Sívota | A | AC | O | A | C | B | • |
| Vasilikí | B | A | B | A | B | B | • |
| **Nísos Meganísi** | | | | | | | |
| Spartakhori | B | AC | O | B | C | C | • |
| Port Vathi | A | AC | O | O | C | C | • |
| Abelike and Kapali | B | C | O | O | O | O | • |
| Port Atheni | B | C | O | O | O | C | • |
| **Nísos Itháki (Ithaca)** | | | | | | | |
| Frikes | B | A | O | B | C | C | • |
| Kióni | B | AC | O | O | C | C | • |
| Port Vathi | A | AC | B | B | B | B | • |
| Pera Pigadhi | B | AC | O | O | O | O | • |
| Áy Andréou | C | C | O | O | O | O | |
| Port Polis | C | C | O | O | C | C | |
| **Nísos Kefallinia (Cephalonia)** | | | | | | | |
| Argostoli | A | AB | A | A | A | B | • |
| Lixouri | B | A | B | B | B | C | • |
| Áy Kiriakis | C | A | O | O | O | C | |
| Assos | C | AC | O | B | C | B | • |
| Fiskárdho | A | AC | B | A | B | A | • |
| Áy Eufimia | B | AC | B | A | C | B | • |
| Sami | C | AB | B | A | B | C | • |
| Póros | B | AC | B | B | B | B | • |
| **Mainland coast adjacent to the inland sea** | | | | | | | |
| Palairos (Zaverda) | B | A | B | A | B | B | • |
| Vounaki | B | A | A | A | C | C | • |
| Mitika | C | AC | B | B | C | C | • |
| **Nísos Kálamos** | | | | | | | |
| Port Kalamos | B | A | O | B | C | C | • |
| Port Leone | B | C | O | O | O | O | • |
| Episkopi | B | AB | O | O | O | O | |
| **Nísos Kastos** | | | | | | | |
| Port Kastos | B | A | O | O | C | C | • |
| **Mainland coast** | | | | | | | |
| Atoko | C | C | O | O | O | O | |
| Marathia | C | C | O | O | O | O | |
| Astakós | B | A | B | A | B | C | • |
| Port Pandelimon | AB | C | O | O | O | O | • |
| Platí Yiali | B | C | O | O | O | O | • |
| Nisís Petalas | B | C | O | O | O | O | • |
| Nisís Oxiá | C | C | O | O | O | O | |
| **Nísos Zákinthos (Zante)** | | | | | | | |
| Áy Nikólaos | B | C | O | O | O | C | • |
| Port Zákinthos | A | A | A | A | A | A | • |
| Porto Roma | O | C | O | O | O | C | |
| Lagana | C | AC | O | O | C | B | • |
| Port Kierí | C | C | O | O | O | C | • |
| Port Vroma | C | C | O | O | O | O | |

1. See 'Prohibited Areas'

# Nisoi Othoní and Erikoússa

When crossing from Italy to Corfu there are two islands, Othoní and Erikoússa, lying off the N end of Corfu island, which have useful anchorages often used by yachts to break the passage between Italy and Corfu.

## NISÍS OTHONÍ (Othonoí Fano)

BA206
Imray-Tetra G11

Nisís Othoní is a bold precipitous island (500m high with a sheer cliff face on the western side), but with the normal summer haze it will often not be seen until two or three miles off. There are two anchorages, Fiki on the N and Ammou on the S. Ammou is the bay normally used in the summer with the prevailing N–WNW winds.

## ÓRMOS AMMOU

### Approach

From the N the lighthouse on the NE corner will be seen. From the W head for the SW tip of the island – the light tower on the SW cannot be seen until closer in. The houses of the hamlet will not be seen until you open the bay.

*Dangers* Care needs to be taken in the approaches of Ifalos Aspri Pétra (1·8m), a reef lying directly in the S approach. Care also needs to be taken of underwater rocks lying off the coast on the E side of the entrance. The approach should be made from a SW direction with a lookout forward conning you in.

### Mooring

Anchor in 2–10m where convenient without blocking the immediate approaches to the small harbour. The ferry charges in here at speed and needs all the space at the entrance to manoeuvre. The bottom is sand and weed, mostly good holding, although there are some anchor-snagging rocks closer in. It is possible to go bows-to part of the quay when the ferry is not due, though care must be taken as the bottom comes up quickly off parts of the

quay. Alternatively anchor and take a long line to the outside of the breakwater.

*Shelter* With the normal NW wind there are mild gusts out of the bay and some swell works its way around into here, but it is secure enough in settled conditions. The new stubby breakwater on the W side of the bay provides some additional shelter from the ground swell that can work its way in. Open S.

### Facilities

Ashore there are several tavernas which often have fresh fish. Limited provisions can be obtained and even small amounts of money can be changed if you arrive from Italy without drachmae. Telephone in the local shop.

*Note* Yachts should not attempt to enter the small fishing harbour to the E (Avlaki) as the entrance is rock-bound and depths in the harbour are variable.

## ÓRMOS FIKI

The bay on the N side of the island offers a good anchorage in the event of winds from the S and SE. Care must be taken of the numerous above and

ÓRMOS AMMOU
⊕39°50'·5N 19°24'·5E

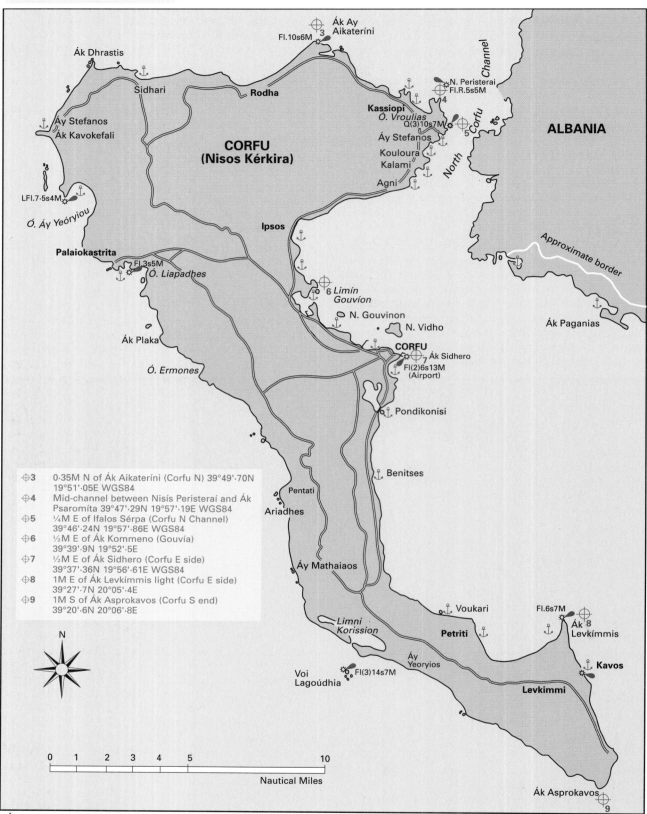

Ák Dhrastis

Sidhari

Rodha

Ák Ay Aikateríni

Fl.10s6M

N. Peristerai
Fl.R.5s5M

North Corfu Channel

ALBANIA

Áy Stefanos
Ák Kavokefali

Kassiopi
Ó. Vroulias
Q(3)10s7M

Áy Stefanos

CORFU
(Nisos Kérkira)

Kouloura
Kalami

LFl.7·5s4M

Agni

Ó. Áy Yeóryiou

Ipsos

Palaiokastrita

Fl.3s5M

Ó. Liapadhes

6 Limín Gouvíon

Ák Paganias

Approximate border

Ák Plaka

N. Gouvinon

N. Vidho

Ó. Ermones

CORFU

Ák Sidhero
Fl(2)6s13M
(Airport)

Pondikonisi

Benitses

Pentati

Ariadhes

**3** 0·35M N of Ák Aikateríni (Corfu N) 39°49'·70N
19°51'·05E WGS84

**4** Mid-channel between Nisís Peristeraí and Ák
Psaromíta 39°47'·29N 19°57'·19E WGS84

**5** ¼M E of Ifalos Sérpa (Corfu N Channel)
39°46'·24N 19°57'·86E WGS84

**6** ½M E of Ák Kommeno (Gouvía)
39°39'·9N 19°52'·5E

**7** ½M E of Ák Sidhero (Corfu E side)
39°37'·36N 19°56'·61E WGS84

**8** 1M E of Ák Levkímmis light (Corfu E side)
39°27'·7N 20°05'·4E

**9** 1M S of Ák Asprokavos (Corfu S end)
39°20'·6N 20°06'·8E

Áy Mathaiaos

Voukari

Fl.6s7M

Ák 8
Levkímmis

Limni Korission

Petriti

Kavos

N

Áy Yeoryios

Levkimmi

Voi
Lagoúdhia

Fl(3)14s7M

0 1 2 3 4 5 10

Nautical Miles

Ák Asprokavos
9

**NÍSOS KERKIRA (CORFU)**

below-water rocks in the vicinity of the bay. When anchoring try to find a patch of sand for plough-type anchors although a fisherman can be hooked on the rocky bottom – attach a trip line. A reef extends a little way from the middle of the bay so caution is necessary close to the shore. I have used this anchorage to ride out a gale from the SE and the shelter from that quarter is excellent.

## ERIKOÚSSA (Merlera, Mérikha)

The island lying about 7 miles due E of Othoní. It is a lower island than Othoní and like Othoní difficult to spot until 1½–2 miles off with the normal summer heat haze. The only village is on the shores of the large sandy bay on the S which affords good shelter from the prevailing NW winds.

## PORT ERIKOÚSSA

BA 206
Imray-Tetra G11

### Approach

The port is on the western side of the large bay on the S side of Erikoússa. The approach is free from dangers except for the reefs running out about 100m from Ák Katergo and Ák Stamoleka on either side of the bay.

*By night* There are no lights, but the lights of the village and the arc lights around the electricity generating plant to the E of the village can be identified.

### Mooring

Anchor off in the bay or go stern or bows-to on the W quay of the small harbour. When the tripper boats are not in you can go alongside the end of the jetty off the village. In the bay anchor in 3-6 metres on a sandy bottom, good holding. In the harbour the bottom is mud and rubble, generally good holding.

*Shelter* Good shelter at anchor from the prevailing NW winds although there are gusts into the bay. Reasonable shelter in the harbour although you are side-on to the gusts. Some shelter from southerlies in the harbour although strong SE winds could make it untenable.

### Facilities

Tavernas ashore, several of which have good fresh fish. Limited provisions. Ferry service to Corfu.

### General

The bay is a useful anchorage, well sheltered from the prevailing summer northerlies, when en route between Greece and Italy. The sandy beach attracts tripper boats from Corfu, but they all disappear by

**LIMÍN ERIKOUSSA**
⊕39°52'·6N 19°34'·8E

1600 and the anchorage is then a peaceful one. The only thing that disturbs the night air is the noise from the electricity generating plant on the shore.

### NOTE

On the E side of the island there are some delightful coves and bights that a yacht can explore in calm weather or with light NW winds.

## NISÍS MATHRAKI

This island off the NW tip of Corfu is surrounded by above and below-water rocks. When navigating in the vicinity of the island every care is needed, especially when the prevailing NW wind is blowing and it can be difficult to pick out the rocks and reefs. If you are heading here it is generally best to do so in the morning before the breeze picks up. On the E side of the island there is the small harbour of Plakes.

### PLAKES 39°46'·9N 19°31'·3E

The harbour lies on the E side somewhat more towards the NW end. Make the approach from a northerly direction as shoals extend out from the shore to the SE of the harbour. Two rough stone breakwaters extend out from the shore enclosing the old mole that protects the fishing boat basin. There are 5m depths in the entrance and 2–2·5m depths on the outside of the mole protecting the inner basin. Go stern or bows-to the mole leaving the space on the end free for the ferry. There is room for perhaps half a dozen yachts here provided no fishing boats are using the outside of the mole. The harbour is very small so you need to have everything ready before you enter. Good shelter and open only NE.

There are several tavernas nearby and basic provisions can be found. Wonderful sandy beaches nearby.

# Nísos Kérkira
## (Corfu Island)

Most people know little of the Ionian but there are few who have not heard of Corfu. The references to Corfu from Homer to the present day praise the island as a lush green paradise spinning a soothing spell over all who visit it. In an age of package holidays the Corfu magic is continuously battered by jets winging in with yet more holidaymakers – and far, far more go to Corfu than to the rest of the Ionian – so it is surprising to find there are still charming and beautiful places on the island.

Corfu lies like a plump sickle off the west coast of Albania and mainland Greece. The channel between the northern end of Corfu and Albania is just one mile across – from Corfu you can see the military outpost at Butrino quite clearly. In contrast to the bare mountains of Albania, Corfu is a luxuriant green island from Mt Pandokrator in the north sloping down to the coastal plains in the south. In the centre are broken slopes cut by green valleys and grassy fields. Seeing cows grazing on the slopes of the hinterland it is sometimes difficult to believe you are in Greece.

## Corfu history

One of the spin-offs of tourism is the proliferation of guides describing the history, places-to-see and things-to-do in Corfu and so rather than attempt to condense the whole history of the island from such guides I have prepared instead a brief synoptic history. This little history also describes, somewhat more loosely, the chain of events and invasions determining the character of the other islands in the Ionian.

*c*.1200BC It is surmised that Homer's Skheria, the island home of the Phaeacians, was Corfu. Palaíokastrita is thought to be the site of the castle of King Alkinoos. The Phaeacians ferried Odysseus home to Ithaca, in so doing arousing the wrath of Poseidon who turned their ship to stone. The island of Gravia off Palaíokastrita is said to be this petrified ship although some say it is the island of Pondokonisi (Mouse Island) near Kanoni.

*c*.734 to 434BC Corfu is colonised by the Corinthians. Corfu, itching for independence from the mother city, called on the Athenians to aid it against the Corinthians who naturally enough asked the opposing Spartans to give them a hand in quelling Corfu. Thus Corfu was indirectly the cause of the disastrous Peloponnesian War that effectively obliterated Athens and classical Greece.

229BC Corfu colonised by Rome.

722AD Corfu passed to the eastern Byzantine Empire.

1080 to 1386 After a collection of Norman and Sicilian rulers, Corfu invites the Venetians to restore order. Corfu remained under Venetian rule until 1797.

1460 The body of St Spiridon is brought to the island and becomes the patron saint of Corfu. Every year there are four processions on which the body of St Spiridon is brought out: Palm Sunday, Easter Saturday, the 11th of August, to commemorate the defeat of the Turks in 1716, and the first Sunday in November to commemorate the end of a plague. Every second male in Corfu seems to be called Spiros after the patron saint.

1431, 1537, 1716 Major assaults by the Turks on Corfu.

1797 Corfu taken over by the French. The French laid out a regular street plan for Corfu and began the construction of the arcaded buildings on the esplanade in Corfu town.

1814 Corfu occupied by the British who began many public works as well as introducing ginger beer, fruit cake and cricket.

1864 Corfu ceded to Greece. Today Corfu reflects many of these influences in its own special Corfiot architecture and culture. The eerie Medusa in the museum, the Venetian forts and galley port, the French architecture raising a second Rue de Rivoli far from Paris, cricket and cake on Sundays, Byzantine churches...yet undeniably Greek, as Lawrence Durrell will tell you:

`A glance at the synoptic history of the place will do nothing to decrease the sense of being out of one's depth, submerged by too much data. But as time goes on, as sunny Greek mornings succeed each other, you will find everything sinking to the bottom of your mind's harbour, there to take up shapes and dispositions which are purely Greek and have no frame or reference to history anywhere else.'

Lawrence Durrell *The Greek Islands*

## North coast of Corfu

**NOTE** Care is needed when approaching the NE corner of Corfu because of the unsettled political situation in Albania. See the note at the beginning of this chapter.

### ÁK AIKATERÍNI

⊕3 0·35M N of Ák Aikateríni (Corfu N) 39°49'·70N 19°51'·05E WGS84

In Órmos Áy Yeoryios on the W side of Ák Aikateríni a small harbour is under construction. Works were in progress in 2001 and at the time of publication the harbour is not useable by yachts. It may be worth investigating in the future.

### ÓRMOS IMEROLIA

39°47'·5N 19°55'·0E

The bay on the W side of Ák Kassiopi. With light NW–W winds it is possible to anchor on the W side of the bay where there is some shelter although some swell still penetrates. In southerlies or in calm weather anchor where convenient. The bottom is sand and mud, good holding.

Tavernas open in the summer.

### KASSIOPI (Avlon Kassapeto)

BA 206

**Approach**

From the W the castle on the headland and a number of houses around Órmos Imerolia will be seen. From the E the buildings of Kassiopi are readily identified. The small harbour itself will not be seen until you are right into the bay.

**Mooring**

Yachts should go stern-to the quay on the E side under the stubby breakwater. Depths here are

KASSIOPI
⊕39°47'·48N 19°55'·40E WGS84

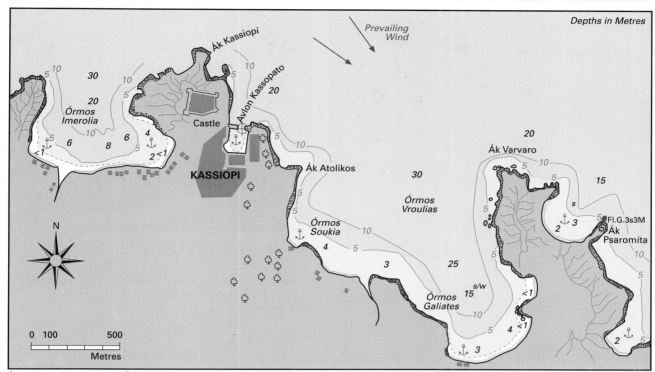

Depths in Metres

Prevailing Wind

**ÓRMOS IMEROLIA TO ÁK PSAROMITA**
⊕ 39°47′·48N 19°55′·40E WGS84

irregular so some care is needed. The bottom is mud and weed, adequate holding once the anchor is in.

*Shelter* Adequate shelter from the prevailing NW-W breeze although some swell penetrates. If the wind goes around to the N or NE it can get very uncomfortable and may become untenable in here.

### Facilities

Water from private sources. A fuel station in the town. Good shopping for provisions and numerous tavernas and restaurants of all types. Bank. PO. Hire scooters.

### General

Kassiopi is a thriving tourist spot with numerous small hotels and self-catering apartments around the original village. In July and August it is crowded with holidaymakers, but outside high season it retains some of the charm of what was a small fishing village.

Nisís Peristeraí and lighthouse at the northern end of North Corfu Channel looking ESE

## ÓRMOS VROULIAS

The large bay immediately E of Kassiopi. In settled weather there are several attractive anchorages on the W side and at the head of the bay. The bottom is mostly sand and weed. On the E side of Ák Varvaro there are two small coves affording reasonable shelter on either side of Ák Psaromíta.

# East coast of Corfu

### NORTHERN CORFU CHANNEL (VORION STENÓN KÉRKIRAS)

BA 206
Imray-Tetra G11

From the N pass between Nisís Peristeraí and Corfu and proceed with caution into the channel until the platform E cardinal beacon on Ifalos Sérpa is sighted. Leave the beacon well to starboard – it is not on the extremity of the reef. When you pass through the channel outside Ifalos Sérpa you are less than a mile from the Albanian coast. At night the light on Nisís Peristeraí Fl.R.5s5M is easily seen from the distance stated and once into the channel the light Q(3)10s7M on the beacon at the end of Ifalos Sérpa will be seen.

*Note* See caution on Albania at the beginning of this chapter.

### AYIOS STEFANOS[1]

A small inlet immediately S of Ifalos Sérpa in the North Corfu Channel. Although just below a military post no objection is normally made to anchoring here.

Áy Stefanos looking SE

The miniature harbour in Órmos Kouloura looking NE

**ÓRMOS ÁY STEFANOU**
⊕39°45'·90N 19°57'·09E WGS84

Proceed into the middle of the bay and anchor in 3–6m depths. The bottom is mud and thick weed which can be difficult to get through. Excellent shelter from the NW wind. On the S side of the bay there is a rough stone mole, but this is usually occupied by local boats.

Some provisions can be obtained and there are numerous tavernas around the shore. Although a number of holiday villas have been built here, the bay retains a calm and beauty well worth the stop for the night.

## KOULOURA[1]

A small bay S of Áy Stefanos. There is a miniature harbour surrounded by shoal water at the SE end of the bay. A yacht drawing one metre or less can enter with care from the N. Excellent shelter inside. Alternatively anchor in 5–10m depths immediately W of the small harbour and take a long line ashore or anchor in the W of the bay in 8–15m. There are two stub jetties off the taverna. The bottom is covered in thick weed. Good shelter from the prevailing NW wind.

1. These harbours lie within an officially prohibited area though the prohibition is disregarded in practice.

Ashore above the small harbour is a taverna which though frequently crowded for lunch is less hectic at night.

## KALAMI[1]

Immediately S of Kouloura is Órmos Kalami. Open to the S and E, it offers good shelter from the prevailing NW wind. Anchor in 4–6m depths in the NW of the bay. There is also a jetty off the taverna on the W side of the bay that can be used. Some provisions and tavernas ashore.

**ÓRMOS KOULOURA, KALAMI AND AGNI**
⊕39°44'·7N 19°56'·6E

**CORFU: NORTH CHANNEL**

⊕3   0·35M N of Ák Aikateríni (Corfu N)
     39°49'·70N 19°51'·05E WGS84
⊕4   Mid-channel between Nisís Peristerai and Ák Psaromíta
     39°47'·29N 19°57'·19E WGS84
⊕5   ¼M E of Ifalos Serpa (Corfu N Channel)
     39°46'·24N 19°57'·86E WGS84
⊕6   ½M E of Ák Kommeno (Gouvía)
     39°39'·9N 19°52'·5E
⊕7   ½M E of Ák Sidhero (Corfu E side)
     39°37'·36N 19°56'·61E WGS84

## AGNI

The bay immediately S of Kalami. Anchor at the N end or at the S end. There are several jetties off the tavernas at the S end of the bay that can be used. Good shelter from the NW wind although it gusts into the bay. Tavernas ashore.

## NOTE

Care is needed if you are using any of the jetties from Kouloura to Agni as a considerable wash is created by the fast ferries steaming in and out of the North Corfu Channel. Several yachts have been damaged by the wash when moored overnight so it may be wise to anchor off rather than going stern-to a jetty.

Ák Sidhero on Corfu looking SW into Órmos Garítsas. Corfu old harbour is just out of the picture right
*Peter Kleinoth/MareTeam*

Ák Sidhero looking S

## IPSOS 39°41'·7N 19°50'·3E

A small harbour has been constructed here consisting of a rough stone breakwater extending in a northerly direction for nearly 200 metres and a short sheltering breakwater extending E. There are 2–3m depths in the entrance and 2–2·5m depths off the E breakwater. The quay running around the head of the harbour is shallow with depths mostly less than 1m and in any case is taken up with local boats. Anchor and take a long line to the rough stone breakwater. You will need to use your dinghy to get ashore. Adequate shelter from the prevailing NW–W wind but open N–NE.

Tavernas and bars ashore. Good shopping for provisions. Ipsos is a pretty noisy resort area and if you are looking for peace and quiet then head elsewhere.

N

0    100    500
Metres

*Prevailing Wind*

<1

1₅

3

m

1₅

1₅

2

1₅

<1

<1

4

1₅

2

<1

2

1₅

2

*Underwater pipeline*

8

Q.R
R

8

Venetian galley sheds

*Órmos Gouvíon*

7₅

7

6

6₅

Yard

Chandlers

WC

4

4

4₅

6 2F.R(vert)3M

6

5

4₅

4

3

3

3

3

GOUVÍA MARINA

To Palaikastrita and Kassiopi

Main road

To Corfu

4₅    3₅    4

3

Marina Office
Supermarket
Restaurant and bar

**Kondokali**

WC

Shops and tavernas

Ipapandi

Q.G
G

Q.R
R

6₅

10

12

10

10

2₅

9

6

9

9

2₂

5

5

4

5

Q.G
G

<1

*Mud bank*

<1

3

5

5

<1

5

Depths in Metres

**LIMÍN GOUVÍON AND GOUVÍA MARINA**
⊕39°39′·53N 19°51′·35E WGS84

## ÓRMOS GOUVÍON (Gouvía)

BA 2406
Imray-Tetra G11

The large enclosed bay NW of Corfu town with Gouvía Marina at the S end.

### Approach

*Conspicuous* Nisís Gouvíon in the S approach and Ákra Kommeno and Vrakhos Foustanopidhima on the N are readily identified. Two large hotels on the N side of the entrance are conspicuous. Once up to the entrance to the bay the red and green buoys marking the channel into the bay are readily seen. Entering the bay keep to the N side of the entrance to avoid the extensive shallows on the S.

*By night* There are no major lights to guide you in, but the conical buoys marking the channel are lit Fl.G and Fl.R, range probably about one mile. The lights on the channel buoys cannot always be relied upon. The end of the marina pier is lit 2F.R(vert)3M.

*VHF* Ch 16, 69 (24/24). Call sign *Gouvía Marina*.

*Dangers* The southern half of the entrance is obstructed by a shallow mud bank. The aforementioned buoys show the channel into the bay clear of the shoal water.

### Mooring

Yachts should head for the marina where they will be directed to a berth. Normally you will be met at the entrance to the marina by an inflatable and guided into your berth.

*Data* 960 berths to be expanded to 1200 berths. Visitors' berths. Max LOA 80m. Depths 2–6m.

*Berths* Berth where directed in the marina where you will be assisted by marina staff on the quay. There are laid moorings tailed to the quay.

*Shelter* The shelter in the marina is now much improved with the construction of new piers and is generally good. However some berths are still uncomfortable with the prevailing wind, especially those on the far west quay, and in strong N–NE winds berths here can get very uncomfortable.

*Authorities* Harbourmaster and marina staff. Charge band 2/3.

**South Anchorage** Can no longer be used as the new pontoons installed by the marina cover most of this area. It is prohibited to anchor in the North Bay.

### Facilities

*Services* Water and electricity (220 and 380V) at all berths. Telephone connections. Shower and toilet blocks. Laundry. 24 hour security.

*Fuel* At the N end of the W quay. Depths are reported to be 3m.

*Repairs* 65-ton travel-hoist. Most yacht repairs can be arranged here including mechanical and engineering repairs, sail repairs, electrical and electronic repairs, GRP and wood repairs. The best policy is to get in touch with the base manager who will organise the necessary repairs. Chandlers in the marina and in Kondokali (Force 5 Chandlers).

Nautilus Yacht Chandlers, Marina Gouvía, 49100 Corfu, GR. ☎ 0661 90343 *Fax* 0661 99277.

*Provisions* There is a supermarket within the marina and supermarkets in Kondokali.

*Eating out* Restaurant at the marina. Others in Kondokali.

IKG Hellenic Marinas, Marina Gouvia, PO Box 29, 49100, Corfu. ☎ (30) 661 91900 *Fax* (30) 661 91829 *E-mail* ikghm@otenet.gr www.gouviamarina.gr

Gouvía Marina looking SE          *IKG Hellenic Marinas*

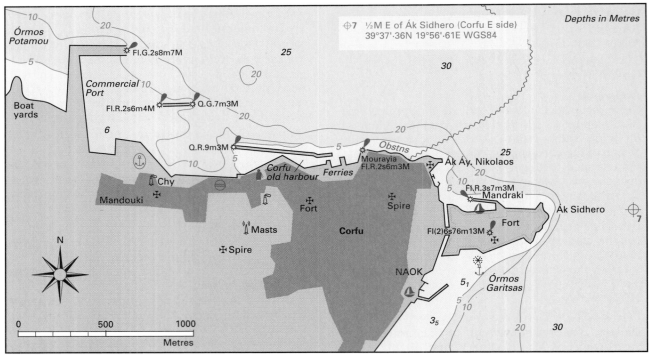

**APPROACHES TO CORFU**

## General

Kondokali was once a small fishing village, but that was long ago before hotels and self-catering apartments were built around the coast. Now it plays host to predominantly English tourists who can find all things English here · – English newspapers, English breakfasts, an English pint, English Sunday lunches – but few things Greek.

The marina was recently sold to the IKG Hellenic Marinas group and is being developed and expanded. The marina is the base for a large number of charter craft and also a popular spot for yachties to spend the winter. It is around 15 minutes from Corfu airport. To get into Corfu either take a bus (every half hour on the main road) or get a taxi.

## NEARBY BOATYARDS

Between Gouvía and Corfu there are several yards which haul yachts. Yachts up to 20–30 tons can be hauled out here on a cradle and slipway. Associated with the yards are various companies who can carry out most yacht repairs including GRP repairs,

**LIMÍN KERKIRA (PALAIO LIMANI)**
⊕39°37'·66N 19°55'·15E WGS84

woodwork, engineering and mechanical work, electrical work, sail repairs and canvas work.

## LIMÍN KÉRKIRA (Corfu Harbour)

BA 2406
Imray-Tetra G11

### Approach

*Conspicuous* From the N Nisís Vidho obscures part of the town. Nisís Vidho and the rock (Vrak Navsika) nearby are conspicuous from the distance. As you near the harbour the buildings of the town will be seen. From the S the Venetian citadel on Ák Sidhero and the lighthouse atop it are clearly visible from some distance off. A red belfry in the town and the two radio masts to the W of the town are also conspicuous.

*By night* Use the light on Ák Sidhero Fl(2)6s13M and closer in the lights of the harbour. The old harbour is lit at the E end Fl.R.3s.3M and the detached breakwater is lit: Q.G.3M and Fl.R.2s4M. The end of the new breakwater is lit Fl.G.2s7M. The red lights atop the radio masts in the town are clearly visible and the citadel is often spotlit in the summer.

*Notes*
1. It is safe to pass between Nisís Vidho and Vrak Navsika.
2. The harbour is used by considerable numbers of ferries from Italy and smaller landing-craft-type ferries from Igoumenítsa. A yacht should give way to these ferries at all times and a good lookout should be kept for them in the approaches to the harbour.

## Mooring

If you require a transit log go on the customs quay. After obtaining your transit log moor in the old harbour to the E of the customs quay. If there is a strong NW wind you can sometimes moor in the old harbour and obtain your transit log from there as the customs quay can be dangerous with the prevailing NW wind. In the summer it is best to arrive early in the morning aiming to be off the customs quay before the NW wind arrives about noon. In the old harbour the most comfortable place is alongside the outer breakwater where the NW wind will hold you off. The old harbour is full of tripper boats and it can be difficult to find a berth. Often you will have to go two or three out from the mole and move when the tripper boats are ready to go.

*Shelter* Good shelter in the old harbour where only southerly gales set up a surge. As mentioned the quay off the customs area is open to the prevailing NW wind which blows straight down onto it.

*Authorities* Customs, immigration, and port police in the customs enclosure. A transit log can be obtained here and as all the relevant authorities are grouped close together this is a comparatively easy process.

*Note* There is talk of turning the old harbour into a marina although no plans are available yet and work had not started at the time of publication.

## Facilities

*Water* On the customs quay and a tap behind the toilet block in the old harbour.
*Fuel* On the customs quay.
*Repairs* Chandlers nearby on the waterfront.
*Provisions* Good shopping for all provisions. There are several small mini-markets on the waterfront, but you are better off going into town where there is a better choice. Ice can be ordered.
*Eating out* A wide choice of tavernas. Those clustered around the square SE of the harbour are as good as any or wander around and find your own favourite. Numerous bars dotted about everywhere.
*Other* PO (open 24 hours and will change foreign banknotes). OTE. Banks and exchange offices. Greek gas and *Camping Gaz*. Hospital. Hire cars, motorbikes, bicycles. Bus service to most parts of the island. Ferry service to Brindisi, Patras and Igoumenítsa. International flights and regular internal flights to Athens.

## General

Corfu town is one of those special places that grows on you the longer you stay. Unfortunately Corfu old harbour is smelly and crowded in the summer which adversely affects your views on the town. Gouvía is too far away unless you have your own land-based transport. The myriad tourists choking the narrow alleys can also put you off. Nonetheless persevere until Corfu charms you. There are many things to do and see in and around Corfu, but as much as anything it is just wandering around that gives pleasure and despite the increase in 'tourist alleys' selling nondescript knick-knacks, there is still much of the old town remaining intact and alive.

## MANDRÁKI

The harbour in Mandráki on the N side of Ák Sidhero belongs to two yacht clubs: POIATH, the Hellenic Offshore Racing Club, and IOK, the Corfu Sailing Club. You may be able to find a berth in here if there is room. The best bet is to go by land to contact the *marinero* in charge or alternatively try approaching the entrance and see if you are directed to a berth.

An L-shaped mole protects the harbour and the masts of the yachts inside are easily identified. There are 3–4m depths in the entrance and mostly 1·5–3m depths inside off the outer mole. Off the quay and on the E side depths are less. Laid moorings tailed to the quay or buoys. Good shelter inside. A charge is made.

The harbour is in an enviable situation under the steep walls of the fort on Ák Sidhero and it is a short walk into the middle of town.

## ÓRMOS GARÍTSAS

A yacht can anchor off on the S side of Ák Sidhero in Órmos Garítsas where there is good shelter from the prevailing NW wind. Anchor in 5–12m on mud, good holding.

## NAOK YACHT CLUB

The yacht harbour on the W side of Órmos Garítsas belongs to NAOK, the Nautical Club of Corfu. There are a limited number of berths for visiting yachts in the summer.

There are 3–4m depths in the entrance and 3m depths on the outer end of the mole decreasing further into the harbour. Off the W quay and piers there are a number of shallow patches. Go stern or bows-to the mole where directed or where convenient. Yachts can also go stern-to the outside of the mole. Good shelter from the prevailing NW winds. In strong southerlies the harbour is reported to be untenable.

Showers and toilets at the clubhouse. Charge band 2. It is a short walk up to the esplanade and the centre of town.

Órmos Garítsas on the S side of Ák Sidhero

**NAOK YC HARBOUR**
⊕39°37'·32N 19°55'·65E

### BENITSES (Benitsai) 39°32'·7N 19°54'·8E

An exposed anchorage 5 miles S of Corfu town. A large white hotel complex is conspicuous N of Benitses. Anchor in 3–10m. The anchorage is only really tenable in calm weather as the prevailing wind funnelled between Corfu and the mainland coast blows down from the N and pushes a swell in. There is a small harbour, but it is always full of local and tripper boats.

Ashore Benitses is a booming resort full of tavernas and bars for the tourists in the hotels and apartments around the original village.

### PETRITI

#### Approach

Seven miles SE of Benitses and just around Ák Voukari is the bay and little fishing port of Petriti. From the N the hamlet will not be seen but an eroded escarpment just S of Ák Voukari is conspicuous. Once the bay is opened the harbour mole and houses will be seen. From the E the houses of the hamlet are easily identified.

*Dangers* In the approach from the E care must be taken of the shoal water extending off the low-lying Ák Levkímmis.

#### Mooring

If there is room in the harbour go stern or bows-to the W quay or on the end of the mole. The harbour is often crowded with fishing boats and it may be difficult to find a berth. Alternatively anchor in the bay in 2–4m on mud, sand, and weed.

*Shelter* Good shelter from prevailing NW wind although some swell creeps around into the anchorage.

#### Facilities

Water on the quay. Limited provisions can be found. Tavernas around the harbour.

#### General

Petriti gets few visitors by land and is one of those sleepy hollows you quickly develop an affection for. It is a green place, watered by a stream, with a good sandy beach and clear water.

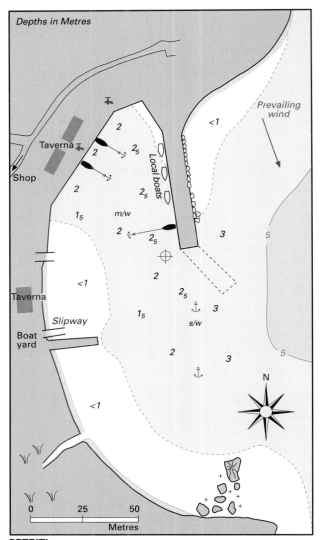

**PETRITI**
⊕39°27'·25N 20°00'·15E

### ÁK LEVKÍMMIS

The low-lying cape E of Petriti. It is difficult to pick out from the distance though the light structure near the end will eventually be seen. Shoal water extends for up to half a mile E and nearly a mile N of the cape and you should keep a healthy distance off.

### LEVKIMMI CANAL

Just S of Ák Levkímmis is the entrance to the canal leading to Levkimmi town (clearly visible). The entrance to the canal has silted and the depths just inside the canal are uneven – reported to be between 1–1·5m.

### LEVKIMMI HARBOUR (Kavos)

39°26'·20N 20°05'·30E

A new harbour just S of Levkimmi. At present it is still under construction though it is in use. The harbour has been built for ferries operating from the mainland and they use the space on the W quay. The harbour has been dredged to 4–5 metres. Berth where convenient clear of the ferry quay. The entrance is open to the prevailing wind and it can get uncomfortable and may be untenable with strong N winds. Strong southerlies cause a surge. At present there are no facilities.

Around Kavos and the adjacent coastline there is much tourist activity and the discos and bars keep going until the small hours.

# West coast of Corfu

### ÁY STEFANOS (Avliotes)

A small harbour on the N side of Ák Kavokefali.

### Approach

Should be made from the W. The breakwater will not be seen until close to the harbour. Care is needed at the entrance which silts and it would be wise to reconnoitre in the dinghy to see if depths are adequate. With the normal NW–W prevailing winds in the summer this can be difficult so if possible try to get here in the morning before the prevailing wind gets up.

*Note* In 2000 depths in the entrance were around 1·5m in approximately the middle of the entrance channel. There are plans to dredge the entrance.

### Mooring

Most of the quay space is occupied by local craft. Anchor and take a long line to the breakwater. The bottom is sand and good holding. Good all-round shelter.

ÁY STEFANOS (AVLIOTES)
⊕39°45'·1N 19°38'·0E

### Facilities

Tavernas and bars open on the beach to the N in the summer. The village of Áy Stefanos is a little further on and here you can find provisions.

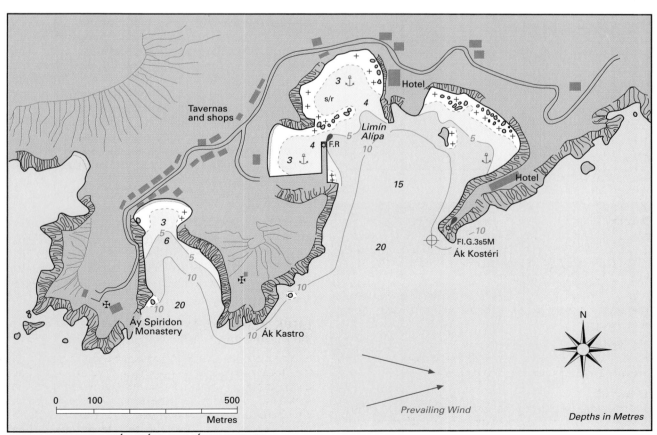

APPROACHES TO LIMÍN ALÍPA (PALAÍOKASTRITA)
⊕39°40'·3N 19°42'·8E

## AYIOS YEÓRYIOU (Agios Georgis)

Ák Arilla light 39°42'·7N 19°39'·3E

A wide sandy bay just N of Palaíokastrita. Anchor in 4–5 metre depths in the N corner of the bay or off Ayios Yeóryiou if it is calm. If the prevailing NW–W wind is blowing with any strength a swell works its way around into the bay. Open S.

Tavernas and bars around the long sandy beach open in the summer.

## PALAÍOKASTRITA (Limín Alípa)

BA 2402
Imray-Tetra G11

### Approach

Difficult by day and night.

*Conspicuous* The village of Lakones on the hill above Palaiokastrita is conspicuous from the distance. Nearer the coast the monastery and the large hotels around the bay are the best marks. You will not see the harbour mole until you are right into the bay.

**PALAÍOKASTRITA (LIMÍN ALÍPA)**
⊕39°40'·4N 19°42'·6E

Palaíokastrita harbour looking SW. Note the rocks off the N side of the entrance

*By night* Use the light on Ák Kostéri Fl.3s5M and the light at the end of the mole F.R.3M. A night entrance is not recommended.

*Dangers*
1. Entering the harbour proper stay close to the head of the moles to avoid the rocky shoal on the N side which is easily visible (rocks awash) by day but not by night.
2. With the prevailing NW wind a heavy swell is pushed onto the coast which rebounds off causing a wicked cross sea.

### Mooring

Go stern or bows-to the mole. The harbour is full of local boats but there is normally space somewhere. Alternatively anchor in the N bay, taking care of the rocks near the entrance to the harbour. The bottom is sand, good holding.

*Shelter* Good shelter from the prevailing NW winds. The harbour is dangerous with strong southerlies when a surge develops and waves break over the mole. If strong southerlies are likely a yacht should vacate the harbour straight away.

### Facilities

Water and fuel in the town. Most provisions can be found. Numerous tavernas and bars although prices can be expensive on account of the captive customers in the large hotels around the bay. Bus to Corfu.

### General

In a watercolour by Edward Lear, Palaíokastrita is depicted as it was before the hotels – a beautiful bay guarded by the monastery of Áy Spiridonos and a few fishermen's houses. Today the giant hotels surrounding the bay considerably mar the landscape, yet the seascape and the view from the monastery are still superb. Now no more hotels are to be built – the authorities consider there are enough here – though service buildings still keep popping up every summer. By the harbour a NATO storehouse is concealed under the hill and theoretically no photographs are allowed to be taken of this, though you can buy a postcard showing the prohibited view!

### PENTATI

At around 39°31'N 19°51'E (approximate co-ordinates) it is reported a small harbour is under construction. Only sketchy details of the harbour are available and care is needed of shallows in the vicinity.

### ÁY YEORYIOS

At around 39°25'·5N 19°57'E (approximate co-ordinates) it is reported a small harbour is under construction. The plan of the harbour does not show a mole or breakwater providing protection from NW–W winds so the usefulness of the harbour is questionable.

**NISOI PAXOÍ AND ANDÍPAXOI**

⊕**11**  ½M N of  Lákka entrance (Paxos)
39°15'·2N 20°07'·7E
⊕**12**  1M S of Ák Ovorós (Andíipaxoi)
39°06'·8N 20°15'·6E

# Nisoi Paxoí and Andípaxoi
### (Paxos and Anti-Paxos Islands)

Seven miles south of Corfu lies Paxoí and its diminutive Andípaxoi. Five miles long and two miles wide, Paxoí until recently produced little else except olive oil for which it is famous. Harrods apparently sells only olive oil from Paxoí. Now tourists from Corfu regularly visit the island and in recent years a large number of villas have been built. The island is also popular with flotilla companies and in the summer the harbours and anchorages are full of yachts.

It was off Paxoí that a significant historical event occurred – little remembered now, but of momentous importance in ancient times. The Egyptian pilot Thamus was bound for Italy when he was becalmed off Paxoí. A voice came over the water commanding him to announce that the great god Pan was dead. Twice he disobeyed until the third command, whereupon he obeyed. Immediately a great wail of lamentation arose from the sea. It is a strange story, recorded for us by Plutarch in the *Moralia*, and yet when Pausanias visited Greece a century later he found Pan was still actively worshipped.

Andípaxoi, immediately south of Paxoí, is only sparsely populated. It has some attractive anchorages but none safe except in settled weather. The few inhabitants cultivate their vines and olives and are dependent on Paxoí for their needs and entertainment.

## ÓRMOS LÁKKA
BA 2402
Imray-Tetra G11
A virtually landlocked bay on the N end of Paxoí.

### Approach
*Conspicuous* The exact location of the bay is difficult to determine from the distance. From the W the lighthouse is conspicuous. From the N and E the light structures at the entrance will be seen when you are closer in.

*By night* Use the main light Fl(3)24s20M and closer in the lights at the entrance: Fl.G.2s3M/Fl.R.2s3M.

### Mooring
Anchor off in the bay where convenient or anchor in the NW corner with a long line ashore. There is some room on the quay for small yachts to go bows-to, but care is needed as the depths are uneven. The bottom is sand and weed, good holding.

**LÁKKA**
⊕39°14'·65N 20°07'·75E

Lákka on the N end of Paxos          *Nigel Patten*

*Shelter* Good shelter from the prevailing winds although if there is more N than W in the wind it can get uncomfortable in here. Uncomfortable and untenable in places with strong NE winds. With NE winds tuck into the E side as far as possible.

*Note* At times it can get a bit smelly from sewage at the SE end of the bay.

**Facilities**

*Water* Sometimes available on the quay. Showers at *Seaside* bar.

*Provisions* Most provisions can be obtained.

*Eating out* Tavernas and bars.

*Other* PO. OTE. Ferry to Parga.

**GAIOS (LIMÍN PAXON)**
⊕₁ 39°12·22N 20°11′·47E WGS84
⊕₂ 39°11·80N 20°11′·32E WGS84

## General

The anchorage is picturesque under olive-clad slopes with the huddle of houses of the hamlet at the head of the bay. The anchorage is popular in the summer and this is a lively place rather than a quiet hide-away.

## LONGOS (Logos)

39°13'·61N 20°09'·75E WGS84
BA 2402

A small harbour on the E coast of Nísos Paxoí between Lákka and Gaios. The harbour is very small and yachts are restricted from berthing inside, where all the space is reserved for local and tripper boats.

Either go stern-to the outside of the mole with a long line to it or anchor and take a long line to the N side of the bay. With the prevailing wind a swell works its way around making these berths uncomfortable. The new breakwater N of the harbour does not yet provide useful berthing space.

Ashore most provisions can be obtained and there are numerous tavernas and bars around the waterfront. It is a pity there is not a comfortable berth to be had at Longos as the small fishing village is an attractive place, with whitewashed houses huddled around the miniature harbour under olive-clad slopes.

## IFALOS PAXOÍ

100m N of Ifalos Paxoí 39°13'·72N 20°10'·27E WGS84

Approximately half a mile E of Longos there is a reef, Ifalos Paxoí, which is difficult to see even in calm weather. It is possible to pass between the reef and the island, though care is needed and it is prudent to have someone up front keeping an eye out for it. Some believe the charted position is in error and it is closer to Nísos Paxoí than shown.

## IFALOS PANAYIAS

A reef lying approximately 2½ miles E of Port Gaios. The reef and shoal water around it is difficult to see with the wind whipping up a chop on the water so it should be given a prudent berth. The reef lies just S of the direct route from Gaios to Parga so care is needed. Some believe it should be closer to the mainland than its charted position, though I think it looks about right.

## PORT GAIOS (Port Gayo, Limín Paxon, Limín Paxoí)

BA 2402
Imray-Tetra G11

## Approach

*Conspicuous* From the N the entrance to the harbour is difficult to see. From the distance the houses and tall chimney at Longos can be seen and as you close the port the lighthouse enclosed by a whitewashed wall on Nisís Panayía marks the entrance to the N channel. From the S the lighthouse on Nísos Andípaxoi is conspicuous and closer to Gaios a number of large white villas S of the town and the

Gaios on Paxos looking NE with Nisís Panayía at the top of the photo *Peter Kleinoth/MareTeam*

lighthouse and wall on Nisís Panayía are visible before the buildings of Port Gaios itself.

*By night* Use the light on Andípaxoi Fl.WR.6s12/9M and on Nisís Panayía Fl.WR.5s10/8M. The N entrance is lit: Fl.R.3s3M and Fl.G.3s3M and the bend in the channel Fl.R.2s3M. The N end of the quay is lit F.G.3M. The S entrance is lit: Fl.G.2s3M and F.R.2M, though the lights should not always be relied on.

*Dangers*
1. Care needs to be taken of Ifalos Panayía in the approach from the E.
2. Ferries and tripper boats are constantly churning in and out of the harbour. In the N entrance care must be taken of the blind bend in the channel where you cannot see what is coming the other way.
3. In the S entrance there are barely 2m depths in the middle and no room to manoeuvre so wait until the way is clear. On either side of the S channel it is shallow.

## Mooring

Go stern or bows-to either side of the town quay leaving the ferry and tripper boat berths clear in the middle. In the summer the town quay is very crowded and the alternative is to berth on the new quayed section in the N channel. The bottom is mud and generally good holding. Large yachts can anchor under the causeway between Nisís Áy Nikólaos and Nisís Panayía although the holding has been reported to be suspect here.

*Shelter* Good shelter from the prevailing summer winds. Strong southerlies cause a surge on the town quay and a yacht may have to move to a berth in the N channel.

*Note* Crossed anchors are a fact of life with all the boats using Gaios and there is not a lot you can do about it except remain cool and use some muscle power in the morning when you leave.

*Authorities* Port police and customs.

**Facilities**

*Water* Water can be delivered by mini-tanker. With so much tourist infrastructure water is scarce on the island.

*Fuel* A mini-tanker will deliver.

*Provisions* Most provisions can be found, though most things are brought in on the ferries and hence may be in short supply at times.

*Eating out* Numerous tavernas.

*Other* PO. OTE. Bank. Hire motorbikes. Ferries to Patras, Parga, and Corfu.

**General**

Gaios is a popular choice for excursions from Corfu making it a very crowded place in the summer. Ferry boats, flotilla yachts and private yachts churn in and out, choking the little harbour. If you want a berth in the height of summer be here early in the afternoon. For all this, Gaios is still an attractive town. Sitting in the cockpit of your yacht you are literally in the middle of town watching the hurly-burly of Gaios life go by. Alternatively, you can sip your ouzo in the square amidst all the activity, probably with a number of cats begging for scraps at your feet (Gaios appears to possess as many cats as tourists), and watch your yacht gently rocking in the harbour.

**MONGONISI (Órmos Spuzzo, Ozias)**

At the S tip of Paxoí, just over a mile SE of Gaios, is the landlocked bay of Mongonisi. The entrance is difficult to determine from the distance, but closer in the entrance will be seen. Once inside go bows-to

the quay on the NE side or on the S side. Alternatively anchor in the middle in 3–5m. The bottom is sand and weed, good holding once through the weed, although getting through the weed can take some doing. Good shelter from the prevailing winds although with a strong N–NW breeze the western side of the anchorage is extremely uncomfortable.

Taverna and bar ashore. Fast speedboat ferry runs to Gaios in the day.

**NÍSOS ANDÍPAXOI**

(Anti-Paxos)

There are two bays on the NE side of the island popular as day anchorages. Approach the coast with care as there are numerous fringing reefs. The N bay here is known as Emerald Bay and the next bay down is Órmos Agrapidia. Anchor where convenient. When the NW wind gets up it can get uncomfortable in here and may become untenable.

There is a miniature harbour at 39°09'·3N 19°55'·2E but it is really too small for most yachts and in any case is usually full of local boats.

Numerous tripper boats run to and from Paxoí, but after the hordes have departed it is a peaceful spot. Several tavernas are reported to open in the NE bays in the summer.

Care is needed of above and below-water rocks off the coast of Andípaxoi especially at the southern end and yachts should keep well out from Nisís Dhaskalia off the southern tip.

# The mainland coast from Corfu to Préveza

**Note** At the time of writing yachts should avoid the bays close to the Albanian border because of the unsettled political situation there. See the note at the beginning of this chapter.

Opposite Corfu the Albanian-Epirote mountains rise to an impressive 1300m. The craggy peaks often have snow on them even in April. Proceeding south the mountain range curves inland and the coastline flattens to salt marsh around Préveza and Levkas. The much-indented coastline has some good harbours and anchorages, some of them much removed from the island tourism.

**FTELIAS** 39°41'·4N 20°00'·5E

Tucked up under the Albanian border is the bay of Ftelias. In the approaches a high rugged island on the Albanian side and a low rocky island on the Greek side will be seen. Leave the Greek island to starboard and enter the bay. There is a fish farm on the N side. Good depths in the entrance decreasing to 10m off the fish farm and 3m around the dogleg. Anchor where convenient on mud. No facilities.

*Note* It is unwise to visit here at the time of writing. See note on Albania at the beginning of the chapter.

**MONGONISI (ÓRMOS SPUZZO)**
⊕39°11'N 20°12·5E

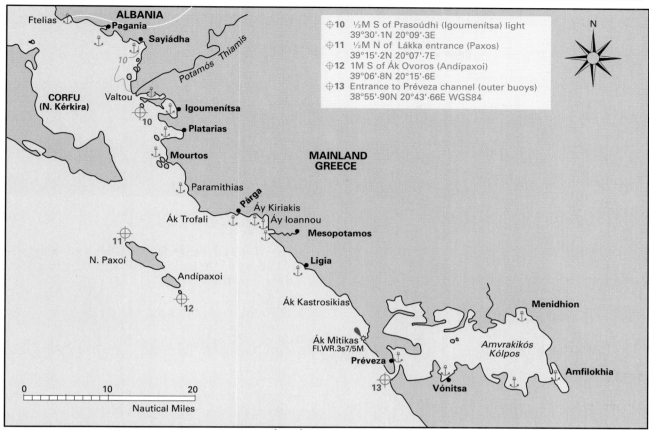

**10** ½M S of Prasoúdhi (Igoumenítsa) light
39°30'·1N 20°09'·3E
**11** ½M N of Lákka entrance (Paxos)
39°15'·2N 20°07'·7E
**12** 1M S of Ák Ovoros (Andípaxoi)
39°06'·8N 20°15'·6E
**13** Entrance to Préveza channel (outer buoys)
38°55'·90N 20°43'·66E WGS84

MAINLAND GREECE FROM PAGANIA TO AMVRAKIKÓS KÓLPOS

## PAGANIA

### Approach

From the S it is difficult to see the entrance. From the distance the road cut into the hill appears to disappear where Pagania headland obscures it. Once into the entrance to the bay the farm buildings will be seen.

*Note* A fish farm extends out from the W side of the bay. It is easily seen by day. There are also other fish farms in the bay.

### Mooring

Anchor in the SW or SE corner. The bottom is mud and weed, good holding. Good all-round shelter.

### Facilities

You may get a few eggs from the farm, but otherwise none.

### General

An idyllic spot little visited by yachts or anyone at all for that matter. The only inhabitants are the farmer and his family on the NE side of the bay. Occasionally a Greek patrol boat will turn up and may order yachts here to leave.

## SAYIÁDHA

### Approach

The buildings of the hamlet can be identified from the distance and closer in the harbour will be seen. The old entrance on the NW side has been closed off and a new entrance on the SE side opened.

### Mooring

Only shallow-draught yachts drawing less than 1·40m should attempt to enter. The new entrance on the SE side is narrow and bordered by rocks. It was probably opened by the simple Greek method of dynamiting a gap in the old wall. It is best to go alongside the outer mole as the holding is poor. Care must be taken of a shallow patch near the middle of the harbour. Shelter in the harbour is much improved with the new entrance. A yacht can also go alongside the quay just outside the entrance where there is reasonable shelter from the prevailing wind.

PAGANIA
⊕ 39°41'·4N 20°00'·7E

**SAYIÁDHA**
⊕39°37'·5N 20°10'·9E

### Facilities
Port police. Water near the quay. A grocery shop, baker, and several tavernas.

### General
A friendly little village untouched by tourism. Alexi's taverna has been recommended as a good place to eat, with fresh prawns and fish at good prices.

**Note** Pagania and Sayiádha fall within the restricted area where theoretically permission should be obtained for a visit. In practice this is not normally necessary.

### ORMISKOS VALTOU (Igoumenítsa Creek)
BA 2406

To the N of Nisídha Prasoúdhi and the entrance to the bay of Igoumenítsa is the deserted bay known as Igoumenítsa Creek. Care must be taken of the shoals off the river mouth (Potamós Thiamis) when entering. In the third cove near the bottom of the inlet there is excellent all-round shelter in 3–8m depths, sand and weed. Care must be taken of shoal water extending out from the shore. Fish traps cut off the very bottom of the inlet.

Just over the neck of the inlet is a long sandy beach and there are some good walks around the area. The high land trapped in the silt of the river delta is thought to be the ancient Sívota Islands where the Corinthians and Corcyreans fought a naval battle in 433BC that eventually led to the Peloponnesian War.

### IGOUMENÍTSA
BA 2406

### Approach
*Conspicuous* Nisídha Prasoúdhi is easily identified and the town of Igoumenítsa can be seen at the head of the bay. The three pairs of buoys marking the channel into the bay stand out clearly. The

Órmos Igoumenítsa looking WNW towards the entrance with Ák Dhrépanon on the right side of the photo

approaches and entrance to the bay can usually be determined by the constant coming and going of car ferries to Corfu.

*By night* Use the light on Nisídha Prasoúdhi Fl(2)9s8M and the light on the S side of the entrance (Ák Kondramoúrto) Fl.3s5M. The buoys marking the channel are lit Q.G/Q.R and a 2F.R(vert)5M is exhibited on the pier head at Igoumenítsa.

*Note* There are massive harbour works in progress to create a new commercial harbour beginning at the southern extremity of the old harbour and extending for virtually the length of the E side of the bay. Along the coast land is being reclaimed and a deep water quay built. These harbour works are obvious from the entrance of Órmos Igoumenítsa and yachts should keep well clear of the area as there are numerous large concrete blocks just under the surface of the water. The S extremity of the works is marked by a 3Q.R.

### Mooring
Go stern or bows-to or alongside the quay. The bottom is mud – good holding.

*Shelter* Reasonable shelter although with strong NW winds it can be uncomfortable here and it may be better to anchor at the N end of the bay. There is a small fishing harbour N of the main pier but it is usually crowded and the depths are uneven (1–2m).

*Anchorage* Yachts can anchor at the N end of the bay where there is good shelter from the prevailing wind. There is also reported to be a good lee under Nisís Áy Dhionisios in attractive surroundings. In calm weather yachts anchor at the S end of Órmos Igoumenítsa.

*Authorities* Port police and customs.

### Facilities
*Water* On the quay.
*Fuel* Near the quay.
*Provisions* Good shopping for provisions.
*Eating out* Numerous tavernas and a number of fast-food places.
*Other* PO. OTE. Banks. Greek gas and *Camping Gaz*. Infrequent buses to Préveza and Athens. Car ferry to Corfu. Ferries to Patras and Italy (Brindisi, Ancona and Bari).

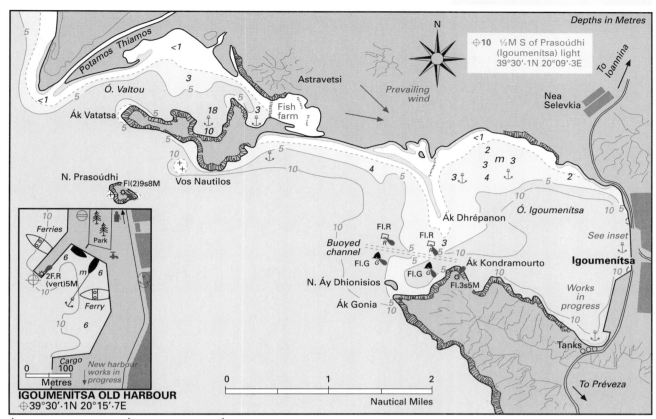

Depths in Metres

⊕10  ½M S of Prasoúdhi
(Igoumenítsa) light
39°30'·1N 20°09'·3E

**IGOUMENÍTSA OLD HARBOUR**
⊕39°30'·1N 20°15'·7E

**ÓRMOS VALTOU AND ÓRMOS IGOUMENÍTSA**

## General

Igoumenítsa is a rather unattractive convenience ferry-terminal town, although the large bay is attractive. In 1979 an earthquake destroyed some of the buildings and 200 people lived in tents for some 6 months after the event. The town is a good place from which to organise a visit to Ioannina and Dodona.

## PLATARIAS

### Approach

A small harbour in the NE corner of Órmos Plataria. The approach is straightforward.

### Mooring

Go stern or bows-to under the short mole or on the village quay.

*Shelter* Good shelter from the prevailing NW wind although it tends to funnel into the bay and kick up a bit of a chop.

*Note* Work is in progress extending the outer mole and it is intended to put a quay under the mole and along the shore.

### Facilities

Water on the quay. Most provisions can be found. Tavernas and bars on the waterfront.

### General

Platarias is a low key resort with good sandy beaches nearby. In the morning calm it is worth anchoring off in the bay for a swim rather than scrumming down on the beach with the other tourists.

## MOÚRTOS AND ADJACENT ISLANDS

Just S of Órmos Plitarias lie the Sívota islands with the village of Moúrtos on the mainland nearby. There are three islands: Nisís Sívota (Sybota), Nisís Áy Nikólaos, and Nisís Mavros Notos.

### Approach

*Conspicuous* From the N the lighthouse on Nisís Sívota and a large three-storeyed house on the mainland are conspicuous. As you close Moúrtos village the houses on the hill above can be easily identified. From the S the islands are more difficult to identify, but the lighthouse on Nisís Sívota will be seen.

*By night* There is only the light on Nisís Sívota Fl(3)20s12M and a light on the pierhead at Moúrtos Fl.R.3M. A night approach is not recommended for the first time.

*Dangers*
1. Do not attempt to pass between Nisís Sívota and Nisís Áy Nikólaos as the channel is obstructed by the reef running across the S end.
2. The passage between the mainland and the islands has only 2m depths at one point (see plan). The deepest part of the bar is approximately one third off Nisís Áy Nikólaos.
3. In the approach from the S keep to the eastern side of the passage to avoid the reef jutting out from Nisís Sívota. Waves break on some of the rocks of the reef.

**NISÍS SÍVOTA AND MOÚRTOS**
⊕₁ 39°24´·66N 20°13´·82E WGS84
⊕₂ 39°23´·88N 20°13´·72E WGS84

## Mooring

There are a number of possibilities.

1. *Moúrtos* Go stern-to the SE quay making sure your anchor is well dug in. There are mostly 2-metre depths along the quay except for the NE end where it shallows. The prevailing wind blows straight down onto the quay making it uncomfortable and at times untenable. There is often damage sustained to boats here both from the wind and swell and also from ferry wash pushing boats onto the quay. It may be possible to get a berth on the charter pontoon under the stubby breakwater if it is not full of the company's boats and here shelter is excellent. Enquire first.

2. *Monastery Bay* The cove NW of Moúrtos quay. Anchor and take a line to the shore or the jetty. Shelter here is better than it looks.

3. *Middle Bay* In the cove on the SE just inside the N entrance to the channel. Anchor in 3–7m and take a long line ashore if possible. The bottom is mud and thick weed, good holding once through the weed. This is the best place to be with good shelter and a short dinghy trip to Moúrtos. The cove opposite on the NW side is mostly too shallow and has underwater rocks fringing it.

4. *Sand Bar Bay* At the S end of the channel there is a cove sheltered by Nisís Mavros Notos. Much of the cove is taken up with moorings for sailing dinghies from the hotel on the slopes above. There are now signs around the bay prohibiting

The N entrance and anchorage in the channel at Nisís Sívota looking across to Nísos Áy Nikólaos *Nigel Patten*

anchoring, although the legality of these is in doubt as anything up to the high water mark is owned by the state and cannot be bought or sold. Although it is possible to anchor here the jet-skis and water-ski boats zooming around make it uncomfortable and the staff at the hotel make any stay here disagreeable. Probably best left alone.

5. ***End Bay (or Fourth Bay)*** On the E side of Nisís Mavros Notos a yacht can find reasonable shelter from the prevailing winds. Anchor in 4–10m on sand and weed. If there are a lot of yachts in here the best thing to do is take a long line ashore to the N or S side rather than swinging to anchor.

*Notes*

1. Depths in the channel between Nisís Áy Nikólaos and the mainland decrease abruptly to a 2m bar before increasing quickly again.
2. There can be a S-going current in the channel with the prevailing wind.

### Facilities

(Moúrtos)

*Services* Water and electricity points on the quay.

*Fuel* In the village about 600m away. It may be possible to get a mini-tanker down to the quay.

*Provisions* Most provisions can be found on the waterfront. There are also grocery shops 600m away in the village.

*Eating out* Good tavernas on the waterfront and up in the village.

*Other* PO. OTE. Bank. Bus to Igoumenítsa.

### General

Moúrtos village is a pleasant place in a wooded setting with friendly locals. The new quayed area and the waterfront development has all been done in a sympathetic way without spoiling the ambience of the place – I wish a few other villages could take some tips from the inhabitants of Moúrtos. Sand Bar Bay is overlooked by a monstrous concrete hotel that has not only cluttered the bay with moorings for

its boats and dinghies, but also disturbs this once tranquil spot with loud music far into the night.

Although called the Sívota Islands these are not thought to be the ancient Sybota Islands off which the Corinthians and Corcyraeans fought their battle in 433 BC. The ancient Sybota Islands are probably the low hills around the creek immediately N of Igoumenítsa.

## PÁRGA

BA 2402

### Approach

*Conspicuous* From the W the fort at Kastelli in the hills NW of Párga is conspicuous and closer in the

**ÓRMOS VALTOU (PÁRGA)**
⊕39°16′·9N 20°23·3E

The harbour in Órmos Valtou looking out to the entrance
*Nigel Patten*

**ÓRMOS PÁRGA**
⊕ 39°16'·75N 20°23'·55E

belfry on Ák Áy Spiridhonos will be seen. From the S the belfry, fort and the buildings of Parga village are conspicuous. The small white chapel on Nisídha Áy Nikólaos also stands out well.

*By night* The light on the fort at Párga Fl(2)6s6M will be seen from the S but is obscured in the approach from the W. The small harbour in Órmos Valtou is not lit.

*Dangers* Care needs to be taken of the reef Voi Spiridhonia lying approximately 100m off Ák Áy Spiridhonos. In calm weather it is easily spotted, but with any whitecaps it can be difficult to pick out.

### Mooring

Most yachts head for the small harbour on the W side of Órmos Valtou. Go stern or bows-to. In general it is better to go bows-to as rock ballasting projects out from the quay in places. Alternatively anchor S of the mole and take a line ashore or to the old mole. Difficult holding so ensure your anchor is well in. The new breakwater S of the old mole provides some shelter if you are tucked right under it with a line ashore – it is likely it will be extended some time in the future to provide additional berths for yachts. Although the wharf at Párga village appears to be adequately protected a swell rolls around into here with the afternoon breeze and in southerlies it is untenable. In any case it is normally occupied by local ferries and tripper boats.

*Shelter* In the harbour at Órmos Valtou is good.

*Anchorage* It is sometimes possible to anchor in the cove under Nisís Panayia. The best policy is to arrive in the early evening when the swimmers have gone home. Anchor fore and aft as there is little room to swing here.

*Note* Of late there have been numerous reports of theft from yachts here. Make sure you lock up well and put any loose items away.

### Facilities

*Water* At the root of the mole in Valtou.

*Provisions* At the eastern end of the beach or in Párga itself.

*Eating out* Numerous tavernas and bars along the beach and in Párga.

*Other* PO. Bank. Taxis. Hire cars and motor bikes. Ferry to Paxos.

### General

Párga has developed into a major resort with the consequence that development spreads all the way around Órmos Valtou and only stops just before the harbour. There are more tavernas and bars than you can shake a stick at and in the day the beach is packed to overflowing. On a yacht you are at least lucky to be just beyond all this in the little harbour.

The castle on the promontory between the two bays is of Norman origin (c.1337). Well defended to seaward and landward by the monolithic rock on which it sits, this castle has always been difficult to capture. The Venetians considered it 'the eye and ear of Corfu' and consequently the Parganiotes enjoyed special trade privileges with Venice. The notorious Ali Pasha attempted to capture the castle many times, finally succeeding in a roundabout way with the help of the English. In 1814, when the French held Párga, British agents managed to persuade the Parganiotes to overthrow the garrison and hand it over to the English. After holding Párga for two years the English then sold it to Ali Pasha to strengthen their claim with the Turks to the Ionian Islands. The inhabitants were evacuated to the islands, only returning generations later. Párga only became Greek in 1913.

## ÓRMOS ÁY KIRIAKIS

A large bay a mile E of Nisídha Áy Nikolao (Kiriakis). A yacht can find reasonable protection from the prevailing wind in the NW corner. Anchor in 3–10m on sand and weed, good holding. Hotel and villas ashore and several taverna/bars open in the summer.

## ÓRMOS ÁYIOU IOANNOU

Three miles east of Párga is Áy Ioannou, affording good shelter from the NW wind although some swell does work its way around into the bay. Anchor in the NW corner of the bay in 4–10m on mud, rock and weed, bad holding in places. The cove in the NW corner is now obstructed by a mussel farm. On the W side of the bay a freshwater spring wells up from the bottom into the sea and the murky slow whirlpool of fresh water is easily spotted.

**ÓRMOS ÁY IOANNOU**
⊕39°16'·2N 20°28'·2E

## ÓRMOS FANÁRI 39°14'·2N 20°28'·5E

Two miles south of Ioannou there is the bay of Fanári. Depths in the bay gradually shelve to the shore with 8–9m depths in the entrance decreasing to 2m around 150–200 metres off the beach at the head of the bay. Anchor under the N side of the bay in 2·5–5m on mud and sand. If the prevailing NW–W wind is blowing strongly the bay is not really tenable as a swell is pushed straight into it.

At the entrance on the S side is the Akheron River and it is possible to navigate up the river to a quay. The river is periodically dredged but often silts to less than 1·5m, so it would pay to reconnoitre in a dinghy first. Tavernas near the quay on the river.

## TWO ROCK BAY

A cove lying approximately 2 miles S of Fanári which offers surprisingly good shelter from the NW wind. Several large rocks just in the entrance identify it. A small yacht can squeeze in – depths are not great, 1·5–2m over a sandy bottom. There are reported to be greater depths on the S side and a yacht can anchor here in 3m.

## LIGIA

A small fishing harbour lying 6M SE of Two Rock Bay. Care is needed of a reef approximately 1M NW of the harbour which is some distance off the coast. The harbour entrance is rockbound and extreme care is needed in the final approach. If any swell is running the entrance can be difficult and it is best approached in calm conditions with someone up front to con the way in. The approach is from the SE between a rocky ledge on either side. Go bows-to on the rough central pier or anchor and take a line ashore to the rough stone breakwater. Good shelter from the prevailing winds. Southerlies may send a swell in.

Taverna near the harbour and others in the village about 20 minutes' walk away. Limited provisions.

**LIGIA**
⊕39°09'·1N 20°33'·9E

## PRÉVEZA

BA 2405

### Approach

*Conspicuous* From the N and S, a low thickly-wooded hill and Fort Áy Yeóryios on the N side of the channel are conspicuous. Aktion Airport is on the S side of the channel and planes will often be seen landing or taking off in the summer. The buoys marking the narrow channel are difficult to see from

0                 1

Nautical Mile

N

To Igoumenitsa

Ó. Vathí
Boatyard

4

10

5

5

13

2

13

1₇

5

1₅

14

5

Préveza
Marina

Fl.R

20

22

Old
earthworks

19

Fl.G
Bn   Vroi
Akri

Préveza

Fl.G.2s4M

24

5

<1

5

23   2

LFl.7.5s5M

Ák Akri

2

Car Ferry

10

<1

Aktion Marine

2₅

1₅

Prevailing
Wind

12

Yards
Préveza Marine

<1

1₅

Cleopatra
Marina

10

10

5

2

Fort Áy
Yeoryios

Road
tunnel

Q.R.

17

Aktion

14

10

Fort

LFl.Y.6s7M

<1

Fort
Pandokrator

10

Órmos
Prevezis

5

<1

5

10

2

15

Q.R.

10

Q.Y.7M

2

5

Q.R.

Q.G.

2

To Levkas

1-3 Knots

Q.R.

Dredged channel to 7m

Q.G.

1₈

5

<1

Stenón Prevesis

Q.R.

Q.G.

1₅

Aktion
airport

2

1₄

2

5

Q.R.

1

10   Q.G.

2

1₅

2

2

5

Depths in Metres

**STENÓN PRÉVEZA**
⊕₁ 38°55′·90N 20°43′·66E WGS84
⊕₂ 38°57′·5N 20°45′·6E (LFl.7·5s5M)

**PRÉVEZA**
⊕38°57′·4N 20°45′·3E (Fl.G.3s4M)

the distance. Closer in the buoys will be seen and the navigable channel is obvious.

*By night* Use the light on Ák Mítikas: Fl.WR.3s7/5M, the red sector covers 078°-135°. There are leading lights into the channel on 066°: Q.Y.7M and LFl.Y.6s7M. The buoys marking the channel are lit Q.G and Q.R. Ák Akrí is lit LFl.7·5s5M and the end of the mole in the harbour is lit Fl.G.2s4M/Fl.R.2s3M.

*Dangers*
1. A current will often be running in the buoyed channel – sometimes as much as 3 knots. The prevailing wind from the NW blowing down over the shallowing water and against the current kicks up a confused swell – uncomfortable rather than dangerous in the summer.
2. The channel is claimed to be dredged to 8m but is only 5–6m in places. Outside the channel the depths can also vary from those shown on the chart due to silting.

3. Keep an eye on the car ferries plying across the channel between Aktion and Préveza, although they will usually wait for you to pass.
4. A new road tunnel is under construction from the ferry terminal to Préveza town. At times there may be workboats from the tunnel construction moored in the channel. Work should be completed by 2001–2.

**Mooring**
Go stern or bows-to in the marina or along the quay inside the basin. While the marina is under construction the situation is somewhat confused with yachts lying alongside, but in the near future moorings will be laid and yachts will go stern or bows-to.

*Shelter* Good shelter in the marina although strong SE winds cause a surge.

*Note* The new marina is basically in place but does not have all facilities. The service boxes for water and electricity are ready to go in and it remains to be seen when everything is finished and up and running.

*Authorities* A port of entry. Port police, customs and immigration. Marina staff when the marina is up and running. A charge will be made.

**Facilities**
*Services* Water and electricity points are being installed. A shower and toilet block is to be constructed.
*Fuel* Can be delivered by mini-tanker.
*Repairs* On Aktion to the N of the ferry pier and road tunnel are three yards.

Yards from S to N
1. *Cleopatra Marina* Not a marina but a boatyard. 50-ton travel-hoist. 350-yacht capacity ashore. Cleopatra Marina has plans to build a mini-marina outside the yard. The small basin will have approximately 80 berths and all services. Work is yet to begin on the project.
   Cleopatra Marina, PO Box 25, 48100 Préveza, Greece ☎ 0682 23015 *Fax* 0682 21414
   *E-mail* clmarina@otenet.gr
2. *Préveza Marine* 50-ton travel-hoist. Large hardstanding area.
   Préveza Marine, PO Box 26, 48100 Préveza, Greece ☎ 0682 24305 *Fax* 0682 29805
   *E-mail* prevmar@otenet.gr
3. *Aktion Marine* Hauling by hydraulic trailer. Large hardstanding area.
   Aktion Marine, Aktion, PO Box 42, Préveza, Greece ☎ 0682 61305 *Fax* 0682 61306
   *E-mail* aktiomar@hol.gr; VHF Ch 09.

All of these yards can carry out most yacht repairs or arrange to have work carried out. I have had various recommendations for stainless steel work, paint jobs and mechanical repairs, but as any of these are dependant on the skills of the local contractor or the staff employed, it is best to enquire locally in case the person who once carried out excellent work has been replaced by someone who is not up to scratch. Overall the three yards attract a fair range of skills and between the yards there are good facilities for the care and repair of yachts. There are some restrictions on outside contractors in some of the yards so check before hauling if you want someone else to do work on the boat. The yards all have water, electricity, showers and toilets, workshops and other facilities.

Chandlers at the Aktion yards and hardware shops in Préveza.

*Provisions* Good shopping for all provisions. Ice can be ordered.

*Eating out* Numerous tavernas on the waterfront and in the back streets.

*Other* PO. OTE. Bank. Greek gas and *Camping Gaz*. Buses to Igoumenítsa (limited), Levkas, and Athens. European charter flights from Aktion Airport in the summer and internal flights.

### General

In the last few years Préveza has cast aside its ugly duckling status and turned into a swan, if not yet a graceful one. The waterfront has been pedestrianised and now has numerous trendy bars and cafés along it. The back streets still have the charm they always had when Préveza was a provincial market town and most people find the place grows on them.

About 3 miles N of the town are the ruins of Nikopolis built by Octavian to commemorate his victory over Anthony in the Battle of Actium. This battle fought in the approaches to Préveza effectively determined the course of the Roman Empire. The ruins are well worth a visit: a large theatre, a villa and the city walls are well preserved and a small museum houses an interesting collection of artifacts.

# Amvrakikós Kólpos
## (Gulf of Amvrakia)

Few yachts enter the Gulf of Amvrakia, yet it offers some good sailing and interesting anchorages. There are also a multitude of ancient sites dotted around the edge of the gulf: Nikopolis, erected by Octavian after his defeat of Anthony; the Venetian castle at Vónitsa built on a Byzantine original; the remains of Limnaea near Karvasarás; ancient Arta and its famous bridge up the Arakthos river.

When entering the gulf from Préveza make for the red buoy (Fl.R) keeping clear of the shallows off Ák Akrí (white beacon LFl.7·5s5M). Then leave the white beacon with a green band (Fl.G.7·5s3M) and the green lightbuoy to starboard. Once into the gulf there are good depths except around the N coast where it has silted in places and shallows may extend further than shown on the chart.

### VÓNITSA
#### Approach
Once into Órmos Vónitsa the buildings of the town and the castle will be seen. The cove on the W side will not be seen until you are in the entrance. The detached breakwater off Vónitsa is easily identified.

#### Mooring
Go stern or bows-to off the town quay. Underwater rubble fringes the quay and it best to go bows-to if possible. The best place to go is between the projecting bit of quay and the short pier. Go slowly and inspect the bit of quay you are going onto. The W end of the quay is also possible with care.

*Shelter* Reasonable shelter from the prevailing NW

**AMVRAKIKÓS KÓLPOS (Gulf of Amvrakia)**

# Nikopolis

After the assassination of Julius Caesar in 44 BC a civil war was intermittently waged until 31 BC when Octavian's victory over Anthony decided the fate of the known world. Anthony had assembled his soldiers and ships at Actium intending to invade Italy. Octavian based his fleet at Mítikas to forestall Anthony and all through the summer the opposing fleets waited for the other to move. Eventually Anthony decided to initiate an action by moving his fleet to the mouth of the estuary. Octavian waited for the afternoon NW wind and when it arrived his swifter and more manoeuvrable galleys attacked the rival fleet. The rout of Anthony's fleet was completed when Cleopatra fled taking her Egyptian ships (Anthony followed leaving his men and ships to be scattered by Octavian).

To commemorate the victory Octavian built Nikopolis (Victory City) on the site from which he commanded his victory. It soon grew to be the capital for the area and to populate it many of the inhabitants of the surrounding countryside were resettled here. The present walls encompass a city about one fifth of the area of the original city which boasted theatres, temples, baths and three harbours – one at Mítikas and two on the Gulf of Amvrakia. Here the Apostle Paul stayed a winter and wrote his Epistle to Titus. Towards the end of AD 4 the city was destroyed by Alaric the Goth and though rebuilt on a smaller scale, it was soon abandoned in the face of the Slavic invasion from the North.

Vónitsa looking E from the fort

**VÓNITSA**
⊕38°55'·39N 20°53'·14E WGS84

**VÓNITSA AND APPROACHES**
⊕38°55'·39N 20°53'·14E WGS84

wind which normally does not blow home. If it does blow strongly from the N then the new detached breakwater provides little additional shelter from the slop set up by the strong northerlies and you may have to leave.

*Anchorage* Anchor in Áy Markou, the cove on the W side of the bay. It is quite deep in here, mostly 8–15m up to the edges, so take a long line ashore. Care is needed in case there is debris on the bottom from the mussel farm that used to be along the N side. It may be better to anchor off the shoal patch in 5m on the S side of the entrance. Good all-round shelter in here.

It is also possible to anchor off on the E side of Nisís Koukouvitsa. The islet, (joined to the mainland by a causeway), provides a good lee from the prevailing wind.

### Facilities

Water on the quay. Fuel in the town. Most provisions can be obtained and there are numerous tavernas. PO. OTE. Bank. The bus to Athens and Levkas stops here.

### General

Above the town is a large Venetian fort (built on the site of a Byzantine fort) which offers excellent views out over the Gulf. According to Alexander Paradissis, Robert Guiscard died here of an epidemic along with 10,000 of his Norman troops . . . however, he is also supposed to have died in Fiskárdho on Cephalonia.

### ÓRMOS PALAIOMILOU
38°54'·0N 21°01'·3E

A bay on the W side of Órmos Loutrakios. There is sometimes a fish farm in here although it was recently reported abandoned. Good shelter from the NW wind.

### LOUTRAKI
38°52'·5N 21°04'·5E

The anchorage under the small village of the same name. Like Palaiomilou this is now obstructed by a fish farm, but you may find somewhere to squeeze into. Limited provisions and taverna in the village.

Menidhion harbour looking E

**MENIDHION**
⊕39°02'·5N 21°07'·1E

## AMFILOKHIA (Karvasarás)

38°52'·1N 21°09'·8E

A small harbour in Órmos Amfilokhia in the SE corner of the gulf. It is possible to go alongside the quay with an anchor out to hold you off. However with a strong afternoon wind a considerable chop is pushed onto the quay and it is better to anchor off. It is very deep in here and you will have to anchor in 12–15m. The harbour is invariably uncomfortable with the prevailing wind and may become untenable.

Fuel and water in the town. Good shopping and tavernas.

Near the town are the remains of the ancient Arcanian city of Limnaea. According to H. M. Denham, in the 19th century a small volcano erupted in this bay (1847 and 1885) killing most of the fish in the gulf.

## MENIDHION (Kópraina)

In the NE corner of the gulf in Órmos Kópraina is the small harbour of Menidhion. There is normally room for small to medium-sized yachts to go bows-to squeezed onto the end of the mole. Alternatively anchor off on a mud bottom – good holding. Shelter is adequate under the mole but it can become bumpy when anchored off here. If it gets untenable head for Ák Kóprainis where you can anchor under the lee of the cape and obtain good shelter from westerlies.

Several tavernas ashore, and limited provisions can be obtained in the village. A taxi can be hired here to visit Arta (18km). Little remains of ancient Arta (Ambracia), but its medieval bridge (with a delightful little museum nearby) and an eccentric Byzantine church are well worth the visit.

### Note

At one time it was possible to ascend the Arakhitkos River near Menidhion to Arta upriver, but the construction of a hydroelectric dam on the river now so restricts the flow of water in the summer that this is virtually impossible and moreover dangerous. Water is sometimes run off from the dam and levels increase very quickly.

## VOUVALOS AND ADJACENT ISLANDS

38°59'·2N 20°55'·0E

Good shelter from the prevailing wind can be found under these islets. The islets are connected by a gravel bar and a yacht should anchor in the lagoon between. There appears to be some confusion over where the entrance is. Reconnoitre with care. Anchor in the middle in 2–3m. Poor holding reported. Good shelter. At one time there used to be lots of mussels around the islets.

## KORONISIA 39°00'·9N 20°54'·8E

A small fishing harbour between Ák Salaóra and Nisídhes Vouvalos. The entrance to the harbour has silted but small yachts can enter with care. Make the approach on a NE course and keep close to the end of the W breakwater where there are 1·5m depths in the entrance. Reconnoitre first if in doubt. Once inside there are 2m depths along the SW mole. Good shelter inside.

Tavernas ashore.

# Nísos Levkas, Nísos Meganísi, and adjacent islands

Levkas is an island only because of the canal which separates it from the mainland. The present canal was built just after the turn of the century by the Greek government, although earlier canals were dug by the Corinthians around the 7th century BC and by Augustus during the Roman occupation. What appears to be an old canal cut can be seen running through the salt marsh just to the E of the present

**NÍSOS LEVKAS**

⊕14  N Entrance to Levkas Canal 38°50'·79N 20°43'·27E WGS84
⊕15  ½M S of Ák Dhoukató (Levkas SW end) 38°33'·4N 20°32'·5E
⊕16  S end of Levkas Canal 38°47'·54N 20°43'·58E WGS84
⊕17  N end Meganísi Channel 38°40'·10N 20°43'·72E WGS84
⊕18  S end Meganísi Channel 38°37'·88N 20°43'·88E WGS84
⊕19  1M SE of Ák Kefáli (Meganísi S end) 38°34'·8N 20°49'·8E

⊕14  N Entrance to Levkas Canal 38°50'·79N 20°43'·27E WGS84
⊕15  ½M S of Ák Dhoukató (Levkas SW end) 38°33'·4N 20°32'·5E

**LEVKAS CANAL AND APPROACHES TO LEVKAS**

canal. The line of ruined stone on the W is the remains of an old Turkish/Venetian bridge.

The main town of Levkas is sited on a bend of the canal and in common with many other towns on this earthquake belt was rebuilt after the 1953 earthquake. Unlike Vathi on Ithaca or Zákinthos, it was not rebuilt to a style and consequently the town is a riotous jumble of corrugated iron and brick houses leaning over narrow streets. It has its own charm despite the chaotic housing and hand-me-down appearance and is in fact a major cultural centre for the area. Every August the town council sponsors bands, folk dancing and exhibitions in the town. The local band practices for weeks before to perfect its cacophonous contributions, storekeepers decorate their shops, the police bedeck the street with flags and banners and Levkas fairly bustles with locals and visitors out to enjoy themselves.

The flat salt marsh and sand spits at the northern end of the island are in marked contrast to the steep-to limestone mountain range forming the rest of the island. Most of the population is around the S and E sides of the island, which are attractively wooded in places. The large fort at the N entrance to the canal, called Santa Maura after a small chapel within its walls, was built in the Middle Ages

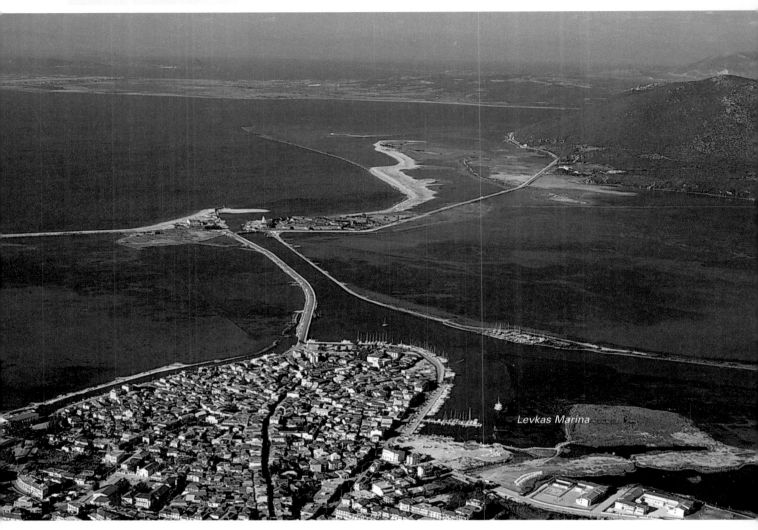

*Levkas Marina*

Levkas canal N end and Levkas town looking N
*Peter Kleinoth/MareTeam*

(c.1300). Later it was used by the Turks and the Venetians. It is worth a visit to wander around the large complex, especially the small galley port adjacent to the E wall. At the S end of the canal is a fort built by the Venetians to guard the approaches to Órmos Dhrepanou.

On the SW corner of the island is a precipitous white cliff called Leukatas from which Levkas takes its name. This is the cliff presumed to be Sappho's Leap from which Sappho of Lésvos, the famous lyric poetess of the 6th century BC, is supposed to have flung herself. After Sappho there are records of criminals being flung from the cliffs; if they succeeded in reaching the sea unharmed, they were recovered and pardoned. There is no anchorage here although the small port of Vasilikí is nearby.

The E coast of Levkas is fringed by a number of small green islands including Skorpios, the private parkland island of the late Aristotle Onassis, and Meganísi, looking like a giant tadpole on the chart and indented on its N coast with half a dozen sheltered anchorages. This area is the setting for Hammond Innes' novel *Levkas Man* which supposes that these islands are the remains of a land

bridge over which primitive man crossed from Africa to Europe. Much of the factual basis of this book is derived from excavations by the German archaeologist Dorpfeldt who discovered Neolithic remains near Evgiros on the S of Levkas. Dorpfeldt also put forward the controversial theory that Levkas fulfills all the requirements for the Ithaca of Homer and indeed he uncovered Mycenaean remains near Sívota and Vasilikí. Dorpfeldt contended that during the Middle Ages the inhabitants of Levkas were driven from their homeland to the more remote Ithaca of today and so transferred their name and cultural identity to that island. However, archaeological opinion still favours the present Ithaca as the original home of Odysseus.

## LEVKAS CANAL

BA 2405
Imray-Tetra G12, G121

Levkas canal, cut through the salt marsh between the island proper and the mainland, effectively severs it from the mainland and provides a passage for boats down the E coast of the island.

The canal is kept dredged to a minimum depth of

The floating bridge at the N end of the Levkas Canal. For small yachts the end section of the bridge lifts up vertically and for larger yachts the whole bridge swivels out of the way, as here

Just beyond this is the floating bridge with a section that can be raised. When the section of the floating bridge is raised it leaves a 9m wide gap on the W side of the canal. For larger craft the floating bridge swivels to lie parallel to the E bank. When the bridge is going to open a siren sounds and theoretically the signal on the bridge is lowered. If that doesn't work the operator will make it plain that you are to go with much waving of the hands.

The canal opens on the hour and traffic heading N from Levkas goes first followed by traffic going S. There may be a current in the canal at times, occasionally up to 1½ knots, which makes manoeuvring difficult. Levkas town is a short distance down the canal.

*Note* The bridge uses VHF Ch 12. Between 2100 and 0600 you will need to call up to get the bridge to open. During daylight hours the bridge opens on the hour as above.

### Approach from the S

Fort Áy Yeoryiou is conspicuous on a summit above the E side of the entrance to the canal. Closer in you will see Nisís Voliós, an islet at the entrance with a light structure on it, and the first set of buoys marking the channel. The channel is then shown by pairs of buoys and beacons and in the salt marsh by poles with red and green triangles atop. The direction of buoyage is from Órmos Dhrepanou.

A yacht should not attempt to cut outside the buoys marking the channel: there is a reef on the E and the remains of an old breakwater on the W.

***By night*** From the N use the light on Ayios Mavros (Santa Maura) fort Fl(2)WR.12s8/5M, (red sector covers 075°-120°) and the light on the end of the short mole sheltering the entrance to the canal Fl.G.1·5s3M. Care is needed as a hotel on the waterfront in Levkas has a quick flashing red and blue neon sign which is easily mistaken for the entrance lights. In the summer the Kastro near the beach has bright spotlights at night and along with the lights of Levkas town this makes spotting the entrance lights difficult. In the summer Fort Áy Yeoryiou at the S end of the canal is spotlit and shows up well.

From the S use Ák Kefáli Fl.4s5M, Nisís Voliós Fl.WR.1·5s5/3M, (red sector covers 293°-335°), and the lights of the buoys and beacons marking the channel Q.G/Q.R.

### LEVKAS TOWN

Levkas town lies a short distance down the canal at the point where the canal turns to run SE. The buildings of the town are easily seen and the location of the harbour is hard to mistake.

### Mooring

Go stern or bows-to the town quay on the NE or S side. Care needs to be taken on the S side as the ballasting runs out underwater in places and a yacht should really go bows-to rather than stern-to. The bottom is sticky mud, good holding, although in places a bit soft, so your anchor pulls through it. If

6m although some of it is deeper than this. The southern end of the canal is buoyed but the rest of the canal is marked by poles with red or green triangles on top. Some of the poles are missing, but normally it is fairly easy to distinguish the shallow brown water marking the edge of the dredged channel from the murky green water of the canal itself.

### Approach from the N

The first approach to the northern end of the canal can be hair-raising. With the prevailing NW wind pushing you down onto a lee shore with just the canal entrance to get you out of it, most people are on tenterhooks the first time around. You should have everything prepared, all sails down and stowed, the engine ticking over and someone up front to keep an eye on any traffic coming out of the canal.

Approaching the island in the afternoon haze it is not easy to identify where the entrance to the canal is. At times the haze can obscure even the high mountains of the island and you may be only 3 or 4 miles off before you see it. Closer in the wine co-op factory and warehouse on the W side of the canal and Ayios Mavros (Santa Maura) fort on the E side will be seen against the flat sandbanks of Yera spit to the W and Pláka spit to the E. From the NW two windmills stand out on Yera spit and behind the buildings of Levkas town will be seen.

On rounding the protecting mole, two rusty 44-gallon drums (sometimes painted red) are the buoys marking the underwater rocks and shallows on the SE side of the canal entrance, though they cannot always be relied on to be in place. A sand bar extends a short distance from the western entrance-point to the canal. Although it is periodically dredged, care must be taken as it silts up and extends rapidly in the summer with the prevailing northerlies.

Levkas town

Local boats

Bridge

Square

Tavernas
and shops

Contract
Yacht Services

Marine Services

Local
boats

To Nidri

Apartments

Wave-breaker pontoon

Levkas Canal (dredged to 6m)

Salt Marsh

Christo's
boatyard

3·5-4m

Levkas
Marina
(Work in progress)
3·5-4m

Yard
(hardstanding)

N

Depths in Metres

0        100        200

Metres

**LEVKAS**
⊕38°50'·1N 20°42'·8E

the harbour is very crowded a yacht can go stern or bows-to the W side of the canal just above the road bridge.

*Shelter* Good all-round shelter. The berths on the S side have the advantage that you are blown off the quay by the prevailing NW–W wind, but care is needed of the underwater ballasting and the wind also blows all the dust from the town across your boat. Berths on the NE quay have the prevailing wind blowing beam-on which is not normally a problem unless it is very strong or your anchor drags. Berths above the road bridge also have the prevailing wind blowing you off the quay. Southerlies set up a considerable surge for a landlocked harbour and care is needed.

*Authorities* A port of entry. Customs, port police and immigration.

## Facilities

*Services* Water on the quay.

*Fuel* On the quay at the E corner.

*Repairs* A boatyard nearby. Most mechanical repairs can be carried out. Light engineering work. GRP and wood repairs. Electrical and minor electronic repairs. Some sail repairs. Chandlers. See Contract Yacht Services or Levkas Marine Centre below.

*Provisions* Good shopping for all provisions. Several supermarkets near the quay and other shops in the town. A good town for restocking the larder. Ice from the supermarket behind Contract Yacht Services.

*Eating out* Numerous tavernas on the waterfront and in the town.

*Other* PO. OTE. Banks. Greek gas and *Camping Gaz*. Hire cars and motorbikes. Occasional buses around Levkas Island. International and internal flights from Aktion.

*Contract Yacht Services* Contract Yacht Services will winter your yacht and get it ready for the summer. All work can be carried out: mechanical and engineering work, wood and GRP work, rigging, sail repairs and life raft servicing including certification. Chandlers and fast order system for spares and equipment from the UK.

Contact Joe Charlton, Petrou Filippa 3a, 31100 Levkas
☎ 0645 24446 *Fax* 0645 24490
*E-mail* c-y-s@aiasnet.gr
www.c-y-s.com

*Yacht Assist* Operated by Contract Yacht Services. Operates a mobile workshop and high speed RIB to attend to yacht breakdowns in the area between Corfu and Cephalonia.
☎ 0645 24446 *Fax* 0645 24490 VHF Ch 08.

*Levkas Marine Centre* Situated down the quay from Contract Yacht Services. Carries out mechanical and engineering work. Also some GRP and wood repairs. Chandlers. *Gardiennage*. Life raft certification.

Contact Theo Georgakis, Golemi 18-20, 31100 Levkas.
☎ 0645 25036 *Fax* 0645 25550 *Mobile* ☎ 093 231595

Chandlers and hardware shops in town.

## General

Levkas town, as I indicated in the introduction to the island, is an odd sort of place that you either like or regard as a convenient stop en route to the north or south. I first came here in 1977 and so I have a long and ongoing association with the place that does not let me regard it objectively. For me it is a real working town that has benefited from a little tourism, but still remains mostly a business hub for the island that does not close down for the winter when the tourists have left. It will be interesting to see how it evolves when Levkas Marina is up and running and whether this substantially changes the nature of the place. I hope not.

Áyios Mavros (Santa Maura) fort at the N end of the canal is not the only fort on Levkas, merely the most obvious. S of present-day Levkas, the remains of ancient Levkas, or Nirikos as it was called in Mycenaean times, can just be discerned. Huge walls surrounded a town that was larger than present-day Levkas.

Levkas town used to be the centre for cigarette smuggling to Italy. Cigarettes were brought by freighter from Belgium or Holland and then run to the Italian coast by fast motorboats. Today the trade has all but disappeared as the Italian police get tougher and the profit margin less.

## LEVKAS MARINA

### Approach

At present care is needed because of ongoing construction work in and around the marina.

*VHF* Ch 69.

### Mooring

*Data* c.350 berths. Possible 800 berths when complete. Visitors' berths. Max LOA c.60m. Depths 3·5–4m.

*Berth* Berth where directed. There will be laid moorings tailed to the quay and pontoons.

*Shelter* Some berths may be uncomfortable with the chop kicked up across the harbour by the prevailing NW wind in the summer. Some berths may be affected by southerlies.

*Authorities* Harbourmaster and marina staff. A charge will be made.

### Facilities

*Services* Water and electricity (220 and 380V) points to be installed. Shower and toilet block to be installed.

*Fuel* Fuel quay to be installed.

*Repairs* A travel-hoist will be installed. Hardstanding area. Workshops.

*Provisions* A mini-market will be licensed.

*Eating out* Tavernas will be licensed in the marina.

*Other* Communication facilities.

### General

The marina structure is basically in place at the time of publication. The plan I have drawn is from an artist's impression of the finished marina and IKG has warned that the finished marina may be different to the artist's impression. In any case rendering a 2D image from a 3D artists impression, even after inspecting the works in progress, leaves some room for error. It is expected that the marina will operate with basic facilities in 2001. Additional infrastructure and facilities will be added as the marina is developed.

## LIGIA

38°47'.3N 20°43'·3E

On Levkas near the southern entrance to the canal is Ligia, a small fishing harbour. A short mole has 2–5m depths, but is normally cluttered with the resident fishing boats. The quay around from the mole is mostly too shallow although there are a few spots a small yacht can go bows-to if there is room amongst the local boats. Most yachts anchor off in 3–7m on mud and thick weed. Make sure you get through the weed as the afternoon breeze gusts down into here and the anchor needs to be well in.

Water on the quay. Ashore limited provisions are available and there are several tavernas. The local fishing boats supply some of the tavernas with good fresh fish and the tavernas here have some of the best fish on the island.

## NIKIANA

A small harbour lying approximately 1½ miles S of Ligia. There are 2–4m depths along the outer half of the breakwater. Go stern or bows-to the mole. Care is needed of old mooring chains fouling the bottom about 30 metres off the quay on the outer end of the mole. A number of charter boats are kept here and between the yachts and the local boats it can be difficult to find a berth. The bottom is mud, sand and weed, good holding once through the weed. Generally good shelter although it sometimes blows into here from the NNE–NE in the late afternoon making it uncomfortable.

Tavernas and some provisions ashore.

## NOTE

In the approaches to Nidri and Órmos Vlikho are three islands: Sparti, Kheloni and Madhouri. Off Nisís Sparti there is a 2m patch where care is

The baroque-style Vallaoritis villa on Nisís Madhouri

**NIKIANA**
⊕38°45'·6N 20°43'·25E

needed. Between Nisís Kheloni and Levkas there are shallow patches off the islet and off the coast of Levkas – care needed.

## NIDRI

BA 2402
Imray-Tetra G121

### Approach

Straightforward and there are no dangers by day. The town is obscured in the approach from the N, but the islands of Sparti, Kheloni and Madhouri make location easy and the town of Nidri will be

**NIDRI**
⊕38°42'·5N 20°42'·8E

seen in the closer approaches. From the S the town will not be seen until you are around the headland opposite Nisís Madhouri. A night approach is not recommended for a first time entry.

*Note* Nidri is a watersports and yacht charter base and there are invariably yachts, motorboats, sailing dinghies, sailboards, water-bikes, tripper boats and ferries to watch out for.

## Mooring
Go stern or bows-to the quay at Nidri. The quay is invariably crowded and you may have to anchor off to the S of the quay in the summer. The bottom is mud and weed, generally good holding.

*Shelter* The prevailing wind tends to blow down onto the quay making it uncomfortable though not usually untenable. The wake from tripper boats and local ferries is also bothersome and berths on the quay are certainly not comfortable.

*Authorities* Port police.

## Facilities
*Water* On the quay.
*Fuel* On the road to Vlikho. A mini-tanker can deliver to the quay.

*Repairs* A boatyard used to hauling yachts just S of the town and others nearby in Vlikho Bay. Hauling here is on a sledge and runners in the old-fashioned way. Mechanical repairs can be carried out. Stainless fabrication to a good standard by Steel Marine ☎ 0645 92243. Sail repairs by Sioux Sails opposite Nidri (look for the sign on the E side of the narrows going into Vlikho). Several well-stocked chandlers in Nidri.
Sioux Sails ☎/*Fax* 0030 (0)645 95525
*E-mail* s_sails@otenet.gr
www.siouxsails.net

*Provisions* Good shopping for all provisions. Ice from the fishmongers in the High Street.
*Eating out* Tavernas and restaurants stretch from one end of the town to the other.
*Other* PO. OTE. Bank. Greek gas and *Camping Gaz*. Hire cars and motorbikes. Occasional bus to Levkas. Ferries to Meganísi.

## General
Nidri is a busy little centre in the summer, something of a crossroads for private and flotilla yachts going N or S. Add a large watersports centre and a lot of land-based accommodation and you

Nidri and Órmos Vlikho on Levkas looking SSW
*Peter Kleinoth/MareTeam*

**PORT VLIKHO AND APPROACHES**
⊕38°42·3N 20°42′·8E

come up with one of the busiest resorts on Levkas. The busy square by the harbour has a superb view out over the bay and across to the islands and the mountains of the mainland opposite.

The Baroque villa on Nisís Madhouri in the approaches to Nidri belongs to the Vallaoritis family, descendants of Aristoteles Vallaoritis (1824–79), Greece's national poet and composer of the national anthem.

## TRANQUIL BAY

Opposite Nidri town there is the large bay called (some time ago when the name was accurate) Tranquil Bay. It provides good all-round shelter in attractive surroundings. Anchor in 8–12m on soft mud and weed, good holding once your anchor is dug in. Yachts often anchor and take a long line ashore to the N side of the bay. Care needs to be taken of a shallow muddy shelf extending around the S and E side of the bay – it can be difficult to see at times. On the edge of the mudbank is the wreck of a small coaster which yachts sometimes tie onto after putting an anchor out.

The slopes around the bay are heavily wooded, mostly with olives and cypress, and there is little habitation to intrude on the peace and quiet, only the numerous other yachts that use it. A number of yachts have wintered afloat here. It is a longish row over to Nidri town for supplies or a cold beer (an outboard helps) but water can be obtained from a tap near the chapel at the entrance to the bay.

Dorpfeldt, the archaeologist who challenged the orthodox theories about the homeland of Odysseus, claiming Levkas to be the original Ithaca of Homer, is something of a folk hero in Nidri. On the N side of the bay an obelisk has been erected to his memory; just above is his beautiful villa, now administered by the Director of Antiquities in Athens. In Levkas town museum some of his finds are exhibited.

## ÓRMOS VLIKHO

From Nidri and Tranquil Bay, Órmos Vlikho extends S through a bottleneck opening and opens up into an oval landlocked bay. There is good all-round shelter here and you can anchor in a number of places. The bottom is everywhere mud and weed, good holding once through the weed.

1. On the NE side of the bay. Anchor in 5–6m. Good shelter from the prevailing wind which tends to gust down from the N. Good tavernas nearby on the E side.
2. On the NW side off the boatyard. Anchor in 5–6m taking care of a shallow ledge off the NW corner. Good shelter.
3. Off Vlikho village. Anchor in 5–6m on mud and weed. Good holding. The wind tends to gust into here but the holding is good and there is no fetch for any chop to build up.
4. On the quay at Vlikho. Where the quay projects there are 1·5–2·5m depths and you can go stern-to here if you can find room. There are a number of yachts which seem to berth permanently alongside taking up most of the quay space. It can be quite uncomfortable on the quay as the prevailing wind tends to push a chop onto the quay. Make sure your anchor is well dug in.

### Facilities

*Water* On the quay, although it has been reported to be non-potable.
*Fuel* Fuel station on the road to Nidri or a mini-tanker can deliver if you are on the quay.
*Repairs* Several yards nearby. Electrics and electronics repair shop on the road to Nidri. Second-hand chandlers. Also see details for Nidri.
*Provisions* Mini-market. Better shopping in Nidri.
*Eating out* Several tavernas dotted around.

### General

After Nidri, Vlikho is a quiet relaxed spot where the tourists seem either to pass by or dally for only a short time. There is talk of improving the facilities at Vlikho, but as yet nothing has happened and it remains a sleepy hollow compared to the booming resort at Nidri.

Vlikho looking NNE from the slopes at the bottom of the bay

## ÓRMOS DESSIMOU

A large bay across the isthmus from Órmos Vlikho and opposite the NW point of Meganísi. It is very deep for anchoring – anchor in the N corner in 10–15m. Good shelter from the prevailing wind. Camping ground and taverna ashore.

## ÓRMOS ROUDA

38°38'·2N 20°42'·0E

A large bay on the SE corner of Levkas. A swimming area is cordoned off with small buoys at the head of the bay and you need to anchor outside this area in 12 to 15 metres. The prevailing wind gusts out of the bay but a swell may still work its way in. A number of tavernas ashore.

In the NE corner is Mikro Yialis and a short quay. The quay has mostly 1·5–2m depths off it and if there is room you could go stern-to. Most of the quay is the preserve of the local fishing boats so if you do berth here, enquire whether or not you are occupying someone's place.

## ÓRMOS SÍVOTA

### Approach

Entrance is easy in all weather. The entrance is difficult to make out from the distance, but closer a number of houses on the slopes on the W side of the entrance will be seen. The houses of the hamlet cannot be seen until you are around the dogleg of the bay.

*Note* With the prevailing wind there will sometimes be strong gusts off the high land in the vicinity of the bay.

### Mooring

Anchor where convenient in 3–10m although when there are large numbers of yachts using the bay you will be forced to anchor further out in 10–20m. The bottom is mud and thick weed, good holding once through the weed though this can take some doing.

The quay along the W and S side has mostly 2–3m depths. If there is room go stern or bows-to, though it is often crowded with charter boats.

**SÍVOTA**
⊕38°36′·87N 20°41′·52E WGS84

*Shelter* Good all-round shelter. With the prevailing wind there are gusts into the bay so make sure your anchor is well in. Yachts are wintered afloat here.
*Dangers* In the SW corner of the bay there are some heavy chains on the bottom which were used as permanent moorings.

Sívota looking SE from the slopes behind

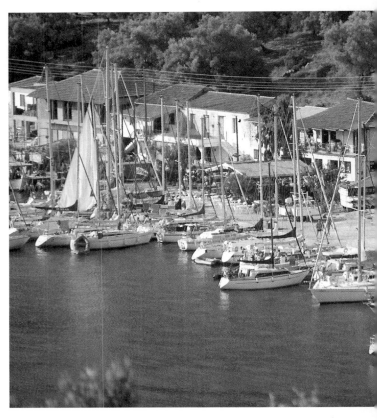

Sívota quay looking SE                    *Peter Sewell*

### Facilities
*Water* Metered water on the quay.
*Provisions* Most provisions can be obtained.
*Eating out* Tavernas around the bay. Make your own choice. Also a number of bars for post dinner drinks.
*Other* Metered telephone. Taxis.

### General
The enclosed bay with olive trees around the steep slopes is a picturesque place, though several new clusters of self-catering apartments threaten the character of the bay. The local community is largely engaged in accommodating the large numbers of yachts visiting the bay – on which the tavernas largely depend for their income.

### ÓRMOS VASILIKÍ (Vasilikas)
BA 2402
Imray-Tetra G121

### Approach
*Conspicuous* The white lighthouse on Ák Dhoukaton is easily identified and once you are into the large bay the houses of Pondi at the W end of the beach will be seen. From the E the houses of Vasilikí village will not be seen until you are right into the bay.

*By night* Care is needed in a night approach. Use the light on Ák Dhoukaton Fl.10s24M and the light on the end of the harbour mole F.G.3M(occas).

*Dangers* With the prevailing wind there are strong gusts out of the bay.

**ÓRMOS VASILIKÍ**
⊕38°37′·7N 20°36′·15E

**VASILIKÍ**
⊕38°37′·7N 20°36′·4E (F.G.3M)

## Mooring

Go stern or bows-to where convenient. The bottom is mud, good holding.

*Shelter* Good shelter although the prevailing wind tends to blow into the harbour. This is usually bothersome rather than troublesome, although some correspondents reckon it can be more dire than that when the wind is really gusting.

*Anchorage* A yacht can anchor in the bay in calm weather or light NW winds. Anchor off Pondi in 2–5m on sand.

*Note* The harbour is prone to silting and since my first surveys depths have already decreased substantially in the harbour.

## Facilities

*Water* On the quay. A natural spring favours this corner of Levkas and keeps the extensive plains watered. Immediately S of the town an outdoor washing house contains four tubs through which cold spring water constantly runs.

*Fuel* On the outskirts of the village. You may be able to get fuel delivered to the quay.

*Provisions* Most provisions can be found.

*Eating out* Tavernas in the village.

*Other* PO. Metered telephone. Exchange office. Ferry to Fiskárdho.

## General

Until the arrival of watersports centres here, Vasilikí was a sleepy little agricultural and fishing village. Now it deals with the summer flock of tourists in its own homespun way without neglecting the fertile agricultural plain behind the beach. For sailboard buffs the regular strong downdraughts into the bay make Vasilikí one of the top ten spots in the world for the sport – so I am told.

This is the nearest secure anchorage to the white cliffs of Sappho's leap close to Ák Dhoukaton. Here also is the site of a temple dedicated to Apollo where in antiquity panhellenic games were held to celebrate the god. Today only a few fragments and shards mark the site.

## NISÍS SKORPIOS AND SKORPIDHI

### (Scorpio Island)

Close E of Órmos Vlikho are the twin islands of Skorpios and Skorpidhi. These are the private islands of the Onassis family, originally bought by the late Aristotle Onassis. Sailing between Skorpidhi and Skorpios you used to see *Christina*, the late Onassis' motor yacht (read ship), moored to two large buoys. The whole of Skorpios has been planted as a park and requires a considerable full-time staff to maintain it. On the SW corner there is a farm to supply fresh milk and meat, on the E side are the generating plant, warehouses and employees' houses. Unfortunately for those who buy islands to gain privacy, the very scale of the acquisition seems to attract sightseers and from Nidri a number of *caïques* run day trips around Skorpios.

You can sail around the islands, you can even anchor off the coast, but you cannot land above the high water mark. All the anchorages are on the S of Skorpios. There is a cove on the SW with a small beach house that Jackie Onassis favoured. Further E is a sandy isthmus and a yacht can anchor on either side of it. The best spot is on the E side of the isthmus off a sandy beach. Anchor in 6–12m on a mud and weed bottom.

# Nísos Meganísi

Imray-Tetra G121

This Rorschach blob of an island lies immediately E of Levkas. The strait between Meganísi and Levkas, Stenón Meganisiou, is one of the loveliest channels in the Ionian, with the high precipitous slopes of Levkas on one side and the lower more gentle slopes of Meganísi fringed by a beach on the other. Winds in the channel are fickle and often you will have wind from a southerly direction at the S end and a northerly wind at the N end.

The N side of Meganísi is much indented with several natural harbours and numerous enclosed bays. Most of the bays are fringed by olive and cypress with clear blue water – a combination that makes them popular with yachts though there is always somewhere to anchor in high season and a little more solitude outside of July and August.

On the SW coast of Meganísi, on the 'tail' of the island, are a number of caves. The most famous of these, 'Papa Nicolis', is quite large and rumoured by the locals to be the hiding place of a Greek submarine during the Second World War.

Further south of this cave are a number of small but deep caves which lead 60 to 70 feet in. There is some good fishing to be had around this part of the island.

## IFALOS HIEROMITI

Between Nisís Skorpios and Nísos Meganísi there is a shoal patch and reef. The reef is scheduled to be marked with a light structure (light characteristic unknown) which will make it a good deal easier to identify. In calm weather the shoal and reef are easily seen, but with the chop from the prevailing wind it can be difficult to see. On a calm day it is possible to anchor off on one of the shoal patches and dive on the reef. If you see any yachts approaching, curious about what you are doing, please stand on the reef to give an indication that there is something there which could stop them abruptly.

## SPARTAKHORI (Port Spiglia)

### Approach

The village of Spartakhori perched on top of a hill on the W side of the bay is easily seen from the N and W. Once you are into the bay the small harbour will be seen.

### Mooring

Go stern or bows-to the quay or short pier where possible. You will have to drop your anchor in quite deep water so ensure you have plenty of scope. The S pontoon has laid moorings tailed to the pontoon to pick up. You can also go stern or bows-to the quay at the head of the bay which also has laid moorings. This quay has recently been extended right around the SE side with a stubby breakwater built out to provide additional shelter. Good shelter with the prevailing winds although the evening NE breeze makes some berths on the W side of the harbour uncomfortable.

*Anchorage* Anchor off the beach at the head of the bay. It is deep here and you will be anchoring in

**NÍSOS MEGANÍSI**

⊕17   N end Meganísi Channel
        38°40'·10N 20°43'·72E WGS84
⊕18   S end Meganísi Channel
        38°37'·88N 20°43'·88E WGS84
⊕19   1M SE of Ák Kefáli (Meganísi S end)
        38°34'·8N 20°49'·8E

**SPARTAKHORI (SPIGLIA)**
⊕38°40'·10N 20°45'·82E WGS84

**SPARTAKHORI**
⊕38°39´.75N 20°45´.6E

**VATHI**
⊕38°39´.8N 20°48´.0E

considerable depths as a buoyed swimming area means you must anchor a fair way out.

### Facilities
Mini-market at the harbour and limited water from the tavernas. Tavernas by the harbour, at the head of the bay, and in the village.

### General
The village is reached by a winding cypress-lined road and is worth the hot walk to reach it. From a bend in the road before you get to the village you have a view over the whole of the N part of the inland sea. Even if you eat at the bottom, it is well worth the steep climb up to the village for both the stupendous view and the enchanting village itself.

## PORT VATHI
### Approach
The entrance to the bay is difficult to determine and you cannot see the houses of the hamlet until you are well into the bay itself.

### Mooring
Anchor in the bay or go stern or bows-to in the harbour. Good shelter from the prevailing winds. A NE wind can blow in the evening making things a bit rolly, although it generally dies down after a few hours.

### Facilities
Water close to the quay, although it is often turned off in the summer. Limited provisions and several tavernas. George's, behind the mole, often has good fish.

### General
The small village is the nominal capital of the island, though the dusty little place hardly acknowledges it. It is a charming place, seemingly half asleep in summer. Good walks inland through the olive groves.

## VATHI MARINA
On the W side of the bay at Vathi a small yacht harbour is under construction. At the time of writing the initial work building the breakwaters had begun and it is anticipated the harbour will be finished around 2002–2003. No details are available on the exact final form of the harbour or what facilities will be available.

## ÓRMOS KAPALI AND ABELIKE
Two large indented bays between Vathi and Atheni. There are no dangers apart from a few reefs, easily seen, extending a short distance off the rocky coast. From the plan it is apparent there are numerous places in which a yacht can anchor.

There are considerable depths in both bays, mostly 10–15m until close to the coast. Anchor where convenient and take a long line ashore – there is little room in the bays to swing to an anchor. The bottom is mud and weed, good holding once through the weed.

The coves in the two bays can get crowded in the summer, but these are peaceful places for all that. There are no facilities and nor should there be. It is about a 10-minute walk from Kapali over the saddle to Vathi.

*Note*

1. In Abelike part of the bay is now buoyed off for swimmers. A road has been cut around the coast from Vathi and it is likely more land-based tourists will use the bays in the future.

2. There have been reports here of bold rats attracted to the rubbish left by yachts on the shore. Since I and a lot of other skippers expended some energy keeping the place clean in

*Prevailing Wind*

*Depths in Metres*

**NÍSOS MEGANÍSI: PORT VATHI TO PORT ATHENI**
⊕₁ 38°40′·26N 20°46′·60E WGS84
⊕₂ 38°40′·17N 20°48′·35E WGS84

years gone by, I'd suggest that anyone visiting here do likewise. It is not a place to dump or bury rubbish.

Meganísi looking SE to Port Vathi and across to Órmos Kapali, Abelike and Port Atheni    *Peter Kleinoth/MareTeam*

## PORT ATHENI

### Approach

From the N and W the two islets of Megálo Nisopoulo and Mikró Nisopoulo are easily identified. From the E the light structure on the E side of the entrance will be seen. Pass to seaward of the two islets as a reef connects them to Meganísi.

*Note* There is a reef running out into the middle of the bay. Most of it is just underwater and numbers of yachts run up on it in the summer. Care needed!

### Mooring

There are several places to anchor.

1. Most boats anchor on the W side of the bay with a long line ashore. Most of the bay is quite deep, 10–20m except at the head of the bay. The bottom is sand and weed, good holding.
2. On the E side of the bay.
3. At the head of the bay. It is quite deep until the very end. The bottom is mud, sand, and thick weed, good holding once through the weed.
4. Bows-to the rough quay off the *Niagas* taverna. It shallows up to the quay so go bows-to rather than stern-to.
5. Bows-to the concrete quay further into the bay. At the time of writing work is in progress extending the quay into deeper water so that there will be 2–3m depths off it.

Port Atheni S end of the bay

*Shelter* There is generally good shelter although a NE wind sometimes blows at night. It usually dies down after several hours.

### Facilities
*Niagas* taverna on the E side. Some provisions and tavernas at Katomeri.

### General
It is about 30 minutes' picturesque walk through the olive groves to the small village of Katomeri, though remember to take a torch if returning at night – there are no streetlights here.

### ÓRMOS EPANO ELIA
The bay tucked under the E side of Ák Elia. Anchor off the beach. The afternoon wind will often not reach here until later and sometimes not at all. A useful lunch stop and in settled weather a possible overnight anchorage.

### ÓRMOS KATO ELIA
The more indented bay further S. Anchor in 6–10m. A few local fishing boats use the bay. You can walk up to Katomeri from here.

# Nísos Ithaca

### (Itháki)
According to Homer this is the island home of Odysseus. Archaeologists can dispute whether or not this is so, but Homer still provides the best description of the island:

'In Ithaca there are not wide courses, nor meadowlands at all. It is a pasture land of goats, and more pleasant in my sight than one which pastureth horses...,

Homer *Odyssey*

The island consists of two peninsulas connected by a narrow isthmus which is the backbone to Kólpos Aetou (Gulf of Molo). The steep-to mountains are bare and rocky, although in a few of the valleys there is a swathe of green fed by some small subterranean spring.

In common with many of the Ionian Islands, Ithaca has a strong seafaring tradition and many of

NÍSOS ITHACA

⊕21 ¼M N of Ák Marmara (Ithaca N end)
38°30'·47N 20°38'·93E WGS84
⊕22 0·10M E of Ák Áy Nikoláou (Ithaca NE end)
38°29'·29N 20°40'·83E WGS84
⊕23 1M S of Ák Áy Íoannis light (Ithaca SE end)
38°18'·3N 20°46'·0E

the young make their living in the merchant navy. Many more have emigrated to Australia or South Africa, although a substantial number do return and it is not unusual to be greeted by an Australian *gidday sport* around the island.

The important port on the island is Port Vathi, although there are a number of other harbours and anchorages. At Port Polis, a bay below the town of Stavrós, the local school teacher looks after a small museum housing a collection of items from excavations on the supposed site of Odysseus' palace. Although the site of the palace has not been conclusively proved, a number of tripods and masks indicating later hero worship of Odysseus have been unearthed. Certainly the fact that Ithaca is on a major fault line may mean that the Homeric palace was completely buried by an earthquake, or perhaps the subject of Homer's epic lived in a comparatively modest dwelling.

### ITHACA CHANNEL (Stenón Ithakis)
*Caution* With the prevailing afternoon W–NW breeze there are strong gusts off the high land into the Ithaca Channel and off the E side of Ithaca. In July and August when the *maistro* is blowing these

## Ithaca and Odysseus

Despite the paucity of archaeological evidence for Ithaca as the island home of Odysseus and despite Dorpfeldt's claim that Levkas is the real Ithaca, the Ithaca of today remains the favoured archaeological choice. Consequently the places on the island mentioned in Homer have nearly all been identified on Ithaca.

Port Polis is the harbour of ancient Polis which stood on the ridge above. Just N on the summit of a hill called Pelikata are the ruins of a Bronze Age settlement which is generally accepted to be the palace of Odysseus. Some of the walls and a section of paved road are all that remain. On the N side of Port Polis there existed a cave, the Cave of the Nymphs, where archaeologists have found Mycenaean pottery and bronze relics including a number of tripods and terra cotta masks indicating later hero worship of Odysseus.

Port Frikes can be identified with the Reithron of the *Odyssey*.

Órmos Pera Pigadhi lies at the bottom of Arethusa's spring. The spring still flows today and above it is the raven's rock (*Korax*) of the *Odyssey*, still called by the same name today. Above here lies the plateau of Marathia and it is probably here that Odysseus met Eumaneus the swine herd.

On Mt Aetos, on the narrow peninsula joining the two halves of the island, are the scanty remains of what may have been a shrine or temple.

All of this is largely speculation, and indeed Dorpfeldt was able to single out equally convincing sites on Levkas.

**FRIKES**
⊕38°27'·60N 20°39'·91E WGS84

gusts can be quite severe. The most notorious spots are the S end of the Ithaca Channel, Órmos Frikou, and Kólpos Aetou (Gulf of Molo).

## FRIKES

Imray-Tetra G121

### Approach

A small harbour tucked into the W corner of Órmos Frikou on the NE of Ithaca. The buildings of the hamlet will not be seen until closer in, when two windmills on a bluff by the hamlet are conspicuous. Care must be taken of above and below-water rocks around the islets under Ák Áy Nikoláou.

*By night* The end of the mole is lit Fl.R.2s3M. The floating pontoon is lit with weak white lights along its length.

Frikes looking W into the harbour

*Note* With the prevailing wind there are strong gusts out of Órmos Frikou and care is needed.

### Mooring

Go stern or bows-to wherever there is room. In the summer many yachts go alongside because of the strong gusts into the harbour and you may well find that you will have to go alongside another yacht if the harbour is crowded. It is intended to install laid moorings at some time. Larger yachts can go stern-to the outside of the mole with a long line to it, keeping clear of the ferry berth.

*Shelter* The prevailing wind gusts down into here but once tied up it is a safe harbour. Strong NE winds could cause a problem. Southerlies cause a surge. Wash from fast ferries now rebounds inside the harbour and can damage yachts.

*Authorities* A charge is to be made. Charge band 2.

*Note* The recently installed pontoon has an alarming undulation with a southerly swell. It is likely that a good southerly blow will damage it in its present exposed position.

### Facilities

*Services* Water and electricity on the quay and pontoon.
*Provisions* Most provisions can be found.
*Eating out* Tavernas around the waterfront.
*Other* Ferries to Fiskardho and Vasiliki in the summer.

### General

The village is a picture postcard place, set at the bottom of a wooded ravine with a stream running down to the sea keeping everything green through the summer. A couple of windmills sit above the village on a rocky crag. Inevitably this once isolated village has begun to attract tourists, but it is still a gem and well worth a visit.

## ANCHORAGES AROUND ÓRMOS FRIKOU

In general the anchorages on the N and W side of Órmos Frikou are the best with the prevailing wind.
*Port Áy Nikólaos* The bay under Ák Áy Nikoláou. Good protection though there are gusts.
*Khondri Pounda* Reasonable shelter though some swell may work its way into here.
*Limenia* A two-headed bay under Ák Khondri Pounda. There is a watersports centre in the W cove. Reasonable shelter.
*Damouri* Immediately E of Frikes. Poor shelter.
*Mavrounas* Calm weather anchorage.
*Vathi Limani* Calm weather anchorage. Ruined monastery ashore.

The bottom is mostly mud, shingle and weed, not everywhere good holding.

## PORT KIÓNI

BA 2402

### Approach

Straightforward, and there are no dangers from N or S. The three ruined windmills on the S point of the bay and the cluster of houses on the saddle of the hill are easily distinguished.

*By night* The end of the short mole in the bay is lit F.G.3M.

*Note* With the prevailing NW wind there are strong gusts down into the bay.

### Mooring

Go stern or bows-to the quay. As the bottom shelves steeply you must drop your anchor in quite deep water, so have plenty of scope ready. Alternatively anchor off, though again, because it is so deep, you will be anchoring in 10+m. Because of limited swinging room it is probably better to anchor and take a long line ashore to the SW side of the bay or to the head of the bay. The bottom is hard mud and weed, uncertain holding in places.

*Shelter* With the prevailing wind there are strong

Kióni looking WNW into the bay　　*Nigel Patten*

Kióni harbour looking NE from just inside the stub mole

KIÓNI
⊕38°27'·0N 20°41'·5E (F.G.3M)

ÓRMOS KIÓNI
⊕38°26'·84N 20°42'·17E WGS84

gusts down into the bay, so ensure that your anchor is well in and holding. In southerlies a surge builds up and the harbour can become untenable. In strong southerlies it is better to head for Vathi.

*Note* In calm weather or light W winds a yacht can anchor off the cemetery in the SE, though again depths are considerable for anchoring.

## Facilities

There is no water supply other than cisterns. Some provisions (baker, grocer) can be found. Tavernas on the waterfront.

## General

Kióni is an attractive huddle of whitewashed houses around the slopes at the head of the bay. If the place seems to have more houses than people, this is because a large part of the population has emigrated to Australia and the USA and many of the houses are still owned by these expatriates. In twenty years the school roll has fallen from some 600 to 20. A *caïque* runs from here to Port Vathi in the season. Pleasant walks over the saddle to a number of small coves.

## VATHI (Itháki)

BA 2402
Imray-Tetra G12

### Approach

*Conspicuous* From the N and S a belfry and the earthworks scar of the road on Mt Korini are conspicuous. Once into Kólpos Aetou (Gulf of

VATHI (ITHACA)
⊕₁ 38°22′·2N 20°42′·8E
⊕₂ 38°21′·95N 20°43′·14E WGS84

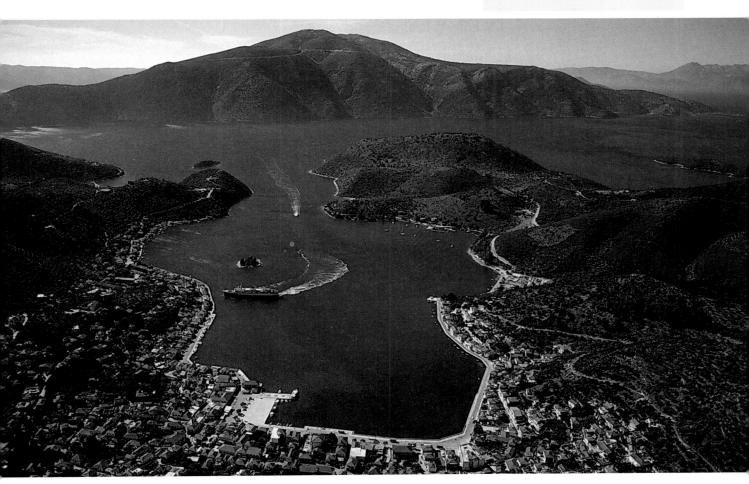

Vathi on Ithaca looking NW out to Kólpos Aetou
*Peter Kleinoth/MareTeam*

Molo) the light structure and the chapel on Ák Áy Andréou are easily distinguished. The light structure on Nisís Katzurbo, the small island at the bottleneck entrance to Port Vathi, will also be seen.

*By night* Use the lights on Ák Áy Andréou Fl.3s5M and on Nisís Katzurbo Fl.G.4s3M. Once into Port Vathi use the light on the small islet in the harbour Q.G.2M.

*Dangers* With the prevailing wind there are severe gusts down into Kólpos Aetou.

## Mooring

Go stern or bows-to the quay on the W under the ferry berths. Alternatively go stern-to the outside of the mole sheltering the basin. Yachts also go stern or bows-to the protruding bit of quay at the head of the bay. In the NE corner the quay has ongoing works at the moment and at the time of writing there were concrete blocks just under the surface so care is needed. No details are available of the planned final shape of the works here. The bottom is everywhere mud and thick weed, not the best holding until you get your anchor through the weed.

*Shelter* The prevailing wind tends to blow into the bay with some force so make sure your anchor is well in and holding. Once the breeze dies at dusk you will have no further worries. No sea enters with the wind and as long as care is taken in anchoring there is good all-round protection.

*Authorities* Port police and customs.

*Anchorage* Anchor off at the head of the bay in 2–5m or in the NE corner in 8–15m. The anchorage at the head of the bay is exposed to the gusts blowing in, but as long as your anchor is in and holding it is safe enough here.

## Facilities

*Water* Can be delivered by mini-tanker to the quay or on the fuel quay (see below).

*Fuel* Fuel quay on the E side of the bay. AVIN fuel quay provides fuel, lubricants and water. ☎ 0674 33316, 33317 *Fax* 0674 33006.

*Repairs* Limited mechanical repairs only.

*Provisions* Good shopping for all provisions. Ice available.

*Eating out* Numerous tavernas in the town. There are also two tavernas in the N bay.

*Other* PO. OTE. Bank. Motorbike and car hire. Ferries to Patras, Corfu and Italy.

## General

Vathi suffered severe damage in the 1953 earthquake, but although most of the town around the harbour is new, it is not an unattractive place. The port hums and bustles with *caïques* coming and going and when the Patras–Brindisi ferry arrives most of the town turns out to watch. Vathi is the best place to leave a yacht and hire a car or motorbike to explore the island – Stavrós, the likely site of Odysseus' palace, is about a one hour drive. In late August there is an Ithaca theatre festival at Vathi.

## ANCHORAGES AROUND KÓLPOS AETOU

*Imray-Tetra G12*

***Órmos Aetou*** In calm weather you can anchor in the SW corner of the gulf. Anchor in 5–10m on the W. Care is needed of the reef about half way along the bay.

***Órmos Dexia*** The bay under Nísos Katzurbo. In calm weather anchor in 5–12m.

***Órmos Skhoinos*** The large bay under Ák Skhoinos. Anchor in 8–12m in the NE corner. You can also anchor in the SE corner in greater depths. Tenable in light W winds.

**KÓLPOS AETOU (GULF OF MOLO)**
⊕1 38°23'·14N 20°42'·01E WGS84
⊕2 38°22'·66N 20°42'·06E WGS84

## ÓRMOS SARAKINIKO

38°21'·9N 20°44'·4E

A bay on the E coast of Ithaca immediately below Ák Sarakiniko. Anchor in 3–10m off the beach on sand, rock and weed. Reasonable protection from the prevailing wind which gusts down from the W. The bay is a delightful spot and in settled weather can be used as an overnight anchorage. Just over the saddle of the ridge is Vathi town, about an hour's walk.

## PERA PIGADHI

*Imray-Tetra G121*

On the SE side of Ithaca the small islet of Pera Pigadhi lies close to the coast. It is difficult to distinguish until you are close to. South of the islet on Ithaca is Órmos Pera Pigadhi.

Anchor in Órmos Pera Pigadhi or just S of the islet. There is room for a few yachts to go alongside the small quay on the islet. There are 4m least depths through the channel between the islet and Ithaca, though the water is so clear it is difficult to

**PERA PIGADHI**
⊕38°20'·15N 20°44'·80E

believe you are not going to touch bottom. Outside the channel depths drop off quickly and you will usually be anchoring in 10–20m in the bay or S of the islet. The bottom is sand and weed, good holding.

The afternoon breeze does not get here until mid-afternoon, when, unless you are tucked right into Órmos Pera Pigadhi or securely on the quay, it may become untenable. There have been a number of reports of very big and bold rats on the island that have no hesitation in invading a yacht moored overnight on the quay.

The steep-to slope above Órmos Pera Pigadhi is called Koraka, corresponding to the *Korax* in the *Odyssey*.

## ÁYIOS ANDREAS

38°18'·2N 20°43'·5E

An impressive deserted anchorage on the S of Ithaca. Anchor in 8–15m at the head of the bay or in the cove on the W with a long line ashore. Some swell enters with the prevailing wind pushing down the Ithaca channel, uncomfortable rather than untenable. Open to the S.

## PORT POLIS

38°26'·4N 20°38'·5E

A large bay on the NW side of Ithaca. Anchor off the beach or go stern-to on the end of the small mole. The bottom shelves steeply, so you will have to anchor in 10–20m. With the afternoon breeze gusting down the channel between Cephalonia and

Ithaca it can be uncomfortable in here, but usually not untenable. Southerlies blow straight into the anchorage and a yacht should go to Fiskárdho in the event of S winds.

# Cephalonia
### (Nísos Kefallínía)

Across the narrow sea strait from Ithaca lies Cephalonia, the largest in area of the Ionian Islands. Like Ithaca, Cephalonia is rugged and steep-to. Starting at the N end of the island a jagged mountain spine runs S to the highest mountain of the Ionian Islands, Mount Nero, standing over 1,600m (5200ft) above sea level. Most of the slopes are bare rock, but in the valleys, particularly on the E side of the island, beautiful pine forests run down to the sea. Much of this forest is composed of a local fir tree, *Abies cephalonica*, a tall slim pine which, despite its name, grows elsewhere in Greece.

In ancient times Cephalonia formed part of the kingdom of Odysseus, and here at least archaeologists have been able to find evidence of the ancient sites mentioned in Homer. There were four important towns: Pale, Krane, Same, and Pronoi. Same or Sami (similarly Pale-Pali and Krane-Krani) was the most important town built on the heights immediately N of the small ferry port of the same name. Extensive ruins of all four towns remain, those at Krani being particularly well preserved relics of Mycenaean occupation. The tombs here are said to be the best examples of Mycenaean tombs in Greece.

Like many of the Ionian Islands, Cephalonia has close links with Italy, and a wartime story is often told which illustrates just how strong this association can be. The Italians invaded the islands in the early days of the Second World War but failed to gain real control. In 1943 the Germans landed in Cephalonia, but the occupying Italian force, some 9,000 troops of the Alpine Division, not only refused to co-operate but actually fought against them for seven days. Of the Italian force only 3,000 survived, and these were brutally lined up and shot, it is said on Hitler's personal orders. Only 34 survived and, so the story goes, one of the survivors swam to Ithaca where he was sheltered by the local Greeks until he escaped. Until recently he was captain on one of the Patras–Brindisi ferries and every time he passed Ithaca gave a long toot on the ship's horn to salute his Greek friends.

*Captain Corelli's Mandolin*, the novel by Louis de Bernières, picks up on this theme and is well worth reading for a fictional account that incorporates this awful bit of Second World War history. Recently it has been made into a film, though interestingly the governor of Cephalonia censored some of the material on the role of the communists in the war, and the film is neutered by this censorship.

Cephalonia produces some good wines, though not from its Italian connection but from local initiative, the French and, surprisingly, an Englishman. Although not cheap by Greek

**NÍSOS CEPHALONIA (KEFALLÍNIA)**

| | |
|---|---|
| ⊕20 | N end Ithaca Channel<br>38°28'·47N 20°35'·73E WGS84 |
| ⊕23 | 1M S of Ák Áy Íoannis light (Ithaca SE end)<br>38°18'·3N 20°46'·0E |
| ⊕24 | 1M S of N. Vardhiánoi light (Cephalonia SW side)<br>38°07'·1N 20°25'·7E |
| ⊕25 | ½M W of Ák Áy Theodhoroi (Kólpos Argostoliou)<br>38°11'·6N 20°27'·6E |
| ⊕26 | 2M SE of Ák Mounda (Cephalonia SE end)<br>38°02'·2N 20°49'·15E |

standards (in fact nearly double the price of the ubiquitous *Demestica*), the *Robola* whites and reds are excellent and for those who like a rosé, the *Manzavino* is also good.

The earthquake belt that blights the other Ionian Islands likewise touches Cephalonia. Edward Lear, when he was touring the Ionian Islands, recorded 43 small tremors in 1863 alone. The major earthquake of 1953 effectively demolished every town on Cephalonia except Fiskárdho, because, it is said, it sits on a bed of soft clay. One inhabitant of Argostoli who experienced the '53 quake described to me how the ground undulated like a three-foot swell on the sea. In some of the rebuilding of Cephalonia there is a sameness about the reinforced concrete architecture that contrasts poorly with the gentle nineteenth-century grace of Fiskárdho.

## ARGOSTOLI (Argostolion)
BA 2402
Imray-Tetra G12

### Approach
*Conspicuous* From the W the large lighthouse on Ák Yero-Gómbos is conspicuous. From the E Nisís Thionisi and a white hotel on Ák Pelagia are easily identified. Closing the low-lying Nisís Vardhiánoi it

is safe to pass between it and Cephalonia, but a more prudent course is to stand off leaving the island to port and then proceed up the Gulf of Argostoli. Once you are in the Gulf of Argostoli, the town of Lixouri and a Doric-style lighthouse on Ák Áy Theodhoroi are conspicuous. Rounding the green wooded slopes of Ák Áy Theodhoroi keep to the middle of the inlet that forms the harbour of Argostoli. Leave the concrete beacon to starboard – although there are three metre depths between the beacon and the docks there are shoal patches close to the docks.

*By night* Use the light on Ák Yero-Gómbos LFl(2)15s24M and closer in the light on Nisís Vardhiánoi Fl.WR.7·5s6/4M (red sector covers 080°-107°). (The range of the light on Nisís Vardhiánoi appears to be less than stated.) Once into the gulf use the light on Ák Áy Theodhoroi Fl.3s5M and the light on the beacon Fl.G.3s3M.

*Dangers* Care is needed of the reef running SE from Ák Pelagia and of the reef running W from Ák Áy Nikólaos.

*Note* With a fresh afternoon breeze blowing down into the approaches to Argostoli (regularly Force 5–6 in the summer) it can be hair-raising entering this dead-end inlet for the first time.

### Mooring
Berth stern or bows-to the S of the ferry quay or on the N end of the W quay. If clearing into Greece go on the S side of the ferry quay within the customs enclosure. The bottom is mud, good holding.

**ARGOSTOLI**
⊕38°10'·90N 20°29'·76E WGS84

The Doric style lighthouse on Ák Áy Theodhoroi

*Shelter* The ferry quay provides a good lee from the prevailing wind whistling down into the inlet.

*Authorities* A port of entry. Port police, customs and immigration.

*Note* See entries which follow for Argostoli Marina and Maistratos harbour.

### Facilities
*Water* On the quay.

*Fuel* Can be delivered by mini-tanker. The nearest fuel station is near the market to the S of the yacht quay.

*Repairs* Mechanical and engineering work can be carried out. Electrical work. According to reports good emergency repairs have been carried out here. Good hardware shops but limited chandlery available. A small boatyard at Maistratos Harbour can haul yachts but there is limited hard-standing.

*Provisions* Good shopping in the town for provisions. Ice can be delivered.

*Eating out* Numerous tavernas in the town.

*Other* PO. OTE. Banks. Greek gas and *Camping Gaz*. Hire cars, motorbikes and bicycles. Buses to most parts of Cephalonia. Regular car ferry to Lixouri. International and internal flights from the airport a short distance out of town.

### General
In previous editions I have described Argostoli as looking 'like a frontier town – a Greek setting for a spaghetti western'. In recent years the town has metamorphosed into something which can almost be called chic. The pedestrianised main street has become all café latte and baguette, with outdoor cafés in between fashionable boutiques and jewellery shops. The residents take their coffee and conversation in a relaxed atmosphere and the hum of conversation lends the place an Italianate feel which of course is not out of place.

On Ák Áy Theodhoroi there is a reconstruction of the mill built by an Englishman, Stevens, in the 19th century. It is powered by the sea pouring into subterranean channels – a team of Austrian scientists, by putting a dye in the water, showed that it eventually reappears at Melissani near Sami. The flow of water is now much reduced after the 1953 earthquake. Also on the headland is the Doric-style lighthouse, which is conspicuous from seawards.

## ARGOSTOLI MARINA
38°10'·90N 20°29'·76E WGS84

**Note** At the time of writing a large sign prohibits any boats from entering and, given that the local boat owners have not moved in, I think we can assume the authorities mean it.

### Approach
The marina is on the E side of the arm running S to Argostoli docks. The light structures on the entrance are conspicuous.

*By night* The light structures are in place but as yet no light characteristic has been assigned.

### Mooring
*Data* c.250 berths. Max LOA c.50m. Depths 3–3·5m.

*Berths* Will be stern or bows-to with laid moorings. The marina has been dredged to 3–3·5m.

*Shelter* All-round shelter.

### Facilities
Yet to be installed. Planned are water and electricity, toilet and shower block, fuel quay, and there is a travel-hoist bay with large hardstanding area nearby.

### General
The structure of the marina is complete but as yet no facilities have been installed. It may be that the marina will be sold to a private operator or that the NTOG will hand the marina over to the local council.

Argostoli Marina looking across to the town quay

## MAISTRATOS HARBOUR
### Approach
This small harbour with a mix of fishing boats and yachts lies approximately 1000m N of the commercial docks. The breakwater and boats inside are easily identified when heading down into the inlet towards Argostoli.

*By night* The entrance is lit Q.Y(occas).

### Mooring
There is little room for visiting yachts. The best policy is to head for Argostoli and then come up and enquire about a berth here. Yachts berth stern or bows-to on the NE and SE quay. The rest of the berths are occupied by fishing boats.

*Shelter* Good all-round shelter.

### Facilities
Water on the quay. Provisions and tavernas nearby. Argostoli town is a short walk away.

Close to the entrance is a yard which can haul yachts. Yachts are craned out but the hardstanding area is relatively small. Mechanical and engineering repairs.

MAISTRATOS HARBOUR
⊕38°11'·4N 20°29'·1E

## LIXOURI
BA 2402
Imray-Tetra G12

### Approach
Directly across the Gulf from Argostoli is Lixouri. The buildings of the town and the harbour moles are easily identified. The entrance is lit: Fl.R.3M and Fl.G.3M.

### Mooring
Berth stern or bows-to the N or W mole. The bottom is soft mud, poor holding until the anchor digs in. The prevailing NW wind sets up a surge in the harbour which can be uncomfortable.

Port police and customs.

### Facilities
Fuel and water near the quay. Shower on the S mole. PO. OTE. Bank. Good shopping and tavernas in the town. Regular car ferry to Argostoli.

**LIXOURI**
⊕38°12'·1N 20°26'·6E

**ASSOS**
⊕38°22'·8N 20°32'·2E

### General

Between the surge with the prevailing wind and the constant smell of sewers, few yachts visit the sister town to Argostoli. The town itself is a likeable place, mostly busy with agricultural concerns and its own little cottage industries.

### ÁY KIRIAKIS

38°18'·6N 20°28'·6E

A small harbour in Órmos Kiriakis is suitable only for small yachts in calm weather. The harbour is very small and partially rock-bound. There are 2–3m depths in the entrance and 1–3m depths inside. Berth under the outer breakwater with a long line to it. Depths inside the harbour are irregular with shallows extending from the middle of the E breakwater and around the shore for approximately 20–30m out.

The little harbour is a gem, with just local fishing boats and a couple of simple tavernas ashore.

### PORT ASSOS

#### Approach

A natural harbour on the W coast 6 miles S of Ák Dafnoudhi (Vlioti). A large Venetian fort on the headland forming the W side of the harbour is not as conspicuous as it might appear on the plan, but can usually be made out from the distance. Closer in the houses of the village and the mole will be seen.

Assos

## Mooring

Go stern or bows-to the mole with a long line ashore, or anchor off. The short mole and the quayed area have mostly 1·5–2m depths, but the ballasting extends a considerable distance underwater, making it difficult to get close in. It is quite deep in the bay, some 7–10m mostly, coming up quickly to the quay. The bottom is mud, shingle, and weed, not everywhere good holding. With the normal NW winds a swell rolls into the harbour – uncomfortable and untenable with strong NW winds. There is no nearby shelter as the swell is just as bad on the S side of the headland in nearby Órmos Mirto.

## Facilities

Good tavernas ashore and some provisions can be found.

## General

The picturesque little harbour is popular with tourists in the summer but few yachts call here on account of the poor shelter from the prevailing NW winds. The Venetian fort which enclosed a sizeable town was built in the 16th century and is well worth a visit.

## FISKÁRDHO (Phiscardo)

BA 2402
Imray-Tetra G121

## Approach

*Conspicuous* It can be difficult to work out just where the bay is, though the general location at the N end of the Ithaca Strait is obvious. From the NE a number of new buildings in the bay immediately N of Fiskárdho are conspicuous. Closer in the twin ruined towers, the large stone lighthouse and the smaller Venetian lighthouse on the N side of Órmos Fiskárdho will be seen, although from the NE they can be difficult to pick out when the sun is low in the sky. The new villas and the hotel on the S side of the bay will also be seen. From the S the houses in the bay are easily discerned once you are past Nisís Dhaskalio which has a small chapel on it.

*By night* Use the light on Ák Fiskárdho (Fl.3s7M) and the light on the end of the short breakwater (F.R.2M).

## Mooring

Go stern or bows-to on the S or W quay or on the new pontoon on the W side. Care is needed on the S quay where the ballasting protrudes underwater in

**FISKÁRDHO**
⊕38°27′·53N 20°34′·94E WGS84

Fiskárdho on Cephalonia looking S    *Peter Kleinoth/MareTeam*

places. Do not berth in the SW corner where local *caïques* moor. In the summer the harbour gets crowded and you may have to anchor with a long line ashore to the N side. The bottom is sand, rocks and weed, reasonable holding.

*Shelter* Excellent shelter from all directions, although strong prolonged southerlies cause a surge, troublesome rather than dangerous.

*Authorities* Port police.

### Facilities
*Services* Water and electricity on the pontoon. You may also be able to get water on the quay from other sources.

*Fuel* Can be delivered by mini-tanker.

*Provisions* Good shopping for all provisions. Ice available.

*Eating out* Good tavernas and bars.

*Other* PO. OTE. Bank. Hire cars and motorbikes. Ferry to Frikes and Vasilikí.

### General
Fiskárdho is a popular spot for yachts, and in the season the quay is stacked two or three deep. The safe port and picturesque 19th-century houses set amid green pine groves remain pretty much original and a historical preservation order will hopefully keep them that way. This was the only place on

Modern lighthouse and Venetian lighthouse (looking NE) on the N side of the entrance to Órmos Fiskárdho

Fiskárdho town quay. The village was virtually the only place on Cephalonia that wasn't damaged in the devastating earthquake of 1953

Cephalonia that escaped damage in the 1953 earthquake that devastated much of the Ionian.

The village is named after Robert Guiscard (thus Guiscardo/Phiscardo/Fiscardho), a Norman adventurer who briefly ruled these parts and who is said to have died of fever here in 1085. Unfortunately for local folk history, it is also recorded that he died in Vónitsa in the Gulf of Amvrakia – also of fever. The ruined Norman towers in the N of the bay are believed to be part of a church built in his memory.

## THE EAST COAST BETWEEN FISKÁRDHO AND AYIOS EUFIMIA

On this green wooded stretch of coastline there are a number of small bays suitable for an overnight stay. Palaiokaravo, Órmos Kakogito and Kalo Limení are all sheltered from the NW wind, although there may be gusts off the high hills above and some swell may roll into some of them. The bays are deserted except for Kalo Limení, where there are a few houses ashore. Exercise some caution when anchoring as the bottom is loose shingle in places.

## ÁYIOS EUFIMIA (Sta Eufemia, Pilaros Cove)

Imray-Tetra G121

### Approach

*Conspicuous* From the N you will not see the town and the mole until you round Ák Agriossiki. From the E the town is conspicuous from the S end of Ithaca and as you close the port you will see the mole.

*By night* Use the light on Ák Dhekalia Fl(2)R.8s5M and closer in the light on the end of the mole Q.G.3M.

*Note* The channel between Cephalonia and Ithaca has a reputation for being very windy. The wind

**STENÓN ITHAKIS (ITHACA CHANNEL)**

⊕20 N end Ithaca Channel
38°28'·47N 20°35'·73E WGS84
⊕21 ¼M N of Ák Áy Íoannis (Ithaca N end)
38°30'·47N 20°38'·93E WGS84

**ÁY EUFIMIA**
⊕38°18'·2N 20°36'·1E (Q.G.3M)

Áy Eufimia looking NNW from the S entrance point

tends to blow either up or down the channel (usually down from the N) and you will also get gusts down the valleys and out of Áy Eufimia.

## Mooring

Go stern or bows-to on the N quay where shown. Alternatively anchor off keeping clear of the area where yachts berth. The bottom is sand, rocks and weed, not everywhere the best holding. In the SW corner there are sandy patches where the holding is better.

*Shelter* Good shelter from the prevailing wind, although it tends to gust down the valley and blow beam on, so ensure that your anchor is well in to hold you off the quay. The wind dies off in the evening. With strong SE winds a swell enters the harbour.

## Facilities

*Services* Water and electricity on the N quay.
*Fuel* Can be delivered by mini-tanker. The fuel station is on the S side of the bay.
*Provisions* Most provisions can be found.
*Eating out* Numerous tavernas. The one around the coast from the root of the mole is worth a visit.
*Other* PO. OTE. Bank. Ferry to Vathi and Astakós.

## General

This used to be the main port for the east of Cephalonia, but after the 1953 earthquake it was abandoned and Sami became the major port for the area. It is a better port than Sami for visiting Lake Melissani and the Cave of Drogarati. Lake Melissani is an underground cave and lake which is fed by seawater entering at Ák Áy Theodoroi near Argostoli and then travelling underground across the island to the lake and the sea on the east coast. A boatman will row you around and although it is crowded in the summer it is still worth a visit, as much for the subterranean cool as for the limpid waters of the lake.

## SAMI

BA 2402

## Approach

*Conspicuous* From the N the double-storeyed buildings lining the quay are easily visible under the green wooded slopes. From the S the harbour will not be seen until you are around Ák Dhekalia. Closer in the outer mole is easily identified.

*By night* Use the light on Ák Dhekalia Fl(2)R.8s5M and the light on the mole head Fl.R.2s4M.

## Mooring

Go stern or bows-to or alongside the new pier inside the basin. The bottom is mud and good holding.

*Shelter* Reasonable shelter from the prevailing N–NW wind although a surge can develop as the sea is pushed through the arches let into the new pier.

*Authorities* Port police and customs.

## Facilities

*Water* On the quay at the root of the mole, though it can be difficult to find the man to turn it on.

**SAMI**
⊕38°15′·3N 20°38′·8E (Fl.R.2s4M)

*Fuel* Near the quay.
*Provisions* Good shopping for provisions near the quay.
*Eating out* Numerous tavernas and bars.
*Other* PO. OTE. Bank. Hire cars and motorbikes. Ferry to Patras.

## General

Sami was completely rebuilt after the 1953 earthquake as the ferry terminal for Cephalonia. The green wooded slopes above Sami are attractive, but the town itself is mostly new, though now mellowing with the patina of a few years' ageing. It is an alternative to Áy Eufimia for visiting the semi-underground Lake Melissani and the Cave of Drogarati. The ruins of ancient Sami (Aegiala) are close to the SE of present-day Sami but there is little to see. Parts of the town and adjacent coast were used during the filming of *Captain Corelli's Mandolin*.

## PÓROS (Pronos Bay)

### Approach

A small harbour tucked under Ák Pronos.

*Conspicuous* From the N the buildings of the village will be seen and closer in the breakwater is easily identified. From the S the village and harbour will not be seen until you round Ák Pronos.

*By night* Use the light on Ák Kapri Fl(3)WR.9s6/4M and on the end of the mole Q.G.3M.

*Dangers* With the prevailing wind there can be strong gusts off the coast.

### Mooring

Go stern or bows-to the new quay in the SW corner. The bottom is mud and weed, mostly good holding.

*Shelter* Uncomfortable but tenable with the prevailing wind which blows down from the N. When the wind dies down at night things become more comfortable although at times it may blow through the night making it difficult to get any sleep.

*Authorities* Port police.

*Note* Yachts should keep well clear of the ferry berth. The ferry normally comes in and drops an anchor and then takes a line to one of the mooring buoys in the harbour.

## Facilities

*Water* On the SW quay.
*Fuel* On the road to the village. A mini-tanker can deliver to the quay.
*Provisions* Mini-market nearby. Other shops in the village.
*Eating out* Tavernas nearby and others in the village and around the road running out to Ák Pronos.
*Other* PO. Bank. Greek gas. Buses to Argostoli. Ferry to Killini.

## General

The village is set in a spectacular position on a strip of flat land between a precipitous gorge and the sea. It has a modest tourist trade, though most people arriving here on the ferry from Killini hardly stop and are on the bus to Argostoli before you even notice they have arrived. Recently a number of villas

**PÓROS**
⊕38°09'·0N 20°46'·9E

Póros looking down onto the harbour from Ák Pronos

and houses have been built around Ák Pronos and the village is expanding as a resort, though still in a low-key sort of way.

## IFALOS KAKOVA

The old BA 203 recommends the following to avoid the Kakova Shoal off the SE tip of Cephalonia: for N–S traffic Ák Kapri kept open of the W end of Nisís Atoko; for E–W traffic Áy Yeoryios castle in line with Ák Koroni clears the shoal. While the marks for E–W traffic are easily located the mark of Nisís Atoko for N–S traffic is difficult to locate with the summer heat haze. Although quite large *caïques* cut across the shoal, it is wise to give it a good offing.

## KATO KATELIÓS

38°04'·0N 20°45'·0E

In the NW corner of the large bay under Ák Mounda a yacht can find some shelter from the prevailing wind which blows from the W around the bottom of Cephalonia. A detached rough stone breakwater shelters fishing boats here, but a reef obstructs the entrance and a yacht is not advised to try to enter. Depths within the harbour are uneven and mostly less than 1m. Anchor off the beach on the N taking care of the off-lying reefs.

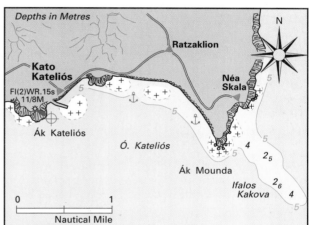

**ORMOS KATELIÓS**
⊕38°03'·8N 20°44'·6E

## PESSADES

38°06'·2N 20°34'·5E

A miniature ferry harbour connecting with Áy Nikólaos on Zákinthos. The tiny harbour and the ferry apron are tucked up in Órmos Lourtha under Ák Sosti. There may be room for a small yacht to tuck in under the end of the short breakwater.

## NOTE

Between Ák Liakas and the entrance to Kólpos Argostoliou there are a number of reefs and shoal water lying up to a mile off the coast. Keep well off when sailing along this stretch coast.

# The mainland coast and adjacent islands to Oxiá Island

Following the east boundary of the inland sea is the steep-to coast of mainland Greece. The eroded brown mountains rise straight out of the sea to some 1550m in places, providing an impressive backdrop to the islands dotting the sea. The two principal islands near the coast and the only inhabited islands are Kálamos and Kastos. Kálamos lies like a great stranded whale in the sea with skinny Kastos alongside. Further S the Dragonera and Echinades (meaning 'sea urchin') islands lie scattered off the marshlands at the foot of the mountains. These numerous small islands are all uninhabited, although sheep and goats are grazed on the larger islands. The southern part of this area is little visited by yachts although it contains a number of safe anchorages and ports, possibly because it is off the yacht 'motorway' to the Gulf of Patras and the Aegean and the few towns in the area are poor in tavernas. For those yachtsmen who like remote anchorages and spectacular, if desolate, scenery, this area makes a good cruising ground.

## VATHI-VALI

Ák Kefáli light 38°45'·4N 20°45'·9E

A small inlet on the mainland coast just S of the Levkas canal around the headland of Ák Kefáli. A fish farm now obstructs most of this inlet though it is still possible to squeeze in. Good shelter except from the S.

## PALAIROS (Zaverda)

### Approach
The buildings of the village straggling down the hillside to the harbour are easily identified. Closer in the harbour mole will be seen. The mole head is lit: Fl.G.1·5s3M.

### Mooring
Go stern or bows-to the quay where convenient. The harbour is used by a charter company and it can get crowded in the summer. The bottom is mud and weed, reasonable holding.

*Shelter* Good shelter from the prevailing wind. At night a katabatic breeze may blow in from the NE, but dies down after 2–3 hours.

### Facilities
*Water* Water on the quay.
*Fuel* A mini-tanker can deliver to the harbour.
*Provisions* Good shopping for provisions in the town.
*Eating out* Numerous tavernas near the harbour and in town.
*Other* PO. OTE. Bank. Irregular bus service to Vónitsa and Mitika.

### General
A largely agricultural village that now adds to its income from the charter company based here. The

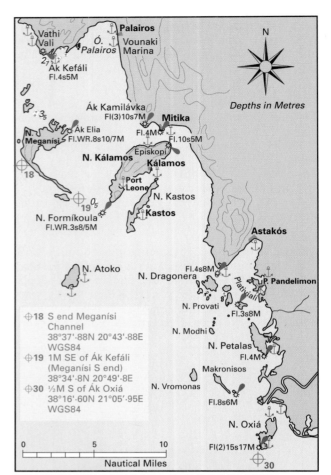

**THE MAINLAND COAST AND ADJACENT ISLANDS**
**(Meganísi to Nisís Oxiá)**

**PALAIROS (ZAVERDA)**
⊕38°46'·9N 20°52'·8E (Fl.G.1·5s3M)

village is attractive in a proper working way, serving the needs of the surrounding farmers, and the inhabitants are a friendly lot. Above the village the slopes of the Arkarnanika rise abruptly to 1,590m (5,167ft) with barren stony slopes bereft of trees and even *maquis*.

## VOUNAKI MARINA

### Approach

Situated just S of Palairos. The harbour is easily identified from the hotel complex behind and the harbour breakwaters show up well closer in. The approach should be from the W as the dinghy mooring area directly N of the harbour is shallow.

*By night* The shelter breakwater is lit Fl.G.3s7m3M.

*VHF* Ch 10.

### Mooring

*Data* 60 berths. Depths 2–6m.

Berth stern or bows-to where directed or convenient. There are laid moorings with lines tailed to the quay.

*Shelter* Good shelter although strong westerlies might cause some bother. It is planned to extend the shelter breakwater further N in the near future and this will improve the shelter in the harbour.

*Authorities* Dockmaster. Charge band 2.

### Facilities

*Services* Water and electricity at or near every berth. Showers and WC.
*Fuel* Fuel dock in the harbour.
*Repairs* 15-ton crane. Mechanical and engineering repairs. GRP workshop. Sail loft. Chandlers.
*Provisions* Mini-market. Better shopping in Palairos 15 minutes' walk away.

*Eating out* Taverna. Others in Palairos.
*Other* Laundry service. Gas available. Telephone and Fax. Car hire. Air tickets.

### General

Vounaki is a major Sunsail charter base in the area but cruising yachtsmen can use the harbour and its resources. The hotel is exclusively for Sunsail clients but the other facilities are available to visiting yachties.

*Sunsail Vounaki Marina*, Palairos, A.K. 30012, Greece. VHF Ch 10. ☎/*Fax* 0643 41944.

## MITIKA

There is a quay on the W side of Ák Mitika in Órmos Mitika, but this is only tenable in the morning calm before the afternoon breeze gets up. On the S side of Ák Mitika a new fishing harbour has been built.

## MITIKA HARBOUR

### Approach

Straightforward. There are no lights for a night entry.

### Mooring

Go stern or bows-to the NE quay or anchor and take a long line to the SW breakwater. Care is needed of the numerous floating mooring lines used by the local boats.

*Shelter* Good shelter from the prevailing NW–W wind.

*Note* The harbour is usually fairly full with local boats, but you can normally find a berth.

*Anchorage* You can anchor off to the E of the harbour, but the prevailing wind pushes swell through the channel between Mitika and Kalamos and the anchorage is not really comfortable.

### Facilities

*Water* Tap on the NE quay.

**VOUNAKI MARINA**
⊕38°46'·0N 20°52'·8E

**MITIKA**
⊕38°39'·90N 20°56'·68E WGS84

103

*Fuel* Some way out of town.
*Provisions* Good shopping for provisions.
*Eating out* Numerous tavernas on the waterfront on the W, some with good fresh fish.
*Other* PO. Bank. Ferry to Ayia Eufemia. *Caïque* ferry to Kalamos and Kastos.

### General

Mitika is a very Greek workaday place with little in the way of tourism and the better for it. It can get a bit dusty in the summer, but once you are safely tucked into the harbour then you can wander around to the western side for a drink and dinner overlooking the sea, in a setting which is just charming.

## Nísos Kálamos

### PORT KÁLAMOS

### Approach

Straightforward. From the N the houses of Kálamos village on the hill will be seen. From the S a number of old windmills, including one on a rocky outcrop before the harbour, will be seen.

*By night* The end of the mole is lit Fl.R.3s3M.

*Note* Care is needed in the afternoon when the prevailing wind gusts up the channel between Kálamos and Kastos.

### Mooring

Go stern or bows-to the mole. In places it is best to go bows-to as there are patches of underwater ballasting extending out from the quay. There are some laid moorings tailed to the quay and if one is available then use one of these. At the head of the

**PORT KÁLAMOS**
⊕38°37'·40N 20°55'·97E WGS84

harbour and around the quay there are insufficient depths. The bottom is mud, sand and weed, mostly good holding.

*Shelter* Good shelter from the prevailing wind. although at night a NE katabatic may blow into the harbour for a while. A strong SE wind can make the harbour uncomfortable and even dangerous if it is a prolonged blow.

*Note* Work is in progress extending the mole at the time of writing and this has been incorporated into the plan as it is expected work will be complete by the publication date.

### Facilities

Mini-market and bakery in the village. Several tavernas. PO.

### General

At Kálamos town and on the NE of the island there are cool green pine glades running down to the sea. The islanders make a living from fishing and a little

**NÍSOS KÁLAMOS AND KASTOS**
⊕₁ 38°34'·0N 20°52'·3E
⊕₂ 38°36'·9N 20°55'·97E

Port Kálamos looking S                    *Nigel Patten*

agriculture and, one suspects, remittances from abroad. Sadly, the village is dying as the young move away to more lucrative jobs on the mainland and the local population is skewed to the elderly.

## PORT LEONE

To the S of the island lies Port Leone, an anchorage sheltered from the prevailing winds and only open to the E. The entrance is difficult to determine from the distance, though closer in two old windmills will be seen on the E side of the entrance. The bay is very deep to anchor in and you will probably be in 10–15m depths. A few yachts will be able to get close in to the ruined piers off the village. The bottom is sand, mud and weed, mostly good holding.

The small village has been deserted since the 1953 earthquake destroyed the local water supply and the inhabitants decided to emigrate rather than rebuild. Every Sunday three or four people from Kálamos come to clean the church and say a few prayers.

**PORT LEONE**
⊕38°35′·96N 20°53′·36E WGS84

## EPISKOPI

38°39′·0N 20°56′·0E

A small harbour on the N side of Kálamos. A few small yachts can get in here though care is needed as there is little room to maneouvre and the depths decrease from 2m on the outer mole to 1·5m in the middle and less towards the beach. No facilities.

# Nísos Kastos

## PORT KASTOS

### Approach

From the N the flat island of Prasonisi and the houses of Kastos identify where the harbour is. From the S a mill on the headland sheltering Port Kastos will be seen, but you will not see the village until you round the headland.

*By night* The end of the mole is lit by a F.R but it should not be relied on. The light will presumably be moved to the end of the new section of the mole when work is complete.

### Mooring

Stern or bows-to the outer end of the small mole, or anchor off in the bay. The bottom is mud and weed, good holding once through the weed.

*Shelter* Behind the mole is good, and anchored off you are safe enough, though the prevailing wind sends in a residual swell that sets yachts rolling. At night a NE katabatic wind may blow but the harbour is usually tenable.

*Note* At the time of writing work is in progress extending the mole and this has been incorporated into the plan.

### Facilities

Several tavernas and a few provisions if you are lucky. Most provisions arrive from Mitika by *caïque*.

### General

The population of Kastos was evacuated in 1976 because of a suspected typhoid outbreak. The islanders are gradually returning, although the population in the winter is still only 80 or so. The village and its setting are beautiful, all prickly pear and olives that supports a surprising assortment of livestock including cows, sheep and the ubiquitous goats. Good snorkelling in the waters around the island.

**PORT KASTOS**
⊕38°34′·2N 20°54′·8E

## ANCHORAGES AROUND NÍSOS KASTOS

***Port Sarakiniko*** 38°34'·0N 20°54'·2E The indented bay on the W side of the island. In calm weather you can anchor in the bay in 5–10m. When the prevailing NW–W wind is blowing a swell is sent into here. At the head of the bay is a short mole (25m long) with 2–3m depths behind it shallowing to less than a metre off the rough quay. If there is space a small yacht may be able to go bows-to or take a long line ashore.

***Prasonisi anchorage*** The rocky islet NE of Kastos harbour. In the channel between the islet and Kastos there are least depths of 4m in the fairway at the N end of the channel and least depths of 7m at the S end in the fairway. In calm weather you can anchor in the bay opposite the islet.

***SE Bay*** On the E side of Kastos and S of the harbour there is an indented bay which affords some shelter from the prevailing wind. It is quite deep in here for anchoring and the best policy is to take a long line ashore in the N arm.

## Nisís Atoko

Around 6 miles E of Frikes on Ithaca lies Nisís Atoko, a dome-shaped island easily identified from the distance.

There are two anchorages on the island. In calm weather or light NW winds Cliff Bay on the S side can be used, although it is very deep (10–15m at either end) to anchor in.

On the SE side One House Bay affords better shelter and more suitable depths for anchoring and consequently is more popular. Anchor in 5–12m on sand, good holding. Shelter from the prevailing NW wind is good and it is possible to stay overnight in settled weather. Clear turquoise water and a solitary house ashore. Sweet water from a well ashore.

## The mainland coast

### ASTAKÓS (Astokos, Dragonmestre)

#### Approach

*Conspicuous* Once you are into Órmos Astakou the buildings of the small town will be seen, and closer in the harbour breakwater is easily identified. Close E of the breakwater is the newly constructed fishing harbour.

*By night* The end of the breakwater is lit: Fl.R.4s3M.

#### Mooring

Go stern or bows-to the N quay, leaving the ferry berth clear. Yachts may have to move off part of the quay when the hydrofoil arrives so if there is a space on the mole it may be worthwhile going there. Care is needed as rock ballasting extends out underwater in places along the mole. The bottom is mud, good holding.

*Shelter* Good shelter from the prevailing winds. Open to southerlies.

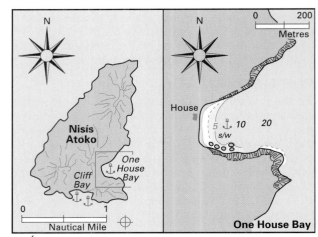

**NISÍS ATOKO**
⊕38°28'·4N 20°49'·1E

#### Facilities

*Water* On the quay.
*Fuel* About 1km out of town.
*Repairs Caïques* are hauled in a yard across the bay. Limited mechanical repairs. Chandlers.
*Provisions* Good shopping for provisions in the town.
*Eating out* Several tavernas on the waterfront and in the town.
*Other* PO. OTE. Banks. Ferry to Ithaca and Póros on Cephalonia.

#### General

Astakós has a little tourist trade, mostly from Greeks on holiday here, but is principally a fishing and agricultural town. Astakós means 'lobster' but despite this promise the restaurants in the town never seem to have the delectable crustacean. Do the locals keep them for themselves or are there really no lobsters in the town called 'Lobster'?

One House Bay on Nisís Atoko                    *Nigel Patten*

**ASTAKÓS**
⊕38°31'·8N 21°05'·6E

## ANCHORAGES NEAR ASTAKÓS

***Port Marathia*** A deserted inlet SW of Astakós tucked in behind Ák Tourkovigla. Good shelter from the prevailing wind. Anchor near the head of the bay on mud. The new coast road running across the N of the bay rather shatters the calm and beauty of the place.

***Boulder Bay*** A bight just before Astakós that can be recognised by the prominent boulder/rock near the shore. Anchor off the beach where convenient. Gusts with the prevailing WNW wind.

## ANCHORAGES AROUND THE DRAGONERA AND ECHINADES ISLANDS

***Nisís Dragonera*** On the SE tip of the island there is a miniature inlet that a small yacht can use. On the N side are two coves suitable in calm weather before the prevailing wind gets up.

***Nisís Karlonisi*** Small yachts can tuck themselves into the narrow channel between Karlonisi and Provati. Care is needed of the reef running out from the W side.

## PORT PANDELIMON

A double-headed inlet now partially obstructed by a fish farm. The perimeter of the two fish farms here is marked by small plastic buoys. At times the fish farm caretakers have objected to yachts anchoring in the inlet, although in recent years this seems not to be the case.

Anchor in the E or the S creek with the latter giving the best shelter. The bottom is mud and weed, good holding once through the weed. The E creek can become uncomfortable with the chop pushed in by the prevailing wind, though rarely dangerous. In the S creek it is a good idea to take a long line ashore. No facilities unless you can get a fish or two from the fish farm.

*Note* The fish farms are often moved because of the debris (uneaten food and excrement) that builds up under them over time. Consequently do not rely on

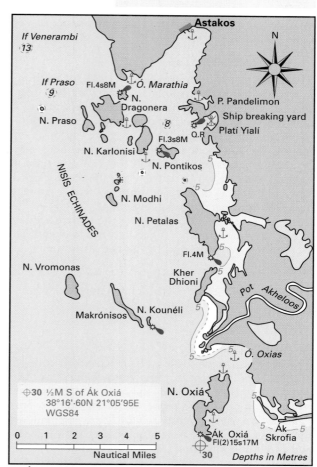

**NISÍS DRAGONERA AND ECHINADES AND ADJACENT COAST**

**PANDELIMON AND PLATÍ YIALÍ**
⊕Karlóglossa light 38°28'·5N 21°05'E

the buoyed off areas for the fish farms being in the exact position shown.

### PLATÍ YIALÍ (Plateali)

The large bay lying immediately S of Pandelimon. For some time massive engineering work has been carried out to create huge concrete aprons and quays and the infrastructure ashore for a ship-breaking yard. Despite the massive amount of money that has been spent it seems that there may be some uncertainty over its future. At one time it appears that hazardous waste was to be re-processed here, but at the time of writing the whole project looks like another EU white elephant.

It is possible to berth alongside the concrete quay in here if you so desire. If the harbour is ever used then no doubt yachts will be banned from here.

### KOMAROS

A small inlet S of Platí Yialí, now effectively obstructed by a fish farm.

### NISÍS PETALAS

Ák Aspro (S end) light 38°23'·7N 21°06'·1E

The large island lying close off the coast 2½ miles S of Platí Yialí. A yacht can find good shelter from the prevailing winds tucked in behind the island. Anchor behind the SE corner of the island in 2–3m. The bottom shelves gently towards the marshland at the N end. Shelter here is much better than it looks and the holding is good in glutinous mud.

Above the anchorage a cave is conspicuous. On one late autumn evening I spied a huge bird sitting by the cave and from a pinion feather retrieved from the cave the breeding pair of vultures here were estimated to have a wing-span of around eight feet. They are shy birds and it is unlikely you will see them through the summer, when they retire to even more remote areas.

### POTAMOS AKHELOOS (River Achelos)

This river, the longest in Greece, empties into the sea about 3 miles S of Nisís Petalas. The exact mouth of the river is difficult to identify and shoal water from the silt brought down extends at least a mile offshore. The shoal water appears to extend further than charted and care is needed to keep a safe distance off.

### NISÍS OXIÁ

⊕30 ½M S of Ák Oxia 38°16'·60N 21°05'·95E WGS84

The high island with a jagged ridge running down the spine at the entrance to the Gulf of Patras. Once seen its spiny outline is unmistakable. The lighthouse on the S end Fl(2)15s17M is conspicuous from the W and E. There are only two indifferent anchorages, both very deep.

1. **North Bay** There is now a fish farm in North Bay, leaving no room to anchor.
2. **East Bay** A bay on the E side affording some shelter from the prevailing westerlies. Anchor in 15–20m with a long line ashore. Spectacular

surroundings and utter isolation except for a few fishing boats.

3. **Órmos Oxias** Some shelter from the prevailing wind can be obtained under the spit of land formed by the river delta of the Akheloos. Anchor in 4–6m on mud, sand and weed.

# Nísos Zákinthos

## (Zante Island)

Zákinthos, the ancient name now officially readopted, is the southernmost of the Heptanesoi. (Kíthera and Andíkithera, although originally part of the Heptanesoi, are now administered separately.) Like a bowl holding something precious, the mountains of Zákinthos enclose the fertile central plain except where it overflows onto the sands of Lagana Beach. The Venetians called Zákinthos 'the flower of the Levant' and looking down on the plain planted with vines, mostly of the dwarf variety for currants, figs, olives, orange and lemon groves, it is easy to see why.

The first time I saw Zákinthos was in the autumn. After the baked islands of the Cyclades, the green slopes dotted with grazing cows were reminiscent of England. Yet despite English rule before Greece became independent, and English commercial interests in the currant trade, there is little apart from the green fields to remind you of England – Zákinthos is an Italianate island. Until the 1953 earthquake destroyed much of the Venetian architecture it must have appeared to be almost a cameo left behind by Venice.

**NÍSOS ZÁKINTHOS**

⊕27　1M N of Ák Skinari light (Zákinthos N end)
　　　37°56'·9N 20°42'·2E
⊕28　1M S of Ák Marathia (Zákinthos SW end)
　　　37°37'·9N 20°50'·0E
⊕29　Limín Zákinthos entrance
　　　37°46'·86N 20°54'·41E WGS84

'Only in Italy itself could one find this sort of baroque style, fruit of the seventeenth and eighteenth-century mind. Then in 1953 came the definitive earthquake which engulfed the whole of the Venetian past and left the shattered town to struggle to its knees once more. This it has done, in a manner of speaking; but it is like a beautiful woman whose face has been splashed with vitriol. Here and there, an arch, a pendent, a shattered remains of arcade, is all that is left of her renowned beauty.'

Lawrence Durrell *The Greek Islands*

Lawrence Durrell goes on to slate the modern town which I personally do not find so distasteful – but then I never saw the old Venetian town.

Zákinthos town overlooks a sheltered bay that has harboured naval fleets since ancient times. Anybody who wanted to move south needed Zákinthos to control the strait into the Gulf of Patras and the route south around the Peloponnisos. First the Athenians, then Philip of Macedon, the Romans, Vandals, Normans, Turks, Venetians, French, Russians and finally the British held the island. While under British rule the island was a constant source of irritation to the Turks, since Greeks could easily escape to it and seek protection under the neutral Ionian flag – only to venture out again to fight the Turks on the mainland.

Twenty-five miles to the south of Zákinthos lie the remote Strophades Islands (Nisídhes Strofadhes). Administered from Zákinthos, the largest island was once a prosperous monastery until the Turks sacked it.

## ÓRMOS ÁY NIKÓLAOS

A bay on the northern tip of Zákinthos partially sheltered by the islet of Áy Nikólaos in the entrance to the bay. Entry can be made on either side of the islet, though care is needed of the reef and shoal water extending N from the N end of the islet and S from the N entrance to the bay. A light is exhibited on the NE side of the islet Fl.2s7M.

Anchor in 5–15m where convenient, leaving the approach to the ferry ramp clear. Yachts can also anchor and take a long line to the outside of the rough stone breakwater. When the afternoon breeze gets up there are strong down-draughts into the bay so ensure your anchor is well in if staying.

Tavernas ashore. Fuel station nearby. Ferry to Pessades on Cephalonia in the summer. Local *caïques* run excursions from here to caves near the northern tip of the island which are said to rival the Blue Grotto on Capri.

## ALIKES

37°50'·6N 20°45'·9E

A small harbour at the S end of Órmos Alikon. A rough stone breakwater encloses a U-shaped basin with the mouth of the U located on the beach side. The end of the breakwater is lit Fl.R.2s3M.

There is no quay to tie up to so you will have to anchor and take a long line to the breakwater. The space inside is largely taken up by local boats so really the best option is to anchor off the beach.

Tavernas ashore.

**ÁY NIKÓLAOS**
⊕37°54'·5N 20°42'·8E

## PORT ZÁKINTHOS (Zante, Zakynthos)

BA 2404
Imray-Tetra G12

### Approach

*Conspicuous* From the N the hills dominated by Mt Skopio (520m) to the E of the central plain look like a separate island from the distance. As you near Ák Krionéri the hotels on the beach to the N of the cape and a tower on the hills immediately above are conspicuous. The buildings of Zákinthos are obscured until you round the cape when the N mole will be easily identified. From the S the buildings of Zákinthos stand out well against the eroded cliffs behind.

*By night* From the N use the lights on Ák Skinári Fl.5s20M, Áy Nikólaos Fl.2s7M and on Ák Krionéri Fl(2)16s6M. From the S use the lights on Ák Kerí Fl(3+1)15s17M and Ák Krionéri

Áy Nikólaos on Zákinthos looking SW into the bay *Nigel Patten*

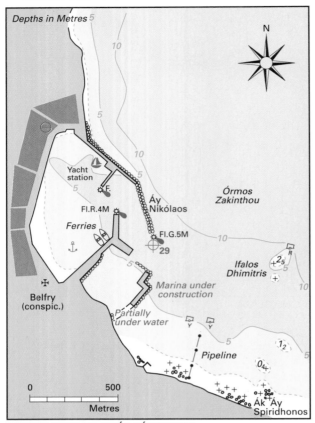

**APPROACHES TO LIMÍN ZÁKINTHOS**

⊕29 Limín Zákinthos entrance
37°46'·86N 20°54'·41E WGS84

Zákinthos looking SE          *Peter Kleinoth/MareTeam*

Fl(2)16s6M. A constant red aerobeacon just W of the town is visible for about 5 miles and two alternate flashing red aerobeacons are also visible for about 3 miles to the W of the town. The entrance to the harbour is lit: Fl.G.1·5s5M/Fl.R.1·5s4M, though in the approach from the S the lights at the entrance are difficult to make out against the lights of the town until you are near the harbour.

*Dangers*
1. Care is needed of Ifalos Dhimitris, a reef and shoal water lying approximately 900m ESE of the harbour entrance. It has been reported that the reef has been removed and least depths here are now more than 2m. Nonetheless care is counselled. It is marked by a red conical buoy.
2. Closer to the coast there is a group of unlit mooring buoys off the end of an oil pipeline.
3. A good lookout should be kept for ferries, which are constantly coming and going from the harbour.

**Mooring**
Moor stern-to the N mole (Áy Nikólaos) on the N side of the protruding loading quay. Keep well clear of the ferry berths on the N mole and the town quay. The bottom is mud and good holding.

*Shelter* Good shelter from the prevailing NW wind.

With strong southerlies a surge builds up in the harbour, and it may be best to anchor off to the W if possible.

*Note* Any craft entering at speed (such as the coastguard boat) creates a significant wash so ensure your anchor is well in and you are pulled far enough off the quay to prevent damage.

*Authorities* A port of entry. Port police, customs and immigration.

*Anchorage* Yachts can anchor in the SW of the harbour keeping clear of the ferry turning area. Anchor in 3–4m on mud. Good holding and good shelter. This is the best place to be if a strong southerly blows when the berths on the N quay may become untenable.

**Facilities**
*Water* On the quay.
*Fuel* A mini-tanker can deliver. Also petrol stations around the waterfront.
*Repairs* Caïques are hauled out at the root of the S mole. Some mechanical repairs. Hardware shops. Chandlers.
*Provisions* Good shopping for all provisions in the town.
*Eating out* Tavernas in the town.
*Other* PO. OTE. Banks. Greek gas and *Camping Gaz*. Hire cars and motorbikes. Ferries to Killini. International and internal flights.

**General**
Until its total destruction in the 1953 earthquake the town consisted largely of Venetian buildings. In the rebuilding of the town a Venetian aura has been retained – spacious boulevards, arcaded shops, central square and imposing public buildings, yet somehow the town cannot be described as anything approaching an aesthetic reconstruction of the pre-'53 town. There is just too much slab-sided reinforced concrete and too little sympathetic detail. A museum in the town houses some of the relics,

**LIMÍN ZÁKINTHOS**

⊕**29**  Limín Zákinthos entrance 37°46'·86N 20°54'·41E WGS84

particularly some fine icons, recovered after the earthquake. Zákinthos is the logical spot to leave a yacht and explore the interior of the island – I suggest you head for the W side where there is some spectacular scenery, small villages, and fewer tourists.

## ZÁKINTHOS MARINA

Construction on the marina on the SE side of the S mole (Áy Dhimitrios) began more than a decade ago and if anything things have gone backwards. A few years ago the basic shape of the marina was in place although concrete blocks had not been laid for the inner quay. Now some of the outer stone breakwater has been washed away by winter storms and lies just under the water.

The basic shape is as shown on the plan, but when the authorities will get around to rebuilding the rock ballasting and letting in the blocks for the quays is anyone's guess. The opinion of some of the locals here was: '10 years to think about it, 10 years to get this far, maybe another 10 years to finish it'.

## PORTO ROMA

A fair-weather anchorage on the SE tip of the island on the E coast. Porto Roma is sheltered from the prevailing NW–W wind, but a swell tends to roll into here. Taverna on the beach and several others a short walk away.

## ÓRMOS YÉRAKAS

The bay lying immediately N of Ák Yérakas. Entry should be made on approximately 040° towards the beach. The rocks which extend on either side of the

Zákinthos yacht quay looking towards the town

entrance are easily identified by day. Anchor where convenient. Good protection from the prevailing NW wind although it will sometimes blow around the bottom of Zákinthos and into the anchorage. Yérakas lies with Zone A of the regulations below.

Tavernas ashore. The beach is a turtle breeding ground and nobody is allowed on the beach after sunset.

## LAGANA BEACH

In settled weather a yacht can anchor off Lagana Beach. The sandy bottom shelves gently to the shore. The anchorage is entirely open to southerlies when a heavy swell sets into the bay. The beach has been much developed for tourism recently and there are numerous tavernas and hotels along it.

The beach is a breeding area for turtles and they are now protected in the breeding season. The area lies within Zone B of the regulations above.

## PORT LAGANA

37°42'·9N 20°51'·8E

The fishing port for the village of Lithakia. The harbour sits under the small islet of Nisís Áy Sostis at the W end of Lagana beach. There are 1·5–3m depths in the harbour but beware of large ropes stretched between the moles just under the water. The harbour is usually packed with fishing boats and local craft. Open to the SE. Taverna and, worse, a disco on the beach.

The harbour lies within Zone B of the regulations above, but is still used by local boats during the prohibited summer season.

## ÓRMOS KERÍ (Kierí)

37°41'·0N 20°50'·2E

An anchorage on the E side of Ák Marathia and to the W of Nisís Marathonisi. Anchor in 2–4m depths on either side of the rough stone mole – the E side is appreciably deeper than the W side. The ballasting on the mole extends a considerable distance underwater making it difficult to moor close to it. Alternatively anchor off outside the harbour. Excellent shelter from the NW–W wind, but open to the S and E.

KÓLPOS LAGANA

Kerí looking W                    *Nigel Patten*

Vroma looking W                    *Nigel Patten*

The famous pitch wells recorded by Herodotus still exist inland.

## ÓRMOS VROMA
37°49'·2N 20°38'·3E

A deep inlet close to the NW corner of Zákinthos. It affords reasonable shelter from the prevailing NW–W wind although there may be gusts down into it. It is dangerous in southerlies when a swell rolls in. Anchor and take a long line ashore as there can be katabatic gusts at night off the high land. Picturesque setting, although the new road takes away some of the solitude of the place. Tripper boats run here and a simple taverna opens in the summer.

In the bay to the N of Vroma is the much photographed 'Wreck Bay' that appears in just about every book on Greece. Numerous tripper boats zip in and out of the picturesque bay bringing tourists with yet more cameras and film.

# II. The Southern Ionian

## Katakólon to Kíthera

The images retained of the northern Ionian are seldom anything but fond memories of rolling green islands and fine sailing days. By contrast the southern Ionian is more rugged and fierce: the shores are for the most part bordered by high mountains, often still snow-capped in spring, under which there is a thin coastal plain washed down over time by the winter torrents. These mountains run irregularly from the centre of the Peloponnisos into the sea in all directions although the two principal mountain ranges, the Taiyetos and the Parnon, run south ending in Cape Matapan (Ák Tainaron) and Cape Malea (Ák Maléas) respectively.

Like the mountains, the peoples of this country have been rugged and tough. It was known in ancient times as the Island of Pelops (hence Peloponnisos or Peloponnisos) after Pelops, son of Tantalus. His bizarre history included being sliced up and stewed for the gods by his father (Zeus later brought him back to life) and outwitting King Oenomaus for the hand of his daughter Hippodamia in a chariot race by removing the pins from the wheels of his competitor's chariot. On a more substantive basis we know that around 2000 BC the Peloponnisos was invaded by the first Greek-speaking peoples, a warrior race from whom the hero legends of Perseus and Pericles were probably derived. Later came the Mycenaeans (the Homeric Achaeans) and later still (around 850 BC), the warrior race supreme, the Spartans, emerged as a power.

Ancient Sparta occupied a spectacular site sandwiched between the Taiyetos and Parnon mountains – in a gorge in the Taiyetos the weak and deformed children considered unfit to belong to this militaristic race were left to die. Nothing much remains of ancient Sparta, but the word 'spartan' has passed into our vocabulary to describe what was a way of life.

With the decline of Sparta the peoples occupying the Mani peninsula formed themselves into the Free Laconian League and their descendants acquired the name Maniotes. The Maniotes have been the most fierce race to people the Peloponnisos – the Spartans notwithstanding. They lived in clans, and feuds within and between clans were common. Families built towers to shelter from reprisals and these strange structures still exist on the Mani peninsula. While the rest of the Peloponnisos was subjugated by a succession of invaders, the Mani remained independent – both Rome and Turkey failed to defeat these fierce warriors.

Along the coastline the forts and castles at strategic points – Pílos, Methóni, Koroni, Kíthera – tell of the importance of the Peloponnisos as part of the trade route between the Aegean and Europe. Until the Corinth canal was cut most of the trade between east and west passed around this lonely stretch of coast. Whoever controlled this route controlled the flow of spices (especially pepper), silk, precious metals and stones, pearls, opium, perfumes – all the exotic wealth of the Indian Ocean – to Europe. The Venetians and, to a lesser extent, the Turks have left the lasting monuments, but often their forts incorporate masonry from more ancient colonists. Even today a lot of the shipping traffic in the eastern Mediterranean travels down this coast rather than through the Corinth Canal.

The forbidding physical geography of the Peloponnisos is perhaps the reason why comparatively few yachts cruise down this coast. Certainly the twin capes at the bottom of the Peloponnisos, Matapan and Malea, have acquired a reputation as minor Cape Horns. Yet the weather is really no worse than that of many other areas of the Aegean and there are sufficient harbours and anchorages to provide refuge in the event of bad weather. Moreover you are off the tourist track and the impecunious will also save the Corinth Canal dues.

## Weather patterns in the South Ionian

In the northern half of the south Ionian, from Katakólon to Methóni, the weather pattern in the summer is very nearly identical to that of the northern Ionian: a NW wind gets up about noon and dies down in the evening. Sometimes it may be more from the W than NW and a little fresher than the Force 3–5 of the northern Ionian.

In the southern half of the south Ionian the wind is more from the W and SW and may last longer into the evening than in the northern Ionian. The wind tends to blow up into Messiniakos Kólpos and Lakonikós Kólpos although it can also gust off the W side of the gulfs. It is rare to get a land breeze in the morning. Around Ák Maléas and Kíthera, and sometimes in Lakonikós Kólpos, there is a NE wind which may blow all day although it rarely exceeds Force 4 – more often Force 2–3. The exception to

# Routes

Routes around the Peloponnese are pretty much a matter of following the coast around from Katakólon to Cape Malea. The prevailing NW–W winds will give you a sleigh ride from the Ionian to the Aegean whereas coming from the Aegean generally means a slog against the wind. For boats needing to get a move on there is a fairly well defined route either way that takes in Katakólon, Pilos or Methoni, Koroni, Porto Kayio, Sarakiniko on Elafonisos and on around Cape Malea. Reverse the route when on passage from the Aegean to the Ionian.

As in the northern Ionian, the prevailing NW–W wind will often not get up until late morning. If you are heading from the Aegean to the northern Ionian then you can make up some miles under engine if you leave early in the morning. When heading S and E it pays to leave a little later in the morning so you get a good downwind sail.

Anyone heading up into the gulfs will get a mixture of weather. Generally the prevailing wind will curve around and blow from the S–SW up into the gulfs. At times the NW wind will gust down through the valleys on the W side of the gulfs and at times these gusts can be severe. At the head of the gulfs there can be a pronounced land breeze and sea breeze effect. The land breeze generally blows from the N–NE and the sea breeze from the S–SW. This means you need to choose anchorages carefully as although the land breeze rarely gets above F4, it can be enough to make it uncomfortable in anchorages exposed to a fetch from that direction.

The biggest problem most people encounter is getting around Cape Malea and into the Aegean. From the E you will usually have a NE wind to help you get around. From the W it is not unusual to sit in Sarakiniko on Elafonisos or at Neapolis waiting for a strong NE wind to die. Yachts have been known to wait a week and I suggest you read my notes for getting around in the section on Cape Malea at the end of the chapter. The advice is not infallible, but I have often found it to work, as have others.

In the winter there are more southerlies and route planning becomes more of a lottery. Really the only thing you can do here is get a forecast and make your plans from there. Remember that many of the harbours which are safe in the prevailing summer northerlies can be less comfortable and even untenable in strong southerlies.

# Data

## PORTS OF ENTRY
Katakólon
Pílos
Kalamata

## PROHIBITED ANCHORAGES
Nisís Skhiza is used for target practice by the air force. Vessels should not navigate in the immediate vicinity and anchoring and landing are prohibited.

## MAJOR LIGHTS
**Ák Katakólon** Fl.4s15M
**Nisís Stamfáni** Fl(2)15s17M
**Nisís Próti** Fl.1·5s6M
**Nisís Pílos** Fl(2)10s9M
**Ák Karsí (Nisís Sapiéntza)** Fl.3s5M
**Nisís Sapiéntza** (SW Summit) Fl(3)20s22M
**Nisís Venétiko** Fl.9s7M
**Ák Kitries** Fl(2)12s7M
**Ák Tainaron** (Cape Matapan) Fl(2)20s22M
**Nisís Kranai** (Yíthion) Fl(3)18s9M
**Ák Xílis** Fl.3s5M
**Órmos Vatíka** Fl.3s7M
**Ák Zóvolo** Fl.7s12M
**Ák Maléas** Fl.10s17M
**Ák Spathí** (Kíthera) Fl(3)30s20M

this is when the *meltemi* is in full swing and you can get strong NE winds from Elafonisos to Cape Malea. (See the weather note in this section). After October and until March–April the winds are predominantly from the SE although there may be strong winds from the N associated with nearby depressions.

There are two problem areas as regards the weather in the south Ionian. The first is to do with the very high mountain ranges down which there can be severe gusts on the lee side. Gusts off the mountains are particularly severe on either side of Ák Maléas and Ák Tainaron (the gusts are coming off the Taiyetos and Parnon mountains) and off Kíthera. At night there may be a katabatic wind which can be quite strong and arrive without warning.

The second problem in this area is that of the six generalised depression tracks over Greece; three of these tracks converge in the strait between Ák Maléas and Crete. Consequently the weather can deteriorate rapidly around the bottom of the Peloponnisos, especially in spring and autumn. It should be borne in mind when seeking shelter in the summer that strong southerlies will often veer to strong northerlies. This is not quite so true in the

spring and autumn when a strong southerly may be prolonged and followed by only a weak northerly.

In the summer there may be thunderstorms around the coast with associated squalls but these seldom last for very long. The temperatures in the summer are marginally warmer than those in the northern Ionian except on Kíthera where the climate is more like that on Crete.

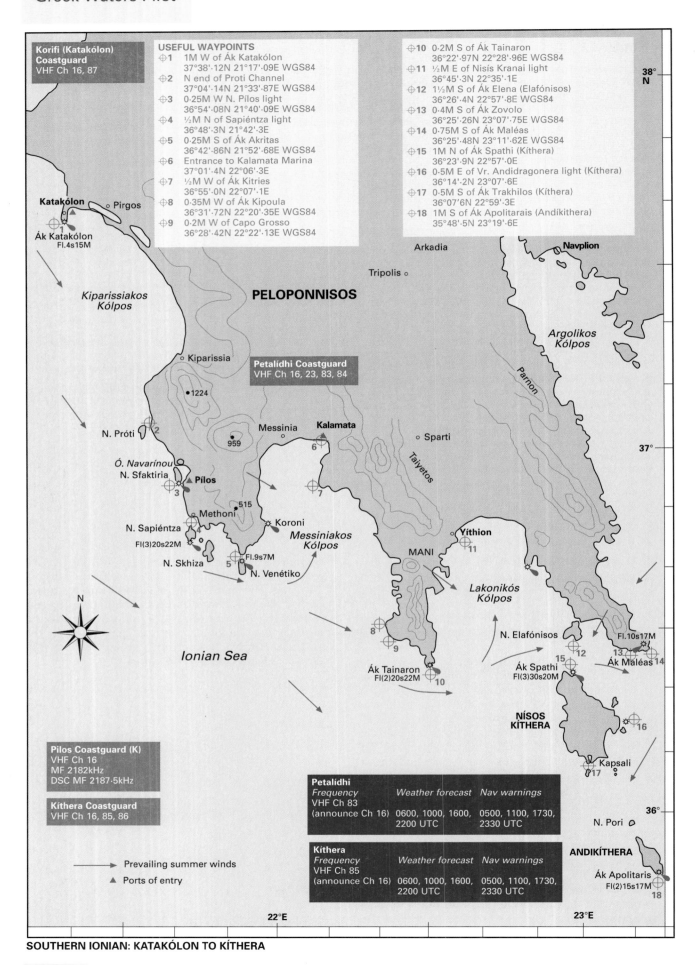

**Korifi (Katakólon) Coastguard**
VHF Ch 16, 87

**USEFUL WAYPOINTS**

⊕1  1M W of Ák Katakólon
37°38'·12N 21°17'·09E WGS84

⊕2  N end of Proti Channel
37°04'·14N 21°33'·87E WGS84

⊕3  0·25M W N. Pílos light
36°54'·08N 21°40'·09E WGS84

⊕4  ½M N of Sapiéntza light
36°48'·3N 21°42'·3E

⊕5  0·25M S of Ák Akritas
36°42'·86N 21°52'·68E WGS84

⊕6  Entrance to Kalamata Marina
37°01'·4N 22°06'·3E

⊕7  ½M W of Ák Kitries
36°55'·0N 22°07'·1E

⊕8  0·35M W of Ák Kipoula
36°31'·72N 22°20'·35E WGS84

⊕9  0·2M W of Capo Grosso
36°28'·42N 22°22'·13E WGS84

⊕10  0·2M S of Ák Tainaron
36°22'·97N 22°28'·96E WGS84

⊕11  ½M E of Nisís Kranai light
36°45'·3N 22°35'·1E

⊕12  1½M S of Ák Elena (Elafónisos)
36°26'·4N 22°57'·8E WGS84

⊕13  0·4M S of Ák Zovolo
36°25'·26N 23°07'·75E WGS84

⊕14  0·75M S of Ák Maléas
36°25'·48N 23°11'·62E WGS84

⊕15  1M N of Ák Spathi (Kíthera)
36°23'·9N 22°57'·0E

⊕16  0·5M E of Vr. Andidragonera light (Kíthera)
36°14'·2N 23°07'·6E

⊕17  0·5M S of Ák Trakhilos (Kíthera)
36°07'6N 22°59'·3E

⊕18  1M S of Ák Apolitarais (Andíkithera)
35°48'·5N 23°19'·6E

Katakólon    ∘ Pirgos

Ák Katakólon
Fl.4s15M

*Kiparissiakos Kólpos*

38° N

Arkadia

∘ Navplion

∘ Tripolis

**PELOPONNISOS**

*Argolikos Kólpos*

∘ Kiparissia

**Petalídhi Coastguard**
VHF Ch 16, 23, 83, 84

•1224

N. Próti

Parnon

**Messinia**    **Kalamata**

∘ Sparti

37°

•959

*Ó. Navarínou*
N. Sfaktiria    ▲ **Pílos**

Taïyetos

N. Sapiéntza    •515
Methoni

☆ Koroni

*Messiniakos Kólpos*

**MANI**    ∘ Yíthion

Fl(3)20s22M

N. Skhiza    Fl.9s7M

N. Venétiko

*Lakonikós Kólpos*

N. Elafónisos    Fl.10s17M

**N**

*Ionian Sea*

Ák Tainaron
Fl(2)20s22M

Ák Spathi
Fl(3)30s20M

Ák Maléas

**NÍSOS KÍTHERA**

**Pilos Coastguard (K)**
VHF Ch 16
MF 2182kHz
DSC MF 2187·5kHz

**Kíthera Coastguard**
VHF Ch 16, 85, 86

Kapsali

36°

N. Pori ∘

**Petalídhi**

| Frequency VHF Ch 83 (announce Ch 16) | Weather forecast | Nav warnings |
|---|---|---|
| | 0600, 1000, 1600, 2200 UTC | 0500, 1100, 1730, 2330 UTC |

**ANDIKÍTHERA**

Ák Apolitaris
Fl(2)15s17M

**Kíthera**

| Frequency VHF Ch 85 (announce Ch 16) | Weather forecast | Nav warnings |
|---|---|---|
| | 0600, 1000, 1600, 2200 UTC | 0500, 1100, 1730, 2330 UTC |

⟶ Prevailing summer winds
▲ Ports of entry

22°E    23°E

**SOUTHERN IONIAN: KATAKÓLON TO KÍTHERA**

## Quick reference guide

| | Shelter | Mooring | Fuel | Water | Provisioning | Tavernas | Plan |
|---|---|---|---|---|---|---|---|
| **Katakólon to Órmos Navarínou** | | | | | | | |
| Katakólon | A | A | A | A | B | B | • |
| Kiparissia | C | C | B | B | B | B | • |
| N. Strofadhes | C | C | O | O | O | O | • |
| Agrilos | B | AB | B | A | C | B | • |
| Nisís Próti | C | C | O | O | O | O | • |
| Marathoupolis | C | A | B | B | C | C | • |
| Voidhokoilia | C | C | O | O | O | C | • |
| Pílos | C | AB | A | A | B | A | • |
| Pílos Yacht Harbour | A | AB | B | B | B | A | • |
| Órmos Navarínou | B | C | O | O | O | C | • |
| **Messiniakos Kólpos (Gulf of Messinia)** | | | | | | | |
| Methóni | B | AC | B | B | B | B | • |
| Port Longos | B | C | O | O | O | O | • |
| Finakounda | B | AC | O | B | C | B | • |
| Maratho | C | C | O | O | O | O | |
| Koroni | B | C | B | B | B | B | • |
| Petalídhion | B | C | B | B | B | B | • |
| Kalamata Marina | A | A | A | A | A | A | • |
| Kitries | C | AC | O | B | O | C | • |
| Kardamila | C | C | O | O | B | B | • |
| Limení | C | C | O | B | C | C | • |
| Diros | O | C | O | B | O | C | • |
| Mezapo | C | C | O | B | C | C | • |
| Yerolimena | O | C | O | B | C | C | • |
| **Lakonikós Kólpos (Gulf of Lakonika)** | | | | | | | |
| Porto Káyio | B | AC | O | O | C | C | • |
| Kotronas | C | AC | B | B | B | B | • |
| Órmos Skoutari | C | C | O | O | O | O | • |
| Yíthion | B | AB | A | A | A | A | • |
| Elaia | B | AC | B | B | B | C | • |
| Plítra | B | A | O | B | O | C | • |
| Nísos Elafónisos | C | C | O | O | O | O | • |
| Elafónisos village | B | AC | B | B | B | C | • |
| Neapolis | C | AC | B | B | B | B | • |
| Palaiokastro | B | ABC | O | O | O | C | • |
| **Kíthera and Andíkithera** | | | | | | | |
| Pelagia | C | AB | B | A | B | C | • |
| Dhiakofti | B | AB | B | A | C | C | • |
| Ó. Áy Nikólaos | C | C | O | O | C | O | • |
| Avelomona | B | AC | O | B | C | C | • |
| Órmos Kapsáli | C | ABC | A | A | B | B | • |
| Órmos Potamóu | O | C | B | O | C | C | • |

# Katakólon to Órmos Navarínou

Approaching Kiparissiakos Kólpos (Gulf of Arcadia) from the north the coastline is low and featureless. The land beyond the wide sweep of the bay is largely salt marsh until the low hills behind. Towards the southern end of the gulf the hills rise abruptly to the mountains behind Kiparissia.

Immediately south of the gulf is the large protected bay of Navarinon – a large natural harbour approximately three and a half miles by two miles. In settled weather a yacht can anchor off the northern end of the bay either near the Sikia channel (not navigable) or further east on the low sandy mainland shore. From here the scene of the Sphakteria incident can be explored and easily visualized in the craggy deserted landscape. The incident described by Thucydides occurred when a group of Athenians under Demosthenes besieged a force of 400 Spartans of which 292 eventually surrendered, thus destroying the myth that Spartans always fought to the death. Later the bay was the scene of the Battle of Navarinon which effectively decided the Greek War of Independence. (See the section on Órmos Navarínou).

## KATAKÓLON (Limín Katakólou)

BA 2404
Imray-Tetra G16

### Approach

*Conspicuous* From the N and S the lighthouse on Ák Katakólon is conspicuous. The low-lying cape

**KATAKÓLON TO METHONI**

**KATAKÓLON**
⊕37°38'·74N 21°19'·14E WGS84

Katakólon looking SE from above the town *Nigel Patten*

Katakólon looking W from the entrance

looking like an aeroplane wing in cross section can be identified a long way off. From the N the harbour breakwater and village will not be seen until around Ák Katakólon, but from the S the breakwater is easily identified.

*By night* Use the light on Ák Katakólon Fl.4s15M and the light on the end of the breakwater Fl.R.3s4M.

*Dangers* Care is needed off the E side of Ák Katakólon not to shave the reef and shoal water here – keep at least 700m off the coast.

*Note* The three small conical buoys on the N side of the harbour mark the limit of the deep water channel for large ships. They are not always in place.

### Mooring

Berth stern or bows-to the quay on the N side of the central loading quay. Alternatively anchor NE of the low mole. The bottom is mud and clay, excellent holding.

*Shelter* Good shelter from the prevailing winds. In unsettled weather go on the S side of the central loading quay.

*Authorities* A port of entry: port police, customs and immigration.

*Note* Work is in progress building a small craft basin on the N side of the harbour. There is talk that this will be a yacht marina, although I suspect it will be for local craft with some yacht berths. At the time of writing the mole sheltering the basin is basically in place and the area around the basin is being dredged. No date has been given for completion.

Ák Katakólon looking W

## OLYMPIA

Although it seems a bit of a trek from Katakólon, the site at Olympia is well worth the effort. The actual site is a rambling muddle of a place with a jumble of ruins overgrown by olive and maquis. The site itself, situated in a wooded valley with the twin rivers of Alfios and Kladhios running through it, is magnificent and even the coach park and tacky souvenir stalls cannot detract from it. It is difficult to imagine that this site hosted the ancient Panhellenic games for over a thousand years and that many of the Greek heroes we read about proved their worth on track and field here.

One of the wonderful things about these ancient games was that a sacred truce, the *Ekeheiria*, was observed for the duration of the games and warring states would put aside their differences to partake in the events, presumably resuming hostilities after the games. It evokes those wonderful moments in the First World War when the British and Germans laid down their arms and played a game of football at Christmas. At the first games the prize for winning was purely symbolic, a palm leaf and an olive branch, but later some professionalism crept in and winners could expect monetary rewards as well as kudos from their home state. Under the Romans large monetary prizes were awarded at the games at Olympia.

The modern Olympic games were revived by Baron Pierre de Coubertin in 1896 and when he died his heart was brought here to be buried at Olympia. There is a small Museum of the Olympic Games in Olympia town and an excellent Archaeological Museum at the site.

### Facilities

*Water* On the quay.

*Fuel* In the town. A mini-tanker delivers to the quay.

*Repairs* Ionian Yacht Services run by Yannis Kalofonos can haul yachts up to 16 tons. Larger yachts can be hauled by arrangement. He uses a crane and puts yachts onto a specially designed trailer to trundle them to the boatyard. The only disadvantage is that your mast must come down. Mechanical and engineering work can be carried out. Some GRP and general repairs.

*Gardiennage* ☎ 0621 21353 (winter) and 0621 21302 (summer). www.pyrgosnet.gr/ionian.yacht

*Provisions* Most provisions can be found in the village.

*Eating out* Numerous tavernas and an inordinate number of pizzerias for the size of the place.

*Other* PO. Telephone. Bus to Pirgos. Taxis. Hire motorbikes and cars.

### General

Katakólon was built in 1875 for the then thriving currant trade. Now it is used by small cargo ships and by cruise ships as a base for the visit to Olympia about 25 miles away. This is the best place to leave a yacht if you wish to visit Olympia – usually you will be accosted by a taxi driver as soon as you arrive. Alternatively hire a motorbike or take the bus to Pirgos and another bus on to Olympia.

## KIPARISSIA (Órmos Kiparissias)

BA 189

Imray-Tetra G16

### Approach

From the N the town of Kiparissia is conspicuous

KIPARISSIA
⊕37°15´.4N 21°40´.0E

under the steep-to Mt Psikro (1350m). From the W the Disneyland castle situated on the seafront at Agrilos is conspicuous.

*By night* There are no lights.

*Dangers* With strong NW–W winds there is a confused swell rebounding off the coast in the approaches. Moreover as shelter is not good in here from strong NW–W winds it is recommended you head for somewhere else.

### Mooring

Go stern or bows-to the quayed section of the breakwater or anchor off. Care is needed of numerous permanent moorings and floating lines on the surface. The bottom is hard sand with some rocks, good holding once the anchor is in though this can take some doing. Shelter from the N and W is only just adequate and with the regular NW–W wind there is a very uncomfortable surge in the harbour. With strong winds from the N the nearest shelter is in Órmos Navarínou or Methóni. With strong winds from the N or W the harbour is untenable – locals report that in the winter of 1990 a northerly gale sank every boat in the harbour.

*Note* The small fishing harbour in the SE corner is normally full of local fishing boats. You may be able to find a berth here although the locals will often wave you away. There are 2–3m depths in the entrance and 1–2m depths in the outer part of the harbour. Better shelter from the NW–W winds than under the outer breakwater.

### Facilities

*Water* On the quay.

*Fuel* In the town about 500m away.

*Provisions* Good shopping in the town.

*Eating out* Tavernas on the waterfront and in the town.

*Other* PO. OTE. Bank. Greek gas and *Camping Gaz*. Buses to Pílos and Patras.

## General

Once an important harbour for nearby Messene, today only a few fishermen keep their boats here because of the poor shelter. This is a pity for yachtsmen because the town and the surrounding countryside are wonderful – as you sail along the coast you realise you are going to miss it all unless you take a chance here. It is worth wandering up to the Byzantine-Frankish castle and the old town below it. The castle and both the old and the new town sit on the lower slopes of Mt Psikro, a conical peak of the Egaleo mountain range rimming the Bay of Kiparissia. The houses of the old town are crumbling now, but this was once a prosperous place of rich merchants. Get up here early in the morning and you can get back before the maistro picks up and makes life uncomfortable in the harbour.

## Nisídhes Strofadhes

Nisís Stamfáni light 37°14'·9N 21°00'·2E

These lonely islands lie approximately 32 miles due W of Kiparissia and 26 miles due S of Ák Yérakas on Zákinthos. A light is exhibited on Nisís Stamfáni: Fl(2)15s17M. On Nisís Arpia, the N island, a church is conspicuous at the N end. On Nisís Stamfáni the lighthouse and the monastery are conspicuous.

The islands once supported a prosperous monastery, but today there is just one monk who with the aid of a tractor looks after a flock of sheep, poultry, a vineyard, and a vegetable garden! At one time the island was plagued by rabbits, but a recent

Órmos Tavernas on the S side of Nisís Arpia. The monastery on Stamfáni is conspicuous behind *Nigel Patten*

The monastery on Nisís Stamfáni *Nigel Patten*

visitor reported there were no rabbits, but a lot of spent cartridges lying around!

**Órmos Tavernas** A bay on the S side of Nisís Arpia. The approach to the bay should be made from the E only – the W side of the channel between Arpia and Stamfáni is obstructed by above and below-water rocks. Anchor in 4–10m. on a sand and rock bottom, good holding once the anchor is in. Good shelter from the prevailing NW wind. Water from a number of wells ashore.

**Órmos Limani** On the W side of Nisís Arpia there is a crescent bay with a tiny rockbound harbour at the N end. The approaches to this bay from either the S or NW are littered with above and below-water rocks. The passage into the bay from the NW can be made on a SE heading, but you should reconnoitre first by dinghy before attempting the approach. Anchor in the N end of the bay where there is only poor shelter from the prevailing NW wind.

**Órmos Panayia** In calm weather you can anchor off the monastery on the N side of Nisís Stamfani. Anchor in 5–6m on sand and rock. When the NW wind gets up it is advisable to

**NISÍDHES STROFADHES**
⊕37°15'·4N 21°00'·7E

leave here and return to the bay on the S side of Arpia. The monastery of Áy Panayia (13th century) ashore is an impressive fortified structure more like a fort than a monastery – not surprising given the certainty of pirate attacks in days past.

***Órmos Prasa*** A bay on the S side of Nisís Stamfáni. Not recommended as an anchorage as the coast is one long, low sea cliff and the sea bed is littered with large boulders.

**Note** In unsettled weather a yacht should not remain at Nisídhes Strofadhes. The waters around the island with gales from any direction have been likened to a giant washing machine swirling around – a potent image that should have you moving as soon as bad weather brews up.

### AGRILOS

A small harbour approximately 5 miles SW of Kiparissia. The harbour is easily identified by the Kastro Paramython nearby. The harbour is very small and mostly 1–1·5m or less, so only small yachts will be able to get in here, much less find a berth amongst the fishing boats. Adequate shelter from the NW–W winds although a bit of a surge can build up.

Nearby the bizarre castle on the coast was built by Haris Fournakis (Harry Fournier), a local boy made good who returned from America to build this and other follies. The Kastro Paramython (Castle of the Fairytales) has battlements, towers and a thirty-five foot statue of Poseidon's horse and another of Athena. The castle is open in the summer

(0900–1400/1700–2000) if you want to visit, or just coast in close for a look.

### ÁY KIRIAKI 37°07'·0N 21°34'·4E

A very small harbour off the village of Áy Kiriaki. It is mostly less than 1 metre and unsuitable for yachts.

### NISÍS PRÓTI AND CHANNEL (Stenón Protis)

On the E coast of Nisís Próti there is a small bay which fishing boats sometimes use to shelter from NW winds. Care is needed of permanent moorings with floating lines on the surface. Depths are considerable and it is not a good anchorage. Above the anchorage is what looks like a restored monastery or a chapel attached to a private villa.

In the bay to the S all that can be seen of the wreck is a single sloping spar about 1m out of the water.

Local fishing boats also anchor on the SW side of Marathoupolis village where there is a surprisingly good lee from NW winds although some swell still penetrates.

**AGRILOS**
⊕37°12'·6N 21°37'·7E

**STENÓN PROTIS**
⊕37°04'·14N 21°33'·87E WGS84

Marathoupolis village on the E side of the Próti Channel looking NE. The small *caïque* harbour is 'around the top' of the headland

**MARATHOUPOLIS**
⊕37°03'·8N 21°34'·5E

## MARATHOUPOLIS

### Approach

A small *caïque* harbour on the NE corner of Próti Channel to the N of Ák Marathoupolis. Suitable for small yachts perhaps up to 10m. The entrance is difficult with rock-bound shallows on either side of the channel. By day enter from the N keeping an eye open for the shallows.

*Conspicuous* A church with two blue cupolas is conspicuous and if the church is lined up with a cream house near the harbour this shows the way in.

*By night* There are no lights and entry at night would be dangerous.

*Dangers* With moderate NW winds there is a considerable swell at the entrance and care is needed. With strong NW–W winds a heavy sea builds up in the approaches and entry is not advised.

*Note* It is reported that much of the new extension to the W breakwater was destroyed recently in a Force 11 winter gale. Care needed in the immediate approaches and the entrance.

### Mooring

There are 2m depths off the extremity of the mole running E–W on the N side of the harbour. Go bows-to tucked just inside the mole. The E side of the harbour is taken up with permanent moorings. The harbour is very crowded with fishing boats and you may have difficulty finding a berth here.

*Shelter* Reasonable shelter from moderate N-NW winds. Good shelter from S winds.

### Facilities

Water in the village. Fuel about 1km away. Taverna and limited provisions in the village.

### General

The village cannot be described as an attractive place, but it is convivial and the situation on the

**ÓRMOS NAVARÍNOU**
⊕3  0·25M W N. Pílos light 36°54'·08N 21°40'·09E WGS84

edge of the channel looking across to Nisís Próti is wonderful.

## VROMONERI

37°01'·0N 21°37'·2E

A miniature cove with a diameter of around 100 metres. In calm weather a small yacht could investigate.

## ÓRMOS VOIDHOKOILIA

36°58'·0N 21°39'·5E

The oval bay located just N of the N end of Nísos Pilos. In calm weather or light NW winds it is an attractive spot to stop over. With strong NW winds a swell is pushed into the bay. Anchor in 2–3m at the N end of the bay on sand.

Above the anchorage to the S is the rocky crag with Palaiokastro on top, a Venetian castle built on the ruins of several other castles.

## PÍLOS (Pylos, Navarino, Neokastro)

BA 2404
Imray-Tetra G16

### Approach

*Conspicuous* Nisís Sfaktiria (ancient Sphakteria) and Nisís Pílos are easily identified. Nisís Pílos has a

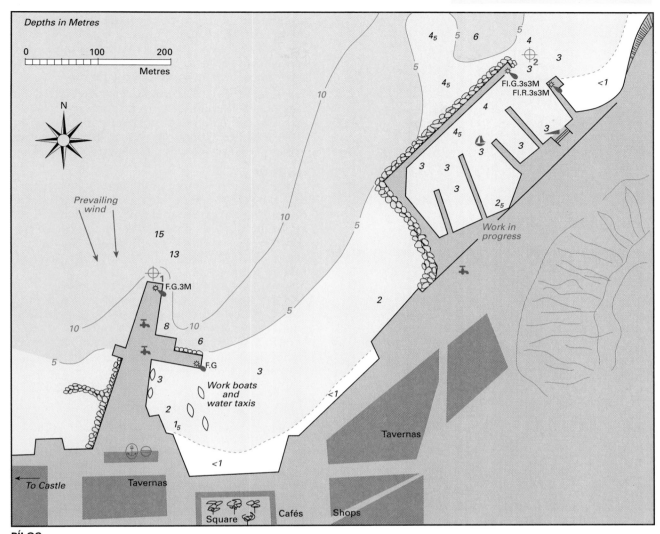

**Depths in Metres**

0    100    200
Metres

N

Prevailing wind

15

13

⊕1 F.G.3M

10

8

6

F.G

3

3

2

1₅

Work boats and water taxis

<1

To Castle

Tavernas

Square    Cafés    Shops

<1

Tavernas

4₅   5   6   4

3

⊕2

3

Fl.G.3s3M
Fl.R.3s3M

<1

5

4₅

4₅

4

4

3

3

3

3

3

2₅

Work in progress

2

5

10

10

5

5

5

**PÍLOS**
⊕1 36°54´·9N 21°41´·6E (F.G.3M)
⊕2 36°55´·2N 21°42´·1E (Fl.G.3s3M)

huge natural arch through it and the lighthouse and a white memorial on it are conspicuous. On entering Órmos Navarínou the large Venetian fort with a conspicuous church on the S side of the entrance is easily identified. Once in Órmos Navarínou the small town of Pílos will be seen.

*By night* Use the light on Nisís Pílos Fl(2)10s9M, the light on Ák Neókastron off the Venetian fort Fl.G.3s6M and the light on the extremity of the pier F.G.3M. The entrance to the new marina is lit: Fl.G.3s3M/Fl.R.3s3M though the lights appear to be unreliable.

*VHF* Ch 12 for Pílos port police.

*Dangers* With moderate to strong W winds a heavy sea piles up in the approaches to Órmos Navarínou. Once inside the bay there is comparative calm although there can be strong gusts off Nisís Sfakteria.

Nísos Pílos looking E into Órmos Navarínou

Pílos town looking E

Pílos Marina looking SW from the slopes above the entrance

*Note*
1. Large ships use Órmos Navarínou to resupply and a good lookout should be kept for ships leaving and entering the bay. There will usually be several ships at anchor in the bay.
2. When approaching the marina entrance you are literally heading straight for the cliffs before you turn hard to starboard to enter the marina. If the prevailing NW wind is blowing there is a bit of slop at the entrance but not really anything to worry about.

### Mooring

*Data* c.180 berths. Visitors' berths. Max LOA c.20m. Depths 2·5–3·5m.

*Berths* At present yachts berth alongside the outer wall and piers of the marina. Laid moorings are to be installed and berthing will then be stern or bows-to.

*Shelter* Good all-round shelter although N–NW winds push a swell onto the cliffs at the entrance which rebounds into the marina and makes some berths near the entrance uncomfortable.

*Authorities* A port of entry: port police, customs and immigration. The authorities are housed in a building at the root of the pier. Charge band 2. Charging for the use of the marina seems to be fairly haphazard at the time of publication although it is likely charges will be applied in the future.

*Note* The future of the marina is uncertain at the moment. A number of private companies have looked at the marina and decided against buying it, but in the future it is more than likely a private company will acquire it and finish the development.

### Facilities

*Services* Water at the root of the marina breakwater. Service boxes for water and electricity are being installed. A shower and toilet block is planned.

*Fuel* In the town. A mini-tanker will deliver to the marina.

*Repairs* 20-ton crane at the marina. Limited mechanical repairs.

*Provisions* Good shopping for all provisions.

*Eating out* A number of good tavernas to the E of the square on the road leading up the hill. Others around the square and waterfront.

*Other* PO. OTE. Banks. Greek gas and *Camping Gaz*. Hire motorbikes and cars. Buses to Methóni, Kalamata, and Kiparissia.

## The Battle of Navarinon

At the very time when the Greek forces were at their lowest ebb during the War of Independence, the fortuitous naval engagement in the Bay of Navarinon changed the whole order of things and effectively won the war. On 6 July 1827, the Treaty of London between Great Britain, France and Russia provided that Greece should be autonomous but under the control of the Turks. This piece of legal chicanery was implemented so that the three powers might remain friendly to both Greece and Turkey and allowed for their fleets to guarantee the treaty. The senior admiral, Codrington, was given wide powers of discretion in the policing of the treaty.

Presented with the terms of the treaty, the Greeks agreed (they had little option) while the Turks did not. Codrington decided to enter the Bay of Navarinon where the Turko-Egyptian fleet was assembled, even though his fleet was outnumbered and outgunned (the allied fleet numbered 26 ships and 1270 guns; the Turko-Egyptian fleet numbered 89 warships and 2450 guns) and despite the fact that his country was not at war with the opposing fleet. The Turko-Egyptian fleet was anchored in a three quarter circle facing the entrance, in theory a trap in which ships sailing in would be caught by fire from all sides before they could sail out again. Codrington led his fleet in, the bands playing on the deck and the gun ports half open, and anchored in the middle of the trap. An Egyptian ship fired a shot and the battle began. 'The bloody and destructive battle was continued with unabated fury for four hours; and the scene of wreck and devastation which presented itself at its termination was such as has been seldom before witnessed', Codrington wrote in his dispatch.

It was an unremitting battle fought at anchor which Codrington won, proving that European gun crews were more efficient in the heat of battle than their eastern counterparts. Codrington was not censured over this action although the English government expressed regret over it. France mopped up any remaining opposition in the Peloponnisos and in the end Greece was free.

## General

Pílos was largely built by the French in the 19th century after the Battle of Navarinon and it shows, with elegant buildings arranged around a large square. The shaded square has a memorial to the three admirals who commanded the fleet which destroyed Turkish sea power – Admirals Codrington, de Rigny and von Heyden. In the evening the locals wander around the square and everyone chooses the café of choice and relaxes as the sun goes down – you could almost be in some provincial French town.

The fort to the W of the harbour, so prominent from seawards, was originally built by the Venetians and added to by the Turks. It has an impressive mosque, now a church, inside the walls. The castle is open from 0930 hours.

Pílos is the place to organise a visit to Ano Englianos and ancient Pílos, the Mycenaean city believed be King Nestor's. There is in fact little to see at the site except the foundations of various buildings and the few artifacts which were not carted off to Athens.

## ÓRMOS NAVARÍNOU – N END

A yacht can anchor at the N end of Órmos Navarínou where convenient. The bottom comes up quickly to the sandy beach so you will have to anchor in 8–12m. The bottom is sand and mud, good holding once the anchor has dug in, though this can take a bit of doing for some reason. Good shelter from the prevailing wind which blows in from between NW and N. At night after the wind has died down it can be a bit uncomfortable here with the residual swell creeping in through the entrance and up into the bay.

There are a couple of snack bars that open in the summer, but little else. If you anchor in the NW corner you can walk across to Nísos Sfaktiria. A shallow bar shuts off the northern entrance to the bay and it is possible to wade across to the island.

The energetic may like to hike up to the summit of Ák Korifasion where a Venetian castle can be seen from the anchorage. The castle is built on the ruins of a former Frankish castle and also on the ruins of the second Pílos built after the first at Englianos was mysteriously destroyed by fire. There is nothing to see, although a cave nearby has been dubbed Nestor's Cave. If you want to visit ancient Pílos and Nestor's Palace, this is best done from Pílos or Methóni.

# Methóni Roadstead and Messiniakos Kólpos

Five miles south of Órmos Navarínou, the once important port of Methóni is tucked behind a small headland dominated by a large fort. Following the coast east for some 12 miles, the wide gulf of

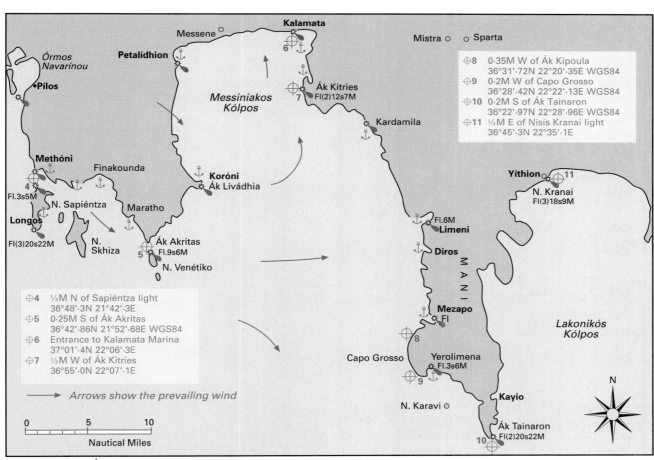

MESSINIAKOS KÓLPOS (GULF OF MESSINA)

Messiniakos Kólpos (Gulf of Messina, Gulf of Kalamata) opens up between Nisís Venétiko and Ák Taínaron (Cape Matapan). Bordered on the west by comparatively tame mountains, the country is for the most part green and wooded down to sandy beaches. The harbours of Koroni and Petalídhion offer reasonable shelter in the summer months. At the head of the gulf lies the low marshland of the Makaria plain with the large port of Kalamata at its eastern end.

Towering above Kalamata is the Taíyetos (2,307m high) running south to the Mani peninsula ending in Ák Taínaron. Tainaron, a.k.a Matapan, was the ancient Tenaron, the entrance to the underworld, and for all that exists around the cape it might as well be the end of the world for yachtsman and ancient alike. Tainaron is very nearly the most southerly cape of mainland Europe and only Cape Tarifa at the entrance to the Gibraltar Strait is further south by just 14 miles.

## METHÓNI (Modon)

BA 1683
Imray-Tetra G15

### Approach

*Conspicuous* From the N and S the Venetian fort and the Turkish tower on the extremity of Ák Soukouli are conspicuous. The silhouette of the Turkish tower is unmistakable once seen. From the W and S the lighthouse on the S end of Nisís Sapiéntza stands out clearly. Once in Methóni Roadstead the small harbour is easily identified.

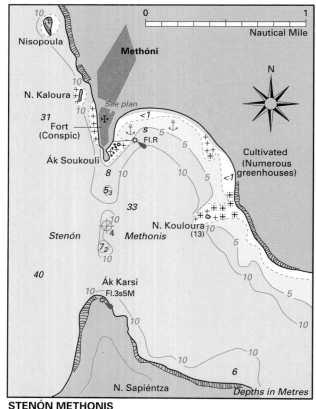

STENÓN METHONIS

⊕4  ½M N of Sapiéntza light 36°48'·3N 21°42'·3E

The conspicuous Turkish tower at Methóni looking SW from the harbour. (It looks pretty much the same from all angles)

*By night* Use the light on S end of Nisís Sapiéntza Fl(3)20s22M, the light on Ák Karsí at the N end of Sapiéntza Fl.3s5M, and the light on the end of the breakwater Fl.R.3s3M.

*Dangers*
1. With westerlies a confused swell piles up between Ák Soukouli and Ák Karsí, but a short distance into the roadstead things quieten down.
2. Care should be taken of the reef around Nisís Kouloura – there is usually broken water around it.
3. A yacht should keep well clear of Nisís Skhiza which is used by the air force for target practice.

### Mooring

Anchor off under the breakwater. The bottom is mud or sand, mostly sand N of the breakwater, good holding.

*Shelter* Good shelter from all but strong SE winds.

Methóni harbour looking E from the castle

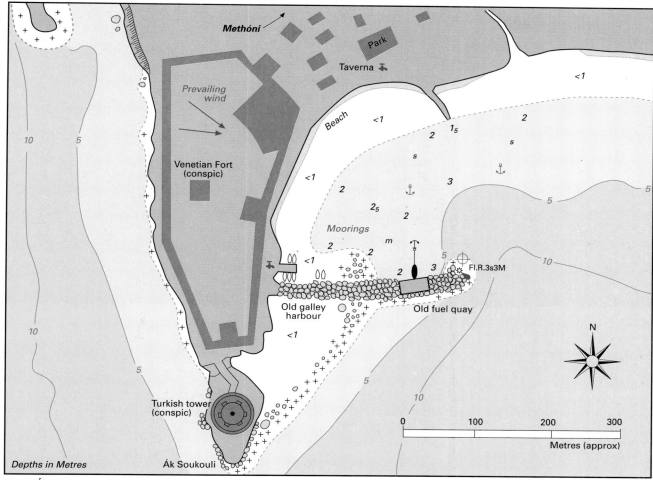

**METHÓNI**
⊕36°48´·9N 21°42´·5E (Fl.R.3s3M)

## Facilities

*Water* At the root of the breakwater or on the beach.
*Fuel* In the town about 500m from the beach.
*Repairs* Limited mechanical repairs.
*Provisions* Good shopping in the village.
*Eating out* Tavernas on the beach and in the town.
*Other* PO. OTE. Bank. Greek gas and *Camping Gaz*.
Bus to Pílos.

## General

The harbour, bounded by the large fort and the
sandy beach, is one of my favourite places on the W
Peloponnisos. Methóni was mentioned by Homer as
being 'rich in vines' and later under the Venetians it
was famous for its wine and pork. Today the
hinterland is still intensively cultivated and you will
see the greenhouses flashing in the sun as you near
the harbour.

The Venetian fort guarded the shipping route
around the Peloponnisos and Methóni, along with
Koroni, was called 'the eye of the Republic'. Later
the Turks captured it and Cervantes was a prisoner
here – the tale in *Don Quixote* of the captive may
relate his experiences as a Turkish prisoner. The
entrance is in the NE wall and the fort is open from
1000–1600.

## PORT LONGOS

On the SE end of Nisís Sapiéntza there is the
deserted bay of Port Longos. The lighthouse is
conspicuous from some distance off. A fish farm
now occupies the E side of the bay, but there is still

**PORT LONGOS**
⊕36°45´·5N 21°42´·5E

Port Longos on Nisís Sapiéntza looking NNE from the lighthouse. Note the fish farm in the S bay
*Neville Bulpitt*

room for 3 or 4 yachts to anchor. Anchor under the saddle between the hills or in the S of the bay in 5–6m on a sandy bottom. The holding has been reported to be bad in places so make sure your anchor is well dug in. Good shelter, although strong easterlies send a swell in and there can be gusts off the land with the prevailing wind.

The lighthouse can be reached by a track from the bay and is now surrounded by an impressive bank of solar cells. Greece was comparatively late in modernising its lights and as a consequence was able to bypass other outmoded 'modern' methods and convert its lights (which used to be mostly powered by bottled gas) to solar power.

## NISÍS SKHIZA

The island is a prohibited area. The air force use it for bombing practice and unless you happen to get a thrill out of F111s approaching at masthead height on a bombing run, it is wise to keep well clear of the whole island. And yes, they do use real bombs and rockets.

Despite the frequent use of the island for target practice, local fishermen can often be seen pottering around the W coast and they sometimes use the cove on the SW end of the island. I have not investigated it (that live ammunition has deterred me somewhat) and would not recommend it.

## ÁK KOLIVRI

With westerlies there is a lee under Ák Kolivri. Local fishing boats sometimes anchor here to sort the catch and in settled weather it might be a useful overnight stop. Open S and E.

## FINAKOUNDA

*Note* At the time of publication it was reported that the end of the breakwater had been damaged and

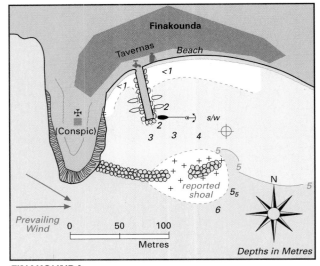

**FINAKOUNDA**
⊕36°48'·3N 21°49'·3E

there was underwater rubble and shoal water surrounding the entrance. Care is needed in the immediate approaches and it would be wise to reconnoitre in the dinghy before entering.

A small harbour in Órmos Finakounda lying approximately 5 miles E of Ák Karsí on Sapiéntza. Once into the large bay the village around the edge of the beach is easily identified. A church on the headland sheltering the harbour is conspicuous. The rough stone breakwater will be seen closer in. There are no lights. With the prevailing wind funnelled W there is often a considerable swell rolling across the entrance to the harbour.

Berth bows-to the end of the pier or anchor off under the shelter of the breakwater. Good shelter from the prevailing W winds but open to the S.

Fuel in the village near the new pier. Water near the root of the pier. Ashore provisions are available and there are numerous tavernas. The once tranquil fishing village has been somewhat shattered by the arrival of a watersports centre and has become something of a backpackers' resort, but retains a likeable character. The setting is wonderful, with the village huddled around the beach under a low rocky bluff and a fertile hinterland.

## PORT MARATHO

36°46'·4N 21°50'·0E

A small inlet 3½ miles NW of Ák Akritas. The inlet is difficult to identify from the distance, but the beach around its head will be seen between the rocky sides to the cove. Care is needed of a group of rocks awash off the N side of the entrance. Anchor in 2–4m on mud and sand, good holding. Reasonable shelter from westerlies and from the N–E winds which sometimes blow out of Messiniakos Kólpos.

## KORONI (Coron)

BA 1683
Imray-Tetra G15

### Approach

*Conspicuous* The fort atop the headland is conspicuous from the N and S. From the N the buildings of Koroni village under the castle are conspicuous. From the S the buildings of the town on the crown of the hill and around the bay to the S are conspicuous. From the S the harbour will not be seen until around Ák Livádhia.

*By night* Use the light on Ák Livádhia Fl.1·5s5M and the light on the end of the harbour breakwater Fl.R.1·5s3M.

### Mooring

Anchor in 2–5m depths on the W side of the bay – the depths come up slowly so you can usually potter in until satisfied and then anchor. The bottom is mostly mud, sand and weed, not everywhere good holding so make sure your anchor is well in. However, very large boulders litter the bottom in places and care should be taken not to snag one of these. Poor holding reported in places. Although there are 2m depths at the extremity of the concrete walkway on the mole where a yacht can moor bows-to, this is not advised as the prevailing wind normally blows onto here and the bottom is littered with permanent moorings.

Koroni castle looking from the harbour. The Venetians called it 'the eye of the Republic'

*Shelter* Good shelter from the prevailing wind which normally blows across the headland from the S or off the hills from the NW–W. At night a NE wind may blow which can be uncomfortable but rarely dangerous.

### Alternative anchorages

1. In calm weather or light westerlies a yacht can anchor off on the E side of the harbour breakwater. This is an idyllic place under the bastions of the castle.
2. A yacht can anchor off on the S side of the headland ending in Ák Livádhia. The beach stretching around the coast from here is wonderful and popular with the locals in the summer.

### Facilities

*Water* Not easily available. Can be delivered by tanker.
*Fuel* 1½km out of the village.
*Provisions* Good shopping in the village.
*Eating out* Good tavernas around the waterfront. Good *ouzeries*.
*Other* PO. OTE. Bank. Greek gas and *Camping Gaz*. Regular bus service to Kalamata.

### General

Built on the steep slopes under and partly inside the Venetian fort, Koroni is an attractive town with

Koroni approach looking E

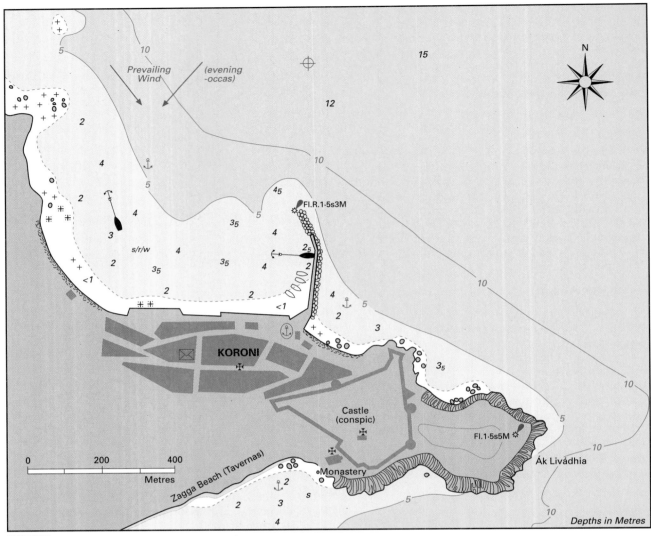

**KORONI**
⊕36°48′·35N 21°57′·6E

some fine old houses. The town acquired the name Korone (corrupted to Coron) via migrants from ancient Korone, now Petalídhion. The Venetians rightly perceived that the headland was the ideal site for a fort to defend their trade route around the Peloponnisos. Much of it is still largely intact and incorporates bits of ancient masonry from nearby Asine. The fort, entered through the massive gateway at the eastern end of the village (follow the road up from the harbour mole), is a wonderfully tranquil place, much overgrown and now mostly occupied by a monastery. This fort was the second 'eye of the Republic' after Methóni.

The harbour front, though a bit smelly in places from the sewage emptying into it, is alive at night with the locals promenading and a few tourists stuffing themselves at the tavernas – there are several good *ouzeries* specialising in charcoal-grilled octopus.

# Koroni to Petalídhion

The coast between Koroni and Petalídhion is pleasantly wooded and there are a number of attractive bays with sandy beaches where a yacht can anchor in calm weather. In Homeric times this was part of ancient Messene and later was conquered by the Spartans. Many of the Messenians fled to Sicily around about this time. Their descendants captured Zancle, renaming it Messana, hence modern Messina and the Messina Strait.

### PETALÍDHION (Petalidi)

An attractive sheltered bay in the NW corner of the gulf. A rough mole has been built a short distance out from the sand spit in a NE direction making the bay safe from all but strong NE and E winds. A church, a two-storeyed building, and the light structure are conspicuous. Anchor in 2–4m depths where convenient – good holding in sand.

Fuel and water in the town. Good mountain water flows from two pipes just N of the old concrete piles. Good shopping and tavernas. The old village on the edge of a sandy beach is attractive and well worth a visit.

**PETALÍDHION**
⊕36°57´·9N 21°56´·2E

The lighthouse on Ák Kitries looking NE

## WEATHER NOTE

In the late summer there are frequently black clouds over the plain behind Kalamata and over the Taiyetos and the Mani. More often than not these come to nothing even though they look threatening, but on occasion there will be some rain and an associated squall. The locals in Kalamata say their summer begins in May and ends in the middle of August.

The weather over the land sometimes affects the weather further out over Messiniakos Kólpos and there may be squalls in the gulf. Normally the prevailing wind blows from the W into the bottom of the gulf and then curves to blow from the SW and finally from the S at Kalamata.

## KALAMATA (Kalami, Kalamón)
BA 2404
Imray-Tetra G15

**Approach**
Straightforward by day and night.

*Conspicuous* The cluster of buildings of the small city is conspicuous. The exact location of the harbour is difficult to see from the distance but closer in a large flour mill at the W end of the harbour and the harbour breakwater will be seen. Yachts should head for the marina and not the commercial harbour.

*By night* Use the light on Ák Kitries Fl(2)12s7M and the lights at the entrance to the marina Fl.G.3s3M/Fl.R.3s3M. The lights at the marina entrance are difficult to make out against the loom of the lights behind. The entrance to the commercial harbour is lit Fl.G.1·5s3M/Fl.R.1·5s3M.

**KALAMATA**
⊕37°01´·4N 22°06´·3E

**KALAMATA MARINA**
⊕37°01'·45N 22°06'·30E WGS84

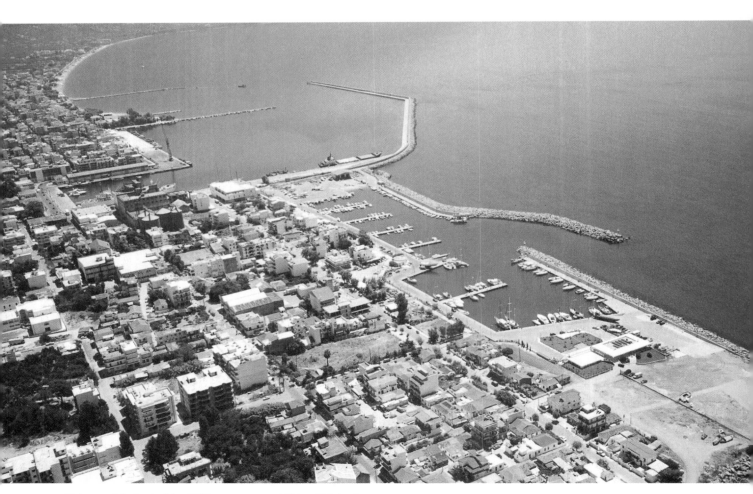

Kalamata Marina looking ESE          *Nikitas Kiriakoulis*

*VHF* Ch 69 for marina office. Call sign *Kalamata Marina*.

*Dangers* With the prevailing onshore breeze blowing there is some confused swell in the narrow entrance – more difficult with a fresh breeze than dangerous.

### Mooring

*Data* 255 berths. Visitors' berths. Max LOA 30m. Depths 2-3·5m.

*Berth* Where directed. Marina staff will assist you to berth. There are laid moorings tailed to the quay. The rope tail is substantial and smaller yachts may need to tie a smaller diameter line to it.

*Shelter* Good all round shelter. The prevailing onshore breeze causes a little surge at some berths near the entrance which can be mildly uncomfortable.

*Authorities* Harbourmaster and marina staff. Port police and customs at the commercial port. Charge band 2.

### Facilities

*Services* Water and electricity at every berth. Shower and toilet block (I rate it one of the best in Greece). Laundry operated by tokens.

*Fuel* Fuel quay near the entrance. Care needed when approaching the quay from the entrance.

*Repairs* 30-ton crane. 50-ton travel-hoist to be installed soon. Hardstanding area for c.130 boats. Most mechanical and engineering work. The marina will carry out *gardiennage* and maintenance on the boat according to what is needed. Chandlers. Hardware shops in town.

*Provisions* Good supermarket a block away heading N from the entrance. Other provisions in town.

*Eating out* A bar and café in the marina. Tavernas close by and others along the waterfront. Some good tavernas in the hills to the E.

*Other* PO. OTE. Banks. Greek gas and *Camping Gaz* (from the service station E of the basin). Hire cars and motorbikes. Buses to Athens and most destinations around the Peloponnisos. Internal flights and some international flights.

*Note* A regular bus service operates past the harbour into the centre of town – Bus No.1.

### General

Kalamata was once the principal port of the Peloponnisos, but now its commercial traffic is much diminished. The harbour and town are more undistinguished than unattractive. The recent earthquake in 1968 caused much damage and consequently parts of the town have an abandoned appearance while the rest is undergoing reconstruction.

Despite this, Kalamata is a place I like, a real Greek place supported by the agricultural hinterland, especially the production of fat black olives famous throughout the world as 'Kalamata olives'. Kalamata Marina is such a friendly well-run marina that it adds to the charm of the place and makes it that much more comfortable when visiting this part of Greece.

There are all sorts of surprises in the town. From the basin if you walk straight up from the W corner you will come to a park you can walk through nearly into the middle of town. The park incorporates the old railway station and on the tracks around it are numerous restored locomotives and carriages from all ages – a must for railway buffs and a pleasant walk into town for the mildly curious.

Kalamata was the capital for the Franks when they controlled the area and the redoubtable Guillaume de Villehardouin (1218–1287) was born and died here – above the town are the remains of the castle he built, though most of what remains are later modifications and additions from the Venetians. Modern Kalamata was built by the French in the 19th century, though many of the old buildings from this period have decayed. Kalamata is the nearest safe harbour to Messene and the safest harbour for visiting Mistra, although Yíthion is also suitable.

Kalamata Marina, 24100, Greece
☎ (0721) 21054/21037 *Fax* (0721) 26079
*E-mail* kalamatamarina@yahoo.com
www.kalamatamarina.tsx.org

### ÓRMOS KITRIES

⊕7 ½M W of Ák Kitries 36°31'·7N 22°07'·1E

On the N side of Ák Kitries lies the large bay of Kitrou. The bay provides good shelter from the prevailing southerlies and reasonable shelter from northerlies which do not normally blow home.

Anchor off in the SE corner off the beach in 5–10m. The bottom is sand and weed, good holding once through the weed.

In the SE corner there is a short mole providing shelter for local boats. Small yachts may be able to find a berth on the end of the mole where there are 1·5–2m depths.

Tavernas ashore. The slopes around the bay are terraced and planted in olive and citrus with villas dotted around the beach and lower slopes. It is an

**KITRIES**
⊕36°55'·7N 22°08'·5E

entrancing spot and in settled weather can be used as an overnight anchorage.

## KARDAMILA

An open anchorage lying about 5 miles SSE of Ák Kitries. There is a small harbour off the village but there are barely 2m depths in the entrance and 1–1·5m depths inside. Anchor off the mole under the islet in 4–8m or in the bay to the S. There is nearly always some swell in here making it uncomfortable, and in unsettled weather it would be untenable.

Numerous tavernas in the village and good shopping for provisions ashore. Fuel available in the village.

The village is an attractive place, all creepers and tiled roofs, though somewhat overrun with visitors with a professorial gait, in search of inspiration from the village's literary inhabitant (though I suspect he escapes from the summer visitors), Patrick Leigh Fermor. For wonderful writing on Greece and all sorts of esoteric information difficult to locate elsewhere, Leigh Fermor's two books on Greece, *Mani* and *Roumeli*, should go on everybody's list of books to read.

KARDAMILA
⊕36°53′N 22°13′.7E

## PORT LIMENÍ (Órmos Limeniou)

### Approach

This large bay lies 18 miles SE of Ák Kitries. The bay is difficult to identify from the distance, but once up to the entrance the ravine splitting the land at the head of it stands out well and closer in the houses around the bay will be seen. The neo-Maniote village above Limení and the church by the light structure on the S entrance point are conspicuous.

LIMENÍ
⊕36°41′·15N 22°22′·3E

*By night* The S side of the entrance is lit Fl.1·5s6M but a night entrance should be made with caution.

### Mooring

Anchor on the E side of Limení cove on the S side of the bay and take a long line ashore or anchor off on the W side of the cove. It is quite deep here and you will have to drop anchor in 10–12m. The bottom is sand and weed with a scattering of rocks over it. In settled weather the prevailing wind tends to blow only lightly in the summer and though it is a little uncomfortable, it is quite tenable.

An alternative anchorage is tucked into the NE corner of the bay. A short stone breakwater runs out from the shore and you may be lucky enough to find a berth on the end. There are 3–4m depths along most of the quay. Shelter here is good although it can get a bit bumpy if it gusts from the NE down the ravine.

### Facilities

Water from local sources ashore. Several tavernas at Limení and around the beach at the head.

### General

The large bay lies approximately halfway down the W side of the Mani peninsula, ideally placed to break the voyage between Kalamata and Porto Káyio. The fact that the bay is open to westerlies puts most people off, but for those willing to chance it, and in the summer you will have no problems most of the time, this is a wonderful place in a magnificent setting. The small hamlet at Limení has a little tourism in the summer, but nothing overwhelming. The tavernas serve simple but good fare with views out over the cove and the bay.

There are two architectural anomalies in the bay. The first is the Maniote village on the hillside above Limení, which is not a Maniote village but a hotel and apartment complex built in neo-Maniote style – only the large windows and the large building at the rear give it away. The second is what appears to be a reproduction of a Scottish Presbyterian church in the village, which is in fact a fortress built in the 19th century by Petros Mavromichalis, a clan leader from Areopolis on the hilltop above.

## DIROS (Dyros)

A bay about 3 miles S of Limení. The entrance is difficult to make out from the distance. A tall tower in Pirgos village N of the bay is conspicuous, but then there are a lot of towers along this stretch of coast. The shelter from the prevailing winds is poor, but in the morning calm a yacht can put in here to visit the Caves of Diros. Anchor in the NE corner or in the SE corner where a few local boats are kept on moorings. The caves and the reception buildings are housed on the SE side of the bay.

The caves are spectacular – one of those sights that stays with you a long time and which few adjectives adequately describe. The viewing of the caves is strictly controlled and it is best to go early before the coaches and cars of other sightseers arrive. The ticket booth is a short distance up the road from the caves. A guide punts and pushes a flat-bottomed boat around the subterranean passages which literally drip with stalactites – unfortunately in recent years the guides have taken to racing through the caves as quickly as possible and a protest is in order if you receive such treatment. The interconnected passages are lit for the convenience of tourists and although the tour is an extensive one, you emerge with the feeling that there are many more passages trailing off into an inky blackness than you have seen from the boat.

The apocryphal story of the discovery of the caves relates that a shepherd, chasing one of his sheep, fell through a hole into one of the caves and thus the cave complex was discovered. In fact evidence of prehistoric occupation has been discovered here and it is likely the caves have been known for a long time. Perhaps this is the real entrance to the underworld rather than Cape Matapan.

Although I am not a speleologist, caves have always fascinated me and I have toured and explored a good number. The Caves of Diros rank with the best of them. Between Limení and Diros and indeed further S of Diros there are a great many caves in the cliffs and it would appear that this whole area is riddled with them. If it is too rough to anchor at Diros, go to Yíthion or Kalamata and take a bus from there.

At Diros there is a small PO and money exchange booth, a bar, café, and taverna.

*Note* There are works in progress in the SE corner of the bay, but no information is available as yet on what the construction is for. I'd plump for a new entrance to the caves.

## MEZAPO (Órmos Mezapou)

A large bay some 10 miles S of Limení. The vast mountainous bulk of Capo Grosso just S is difficult to miss. On the thin peninsula partially sheltering the bay (Tigani = frying pan, because of its shape) the remains of a fort will not be seen until close in. Once at the entrance to the bay the village of Mezapos is difficult to make out until closer in.

Anchor off the small harbour and take a long line ashore. Very small yachts may find a space in the harbour, though care is needed as the bottom is uneven. The bay affords some shelter from the prevailing winds but at night a strong katabatic wind may blow in from the N–NE making it uncomfortable and possibly untenable. Tavernas ashore and limited provisions are available.

The small fishing harbour under vertical cliffs is a spectacular spot. Mezapo for a long time had a reputation as a local pirating and smuggling village and it continues to give that impression. Tim Severin on his voyage to retrace the route of Odysseus identified the place with the harbour of the Laestrygones, the cannibal giants who threw stones down on Odysseus and his men, killing many of them and sinking all but the galley of Odysseus. Formerly Bonifacio on Corsica was identified with the harbour of the Laestrygones. Make up your own mind on the matter.

**DIROS**
⊕36°38′·8N 22°22′·5E

**MEZAPO**
⊕36°32′·9N 22°22′·6E

Ák Tainaron (Matapan) and lighthouse looking W

## CAPO GROSSO

Immediately SW of Mezapo lies the vast bulk of Capo Grosso, a huge precipitous mass of rock that is unmistakable once seen – if any large cape should be called 'gross' it is this one. The cliffs rise sheer from the sea to 250m (800ft) and more, split by ravines and peppered with caves. Some of the caves have been walled up and it is said these contained the wealth of the Mezapo pirate families, but you would need to be a rock climber to get to them.

On the S side of Grosso just before Yerolimena there is a huge natural cave in the cliffs, easily identified from seawards, and this cave would be a natural choice for the ancients' entrance to Hades, said to be situated at Tainaron (Matapan).

## YEROLIMENA

36°28'·9N 22°24'·04E

A bay tucked in S of Capo Grosso. There is a small

**YEROLIMENA**
⊕36°28'·8N 22°24'·0E

quay for fishing boats where two or three small yachts could berth with care. The bay is open W and S and invariably has some swell rolling into it. In calm weather anchor off in 4–6m on sand and rock, poor holding in places. If there is a hint of strong winds from almost any direction then you should leave and seek shelter elsewhere. In strong southerlies head for Porto Káyio or Kalamata.

Provisions and tavernas ashore.

At one time this was the principal ferry port for the Mani.

# Lakonikós Kólpos
## (Gulf of Lakonika, Gulf of Kolokythia)

Around Ák Tainaron (Cape Matapan) lies the steep-sided and heavily indented Lakonikós Kólpos. Bordered on the west by the Taiyetos and on the east by the Parnon, it is a forbidding place, although the weather at the head of the gulf is often more settled than around the southern end. On the eastern side Nísos Elafónisos must be rounded before Ák Maléas is encountered.

Now, as in ancient times, the channel between Ák Maléas and the island of Kíthera is an important channel for ships leaving and entering the Aegean. The chances are you will encounter a fair number of large ships in this channel and a sharp lookout must be kept.

Ák Maléas is a mountainous headland some 780m high. It has a formidable reputation and mariners leaving Greece coined the saying: 'Round Malea, forget your native country'. It was the *Formidatum Maleae caput* of the Roman poet Statius and the cape where Odysseus was blown south to the land of the Lotus Eaters.

'I might have made it safely home, that time, but as I came round Malea the current took me out to sea, and from the north a fresh gale drove me on, past Kythera.'

*Odyssey*

Today, even with the aid of weather forecasts, it pays to treat the cape with respect.

### PORTO ASOMATO AND ÓRMOS VATHI
**Porto Asomato** 36°24'·4N 22°29'·4E
**Órmos Vathi** 36°23'·8N 22°29'·4E

These two inlets on the E side of Ák Tainaron are suitable overnight anchorages in calm weather. Both are subject to severe gusts with W–SW winds and are open to the SE whence a heavy swell rolls in. Only one mile N is the better shelter of Porto Káyio.

It was off here on 29 March 1941 that the British fleet from Alexandria surprised the Italian fleet and sank five Italian ships for the loss of only one plane. Despite this success the Axis powers soon pushed down through Greece and two months later Crete fell and British troops were hurriedly evacuated to Alexandria.

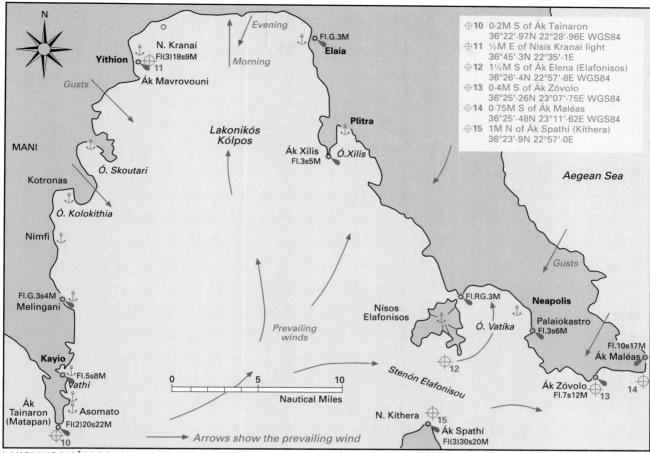

⊕10 0·2M S of Ák Tainaron
36°22'·97N 22°28'·96E WGS84
⊕11 ½M E of Nisís Kranai light
36°45'·3N 22°35'·1E
⊕12 1½M S of Ák Elena (Elafonisos)
36°26'·4N 22°57'·8E WGS84
⊕13 0·4M S of Ák Zóvolo
36°25'·26N 23°07'·75E WGS84
⊕14 0·75M S of Ák Maléas
36°25'·48N 23°11'·62E WGS84
⊕15 1M N of Ák Spathí (Kíthera)
36°23'·9N 22°57'·0E

**LAKONIKOS KÓLPOS (GULF OF LAKONIKA)**

## PORTO KÁYIO (Kaio)

BA 1092

### Approach

*Conspicuous* The Maniote towers of the two small villages on the hilltops and the ruined monastery on the NW side are conspicuous. Closer in a small church on the S entrance point and the light structure will be seen. The houses of the hamlet will not be seen until into the bay.

*By night* Use the light on Ák Tainaron Fl(2)20s22M and the light at the entrance Fl.5s8M.

*Dangers* With strong westerlies there can be strong gusts out of the bay and off the high land in the approaches.

### Mooring

With the normal W–SW wind anchor in 4–10m in the S cove of the bay. The gusts off the hills are not violent or frequent here. The holding in the S cove is not always to be relied upon. The bottom is hard sand with weed and some rocks. It is also possible to anchor and take a long line ashore to the quay in the SE corner where you are nicely tucked into the coast with good shelter from E–NE winds. The quay has only 1m or less depths off it so it is not possible to berth here. Strong NE winds may blow in unsettled weather and in that case the N cove is the best place to be. Here the bottom comes up very quickly from 30m to the shore so there is really only space for 2 or 3 yachts to anchor in reasonable depths. The bottom here is sand and weed, good holding.

*Shelter* Good shelter from the prevailing W–SW winds. Good shelter in the N cove from NE winds.

### Facilities

Water from local sources. Several tavernas in the summer. Fruit and vegetables from a small truck that calls at the bay.

Porto Káyio looking E down onto the anchorage    *Nigel Patten*

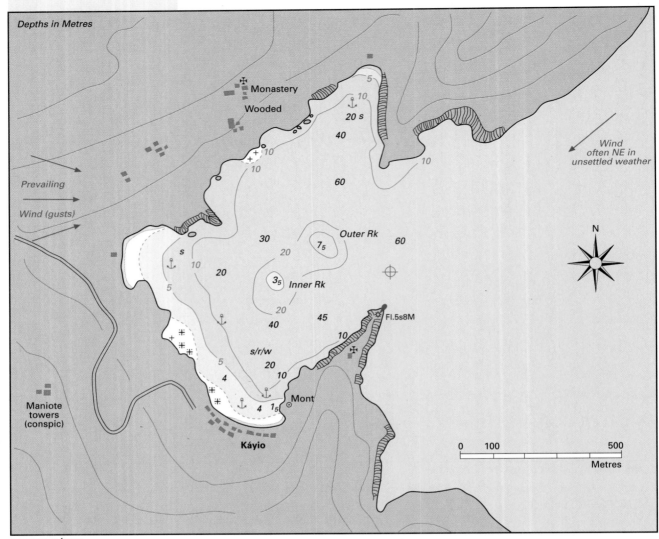

*Depths in Metres*

Monastery

Wooded

Prevailing

Wind (gusts)

20 s

40

60

10

10

Wind
often NE in
unsettled weather

N

Outer Rk

30

20

7₅

60

s

10

20

3₅ Inner Rk

5

20

40

45

10

Fl.5s8M

s/r/w

20

10

5

4

10

Maniote
towers
(conspic)

4 1₅ Mont

Káyio

0   100               500
Metres

**PORTO KÁYIO**
⊕36°25′·98N 22°29′·48E WGS84

## General

The bay was called Psamathous in ancient times and
Porto Quaglio by the Venetians, from which the
present name probably comes – 'Quaglio' means
quail and apparently great numbers of quail were
caught here and salted for export. The bay was used
by the Venetians, the Turks, and by various Maniote
pirates of whom the most famous was Katsonis – a
monument to the freedom fighter-cum-pirate stands
near the quay in the SE corner.

In 1980 there were only a few families including
the fishermen living in the small hamlet in the S of
the bay. Since then the summer arrival of yachts on
passage around the Peloponnisos and numbers of
camper-vans has rejuvenated the hamlet.

## ÓRMOS MELINGÁNI

36°30′·5N 22°29′·5E

Five miles N of Porto Káyio is the bay of Melingáni
offering indifferent shelter. It is easily identified by a
few houses at its head and the white light structure
Fl.G.3s4M on the N side of the bay.

## PORTO NIMFI (Nymphi)

Four miles N of Melingáni is a narrow inlet open to
the E. The village is situated on the hill above the
inlet. Subject to squalls with W winds.

## KOTRONAS

A small village at the head of Órmos Kolokithias
under Ák Kolokithia. There are often severe gusts
out of the bay, but when the gusts are not severe it
is possible to anchor in the bay for a lunch stop or
overnight if the weather remains calm. Open S and
if southerlies blow you should vacate the bay.
Anchor in 5–8m off the village and mole. The
bottom is sand and gravel, not everywhere good
holding. It may be possible to find a spot on the end
of the pier to go alongside. There are 2–3m depths
on the outer half of the mole.

Some provisions and tavernas ashore in the
village. The fishing village tucked under the steep
slopes is an attractive spot that has inevitably
developed into a small resort. On the headland to
the W are the remains of a prehistoric settlement.

Pórto Káyio in Lakonikós Kólpos looking WNW into the
anchorage                    *Peter Kleinoth/MareTeam*

**KOTRONAS**
⊕36°36'·5N 22°30'·5E

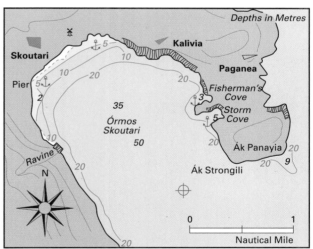

**ÓRMOS SKOUTARI**
⊕36°38'·6N 22°31'·9E

## ÓRMOS SKOUTARI (Scutari Bay)

The large bay between Ák Stavri and Ák Pagania.
There are several anchorages around the large bay
which can be used in settled weather.

*Skoutari* Anchor off the beach below the village or
in the rocky cove by a prominent cave in the N.

Generally you can anchor in 3–5m on a sand and
weed bottom, adequate holding once the anchor
is in. There can often be severe gusts down off the
high land onto these anchorages and if staying for
a while it would be prudent to lay a second
anchor.

*Fisherman's Cove* A cove with a beach at the head
on the E side of Órmos Scoutari. Anchor in 3–6m
on a sandy bottom. Depending on the severity of
the gusts off the land, this is an attractive
anchorage open W–NW.

*Storm Cove* A cove immediately S of Fisherman's Cove. Anchor in 4–5m on sand. It may be useful to anchor and take a long line ashore to the N side depending on the wind and sea. Reasonable shelter tucked into here.

### Weather note

The severity of gusts off the land in the vicinity of Skoutari varies greatly. Sometimes there may be next to no wind at all and another time there can be severe gusts. The latter usually arrive in the afternoon and continue until dusk. If on passage between Yíthion and Melingáni exercise some caution or leave early in the morning. The two last mentioned coves afford good shelter from the NE winds which sometimes blow in the gulf.

### YÍTHION (Githion, Gytheoin)

BA 1683
Imray-Tetra G15

### Approach

*Conspicuous* From the SE, especially if you are approaching at dusk, it is difficult to pick out just where Yíthion town is. By day the village of Mavrovouni atop Ák Mavrovouni and the tall white octagonal lighthouse on Nisís Kranai are conspicuous. From the S the buildings of Yíthion town are not visible until you round Ák Mavrovouni.

*By night* Use the light on Nisís Kranai Fl(3)18s9M and the light on the extremity of the mole Fl.R.3s3M.

*Dangers* Care needs to be taken of gusts off the high land in the approaches.

**YÍTHION**
⊕36°45´·6N 22°34·2E (Fl.R.3s3M)

### Mooring

Go stern or bows-to the mole. Good depths and good holding in mud.

*Shelter* Good from the prevailing winds. With strong winds from the NW (not common in my experience) there may be strong gusts off the Taïyetos mountains – in this case the best place is bows-to the W quay where you will be held off the quay by the wind. Strong NE winds are reported to cause a surge.

*Authorities* Port police and customs.

*Note* There are plans to build a mole out from the coast to the E to improve the shelter in the harbour.

### Facilities

*Water* On the quay.
*Fuel* Some distance out of town. A mini-tanker may deliver.
*Repairs* Limited mechanical repairs.
*Provisions* Good shopping for all provisions close by.
*Eating out* Good tavernas nearby including good fish restaurants.
*Other* PO. OTE. Banks. Greek gas and *Camping Gaz*. Buses to Sparta and Athens. Ferry to Piraeus twice a week calling at Yerolimena, Neapolis, Monemvasía and Kíthera.

### General

Yíthion is seldom visited by yachts, yet it is an excellent base for exploring Lakonikós Kólpos and a pleasant low-key place in itself. Yíthion has a long pedigree: claimed to have been founded by Heracles

Yíthion in the NW corner of Lakonikós Kólpos looking WNW across Nisís Kranai in the foreground

*Peter Kleinoth/MareTeam*

Yíthion from above the town      *Nigel Patten*

**ELAIA**
⊕36°45′·2N 22°48′·0E

and Apollo, it has seen Mycenaean and Phoenician colonists and was the chief port of Sparta. With the decline of Sparta, Yíthion became the most important town of the Free Laconian League and later of the Maniotes. Before all this Kranai was the island mentioned by Homer in the *Iliad* where Paris and Helen spent their first night after eloping together.

'...when I snatched thee first
From lovely Lacedaemon's vale, put out to sea in hollow ships,
And on Kranai lay with thee upon a couch of love'
Homer *Iliad* Book 3

The result was of course the siege of Troy and the battle of the heroes, not to mention the birth of Greek literature.

Yíthion makes a good base for exploring the medieval town of Mistra – a remarkable fortified town of narrow streets crowned by a large castle. It is the completeness and size of the town in a forbidding setting that visually impresses one, although here some of the finest Byzantine architecture is preserved. Mistra can be visited by taxi or bus from Yíthion.

## ELAIA (Elea)

Across the gulf directly E of Yíthion the large village of Elaia is conspicuous.

There is a short mole off the village but this is often crowded with local boats. Anchor off the beach in 2–4m on sand and weed. There are some patches with rock under the sand where it is difficult to get the anchor to hold. If there is room go stern or bows-to the end of the mole. Good shelter from all but strong NW–W winds.

Some provisions and tavernas ashore. Additional facilities in Yithion or Molaous.

## ÓRMOS XÍLIS AND PLÍTRA (Xyli Bay, Plythra)

### Approach

*Conspicuous* From the W and S the steep-to craggy Ák Xílis is conspicuous. Nearing Plítra the buildings of the small village and the mole are easily identified.

*By night* Use the light on Ák Xílis Fl.3s5M and the light on the end of the mole Q.G.3M.

*Dangers* Caution is called for to avoid the above and below-water rocks lying approximately 30m N of the extremity of the mole. The rocks are marked by an iron pipe beacon. A night entry is possible, but care must be taken of the rocks N of the mole as the beacon is not lit.

### Mooring

Go stern or bows-to the outer end of the mole. The bottom is largely rock and there are numerous permanent moorings on the bottom. Care is needed and it may be wise to use a trip-line on the anchor.

*Shelter* Good protection from all but strong southerlies although the fishermen say they leave their boats here all year round. With the normal SW wind a limited swell of no consequence creeps around the end of the mole making it a bit uncomfortable.

*Anchorage* Depending on the weather you can anchor off the beach at the head of Órmos Xíli. Anchor in 3–5m on sand and rock, once you find a good sandy patch that the anchor will dig into. Taverna ashore.

### Facilities

Water from local sources only. In the summer there are several tavernas around the shore. The nearest village for supplies is 4km away.

### General

Plítra is an unprepossessing village but manages to attract a few tourists to its sandy beaches in the

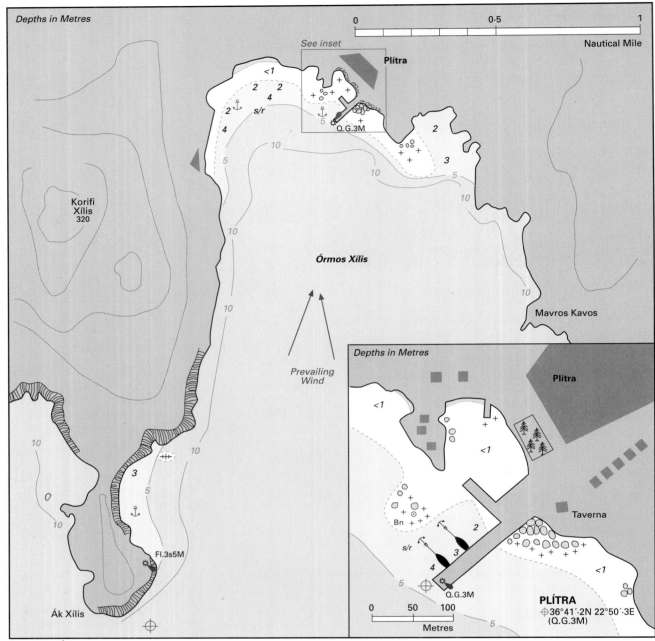

Depths in Metres

0          0.5          1

Nautical Mile

See inset

Plítra

Korifi
Xílis
320

Órmos Xílis

Prevailing
Wind

Mavros Kavos

Q.G.3M

Depths in Metres

Plítra

Taverna

PLÍTRA
⊕36°41′·2N 22°50′·3E
(Q.G.3M)

0    50    100

Metres

Bn

s/r

Fl.3s5M

Ák Xílis

**ORMOS XÍLIS**
⊕36°39′·15N 22°49′·0E

summer. It is a pleasant sleepy little place that grows on you. On the seaward side of the mole are the remains of the ancient town of Plithra, now mostly submerged. You can snorkel over the remains that are scattered around the sea-bed in shallow water.

**Note**
Some yachts use Arkhangelos in the SE corner of Órmos Xíli. It is open N–NW but may be tenable with the prevailing wind which tends to curve and blow from the W–SW into Órmos Xíli. The bottom here is reported to be mostly rock so unless you find a sandy patch and the weather is relatively calm, it is better to move elsewhere.

# Nísos Elafónisos and channel

Nísos Elafónisos is the island on the N side of the channel between Nísos Kíthera and the Peloponnisos. It is separated from the Peloponnisos by a shallow boat channel that those with iron nerve can negotiate if they so desire. Elafónisos means 'deer island' although nobody, myself included, has ever seen any here. In antiquity there was a trading post here and the island was known as Onugnathos, 'ass's jaw', which with a little imagination the island can be seen to resemble.

There are a number of anchorages around the island and a small harbour at the village of Elafónisos on the NE corner.

Elafónisos fishing harbour looking across to the church which is conspicuous in the approaches

Elafónisos *caïque* harbour

### Anchorages around Elafónisos

1. **W coast** There are several anchorages in and around Nisís Pori and Nisís Elli. Anchor where convenient on sand. Good shelter from the S–SE and from E–NE.

2. **Órmos Sarakiniko** The large bay on the S of the island. Anchor off the beach on the E side on sand, good holding. In the summer there will often be a NE–E wind blowing over Elafónisos and around Ák Malea. Good shelter here from NE–E and in fact you will often be in company with those waiting to get around Malea. A beach taverna/bar in the summer.

3. **Ormiskos Frangos** The bay immediately E of Sarakiniko. Anchor off the beach on sand. Good shelter and suitable as an overnight anchorage in settled weather.

4. **Órmos Levki** The bay on the E side of the island. It affords good shelter from the prevailing wind. The bottom is sand and rock with good holding reported at the S end of the bay, although bad holding has been reported in other parts of the bay.

The attractions of all these anchorages are wonderful sandy beaches and translucent water in

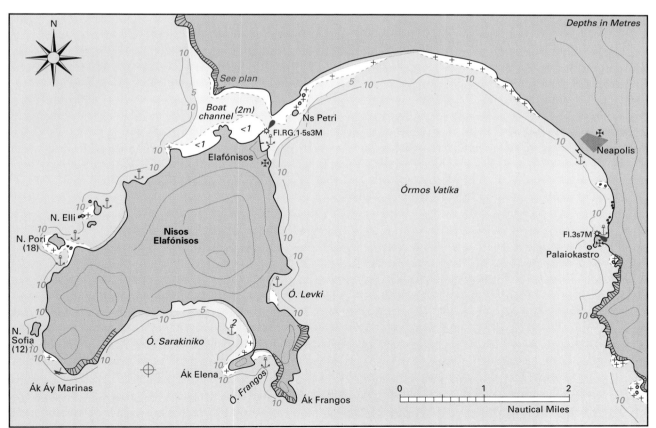

**ELAFÓNISOS AND ÓRMOS VATIKA**
⊕36°27′·9N 22°56′·8E

143

deserted surroundings, although camper vans somehow seem to have penetrated to Sarakiniko and Frangos in the summer.

## WEATHER NOTE

The normal summer breeze is from the W curving up to blow from the S in Órmos Vatíka. At night a NE wind may blow and may continue to do so through the day. In unsettled weather care is needed as there can be violent winds around this area.

## ELAFÓNISOS VILLAGE

### Approach

*Conspicuous* From the S the church sitting out in the channel is conspicuous. The houses of the village will also be seen, but the rough stone mole of the harbour will not be seen until closer in.

*By night* Use the light on the E side of Órmos Vatíka Fl.3s7M and the light on the beacon (Vrakhos Stavrós: Fl.RG.1·5s3M). The harbour entrance is not lit.

### Mooring

Anchor in the bay or go stern or bows-to the mole at the S entrance. The bottom is rock covered by a minuscule amount of sand, bad holding. Snorkel over your anchor to make sure it has snagged on something and preferably use a fisherman anchor.

*Shelter* Good shelter from the prevailing winds. The harbour is open E and in strong southerlies I would expect a surge in here.

*Note* The fishermen's harbour N of the ferry harbour is shallow and packed full of local boats.

### Facilities

Water tap near the fishing harbour. Most provisions can be found in the village. Tavernas and bars around the waterfront. OTE. Ferry to the mainland opposite. Ferry to Kíthera.

### General

The village is a ramshackle sort of place, but convivial. Greek tourists come here and camp on the mainland opposite off the magnificent beach fronted by the turquoise waters of the boat channel. At night

**ELAFÓNISOS VILLAGE**
⊕36°30'·8N 22°59'·0E

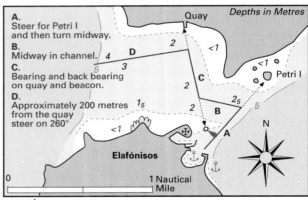

**ELAFÓNISOS BOAT PASSAGE**

the entertainment for the locals and tourists can reach fairly high decibel levels.

## ELAFÓNISOS BOAT PASSAGE

Separating Elafónisos from the Peloponnisos is the shallow boat channel which can be seen as the expanse of turquoise water N of Elafónisos village. Passage through the channel is possible for yachts drawing less than 2m in calm weather, but with any swell a yacht should go S of the island. It is essential to have someone up front conning you through and a careful eye should be kept on the depth sounder. Even so the passage requires an iron nerve and a calm day. Every feature on the bottom can be clearly identified and the depths are such that you are never out of 2–2·5m for nearly a mile.

Órmos Sarakiniko and Órmos Frangos abut one another on the S end of Elafónisos

Ák Áy Ilías, the S entrance point to Órmos Vatíka, looking NW

## NEAPOLIS

The large town on the E side of Órmos Vatíka is visible from some distance off. A large church is prominent behind the town. Shelter off here is rarely comfortable and depends on what has been happening with the weather outside Órmos Vatika. If there has been a lot of wind from almost any direction then it will not be that comfortable in here. With southerlies of any sort it will be uncomfortable and can be untenable. With the E–NE wind that often blows in the summer it is tenable but a swell is pushed around into Órmos Vatika.

Anchor to the S of the ferry pier in 4–8m on mud and weed, generally good holding. The ferry pier is quite high to go alongside or stern or bows-to, but in calm weather it is possible. The S side is used by the ferry to Kíthera.

Water and fuel in the town. Good shopping for provisions and numerous tavernas. PO. OTE. Banks. Ferry to Kíthera and Piraeus.

Neapolis is an interesting place which has a little local tourism, but otherwise functions as the main town for the area. It is not the most attractive place with a lot of 'pour-and-fill' buildings, but it is a proper working town serving this outpost of the Peloponnese. The Bay of Vatika takes its name from ancient Voiai (the Voiatic Gulf), the remains of which are said to be underwater somewhere S of Neapolis.

Nearby to the NW the tiny fishing harbour of Neapolis is too small and shallow for a yacht. The entrance is rock-bound with around 1·7m depths in the entrance and less inside. A rock with less than

**NEAPOLIS**
⊕36°29'·6N 23°03'·9E

2m over it is reported to lie in the immediate approaches. Not recommended for yachts, though very small motorboats drawing less than a metre might find some shelter inside. Extreme care needed here.

## PALAIOKASTRO

About 1½M S of Neapolis, a new quay has been built under the headland on which stands a conspicuous church. The headland (Ák Vatíka or Palaiokastro) is lit Fl.3s7M and the end of the mole is lit Fl.G.3s3M.

At the time of writing an old ferry occupies much of the quay and it looks as if it has been abandoned here. There is still some quay space left that can be used. Alternatively anchor off in 3–10m tucked as far under the headland as you can. Good shelter from southerlies and from the E–NE winds which often blow. On the quay there is also good protection from westerlies.

The name Palaiokastro (old castle) indicates there has been ancient occupation here although little is recorded.

**PALAIOKASTRO**
⊕36°29'·4N 23°03'·8E

## ÁK MALÉAS

Ák Maléas has a bit of a fearsome reputation and at times it lives up to it. At other times you can motor around it in a flat calm. Coming from the W most yachts will hole up in Órmos Sarakiniko or nearby if there are strong adverse winds in order to wait for the wind to die down. Often in the summer a whole gaggle of yachts can build up here waiting for the right time to leave. The problem is that the winds around Elafónisos are not always a good indication of the wind around Maléas and I have left here (watched curiously by all the other yachts) with two reefs down and a pocket handkerchief for a jib, only

The lighthouse on Ák Maléas

to end up motoring around Maléas and up to Monemvasía. I have also left here and returned to Elafónisos after being battered by 40-knot gusts near the cape. There is no accurate method of judging what the wind is doing around the cape in the summer and you can only use your nose to sniff things out as best you can.

In spring and autumn any depressions in the vicinity of Maléas will bring strong winds and confused seas. It is quite simply a windy place to be when depressions are nearby and if in doubt hole up somewhere secure. While this is not much consolation, I can assure you, having hurtled around here in a winter gale when en route from the Saronic to the Ionian, that once bitten you treat this place with respect. And don't forget to wave to the monks in the hermitage who watch over ships large and small rounding this lonely place.

# Nísoi Kíthera and Andíkithera

**(Kythera, Cerigo and Anti-Kíthera, Cerigotto, Lious)**

Kíthera and Andíkithera form an island bridge between the Peloponnisos and Crete. As a convenient lee or port of refuge, the islands have played an important part as stepping-stones on the ancient trade routes around the Peloponnisos to the Aegean and east along Crete. Near Avelomona, a small village on the south of Kíthera, a Minoan trading post (c.2000–1450 BC) has been excavated. Later the Phoenicians (the island was reputed to be rich in murex from which the Phoenicians extracted their famous purple dye), Mycenaeans, Romans and Venetians used the island.

Kíthera has another claim to classical fame and it is that Aphrodite was born here, though other islands, notably Cyprus, also lay claim to the goddess. Her worship was probably introduced to this lonely rocky island by the Phoenicians and when she was later adopted by the Greeks, her birthplace

was assumed to be Kíthera. This seems as good a place as any to let Lawrence Durrell describe this most human of goddesses:

'Under her title Urania, she stood for pure and ideal love; as Genetrix or Nymphia, she was the protector of lawful marriage and favoured all serious unions; as Pandemos or Porne she was the patron of all prostitutes and favoured all lust and venal love. Everything to do with passion, from the noblest to the most degraded, came within her scope. It is her completeness, compounded of many attributes, which wins our hearts. Her loving had a comprehensiveness that accepted every human foible, good or bad.

Nor was she averse to using her powers mischievously – as when she took it into her head to light a short fuse under the chair of Zeus in Olympus, which gave him one of the worst attacks of skirt-fever ever to win a place in the Olympian version of 'The Guinness Book of Records'. Was there nothing sacred, he asked her, all lit up like a Christmas tree? Yes, she must have answered, everything is sacred, without distinction, even laughter. Especially laughter.'

Lawrence Durrell *The Greek Islands*

When the Union of the Seven Islands was declared, Kíthera and Andíkithera were declared to be part of the Heptanisoi, despite the distance separating them from the other Ionian islands. After the War of Independence the islands gradually came under the administration of Athens. Today a few tourists who enjoy quiet places visit Kíthera, but on the whole the island remains a comparatively untouched spot.

Eighteen miles south of Kíthera lies its diminutive Andíkithera (Anti-Kíthera) – a pitted rocky island rising sheer from the sea and inhabited by around fifty hardy souls. Few yachts call here as the only harbour is unsafe in all except calm weather. Early this century a wreck of the 1st century BC was discovered near the island and a number of valuable bronze and marble statues recovered. These are now displayed in the National Museum in Athens.

## PLATIA AMMOS

36°22'·0N 22°57'·7E

A small bay approximately 2 miles SE of Ák Spathi. A short mole provides some shelter from NE winds, although even a moderate NE breeze makes it uncomfortable in here and if it blows strongly from the NE it is untenable. With westerlies there are strong gusts into the bay.

## PELAGIA

### Approach

The old ferry port lies approximately 4 miles SE of Ák Spathi. The mole for the ferry is easily located.

*By night* The end of the mole is lit Fl.R.1·5s3M.

*Dangers* When close, care is needed of the shoal water off the coast in the vicinity of the mole.

### Mooring

If there is room go alongside or stern or bows-to the mole. Alternatively anchor off on either side of the mole. The bottom is sand and weed, good holding.

**KÍTHERA AND ANDIKÍTHERA**

**PELAGIA**
⊕36°19'·7N 22°59'·1E

*Shelter* The harbour is useful only in calm weather or light offshore winds. With westerlies there are strong gusts into the harbour and it is completely open to NE winds. With any wind from the NE you should vacate the harbour and go elsewhere.

*Authorities* Port police.

**Facilities**
*Water* At the root of the mole.
*Provisions* Mini-market near the mole.
*Eating out* Tavernas around the waterfront.

**General**
The harbour and village have become a bit of a ghost town now that the new ferry port at Dhiakofti has opened, although there is still a modest tourist trade here.

**DHIAKOFTI**
The new ferry port for Kíthera, situated on the W side of Makrónisos.

**Approach**
Makrónisos joined by a causeway is easily recognised from the N and closer in the breakwater sheltering the ferry quay will be seen.

*By night* Use the light of Makrónisos Fl.10s7M and the light on the end of the breakwater Fl.R.3s3M.

**Mooring**
Go alongside or stern or bows-to the S side of the quay. Most of the W quay is for the ferries and

147

**DHIAKOFTI**
⊕36°16′·6N 23°04′·8E

hydrofoils running to Kíthera. An alternative in W–N–E winds would be to anchor on the E side of Makrónisos tucked under Vrakhoi Mikro. The bottom is sand and weed with some rock, mostly good holding.

*Shelter* Adequate shelter from all winds when tucked under the S quay although with strong NE winds it is likely to get uncomfortable and might be untenable in here.

*Authorities* Port police. Customs.

### Facilities
*Water* On the quay.
*Fuel* Outside the village.
*Provisions* Mini-market.
*Eating out* Tavernas on the waterfront, some of which have good fresh fish.
*Other* Exchange. Ferries and hydrofoil to Neapolis and Yíthion.

### General
Until the construction of the ferry port this was a sleepy little fishing hamlet. Inevitably the construction of the port has meant the usual rash of reinforced concrete to cater for the captive ferry arrivals.

## ÓRMOS ÁYIOS NIKOLAOS

A large bay immediately SE of the Dragonera and Andidragonera islets. In calm weather or light NE winds anchor off the beach in 7–10m on sand, mud and weed, good holding. With wind from any direction there is inevitably some swell in the bay making it uncomfortable and with fresh to strong winds (especially S–E–NE) the bay is untenable.

**ÓRMOS ÁY NIKOLAOS**
⊕36°12′·9N 23°04′·5E

## AVELOMONA

### Approach
The twin-headed inlet lies in the NE corner of Órmos Áy Nikolaos.

*By night* Use the light on Andidragonera Fl(3)15s7M and the light on the E side of the entrance to Avelomona Fl.G.1·5s3M.

**AVELOMONA**
⊕36°13′·4N 23°05′·0E

*Note* The two coves are very small and you should have everything ready before entering.

## Mooring

Go stern or bows-to where possible on the stubby mole or on the quay just inside the mole. Alternatively anchor and take a long line ashore to the NE side. If you cannot get into the cove then it is possible to anchor off outside in 6–12m if the weather is settled. The bottom is sand and weed, good holding.

*Note* There are some permanent moorings on the bottom which can foul an anchor so care is needed where you drop the anchor. It may be useful to rig a trip-line.

*Shelter* Reasonable shelter from NE and W winds although there is often a surge in here if NE winds are fresh. Open S.

## Facilities

Some provisions available and several tavernas ashore.

## General

The little hamlet tucked into the corner of Áy Nikolaos is a sweet little place that has experienced something of a renaissance in recent years and has now been smartened up. There is evidence that the harbour has been used since antiquity and around the bay at Kastrí a Minoan settlement has been excavated which was occupied from c.2000–1450 BC. The Venetians too used it as they built the small fort on the W headland of Avelomona.

## ÓRMOS KAPSÁLI (Kíthera)

### Approach

*Conspicuous* From the distance Vrak Avgo (Ovo Island) which means Egg Island – it is roughly egg-shaped – is conspicuous. From the S and E a windmill on Ák Grosso and the fort above the *chora* are conspicuous. From the W the fort can be seen as you near Ák Trakhilos. Once into the large bay, two large white villas to the W of the harbour and the lighthouse on the bluff above the harbour are conspicuous.

*By night* Use the light on the bluff (Fl.3s10M) and the light on the end of the quay (F.G.3M).

*Dangers* With strong westerlies there are gusts off the high land and a considerable swell around the coast.

## Mooring

Only the W cove is deep enough for a yacht. The E cove is shallow and rock-bound. Moor stern-to or alongside the outer half of the quay if there is not a swell. The bottom is sand, rock and weed, reasonable holding once the anchor is in.

*Shelter* Whatever the wind direction I have invariably encountered a swell in the harbour, making it uncomfortable. With strong S winds the harbour is untenable.

*Note* It is reported that it is prohibited to anchor in the harbour without permission from the port police. A yacht can be fined for contravening this regulation.

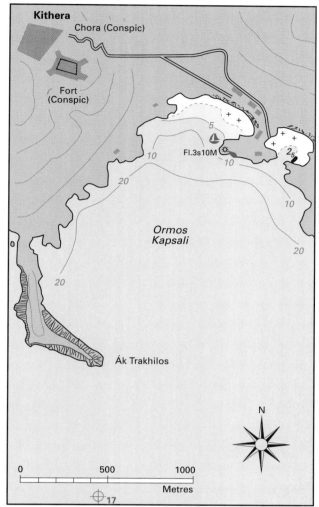

**APPROACHES TO ORMOS KAPSALI**

⊕17 0·5M S of Ák Trakhilos (Kíthera)
36°07′6N 22°59′·3E

*Authorities* Port police and customs.

## Facilities

*Water* From a café on the quay, by hose.
*Provisions* Limited provisions at the harbour, better shopping in the *chora*.

Órmos Kapsáli looking SW onto the quay

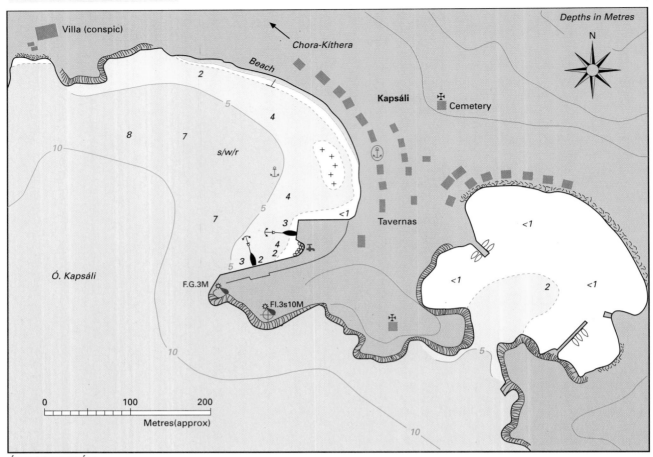

**ÓRMOS KAPSÁLI**
⊕36°08´·6N 23°00´·0E

*Eating out* Tavernas on the waterfront.
*Other* PO and OTE in the *chora*.

### General

Órmos Kapsáli is picturesque as are the walled *chora*
and fort, a steep climb above. The walled *chora* is
the capital of Kíthera, although nowadays Potamós
is the commercial centre. The fort, on what looks
like an impregnable rocky bluff, was first built by the
Venetians in 1316 to protect their new trade route
around the Peloponnisos. Despite the poor shelter
in the harbour it is well worth a visit to this
picturesque place – most of the time in the summer
it is tenable, if uncomfortable.

### ÓRMOS POTAMOU (Andíkithera)

At the northern end of Andíkithera the natural
harbour of Órmos Potamou is a narrow inlet
running southwards and open to the N. Anchor in
6–12m at the S end of the inlet. At the head of the
bay there are above and below-water rocks. The
bottom is sand and rock. There is invariably a swell
in the bay and with even moderate N winds the
harbour is untenable. With SW–W winds there are
gusts into the harbour.

Meagre supplies can be obtained ashore. Despite
the unsafe anchorage the island is attractive in a
barren desolate sort of way.

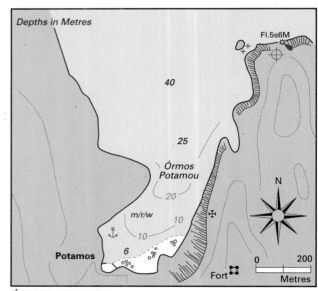

**ÓRMOS POTAMOU**
⊕35°53´·5N 23°17´·7N (Fl.5s6M)

# III. The Gulf of Patras and the Gulf of Corinth
## (Patraikos Kólpos and Korinthiakós Kólpos)

Approaching the Gulf of Patras from the west, the coast is low-lying although backed by high land. Much of this coast is shallow salt marsh and shoal water extends some distance offshore, particularly on the north side of the gulf. Approaching the narrow western entrance to the Gulf of Corinth, the coast rises abruptly to high mountains. The sides of the Gulf of Corinth are flanked by two high mountain ranges scarred by winter torrents and split by deep gorges. On the south coast Mt Killini (Zyria) rises to 2,377m (7,800ft) and on the north coast Mt Parnassos reaches 2,454m (8051ft). Well into late spring these mountains are capped with snow.

The Gulf of Corinth is 60 miles long from the Straits of Ríon and Andírrion (once known as the 'little Dardanelles') to the Corinth Canal. Surrounded by high mountains, the gulf is much like a large lake and indeed the scenery resembles that of an Alpine lake. The narrow alluvial plain on the south coast is extensively cultivated with vineyards and citrus and fringed by attractive beaches. On the north coast the mountains are for a large part bare of vegetation although in places, particularly Návpaktos and Itéa, there are patches of green contrasting with the barren mountains behind.

The history of the gulfs has largely revolved around the fortunes of Corinth. Using the Corinth Canal saves a distance of approximately 150 miles between the Ionian Sea and Athens. In antiquity, vessels were transported across the isthmus on rollers on a road called the *diolkos* and Corinth controlled this passage between the Ionian and the Aegean. From the Archaic period right up to the end of Roman rule the city flourished and grew fat on its income from the *diolkos*. In 522 and 551 AD earthquakes destroyed the city and it never regained its former prosperity.

The city and control of the gulf passed through successive invaders: the Normans sacked it in 1147; Villhardouin captured it in 1212; the Turks took it in 1458; the Knights of Malta in 1612; the Venetians in 1687; and, in 1715, the Turks acquired it yet again until it finally became a part of Greece at the beginning of the War of Independence. Today Corinth has little to exercise the perceptions, but its former feats and glories have passed into our language and culture.

At the entrance to the Gulf of Patras two maritime incidents took place – one of historical note and the other just a footnote to history.

Proceeding down the channel between Oxiá Island and Ák Scrofa the coast becomes low-lying for some 25 miles before the town of Mesolóngion appears hovering over the salt marsh. In and around the channel off Oxiá the Battle of Lepanto took place. The Turks prepared their fleet in Návpaktos, then known as Lepanto, and engaged the combined Christian fleet under Don John of Austria in this desolate spot. The Christian fleet with galleys from Venice, Genoa, the Papal States, Spain, Sicily and Naples defeated the Turks, sinking and capturing some 250 galleys and freeing 15,000 galley slaves. This was the last major sea battle fought with galleys rowed by slaves and effectively demolished Turkish control of the sea. It is recorded that Cervantes, the author of *Don Quixote*, lost the use of his left hand here. The late Peter Throckmorton attempted to locate some of the galleys lost in this action but uncovered nothing from the thick silt that covers the bottom.

It was also here under the lee of Scrofa that a small ship Byron was on put in to evade a Turkish brig-of-war on New Year's Eve in 1823. En route to Mesolóngion from Cephalonia, his Ionian skipper elected to anchor until the Turks passed. Apparently feeling unsafe they later went further north to Astakós, then called Dragomestre. Eventually three ships from Mesolóngion found Byron's ship and escorted it safely into the marshy fortress. Although Byron liked the sea and ships he knew very little about them and his companions were even more ignorant of matters nautical. David Howarth records this amusing episode on the trip to Mesolóngion in his *The Greek Adventure*:

'The passengers in this boat were a land-lubberly lot, except perhaps Tita the gondolier, and the crew seems not to have been much better. Fletcher the valet had caught a cold and had to lie down on the only mattress on board, Dr Bruno was prone to wring his hands and weep at any threat of disaster, and Loukas could not swim. Byron himself liked boats, but had never learned much about them. And as they returned through the Oxiá channel, the boat missed stays and ran aground in a squall. Two thirds

## Quick reference guide

| | Shelter | Mooring | Fuel | Water | Provisioning | Tavernas | Plan |
|---|---|---|---|---|---|---|---|
| Killini | B | AB | B | A | B | B | • |
| Kato Achaia | A | A | B | B | C | C | • |
| Missalonghi | A | ABC | B | A | B | B | • |
| Krionéri | O | C | O | O | O | C | |
| Patras | B | A | A | A | A | A | • |
| Patras Yacht Harbour | A | A | B | A | A | B | • |
| Návpaktos | B | A | A | A | A | A | • |
| Khiliadhou | B | AB | O | B | C | C | • |
| Monastiraki | C | C | O | B | C | C | |
| Nisís Trizónia | A | ABC | O | B | C | C | • |
| Aiyíon | C | AC | B | B | B | A | • |
| Kallithea | B | C | O | B | C | C | • |
| Eratini | C | C | B | B | B | C | • |
| Panormos | C | C | O | O | O | C | • |
| Vidhavis | C | C | O | O | O | C | • |
| Anemokambi | B | O | O | O | O | C | • |
| Galaxidhi | A | A | B | B | B | A | • |
| Itéa | A | A | B | B | B | B | • |
| Andíkiron | B | ABC | B | A | C | B | • |
| Áy Saranda | B | C | O | B | C | C | • |
| Kólpos Domvrainis | B | C | O | O | O | O | |
| Porto Germeno | A | AB | O | A | O | C | • |
| Kato Alepochori | A | A | B | B | C | C | • |
| Nisídhes Alkonidhes | C | C | O | O | O | O | • |
| Agriliou | O | C | O | O | O | O | |
| Loutráki | O | C | B | B | B | B | |
| Corinth | A | AB | B | B | A | B | • |
| Corinth Canal | O | O | O | O | O | O | • |
| Posidhonía | C | AC | O | B | O | C | • |
| Isthmia | B | A | O | B | O | C | • |
| Vrakhati | B | A | O | B | C | C | • |
| Kiato | B | A | B | A | A | B | • |
| Xilokastro | A | A | O | A | C | C | • |

of the crew climbed out on the bowsprit and jumped ashore, Byron told Loukas he would save him, and Dr Bruno stripped to his flannel waistcoat and running about like a rat (it was Byron's description) shouted 'Save him indeed! By God, save me rather – I'll be the first if I can.' Thereupon, after striking twice, the boat blew off again. The crew was removed from the rocks by one of the escort ships, and that evening, without any more alarms, Byron reached the entrance of Missalonghi.'

Byron accomplished little in Mesolóngion. The guerrilla chiefs assembled around him for the money he had brought. The collection of Philhellenes gathered in Mesolóngion for the most part grumbled and argued amongst themselves and with the Greeks. Byron was appointed a 'commander' but could do little to organise the ill-assorted groups around him. It was more his death of fever on 19 April 1824 that inspired the world and focussed

## Data

**PORTS OF ENTRY**
Patras
Itéa

**PROHIBITED AREAS**
A small harbour on the E side of Órmos Andíkiron and the area immediately surrounding it.

**MAJOR LIGHTS**
**Ák Oxiá** Fl(2)15s17M
**Nisís Kavikalidha** (Cape Killini) LFl.WR.10s12/9M
**Ák Páppas** LFl(2)20s10M
**Ák Áy Sóstis** Fl.WR.5s17/14M
**Ríon** Fl.6s6M
**Andírrion** Fl(2).10s10M
**Ák Mórnos** Fl(3)15s7M
**Ák Dhrépanon** Fl.10s22M
**Nisís Trizónia** Fl.4s4M
**Ák Psaromíta** Fl(2)15s21M
**Ák Andromákhi** Fl(3)15s10M
**Nisís Apsifía** (Galaxidhi) Fl.7s5M
**Ák Mákri-Nikólaos** Fl.4·5s5M
**Ák Likoporiá** Fl(2)16s10M
**Ák Kefálí** Fl.3s4M
**Ák Melangávi** Fl.10s17M

## Routes

Given the confines of the two gulfs, yachts will pretty much be heading east or west most of the time.

When heading E into the Gulf of Patras the prevailing wind in the summer is the NW breeze which is funnelled into a W wind and blows right through the Gulf of Patras and into the Gulf of Corinth from a westerly direction. The funnelling effect can substantially increase the strength of the wind, especially where it is squeezed by the land at the Strait of Rion and Andírrion and for some distance into the narrow W part of the Gulf of Corinth. For yachts headed E this is no real problem as once into the gulfs the seas are relatively slight and you are on a downwind run to Corinth.

When heading W from Corinth you will pretty much be plugging into the wind most of the time. As the prevailing summer wind tends to gradually extend into the gulfs from the Ionian, if a yacht leaves early in the morning it will generally be able to motor some of the way in the morning calm. If you are beating into the wind when headed W then it pays to stay on the N side of the gulfs where you will often pick up a bit of a lift with the wind getting a bit of northerly in it. You will also have less sea under the N side of the gulfs.

When heading out of the Gulf of Patras into the Ionian, care is needed not to get too close to the shoal water on the N side of the gulf. Keep an eye on the depthsounder and on your position. Once up to Oxiá it is better to continue out past the S end of the island for a bit before putting a tack in as the wind tends to follow the contours of the inside channel between Oxiá and the coast.

At times in the summer you will have N–NE winds at the E end of the Gulf of Corinth and there can be fierce gusts off the high land on the N side. In this case stick close in to the N coast before turning down to Corinth. If you arrive off the Corinth Canal with strong westerlies it is often better to stay overnight in Corinth harbour and venture out in the morning calm to transit the canal.

| For weather for the Gulf of Patras listen to **Cephalonia** | | | For weather for the Gulf of Corinth listen to **Perama** | | | **Patras Coastguard (K)** |
|---|---|---|---|---|---|---|
| Frequency | Weather forecast | Nav warnings | Frequency | Weather forecast | Nav warnings | VHF Ch 16, 85 |
| VHF Ch 27 | | | VHF Ch 86 | | | MF 2182kHz |
| (announce Ch 16) | 0600, 1000, 1600, 2200 UTC | 0500, 1100, 1730, 2330 UTC | (announce Ch 16) | 0600, 1000, 1600, 2200 UTC | 0500, 1100, 1730, 2330 UTC | DSC MF 2187·5kHz |

**GULF OF PATRAS AND GULF OF CORINTH**

**USEFUL WAYPOINTS**
- ⊕1  ½M S of Ák Oxiá
  38°16'·60N 21°05'·95E WGS84
- ⊕2  2M N of Ák Papas light
  38°14'·9N 21°22'·4E
- ⊕3  0·2M S of lightbuoy off Ák Evinos
  38°16'·86N 21°29'·16E WGS84
- ⊕4  Mid-channel of Rion – Andírrion Strait
  38°19'·25N 21°46'·45E
- ⊕5  Mid-channel between Ák Mórnos and Ák Dhrepanon
  38°21'·22N 21°52'·19E WGS84
- ⊕6  SE end of Nísos Trizónia
  38°21'·49N 22°05'·47E WGS84
- ⊕7  ½M S of Ák Psaromíta light
  38°18'·9N 22°11'·1E
- ⊕8  ½M S of Ák Andromákhi light
  38°19'·5N 22°22'·7E
- ⊕9  1M S of Ák Mákri Nikólaos light
  38°16'·0N 22°33'·1E
- ⊕10 ½M E of Ák Kefáli (Andíkiron)
  38°21'·6N 22°39'·4E
- ⊕11 1M N of Ák Likoporia light
  38°09'·2N 22°29'·5E
- ⊕12 1M S of Ák Melangávi light
  38°00'·8N 22°51'·0E
- ⊕13 ½M W of Corinth Canal entrance (Posidhonia)
  37°57'·29N 22°56'·88E WGS84

attention on the Greek struggle than his presence – as he lay dying he is reported to have said: 'I do not lament for to terminate my wearisome existence I came to Greece. My wealth, my abilities, I devoted to her cause. Well, there is my life to her.'

Many yachts pass through the Gulf of Patras and the Gulf of Corinth – most are using it simply as a short cut to the Aegean, saving 150 miles on the trip around the Peloponnisos. For the yachtsman who is not in a hurry to reach the Aegean, the two gulfs, in particular the Gulf of Corinth, are good cruising areas with a lot of attractive harbours and anchorages. In the Gulf of Corinth the south coast is relatively straight and offers few secure anchorages, but the north coast is much indented with many attractive and safe anchorages separated by short distances.

## Weather patterns in the Gulf of Patras and the Gulf of Corinth

The prevailing winds in the summer are from the W. Across the low salt marsh on the N of the Gulf of Patras the wind is from the NW to WNW. In the Gulf of Corinth the high mountains funnel the wind so it comes from the W. It normally blows from midday until well into the evening and may reach Force 5–6 in July or August. The wind may also blow from the NE at Corinth and sometimes blows right down to the Gulf of Patras. Again it is funnelled into an E wind in the two gulfs. In Krissaíos Kólpos (Gulf of Krissa) and Órmos Andíkiron (Antikyrra) there is frequently no wind even when it is blowing strongly in the middle of the gulf.

In the spring and autumn the winds vary between W and E – depending largely on the winds in the Ionian and the Aegean. In the Gulf of Patras there are frequently violent thunderstorms which may last for some time in the spring and autumn. Waterspouts are fairly frequent here in unsettled weather and, believe me, you don't want to see a big waterspout in action.

Although gusts off the high mountains could be expected, in my experience they have been little stronger than the winds in the middle of the two gulfs. The mountains appear to funnel the wind (W or E) for the length of the gulf rather than act as obstacles off which gusts might blow. Only at the

Corinth end is this not the case with NE winds, where gusts blow off the high land with some violence.

# Gulf of Patras
(Patraikos Kólpos)

### KILLINI (Kyllini, Glarenza)
BA 2404
Imray-Tetra G16

### Approach
The harbour actually lies outside the Gulf of Patras 20 miles SW of the entrance. Castel Tornese on a hill inland of Killini is conspicuous from some distance away. The lighthouse on Nisís Kavikalidha is also conspicuous. Closer in the buildings of Killini and the harbour mole will be seen against the low-lying coast.

*By night* Use the light on Nisís Kavikalidha LFl.WR.20s12/9M (red sector 059°-092°) and the light on the buoy at the entrance Fl.G.3s. Castel Tornese above Killini is floodlit in the summer and can be seen from a considerable distance, up to 20M depending on visibility.

*Dangers* A reef runs out from the headland immediately NW of the harbour and it should be given a good offing as it can be difficult to see. Make the immediate approach to the harbour from the NE.

**KILLINI**
⊕37°56'·3N 21°09'·2E

### Mooring
Berth stern or bows-to the quay on the W side of the harbour. Care is needed of works in progress (see *Note* below). The bottom is mud, good holding.

*Shelter* Good shelter from the prevailing NW–W winds. Open to the E.

*Authorities* Port police and customs.

*Note* Work is in progress building the new quay on the W and the breakwater on the SE side of the harbour. Care is needed when entering and berthing.

### Facilities
*Water* On the quay.
*Fuel* In the village.
*Provisions* Most provisions can be obtained.
*Eating out* Tavernas along the waterfront.
*Other* PO. OTE. Exchange. Bus and train to Patras. Ferry to Zákinthos and Cephalonia.

### General
Known in Venetian times as Glarenza, the port was once an important link in the trade route around the Peloponnisos. It is difficult to think of this dusty little place, now the ferry terminal for Zákinthos and Cephalonia, being a thriving cosmopolitan place full of the sights and sounds of foreign sailors and merchants en route to or from the Orient. The port is not exactly a 'glam' spot to visit, but it can be a useful harbour en route to and from the Ionian.

The castle on the heights to the S was built in 1220 by Geoffrey Villehardouin and later passed to the Venetians who named it Castel Tornese. It was taken by the Turks during their occupation of the Peloponnisos and finally partially destroyed by Ibrahim Pasha in 1825. It is now being restored and is worth a visit – it commands superb views over the surrounding countryside and the approaches to the Gulf of Patras.

### ÁK SKROFA
On the northern entrance to Patraikos Kólpos around Ák Skrofa extensive works have been in progress for some years. The purpose of the land reclamation here is not known but may be linked to the huge harbour works at Plátiyiali or may be a separate project altogether. The results are unlikely to be of use to yachts.

### KATO ACHAIA
A small fishing harbour lying approximately 9M ESE of Ák Páppas. It is quite shallow and only yachts drawing less than 1·5m should attempt to enter it. The approach to the harbour should be made with caution and in calm weather as there is shoal water in the vicinity. Make the approach on a SSE course keeping an eye on the depthsounder and colour of the water. The end of the mole is lit Fl.WR.3s5/3M, but the light should not be relied on.

The entrance to the harbour is very narrow so have everything ready for berthing before entering. The harbour is usually quite full of fishing boats so berth stern or bows-to where possible. Catwalks

**KATO ACHAIA**
⊕38°09'·6N 21°32'·4E

have been built out from the rubble along the inside and if you cannot find one of these free you will have to take a long line to the shore. Good shelter.

Ashore there are a couple of tavernas which have good fresh fish.

## MISSALONGHI (Mesolóngion)

Imray-Tetra chart G13

### Approach

*Conspicuous* The white lighthouse on Nisís Áy Sóstis and the group of houses at the entrance to the canal will be seen first. The red and green buoys marking the entrance to the dredged channel are difficult to pick out from the distance and in bad visibility it can be quite a job finding them until close to. Once the buoys are located the canal is marked out by four pairs of beacons.

*By night* Use the light on Nisís Áy Sóstis Fl.WR.5s17/14M (red sector 293°-010°) and the lights on the outer buoys Fl.R.4·5s and Fl.G.4·5s. The channel beacons are lit (all Q.R and Q.G.3M). The lights on the buoys at the seaward end can be very difficult to locate and the lights of the beacons marking the channel are not easily seen against the lights of the town.

*Note* The canal is dredged to a least depth of 6m. In parts there are depths of 8m. At the entrance to the basin don't cut the corner but head for the middle of the basin to clear the shallows on the E.

### Mooring

Stern or bows-to or alongside the N quay. Most yachts elect to go alongside. The bottom is mud, excellent holding.

*Shelter* Excellent shelter from all winds although the prevailing wind pushes a chop across the large basin into the NE corner.

*Authorities* Port police and customs.

*Note* The W end of the harbour now has a quay

**MISSALONGHI**
⊕38°18'·75N 21°25'·0E

*Stilt houses at the entrance to Missalonghi*

along it with a stub pier in the middle. There is talk of this becoming a marina, but at the time of publication no further works were in evidence. At present yachts can berth alongside where there is good shelter with the prevailing wind blowing you off the quay.

*Anchorage* Yachts can anchor in the SW corner where there is good shelter.

### Facilities
*Water* On the quay. Showers in the hotel SE of basin.
*Fuel* In the town a considerable distance (30 minutes' walk) away. You may be able to arrange for a mini-tanker to come to the quay.
*Repairs* Some mechanical repairs. Hardware shops.
*Provisions* Good shopping for all provisions. Ice available.
*Eating out* Hardly a good taverna for a town of this size. Avoid any in the town that are labelled 'Self Service Caféteria'. The taverna at the harbour is as good as any. The cafés around the central square are pleasant enough.
*Other* PO. OTE. Bank. Bus to Athens.

### General
Neither the harbour nor the town of Missalonghi has much charm, but the locals are friendly and somehow Missalonghi grows on you. When you eventually get through all the reinforced concrete and dust to the town square and sit down in a café for a beer or two, Missalonghi seems a little more charming and after a while you quite get to like the place.

The entrance to the canal has some interesting fishermen's houses standing on stilts in the shallow water, looking like something out of SE Asia. The picture is reinforced by locals up to their knees in the salt marsh pushing rakes through the mud to collect shellfish, mostly the enormous golden-shelled fan mussel. The surrounding salt marsh supports a variety of water birds.

Those visiting Missalonghi for its associations with Byron will be disappointed for there is little to see and little to remind us that Byron died here. There is a statue of the poet and a small museum houses a few relics from the War of Independence,

but just as it had never been heard of before Byron died here, so it seems to have slipped back into an anonymity fostered by the featureless salt marsh all around it.

## KRIONERI
38°20'·5N 21°36'·5E
Situated under the steep slopes of Mt Varasavon (922m) the open bay offers limited protection from the prevailing winds. There are 2–5m depths in the middle section of the short pier off the village where some shelter from E winds can be gained. The extremity and E side of the pier is shallow. Taverna on the waterfront.

**Caution** The shoal water off Ák Evinos between Missalonghi and Krionéri is marked at its extremity by a S cardinal lightbuoy Q(6)+LFl.15s.

⊕3  0·2M S of lightbuoy off Ák Evinos 38°16'·86N 21°29'·16E WGS84

## PATRAS (Limín Patron, Pátrai)
BA 2404
Imray-Tetra G13

### Approach
*Conspicuous* The buildings of the city are easily identified from some distance off. The dome of Áy Andreas church is conspicuous close to the S entrance to the harbour. A chimney is conspicuous just inland from the N entrance. The outer breakwater is quite low and it can be difficult to identify until closer in, but the cargo ships and ferries within the harbour show up well.
*By night* The S entrance is lit: Fl.G.3M on the inner breakwater/Fl.R on the buoy off the breakwater. The N entrance is lit: Fl.G.5s8M and F.R on the buoy off the yacht 'marina'. The elbow of the detached breakwater is lit Fl.G.1·5s3M. The harbour lights are difficult to distinguish against the lights of the city until 1–2 miles off. On calm nights there are numerous fishing boats with bright lamps outside the harbour whose bright lights bobbing up and down in the swell give the appearance of navigation lights. The aero beacon Fl.R on Profitis (6½ miles SE of Ák Páppas) shows up well.
*VHF* Ch 16, 12 for port authorities. Ch 12 for Nautilus Yachting (call sign *Nautilus*).
*Dangers*
1. With the brisk prevailing breeze from the W there can be a confused sea off the breakwater, bothersome rather than dangerous.
2. Large ferries are constantly coming and going from the port and a good lookout must be kept in the approaches and the harbour itself.

*Note* Yachts should make for the yacht harbour at the N end of the commercial harbour. Large yachts should call up the harbour authorities in advance to arrange a berth in the commercial harbour.

### Mooring
*Patras Yacht Harbour*
The entrance to the yacht harbour is difficult to

**PATRAS**
⊕38°15′·6N 21°44·0E

**PATRAS YACHT HARBOUR**
⊕38°15′·7N 21°44′·2E

identify until close to. Once into the entrance keep close to the breakwater as the harbour shallows towards the quay. Go stern or bows-to where directed or where convenient. Most berths have laid moorings tailed to the quay or to a small buoy.

*Shelter* All round shelter.

*Authorities* Harbourmaster. Charge band 2.

### Patras commercial harbour

Go alongside or stern-to the central pier. It is often difficult to find a berth here as workboats and tugs occupy much of the quay space. Large yachts should arrange a berth in advance.

*Shelter* Adequate shelter although the coming and going of tugs, workboats and ferries creates a lot of wash in the harbour.

*Authorities* Port police. Customs. Immigration. A port of entry.

### Facilities

*Services* Water and electricity in the yacht harbour. Toilets and showers in the yacht harbour.

*Fuel* Near the central pier in the commercial harbour. A tanker can deliver to the commercial harbour. A mini-tanker may deliver to the yacht harbour.

*Repairs* A yard near the yacht harbour can haul up to 20 tons. Most yacht work can be arranged but for specialist work you will need to go elsewhere. Hardware shops and chandlers in town.

*Provisions* Excellent shopping for all provisions in town. Supermarket about 500m going towards Patras from the yacht harbour.

*Eating out* Tavernas and restaurants of all types in town. Bars and cafés near the waterfront.

*Other* PO. OTE. Banks. Greek gas and *Camping Gaz*. Hire cars and motorbikes. Regular buses to Athens, around a 2½ hour trip. Ferries to Ithaca, Cephalonia, Corfu and Italy.

S entrance to Patras commercial harbour

## General

Patras is the largest city in the Peloponnisos and the third largest in Greece. The city and the harbour are noisy and grubby but lively. You enter Patras thinking you will dislike it and slowly you end up quite liking it. The carnival (in late February and early March – traditionally ten days before Lent) is celebrated with as much gusto as Easter in Patras. The first time I entered Patras it was 0100 in early March and it was rather an odd experience to be handed sweets and hit on the head by masked strangers after a gruelling slog to windward. What do you do? Buy your own plastic club and mask and walk around hitting other strangers on the head as this seemed the proper thing to do during carnival?

Historically the city has always been important as a commercial centre and the western gateway to Greece. The city was celebrated during the War of Independence when the Bishop of Patras first raised the Greek flag here. This patriotism was remembered all over Greece for many years and was the subject of countless illustrations which can be seen in many of the museums. The Turks retaliated by razing the town, and the present city was laid out on a grid system.

The wine from the region is excellent despite the ubiquitous *demestica*, and a visit to the Achaia-Klauss wine factory that makes this and other wines is well worth while.

*Yacht harbour guardian* Llanos Vasilli ☎ 061 429130

*Nautilus Yachting* Can assist with berthing at the marina and provides other services including clearing yachts in and out of Greece (non-EU flags), fuel, water, provisioning and so on. A charge is made for services and it is mostly concerned with larger yachts.

Contact on VHF Ch 12. ☎ 061 622676/270019
*Fax* 061 621400.

## DHIAVOLOS RÍON AND ANDÍRRION
### (Strait of Rhion and Anti-Rhion)

This narrow strait, only one mile wide, is the western entrance to the Gulf of Corinth. A Venetian fort stands on Ríon (conspicuous) and another on Andírrion. A current of up to 2 knots has been reported to flow either way through this strait depending on the wind direction, though in my experience there is normally a W–going current despite the prevailing W winds. If the wind is against the current it is easily seen as a small patch of troubled water. Care needs to be taken of the numerous car ferries plying between Ríon and Andírrion.

The strait is lit on either side: Ríon Fl.6s6M and Andírrion Fl(2)10s10M.

In 1999 construction began on the Ríon Andirrion suspension cable bridge across the strait. At the time of writing construction is in full swing with two of the cable columns in place. The bridge will be a five span cable suspension structure with a total length of 2,290 metres. Air height for the bridge is not known at this stage but will probably be

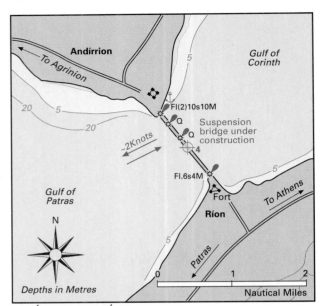

**ANDÍRRION AND RÍON**

⊕4　Mid-channel of Rion – Andírrion Strait 38°19'·25N 21°46'·45E

in the vicinity of 80–100 metres under the main navigable span.

At present the cable columns are lit by quick flash lights atop the structures or the cranes and are visible for a considerable distance off. The navigable channel will change as work proceeds but is at present about mid-channel.

Communication with bridge coastguard VHF Ch 08.

## ANDÍRRION 38°19'·7N 21°46'·0E

Immediately E of the car ferry ramps there is a very small basin. The entrance is around 20m wide and the basin itself is approximately 100m by 30m wide. There are 2m depths in the entrance and 1·5m depths in the outer part of the basin. It is recommended you do not use the basin as a matter of course, but in an emergency it could be useful for very small yachts. At the time of writing it is in the middle of the construction site for the bridge project.

# Gulf of Corinth
## (Korinthiakós Kólpos)

The Gulf of Corinth extends from Rion and Andírrion to the Corinth Canal. It is considerably indented on the N side with numerous natural bays and gulfs in which a yacht can find shelter. There are also man-made harbours on both the N and S sides of the gulf. Many yachts charge through the gulf intent on getting to or from the Aegean, and miss out on the delights of the places around the coast. You can usefully spend a couple of weeks dawdling around the gulf should you decide to take it easy and there are a number of sites ashore (Delphi and Corinth spring to mind) which are well worth a visit.

*Depths in Metres*

**NÁVPAKTOS**
⊕38°23´·55N 21°49´·72E

## NÁVPAKTOS (Lepanto)

### Approach

*Conspicuous* From the distance the castle walls on the hill above the town and the buildings of the town are conspicuous. Closing the town, the castellated walls of the harbour will be seen.

*By night* The entrance is lit Fl.G.2s3M.

*Note* The medieval harbour is very small so a yacht should have everything ready for berthing before entering. A large yacht should not attempt to get in here as there simply isn't room.

### Mooring

Go stern or bows-to on the S side of the harbour or off the fuel jetty or wherever there is room. Beware of floating lines from the local fishing boats. The bottom is soft mud, not always the best holding. The small harbour gets very crowded in July and August so you may not be able to find a berth – after all it doesn't take too many yachts to fill a harbour of this size. Crossed anchors are also something you can do little about given the difficulties of manoeuvring once inside and the lack of space.

*Shelter* Reasonable shelter from the prevailing wind although a prolonged westerly sets up a surge. Winds from the SW and SE funnelling into the bay cause a surge, though in the summer this is more uncomfortable than dangerous.

*Anchorage* If the harbour is impossibly full then you can anchor off the beach in settled weather. This is not the most comfortable place to be with the prevailing westerlies although they will usually die down at night. Large yachts (over c.18m) should anchor off anyway or they will simply block access to most parts of the miniature harbour. Off the beach the bottom is sand or mud, good holding.

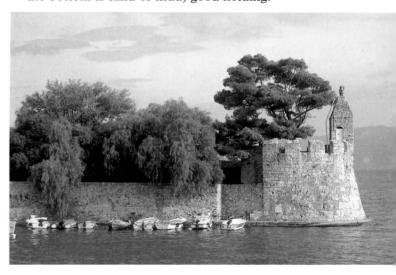

Návpaktos looking out to the E side of the harbour

159

Návpaktos looking NW

## Facilities

*Water* On the quay.
*Fuel* Close to the quay – a hose can be led down to the fuel quay.
*Repairs* Minor mechanical repairs. Hardware shops.
*Provisions* Good shopping for all provisions. Ice available.
*Eating out* Numerous tavernas in the town.
*Other* PO. OTE. Bank. Greek gas and *Camping Gaz*. Bus to Andírrion where you can get a ferry across to Ríon and catch the bus to Athens or Patras.

## General

The minute medieval harbour bordered by old plane trees and under the shadow of the Venetian castle (now a park) is a captivating place. It is a pity the same cannot be said for the reinforced concrete sprawl on either side of the old town. Nor is the harbour a quiet place – traffic rumbles and buzzes around the road by the harbour, the locals are an animated lot and it all goes on in the square by the harbour. Around the harbour some of the old houses have been turned into convivial cafés and restaurants. Take a wander around the E side of the harbour.

It is well worth a walk up to the castle to escape the hubbub. Návpaktos is well-watered and in the summer heat it is strange to hear water bubbling away when not so far away it is scarce. The town was known in medieval times as Lepanto and it was here that the Turks refitted before the disastrous (for them) Battle of Lepanto. The medieval harbour is one of the best examples of its type in the Mediterranean and should not be missed.

## ÁK DHREPANOU

At Ák Dhrepanou there is a cement loading quay used by coasters. Entrance is from the W by a buoyed channel. With the prevailing westerlies a swell is pushed directly onto the quay.

Off Ák Dhrepanou a lightbuoy (Fl.G.3s) marks the extremity of an old sunken pier and shoal water off the cape.

## KHILIADHOU

A small harbour on the E side of the low land running out to Ák Mornos. The entrance is prone to silting so care is needed in the immediate approach. Go stern or bows-to or alongside in the outer part of the harbour where possible. Care is needed as depths are uneven in the harbour and only yachts drawing 1·5m or less should try to get in here. Good shelter from all but strong S–SE winds.

Water in the village square and several tavernas ashore.

**KHILIADHOU**
⊕38°23'·4N 21°55'·0E

## MONASTIRAKI 38°24'·2N 21°56'·4E

With the prevailing westerlies you can anchor off the village here. Anchor in 5–8m on mud. Generally some swell tends to creep around into the bay and it is not the most comfortable place to stay for the night. The short pier and quay off the village has mostly less than 1m depths except near the end of the pier where there are 1–1·5m depths.

Water tap near the quay. Several tavernas.

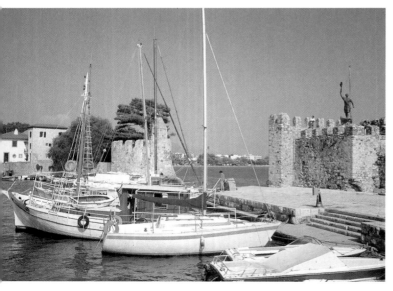

Návpaktos harbour looking NE to the entrance and E side

**RÍON TO TRIZÓNIA**

**TRIZÓNIA TO KRISSAÍOS KÓLPOS**

## MARATHIAS 38°23'·3N 22°00'·7E

Marathias village sits tucked under the W side of Ák Marathias approximately halfway between Monastiraki and Trizonia. Off the village there is a very small harbour in which a small yacht drawing 1·5m or less may be able to find a berth. There are 2m depths in the entrance decreasing to 1–<1m further in. Good shelter.

Tavernas ashore.

## GLIFADHA 38°22'·8N 22°04'·5E

A very small harbour on the mainland opposite Trizonia. The harbour is around 80m long by 40m wide. Entrance is at the SE end with around 2m depths in the entrance. A very small yacht may be able to go alongside the end of the outer mole where there are 1·5–2m depths.

Mini-market and taverna ashore.

161

# NISÍS TRIZÓNIA

## Approach

From the distance the island is difficult to make out against the nearby hills of the mainland. From the W a villa on the saddle of Nisís Trizónia stands out well and several other villas on the S side will be seen. From the E an escarpment on Nisís Áy Ioánnis is conspicuous. Closer in the village on the mainland opposite the island will be seen, but the small hamlet on the island and the entrance to the bay are not visible until you are near the anchorage.

*By night* With care a night approach is possible. The N entrance is lit Fl.4s4M. The fish farm in the bay opposite the SE end of Trizónia is lit by bright arc lights. The marina is unlit.

*Dangers* If proceeding between Trizónia and the mainland coast care is needed of the reef running out from the island for around 300m off the N side of Trizónia. Keep closer to the mainland coast than to Trizónia.

## Mooring

At present yachts go alongside in the marina. In the summer when it gets more crowded yachts should go stern or bows-to. Care is needed off the two jetties running out from the shore as it has been reported that there are large mooring chains running parallel to them ready to take mooring lines. If going alongside on the outside of the moles care is needed of ballasting and rubble near the mole although I found mostly 2·5–3·5m depths despite the rubble.

*Shelter* All round shelter in the marina. There are gusts down into the marina from the W–NW with the prevailing summer wind.

*Anchorage* Anchor in the bay keeping clear of the entrance to the marina. The bottom is mud and weed – good holding once through the weed although it can be difficult to do this in places. Keep

Trizónia 'marina' looking E towards the entrance to the bay

persisting. Good shelter although there are gusts into the bay from the W–NW.

*Note* Work appears to have come to a halt on the marina, although in its present state it is perfectly usable.

## Facilities

*Water* Available from Christo on the N side of the marina near the hotel. You will have to be in a berth on the N side of the marina.

*Fuel* Some distance from Glifadha, the village on the mainland opposite.

*Repairs* Christo in the house near the hotel can carry out *gardiennage* including engine and boat maintenance, and he has acquired a good reputation. He also has the metered water hose.

*Provisions* Mini-market in the village. Navpaktos is the nearest place for all provisions.

*Eating out* Several tavernas in the village and a restaurant at the Hotel Dryma and Lizzie's below.

*Other* Caïque ferry to the mainland opposite.

***Lizzie's Yacht Club*** Actually run by Alison. Not really a yacht club as such but a convivial restaurant and bar. Also showers, laundry, book-swap library and they will hold mail. Reached by road from the 'marina' or take your dinghy across to a small wooden landing stage.

Lizzie's Yacht Club, Trizónia Island, Gulf of Corinth, 33058 Doridos, Greece.
☎ 0266 71580.

## General

The land around the bay is green and lush – mostly vines and olives. The small fishing hamlet has changed little over the years despite the number of yachts using the sheltered bay. A few more villas have now been built on the island, but as yet it is still an out-of-the-way spot that has now attracted a surprising number of yachts for the winter.

Even if you do not eat ashore it is well worth your while to go ashore for an *ouzo* or brandy and coffee – sitting around the little square overlooking the small harbour you'll easily lose an evening.

**NISÍS TRIZÓNIA**

⊕6   SE end of Nísos Trizónia
38°21'·49N 22°05'·47E WGS84

**TRIZÓNIA**
⊕₁ 38°22'·06N 22°04'·77E WGS84
⊕₂ 38°22'·10N 22°04'·57E WGS84

## NISÍS ÁY IOÁNNIS

In calm weather you can anchor off this delightful islet in the eastern approaches to Trizónia. Anchor on the N side taking care of the rock off the N and E ends. With the prevailing westerlies it is usually too bumpy to stay here.

## AIYÍON (Aigion, Vostitsa)

BA 2404
Imray-Tetra G13

Opposite Nisís Trizónia on the S side of the Gulf of Corinth, the open bay of Aiyíon is the terminus for the ferry from Kallithea. There are a number of options for mooring here.

1. In calm weather go stern-to or alongside the E end of the ferry quay. If it blows strongly from the W or E it is not secure here.
2. Anchor in the bay on the W side under the small fishing harbour. Depths here are less than

**AIYÍON**
⊕38°15'·3N 22°05'·0E

163

elsewhere and you will be able to anchor in 4–6m on mud and weed. Exposed to E winds and only moderate shelter from W winds.

3. Small yachts may be able to get into the small fishing harbour on the W side. There are 1·5m depths in the entrance and 1–1·5m depths inside. Good shelter here.

Ashore there is good shopping for provisions and tavernas and cafés. Aiyíon is something of a provincial centre and generally has good facilities ashore.

## SKALA KALLITHEA (Áy Nikoláos)

Situated 4 miles SE of Nisís Trizónia. On the E side of the entrance is the small islet of Lagonisi and further into the bay there is another small islet with a chapel on it. Care is needed of the above water rock off Lagonisi. The bay hooks NW to give good

**KALLITHEA**
⊕38°20'·8N 22°09'·6E

shelter from W winds although E winds send in some swell. Open to the S. Anchor in 3–6m where convenient. The bottom is sand – good holding.

Some provisions ashore. Tavernas. Ferry to Aiyíon.

## ÁK PSAROMITA

The lighthouse on the cape is easily spotted from some distance off. On the E side there is reasonable shelter from the prevailing westerlies. The best place to be is tucked up in the NW corner where there are 5–10m depths to anchor in.

On the beach nearby is a large hotel with a taverna.

## ERATINI

A bay situated situated 3 miles NE of Ák Psaromíta. The large white hotel behind the beach to the W of Eratini is conspicuous and closer in a church in the village stands out well. The bay affords reasonable shelter from the prevailing winds though some swell rolls into it. It is not a secure spot in unsettled weather. Anchor in 5–10m off the village. A small pier has 3m depths at its extremity and a yacht can go bows-to if there is room.

On the E side of the bay a small *caïque* harbour has been built. There is usually room in here for a small

**ERATINI AND PANORMOS**
⊕38°21'·0N 22°14'·2E

Kallithea looking NW towards the town and islet

**KALLITHEA TO GALAXIDHI**

**ERATINI**
⊕38°21′·6N 22°13′·8E

Ák Psaromíta and lighthouse looking E

Eratini *caïque* harbour looking down from above the town

to medium size yacht to go stern or bows-to or alongside. Good all-round shelter in the *caïque* harbour.

Most provisions can be found and tavernas open in the summer. PO. OTE.

## ÓRMOS PANORMOS

The bay situated over the headland immediately E of Eratini. Anchor in 5–10m tucked up into the NW side. The bottom is sand and weed, good holding. Adequate shelter from the prevailing westerlies. E winds send in a swell. If anchoring in the NE corner care is needed of shoal water off the coast – easily seen in calm weather.

Tavernas open in the summer and limited provisions are available.

## ÓRMOS VIDHAVIS (Áy Pandes)

Lying 2 miles to the E of Panormos on the E side of Ák Dounos. The islet of Xeronisi off the cape is easily identified and Vidhavis lies at the W end of the conspicuous escarpment dropping down into the sea along this stretch of coast. Vidhavis affords good

165

Ák Andromákhi looking E. The light structure is difficult to make out until close-to

Órmos Anemokambi looking S

**VIDHAVIS**
⊕38°21′·2N 22°17′·9E

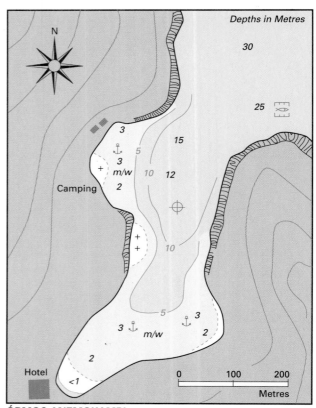

**ÓRMOS ANEMOKAMBI**
⊕38°21′·0N 22°22′·9E

shelter from W winds but E winds send in some swell. Open to the S. Anchor in 3–6m at the head of the bay. Good holding. A small harbour at the E end has just 2m depths at the end of the quay. Minimarket, telephone and tavernas ashore.

The bay is marred by the awful road scar right around it, but otherwise is an attractive place. In calm weather there is a pleasant anchorage in the bay just N of Xeronisi.

## ÓRMOS ANEMOKAMBI (Andromákhi)

An almost landlocked bay lying just N of Ák Andromákhi. The light structure on the cape is difficult to see until close to. In the approaches Ifalos Trakhilou lying 0·4 miles E of Ák Trakhilou, the S entrance point of Anemokambi Bay, has 3m depths over it. It is easily seen in calm weather. In the bight before Anemokambi inlet and on the N side of the bay there are now fish farms. Large buoys mark the limits of the fish farms and by day entry to the bay is straightforward, but at night care is needed.

Anchor where convenient in 3–12m. The bottom is mud and weed, good holding. Good shelter. There is a hotel at the head of the inlet with a restaurant. The new road around the bay has brought the hotel and campers in the summer, but it is still an attractive place and worth a visit.

## GALAXIDHI
Imray-Tetra G13

### Approach

The approach to the harbour should be made between Nisís Apsifiá and Nisís Áy Yeóryios until past the stone beacon on the reef E of the entrance and then into the harbour as shown on the plan.

*Conspicuous* Once up to Ák Pounda, Nisís Apsifiá and Nisís Áy Yeóryios can be distinguished. Apsifiá has a single tree on it and a white shed next to the light structure. Áy Yeóryios has a church on the S end and another on the NW end. On the headland sheltering Galaxidhi the buildings of the naval college are conspicuous. The beacon (roughly rectangular) marking the reef off the entrance to Galaxidhi is easily identified. Once up to Áy Yeóryios the buildings of Galaxidhi (the cathedral is conspicuous) will be seen.

*By night* There is a light on Nisís Apsifiá Fl.7s5M and a light off the W side of the entrance to the harbour (Fl.RG.1·5s3M  080°-R-216°-G-347°). A night entry is not recommended.

*Dangers*
1. Care needs to be taken of the reefs fringing Nisís Apsifiá and Nisís Áy Yeóryios – see plan.
2. Care needs to be taken of the reef off the E side of the entrance marked by a stone beacon. Although local boats pass between this reef and the coast, this passage is not recommended even with local knowledge.

### Mooring

Go stern or bows-to the quay on the W. It is better to go bows-to as ballasting extends some distance under the water. The bottom is mud and weed, good holding.

*Shelter* Good all-round shelter. NE winds send some swell in – more uncomfortable than dangerous. It has been reported that there can be a tidal surge similar to the *marrobio* experienced in some harbours on the S of Sicily, but I have yet to encounter any reliable reports of its occurrence here.

*Authorities* Port police.

**GALAXIDHI APPROACHES**
⊕38°22'·8N 22°24'·45E

Nisís Áy Yeóryios with the church conspic looking NE

Approach to Galaxidhi harbour looking SW. The rectangular beacon marking the reef (left) and the cathedral in the town are easily identified

Depths in Metres

N

Fl.RG.3M

Cathedral
(conspic)

Museum

Shops

Tavernas/bars

s/r/w

Pine

Kronos
Tomb

0          100          200
Metres

**GALAXIDHI**
⊕38°22´·7N 22°23´·4E

Galaxidhi looking from the E side of the inlet

### Facilities

*Water* On the quay.

*Fuel* Can be delivered by mini-tanker.

*Repairs* Limited mechanical repairs. Hardware shop.

*Provisions* Good shopping for most provisions.

*Eating out* Tavernas around the waterfront and others in the village. *Pension Gannymede* does an excellent luxury breakfast in the garden.

*Other* PO. OTE. Exchange. Greek gas. Bus to Itéa and then on to Delphi. Taxi to Delphi.

### General

From the distance the rocky islets and stony hills hide the tranquil narrow inlet of Galaxidhi harbour. Hemmed in by a pine-studded peninsula to the E and the town hunched on a rocky mound to the W, this harbour is one of the most pleasing in the Gulf of Corinth. In the 18th and early 19th centuries it was a prosperous port until the Turks occupied the area and captured the fleet. Near the harbour there is an interesting small museum displaying curios including some fine figureheads from its heyday as a thriving shipping town.

Today it lies as quietly as it has done for over a century and offers shelter only to yachts. It has a modest amount of tourism and some fairly sophisticated restaurants and gift shops (with sophisticated prices) will be found on the waterfront. This is a useful safe harbour near Delphi, which can be reached by the local bus or by taxi.

## ITÉA

Imray-Tetra G13

### Approach

*Conspicuous* The buildings of Itéa are easily identified. A large church on the waterfront and the silos of a flourmill near the W end of the marina are conspicuous.

*By night* The end of the pier is lit Fl.RG.3s4M (295°-G-355°-R-030°-G-111°).

**ITÉA**

⊕38°25′·8N 22°25′·5E

Approach to Itéa looking NE

Itéa Marina looking in through the entrance

*Dangers* In the approaches keep well clear of the islets of Molimenos and Stafidha which have reefs and shoal water around them.

*Note* Yachts should make for the marina. The entrance is difficult to see until close to, but it is obvious where it is.

### Mooring

*Note* At the time of publication work is still in progress on parts of the marina, although the harbour works are basically complete.

At present yachts go alongside where convenient. In the future laid moorings will be installed and yachts will go stern or bows-to.

*Shelter* Good all-round shelter although a surge can build up with southerlies.

*Authorities* Port police. Customs.

### Facilities

*Services* Water and electricity points to be installed. There are some water points near the marina where you may be able to get water.

*Fuel* In the town. Can be delivered by mini-tanker.

*Repairs* Basic mechanical and engineering repairs.

*Provisions* Good shopping for all provisions nearby. Ice available.

*Eating out* Numerous restaurants and bars along the waterfront. Some more ethnic haunts in the back-streets.

*Other* PO. OTE. Banks. Bus to Athens which stops at Delphi.

### General

Itéa is an odd little town. It survives on the dark red haemetite iron ore extracted just around the coast and also services the agricultural hinterland. The waterfront is a line of tavernas and bars and a thoroughly pleasant spot to stroll along if the wind is not blowing its usual cloud of gritty red dust over the town. Itéa is a dusty spot and everything gets covered by the greasy red dust, including any yachts in the marina.

Behind the waterfront the town is a pleasantly old-fashioned place as it gets few tourists except those stranded here en route to or from Delphi.

### ITÉA FISHING HARBOUR

On the W side of the town there is a fishing harbour affording good all-round protection. However there are only 1–1·5m depths in the entrance and along the outer breakwater. Most of the harbour is very shallow. Small craft drawing less than 1m could get in here with care. Good all-round shelter inside.

### ÓRMOS SALONA (Krissa)

BA 2405
Imray-Tetra G13

Lying at the NW extremity of Krissaíos Kólpos, there are a number of sheltered coves bordering the bay, but the opencast mines on the coast hideously scar it and with any wind a haematite red stains the sea and the surrounding land. Recently fish farms have been built in some of the coves so there is really little point in heading up into the bay.

It was in this bay that Frank Abney Hastings proved the worth of a steam-powered ship in more ways than one. With a small escort he steamed into the bay and destroyed a much bigger Turkish fleet.

## DELPHI

Ancient Delphi is easily visited from Galaxidhi or Itéa and although acknowledged as one of the most spectacular and beautiful classical sites in Greece, it is for my taste, also spectacularly overcrowded in summer, when there are frequently twenty to thirty coaches lining the road. It is best visited in spring or autumn.

Delphi was regarded by the ancients as the centre of the world. Its spectacular site amidst ravines, rocky bluffs and sheer cliffs on the side of Mt Parnassos contributes for a large part to its air of mystery. It takes its name from Apollo Elphinos when the god was worshipped in the shape of a dolphin. As well as Apollo other gods were associated with Delphi, notably Dionysus and Athena. The Delphic oracle was famous throughout Greece - it is interesting to note that the interpretations were vague and often obscene but had the reputation of being more truthful than elsewhere. Its fame diminished during the Roman times.

The French school began excavating the site in 1892 and have continued to do much of the work. A museum houses most of the important finds.

Not only could he manoeuvre under power but his iron hull was less susceptible to damage. According to H. M. Denham he used hot shot (heated in the boilers) because he feared solid shot would simply go straight through an enemy ship without doing any real damage. It is somewhat ironic that the place where an iron ship was first used for combat in Greece is now a mass of mines extracting iron ore.

## ÓRMOS ANDÍKIRON (Antikyrra)
BA 2405
Imray-Tetra G13

This large bay to the E of Ák Mákri-Nikólaos has a number of anchorages around it that can be used by a yacht depending on wind and sea. The whole bay is surrounded by steep slopes and split by spectacular ravines. It is an impressive coast to sail around although the high mountains mean that there can be severe gusts at times.

Andíkiron looking NE onto the town quay

**ÓRMOS ANDÍKIRON**

⊕**10** ½M E of Ák Kefáli (Andíkiron)
38°21'·6N 22°39'·4E

*Órmos Veresses* Lies immediately NW of Ák Trakhilos. Affords good shelter with W winds. Untenable with NE–E winds. Anchor in 3–10m.

*Órmos Isidhorou* Lies on the S side of Kefalí, the high headland on the W side of Andíkiron proper. Good shelter from W and NE–E winds, although westerlies may creep around Ák Pangalos and up into here. Anchor in 5–10m. Care needs to be taken of large concrete mooring blocks on the bottom off the beach by the café. Café ashore.

Immediately W of Isidhorou are two other bays worth exploring.

*Andíkiron* The large bay entered between Kefalí on the W and Ák Mounda on the E. The town of Andíkiron (Aspra Spitia) around the head of the bay and the factory 'suburb' on the NE (tower blocks conspicuous) is easily identified. On the W side of the bay there is a military base and on the SW side two large red and white mooring buoys

**ANDÍKIRON**
⊕38°22'·6N 22°37'·9E

**ÁY SARANDA**
⊕38°14'·2N 22°53'·2E

171

**KÓLPOS ALKIONÍDHON AND ÓRMOS KORINTHOU**

Within the map:

0     5
Nautical Miles

Ó. Vourlias

Paralia
Fl.R.3s3M
40
Vr
Alatonisi
Ó. Saranda

Ó. Vathi
Ó. Áy Ioannou

Áy Nikoláou
Aliki
Fl.R.3s3M
Kalamaki

Kólpos
Domvrainis
Ó. Alikis

Órmos
Livadhostrou
Á. Vasilios
Fl.G.3s3M

Porto
Germeno

N. Vroma

Ák.
Petritis
Á.
Panayia
Ák. Pounda

Órmos
Germenou
Fl.R.2s3M

N.
Tambourlo

N. Fonias

N. Gromboloura

Ák. Germenou

N. Makronisos

Ák. Psathas

Depths in Metres

N. Alkionidhes
(Kala Nisia)

Kólpos
Alkionídhon

Órmos Psathas

Psatha

N. Dhaskalio
N. Praso
N. Glaronisi

N. Zoodhokhos
Pigi

Kato
Alepokhori

Ó. Skalosia

Ó.
Skhoinou Mavrolimnos

Ák. Sterna

Kiato
Fl.G.6M

Lt Ho.
Ák. Melangávi
Fl.10s58m17M

Ln Vouliagmeni

12

Órmos
Korinthou

Ó. Agriliou

Panayia

YERANEIA ORI

Ó. Loutrakiou
Loutraki

Vrakhati

Iso.G.2s10M

Iso.R.2s10M

Fl.G.3s3M

13

CORINTH

Corinth
Canal

⊕12  1M S of Ák Melangávi light
38°00'·8N 22°51'·0E
⊕13  ½M W of Corinth Canal entrance
(Posidhonia)
37°57'·29N 22°56'·88E WGS84

---

(lit: Q.R). Yachts can go stern or bows-to on the W side of the new pier. Care is needed of some underwater rubble, but on the outer end depths are deep enough so that you can easily get close to the pier. Good shelter behind the pier.

Alternatively anchor off although the depths drop off considerably so you will be anchoring in 10–15m.

Water and electricity points on the pier. Fuel in the town. Good shopping for provisions and tavernas and cafés on the waterfront. PO. Bank.

**Órmos Grammatikon** The bay in the SE of Andíkiron. The bay is designated as a military zone and although a yacht may anchor here, photographs of the area are forbidden.

## ÓRMOS ÁY SARANDA (Saranti)

The large bay lying 6 miles E of Ák Velanidhia. The bay affords reasonable shelter from westerlies, but with easterlies a swell runs into the bay and unless you can get into the small harbour it can be uncomfortable. Depths are considerable right up to the head of the bay and you will usually have to anchor in 12–15m. It is difficult to tuck right up into

the NW corner because of the local boats on permanent moorings here. If you can get in go stern or bows-to or alongside the end of the mole of the small harbour in the NW corner. Good shelter in here from W and E winds.

Some provisions available ashore and several tavernas.

## KÓLPOS DOMVRAINIS (Dobrena)

The much-indented gulf lying E of Ák Tambourlo. A number of small islands are peppered across the entrance. In the gulf the prevailing wind is often an E–NE wind which can gust down off the steep slopes around the gulf. There are a number of anchorages around the gulf.

**Órmos Vathi Naoussa** A deeply indented bay in the NW corner of the gulf. Harbour works are reported to be in progress at the head of the bay, but as yet there is no indication of what is to be built. Anchor in 5–10m near the head of the bay. Good shelter from the E–NE although there are often gusts down into the bay.

**Órmos Áy Ioannou** A double-headed bay immediately E of Vathi. Anchor off the hamlet in the NW arm of the bay in 5–10m. The setting of the bay is spectacular under steep slopes. You can also anchor in the NE arm of the bay in 6–10m.

*Áy Nikoláou* An exposed anchorage off the beach in the NE corner. Suitable in calm weather.

*Aliki* 38°11'·9N 23°02'·8E The bay on the E side of the gulf. A light is exhibited at the end of a stub mole: Fl.R.3s3M. Anchor off the village in 6–12m. The bottom drops off quickly. Good shelter from all sectors except the W. There can be gusts from the N–NE into the bay. The stub mole has just 2m depths at the end decreasing to 1m near the root.

Provisions and taverna ashore.

## ÓRMOS LIVADHOSTROU

A large bay immediately E of Kólpos Domvrainis. On the E side Órmos Áy Vasilios affords shelter from E–NE winds. The bay is open W. Anchor in 6–12m depths in the SE corner off the village. Taverna ashore.

At 38°10'·9N 23°08'·5E the stub mole off the village has 1·5–1m depths off it, but is full of local boats. The end of the mole is lit Fl.G.3s3M.

## PORTO GERMENO

### Approach

Órmos Germenoú is the large bay at the NE end of Kólpos Alkionidon. At the head of Órmos Germenoú is Porto Germeno.

*By night* The entrance is lit Fl.R.2s3M/Fl.G.2s3M.

### Mooring

If there is room go alongside the end of the outer mole. There are good depths here up to the dogleg, but further in it quickly becomes shallow and depths are irregular.

*Shelter* Good shelter under the outer mole.

*Anchorage* You can anchor off in 5–10m. The bottom is reported to be shingle and rock, poor holding.

**PORTO GERMENO**
⊕38°09'·5N 23°13'·2E

### Facilities

A water tap near the root of the mole. Tavernas open in the summer. Bus to Athens.

### General

Porto Germeno is a local resort that attracts a fair number of Athenians in the summer. One reason to make the voyage up here is to look at the 4th-century BC fort of Aegosthena above the mouth of a valley to the S. The ancient walls are impressive with two towers still standing. The site was not historically that important, which may account for why it has remained intact for so long. (Important sites tended to be rebuilt using state-of-the-art military architecture.) Inside are the remains of a medieval monastery.

## ÓRMOS PSATHAS

The large bay in the SE corner of Kólpos Alkionidhon. Depths are considerable right up to the shore. On the S side of the bay is Kato Alepochori which has a small harbour off it.

*Kato Alepochori* The harbour is small and cramped so have everything ready before entering. Most of the quay is occupied by local boats and depths off the quayed areas are mostly 1m or less. You may be able to go stern or bows-to on the E quay. Alternatively anchor and take a long line ashore to the rough stone breakwater. Good shelter.

Ashore provisions can be found and there are several tavernas.

**KATO ALEPOCHORI**
⊕38°05'·4N 23°11'·2E

## MAVROLIMNOS 38°03'·7N 23°06'·4E

A large harbour on the S side of Kólpos Alkionidhon. Depths inside are unknown, although reported to be adequate for small to medium-sized yachts. Probably the best thing to do is send someone in with a dinghy to reconnoitre.

## NISOI ALKONIDHES (Kala Nisia)

A group of three small islands lying to the S of Kólpos Domvrainis in Kólpos Alkionidhon. With W or E winds shelter can be found anchored between Dhaskalio and Zoodhokos. A bar with depths of 1m or less connects the southernmost tip of Dhaskalio

**NISOI ALKIONIDHES**
⊕38°06'·7N 22°59'·4E

to the middle of Zoodhokos. Anchor in the cove to the S of the bar off the monastery on Zoodhokos (sheltered from the E and NE) or on the N side of the bar between Dhaskalio and Zoodhokos (sheltered from the W). The bottom is sand – good holding.

Once the islands supported a prosperous monastery, the buildings of which still stand on these lonely islands.

## ÓRMOS AGRILIOU

38°00'·5N 22°55'·4E

A shallow bight lying 3 miles E of Ák Melangávi (the lighthouse on the cape is conspicuous from the distance), this open anchorage has been used by some yachts waiting to go through the canal. It offers some shelter from the NE but is open to all other directions.

## ÓRMOS LOUTRAKIOU

37°58'·8N 22°58'·4E
BA 2404
Imray-Tetra G13

The open bay lying N of the Corinth Canal. Used by some yachts while waiting to go through the Corinth Canal. Large hotels conspicuous from the distance line the edge of the bay. It offers shelter from the NE but is open to the W and S. Anchor where convenient in 3–6m. The bottom is sand and weed with some rocks – the holding is uncertain in places.

# Corinth Canal

## (Dhiórix Korínthou)

BA 1600
Imray-Tetra G13

The canal is 3·2 miles long, 25m (81ft) wide, the maximum permitted draught is 7m (23ft) and the limestone from which it is cut rises to 76m (250ft)

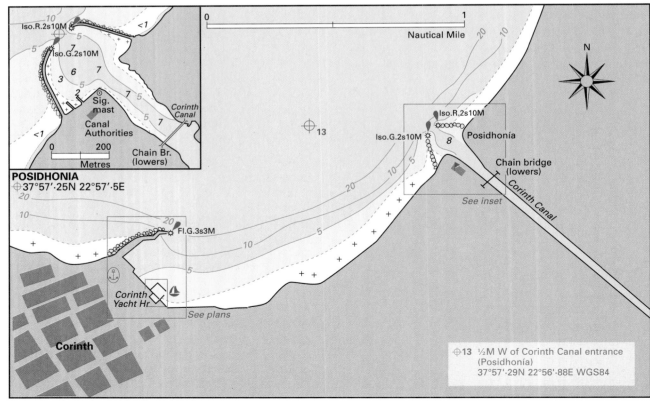

**POSIDHONIA**
⊕37°57'·25N 22°57'·5E

⊕13 ½M W of Corinth Canal entrance (Posidhonía)
37°57'·29N 22°56'·88E WGS84

**CORINTH CANAL - WEST ENTRANCE**

above sea level at the highest point. The canal is closed on Tuesdays to repair the crumbling limestone sides and for dredging.

A current of 1–3 knots is stated to flow either way in the canal depending on the wind direction. Certainly I have been through when strong westerlies have been blowing for several days and there was at least a 2 knot current. If you happen to get stuck behind a large ship in the canal further complications can ensue from the wash produced by its propellers which create a washing machine effect behind it.

There are two chain bridges across the canal near either end. The bridges are lowered down into the water and traffic lights indicate when to go or stop. When you are clear to transit the canal the bridges will be ordered to lower from the canal offices. The following signals concerning entry into the canal are displayed on a signal mast at either end of the canal.

| By day | By night | Signal |
|--------|----------|--------|
| Blue flag | One white light | Entry permitted |
| Red flag | Two vertical white lights | Entry prohibited |

The canal zone authorities use VHF Ch 11.

A yacht may have to wait up to three hours before entering the canal. Yachts normally go through at the end of the ship convoy heading in their direction. The paperwork and canal fees are done at Isthmia at the Aegean end of the canal. Moor alongside the quay on the S side of the canal. Large yachts may pay the pilot outside the canal – he will come alongside in a launch.

The ancients used to drag ships across the isthmus on a paved road (the *dhiolkos*), parts of which can still be seen on the N side. Octavian in pursuit of Antony after the Battle of Actium had his ships dragged across here. At various times the Greek and Roman rulers worked out schemes for a canal but Nero was the only one to start digging. Using 6,000 Jews, he didn't even get to the rock before insurrection in Gaul diverted his energies. The

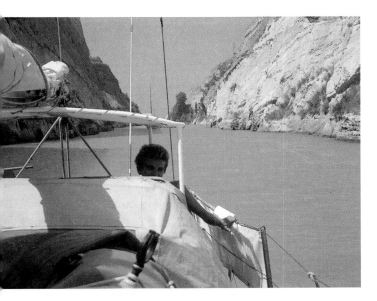

Corinth Canal going E

---

### CORINTH CANAL DUES

The Corinth Canal is probably one of the most expensive canals per mile in the world. Yachts are now charged on LOA. The charge is calculated using the following components:

Fixed dues
Passage dues based on LOA
VAT

In 2000 canal dues were around GBP£50 (US$105) for an 11m yacht and around GBP £80 (US$150) for a 13m yacht. Rates do of course vary according to the exchange rate as all calculations are in Greek drachmae.

Payment can be made in hard cash (Dx or US$) or by Eurocheque. Credit cards are not accepted.

On Sundays and holidays 30% is added and for night passages 25% is added. Yachts which attempt to alter their certificates or present photocopies will find themselves charged at a higher rate, which may explain some of the letters I get from irate owners complaining about the charges. It is difficult to predict what costs will be in advance due to fluctuations in the exchange rate and variations in the percentage increase of canal fees by the authorities.

---

present canal was started by a French company and finished by the Greeks in 1893. It was enlarged after damage suffered in the Second World War. Three bridges, a railway bridge and two road bridges, cross it at the maximum height of the cut.

*Caution* Severe gusts blow off the surrounding high land at either end of the canal. They are particularly bad at the Aegean end with NE winds.

### POSIDHONÍA

(Corinth Canal W end)

From the Gulf of Corinth the breakwaters protecting the W end of the canal are difficult to see. Closer in the canal office buildings for the W end and the signal mast will be seen. The entrance is lit Iso.R.2s10M/Iso.G.2s10M although the effective range seems much less.

When waiting to transit the canal the normal procedure is to potter around outside. This can be uncomfortable if westerlies are blowing strongly, but there are few alternatives. I have anchored inside the S breakwater, but the holding is bad here and the authorities frown on the practice. It is also possible to go alongside the very end of the N pier where there are just 2m depths at the end quickly becoming less.

**Note** When crossing between Posidhonía and Corinth Harbour, keep a reasonable distance off the shore as it is reported that shallows extend further than shown on the chart. A sort of semi-circle route is best.

### ISTHMIA

(Corinth Canal E end)

In effect you head for the NW corner of Kenkhreon Kólpos. When closer in the tower of the canal office and the breakwater protecting the entrance will be seen. The entrance is lit Iso.G.2s10M/Iso.R.2s10M.

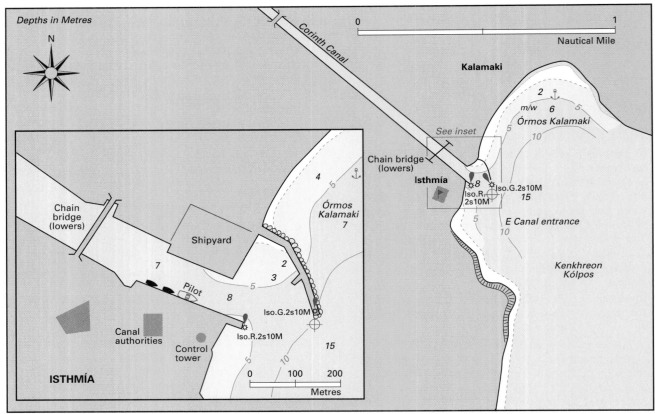

**CORINTH CANAL - EASTERN ENTRANCE**
⊕37°54′·9N 23°00′·6E

Small to medium yachts proceed into the entrance and tie up alongside the quay on the S side. This is fendered with large rubber bumper rails, but the quay itself is quite high and the black rubber bumper fenders are pretty unforgiving to topsides, so you should hang out every fender you have. Large yachts (25m plus) should call up the control tower and request the pilot boat to come out so the paperwork can be completed. You can also arrange an agent in Piraeus to do the necessary paperwork and pay on account.

Once tied up, go to the office in the tower and fill in the requisite paperwork and pay the canal fees. You then hang around until you can transit the canal. If a large ship is transiting either way pay attention to your warps as the water pushed by large ships in the confines of the canal significantly adds and then removes a large mass of water as the ship passes. This can snap mooring lines, with dire consequences. It may be better, if a large ship is going to pass, to go outside the canal entrance and hang around until it is time for you to enter the canal.

The small harbour on the N side under the breakwater does not have berths for transiting yachts. If you do decide to berth here for any reason care is needed of the ballasting which extends underwater for a short distance.

## Ancient Corinth

Ancient Corinth sits on a plateau behind modern Corinth, and the ruins of this infamous city deserve a visit. The ancient city commanded the passage of trade between the mainland and the Peloponnisos and across the isthmus between the Ionian and the Aegean. Consequently it was an important and rich city. The Corinthians were fine seamen and possessed a large fleet with which they founded and protected colonies in Corfu and Syracuse. Some believe the first trireme was built here. They paid particular attention to the gods of the sea, Poseidon and Palaimon. The latter was the protector of harbours and myth has it that he was originally Melikertes who was transported to Corinth on a dolphin.

The hard-living Corinthians were evidently hard-working as well. Their pottery was esteemed throughout the Mediterranean and from the 5th century BC the Corinthian style of architecture embodied in the Corinthian column became one of the most popular styles – continuing on through Byzantium and to the present day. From the 4th to the 2nd centuries BC Corinth earned a reputation for itself of a fast-living city where (in an age of loose living) the inhabitants were notorious for their vices. From this hedonistic age we get the term Corinthian, used in the early 19th century to describe a hard-living sportsman devoted to pugilism, horse racing and yachting! The term survives today as the name of various yacht clubs and football teams.

## CORINTH HARBOUR

BA 1600
Imray-Tetra G13

### Approach

*Conspicuous* The harbour is difficult to locate from the distance. The high-rise buildings of Corinth city are easily identified and the harbour lies immediately NE of the cluster of buildings. The harbour mole will be seen closer in.

*By night* Use the light on Ák Melangávi Fl.10s17M and the lights at the entrance to the Corinth Canal Iso.R.2s10M/Iso.G.2s10M (although the range of the canal lights appears less). The harbour mole is lit

**CORINTH**
⊕37°56′·8N 22°56′·1E

**CORINTH YACHT HARBOUR**
⊕37°56′·6N 22°56′·0E

on the extremity (Fl.G.3s3M) although it is difficult to pick up against the loom of the town lights. There are four large floodlights along the quay. The yacht harbour is lit F.R.3M and F.G.3M, though these should not be relied on.

### Dangers

1. With strong NE winds there can be severe gusts down into this end of the Gulf of Corinth.
2. With strong westerlies a swell piles up at this end of the gulf although once behind the mole you are out of it.

*Note* Yachts up to 20m or so should head for the yacht harbour. Yachts over 20m may have to berth in the commercial harbour and should contact the port authorities on VHF Ch 12 or 16 to obtain permission.

Corinth harbour looking S          *Claude Mauge*

Corinth yacht harbour looking towards the entrance

## Mooring

Go stern or bows-to under the outer mole where possible. Yachts sometimes go alongside, but this is just impolite and takes up quay space. If yachts are alongside ask permission to go alongside one of them. The bottom is mud, good holding. Very large yachts should berth alongside in the commercial port where possible.

*Shelter* Good all-round shelter in the new yacht harbour. The outer harbour is considered dangerous in strong NE winds.

*Authorities* Port police and customs.

## Facilities

*Water* On the quay. You will need to find the waterman.

*Fuel* In the town. A mini-tanker can be arranged to deliver fuel to the quay.

*Repairs* Mechanical and engineering repairs possible. Good hardware shops in the town.

*Provisioning* Good shopping for all provisions. Several large supermarkets in the town and a small fruit and vegetable market at the N end several streets in from the quay.

*Eating out* Tavernas in the town.

*Other* PO. OTE. Banks. Greek gas and *Camping Gaz*. Hire cars and motorbikes. Bus to Patras and Athens.

## General

Corinth is a bustling modern and thoroughly nondescript city – just the sort of place you would expect of a city that has been hastily erected after a series of earthquakes demolished previous cities here. It seems to be more of a crossroads for people going elsewhere than a centre for anything.

## VRAKHATI

A harbour lying approximately 7 miles W of Corinth on the S side of Órmos Korinthou. Off Vrakhati the mole extends out from the coast providing shelter from westerlies. The harbour is completely open to E–NE winds and you should not attempt to shelter here in these conditions. Go stern or bows-to or alongside the outer end of the mole. Care is needed as ballasting extends underwater from the quay in places. The inner part of the harbour is shallow.

Provisions in the village about 10 minutes' walk away. Taverna nearby.

## KIATO

Imray-Tetra G13

## Approach

*Conspicuous* The town of Kiato can be seen from the distance and closer in the high retaining wall of the harbour mole is easily identified. A cathedral with a red tile cupola and belfry is conspicuous behind the harbour.

*By night* The end of the breakwater is lit Fl.G.6M. A green neon light to the E of the harbour also has a good range!

**VRAKHATI**
⊕37°58′·0N 22°48′·8E

## Mooring

Go stern or bows-to or alongside the mole wherever there is sufficient room. The harbour is 15m deep near the extremity of the mole so if possible go alongside.

*Shelter* Good protection from W winds although some swell works its way around the end of the mole. Open to the E and dangerous with winds from that direction. With strong N winds it has been suggested yachts go under the high part of the sea wall rather than the low part near the root of the mole as sheets of spray come over the low part drenching any yacht berthed there.

*Note* Part of the quay is reported to have detached itself from the outer part of the end of the mole and to have subsided to sea level. Attention is needed on

**KIATO**
⊕38°00′·9N 22°45′·3E

entry and yachts should berth elsewhere in the harbour.

*Authorities* Port police and customs.

***Kiato fishing harbour*** The small fishing harbour immediately E of Kiato commercial harbour is usually full of local boats. The outer part of the harbour has 1·5–2·5m depths, but off the shore it is <1m. Small yachts may be able to find a berth in here although usually the locals or the port police will wave you away. If you manage to tie up, just feign incomprehension. Go stern or bows-to off the end of the outer mole taking care of depths off the quay. Good shelter from E–NE winds in here.

### Facilities
*Water* Close to the quay.
*Fuel* In the town. A mini-tanker can be arranged to deliver to the harbour.
*Provisions* Good shopping for all provisions in the town.
*Eating out* Tavernas near the waterfront.
*Other* PO. OTE. Bank. Greek gas and *Camping Gaz*. Hire cars. Bus to Athens.

### General
Kiato is developing into a popular tourist resort based on the good bathing beaches nearby. The surrounding land is intensively cultivated with citrus and the vine.

## XILOKASTRO

A private yacht harbour situated at the E end of Xilokastro village. The harbour is small with a difficult narrow entrance. Depending on members' boats in here you may or may not find a berth. The inner part of the harbour is 1–<1m, so berth in the outer part of the harbour. Good shelter inside.

Water on the quay. Tavernas at the harbour. It is around a 5-minute walk into Xilokastro to the E.

**XILOKASTRO**
⊕38°05'·0N 22°37'·5E

# IV. The Saronic and Eastern Peloponnisos

The Aegean Sea is entered from the west round Cape Malea or through the Corinth Canal, the southwestern and northwestern limits of the sea area covered in this chapter.

The Aegean takes its name from Aegeus, the father of Theseus, who flung himself into the sea when he believed his son to have been killed in Crete. Theseus had gone to Crete as part of the annual tribute of young Athenian men and women to the Minotaur, but with the help of Ariadne slew the monster and escaped. Ariadne was unceremoniously dumped on Naxos and perhaps the gods clouded his memory after this foul deed, because he forgot the prearranged signal to his father to tell him that all was well. If his ship carried a black sail then Aegeus would know his son had perished; a white sail would mean he was alive. Aegeus, seeing the black sail on the approaching ship, was overcome with grief and leapt to his death.

The Aegean geographically divides Europe from Asia, although the islands in the sea form a bridge between the two continents. Between the islands, without compass or sextant, the merchants of ancient times could cross the Aegean and be out of sight of land for only a few hours. Almost as important as the island bridge across the sea were the regular summer winds blowing from the north. These winds, now called by the Turkish name, the *meltemi*, were then called the *etesian* winds from the Greek *etos*, a year, because they blow regularly every year. Traders could sail across the Aegean with this wind and return in the spring or autumn when the northerlies are light and southerlies sometimes blow. The winter winds can be fierce and some ancient states forbade traders to cross the sea in the winter months.

The area covered in this chapter encompasses three significant historical centres. Mycenae at the head of the Argolic Gulf was the centre of the Mycenaean period, which succeeded the Minoans and provided the material for Homer's epics. Athens was of course the centre of Classical Greece, although it is all too easy to attribute too much to this ancient city and forget the contributions to art, oratory, science, and commerce from other city-states all over Greece. Lastly, the fleets of Ídhra (Hydra) and Spétsai were of key importance in determining the outcome of the War of Independence and both Navplion and Aigina were at different times the capitals of the newly liberated Greece.

## Weather patterns in the Saronic and Eastern Peloponnisos

The normal summer wind differs radically depending on where you are in this area. Along the mainland coast from the Corinth Canal to Ák Sounion and the sea area between the mainland coast and Methana, the *meltemi* is the normal wind. It blows from the NNE to NE at about Force 4–6, although it may be stronger around Ák Sounion. Around the Methana peninsula and Póros it is usually less. The *meltemi* starts blowing in July and dies in October. If the *meltemi* does not blow, (and it is not as regular here as in the Cyclades or the Dodecanese), the wind in this sea area is generally from the south, usually getting up about midday, blowing Force 2–4, and dying off about sunset.

Moving south and east, in Kólpos Idhras (Gulf of Hydra) and Argolikós Kólpos (Argolic Gulf), the prevailing wind is from the SE. It gets up about midday, blows Force 3–5, occasionally more, and dies down at night. In Argolikós Kólpos this wind can be relied upon in the summer for 90% of the time. Down the eastern Peloponnisos the wind may be a weak *meltemi* from the NE or a southerly from the SE or SW. In the spring and autumn the wind is predominantly from the S over the whole area and is generally weak.

In general there are few weather problems in the area. When the *meltemi* is blowing there are strong gusts off the high land near the entrance to the Corinth Canal and around Ák Sounion. Along the eastern coast of the Peloponnisos there may be a katabatic wind at night. Ástrous is particularly notorious for this wind which arrives without warning and often reaches Force 6–7 where previously there was no wind. It usually lasts for 4–6 hours. In the spring and autumn there may be thunderstorms accompanied by a squall, but these last only one or two hours on average. In the winter the Saronic and Argolic Gulfs have a mild sunny climate, making them popular places for yachts to spend the winter.

# Routes

Routes in the area covered by this chapter can be divided into three categories.

In the Saronic Gulf the yachtsman will come upon the greatest concentration of yachts in Greece. Most of these are based at the marinas along the Attic coast from where a considerable number of charter companies operate. Many charter yachts follow the Saronic trail to Aígina, Póros, Ídhra and Spétsai and to nearby harbours and anchorages, so if you wish to avoid the crowds in the summer stay away from the charter yacht milk run and head for the eastern coast of the Peloponnisos where there are less crowded harbours and anchorages.

1. **From the Corinth Canal heading E along the Attic coast and down towards the Argolic Gulf and Cape Maléa**

The prevailing wind in the Saronic Gulf is the *meltemi* blowing from the N–NE. To get to the marinas around Athens it is best to stick close to the Attic coast. Gusts can be fierce off the coast but the sea is generally fairly flat. Heading down towards Aígina and Póros you will be close or beam reaching and as you get towards Póros the wind usually moderates and may even turn to the S–SE.

If you are heading towards the Cyclades from Athens then stick to the Attic coast until Sounion before departing for the islands. It can get very windy and bumpy around the Kea Channel and will get no better further E if the *meltemi* is at full strength. When I used to skipper charter boats from Athens it was not unusual for charterers who just had to visit the Cyclades to change their minds and enquire if there was somewhere a little less windy to go to. It was a relief to jibe over and head to Póros and the 'milk run'.

From Póros to the Argolic Gulf the prevailing summer wind is the SE sea breeze and in general seas are slight to moderate. As the breeze does not get up until midday or so you can motor in the morning calm if you need to. Down the coast of the Peloponnisos the wind will often be variable or a light S–SE wind or, if the *meltemi* gets through, a fresh NE breeze.

2. **The reverse route from Cape Maléa to the Argolic Gulf and the Attic coast**

See the notes on rounding Cape Maléa at the end of Chapter II. Often you will find that once around Cape Maléa the *meltemi* is light and often variable up the coast to Monemvásia. At times it does blow hard and if that is the case you have few options except to bash up against it. It is worth trying to leave early in the morning when the wind is often lighter although there is usually a residual swell from the central Aegean making things uncomfortable. As you get closer to the Argolic Gulf the wind will become fluky and then eventually turn to the SE sea breeze. It is worth threading your way up through Kólpos Idhras to Póros and Aígina as although the SE breeze can be brisk, the sea is usually moderate.

To get from Póros and Aígina back to the marinas around Athens will entail either a wet and bruising beat against the *meltemi*, or if it is not blowing too hard, a more pleasant sail but still a beat to windward. At either end of the summer there is a higher frequency of southerly sea breezes and this makes the return to Athens an altogether more pleasant experience.

3. **Routes coming W from the Cyclades**

This is probably the most debated of routes by charter skippers. When the *meltemi* is blowing strongly I think it is worth doing a bit more distance and heading for Ídhra or Póros from the Cyclades. Generally you will get a good close reach from the southern Cyclades or a beam reach from the middle Cyclades. Once up to Ídhra or Póros you can run up to Aígina and on back to Athens.

Some charter skippers disagree and reckon you may as well beat back to Athens, though if you question them closely, what they mean is motorsail back to Athens. It really depends on how hard the *meltemi* is blowing as to whether it is worth beating back directly or taking the circular route via Ídhra, Póros and Aígina.

# Data

## PORTS OF ENTRY
Zéa Marina
Vouliagméni
Navplion

## PROHIBITED AREAS

1. It is prohibited to navigate in Órmos Salamís in an area half a mile off the southern shore between a point one mile and a point two miles E of Ák Petritis.
2. It is prohibited to enter an area NE of Órmos Elevsinos, one mile E of Limín Elevsis.
3. It is prohibited to navigate between Salamís and the NE side of the mainland except in a narrow channel in the fairway. It is prohibited to navigate in this channel at night.
4. It is prohibited to anchor outside the channel mentioned above.
5. It is prohibited to navigate and anchor in the northern part of the bay immediately N of Póros town where there is a naval college.
6. Nisís Ipsilí is used for target practice by the Greek Navy.
7. Although not listed as such, Nisídhes Karavi (36°46'N 23°36'E), three barren islets lying off the eastern Peloponnisos, are also used for target practice by the Greek air force.

## MAJOR LIGHTS
**Corinth Canal** (W side) Iso.R.2s10M
**Corinth Canal** (mole head) Iso.G.2s10M
**Órmos Sofikoú** (Korfos) Fl.4s5M
**Ák Kalamáki** Fl.2s6M
**Mainland coast**
**Ák Sousáki** Fl.G.10s12M
**Ák Káras** Fl.4s8M
**Ák Kónkhi** Fl.4s9M
**Nisís Psittália** Fl(2)15s25M
**Ák Filatoúri** Fl(2)14s5M
**Póros Themistokléous** LFl.G.6s9M
**Piraeus Harbour** LFl.R.6s9M
**Zéa Marina** (S mole) Fl(2)R.6s7M
**Mounikhías** (N mole) Iso.G.2s6M
**Mounikhías** (S mole) Iso.R.2s8M
**Ellinikón** (aero beacon) AlFl.WG.6s15M
**Nisís Fléves** Fl(3)10s8M
**Vouliagméni** (mole head) Fl(3)R.12s7M

**Aigina**
**Ák Plakákia** Fl(2)15s7M
**Ák Toúrlos** Fl.3·6s5M
**Nisís Moní** Fl(2)WRG.10s11·8M
**Nisís Lagoúsa** LFl.7·5s5M

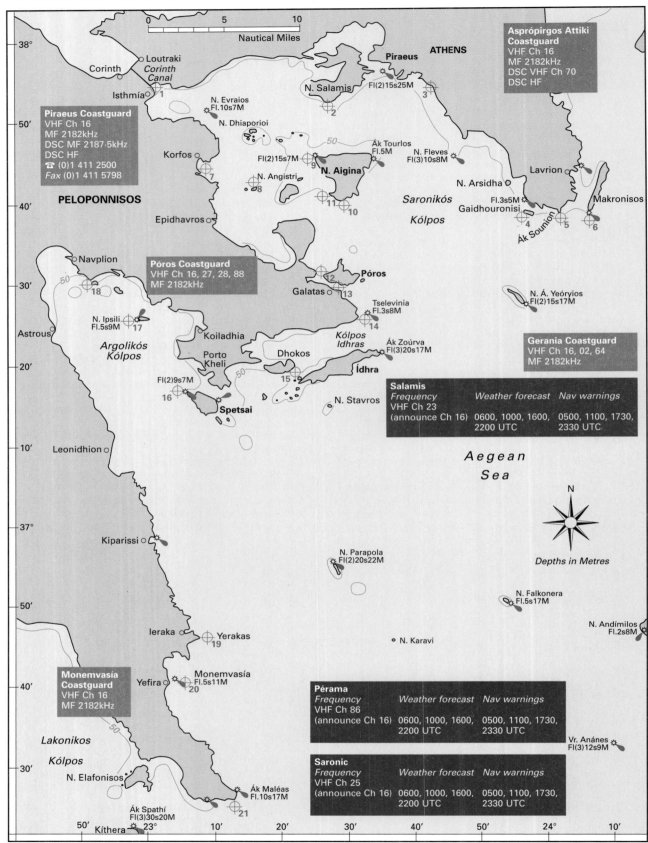

**THE SARONIC AND EASTERN PELOPONNISOS**

**Póros**
Ák Dána (N entrance) Fl.WR.4s8/5M
Ák Stavrós S Point Fl.RG.3s4/4M

**Ídhra**
Ák Zoúrva Fl(3)20s17M
Nisís Dhokós (SE point) Fl(2)WR.12s6/4M
Nisís Áy Yeóryios (SE end) Fl(2)15s17M

**Spétsai**
Ák Fanári (Báltiza) Fl.WR.5s18/14M
Ák Mavrókavos Fl.WR.2s5/3M
Nisís Petrokáravo Fl(2)9s7M

**Argolikós Kólpos**
Ák Kórakas Fl.7s11M
Nisís Ipsilí (SW point) Fl.5s9M
Limín Khäidhari (E point) Fl(3)WR.15s5/3M
Ák Skála (Nisís Toló) Fl(2)WR.10s6/4M
Ák Panayítsa Fl.1·5s5M
Ák Ástrous Fl.3s5M
Ák Sambateki LFl.7·5s6M

**E Peloponnisos**
Nisís Parapóla Fl(2)20s22M
Nisís Falkonéra (S end) Fl.5s17M
Nisís Monemvasía Fl.5s11M
Ák Maléas Fl.10s17M

**USEFUL WAYPOINTS**
⊕1 Eastern entrance to Corinth Canal
37°54'·9N 23°00'·5E
⊕2 ½M S of Ák Kónkhi (Salamina SW end)
37°52'·0N 23°27'·2E
⊕3 Marina Alimos (Kalamáki/Athens)
37°54'·8N 23°42'·1E
⊕4 ½M S of W end of Gaidhouronisi
37°38'·45N 23°56'·04E WGS84
⊕5 ¼M S of temple on Sounion
37°38'·63N 24°01'·31E WGS84
⊕6 0·15M S of S end of Makronisos
37°38'·56N 24°06'·25E WGS84
⊕7 1M S of Ák Trelli (Órmos Sofikou)
37°44'·49N 23°08'·93E WGS84
⊕8 ¼M N of N. Kira
37°42'·82N 23°16'·38E WGS84
⊕9 ½M W of Ák Plakákia (Aigina)
37°45'·8N 23°24'·6E
⊕10 0·10M S of Ák Pirgos (Aigina)
37°40'·29N 23°28'·82E WGS84
⊕11 S end Stenón Monis (Aigina)
37°41'·26N 23°26'·82E WGS84
⊕12 N Channel into Póros

37°31'·62N 23°25'·31E WGS84
⊕13 SE Channel into Póros
37°29'·61N 23°27'·74E WGS84
⊕14 S end of Tselevinia Channel
37°26'·05N 23°32'·15E WGS84
⊕15 ½M S of Dhokós SE light
37°19'·30N 23°21'·48E WGS84
⊕16 0·1M W of Petrokarovo light
37°17'·08N 23°04'·67E WGS84
⊕17 1M W of Nisís Ipsilí light
37°25'·9N 22°57'·1E
⊕18 1M W of Ák Megalí (Toló)
37°30'·6N 22°50'·3E
⊕19 ¼M E of Ák Yérakas
36°46'·17N 23°06'·90E WGS84
⊕20 ¼M E of Monemvásia headland
36°41'·52N 23°03'·89E WGS84
⊕21 ¾M S of Ák Maléas
36°25'·48N 23°11'·62E WGS84

# Athens and the mainland Attic coast

This section from the Corinth Canal to Ák Sounion is mostly mountainous barren terrain. Around Athens there is the large flat Attic Plain, much of which is covered by Athens and Piraeus and their outlying suburbs. There are a considerable number of industrial installations along the coast: the large petrochemical refinery near the canal (the gaseous by-products burning off are conspicuous at night); the shipyards and naval base near Pérama and on Salamínas; and numerous factories and mills between Pérama and Piraeus – in fact some 60% or more of Greek industry surrounds the capital. Between Piraeus and Glifadha the coast is lined by high-rise apartment blocks. A motorway and railway run parallel to the coast between Athens and the canal.

Athens is a comparatively modern city whose modern architecture compares badly with the

CORINTH TO SOUNION

## Quick reference guide

| Attic Coast | Shelter | Mooring | Fuel | Water | Provisioning | Tavernas | Plan |
|---|---|---|---|---|---|---|---|
| Órmos Kalamáki | C | C | B | B | C | C | |
| Salamís | B | AC | B | A | B | B | • |
| Ambelakia | A | AB | B | A | C | C | |
| Pakhi | B | AB | B | A | C | B | |
| Elefsina | A | AB | B | A | B | B | |
| Zéa Marina | A | AB | A | A | A | A | • |
| Mounikhías | A | A | B | A | A | A | • |
| Faliron | B | A | B | A | A | A | • |
| Kalamáki (Alimos) | A | A | A | A | A | A | • |
| Glifadha 4 | A | A | B | A | B | A | • |
| Glifadha 1, 2, 3 | A | A | A | A | B | A | • |
| Voula | B | AB | B | A | B | B | |
| Vouliagméni | A | A | A | A | C | B | • |
| Várkiza | B | A | B | A | B | B | • |
| Órmos Anavíssou | B | C | B | B | C | B | • |
| Sounion | C | C | O | O | O | B | • |
| **Peloponnisos and off-lying islands to Póros** | | | | | | | |
| Órmos Linari | C | C | O | O | O | O | |
| Frangolimani | C | C | O | O | O | O | |
| Órmos Dimani | C | C | O | O | O | O | |
| Korfos | A | AC | B | A | B | B | • |
| Órmos Selonda | B | C | O | O | O | O | |
| Néa Epidhavros | B | AC | O | B | C | C | • |
| Epidhavros | B | AC | B | A | B | B | • |
| Vathi (Methana) | A | AC | O | O | O | C | • |
| Limín Aigina | A | A | B | A | A | A | • |
| Perdika | C | AC | O | B | B | B | • |
| Skála (Angistri) | C | C | O | B | C | C | |
| Áy Marina | O | C | O | O | O | B | |
| Souvalas | C | A | O | O | C | C | |
| Angistri | C | A | O | B | C | C | • |
| Dhoroussa | B | C | O | O | O | C | |
| Áy Yeoryios | B | A | O | B | O | C | |

| | Shelter | Mooring | Fuel | Water | Provisioning | Tavernas | Plan |
|---|---|---|---|---|---|---|---|
| Methana | A | A | B | A | A | B | • |
| Póros | A | ABC | A | A | A | A | • |
| **Kólpos Ídhras and Argolikós Kólpos** | | | | | | | |
| Nisís Soupia | C | C | O | O | O | O | |
| Hydra Beach Hotel | A | AB | O | A | O | C | |
| Ermioni | A | AC | B | A | A | B | • |
| Órmos Kapari | C | C | O | O | O | C | |
| Limín Idhras | B | A | O | A | A | A | • |
| Mandráki (Ídhra) | C | C | O | O | O | C | • |
| Órmos Skindos (Dhokós) | B | C | O | O | O | C | |
| Báltiza (Spétsai) | A | AC | A | A | A | A | • |
| Dápia (Spétsai) | C | A | B | B | A | A | • |
| Órmos Zoyioryia (Spétsai) | B | C | O | O | O | C | |
| Porto Kheli | A | AC | B | B | A | B | • |
| Nisís Korakonisia | C | C | O | O | O | O | |
| Iria | B | A | O | B | O | C | |
| Koiládhia | A | AC | O | B | B | C | • |
| Khäidhari | A | C | O | B | B | B | • |
| Toló | C | AC | B | B | A | A | • |
| Navplion | A | AB | B | A | A | A | • |
| Ástrous | A | A | B | A | B | B | • |
| Tíros | B | A | B | B | B | C | • |
| Leonídhion | C | A | O | A | C | B | • |
| Poúlithra | C | A | O | O | C | C | • |
| Fokianas | C | C | O | O | O | O | |
| **Peloponnisos** | | | | | | | |
| Kiparíssi | B | AC | B | B | C | B | • |
| Ieraka | A | AC | O | O | C | B | • |
| Monemvasía | AB | AC | B | B | A | A | • |
| Palaio Monemvasía | B | C | O | O | O | O | • |

ancient monuments in the centre. It has grown rapidly as the young from the islands and rural mainland have arrived here by the thousands looking for work. Consequently the outlying suburbs have been built to house these migrants with little planning or thought and are particularly unattractive. The geographical situation is similar to that of Los Angeles, so Athens has a smog problem that is often worse than that of the smog capital of the USA – at times you will see the green-grey cloud of the dreaded *nefos* hanging over the city as you approach from seawards. It is not surprising that many have voted Athens the worst capital city in Europe. The city's population is over three million, about one third of the total population of Greece.

Although the natives of a particular island or region will always run down the natives of another island or region ('they are liars/cheats/thieves/etc.'), between the natives of Athens and the rest of the population there is a very real enmity. There are effectively two races in Greece: those Greeks who live in Athens and the others. I well remember being introduced to an Athenian on Spétsai with the admonition that he was an Athenian, but a 'good person' despite that handicap.

Athens, partly because of its position and communications and partly because much of the wealth is concentrated here, is the Greek equivalent of the Hamble or the French Riviera. Along the coast there are six marinas. The marinas are all crowded and although many of the yachts are owned by Greeks, still a very small percentage of the overall population takes to the water purely for pleasure. Most of the bareboat charter companies and the skippered yachts for charter are based at Zéa or Kalamáki. A yacht entering the Aegean will inevitably home in on Athens and its string of marinas for the facilities and availability of spares and nautical items which will only be found there. Apart from that, there is little point in going there as the surrounding sea is dirty and polluted and the scenery quite unrepresentative of the rest of Greece. You will have seen Athens but not Greece.

**CORINTH CANAL See Chapter III Gulf of Patras and Corinth.**

## ÓRMOS KALAMÁKI

While waiting to proceed through the canal or after coming through from the Gulf of Corinth, a yacht can anchor in Órmos Kalamáki immediately N of the canal entrance. Anchor in 4–6m at the head of the bay. Good shelter from the *meltemi* although there are strong gusts off the high land above. The bottom is sand and weed – only mediocre holding. Tavernas ashore. Fishing boats are kept on moorings here all year round.

## ÁK SOUSAKI BOATYARD

On the W side of Ák Sousaki approximately 2 miles E of Órmos Kalamáki there is a large boatyard. Anchor in the bay and go ashore to enquire at the boatyard. Boats are hauled from a concrete apron on the E point which has a reported depth of 4m. Hauling is by crane and the yacht is then stored ashore.

The yard is somewhat remote, but has become increasingly popular and there are now good facilities ashore. Most yacht repairs can be arranged. Taverna and café nearby.

# Nísos Salamís

## (Nísos Salamina)

An arid rocky island devoid of vegetation. It is much indented, but there are few anchorages available to yachts because of the extensive naval installations around the coast near which anchorage is prohibited. This is no great loss as the water is very polluted (a dirty oily brown colour with all sorts of objectionable flotsam) and the nearby coast is an industrial wasteland.

**Caution** For about 6 miles E of the Corinth Canal in Kólpos Kenkhreon (Gulf of Kenkhreo) there are strong gusts off the mountains on the N side of the

SALAMÍS TO PIRAEUS

⊕2   ½M S of Ák Kónkhi (Salamís SW end)
37°52'·0N 23°27'·2E

gulf when the *meltemi* is blowing. The gusts become less fierce the further E and S you go.

## NAVY PRACTICE AREA

The sea area between the Corinth Canal and Salamís is often used by the navy for exercises. Nisís Ipsilí in this area is used for target practice.

## ÓRMOS SALAMÍS (Salaminos)
### Prohibited Areas

1. In Órmos Salamís navigation is prohibited within half a mile of the shore between one and two miles E of Ák Petritis (the southern entrance of the bay).
2. Navigation is prohibited in an area around Elevsis in the Kólpos Elevsinos.
3. Except for a narrow channel in the fairway, navigation is prohibited between the NE side of Salamís and the mainland coast opposite. Navigation at night is prohibited. Large ships are not permitted to navigate (without special permission) in the area enclosed by Nisís Psittália, Salamís and the mainland (Órmos Keratsiniou). Anchorage is prohibited in the area.

## SALAMÍS (Salamina)
### Approach

Salamís village lies at the head of Órmos Salamís. The boatyard on the N side of the bay and the houses of the village are easily identified.

*By night* Use the light on Ák Káras Fl.4s8M and the light on the pier head at Salamís 2F.R(vert)3M.

### Mooring

Go alongside or stern or bows-to in the inner basin if you can find a berth. The mole and the pier are usually crowded with fishing boats.

*Shelter* Good shelter from the *meltemi*. Southerlies whip up a short chop across the large bay.

*Anchorage* Anchor in 3–5m in the bay clear of the

**LIMÍN SALAMÍS**
⊕37°57'·7N 23°29'·6E

approaches to the harbour. In the summer the anchorage is well protected although there can be gusts with the *meltemi*. The bottom is mud, sand and weed, good holding.

### Facilities
*Services* Water on the quay in places. You may be able to get a connection for electricity.
*Fuel* Close to the mole.
*Provisions* Good shopping for provisions.
*Eating out* Tavernas.
*Other* PO. OTE. Bus to Paloukia and ferries to the mainland (Pérama and Piraeus).

### General
The village has a run-down appearance, but the locals are friendly and it is a convivial enough place if you are hauled out at the boatyard. There are some good local tavernas nearby which often have fresh fish.

## BOATYARDS

To the W of the village there are a number of yards which can haul out yachts up to 40 tons. Hauling is by cradle and sledge in the old-fashioned way. They can carry out general repairs including some engine repairs and welding and machining jobs. Anchor off the boatyard where there is reasonable shelter from all but strong SW winds.

## ANCHORAGES AROUND SALAMÍS

*Kanákia* N. Kanákia light 37°54'·3N 23°23'·5E The bay on the SW end of Salamís with the islet of Kanákia lying off it. Care is needed of the reef and shoal water off the N and SE side of Nisís Kanákia and off the shore of the bay. Anchor at the N or S end of the bay where convenient. Good shelter from N–NE winds in the N end of the bay. The bay is a pleasant spot with pine down to the shore. Taverna opens in the summer.
*Kolones* 37°52'·6N 23°26'·5E A very small harbour

under the cliffs. The entrance is rockbound and you should reconnoitre first by dinghy. There are 3m depths in the entrance, but the inner part of the harbour has <1m depths.
*Aias* 37°53'·4N 23°28'·9E This small bay affords good shelter from the *meltemi*. Anchor off the beach in 4–6m on sand. Care is needed of the reef running out from the shore in places. There is a short mole in the NE corner, but this is used by the local fishing boats. Tavernas ashore.
*Órmos Peranis* 37°53'·7N 23°29'·4E The large bay immediately E of Aias. Anchor on the NW side or in the NE cove. Care is needed of the reefs on the W and N sides of the bay. Good shelter from the *meltemi*. Tavernas in the summer.
*Kaki Vigla* 37°54'·6N 23°30'·7E The large bay under Ák Tourlos. Anchor in N of the bay. Mediocre shelter only. Tavernas ashore.

## AMBELAKIA BOATYARD
37°57'·1N 23°32'·9E

At Ambelakia, on the E side of Salamís there is a large boatyard with the capacity to haul craft up to 100 tons. The yard is located in the SW corner of the bay with a quayed area and short pier where yachts can berth. The yard has a 100-ton travel-hoist and hardstanding ashore. All manner of repairs including steel and stainless steel fabrication, wood and GRP repairs, mechanical and general engineering repairs are undertaken and other work can be arranged in Piraeus.

Contact Theo Bekris, Bekris & Co Ltd, 18902
Ambelakia, Salamís (office) ☎ 1 412 5111, (yard)
☎ 1 467 1588/1 467 4120 *Fax* 1 453 2858

## ATTIC COAST OPPOSITE SALAMIS

Before pottering up around Salamis read the notes
on 'Prohibited Areas' at the beginning of the
chapter. Around the Attic coast there are two fishing
harbours where you may find a berth.

*Pakhi* 37°58'·4N 23°21'·7E A small fishing harbour
on the mainland coast N of Nisídhes Pakhi.
There are 5m depths in the entrance and 1·5–7m
depths inside. If there is space go alongside the
outer end of the mole. Good shelter. Water on
the quay. Tavernas ashore.

*Elefsina* 38°02'·3N 23°33'·1E A small fishing
harbour off Elefsina which is virtually a suburb of
Athens. There are 5m depths in the entrance.
Care is needed off the quayed areas which have
<1m in places. Go stern or bows-to where
possible. Good shelter. Water and electricity on
the quay. Provisions ashore. Tavernas.

## PERAMA

Perama is largely the industrial area on the E side of
Piraeus. There are a number of shipyards here with
associated facilities for engineering and mechanical
work. One of these yards is equipped for work on
yachts.

*Halkitis Urania Boatyard* Uses a 280-ton travel-
hoist. Max capacity is as follows: Weight 280-
tons/LOA 45 metres/Breadth 9 metres/Draught 5·2
metres.

All facilities at the yard including water,
220/380V, compressed air, showers and toilets,
communications, 24 hour security. All yacht repairs
carried out or arranged.

Halkitis Urania Boatyards, 104-6 Dimokratis Av, 18863
Perama, Piraeus ☎ 1 441 0182/402 0256
*Fax* 1 402 0262.

## PIRAEUS COMMERCIAL HARBOUR

This large harbour is for ferries and commercial
cargo ships only. A yacht should not attempt to
enter or berth here.

## ZÉA MARINA

BA 1596
Imray-Tetra G14

### Approach

The roadstead between the coast of Salamís and
Piraeus is crowded with ships (cargo and ferries) at
anchor and under way. Care is needed when
navigating through this maze, especially at night.

*Conspicuous* The multi-storey apartment blocks of
Piraeus and the outlying suburbs of Athens are
spread along the coast, making it difficult to identify
exactly where Piraeus and Zéa Marina are. A tall
chimney with red and white bands is conspicuous W
of Piraeus and the stadium at Faliron to the E is
easily identified. Between Piraeus and Zéa there is a
rocky bluff covered in apartments. Closer in,

Piraeus Commercial Harbour (there are always
ferries coming and going) and the outer mole of Zéa
can be identified.

*By night* The lights which stand out are: Ák Khónkhi
light on the SE tip of Salamís Fl.4s9M; the light on
Nisís Psittália Fl(2)15s25M; the lights at Piraeus
Commercial Harbour LFl.R.6s9M; the light on the
extremity of the outer mole of Zéa Fl(2)R.6s7M;
and the light on Nisís Fléves Fl(3)10s8M. The lights
are not always easy to pick up against the loom of
the lights of Athens and Piraeus. The entrance to
Zéa is lit: Fl(2)R.6s7M and Fl(2)G.6s4M. The
channel into Paşalimani is lit: Fl.G.1·5s4M,
Fl.G.1·5s3M and Fl.R.1·5s3M.

*VHF* Ch 09 for Zéa Marina and Sea Trade Marine.

*Dangers*
1. Care is needed of the large amount of shipping
coming and going from Piraeus and the
anchorage off it. Some of the new ferries and the
hydrofoils approach at considerable speed (25–30
knots) so keep a good lookout aft. There are
traffic separation zones for ships coming and
going from the Aegean, but do not count on
shipping sticking to the correct zone.
2. With the *meltemi* there can be gusts in the
approaches.

### Mooring

A marina attendant will direct you to a berth,
probably alongside the outer end of the outer mole
if you are only staying for a short period. The inner
harbour (Paşalimani) is generally full as most of the

**ZEA MARINA**
⊕37°56'·0N 23°39'·2E

berths are permanently occupied by Athens-based yachts.

*Shelter* Paşalimani has excellent all-round shelter. The outer harbour can be uncomfortable in strong southerlies when a reflected swell causes a surge to develop.

*Authorities* A port of entry: port police, customs, and immigration. Port captain and marina staff. Charge band 2.

### Facilities

*Services* Water and electricity (220v) can be connected to all berths. Showers and toilets.

*Fuel* Close to the quay or a tanker will deliver.

*Repairs* Mechanical repairs. All types of engineering work possible. Wood and GRP repairs. Most spares for marine engines and boat gear can be found or ordered. All repairs can be carried out including specialist marine diesel repairs, GRP work and electrical and electronic work. Marine grade stainless steel can be purchased and work carried out. Most types of exotic hardwood can be found. Galvanizing work. Propellers can be made to order. Masts and rigging can be made and repaired. Sailmakers. Good chandlers near the marina. Most charts and relevant nautical publications can be obtained. Excellent hardware and tool shops. If repair work cannot be carried out or organised from here it is unlikely it can be done elsewhere in Greece. Yachts are not generally hauled out at Zéa although a few occasionally are.

*Sea Trade Marine* offer a range of services to yachts including arranging a berth in Zéa, spares and repairs, chandlers, provisioning, bunkering and related services. All repairs and *gardiennage* can be arranged.

Contact: Sea Trade Marine, 4 Akti Themistocleous, Zéa Marina, 18536 Piraeus ☎ 1 451 1322, 451 1334 *Mobile* 0944 315970 (A Polemis), 0944 318353 (Mike Brewer) *Fax* 1 452 3629
*E-mail* sea-trade@ath.forthnet.gr

Zéa Marina entrance looking S

Paşalimani in Zéa Marina

*Provisions* Excellent shopping for all provisions. Several markets nearby. Ice can be ordered.

*Eating out* All types of tavernas and restaurants nearby.

*Other* PO and OTE at the marina. Banks nearby. Consular offices in Athens for all European and most overseas countries. Greek gas and *Camping Gaz*. Hire cars and motor bikes. Bus to Athens and from there to all over Greece. Underground to Athens. Ferries to most destinations in the Aegean. Hydrofoils to the islands in the Saronic Gulf and to ports on the eastern Peloponnisos.

*Enquiries* Zéa Marina ☎ 1 451 1480/451 3944/451 3623.

### General

Zéa is a dirty, noisy, crowded harbour and if you don't have a headache after arriving from some comparatively peaceful island you will be one of the lucky few. Yet Piraeus city grows on you. It has many amenities not found elsewhere in Greece: movie theatres with the latest films from the West End; a choice of restaurants (Chinese, Indian, steak houses, French, Italian); bars and nightclubs; English magazines and newspapers only a day old; and shop windows crammed with all the consumer goods you don't need (especially on a boat), but like to look at.

Near the commercial harbour over the hill from Zéa the markets and a warren of alleys with tiny shops stocked with a miscellany of wares are intriguing places to wander around. In the outer harbour of Zéa the luxury yachts of the very rich line the quay outside the marina offices – the brass gleams, the brightwork is immaculate despite the blistering sun, and the flower arrangements on the saloon table would probably pay for a week's mooring of a small yacht. And when you have finished with Piraeus then a trip into Athens – at the very least to visit the Acropolis and the National Museum – must be made now that you are here.

### MOUNIKHÍAS (Turkolimani, Mikrólimani)
Imray-Tetra G14

The almost circular harbour immediately east of Zéa. The harbour is administered by the Royal

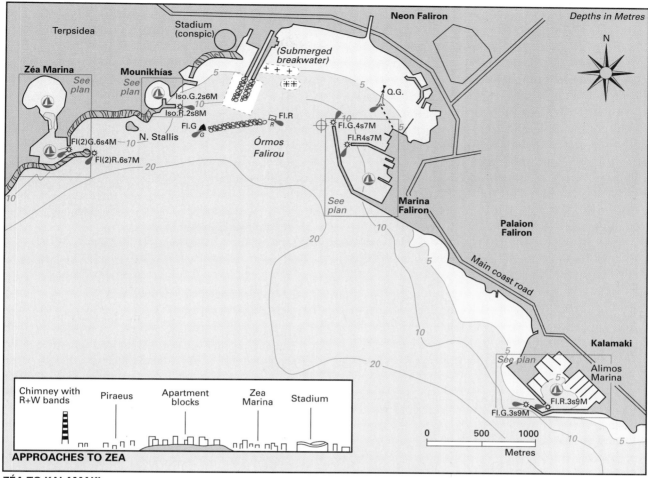

Depths in Metres

**APPROACHES TO ZEA**

**ZÉA TO KALAMAKI**
⊕37°57´·1N 23°40´·8E

Hellenic Yacht Club and foreign yachts are not always welcome here. The best policy is to go to Zéa and then check with the authorities at Mounikhías to see if there is a berth available.

### Approach
The entrance is straightforward.

**MOUNIKHÍAS**
⊕37°56´·3N 23°39´·7E

*By night* The entrance is lit Iso.G.2s6M/Iso.R.2s8M.

*VHF* Ch 09.

### Mooring
Moor where directed by the marina attendant. There are laid moorings to all berths. A lot of yachts are kept on fore and aft moorings in the middle of the harbour. Good all-round shelter.

### Facilities
Around the marina are numerous, mostly expensive, restaurants (specialising in sea food) and cafés. Provisions nearby. Yacht club.

### FALIRON (Flísvos)
BA 1599
Imray-Tetra G14

### Approach
The harbour on the E side of Órmos Falírou. The outer breakwater is easily identified.

*By night* The outer breakwater is lit on the extremity Fl.G.4s7M and the N breakwater is lit on the extremity Fl.R.4s7M.

*VHF* Ch 09.

Mounikhías looking ESE

## Mooring

Go stern or bows-to where directed or where convenient. Large yachts berth along the outer mole on the S. There are few berths for visiting yachts and most prefer to go to Zéa or Kalamáki.

*Shelter* The harbour is open to the N–NW and with strong N–NW winds it can get very choppy in the harbour.

## Facilities

*Services* Water and electricity can be connected to most berths.

*Fuel* Can be delivered to the quay.
*Provisions* Good shopping for provisions in Faliron.
*Eating out* Tavernas in Faliron.
*Enquiries* ☎ 1 982 9218/982 8537.

## ALIMOS MARINA (Kalamáki)

Imray-Tetra G14

### Approach

The marina lies about 1½ miles to the SE of Faliron.

*Conspicuous* A large blue hangar at the airport to the SE is conspicuous. Following the coast, the outer moles and masts of yachts moored within will soon be seen. Immediately W of the marina a green lawn in a cemetery with a conspicuous white cross can be identified. The entrance is not apparent until you are right up to the marina.

*By night* The entrance is lit: Fl.G.3s9M/Fl.R.3s9M. Despite the range of the lights they can be difficult to see against the bright flashing lights along the waterfront.

*VHF* Ch 09, 16.

FALIRON
⊕37°56′·1N 23°40′·8E

ALIMOS MARINA (KALAMAKI)
⊕37°54′·8N 23°42′·1E

*Dangers* Care must be taken of the reef running SW from Ák Áy Kósmas about 1 mile S of the Marina. A light tower stands towards the end of the reef: light Q(9)15s5M.

## Mooring

Go stern or bows-to under the W mole wherever you can. There are laid moorings tailed to a buoy or to the quay. The visitors' quay is theoretically along the inner W mole (berths A–E), but it is so congested here with permanent berth holders that it can be exasperating trying to find a berth. Asking at the office normally doesn't help at all.

*Shelter* Excellent all-round shelter.

*Authorities* Port police and customs. Port captain and marina staff. Charge band 2.

*Note* The marina has little security and a number of yachtsmen have asked me to mention that a 'minder' is virtually mandatory. Lone females should be wary of wandering around at night.

## Facilities

*Services* Water and electricity (220v) near every berth. Showers and toilets near the office.

*Fuel* On the quay.

*Repairs* Most mechanical repairs. Light engineering work including stainless steel work can be arranged. Wood and GRP repairs. Electrical and electronic repairs. Sailmaker. Chandlers along the main coast road. Yachts can be craned onto the hard in the marina if there is room.

*Provisions* Good shopping for provisions nearby. Ice available.

*Eating out* Tavernas along the coast road and also on the beach side. There are some good local tavernas tucked up in the streets behind the main coast road.

*Other* PO, OTE, and banks in Faliron. Greek gas and *Camping Gaz*. Hire cars and motorbikes. Regular buses into Athens and Piraeus from outside the marina.

*Enquiries* ☎ 1 982 8642/981 3315/982 1850.

## General

Kalamáki is a comparatively new marina and has quickly filled up with yachts. The surrounding suburbs are drab apartment blocks and the marina is not much better. One of the things which has blighted Kalamáki and its environs, the noise of large jet aircraft taking off from the nearby airport, has disappeared now the new airport at Sparta has opened. At night a disco within the marina blasts out enough decibels to shiver your GRP. If you get the impression I don't much like the place you are right and neither, for that matter, do most people who visit here.

## GLIFADHA MARINA 4 (Glyphada)

Although called 'Marina 4', this is in fact the first of the Glifadha marinas to be encountered when bound down the coast from Athens.

## Approach

The harbour lies approximately 3 miles SE of Kalamáki. Care must be taken of the reef running SW of Ák Áy Kósmas.

**GLIFADHA MARINA 4**
⊕37°52´·3N 23°44´E

*By night* Áy Kosmás is lit Q(9)15s5M. The entrance is lit: F.G.3M/F.R.3M.

*VHF* Ch 09.

## Mooring

Go stern or bows-to where directed. There are laid moorings tailed to the quay. The harbour is normally very crowded and you will be lucky to find a berth.

*Shelter* Good all-round shelter.

*Authorities* Port police and a port captain. Charge band 2/3.

## Facilities

*Services* Water and electricity at every berth.

*Fuel* A mini-tanker can deliver to the quay.

*Repairs* Most repairs can be arranged.

*Provisions* Good shopping for provisions nearby in Glifadha.

*Eating out* Tavernas and restaurants in Glifadha.

*Other* PO. OTE. Banks. Hire cars and motorbikes.

*Enquiries* ☎ 894 1967/894 7979.

## General

If you can arrange a berth here this is one of the more agreeable marinas near Athens. You are far enough away from the main coast road for it to be comparatively peaceful and yet it is a short hop into the hurley-burley of downtown Athens.

**GLIFADHA MARINA 1,2,3**
⊕37°51′·8N 23°44′·6E

## GLIFADHA MARINA 1, 2, 3 (Glyphada)

### Approach

*Conspicuous* The large hotels around Ormiskos Glifadha and a church with a blue cupola behind the harbour are conspicuous. Closer in, the masts of yachts in the marina and a hoarding on the extremity of the mole of Marina 3 are conspicuous.

*By night* The entrances to all three marinas are lit F.G.3M and F.R.3M which could conceivably lead to confusion. The loom of the lights behind makes identification of the lights difficult anyway.

### Mooring

Go stern or bows-to where directed in Marina 3. There are laid moorings tailed to the quay. The marina is small, crowded, and you will be lucky to find a berth here.

*Shelter* Good shelter although strong southerlies send in an uncomfortable swell.

*Authorities* Port police and port captain. Marina charges are made.

### Facilities

*Services* Water and electricity at or near every berth.
*Fuel* On the quay.
*Repairs* Some mechanical repairs. Chandlers.
*Provisions* Good shopping for provisions in the town.
*Eating out* Tavernas in Glifadha. Buses to Piraeus and Athens.

### General

The marinas are essentially private with few places for visitors.

*Note* For some time it has been planned to redevelop Glifadha Marinas 1, 2 and 3 and incorporate them into a large complex with a total capacity of 1800 berths. A development ashore is intended to complement the 'super-marina'. At the time of writing, work has not started and it is now more than ten years since the project was first mooted.

## VOULA 37°50′·3N 23°45′·7E

A small harbour S of Glifadha. A mole running S from the coast and curving around to the E has 2–3m depths behind it. A small buoy marks the shallows beyond the channel into the entrance. The harbour is full of local yachts and it can be difficult to find a berth. Good shelter if you can get in here. Tavernas and shopping nearby.

## VOULIAGMÉNI

### Approach

*Conspicuous* A large white hotel on the hill above the marina is conspicuous. Once into Órmos Vouliagmenos the marina will be seen on the W side of the bay.

*By night* Use the light on Nisís Fléves (Fl(3)10s8M) and the lights at the entrance: outer entrance Fl.G.1·5s2M/Fl.R.1·5s2M and inner entrance Fl.G.1·5s2M/Fl(3)R.12s7M.

*VHF* Ch 09 (don't rely on getting a reply).

*Dangers* Care must be taken of Vrak Kasidhis, the reef lying approximately 350m S of the W entrance to Órmos Vouliagménos. There is an inside passage but the prudent course is to pass to seaward of the rock.

### Mooring

Berth stern or bows-to where directed. There are laid moorings tailed to the quay or a small buoy. The marina is usually fully booked although for a short stay there may be a vacant berth.

**VOULIAGMÉNI**
⊕37°48′·3N 23°46′·6E

Vouliagméni looking S into the entrance

*Shelter* Good shelter although strong southerlies cause a reflected swell that makes it uncomfortable inside.

*Authorities* A port of entry: port police, customs, and immigration. Port captain and marina staff. Charge band 3.

## Facilities
*Services* Water and electricity at or near every berth. Shower and toilet block.
*Fuel* On the quay.
*Repairs* Most repairs can be arranged.
*Provisions* Most provisions can be obtained. Ice available.
*Eating out* Tavernas nearby.
*Other* Taxis available at the marina.
*Enquiries* ☎ 1 896 0012/896 0415.

## General
Vouliagméni was the first marina to be built in Greece and the developers chose a wonderful site in the bay away from the hustle and bustle of Athens and Piraeus. The peninsula on the W side of the bay is an up-market suburb with very expensive bits of real estate discreetly scattered around the wooded slopes. Likewise the marina is an up-market place full of millions of dollars' worth of little ships.

## VÁRKIZA (Varkilas)
### Approach
A small harbour in the NW corner of the large bay immediately E of Órmos Vouliagmenos.

*By night* The entrance is lit: F.R.3M.

### Mooring
Berth stern or bows-to the outer mole or inside the basin if there is room. The bottom is sand, rocks and weed, poor holding.

*Shelter* Good shelter in the basin. Mediocre shelter from the *meltemi* on the mole.
*Anchorage* Depending on wind and sea it is possible to anchor off the beach or on the SW side of the breakwater of Varkiza. Anchored off the beach there is reasonable shelter from the *meltemi*.

**VÁRKIZA**
⊕37°49´·1N 23°48´·3E

Várkiza looking E towards the entrance

193

## Facilities

*Water* On the quay.
*Fuel* A mini-tanker can deliver to the quay.
*Provisions* Most provisions can be found nearby.
*Eating out* Tavernas nearby.

## General

The small harbour is crowded with local boats, but a small yacht may find a berth here. Várkiza is an outer suburb of Athens, mostly bland apartment blocks and the wide coast road to whisk commuters in and out of Athens.

## LAGONISI 37°47'·0N 23°53'·2E

A small harbour at the S end of the beach. There are 3–4m depths off the end of the mole, but it is usually crowded with local boats. Anchor off the beach in 3–6m. Good shelter from the *meltemi*. Tavernas.

## ÓRMOS ANAVÍSSOU

The large bay with Nisís Arsidha lying off the entrance. There are a number of anchorages around the bay.

1. ***Chapel cove*** The enclosed bay on the W side of Órmos Anavíssou. Much of the cove is taken up by boats on permanent moorings. Anchor clear of any permanent moorings where possible. Good shelter from the *meltemi*. A *cantina* opens in the summer.
2. In the NW corner where a number of boats are kept on permanent moorings. The holding is reported to be poor. Reasonable shelter from the *meltemi*.

Chapel Cove on the W side of Órmos Anavíssou. Some yachts are kept here on permanent moorings throughout the summer

Looking S across Palaia Fokaia harbour to the anchorage outside

3. ***Palaia Fokaia*** The small harbour has 2–3m depths along the outer half of the mole, but it is usually full of local boats. The inner part of the harbour has <1m. Care is needed in the approach to the harbour as the depths are uneven and there are areas of underwater rocks protruding up to 2–2·5m in the vicinity of the harbour. The best policy is to anchor off the harbour in 3–6m. Care must be taken of patches of coral-like rock that can foul an anchor. Good shelter from the *meltemi* although there are gusts into the bay.

Water and electricity on the mole. Fuel nearby. Good shopping for provisions and tavernas in the village.

A word of warning about the tavernas on the waterfront. In one of these I had one of the most expensive and least satisfactory meals in Greece. Touts outside will promise you everything gastronomic, but deliver awful food. Choose your own taverna with care.

**ÓRMOS ANAVÍSSOU**
⊕37°43'·2N 23°56'·7E

### NISÍS GAIDHOURONISI (Patróklou)

⊕**4** ½M S of W end of Gaidhouronisi 37°38'·45N 23°56'·04E
WGS84

The humpbacked islet lying close off the coast S of
Ák Katafiyí. It is lit on the NE side: LFl.10s6M. It
is possible to pass inside the islet though care must
be taken of the reef just under the water lying near
the middle of the fairway at the eastern end.

There is a useful anchorage on the NE end if
W–SW winds are blowing. There is a fish farm in
here but still room for a number of yachts to anchor.

### SOUNION

The bay under Ák Sounion is often used by yachts
waiting for the *meltemi* to die before proceeding into
Kólpos Petalíon or returning to Athens.

The temple on the cape is conspicuous from the
distance. Anchor where convenient. The bottom is
sand and weed – bad holding. In the N of the bay

The anchorage at Sounion looking W

**SOUNION**

⊕**5** ¼M S of temple on Sounion
37°38'·63N 24°01'·31E WGS84

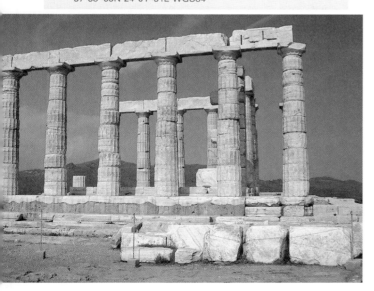

The temple at Sounion

there is a 3·5m patch of sand off the chapel which is
good holding. Make sure your anchor is well in and
holding as the gusts into the bay have caused
numerous yachts to drag anchors here. Good shelter
from the *meltemi* although there are strong gusts into
the bay. Tavernas on the shore.

The temple of Poseidon on the cape is easily
reached after a short walk from the shore. It was
built around 444 BC, probably to a design by
Hephaisteion of Athens. Visit it in the morning as in
the afternoon and evening it is overrun by day-
trippers from Athens. The young Byron is supposed
to have carved his name on one of the columns and
afterwards he penned a few lines on his visit:

'Sunium's marbled steep
Where nothing save the waves and I
May hear our mutual murmurs sweep.'

# The Saronic Islands and the adjacent coast

## The coast

This section covers the coast from the Corinth
Canal down to Ák Skillaion and around the corner
to Ák Mouzaki opposite the NW tip of Nísos
Dhokós. It is mostly mountainous with a ridge
running along the coast between 600 and 900m
(2,000–3,000ft) high reaching the summit at
Ortholithi (112m/3,625ft) opposite Methana
peninsula. The upper slopes are rocky and devoid of
vegetation, but the lower slopes along the coast are
densely wooded in pine. Methana peninsula,
properly Khersónisos Methanon (almost an island
but for a narrow isthmus), is an extinct volcano.

### ÓRMOS LINARI

37°50'·6N 23°04'·8E

Lies on the S shore of Kólpos Kenkhreon 5 miles SE
of the canal. Poor shelter as a swell enters with
strong northerlies. Open to the NW–W. No
facilities.

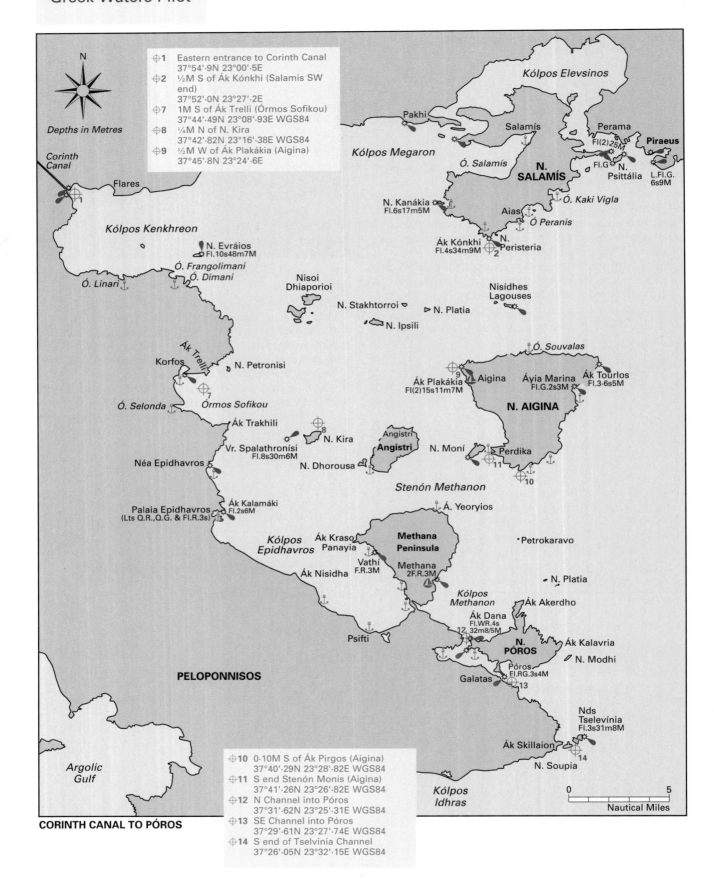

N

Depths in Metres

**1** Eastern entrance to Corinth Canal
37°54'·9N 23°00'·5E
**2** ½M S of Ák Kónkhi (Salamis SW end)
37°52'·0N 23°27'·2E
**7** 1M S of Ák Trelli (Órmos Sofikou)
37°44'·49N 23°08'·93E WGS84
**8** ¼M N of N. Kira
37°42'·82N 23°16'·38E WGS84
**9** ½M W of Ák Plakákia (Aigina)
37°45'·8N 23°24'·6E

Corinth Canal

Flares

*Kólpos Kenkhreon*

N. Evráios
Fl.10s48m7M

*Ó. Frangolimani*
*Ó. Dimani*
*Ó. Linari*

*Ák Trelli*
Korfos
N. Petronisi

*Ó. Selonda*
*Órmos Sofikou*
Ák Trakhili
Vr. Spalathronísi
Fl.8s30m6M
N. Kira

Néa Epidhavros
N. Dhorousa

Ák Kalamáki
Fl.2s6M
Palaia Epidhavros
(Lts Q.R.,Q.G. & Fl.R.3s)

*Kólpos Megaron*

Pakhi

Salamís
Perama

Fl(2).25M
**Piraeus**

Fl.G
N.
Psittália
L.Fl.G.
6s9M

*Ó. Salamís*
**N. SALAMÍS**

N. Kanákia
Fl.6s17m5M

Aias
*Ó. Kaki Vigla*

Ák Kónkhi
Fl.4s34m9M
N.
Peristeria
*Ó Peranis*

*Kólpos Elevsinos*

Nisoi
Dhiaporioi

N. Stakhtorroi
N. Platia

N. Ipsili

Nisídhes
Lagouses

*Ó. Souvalas*

Ák Plakákia
Fl(2)15s11m7M
Aigina

Áyia Marina
Fl.G.2s3M
Ák Tourlos
Fl.3·6s5M

**N. AIGINA**

Angistri
**Angistri**
N. Moní
Perdika

Stenón Methanon

Á. Yeoryios

Petrokaravo

*Kólpos Epidhavros*
Ák Kraso
Panayia
Vathí
F.R.3M
**Methana Peninsula**
Methana
2F.R.3M

Ák Nisidha

N. Platia

*Kólpos Methanon*
Ák Akerdho

Ák Dana
Fl.WR.4s
32m8/5M
**N. PÓROS**
Ák Kalavria
N. Modhi

Psifti

Galatas
Póros
Fl.RG.3s4M

Nds
Tselevínia
Fl.3s31m8M

Ák Skillaion
N. Soupia

**PELOPONNISOS**

*Argolic Gulf*

*Kólpos Idhras*

**10** 0·10M S of Ák Pirgos (Aigina)
37°40'·29N 23°28'·82E WGS84
**11** S end Stenón Monis (Aigina)
37°41'·26N 23°26'·82E WGS84
**12** N Channel into Póros
37°31'·62N 23°25'·31E WGS84
**13** SE Channel into Póros
37°29'·61N 23°27'·74E WGS84
**14** S end of Tselvinia Channel
37°26'·05N 23°32'·15E WGS84

**CORINTH CANAL TO PÓROS**

0                    5
Nautical Miles

## FRANGOLIMANI

37°50'·7N 23°07'·0E

A bay 3½ miles E of Linari. It is steep-to until close to the shore. A beach around the SW side. You will have to drop your anchor in 15–20m and take a line ashore. The bottom is hard sand and weed – bad holding. A swell enters with strong northerlies and shelter is not as good as it looks. The slopes above are being developed for summer villas.

## ÓRMOS DIMANI

A bay approximately 1M E of Frangolimani. Suitable in settled weather. From here on in the coast is littered with fish farms tucked into any and every cove until Korfos. It could be renamed Fish Farm Coast.

## NISOI DHIAPORIOI

A group of uninhabited islands lying to the E of Ák Spiri. The channel between the two largest islands, Áy Thomas and Áy Ioánnis, does not have the depths shown on BA 1657. A reef joins the two islands with the deepest part (3–4m) nearest to Nisís Áy Ioánnis.

## NISÍS ÍPSILI

Lies to the ESE of Nisoi Dhiaporioi and is used for target practice by the Greek Navy.

## KORFOS (Limín Sofikoú)

### Approach

A nearly landlocked bay 1½ miles W of Ák Trelli. The islet of Petronisi with fish farms around it is easily identified in the approaches. The houses of the village will not be seen until into the bay.

*By night* The E side of the entrance is lit: Fl.4s5M. With care a night entry is possible.

*Dangers*
1. Care must be taken of the reef running out from Ák Trelli for nearly 400m. With any chop on the water it can be difficult to see and because Ák Trelli is low-lying it is difficult to determine where the reef starts and finishes.
2. With W–NW winds there are fierce gusts off the land.

Korfos waterfront looking N from the anchorage

**KORFOS**
⊕37°45'·32N 23°07'·72E WGS84
(0·15NM S of light)

### Mooring

Anchor in the bay in 10–12m or go stern or bows-to off the quayed area on the N side just off several tavernas here. Two of the tavernas each have a concrete quay with 2–3m metre depths off them. Between the two concrete quays depths are shallow and even off the quays depths are variable. The bottom is mud and weed, poor holding in places, so make sure your anchor is well in.

*Shelter* Good all-round shelter although there are strong gusts with westerlies.

### Facilities

*Water* On the quay.
*Fuel* A mini-tanker can deliver to the quay.
*Provisions* Good shopping for provisions in the village.
*Eating out* Good tavernas along the waterfront.
*Other* PO. OTE. *Camping Gaz.*

### General

The bay is attractive enough, but the same cannot be said for the awful concrete villas that have been thrown up around the slopes. The best part of Korfos is the waterfront and the tavernas with views out over the bay.

## ÓRMOS SELONDA

37°43'·8N 23°07'·8E

A deep inlet 2 miles S of Korfos. It is now largely obstructed by a fish farm, but it is possible to find a space to anchor in. It is mostly very deep for anchoring. Even with the fish farm here it is a tranquil pleasant spot. Open to the E–SE only.

**NÉA EPIDHAVROS**
⊕37°40'·8N 23°09'·3E

## NÉA EPIDHAVROS

### Approach

A small harbour off the hamlet set at the foot of a flood plain. The approach is straightforward with good depths up to the entrance.

*By night* The entrance is lit Fl.G.3s.3M and Fl.R.3s3M.

### Mooring

Go stern or bows-to the pontoon off the taverna in the NE of the harbour. The pontoon is a bit rickety and semi-sunk in places so care is needed. Alternatively go alongside the end of the stubby mole.

*Shelter* Good shelter from the prevailing NE wind although there can be a bit of a surge.

*Anchorage* In calm weather anchor off the beach in 2–4m on sand and weed, good holding.

### Facilities

Water at the taverna. Limited provisions. If you berth on the pontoon then really you should eat in the taverna above which has wonderful views.

### General

The hamlet on the small flood plain is a convivial place that has a little tourism to augment the income from the citrus groves extending back from the beach into the valley. The harbour here is like some secret place locked in by the cliffs and the steep-sided valley. The river that formed the flood plain now runs under the cliffs and empties into the N corner of the harbour.

## EPIDHAVROS (Old (Palaia) Epidavros, Epidhavro, Epidauros)

### Approach

*Conspicuous* The entrance to Órmos Palaia Epidhávrou is difficult to see from seaward. A road scar on the hill on the S side of the bay is conspicuous. Closer in, the light structure and a church on the N side of the bay will be seen. The village of Palaia Epidhavros at the head of the bay will not be seen until you are in the entrance. Once into the bay proceed between the two beacons marking the channel to the quay.

*By night* Use the light on the N side of the entrance Ák Kalamáki Fl.2s6M, on the two beacons Q.G.3M, Q.R.3M and on the pierhead Fl.R.3s3M.

**APPROACHES TO PALAIA EPIDHAVROS**
⊕37°38'·5N 23°10'·2E

**PALAIA EPIDHAVROS**
⊕37°38′·3N 23°09′·5E

## Mooring

Go stern or bows-to the pier or the quay or anchor in the bay. The bottom is mud and weed, reasonable holding.

*Shelter* Good shelter. Although the bay is open E, winds from the E rarely blow in the summer with any force.

*Authorities* Port police.

*Note* The port police and local hoteliers do not like you anchoring too close to the beach. This is understandable as boats have loos and I for one don't like swimming in pumped out liquid goo.

## Facilities

*Water* On the quay.
*Fuel* In the town.
*Provisions* Good shopping for most provisions.
*Eating out* Tavernas on the waterfront and in the town.
*Other* PO. OTE. Bank. Greek gas. Hire motorbikes. Taxis can be hired to go to Epidhavros theatre.

## General

Set at the base of steep wooded slopes, Palaia Epidhavros is an attractive small village. However the real attraction is Epidhavros theatre about 30 minutes away by taxi – the easiest way of getting there.

The theatre is accepted as the best preserved of all Greek theatres and one of the finest pieces of classical architecture in existence. Some sensible restoration has been carried out, but the theatre is mostly original. The acoustics of the theatre are perfect: a piece of paper rustled on the stage or a coin dropped on the floor can be clearly heard from any one of the 14,000 seats. There is a festival of ancient Greek drama in the summer and seats and transport can be booked at Palaia Epidhavros.

The site was renowned in ancient times not for its theatre but as a sanctuary of the Askeplion: a religious centre for curing the sick and infirm. Extensive temples, hospitals, sanatoriums and the bath-houses covered a site comparable to Delphi. Little remains of the buildings today but the site on

**VATHÍ**
⊕37°35′·7N 23°20′·3E

Epidhavros looking S into the bay

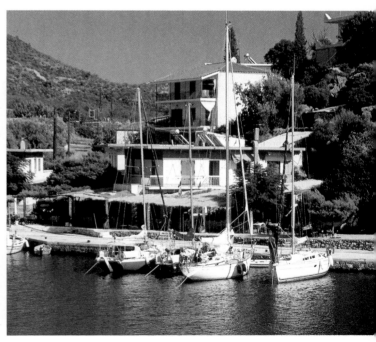

Vathi looking SE from the NW side of the harbour

199

the pine-clad slopes has a certain feeling of quiet and calm about it. A museum on the site houses local finds.

## VATHÍ (Methana)

### Approach

Vathi is a small fishing harbour on the W coast of the Methana peninsula. The rough stone breakwater and houses of the village will not be seen until close to in the approach from the N.

*By night* A F.R.3M is exhibited on the end of the breakwater.

### Mooring

Go stern or bows-to the quay off the tavernas on the S side. Alternatively anchor and take a long line ashore to the rough stone breakwater. The bottom is mud and weed, mostly good holding, although a bit soft in places.

*Shelter* Good shelter, although strong N–NE winds gust into the harbour, more bothersome than troubling.

### Facilities

Several café/tavernas ashore. Infrequent bus to Methana town.

### General

The hamlet is a delightful spot and well off the Saronic charter milk run. On the black basalt slopes a short distance N there is an old caldera, betraying the peninsula's recent volcanic origins.

## NEARBY ANCHORAGES

To the S of Vathi there are several deserted bays that can be used in calm weather. A yacht can also anchor off on the SW side of Kólpos Epidhávrou in calm weather.

# Nísos Aigina

## (Aiyina, Aegina, Egina)

Aigina is the roughly triangular island lying some 12 miles SW of Zéa Marina. The summit of Aigina, Oros (532m/1,745ft), is near the southern end of the island. The island is mostly rocky and barren, but there are a few wooded areas around the coast.

The position of Aigina guarding the northwestern approaches to the Aegean has meant that it was important from the very early days of trade. It was occupied by a Neolithic people who were in turn supplanted by a Bronze Age people around 2000 BC. The Mycenaeans occupied it about 1400 BC, but appear to have abandoned it after a couple of centuries. Later it was recolonized and the inhabitants began to build up their own merchant marine fleet. In the Battle of Salamís the fleet from Aigina was said by Herodotus to have distinguished itself above all others. The growth of the maritime fleet aroused the envy of the Athenians to the extent that Aristotle remarked that the island was 'the eyesore of Piraeus'.

At the beginning of the Peloponnesian War the island opted for the Spartan side (its relationship with Athens had never been a happy one), and was subsequently subdued by Athens. It never recovered and thereafter endured the usual succession of invaders: the Romans, Byzantines, the Saracens, Venetians and Turks. From 1826–28 the city was the capital of the newly liberated Greece and the first modern Greek coins were minted here and the new Greek national flag flown.

The island is very popular with tourists and Athenians alike. By hydrofoil from Zéa it is only 20 minutes away and is a popular excursion for the smog-bound Athenians. Tourists visiting Athens

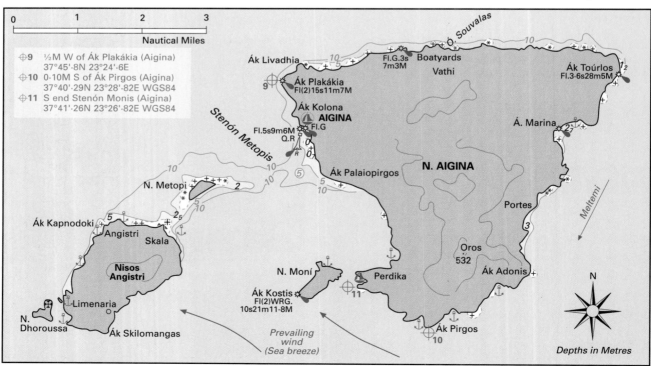

AIGINA AND ANGISTRI

often come on a day trip here. Consequently the strip of water between Aigina and Athens is constantly churned up with ferries and hydrofoils hurrying back and forth, and at the weekends with Athens-based pleasure boats scurrying to get out or back to the capital.

## AIGINA (Aegina, Egina)

Imray-Tetra G14
BA 1657

### Approach

*Conspicuous* The town of Aigina is conspicuous from the distance. Closer in a Doric column on Ák Kolóna immediately NW of the town and a white chapel near the outer end of the W mole are conspicuous. A red conical buoy marks a rock with 3m over it off the marina and another red conical buoy marks a shoal patch with 2·4m least depths just W of the entrance.

*By night* Use the light on Ák Plakákia Fl(2)15s7M, Nisís Moní (Ák Kóstis Fl(2)WRG.10s11-8M; the white sector 296°-322° covers the safe passage across the shoal water between Aigina and Angistri), and the lights at the entrance: Fl.5s6M, Fl.R.2s4M and Fl.G.1·5s3M. The entrance to the marina is lit Fl.G.2s.

### Dangers

1. Care should be taken when making an approach from the S as shoal water extends E from Nisís Metopi across to Aigina. There are least depths of 8–9m through the fairway of the channel.
2. Care is needed at the entrance to the harbour as numerous ferries and hydrofoils use it and they enter and leave at speed. A good lookout is needed.

### Mooring

Go stern or bows-to the town quay. The S mole is taken up with private and charter company berths. Berths in the marina are allocated for longer stays. If you want to berth here then apply to the port police for a berth. The harbour gets very crowded with yachts in the summer months.

*Shelter* Good all-round shelter although strong southerlies send in an uncomfortable swell. The bottom is mud with some rocks – poor holding in places. Some yachts winter afloat here.

*Authorities* Port police and customs.

***Aigina Marina*** The marina is now in use and yachts berth stern or bows-to the pontoons. There are laid moorings tailed to the quay. If you use your anchor then a trip line is advisable. At the time of

AIGINA
⊕37°44'·7N 23°25'·5E

Entrance to Aigina harbour looking NE

writing many of the berths are occupied by local boats and yachts permanently based here. The marina is still not finished and the situation is in a state of flux. If you can find a berth here use it. Otherwise it is really better to be on the town quay if space is available. Shelter in the marina is generally good and only NW winds cause a swell to enter.

## Facilities

*Services* Water and electricity points on the town quay and in the marina. The service points in the marina are not yet connected.

*Fuel* Some distance from the harbour. A mini-tanker can deliver to the quay.

*Repairs* Limited mechanical repairs. Chandlers. For hauling see section on Boatyards on the N side of Aigina.

*Provisions* Good shopping for provisions. Large supermarket on the coast road going S out of town (turn left at Miranda Hotel). Fruit and vegetables can be bought from *caïques* moored on the town quay. Ice available.

*Eating out* Good tavernas around the waterfront.

*Other* PO. OTE. Banks. Greek gas and *Camping Gaz*. Hire motorbikes and bicycles. Buses to the other villages on the island. Ferries to Piraeus and to the other islands in the Saronic Gulf.

Aigina looking NW with the new 'marina' in the foreground.
This picture does not show the later additions to the 'marina'
*Peter Kleinoth/MareTeam*

## General

The small town around the harbour is a pleasant homely sort of place despite the large numbers of tourists deposited here in the summer months. It has the distinction of being the first place in Greece where the Greek flag was raised at the end of the Greek War of Independence. This flag differed from the present-day one, being red and gold in colour. The single column on Ák Kolóna is all that remains of the Temple of Aphrodite that formerly stood on the cape.

## PERDIKA

### Approach

The small bay on the SW end of Aigina. The small village on the N side of the bay is easily identified from seaward.

*By night* Use the light on Nisís Moní Fl(2)WRG.10s11-8M and the light on the end of the outer mole Fl.R.1·5s2M.

### Mooring

It's always a bit of a squeeze trying to get into Perdika in the summer. Go stern or bows-to either side of the centre mole, the new pontoon immediately E or on either side of the outer mole where possible. Depths are variable around the centre mole and in general you are better off trying to go bows-to.

*Note* Do not obstruct the end of the centre mole where the water tanker berths alongside.

*Shelter* Good shelter from the normal summer winds. The bay is open to the W and with fresh to strong NW–W winds the outer part of the harbour is very uncomfortable and may become untenable.

*Anchorage* There is room for a few yachts to anchor and take a long line to the stubby mole on the S side.

### Facilities

Water on the quay. Fuel 500m out of the village, although he may deliver to the quay. Several mini-markets. Good tavernas on the waterfront, some of which specialise in seafood.

**PERDIKA**
⊕37°41′·43N 23°27′·06E WGS84

Perdika pier looking SW

## General

The bay is an attractive place, but fills up quickly in the summer with visiting yachts. Get here early and take some time off for a wander around the village and a beer on the seafront.

## NISÍS MONÍ

In calm weather a yacht can anchor in the bay on the N side of the island. Anchor in 8–10m. A taverna opens in the summer. The S side of the island is bare weathered rock, but on the N side it is partially wooded.

## SOUTH SIDE ANCHORAGES

In settled weather yachts can anchor off in the bays on the S side of Aigina. Órmos Mourioti and Órmos Klima afford the best shelter. Órmos Ligia and Órmos Kipos can be used in calm weather.

## AYIA MARINA

Ayia Marina light (Fl.G.2s3M) 37°44′·7N 23°32′·4E

An open bay near the NE corner of the Nísos Aigina. A large hotel on the waterfront is conspicuous. In calm weather anchor near the NW corner of the bay in 4–6m. Sand and weed bottom. A small quay in the NW corner is reserved for *caïque* ferries bringing tourists to see the Temple of Aphaia. It would be prudent to leave someone on board the yacht while visiting the temple in case there is a sudden change in the weather.

The Temple of Aphaia (5–6 BC) on the NE corner of the island has been called the most perfectly developed classical temple in Greece. Cruise ships anchor in Ayia Marina to disembark passengers wishing to view it. In calm weather this is the nearest anchorage to the temple for a yacht – alternatively buses run from Aigina town to Ayia Marina.

## ÁK TOÚRLOS

The NE corner of Aigina. Care is needed of two patches of shoal water and rocks lying approximately 250 metres off the cape. Give it a wide berth when rounding it.

## SOUVALAS

37°46'·4N 23°29'·3E

A small harbour situated midway along the N coast. A short mole (50m long) runs W from the E side of the coast and has 2m depths just inside. If there is room moor bows-to the mole. Care must be taken as the depths inside are uneven and there is little room for manoeuvring. Care is also needed not to obstruct the ferry berth. Tavernas ashore.

## BOATYARDS

On the N of Nísos Aigina to the W of Souvalas are two boatyards.

*Asprakis Boatyard* 60-ton travel-hoist. 2·5m depths. Limited yacht repairs. Few facilities. A bit out of the way but transport can be arranged.
☎ 0297 23925 *Fax* 0297 26112

*Kanonis Boatyard* 37°46'·3N 23°27'·6E 50/20-ton hydraulic trailers. 2m max depths.
☎/*Fax* 0297 24151.

## METOPI SHOALS

Between Aigina and Angistri lies Nisís Metopi, a low flat islet, with shoal water extending from either side. Between Metopi and Angistri there is a passage with 2·5-3m least depths on a course of approximately N–S around the mid-channel point. This passage is not recommended and in general a yacht should not attempt to pass in between Metopi and Angistri where the depths are variable and there are numerous underwater rocks either side of the passage. Between Metopi and Aigina the channel has 8–9m depths approximately one third of the way across from Aigina.

# Nísos Angistri

## (Aykistri)

Angistri is the small island lying 4 miles to the west of Aigina and connected to it by the strip of shoal water. Angistri is hilly, with the summit on the eastern side (296m/965ft). It is covered for the most part in pine and supports a small population.

There are two harbours on Angistri, but only Angistri harbour on the NW is really suitable for yachts, whereas Skala on the NE side is not.

## ANGISTRI (Miloi, Megalohorio, Saint Georgis)

### Approach

A small harbour on the NW corner of Angistri. Care must be taken when approaching the harbour from the E because of the reefs and shoal water between Angistri and Nisís Metopi.

*By night* The entrance is lit Fl.G/Fl.R.

### Mooring

Go stern or bows-to the quay if there is room. More usually you will have to anchor and take a long line to the rough stone breakwater on the NE side. Care is needed of large mooring chains fouling the bottom.

*Shelter* Local ferries spend the night on the quay, taking up most of the room available. Good shelter except for strong NE–E winds when it can get very uncomfortable.

### Facilities

Tavernas and cafés at the harbour. Provisions available in Angistri village.

### General

Tripper boats run across to here from Aigina in the summer, but the island retains a simplicity and charm of its own. Recently a number of villas have been built on the slopes around the harbour.

ANGISTRI
⊕37°42'·8N 23°20'·9E

## SKALA

37°42'·5N 23°22'·1E

This ferry harbour lies on the S side of the shoal water connecting Angistri to Metopi. The ferry pier is constantly in use and should not be approached. The small harbour to the NW of the ferry pier offers poor shelter from N–NE winds. There are 2–2·5m depths in the entrance and mostly 2m depths along the outer part of the rough stone breakwater. Anchor and take a long line to it. Care is needed of permanent mooring chains on the bottom.

## NISÍS DHOROUSSA ANCHORAGES

N end of Dhoroussa Channel 37°41'·08N 23°19'·18E WGS84

Nisís Dhoroussa lies off the SW tip of Angistri. The narrow channel between the two islands is deep and clear of dangers. Opposite Nisís Dhoroussa there are a number of small bays offering good shelter from the normal summer winds (SE or NE) in attractive wooded surroundings. Anchor where convenient. A delightful little corner, with a taverna opening in the summer.

## Methana Peninsula

### ÁY YEORYIOS (Áy Georgis)

37°38'·38N 23°23'·72E WGS84

A small harbour on the NE corner of the Methana peninsula. A large church is conspicuous close behind the harbour and closer in the outer breakwater, an old coaster that has been sunk and filled with ballast will be seen. There is room for a few yachts to go stern or bows-to behind the outer breakwater where there are 2–3m along the outer half of the quay. Further into the harbour it becomes progressively shallow. Care is needed off the quay as depths are uneven. Good shelter from the prevailing winds although with strong northerlies it can get bumpy in here.

Limited provisions and tavernas ashore.

### METHANA

#### Approach

*Conspicuous* The town of Methana is easily identified from some distance off. The marina lies near the S end of the town and it is difficult to identify the entrance tucked under the wooded headland until close to.

*By night* Use the light on the headland Fl.G.3s3M and the lights at the narrow entrance Q.G.3M/Q.R.3M – care needed.

*Dangers* Care is needed negotiating the narrow entrance into the harbour.

#### Mooring

Go stern or bows-to the quay on the W or N. Depths off the quay are variable, between 1·5–2·5m, but if you touch bottom it is all mud. The bottom of sticky black mud is excellent holding, but messy when you haul the anchor up again. Some yachts use rope rather than chain because of the corrosive action of the sulphurous water on chain.

*Shelter* Good all-round shelter. A number of yachts are wintered afloat here.

*Authorities* Port police and customs. Charge band 2.

#### Facilities

*Services* Water and electricity points around the quay.
*Fuel* Near the quay. A mini-tanker can deliver to the quay.
*Repairs* Some mechanical repairs. Hardware shops.
*Provisions* Good shopping for provisions. Ice available.
*Eating out* Tavernas in the town.
*Other* PO. OTE. Greek gas and *Camping Gaz*. Ferries to Piraeus and to the islands in the Saronic Gulf.

### General

The lasting impression of Methana is not visual but olfactory. The characteristic rotten-egg smell of the sulphuretted hydrogen bubbling up into the harbour is so pungent that the village above Methana is called Vromolimani or 'stinking shore'. The buildings on the west side of the harbour house sulphur baths to which people suffering from rheumatic diseases come. You can have a free bath in the harbour if you fancy it. Boats moored here are said not to have fouling problems as the sulphur in the water kills off weed and barnacles.

METHANA
⊕37°34'·6N 23°23'·5E

Methana looking NW                    *Peter Kleinoth/MareTeam*

Petrokaravo looking N with Nísos Aigina behind

## PETROKARAVO

The group of jagged rocks (the highest is 15m/49ft), lying 3½ miles S of the southern tip of Aigina. There are considerable depths close to the rocks. They are covered by one of the red sectors of the light on Nisís Moní (Fl(2)WRG.10s11-8M) and the red sector of the light on the W tip of Póros (Ák Dána Fl.WR.4s8/5M).

## NISÍS PLATIA

The small island (7m/23ft high) approximately 1½ miles NE of the northern tip of Póros. It is surrounded by a reef and is unlit.

Ák Nédha looking SE to Póros in the N Channel

# Nísos Póros

The Rorschach blob island of the Saronic. It lies close to the coast of the Peloponnisos, separated from it by a narrow and in places shallow channel. The island is extensively wooded (mostly pine but also olive and citrus groves) and is cultivated in places.

In ancient times the island was known as Kaularia and was the centre of the Kaularian league, a maritime confederacy of the 7th century BC amongst whose members were Athens, Aigina, Epidhavros, Troezein, Ermioni, Navplion, Praisiai and Póros. Its patron was Poseidon and a few remains of a temple to Poseidon (about 6 BC but built on an earlier site) can be found on a picturesque site on the east coast of the island.

In 1831 at the end of the Greek War of Independence the islanders opposed the first Greek government and formed a constitutional committee to replace it which had widespread support from the surrounding islands. The Greek ships *Hellas* and *Hydra* were blown up in the harbour by Admiral Miaoulis in defiance of the new government when it sent forces to crush the rebellion. A Greek naval establishment and naval cadet school are situated immediately north of Póros town, perhaps to ensure that there are no further insurrections on the island.

## PÓROS

BA 1599
Imray-Tetra G14

### Approach

*Conspicuous* From the N the narrow channel leading into the large landlocked bay is difficult to see from the distance. The numerous ferries plying this stretch of water will seem to disappear or appear from nowhere. Closer in the lighthouse on the E side of the entrance will be seen. Once in the large bay, the town of Póros will be clearly seen. A light blue clock-tower is conspicuous.

From the S the buildings on the low-lying isthmus can be seen, but it is difficult to see the entrance to the narrow channel. Keep close to the Póros side of the channel and keep a good lookout for the numerous ferries which come rocketing out of the narrow channel.

*By night* From the N use the two lights on the E side of the entrance: Ák Dána Fl.WR.4s8/5M and Ák Nédha Fl.R.2s2M.

From the S a night entrance is difficult because of the unlit islands in the approaches. The red sector of the light on the S point of Póros covers the islands: Ák Stavrós Fl.RG.3s4M: 284°-R-309°.

*VHF* Ch 16, 27, 28, 88 for port authorities.

*Dangers*
1. Care is needed of the shallows on the Peloponnisos side of the channel through Póros town. Stick close to the Póros side. Local *caïques* make a good living pulling inattentive yachtsmen off the sticky mud.
2. Care is needed of the ferries and hydrofoils entering and leaving at speed.

**APPROACHES TO PÓROS**

## Mooring

Go stern or bows-to the quay on the N side of town or stern-to the quay on the S in the narrow channel. The wash from ferries, particularly the hydrofoil, can be uncomfortable and you must ensure your anchor is well in so that you are not violently pushed onto the quay. The holding off the N quay is patchy. The bottom in the channel is mud – excellent holding.

*Note* Mooring blocks and chains have been laid in the places shown on the plan. The mooring lines were long ago removed, allegedly by the local diver who thought he would lose out on charging for recovering fouled anchors. On the S quay the chains are around 20m off the quay at the W end and around 30m off at the E end. On the N quay there is only a short section of chain on the W side around 25m off.

*Shelter* Good all-round shelter although strong westerlies cause some slop on the N quay. There are strong gusts off the hills of the Peloponnisos with strong southerlies.

*Authorities* Port police and customs. A charge is sometimes made.

*Note* A current normally flows through the Póros Strait, usually from W to E though it can reverse and flow in the opposite direction. The current can be up to 1 knot although usually less. The only real problem with the current is when berthing on the town quay in the strait when it can push you about as you go stern-to at slow speed. Likewise when you leave you may have to be a bit snappy about it so you do not get pushed down onto your neighbours.

## Facilities

*Water* On the quay. The waterman usually does the rounds in the morning and evening. Showers available in several of the bars on the waterfront.

*Fuel* A mini-tanker delivers to the quay.
*Repairs* Some mechanical repairs. Hardware shops. Two chandlers. *Greek Sails*, the charter company which operates from the quay at the SE end of the channel, can arrange various repairs including engine, engineering and sail repairs.

Greek Sails, Punta Póros, 18020 Greece ☎ 0298 22332 *Fax* 0298 23147 *Mobile* 0944 561016
*E-mail* Grsails@x-treme.gr.

*Provisions* Good shopping for all provisions. Ice available.

*Eating out* Numerous tavernas on the waterfront and behind. Also tavernas at Galatas across the strait. Yorgiou at the *Café Remetzo* on the waterfront serves a good breakfast or a cool beer in the evening.

*Other* PO. OTE. Banks. Greek gas and *Camping Gaz*. Laundrette close to the N quay. Hire cars, motorbikes and bicycles. *Caïque* ferries across to Galatas. Ferries to Piraeus and the other islands in the Saronic Gulf.

## General

The small volcanic peninsula on which Póros town is built was known in ancient times as Sphaeria. Póros means a 'strait' or 'ferry' and is a later name. The town built on the rocky slopes is attractive and the approach by sea one of the most beautiful in Greece. Póros is a popular tourist spot as well as being popular with day-trippers from Athens. In the season they pour into Póros, yet it somehow manages to stand up to it all and remains a likeable place.

If you are berthed on the S quay it can get smelly at the height of the season from the sewage emptying into the harbour. If the smell doesn't prevent you from sleeping, the latest in popular music will assail your eardrums from the numerous bars along the waterfront.

*Depths in Metres*

Ferry to Galatas

Clock tower (conspic)

Póros

Ice

Fishing boats

Ferry

Moorings

Shallows 1-<1

Galatas

dries occas.

Charter boats (private)

Disco

Órmos Pórou

Ák Stavros
Fl.RG.3s4M

.......... laid mooring chains

**PÓROS**

⊕13 SE Channel into Póros
37°29'·61N 23°27'·74E WGS84

## ANCHORAGES NEAR PÓROS

1. ***Órmos Vidhi*** Anchor in the bay or any of the coves on the N side. A fish farm obstructs one of the bays, but you can still get in. The water here is a bit murky. Taverna on the beach at the head of the bay.
2. ***Ák Dána*** Anchor in the cove tucked under the cape. Good shelter from the prevailing winds and clear water.

3. ***Russian Bay*** Nisís Dhaskalia under Ák Nédha is easily recognised by the conspicuous white chapel on it. Care is needed of the reef running out for approximately 50m from the E side of the islet. Anchor in the bay under the islet. The bottom is mud and weed, good holding once through the weed. Good shelter from the prevailing winds.
4. ***Órmos Neorion*** In the bay SE of Russian Bay where a number of charter yachts have permanent moorings there is good shelter.
5. ***Aliki*** A reef connects the small islets to the SE of Póros Channel to the mainland. Pass between the islets and Nisís Bourtzi. Good shelter. Sandy bottom. Taverna on the beach.
6. ***Órmos Pórou*** Is quite deep until a short distance off. Poor holding. Taverna on the beach.
7. ***Monastery Bay*** As for Órmos Pórou.

## ALIKI BOATYARD

At Aliki Beach Póros Marine can haul yachts up to 17 tons. There is around 2m off the short quay where hauling takes place. Hauling is by crane and then yachts are shored up on the hard. Most yacht repairs can be arranged. Go around to Aliki Beach or contact Richard at *Greek Sails* in Póros.

Póros town looking ESE towards the yacht quay on the N side of the peninsula

Póros looking SE out to the SE entrance and Órmos Pórou
*Peter Kleinoth/MareTeam*

## NISIDHES TSELEVINIA

⊕14  S end of Tselevinia Channel 37°26'·05N 23°32'·15E
WGS84

These two islands, Spathí and Skilli, lie to the S of
Póros just before you 'turn the corner' to head into
Kólpos Idhras (the Hydra Gulf). The passage
between the two islands is deep and clear of dangers
in the fairway. However, great care is needed of the
numerous ferries and hydrofoils which charge
through the narrow channel at full speed (the ferries
come through at 15–20 knots, the hydrofoil at
around 30 knots).

The passage between Nisís Spathí and the
Peloponnisos is obstructed by a reef just below the
water. Off the SW tip of Spathí there is a small islet
and behind it a secluded anchorage.

## NISÍS SOUPIA

37°25'·00N 23°29'·60E WGS84 (0·2M S of N.
Soupia)

An islet lying close off the coast about 1½ miles W
of Nisís Spathí. The islet looks like a crouching frog
when viewed from the E. Anchor behind the islet
where convenient. Good shelter in settled weather.
The bottom is covered in thick weed and is poor
holding in parts. Mulberry trees around the shore
and a villa development above.

## HYDRA BEACH HOTEL

37°24'·8N 23°20'·4E

This large hotel complex lies approximately 8½
miles W of Nisís Spathí. It is easily identified from
seaward. There is a small boat harbour attached to
the complex, but it is usually crowded with *caïque*
ferries.

Small yachts may find a berth here, but the
entrance is barely 20m wide and the basin itself is
very small. There are 3·5m depths in the entrance
and 2–3·5m depths on the W side of the basin. Bar
and tavernas ashore, although the complex has a
run-down feel to it.

Nisís Soupia looking NE

209

Nisís Soupia and the anchorage behind looking S to Ídhra

## ERMIONI (Hermioni, Kastrí)

### Approach

*Conspicuous* The village of Ermioni saddling the headland is easily identified from seaward. The end of the headland is wooded (mostly conifers).

*By night* Use the light on Ák Kastrí Fl.1·5s4M and on the mole head F.R.2M. The new breakwater head is lit Fl.G.2s3M.

*Dangers* Care needs to be taken of the remains of the ancient mole on the N side of the headland.

### Mooring

Go stern or bows-to behind the outer mole if there is room. Larger yachts can anchor in the bay. The harbour can get crowded in the summer. The bottom is mud and weed with some rocks – poor holding in patches.

*Shelter* Good all-round shelter behind the mole. One or two yachts have wintered afloat here. The new stone breakwater running out from the shore on the W provides additional shelter from northerlies though not from northeasterlies which can blow fiercely off the hills.

*Authorities* Port police.

*Note* On the S side of the peninsula there is a protruding quayed area with 2–5m depths off it. The bottom drops off quickly to 10m and more. The rest of the quayed area is bordered by underwater rubble. The S quay is entirely open to southerlies and easterlies so does not provide all-round shelter. However, with offshore winds it is a delightful spot and comparatively peaceful in the summer compared with the other side of the headland.

### Facilities

*Water* On the quay.
*Fuel* In the town.
*Repairs* Limited mechanical repairs. Hardware shop.
*Provisions* Good shopping for most provisions. Ice available.
*Eating out* Tavernas on the waterfront and on the S side of the headland.
*Other* PO. OTE. Bank. Greek gas. Car and

Ermioni in Kólpos Idhras looking NE across Ák Kastrí with the
harbour middle-left          *Peter Kleinoth/MareTeam*

Ermioni approaches to the harbour looking W

motorbike hire. Ferries to Piraeus and the islands in the Saronic Gulf.

### General

The village has been relatively untouched by tourism although there are now several small hotels of what has been called the 'pour and fill' variety. Walk over the saddle of the town to the S side of the headland where things are peaceful and you can sit in a bar on the waterfront with wonderful views over the water.

In ancient times Ermioni was of some importance. The remains of an ancient mole and parts of a wall can be seen on the N side of Ák Kastrí. Pausanias records that a festival in honour of Poseidon was held here and depending on your interpretation of the ancient Greek, either swimming or boat races were held – it is possible Ermioni was the site of the first small boat regatta in recorded history.

### ÓRMOS KAPARI

The large bay immediately S of Ermioni. In the SW corner there is good shelter from the normal summer winds. Anchor in 2–5m. The bottom is sand and weed – good holding. Care must be taken of Vrak Kapari, an islet and rocks lying to the E of the southern entrance point. Some of the rocks are only just above water and are difficult to see.

ERMIONI HARBOUR

Órmos Kapari

Depths in Metres

**ERMIONI**
⊕37°23´·2N 23°15´·0E

# Nísos Ídhra

## (Hydra)

The long narrow island lying parallel to the Peloponnisos coast and bordering the south side of Kólpos Ídhras. It is mountainous throughout, rising to the summit, Mt Eros (590m/1935ft), near the centre. It is everywhere arid and sterile and devoid of vegetation.

Ídhra appears not to have been of any importance in ancient times. It was during the centuries of Turkish rule that it prospered and built up a large mercantile marine fleet. It paid no taxes but supplied sailors for the Turkish fleet. In 1821 it was the first of the islands to pledge its sizeable fleet (some 150 ships) to the Greek cause. Admiral Miaoulis, admiral of the Greek fleet, was an Hydriot as were many of the other captains and sailors who distinguished themselves against the Turks. It has been said that but for the Hydriot fleet and sailors, the War of Independence would not have been won.

The Hydriot fleet never recovered from the war effort and Ídhra declined in importance to become a backwater of the Saronic until it was discovered by discerning travellers. It became a fashionable resort, and in the early days of tourism the rich and famous holidayed in Ídhra, though now it is visited by larger numbers ferried in daily from Piraeus.

## LIMÍN ÍDHRAS (Hydra, Ydra)

### Approach

*Conspicuous* A white monastery on the hill above the harbour is conspicuous from some distance off. Closer in the small town of Ídhra built around the natural amphitheatre above the harbour will be seen.

*By night* Use the light on the E side Fl.R.1·5s3M and the lights at the entrance F.R.2M/F.G.2M.

*Dangers* Care is needed of the numerous craft, ferries and hydrofoils and pleasure craft, entering and leaving the narrow entrance, often at speed.

### Mooring

Go stern or bows-to the town quay or the N mole. The latter has underwater ballasting projecting a short distance out in places so care is needed when berthing there. If possible go on the N mole in case N–NW winds blow. In the summer the harbour is very crowded and it is not unusual for yachts to be berthed three out from the quay. Crossed anchors are a fact of life here and there is little you can do about it. The bottom is mud and weed with some rocks – poor holding in places.

*Shelter* With strong N–NW winds a dangerous surge develops and the only safe place is on the N mole.

*Authorities* Port police and customs.

### Facilities

*Water* On the quay.

*Provisions* Good shopping for most provisions. Ice from the market.

**KÓLPOS ÍDHRAS**

**LIMÍN ÍDHRAS**
⊕ 37°21´·1N 23°28´·0E

*Eating out* Tavernas on the waterfront and in the town. I suggest you go into the town away from the overpriced tavernas and bars on the waterfront.

*Other* PO. OTE. Bank. Greek gas and *Camping Gaz*. Ferries to Piraeus and the other islands in the Saronic Gulf.

### General

Among the buildings of the town there are many large stately houses built in the time when Ídhra was a prosperous town and possessed a large mercantile fleet. In the 1950s and '60s Ídhra became a fashionable artists' colony attracting, amongst others, songwriter and performer Leonard Cohen, the champion of depressive and suicidal ballads. He still has a house here.

Limín Ídhras looking N                    *Nigel Patten*

213

Ídhra (Hydra) harbour looking SE     *Peter Kleinoth/MareTeam*

Later it became a popular tourist island, but it has not experienced the extensive development of Míkonos or Rhodes and remains architecturally very much of the 18th and 19th centuries. In the summer months there are about 10 ferries a day and perhaps one or two cruise ships anchored off or berthed in the tiny harbour.

## MANDRAKI

A bay about ¾ mile E of Hydra. A hotel at the head of the bay is conspicuous. Good shelter from southerlies but open to northerlies. Anchor in 3–6m. The bottom is sand, mud and weed – good holding. Tavernas ashore. Water taxi to Ídhra.

*Note* The breakwaters I was assured would be built out from either side were not built as indicated in my last edition. Apologies to those of you who arrived here expecting to see two breakwaters. It just goes to show that you cannot always believe your most trusted correspondents. It is not known if the breakwaters will be built at some future date.

## ANCHORAGES SW OF LIMÍN IDHRAS

Along the northern side and at the SW end of Ídhra there are several anchorages affording some shelter from the prevailing SE wind. At times there may be

**MANDRAKI**
⊕37°21′·5N  23°28′·8E

214

gusts off Ídhra though they vary in strength and duration.

1. *Vlikhos* Anchor off the hamlet. Taverna ashore.
2. *Órmos Molos* A small bay opposite Nisís Kivolos. Taverna ashore.
3. *Petassi* Opposite the NE end of Nisís Petassi there are several small coves that can be used.
4. *Bisti* Under Ák Bisti there is a bay that can be used though it is quite deep.
5. *Áy Nikólaos* NE of Nisís Áy Nikólaos there is a large bay that can be used in calm weather. Marvellous surroundings and clear water. When the prevailing wind gets up a swell is pushed in here.

## NISÍS DHOKÓS

The bluff barren island off the SW end of Ídhra. Stenón Petassi, the channel between Ídhra and Dhokós, is deep and clear of dangers. The winds in this channel are variable and often die away altogether so it is best to motor through until they pick up again. One or two families live in Órmos Skindos on the north side of the island.

The island has a number of archaeological remains around Órmos Skindos E side and at times parts of it are closed off for archaeological digs. The remains here date from Mycenean and the early Hellenistic period. In the bay at the top there has been some excavation of an early Hellenistic trading ship.

## ÓRMOS SKINDOS

A large bay with a number of coves around the edges providing good shelter from the normal summer winds.

*Órmos Skindos E side* On the E side where possible. Anchor in 2–5m with a line ashore if necessary. Yachts also anchor SW of this anchorage. Reasonable shelter from the prevailing wind although at times it can be uncomfortable. The bay is popular as a lunch stop but is often deserted at night. Open W across the bay and NW.

*Derrick Cove* In the NW corner a small inlet with

**ÓRMOS SKINDOS**
⊕37°20′·8N 23°20′·2E

Nisís Dhokós. Anchorage in the NW cove of Órmos Skindos

a number of houses around the shore provides good shelter. Anchor in 7–10m. Sand and weed bottom. The large buoy formerly in here has been moved but its substantial mooring chain is still on the bottom.

## NISÍS TRIKERI

The islet midway between Ídhra and Spétsai. Fishing boats will often be seen around it. Between Tríkeri and Ídhra there is a chain of islets and islands: Asteri, Dhrápi, Strongiló, Dhisakki, Tagari, Karteli, Ventza and Alexandros. The red sector of the light on the E side of Báltiza Creek (Ák Fanári Fl.WR.5s18/14M red sector covers 254°-278°) covers these islands and rocks as well as Ifalos Tríkeri (least depth 5m) and Ifalos Milianós (least depth 7m) lying between Nisís Tríkeri and Spétsai.

# Argolikós Kólpos

Argolikós Kólpos reaches back up to the north from the more southerly Saronic Islands of Spétsai and Ídhra. It is surrounded by high mountains except at the head of the gulf where there is the flat plain of Argos. The mountains on the western side of the gulf are the first of the Parnon range which continues right down the eastern side of the Peloponnisos to Ák Maléas. The mountains are rugged and barren and the shore inhospitable. Generally there are good depths close off the coast as the mountains drop sheer into the sea. The highest peaks are covered with snow in the winter and often well into the spring.

## ÁK MILIANÓS (Áy Amilianós)

Ák Milianós light 37°17′·4N 23°12′·0E

A reef partly under the water on which the sea breaks extends about ¼ mile S of the cape. A white church on the cape is conspicuous. A small light structure marks the extremity of the reef (Fl.WR.10s8/6M red sector covers 314°-357° over Ifalos Milianós and Ifalos Tríkeri).

In the bay immediately W of Ák Milianós there are several attractive calm-weather anchorages.

Ák Milianós looking NE

# Nísos Spétsai

The roughly oval island lying in the eastern approaches to Argolikós Kólpos. It has a gentler aspect than either Ídhra or Dhokós and the climate is described by the Admiralty *Pilot* as 'exceedingly healthy'. Much of the island is covered by pine trees planted in an inspired afforestation programme implemented in the early part of the last century. Unfortunately with the dawn of this century much of the forest has been destroyed by forest fires, many apparently caused deliberately. Most of the population lives in Spétsai town on the northern coast (conspicuous from the east).

Spétsai has the distinction of being the first island (with Ídhra) to revolt against the Turks and commit her merchant fleet to the Greek cause. The local heroine was Boubalina (many of the local boats are named after her) who commanded the Spétsai fleet – her most daring deed was the destruction of part of the Turkish fleet at Navplion with fire ships. The deed is commemorated by a regatta in September when a small *caïque* rigged out as an old trader is set on fire in the harbour accompanied by a noisy fireworks display and much merriment. Like Ídhra, the mercantile power of Spétsai declined after the War of Independence.

Spétsai town is more akin to the Italian Riviera than a Greek town although recent architectural additions have reduced the effect. Of late a number of large hotels have been built in the town to cater for the large numbers of tourists who descend on the island in the summer.

Just outside the town the large public school, the Anarghyrios and Korghialenios School of Spétsai, is modelled on an English public school. John Fowles taught at the school for a time and his novel *The Magus* is set on the island – most of the places in the novel can be easily identified including the Villa Yasemia on the west coast where most of the action in the novel takes place.

## SPÉTSAI (BALTIZA CREEK) (Spetses, Balza, Palaio Limani)

BA 1683
Imray-Tetra G14

### Approach

*Conspicuous* From the distance the houses of Spétsai town around the northern shores and on the gentle slopes are easily seen. Closer in, the lighthouse on Ák Fanári, the headland forming the E side of the harbour, and a number of whitewashed windmill towers (now converted to houses) are conspicuous.

*By night* Use the light on Ák Fanári Fl.WR.5s18/14M and the light on the extremity of the headland Q.R.3M.

*Dangers*
1. Care should be taken rounding the extremity of the headland where there are some above-water rocks and a short reef.
2. There is often a confused swell at the entrance with S winds.

### Mooring

Anchor in the bay with a long line ashore or stern or bows-to in the inner harbour if there is room. Báltiza Creek is a popular destination for yachts in the season and the inner harbour will usually be full to bursting and the outer harbour too crowded for you to swing at anchor. In the outer harbour the bottom is sand and weed (poor holding in patches) and in the SW corner there is a large permanent mooring chain fouling the bottom. In the inner harbour the bottom is mud – excellent holding.

*Shelter* With strong NW winds the outer harbour is uncomfortable and possibly dangerous for small yachts. The inner harbour has excellent all-round protection and a number of yachts are wintered afloat here.

*Authorities* Port police and customs in the new harbour.

### Facilities

*Water* On the quay.
*Fuel* On the quay.
*Repairs* Yachts can be hauled out in any one of the yards around the harbour, though you will need to

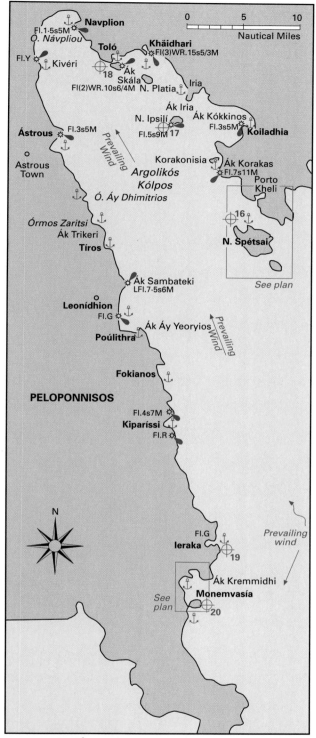

**ARGOLIKOS KÓLPOS AND THE EASTERN PELOPONNISOS**

⊕16 0·1M W of Petrokarovo light
37°17'·08N 23°04'·67E WGS84
⊕17 1M W of Nisís Ipsilí light
37°25'·9N 22°57'·1E
⊕18 1M W of Ák Megalí (Toló)
37°30'·6N 22°50'·3E
⊕19 ¼M E of Ák Yérakas
36°46'·17N 23°06'·90E WGS84
⊕20 ¼M E of Monemvásia headland
36°41'·52N 23°03'·89E WGS84

**STENÓN SPÉTSAI**

⊕16 0·1M W of Petrokarovo light
37°17'·08N 23°04'·67E WGS84

book early to get a place. Some mechanical repairs. Old-fashioned wood repairs. Small chandlers. Hardware shops.

*Provisions* Good shopping for provisions near the harbour and in town. Ice available.

*Eating out* Good tavernas near the harbour and others in town.

*Other* PO. OTE. Banks. Greek gas and *Camping Gaz*. Hire motorbikes and bicycles. Horse drawn gharries. Car ferry to Kósta across Spétsai Strait and ferries and hydrofoils to Piraeus and the other islands in the Saronic Gulf.

**General**

Spétsai is an attractive town popular with tourists and Athenians alike. Spétsai restaurants often have an excellent dish peculiar to the island, fish *á la Spetsiosa*, a casserole of fish, tomatoes and green peppers covered in cheese – which is well worth sampling.

Spétsai old harbour and environs is a wonderful place to wander around. There are several yards building *caïques* and Spetsiot boats are said to be among the best in Greece. Tim Severin had his replica galley built here for his voyages tracing the routes of Jason and the Argonauts and Odysseus wandering home from the Trojan War.

Around the harbour are many grand old houses

Depths in Metres

10

0   50   100   200
Metres

5

Care needed of reef
and shoal water
350m NW

8

7₅

7

⁜ Church

7

Prevailing
Wind

3

Q.R.3M

4

5

Fl.WR.5s18/14M
LtHo(conspic)

2

2

<1

New
Church

6

s/w

2₅

4

4

2₅

4

3

5

5

4

Taverna

4

2

5

Large houses

Foul

3

5

1₅

2

<1

Yard

5

Mill

4

Supermarket

Bar

Boatyard

4

2

2

<1

Houses

m/w

4

Bar

3

3₅

Yard

2

2

SPÉTSAI NEW HARBOUR (DÁPIA)
⊕37°16′·2N 23°09′·5E

5

5

5

2

10

2

<1

3

10

2

F.R.3M

Ferry   Ferry

N

Bars and
Tavernas

Trip
boats

<1

Dapia

Mill

N

0   100
Metres

Depths in Metres

**SPÉTSAI - BÁLTIZA CREEK**
⊕37°15′·9N 23°10′·0E

Báltiza Creek on Spétsai looking NE out to the conspicuous lighthouse on the headland sheltering the E side of the creek
*Peter Kleinoth/MareTeam*

built in the prosperous era of the 18th and 19th centuries when Spetsiot ships traded all over the eastern Mediterranean, and because no cars are allowed on the island (motorbikes unfortunately are) walking around the old quarter is a delight.

## SPETSAI REEF

Between Baltiza Creek and Spétsai New Harbour (Dápia), a reef projects nearly 200m from the coast with 1m depths over it. Make sure when you are moving between the Dápia and Baltiza you do not cut the corner and come to grief on it.

## SPETSAI NEW HARBOUR

Off the Dápia at Spétsai town there is a mole and a small boat harbour. The mole is reserved for ferries and the small boat harbour for local *caïque* ferries. A yacht will be turned away by the port police.

On the W side of the ferry mole and boat harbour there is a short mole and a quay. There are underwater rocks off the quay, but on the W side of the mole there are 2–5m depths. Go stern-to where convenient. There is usually an uncomfortable swell with the normal summer winds and it is untenable with northerlies.

## ÓRMOS ZOYIORYIA

37°17'·0N 23°06'·4E

A large bay on the NW corner of Spétsai. Anchor in the bay in 5–8m. On the W side of the bay there is a small cove offering good shelter from all but NE–E winds. The bottom is sand with some rock – good holding. Sometimes at night a katabatic wind will blow out of Argolikós Kólpos from the NW making the bay uncomfortable and sometimes untenable. The cove on the W affords shelter from this wind.

The surroundings here are attractive with a wooded foreshore and clear water. A taverna on the shore.

## NISÍS PETROKÁROVO

⊕16 0·1M W of Petrokarovo light 37°17'·08N 23°04'·67E WGS84

The islet off the NW tip of Spétsai. It is lit: Fl(2)9s7M. Between the islet and Spétsai there is a reef which has a deep passage through it nearer to Spétsai than Petrokárovo. The reef is sometimes marked by 3 red buoys along its length although this cannot be relied upon. The prudent course is to go around the outside of Petrokáravo.

## SPETSOPOULA

The small island lying off the SE tip of Spétsai. It is the private property of Stavrós Niarchos, (the ship owner whose fleet rivals that of the late Onassis), and landing is prohibited on it. There is a private harbour on the N end of the island where Niarchos' large yacht is sometimes moored. Care must be taken when navigating between Spétsai and Spetsopoula as there are a number of reefs in the general vicinity.

## PORTO KHELI (Heli)

BA 1683
Imray-Tetra G14

### Approach

*Conspicuous* A large white hotel on the SE side of the entrance and a number of large villas on the E side of the channel are conspicuous from the W. From the E Nisís Khinitsa is easily identified. Closer in the

Nisís Petrokárovo off the NW tip of Spétsai looking SE

Porto Kheli looking out to the W side of the channel

Porto Kheli anchorage and moorings on the NW side of the bay

be uncomfortable with the slop that is kicked up across the bay. Numbers of yachts are wintered afloat here.

*Authorities* Port police and customs.

*Anchorages* On either side of the entrance channel into Porto Kheli there are numerous coves where a yacht can anchor depending on the wind direction (see plan). Shelter in the coves is generally good enough to overnight in most of them.

**Facilities**

*Water* Local water is brackish. Drinking water is delivered by tanker.

*Fuel* Near the quay. A mini-tanker delivers to the quay.

*Repairs* Yachts are hauled at the boatyard here. Some mechanical repairs. Two chandlers. Frank's Yacht Station is a German-run company that will look after yachts afloat (on moorings) or ashore. Wintering and repair work can be carried out. Most mechanical and light engineering work can be arranged. Life raft servicing. Yachts up to 20 tons can be craned out.

*Contact* Frank's Yacht Station, Frank Wenzloff, Odos Costa 2, Porto Kheli, 21300 Greece ☎ (0754) 52380 *Fax* (0754) 51364

*Provisions* Good shopping for provisions. Ice available.

*Eating out* Tavernas around the waterfront and in the village. There seems to be a paucity of good tavernas, given the numbers of tourists here.

*Other* PO. OTE. Bank. Greek gas, *Camping Gaz*. Bus to Athens. Ferry (hydrofoil) to Piraeus and the islands in the Saronic Gulf.

light structure on the W side and the beacon (white with a red band) marking the reef off the E side of the entrance will be seen.

*By night* Use the lights at the entrance: Fl.1·5s5M on the N side and Fl.G.3s3M on the beacon on the E side.

*Caution* The channel between Nisís Khinitsa S of the entrance and the mainland has 2m depths in the fairway, but the bottom is uneven and extreme caution is needed when navigating through the channel. The prudent course is to keep to seaward of the island.

**Mooring**

Go stern or bows-to the quay or anchor off. The area in which you can anchor is marked by buoys around the outer limits. In fact much of this area is taken up by permanent moorings and in the summer yachts anchor outside the buoyed off area. The bottom is sticky mud – excellent holding.

*Shelter* Excellent all-round shelter. However, with the regular SE day breeze the berths on the quay can

**ÁK KÓRAKAS TO ÁK ÁY NIKÓLAOS**
⊕37°21´·2N 23°04´·1E

221

## General

The long quay was built in the 1960s when Porto Kheli was zoned as a NATO base. The plan was eventually shelved and the unfinished harbour and airstrip nearby, used today by small planes, are all that remain of the scheme. Over the years trees have been planted and roads laid so that what was a dust bowl is now more convivial.

Kheli or heli means eel in Greek, probably referring to the numbers of eels which once lived here, especially in the landlocked saltwater lagoon on the W side. The landlocked bay is not unattractive and is custom-made for water sports, so it is not surprising that a number of hotels have been built – in the summer the bay is busy with sailboards, dinghy sailors, paragliding, jet skis, water skiers, and a few swimmers taking their chances amongst the flotsam of skimming plastic and whirling propellers.

## NISÍS KORAKONISIA

Ák Kórakas light 37°21'·2N 23°04'·1E

A small island lying immediately N of Ák Kórakas (light: Fl.7s11M). On the coast just N of the island there is a small bay sheltered from the normal summer wind. Anchor where convenient. The bottom is sand and rock – good holding. A few houses around the shore. You can also anchor in the cove on the E side of the island. Wonderful surroundings.

## ÁK ÁY SPIRIDHION

Just N of this headland with a white church on it there is a bay affording reasonable shelter from the prevailing wind. Anchor in 4–5m off the beach. Taverna ashore in the summer.

In calm weather there are several other anchorages off sandy beaches in the vicinity.

## KOILÁDHIA (Koilas, Kilas)

### Approach

The large bay in the easternmost part of the gulf with the islet of Koiládhia in the entrance.

*Conspicuous* The white church on Ák Kókkinos is conspicuous and closer in the large church in the village will be seen. Nisís Koiládhia in the entrance is easily identified.

*By night* A night entrance should be made with care. Use the light on Ák Kókkinos Fl.3s4M and the light on the pierhead 2F.G(vert)3M.

*Dangers* Care must be taken of the reefs bordering the channel off Ák Kókkinos and Nisís Koiládhia.

### Mooring

Anchor off the village in 2–3m. The short pier off the village is usually crowded with fishing boats, but there may be spaces available. The bottom is mud – excellent holding.

*Shelter* Good all-round shelter in the bay. Boats are left on moorings here all year round.

*Note* Nisís Koiládhia is privately owned by a ship owner and the small harbour on the SE side is private.

### Facilities

*Water* On the quay.

*Fuel* Out of town.

*Provisions* Most provisions can be found. Ice available.

*Repairs* The boatyard round from Koiladhia still builds wooden *caïques and* can arrange to haul yachts. It has been reported that a 2m channel has been dredged to the yard and a crane then hauls yachts out onto hardstanding. Go round from Koiladhia to check first.

**KOILÁDHIA**
⊕37°25'.4N 23°06'·8E

Koiládhia looking NW towards the village and conspicuous church

*Eating out* Several tavernas on the waterfront which often have good fresh fish.

*Other* PO. OTE. Greek gas. Taxis.

## General

Koiládhia is very much a proper working and fishing village with a large resident fleet. The look-alike reinforced concrete houses are not the image you may have of a Greek village, but the place grows on you and the locals are a friendly bunch.

In the Franchthi Cave, prominent on the E side of the anchorage, numerous prehistoric remains have been found, including a skeleton from the Mesolithic period, the oldest found in Greece.

**ÁK IRIA TO TOLÓ**

⊕17  1M W of Nisís Ipsilí light 37°25'·9N 22°57'·1E
⊕18  1M W of Ák Megalí (Toló) 37°30'·6N 22°50'·3E

## NISÍS IPSILÍ AND NISÍS PLATIA

On the NE side of the gulf there are two islands. Nisís Ipsilí, the southern of the two, is a bold crescent-shaped island. Nisís Plátia to the N is of lower aspect.

There are no anchorages around Ipsilí as the depths are considerable right up to the edge. On Plátia there is an anchorage on the N side sheltered from the afternoon breeze blowing up the gulf, but fish farms now obstruct much of the anchorage.

## OTHER ANCHORAGES

On the E side of Ák Iria there is a solitary anchorage in a cove worth exploring. In settled weather a yacht can anchor off the long sandy beach by the hamlet of Kantia. The anchorage is exposed to the afternoon breeze so be prepared to move off when the wind gets up. Taverna ashore.

## IRIA 37°28'·7N 22°59'·9E

A small harbour off the village of Iria. The harbour is very small and mostly occupied by local boats. There are just 2m depths in the entrance and 1–1·5m depths inside. With the normal SE sea breeze there is a swell at the entrance and it would be tricky trying to get in. Taverna ashore.

## KHÄIDHARI (Dhrepano Vivari)

### Approach

The entrance to the inlet is difficult to make out from the distance. When closer in the ruins of the fort on the W side and the light structure on the SE side will be seen. The entrance is deep and free of dangers.

*By night* The SE point is lit Fl(3)WR.15s5/3M. There are no other lights but with care a night entrance is possible.

### Mooring

Go stern or bows-to the pier if there is room. There are 3m depths on the end and 1·5–2·5m depths on either side although care is needed as the depths are irregular in places. Alternatively anchor in 6–12m keeping clear of the permanent moorings in the W corner. The bottom is mud and weed, good holding.

*Shelter* Good all-round shelter.

**KHÄIDHARI**
⊕37°31'·4N 22°56'·1E

Khäidhari looking E to the pier

223

## Facilities

Water on the pier. Limited provisions in the village. Numerous tavernas on the waterfront.

## General

Most people like Khäidhari and the entrance into the long inlet under the cliffs on either side makes it an impressive natural anchorage. The fort on the point is of Venetian origin signifying the harbours importance to Venetian trading ships.

## TOLÓ (Tolon)

### Approach

*Conspicuous* Nisís Plátia and Nisís Toló lying close off the coast are easily identified. A white chapel on a conical peak behind Toló village is conspicuous. The small harbour lies in Stenón Toló at the SW end of the village.

*By night* Use the light on the S end of Nisís Toló (Ák Skála Fl(2)WR.10s6/4M), on Ák Khäidhari (Fl(3)WR.15s5/3M) and on Ák Megalí (Fl.2s3M). The end of the mole is lit: 2F.R(vert)3M.

*Dangers* Ifalos Toló is a reef approximately ¾ of a mile SE of Ák Skála, the SE extremity of Nisís Toló. The reef has 3·5m least depth over it and is covered by the red sectors of the light on Ák Skála (315°-343°) and on Ák Khäidhari (046°-058°).

## Mooring

Anchor off the village or go alongside or stern or bows-to the outside of the S mole. Inside the little harbour is usually crowded with fishing boats whose

Toló looking SW to Nisís Toló

owners take exception to visiting yachts taking their spaces. The bottom is sand, good holding.

*Shelter* Off the village it can get bumpy with the afternoon breeze, but the holding on sand is good. Alongside the outside of the mole you are protected from the afternoon breeze, but completely exposed to westerlies.

## Facilities

*Water* On the quay in the small harbour.
*Fuel* In the town.
*Provisions* Good shopping for provisions.
*Eating out* Numerous tavernas on the waterfront.
*Other* PO. OTE. Bank. Greek gas and *Camping Gaz*. Hire cars. Bus to Navplion. *Caïque* ferry to Ástrous. Hydrofoil to Piraeus.

## General

Toló was a small fishing village that has developed into a tourist resort on the strength of its sandy beach. Of late it has become very crowded with tourists on package holidays and little remains to remind you that fish, and not people, was once the principal industry here.

## ÓRMOS KARATHONA

The large bay between Toló and Navplion. A yacht can anchor at the southern end of the bay where there is some protection from the prevailing southerlies blowing up the gulf. A breakwater at the S end provides additional shelter if you can get under it and take a long line to it. Taverna ashore.

## NAVPLION (Nauplion, Nauplia)

BA 1683

### Approach

*Conspicuous* The large town will not be seen until around Akronavplia. A chapel on Ák Khondrós and a hotel on Akronavplia will be seen. The fortress of Palamidi will also be seen. Once close to the point the small fort on Nisís Bourtzi will be seen.

**TOLÓ**
⊕37°30′.9N 22°51′.5W

*By night* Use the light on Ák Panayítsa Fl.1·5s5M and the lights at the entrance (light buoy Q.R and Fl.G.3s3M).

*VHF* Ch 12, 16 for port authorities.

### Mooring

Go alongside or stern or bows-to the quay in the large inner basin. The bottom is gooey mud which plough anchors will sometimes pull through.

*Shelter* Good shelter although strong NW winds cause an uncomfortable slop. If the swell becomes dangerous anchor off.

*Authorities* A port of entry: port police, customs, and immigration.

*Note* Sewage empties into the harbour and with the summer heat it can get very smelly.

### Facilities

*Water* On the quay when you can find the waterman.
*Fuel* In the town.
*Repairs* Some mechanical repairs. Good hardware shops.
*Provisions* Excellent shopping for provisions. Ice available.
*Eating out* Numerous tavernas in the town, including some quite sophisticated places in and around the old streets.
*Other* PO. OTE. Banks. Greek gas and *Camping Gaz*. Hire cars and motorbikes. Buses to Athens. Ferry (hydrofoil) to Piraeus.

### General

The large town of mostly 18th and 19th-century buildings, mainly two or three-storeyed and shuttered and balconied, is a gem. The stone houses

Navplion quay looking NW to Nisís Bourtzi

seem to be engulfed in vegetation as they vie with each other to grow the biggest swathe of bougainvillea or clematis. The narrow cobbled streets wind in and out of modest mansions and less modest public buildings, many of them built in a golden sandstone that seems to absorb colour from the sun. Shops and tavernas are tucked away in streets everywhere. It is the sort of place you could willingly live in and has always been the most important city of the Argolid. At the beginning of the fledgling Greek Republic after the War of Independence, Navplion was briefly capital before Athens was chosen.

In the square the museum is the large building, originally built by the Venetians as a naval arsenal. It has a number of interesting exhibits including a suit of Mycenaean armour, a reminder that this whole area was the heartland of the Mycenaeans and in fact Navplion may have been a Mycenaean naval base at one time. Navplion is also thought to be the birthplace of Palamedes who is credited with the invention of lighthouses, the art of navigation, and the games of dice and knucklebones.

The Venetian citadel, Palamidi, is reached by a winding track of about 1000 steps. The hot climb is worthwhile, not only to view the most finely-preserved piece of Venetian military architecture in existence, but also for the view over the Argolic Gulf. Alas, the vast structure was out of date not long after it was completed. The citadel is open 0800–1845.

### KIVERION 37°31'·4N 22°44'·0E

A bight on the coast opposite Navplion which is really only suitable before the afternoon breeze gets up. There is a short mole here with 1·5–3m depths off it, but it is usually occupied by fishing boats. If you can tuck behind it there is good shelter from the SE breeze. Alternatively in calm weather anchor off in 3–5m on mud and weed.

Good fish tavernas ashore.

**NAVPLION**
⊕37°33'·8N 22°47'·6E

## ÁSTROUS (Astros, Paralion Astros)

### Approach

*Conspicuous* The rocky headland, connected by a low isthmus (on which the village is built) to the Peloponnisos, looks like an island from the distance. Closer in, the castle and some houses on the headland and the lighthouse are conspicuous. From the N and E the village will not be seen until you are around the headland.

*By night* Use the light on Ák Ástrous Fl.3s5M and the lights at the entrance F.R.5M/F.G.5M.

### Mooring

Go stern or bows-to either mole where convenient. Along the S mole the ballasting projects some

**ÁSTROUS**
⊕37°24′·9N 22°46′·1E

Ástrous looking NW from the castle

---

# Mycenae
## (Mikinai)

This ancient city situated some nine miles from the head of Argolikós Kólpos was the centre of a great Helladic civilization between about 1650 and 1100 BC. Despite scholarly conjecture, it is widely accepted that the period dominated by Mycenae (and therefore called the Mycenaean period) fits in with the Achaeans of Homer's *Odyssey* and *Iliad*, although he probably telescoped events occurring over five centuries into a smaller timescale.

The site was occupied very early on, but not until 1700–1650 BC did it become important. Its position guards the approaches to the Argolic Gulf and the natural land route through the mountains to Corinth. The Mycenaeans were a militant race that quickly came to dominate Greece: their domain covered the whole of the Peloponnisos, the Aegean Islands, the Greek mainland and Crete.

Their cultural influence spread even further, to Asia Minor, Cyprus, Egypt and the Ionian Islands. The wealth of Mycenae was legendary and the dead were buried with lavish amounts of treasure, much of which was lost to grave robbers in later centuries. Particularly notable are the gold death masks, of which the mask of Agamemnon found by Heinrich Schliemann is the most famous. The Mycenaean period came to an abrupt end around 1000 BC and scholars are still at a loss to explain just what it was that stopped a great civilization in its tracks and put the clock back for four centuries in the Greek 'Dark Ages'.

The site can be conveniently visited from Navplion (by taxi or bus) and there is enough for the layman to make it a worthwhile excursion. The site on a virtually treeless hill can be unbearably hot in the summer and it is recommended you go early in the morning and take a hat and water.

---

distance underwater in places. The bottom is mud and weed – poor holding in places.

*Shelter* Good shelter from the prevailing southerlies. Care is needed at night as Ástrous is notorious for katabatic winds which blow strongly off the mountains from the NW–W in the evening – it is generally over in 3–4 hours.

*Authorities* Port police.

### Facilities

*Water* On the quay.

*Fuel* On the outskirts of the village.

*Provisions* Most provisions can be obtained. Ice available. Better shopping in Ástrous town about 2½ miles away.

*Eating out* Good tavernas on the waterfront and in the village.

*Other* PO. OTE. Irregular bus service to Ástrous town and Tripolis. Hydrofoil to Navplion and Piraeus.

### General

Ástrous is a bustling fishing village and tourist resort. The village is built around the slopes above the harbour with the new development along the long sandy beach around the bay. The harbour is one of my favourite places in the gulf and even with its tourism remains a likeable and very Greek village.

The medieval castle on the top of the hill is in reasonable condition and well worth the short walk up to it for the views over the gulf. Local folklore tells of a subterranean passage leading from the castle to the cave at sea level on the S side of the headland, but I haven't been able to find any trace of it. On the tip of the headland are the ruins of a large classical building.

The village around the harbour is properly called Paralion Ástrous and the main village of Ástrous is some 2½ miles inland. It is a down-to-earth agricultural town in the middle of a region which is noted for its orchards and particularly for its peaches. Also nearby is Moní Loukous, a large monastery approximately 2½ miles from the village, which is worth a visit.

## ANCHORAGES BETWEEN ÁSTROUS AND TIROS

Along the steep-to coast between Ástrous and Leonídhion are several anchorages suitable as lunch stops in calm weather.

*Áy Dhimitrios* 37°20'·0N 22°48'·5E The bay under Ák Áy Dhimitrios. Tucked into the cove on the S you can overnight with care although any northerlies will mean you must leave.

*Órmos Krionéri* Anchor in the SW corner. Really only a lunch stop.

## TIROS

### Approach

A short mole on the S side of Órmos Tiros. From the S it will not be seen until you are around Ák Tiros which has 3 windmills running down the ridge.

*By night* The end of the mole is lit Fl.R.3s3M.

### Mooring

If you can find a space behind the mole go stern or bows-to. Make sure you do not obstruct the hydrofoil quay although I have been told it no longer runs. Care is needed of a patch of rock ballasting about one third up from the root of the mole. Care is also needed of permanent mooring lines everywhere.

*Shelter* Good shelter from the SE sea breeze.

*Anchorage* In calm weather anchor in the S part of the bay tucked under the mole as much as possible and take a long line ashore.

### Facilities

*Water* On the mole.
*Fuel* Some way out of town.
*Provisions* Good shopping for provisions
*Eating out* Tavernas and cafés along the waterfront.
*Other* PO. Bank. Hire cars and motorbikes. Hydrofoil to Piraeus.

### General

Tiros is a busy resort popular with the Germans and French. The long sandy beach is permanently occupied and the waterfront hums with the sounds of drinking and eating, but it is too much of a resort for my liking.

## LEONÍDHION (Leonideon, Pláka)

### Approach

*Conspicuous* The harbour is difficult to locate from the distance. A mill converted to a house on the beach to the N of the harbour and a white church behind the harbour can be identified closer in. The hotel in the village will also be seen. Only a small part of the mole is visible as most of it is behind a continuation of the beach.

*By night* Use the light on Ák Sambateki LFl.7·5s6M and the light on the extremity of the mole Fl.G.1·5s3M.

*Dangers* With the normal southerly sea breeze there is a confused swell in the entrance.

**TIROS**
⊕37°14'·8N 22°52'·1E

**LEONÍDHION**
⊕37°08'·8N 22°53'·6E

Leonídhion (Pláka) looking NE

## Mooring

Go stern or bows-to the mole. The bottom is hard sand with some rocks – poor holding in patches.

*Note* At the time of publication work was going on to repair and extend the mole at Leonídhion after damage from a winter gale in 1998. This made berthing on the mole somewhat difficult, but hopefully the work will be complete by 2001–2002.

*Shelter* With the regular SE day breeze there is an uncomfortable surge in the harbour. With southerly gales it could be untenable in here.

*Authorities* Port police.

## Facilities

*Water* On the quay.
*Provisions* Some provisions.
*Eating out* Good tavernas on the waterfront.
*Other* Bank in Leonídhion town. Taxis. Hydrofoil to Piraeus.

## General

The small hamlet under the towering cliffs is a pleasant, mostly unspoilt spot. The fertile valley (citrus, olives, figs and market gardening) winds between the high mountains to Leonídhion town – a modest place untouched by tourism. About 30 minutes away by taxi is the small monastery of Elonas, on a spectacular cliffside site reminiscent of those at Meteori. It is well worth visiting. The surrounding Parnon range is rugged and steep-to with cliffs dropping sheer for 600–700m (2,000–2,300ft).

In the region around Leonídhion a dialect known as 'Tsakonika' used to be spoken by the older inhabitants and is considered to be a link between ancient (Doric) and modern (Demotic) Greek.

## POÚLITHRA

Poúlithra light F.R.3M 37°07'·1N 22°54'·2E

A small fishing harbour 2 miles S of Leonídhion. A white church near the harbour is conspicuous. Go stern or bows-to the short mole. Care is needed of rock ballasting extending underwater from the quay so it is best to go bows-to here. Good shelter from the normal summer southerlies. With northerlies a swell works its way into the harbour. Tavernas ashore. The hamlet of Poúlithra is about 15 minutes' walk away and enjoys a modest tourist trade in the summer.

## FOKIANAS (Phokianos)

37°04'·1N 22°59'·2E

A bay lying just S of Ák Turkoviglia. With the normal summer wind from the SE it is untenable, but it affords good shelter from the northerlies. A cove in the NE corner has reasonable shelter. Care is needed of large permanent moorings on the bottom which may foul an anchor. Permanent bottom nets have also been reported. A beach runs around the head of the bay under the steep slopes behind – wonderful wild surroundings.

## KIPARÍSSI (Kyparissi)

### Approach

This large bay lies about 5 miles S of Fokianas. On the N side of the entrance a conspicuous road scar runs around the coast and on the S side a pylon communications tower is conspicuous. The houses of the hamlet cannot be seen until you are in the entrance to the bay and it can be difficult to identify just where it is from the distance.

*By night* There are lights on either side of the entrance: N side (Ák Aspro Kórtia) Fl.4s7M and S side (Ák Nisáki) Fl.R.1·5s3M.

### Mooring

There are several places a yacht can go, depending on wind and sea.

1. *Kiparíssi town pier* When southerlies are blowing the ferries and hydrofoil use the town pier. Care is needed of the reef running out from the shore approximately 50 metres NW of the pier. Go alongside the SW side of the pier. Alternatively you can anchor off the village in 3–8m keeping clear of the pier. Adequate shelter in calm weather or light southerlies. Untenable with strong NE winds.

**KIPARÍSSI**
⊕36°59′·1N 23°00′·4E

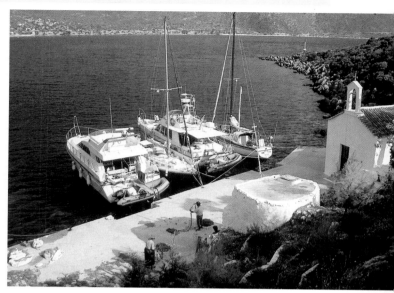

The short quay off the chapel on the SE side of Kiparíssi

2. **N ferry pier** If the N pier is not being used by the ferry go alongside. Alternatively anchor to the W of the pier keeping clear of the approaches for the ferry. Reasonable shelter when it blows from the NE.

3. **Chapel Cove** In the SE corner of the bay there is a short quay close off the chapel here. Go stern or bows-to if there is room. It is very deep (15–20m) a short distance off so you will be dropping the anchor in fairly deep water. Good shelter from southerlies and adequate from NE winds.

**KIPARÍSSI: TOWN PIER**
⊕36°58′·3N 22°59′·7E

**KIPARÍSSI: NORTH PIER**
⊕36°59′·0N 23°00′·0E

*Note* The bottom is mostly sand and thick weed, not everywhere good holding.

**Facilities**
Provisions and tavernas in the village. PO. OTE. Hydrofoil and ferry to Piraeus and Monemvasía.

**General**
The small village is quite unspoilt and the bay, surrounded by mountains, a spectacular spot. Chapel Cove in the SE corner is my favourite spot in Kiparíssi with good shelter and just a few fishermen cleaning their nets under the chapel for company.

## IERAKA (Yérakas)
**Approach**
The narrow entrance between the high cliffs is difficult to locate even quite close in.

*Conspicuous* From the N a church on a knoll about one mile NW of Ák Vathi is conspicuous. The light structure will only be seen from a short distance off when approaching from the N.

Kiparíssi. The anchorage off the village     *Nigel Patten*

Ieraka looking W from Ák Kástro

*By night* The approach is difficult as the light at the entrance (Ák Kástro Fl.G.3s5M) is obscured except between 240°-200°.

*Dangers* With strong northerlies there is a confused reflected swell in the approaches and in the entrance.

## Mooring

Go bows-to the quay. Some care needs to be taken as the depths are uneven and underwater rocks litter the bottom off the quay. Shallow-draught craft can go through the bottleneck and anchor at the entrance to the lagoon. The bottom is mud with some rocks and weed, reasonable holding.

*Shelter* Good all-round shelter, although a surge develops with strong northerlies – uncomfortable, but not normally dangerous. If you are on the quay the surge causes yachts to roll considerably, making things uncomfortable – go ashore for a meal!

## Facilities

Tavernas and a café ashore. The tavernas have limited fare and you will probably be asked whether you want pork chops or fish. Some provisions from a little shop. Ferry to Piraeus.

## General

The small hamlet surrounded by the hostile mountains of the Parnon is hardly touched by outside influences. In the hot afternoon sun out of the cooling reach of the *meltemi* the whole hamlet snoozes until the cool of evening when things come

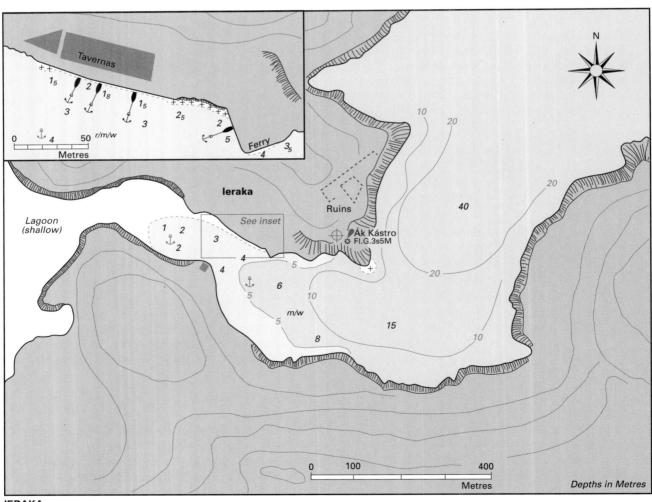

**IERAKA**
⊕36°47′·2N 23°05′·3E

to life again. On the summit of the entrance is an extensive ruined acropolis, probably of Mycenaean origin.

## MONEMVASÍA (Monemvassi)

BA 1683
Imray-Tetra G15

### Approach

*Conspicuous* The humpbacked island of Monemvasía (likened to a little Gibraltar) connected to the Peloponnisos by a causeway is easily identified from the distance. Closer in the village of Yefira on the mainland will be seen.

From the S the old village of stone houses on the S side of Monemvásia tends to blend into the rocky background and is difficult to see until closer in. If heading for the marina it can be difficult to pick out the breakwater. Head for the last white house on the outskirts of Yefira.

*By night* Use the light on the end of Nisís Monemvasía Fl.5s11M and the light on the end of the mole Fl.R.2s3M. The end of the marina breakwater is not lit.

*Dangers* With the *meltemi* there are fierce gusts in the approaches to the bay.

### Mooring

If there is space in the marina then go alongside the outer breakwater or alongside the end of the pontoons. The outer pontoon is partially sunk but still usable. Inner berths at the marina are occupied by local boats. If the marina is full, as it often is in the summer, then there may be space on the inside of the ferry mole on the N side of the causeway or anchor off on the S side of the causeway.

**MONEMVASÍA APPROACHES**

⊕20 ¼M E of Monemvásia headland
36°41'·52N 23°03'·89E WGS84

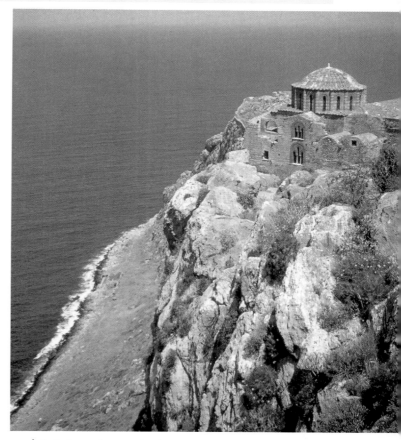

Áyia Sofía on the summit of Monemvasía          *Nigel Patten*

*Note* The square concrete mooring blocks for the pontoons have just been laid on the bottom and reduce depths by around 0·4–0·6m. They are easily seen.

*Shelter* Good shelter in the marina. Good shelter from southerlies under the ferry mole and adequate with the NE *meltemi*. The *meltemi* causes a surge behind the ferry mole and you will roll around, so make sure you have plenty of fenders out to avoid damage to the topsides from boats on either side. The anchorage on the S side of the causeway is adequate with light southerlies and provides reasonable protection from the *meltemi*, although some swell works its way around the headland and you will roll at anchor.

*Authorities* Port police and customs in Yefira.

*Anchorage* If anchoring under the causeway you will be in reasonably deep water, typically around 12–15m. Try to anchor as close towards the fishing harbour as possible. The bottom is sand, rocks and weed, poor holding in patches.

### Facilities

*Water* On the breakwater quay in the marina.
*Fuel* Near the root of the mole. A mini-tanker can deliver.
*Repairs* Minor mechanical repairs. Hardware shop.
*Provisions* Good shopping for all provisions. Ice available.
*Eating out* Good tavernas. In the old village on the

*Depths in Metres*

N

**Yefira**

Baker

Bars/tavernas

Fishing boats

Bridge

Kástro

Hydrofoil and ferry

Fl.R.2s3M

2nd phase

Lifeboat

Monemvasía Marina

White hse.

Local boats

0    50    100    200
Metres

**MONEMVASÍA**
⊕36°41′·03N 23°02′·38E WGS84

island there are a number of excellent tavernas in a romantic setting between the steep slopes and the sea. Good *ouzeries* around the fishing harbour, serving octopus mezes.

*Other* PO. OTE. Bank. Greek gas and *Camping Gaz*. Ferry (hydrofoil and regular ferry) to Piraeus.

### General
Monemvasía Island was called Minoa in ancient times suggesting a Cretan influence. Until the 20th century it was an important port, the last port of call before setting off around Cape Malea. The old fortified village is of Byzantine origin although the Venetians rebuilt much of it.

You should not miss an opportunity to visit the old village which is slowly coming to life again in a sympathetic way. The gift shops and restaurants do not detract from its character if you squint your eyes and don't dally too long. There are a number of interesting churches in the village, but to get to the

Monemvasía 'marina' looking ENE towards Monemvasía

best of them, Ayia Sofia, you will have to climb up the zig-zag path behind the village to the summit. The fortified path and tunnel into the fort with its iron gates still intact is as impressive as the fortifications at the top, and if you run out of breath on the way up it is a good excuse to sit down and enjoy the superb views down onto the roofs of the old village and out over the sea.

Ayia Sofia stands on the very edge of a sheer cliff on the N side with what the *Blue Guide* quaintly describes as a 'view of wild grandeur at sunset'. The church has interesting frescoes and its situation on the edge of the cliff affords a view of the wild hinterland of the Peloponnisos and the grand sweep of Kólpos Monemvasías.

In the past Monemvasía was called Malmsey or Malvoise by the French, hence the name of the famous red and white wines shipped (but not necessarily grown in the region) from the port in its heyday. The strong sweet red wine was known to travel well and hence was much in demand on the extended voyages in the age of sail – and from this we should learn the lesson that a small yacht is not the place for good wine, especially delicate whites and some of the more fragile reds, so drink up before any of that good wine you have on board goes off.

### ANCHORAGES IN KÓLPOS MONEMVASÍA

**Órmos Palaio** Palaio light 36°43'·9N 23°02'·4E
In the NW corner of Kólpos Monemvasía this small bay offers good shelter from all but W–SW winds. Care must be taken of the reef off the southern entrance. The S entrance is lit: Fl.G.1·5s3M. Anchor in 6–8m on a sandy bottom. From about the 6m line into the head of the bay large permanent moorings foul the bottom. There are a few villas and fishermen's houses around the bay.

**Órmos Kremmidhi** Lies just around the cape from Órmos Palaio. Open to the S–SE. Anchor in

5–8m on a sandy bottom. The severe gusts into the bay with the *meltemi* mean you must be sure your anchor is in. If in doubt lay a second anchor.

## Islands lying off the Peloponnisos

Between the Peloponnisos coast and Mílos and Sífnos there are several small and uninhabited islets.

**Nisís Parapóla** (Belopoula) light 36°55'·8N 23°17'·2E
An islet lying approximately 21 miles off the coast from a point midway between Kiparíssi and Ieraka. It is quite high at 227m (745ft) and easily seen by day. It is lit on the N: Fl(2)20s22M. It is reported that the bay on the SW side affords some shelter from NE winds.

**Nisídhes Karavi** 36°46'N 23°36'E
A group of three small islets that look like one from the distance. Although the maximum height is only 33m (110ft) they are easily identified by day. Care is needed to give the islets a wide berth as they are sometimes used by the Greek air force for target practice and I would suggest, having been one mile off while live rockets were used, that a yacht keep at least 3 and preferably more miles off the islets. (There is no mention in the relevant publications of the fact that it is a prohibited zone.)

**Nisís Falkonéra** 36°50'·4N 23°53'·4E
The high bold islet lying approximately midway between Parapóla and Mílos. It is easily identified by day and is lit on the S end Fl.5s17M. It is reported that a bay on the SW side affords shelter from N winds, but as with other islands in the vicinity, there are likely to be fierce gusts off the lee side.

# V. The Cyclades
## (Kikladhes Nisoi)

This is the central group of islands in the Aegean, so named because they more or less surround Delos, the ancient centre of trade and worship (*kukloi* = rings). I will not attempt to describe the islands here, but describe each separately when I come to them. To impose some order on the scattered islands they are broken down into three sections: northern, middle and southern Cyclades.

***Northern Cyclades*** Kéa, Kíthnos, Síros, Andros, Tínos, Míkonos, Delos and Rinia.

***Middle Cyclades*** Sérifos, Sífnos, Andíparos, Páros, Naxos, Dhenoussa, Iráklia, Skhinoússa, Koufonisia, Amorgós and Lévitha.

***Southern Cyclades*** Mílos, Kímolos, Folégandros, Síkonos, Ios, Thíra and Anáfi.

## Weather patterns in the Cyclades

The prevailing wind in the summer is the infamous *meltemi* blowing from the N–NW. The *meltemi* begins to blow fitfully at first in June, blows strongest in July, August and September, and dies during October. In July and August the *meltemi* blows at Force 5–6 and may reach Force 7–8 on occasions. It may blow for 1–3 days or it may sometimes blow for 2 weeks at a time. There is no way of knowing just how long it will blow. It has a

| Síros<br>Frequency<br>VHF Ch 04<br>(announce Ch 16) | Weather forecast | Nav warnings |
|---|---|---|
| | 0600, 1000, 1600, 2200 UTC | 0500, 1100, 1730, 2330 UTC |

| Saronic<br>Frequency<br>VHF Ch 25<br>(announce Ch 16) | Weather forecast | Nav warnings |
|---|---|---|
| | 0600, 1000, 1600, 2200 UTC | 0500, 1100, 1730, 2330 UTC |

| Pérama<br>Frequency<br>VHF Ch 86<br>(announce Ch 16) | Weather forecast | Nav warnings |
|---|---|---|
| | 0600, 1000, 1600, 2200 UTC | 0500, 1100, 1730, 2330 UTC |

Map labels: Athens, Kólpos Petalion, Andros, Piraeus Coastguard VHF Ch 16 MF 2182kHz DSC MF 2187·5kHz DSC HF ☎ (0)1 411 2500 Fax (0)1 411 5798, VIII. EASTERN SPORADES, Ándros Coastguard VHF Ch 16, 24 MF 2182kHz, Saronikós Kólpos, Aigina, Kéa, Yiaros, Tínos, Ikaria, Míkonos, Síros, NORTHERN CYCLADES, Kíthnos, Rinia, Delos, Síros Coastguard VHF Ch 16, 03, 04 MF 2182kHz, Idhra, Aegean Sea, Sérifos, Dhenoussa, MIDDLE CYCLADES, Andíparos, Naxos, Lévitha, Sífnos, Páros, Kinaros, Kimolos, Amorgós, Síkonos, Ios, Mílos, SOUTHERN CYCLADES, Folégandros, Anidhros, Mílos Coastguard VHF Ch 16, 82 MF 2182kHz, Thíra Coastguard VHF Ch 16, 26, 87 MF 2182kHz, Astipalaia, Thíra, Anáfi, IX. DODECANESE, N.

thermal component in that it loses some strength at night and increases again in the day.

In June and again in late September the wind strength is considerably less at about Force 4–5 and there may be wind from other directions. The direction of the *meltemi* varies down through the Cyclades. In the northern Cyclades it blows from the NE, curving to blow from the N in the middle Cyclades and curving again to blow from the NW–WNW in the southern Cyclades. In the SW islands of the Cyclades the wind is marginally less strong than in the northern and eastern islands.

In the spring and autumn the wind is predominantly from the N although there are also winds from the S. Gales are commonly from the N or the SE.

**Note** Care must be taken of violent gusts off the high land on the lee side of the islands when the *meltemi* is blowing. These gusts may be considerably stronger than the wind strength on the open sea – gusts of Force 7–8 may be experienced when the wind on the open sea is Force 5–6. At times small whirlwinds may accompany the gusts which strike with great force and very quickly. Places noted for these squalls are the Doro Channel between Evia and Andros, the south coasts of Andros and Tínos, Yiaros, the Kéa Channel, Míkinos, Naxos and the islands S of it, the S coast of Amorgós, Kímolos, Folégandros, and the S side of Ios.

In the summer months the Cyclades are hot and temperatures average 25°–26°C (79°F) and often reach 33°–35°C (95°F). In the summer there is very little if any rain and many of the islands run short of water towards the end of the season. Snow will only fall on the peaks of Andros and occasionally Tínos in the winter.

## Routes

Route planning in the Cyclades is really a matter of going E or W. Anyone who has sailed there will know that getting back through the islands from the E against the *meltemi* is the problem. If you are going E the *meltemi* blowing down from the NE–N–NW will give you a sleigh ride to the Dodecanese or Crete. At times there will be too much wind even for a beam reach and you may have to bear off under headsail alone, but overall choosing the route to the E is more a matter of personal choice than of weather considerations.

How to get back to windward through the Cyclades is a much debated point. I favour going S in a great semicircle around the southern Cyclades where the wind is less strong and you can make to the N through the Saronic islands. From Kós or Kalimnos head for Astipálaia, Anáfi, Thíra, Íos, Folégandros, Kímolos and Mílos. At times the *meltemi* can be just as strong around Íos/Folégandros/Mílos as elsewhere, so you may need to keep going to the Peloponnisos! Others maintain that you should go N in the eastern Cyclades or the Dodecanese and then W through the northern Cyclades. One thing is clear – going E through the Cyclades is infinitely preferable to going W when the *meltemi* is blowing.

## Data

### PORTS OF ENTRY
Ermoúpolis (Síros)

### PROHIBITED AREAS
2M offshore around Nísos Yiaros. Nisídhes Karavi is sometimes used for target practice by the air force.

### MAJOR LIGHTS
**Kéa**
**Áy Nikólaos** Fl(2)10s15M
**Ák Tamélos** Fl(2)15s17M

**Kíthnos**
**Ák Kéfalos** Fl.4s9M
**Ák Áy Dhimítrios** Fl.10s12M
**Ák Mérikha** Fl.WR.5s5/3M

**Síros**
**Nisís Gáïdharos** Fl.6s12M
**Ermoúpolis** Fl.G.3s6M
**Ák Trímeson** Fl(2)14s12M

**Ák Velostási** Fl(3)12s6M

**Andros**
**Ák Fássa** Fl.10s25M
**Ák Kastrí** Fl.6s8M
**Ák Kolóna** Fl.3s5M
**Órmos Kástrou** Fl(2)15s6M
**Ák Griá** Fl.20s25M
**Vrákhoi Kalóyeroi** (Kaloyeri Reef) Fl(2)15s17M

**Tínos**
**Nisís Dhisvaton** Fl.10s16M
**Ák Livádha** Fl.15s7M
**Limín Tínou** Fl.R.3s7M

**Míkonos**
**Ák Armenistís** Fl.10s22M
**Nisídhes Prassonisía** Fl.3s6M
**Nisís Náta** Fl.3s6M

**Sérifos**
**Ák Spathí** Fl(3)30s19M
**Ák Kíklops** Fl(2)14s9M

**Sífnos**
**Ák Fílippos** Fl.5s9M

**Ák Kokkála** Fl(3)12s9M

**Andíparos**
**Ák Kórakas** LFl.12s14M

**Páros**
**Ák Áy Fokas** Fl.3s6M
**Ák Kratzi** Fl(3)WG.15s12/10M

**Naxos**
**Limín Náxou** Fl.R.4s7M
**Ák Stavrós** Fl(2)16s13M
**Vrákhoi Amarídhes** Fl.WR.4s5/3M
**Vrakhónisos Kopriá** Fl(2)12s10M

**Dhenoussa**
**Ák Kalota** Fl.1·5s5M

**Iráklia**
**Nisís Mikró Avélos** Fl(3)10s6M

**Skhinoússa**
**Mirsini** Fl.4s6M

**Amorgós**
**Ák Goniá** Fl.8s11M
**Órmos Katápola/Ák Áy Ilías** Fl(2)10s12M
**Áy Annas/Ák Langadhia** Fl.5s8M
**Nisídhes Liadhi (N)** Fl(2)20s9M

**Lévitha**
**Ák Spanó** Fl.10s11M

**Mílos**
**Nisídhes Akrádhia** Fl.10s10M
**Ák Bombárdha** Fl.5s12M
**Andímilos** Fl.2s8M
**Nisís Paximádhi** Fl(2)15s12M
**Nisís Anánes** Fl(3)12s9M

**Políagos**
**Ák Máskoula** Fl.5s19M

**Folégandros**
**Ák Asprópounda** Fl(3)30s17M

**Síkonos**
**Órmos Skála** Fl.1·5s5M

**Íos**
**Ák Fanári** Fl.4s7M

**Thíra**
**Ák Akrotíri** Fl.10s24M
**Epanomeria** Fl.4s7M
**Nisídhes Khristianá** Fl(3)9s10M

# Quick reference guide

| Northern Cyclades | Shelter | Mooring | Fuel | Water | Provisioning | Tavernas | Plan |
|---|---|---|---|---|---|---|---|
| **Kéa** | | | | | | | |
| Áy Nikólaou | B | AC | B | A | B | B | • |
| Órmos Pisa | C | C | O | O | O | O | |
| Órmos Kavia | B | C | O | B | C | C | • |
| Khalidhoniki | B | C | O | O | O | C | • |
| Órmos Polais | O | C | O | O | O | O | • |
| **Kíthnos** | | | | | | | |
| Órmos Fikiadha | B | C | O | O | O | O | • |
| Órmos Kolóna | B | C | O | O | O | O | • |
| Mérikha | B | AC | B | B | B | B | • |
| Loutra | A | ABC | B | A | C | B | • |
| Áy Stefanos | B | C | O | B | O | C | • |
| Kanala | O | C | O | O | O | O | |
| **Síros** | | | | | | | |
| Ermoúpolis | AB | AB | B | A | A | A | • |
| Nisís Gáïdharos | B | C | O | O | O | O | • |
| Órmos Varis | B | C | O | B | C | C | • |
| Finikas | A | AC | B | A | B | B | • |
| Posidhonía | C | C | O | B | C | C | • |
| Órmos Galissas | C | C | O | B | C | C | • |
| Órmos Kini | C | C | O | B | C | C | • |
| Órmos Delfino | B | C | O | O | O | O | • |
| Órmos Aetou | C | C | O | O | O | O | • |
| Órmos Grammata | B | C | O | O | O | O | • |
| **Andros** | | | | | | | |
| Gavrion | B | AC | B | A | B | B | • |
| Órmos Petros | C | C | O | B | O | C | |
| Órmos Fournos | C | C | O | B | O | C | |
| Batsí | B | AC | B | A | B | B | |
| Palaioupolis | O | C | O | O | O | C | |
| Órmos Plaka | C | C | O | O | O | O | |
| Kástro | B | AC | B | A | B | B | • |
| Korthion | C | AC | O | B | C | C | • |
| **Tínos** | | | | | | | |
| Tínos | A | A | B | A | A | B | • |
| East coast anchorages | C | C | O | O | O | C | |
| Órmos Panormou | C | C | O | B | C | C | • |
| Órmos Kolombithra | C | C | O | O | O | O | |
| **Míkonos** | | | | | | | |
| Míkonos Marina | A | AB | B | B | C | C | • |
| Órmos Ornos | B | C | O | O | O | C | • |
| Órmos Áy Annas | B | C | O | O | O | C | • |
| Panormos | C | C | O | O | O | C | |
| **Rinia** | | | | | | | |
| Órmos Skhinou | C | C | O | O | O | O | • |
| South Bay | B | C | O | B | O | O | • |
| Órmos Miso | B | C | O | O | O | O | • |
| Órmos Kormou Ammos | C | C | O | O | O | O | |
| **Middle Cyclades** | | | | | | | |
| **Sérifos** | | | | | | | |
| Livádhi | A | AC | B | A | B | B | • |
| Órmos Koutala | B | C | O | B | C | C | • |
| Mega Livádhi | B | C | O | O | O | O | |
| **Sífnos** | | | | | | | |
| Áy Yeóryios | B | C | O | O | O | C | • |
| Kamáres | B | AC | O | A | B | B | • |
| Órmos Vathí | B | AC | O | O | C | C | • |
| Órmos Fikiadha | C | C | O | O | O | O | |
| Órmos Platí Yialos | C | C | O | O | C | C | • |
| Faros | B | C | O | B | C | C | • |
| Kástro | O | C | O | B | B | C | • |
| **Andíparos** | | | | | | | |
| Órmos Dhespotico | B | C | O | O | O | O | • |
| Andíparos | C | C | O | O | B | C | • |

| Páros | Shelter | Mooring | Fuel | Water | Provisioning | Tavernas | Plan |
|---|---|---|---|---|---|---|---|
| Paroikía | B | AC | B | B | A | A | • |
| Órmos Naoúsis | A | C | O | O | A | C | • |
| Náoussa | B | AC | B | A | B | B | • |
| Órmos Filizi | C | C | O | O | O | O | • |
| Órmos Marmara | C | C | O | O | O | O | |
| Piso Livádhi | B | AC | O | A | C | B | • |
| Órmos Faranga | C | C | O | O | O | O | • |
| Aliki | B | C | O | O | O | C | • |
| **Naxos** | | | | | | | |
| Naxos | A | ABC | B | A | A | A | • |
| Órmos Áy Prokopiou | C | C | O | O | O | C | • |
| Áy Annas | B | AC | O | A | C | B | • |
| Órmos Kouroupa | C | C | O | O | O | O | • |
| Órmos Kalando | C | C | O | O | O | O | • |
| Órmos Panormou | C | C | O | O | O | O | • |
| Órmos Moutsouna | O | C | O | O | O | C | • |
| Apollonia | O | C | O | B | C | C | • |
| **Dhenoussa** | | | | | | | |
| Órmos Roússa | C | C | O | O | O | C | • |
| Órmos Dhendhro and Stavrós | B | C | O | O | C | C | • |
| **Iráklia** | | | | | | | |
| Áyios Yeóryios | C | C | O | O | C | C | • |
| Órmos Livadhi | C | C | O | O | O | C | |
| Órmos Pigadhi | C | C | O | O | O | O | |
| **Skhinoúsa** | | | | | | | |
| Órmos Mirsini | B | C | O | O | C | C | • |
| Agrilos | C | C | O | O | O | O | • |
| **Koufonisia** | | | | | | | |
| Koufonisia | C | C | O | B | C | C | • |
| Parianós | B | AC | O | O | O | O | • |
| Dhrima and Andíkaros | C | C | O | O | O | O | • |
| **Amorgós** | | | | | | | |
| Katápola | B | AC | B | A | B | B | • |
| Órmos Kalotaritissa | B | AC | O | O | O | C | • |
| Órmos Akrotíri | O | C | O | O | O | C | • |
| Kalotiri | C | C | O | O | O | C | • |
| Órmos Áy Annas | B | AC | O | B | C | C | • |
| Órmos Vilakardha | O | C | O | O | O | O | |
| **Lévitha** | | | | | | | |
| Órmos Lévitha | A | C | O | O | O | C | • |
| Órmos Vathi | B | C | O | O | O | O | • |
| Órmos Pningo | B | C | O | O | O | O | |
| **Southern Cyclades** | | | | | | | |
| **Mílos** | | | | | | | |
| Adhamas | B | AC | B | A | A | A | • |
| Apollonia | B | AC | O | B | C | B | • |
| Voudhia | C | C | O | O | O | C | • |
| **Kímolos** | | | | | | | |
| Sikia | C | C | O | O | O | O | • |
| Psathi | C | AC | O | O | C | C | • |
| Sémina | C | C | O | O | O | O | • |
| Pirgonisi | B | C | O | O | O | O | • |
| Prasonisi | O | C | O | O | O | O | |
| **Políagos** | | | | | | | |
| Nisís Manolonisi | C | C | O | O | O | O | • |
| **Folégandros** | | | | | | | |
| Karavostási | B | ABC | O | O | C | B | • |
| Vathi | C | C | O | O | O | O | • |
| **Síkinos** | | | | | | | |
| Skála | B | C | O | B | C | C | • |
| **Íos** | | | | | | | |
| Íos | A | A | B | B | B | B | • |
| Órmos Koumbaras | C | C | O | O | O | C | |
| Órmos Milopotamou | C | C | O | O | O | C | • |

| | Shelter | Mooring | Fuel | Water | Provisioning | Tavernas | Plan |
|---|---|---|---|---|---|---|---|
| Órmos Manganari | B | C | O | O | O | C | • |
| Órmos Tris Klises | B | C | O | O | O | O | • |
| **Thíra** | | | | | | | |
| Áy Nikólaos | C | C | O | O | C | C | |
| Finikia | C | C | O | O | C | C | |
| Skála Thíra | C | A | O | O | A | A | • |
| Vlikadha | A | AB | O | A | C | C | • |
| Monolithos | C | A | O | B | O | C | • |
| **Néa Kammeni** | | | | | | | |
| (SE cove) | B | AB | O | O | O | O | • |
| **Anáfi** | | | | | | | |
| S Coast | C | C | O | O | O | C | • |
| Skála | C | C | O | O | C | C | • |

In ancient times the island was considerably more important than it is now. It had four cities and produced the lyric poets Simonides and Bacchlides and the physician Erasistratos. A few ruins of the cities remain and there is a large lion with a face like a big pussy cat carved out of a rock face (about 6m/20ft long) to the east of the *chora*. The ancient Kéans were apparently noted for their modesty and temperance. Today the population is much diminished (about 2,000), as the young leave the island to find work in Athens.

**USEFUL WAYPOINTS FOR N. CYCLADES**
Note: waypoints follow the order of the islands in this chapter.
⊕1  **1M N of Ák Perlevos (Kéa)**
    37°42'·3N 24°21'·0E
⊕2  0·2M S of Ák Tamelos (Kéa)
    37°31'·14N 24°16'·50E WGS84
⊕3  ¼M N of Ák Kéfalos (Kíthnos)
    37°29'·21N 24°26'·01E WGS84
⊕4  1M S of Ák Áy Dhimítrios (Kíthnos)
    37°17'·1N 24°21'·9E
⊕5  ½M N of Ák Trímeson (Síros)
    37°31'·4N 24°53'·0E
⊕6  0·2M S of Ák Velostási (Síros)
    37°21'·58N 24°52'·53E WGS84
⊕7  0·2M S of Ák Khondra (Síros)
    37°22'·75N 24°56'·60E WGS84
⊕8  Mid-channel Stenón Kafirevs (Andros/Evia)
    37°58'·4N 24°37'·7E
⊕9  Mid-channel Stenón Dhisvaton (Andros/Tínos)
    37°40'·6N 24°58'·0E
⊕10 Mid-channel Stenón Mikonou (Tínos/Míkonos)
    37°30'·9N 25°16'·4E
⊕11 ¾M N of Ák Via (Rinia)
    37°27'·12N 25°13'·58E WGS84
⊕12 ¼M off Delos E side (Prasonísia channel)
    37°23'·63N 25°17'·11E WGS84
⊕13 1M S of Nisís Khatapodhia light
    37°23'·7N 25°33'·8E

# Northern Cyclades

## Nísos Kéa

### (Zéa, Tzia)

A craggy and mountainous island lying a little over 12 miles east of Ák Sounion in the approaches to the Kólpos Petalíon. A high mountain ridge runs down the east coast with the summit, Mt. Ayias Ilías (561m/1,840ft), near the east coast 4 miles south of the northern extremity of Kéa. Most of the inhabitants live in the *chora* (Kéa) or at Áy Nikólaos. The island is mostly barren although there are patches of cultivated and wooded ground near the coast.

**NORTHERN CYCLADES**

237

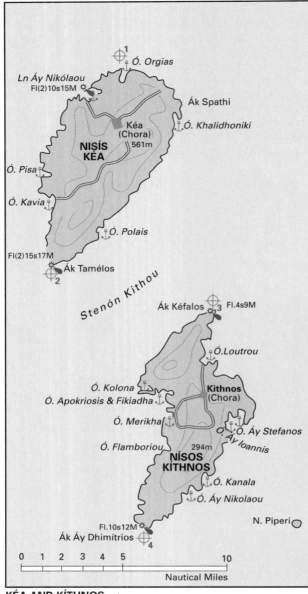

**KÉA AND KÍTHNOS**

⊕1 1M N of Ák Perlevos (Kéa)
   37°42'·3N 24°21'·0E
⊕2 0·2M S of Ák Tamelos (Kéa)
   37°31'·14N 24°16'·50E WGS84
⊕3 ¼M N of Ák Kéfalos (Kíthnos)
   37°29'·21N 24°26'·01E WGS84
⊕4 1M S of Ák Áy Dhimítrios (Kíthnos)
   37°17'·1N 24°21'·9E

## LIMÍN ÁYIOS NIKÓLAOU

### (Aghiou Nicolaou, Livádhi, Vourkari)
BA 1538
Imray-Tetra G31

### Approach

*Conspicuous* The village or *chora* (Kéa) on the hill behind the harbour is visible from the N. The entrance is not easy to spot from the distance but the general location on the NW end of the island is obvious. From the W the cluster of houses on the slopes behind Vourkari will be seen. Closer in the chapel and light (on top) on the N side of the

entrance and a church on the S side are conspicuous.

*By night* Use the lights on either side of the entrance: N side Fl(2)10s15M/S side Fl.1·5s5M. The mole at Korissía is lit: Fl.G.3s3M.

*Note* With the *meltemi* there are strong gusts off the high land in the vicinity of the harbour.

### Mooring

There are three possibilities:
1. ***Órmos Livádhi*** The S arm of the bay. Moor stern or bows-to the quay at Korissía keeping clear of the ferry berth behind the mole. Reasonable shelter from the *meltemi*. Alternatively anchor off in the bay in calm weather. The bottom is mud and weed, not everywhere good holding.
2. ***Vourkari*** The NE arm of the bay. Anchor in the bay or go stern or bows-to the quay in the space indicated between the hatched lines on the plan. The bottom comes up quickly just before the

The chapel-cum-lighthouse on the N side of the entrance to Limín Áy Nikólaou

Áyios Nikólaou on Kéa looking W with Voukari in the foreground and Órmos Livádhi top left

*Peter Kleinoth/MareTeam*

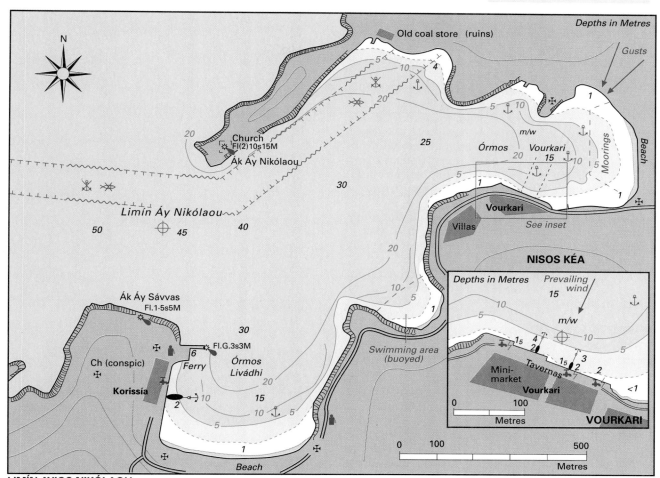

**LIMÍN AYIOS NIKÓLAOU**
⊕ 37°39′·89N 24°18′·67E WGS84

quay and consequently it is best to go bows-to if possible. On either side of this space it is too shallow off the quay. The bottom drops off quickly here (over 10m depths 30m out from the quay) so make sure you have an adequate length of chain or line to let go. The bottom is mud and weed and not everywhere good holding. It is reported there is a cable fouling the bottom about 30m off the quay. As the *meltemi* blows straight on to the quay ensure your anchor is holding before tying up to the quay. If you are anchoring off there are laid moorings off the E side of the bay, but you can anchor amongst the moored boats with care. Alternatively anchor outside the area with laid moorings in 8–12m.

In the summer there are a lot of yachts using this bay.

3. **Coal Bunker Bay** Anchor off the old coal bunkering depot in the N arm of the bay. Good shelter from N winds. The bottom is mud and weed, indifferent holding.

*Authorities* Port police at Korissía.

### Facilities

*Services* Water and electricity points on the quay at Vourkari. Water on the quay at Korissía. Water is often in short supply in the summer and may be rationed.

*Fuel* Near the quay at Korissía. A mini-tanker can deliver to the quay (☎ 24100).
*Provisions* Some provisions available at Vourkari and Korissía.
*Eating out* Tavernas at Vourkari and Korissía.
*Other* Telephone. Irregular bus to the *chora*. Ferry to Lavrion.

The quay at Vourkari

## General

Áyios Nikólaos is more often than not crowded in the summer with Athens-based yachts, the picturesque hamlet of Vourkari being the most popular.

The bay was once important as a coaling station for steamers plying between Black Sea ports and western Europe. Recent excavations on the N side of the bay by the American school have unearthed an important Bronze Age settlement inhabited from around 2000 BC to 1400 BC. Pottery, domestic and ornamental, and the classic Cycladic figurines have been unearthed amongst the buildings, many of which are now just under the sea.

The *chora* on the hill, a huddle of glaring white houses, is picturesque and well worth a visit – enquire about the bus to get there and walk back downhill. About 20 minutes' walk to the E of the village is the large lion (the 'pussy cat') carved from the rock face and attributed to an Ionian sculptor from around 600 BC.

## ÓRMOS PISA (Pisses)

37°36'·1N 24°16'·6E

A small bay on the W coast about 1½ miles N of Ák Makropoundha. Open to the W and S. With the *meltemi* some swell creeps into the bay making it uncomfortable. Anchor in 4–8m near the head of the bay. Sandy bottom.

Tavernas ashore. The valley behind is a startling green in comparison to most of the island. There are a few ruins of ancient Piessa here, a comparatively minor ancient town of the island.

There is a cove immediately N of Órmos Pisa that looks good, but it is very deep even close in.

## ÓRMOS KAVIA (Koundouros)

A small bay lying approximately one mile to the E of Ák Makropounda. Care must be taken of a reef lying about ¼M SSW of Makropoundha. Waves break on it with a slight swell and it is relatively easy to spot. A number of windmills on the slopes around the bay are conspicuous as well as a large building on the N side of the entrance to the bay.

Anchor in 3–6m on a sandy bottom. Good shelter from the *meltemi*, although some swell creeps around into the bay making it uncomfortable. A number of old mooring blocks and chains have been

**ÓRMOS KAVIA**
⊕37°34'·44N 24°16'·13E WGS84

reported on the bottom so it may be wise to use a trip-line on the anchor.

The bay is being developed with new hotels and houses which, with the exception of a brown blob of a building, fit reasonably well into the landscape. Manos, who used to be here, seems to have moved on. Limited provisions and tavernas ashore.

## ORGIAS (Otzias) 37°40'·5N 24°21'·3E

A small cove on the N side of Kéa suitable in calm weather only. Anchor in 5–6m near the head of the inlet. A line of small buoys marks the limit of the swimming area at the head of the cove. There are a few houses around the slopes and a taverna opens in the summer.

*Note* A rock above water has been reported 0·4M E of the entrance to Orgias.

## KHALIDHONIKI

A small cove on the NE corner of the island under Ák Spathí. Anchor near the head of the cove in 3–5m on a sandy bottom. Good shelter from the

Órmos Kavia looking NNE from the entrance

**ÓRMOS KHALIDHONIKI (Spathi)**
⊕37°38'·6N 24°24'·5E

*meltemi* although some swell is pushed into the cove. Open S. A small hamlet ashore and a taverna at the head of the bay.

## ÓRMOS POLAIS

An open bay on the SE coast of Kéa 3 miles NE of Ák Tamélos. In the middle of the bay there is a small islet joined by a reef to the shore. Anchor to the E of the islet and the reef in 3–4m. The bottom is sand and weed with some rock and not everywhere good holding. Poor shelter from the *meltemi*.

**ÓRMOS POLAIS**
⊕37°33´·4N 24°20·05´E

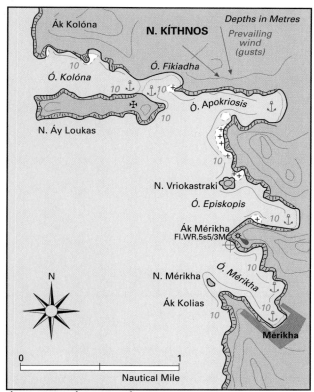

**ÓRMOS KOLÓNA TO MÉRIKHA**
⊕37°23´·65N 24°23´·5E

There are a few ancient ruins ashore including the remains of a temple belonging to ancient Karathia. Some of the ancient city walls and the theatre can also be found. The site is best visited in calm weather as the anchorage is not the best with the *meltemi*.

# Nísos Kíthnos
## (Kythnos, Thermia)

A barren rocky island lying a little over 6 miles SE of Kéa. The hump of the island is highest in the middle where the summit reaches 294m (965ft). Despite its modest height, the island is so folded and steep-to that it gives the impression of being more savage and higher from seawards than figures suggest. The population mostly lives in the *chora* (Kíthnos) on the hill above Órmos Apokriosis and in Mérikha. The island has some tourist trade in the summer, but on the whole is little touched by tourism.

### KOLÓNA, APOKRIOSIS AND FIKIADHA
#### Approach

These bays are situated about one mile to the N of Mérikha where the huddle of houses around the harbour is conspicuous. Care should be taken of the underwater rocks on the S side of the entrance to Órmos Apokriosis and on the NE side of the entrance to Fikiadha.

*By night* There are no lights.

*Dangers* With the *meltemi* there are strong gusts into the approaches and the bays.

#### Mooring

*Órmos Kolóna* (Sand Bar Bay) Anchor in the NE corner in 3–6m on sand. In the summer the bay is popular so it is common practice to take a long line ashore. The bottom is sand and good holding. Good shelter from the *meltemi*. Open W.

*Órmos Fikiadha* Anchor in 3–5m on sand and weed, good holding once the anchor is through the weed. Good shelter from the *meltemi* although there are gusts into the bay. Open S for a limited sector.

*Órmos Apokriosis* Anchor in 5–10m on sand and weed. You can take a long line ashore to the N side for added security. Good shelter from the *meltemi*. Open SW–W.

#### Facilities
Taverna at Apokriosis.

#### General
The bays provide good shelter in pleasant surroundings. Development has slowly been extending northwards from Merikha, but has not really affected these bays yet.

On Nisís Áy Louka, the islet connected to Kíthnos by the sand bar, are a few ancient remains including traces of walls, a temple and *agora*. On the N side of Órmos Kolona it is reported there is a hot spring.

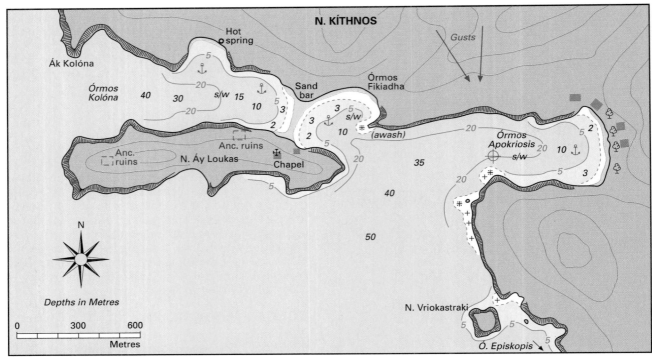

**Ó. KOLÓNA, FIKIADHA AND APOKRIOSIS**
⊕37°24'·9N 24°23'·5E

## EPISKOPIS

Lies in between Mérikha and Órmos Apokriosis. With the *meltemi* some swell enters the bay. In calm weather or with SE–E winds anchor in 3–10m where convenient. Open to the W. A taverna opens in the summer.

## MÉRIKHA (Merikhas)

### Approach

A small harbour on the W coast and the ferry port of Kíthnos. The buildings of the town are conspicuous from seaward.

*By night* Use the light on Ák Mérikha Fl.WR.5s5/3M: the red sector covers Vrak Mérikha on the S side of the entrance 340°-R-030°. The end of the ferry mole is lit Fl.R.3s3M.

### Mooring

Go stern or bows-to the quay inside the ferry berth or anchor off. Make sure you let out plenty of scope and that the anchor is well in to cope with the ferry and the fast ferry which will often use the propellers to keep them off the quay and in so doing create a lot of wash.

*Shelter* Reasonable shelter from the *meltemi* although there are strong gusts into the bay that can be most uncomfortable. Any wind with any W in it sends a swell into the harbour. Strong SW–W winds may make it untenable.

*Authorities* Port police and customs.

### Facilities

*Water* On the quay, but you will need to track down the waterman
*Fuel* Can be delivered by taxi.
*Provisions* Most provisions can be found although

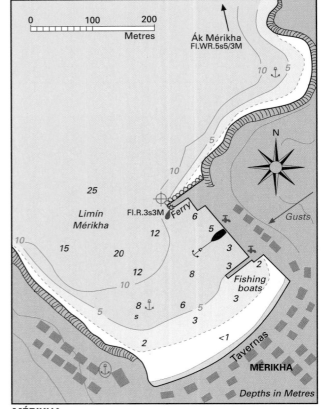

**MÉRIKHA**
⊕37°23'·45N 24°23'·75E WGS84

supplies are much dependent on the ferry. Ice.
*Eating out* Tavernas on the waterfront.
*Other* Telephone. Greek gas. Bus to the *chora*. Ferry to Lavrion.

Mérikha on Kíthnos looking NW with Fikiadha and Apokriosis
at the top of the photo          *Peter Kleinoth/MareTeam*

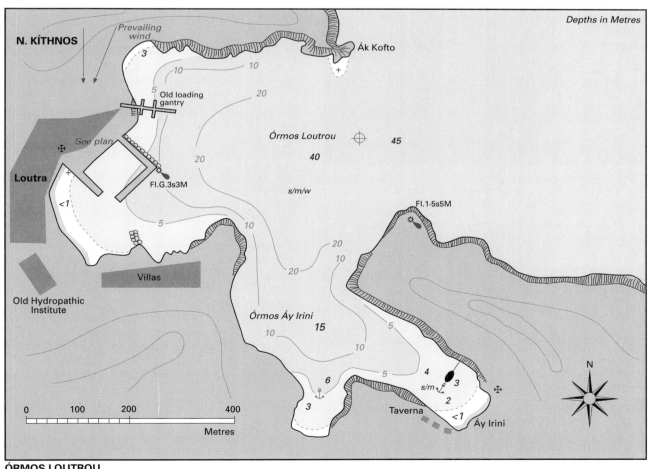

Depths in Metres

N. KÍTHNOS

*Prevailing wind*

3

Ák Kofto

10          10

20

5     Old loading gantry

*See plan*

Órmos Loutrou          45

40

20

Loutra

s/m/w

Fl.G.3s3M

Fl.1·5s5M

<1

5

10

20

5

20

Villas

10

Old Hydropathic Institute

Órmos Áy Irini          15

10

10

5

10

4     3

6          5     s/m     2

3          Taverna     <1     Áy Irini

N

| 0 | 100 | 200 | 400 |

Metres

**ÓRMOS LOUTROU**
⊕37°26´·66N 24°25´·97E WGS84

## General

Mérikha is a comparative newcomer of a village, really built to service the ferry port. It is effectively the biggest place on Kíthnos (the *chora* has more houses but less in the way of services) and the tavernas on the beach are pleasant enough places to while away an evening while the *meltemi* screams down into the bay.

It is worth hiring a motorbike from here to look around the island, though care is needed on the roads which are both steep and in poor repair in many places.

## LOUTRA (Loutron, Port Irene)

### Approach

The entrance to the bay is difficult to pick out from the distance until close to. The light structure on the S side of the entrance is difficult to spot. Once up to the entrance some of the houses on the S side of Loutra will be seen.

**LOUTRA**
⊕37°26′·6N 24°25′·7E

Loutra on Kíthnos looking NNW with Órmos Áy Irini bottom right and the yacht quay off the village middle left (taken before the new basin was built) *Peter Kleinoth/MareTeam*

Loutra harbour looking NW

*By night* Use the light on Ák Kéfalos Fl.4s9M and the light on the S side of the entrance Fl.1·5s5M. The dogleg corner of the basin at Loutra is lit Fl.G.3s3M.

*Caution* With the *meltemi* there is a considerable amount of wind and sea pushing you into the bay. As the basin has limited manoeuvring space it is prudent to prepare the boat for berthing in the outer part of the bay.

### Mooring

*Loutra* Go alongside either side of the outer arm of the basin or stern or bows-to the NE mole. Yachts normally go alongside the outer quay because otherwise anchors would be criss-crossed inside the small basin. Excellent shelter inside the basin although there are gusts with the *meltemi*. In settled weather or when the basin is full yachts can go stern or bows-to the quay N of the basin. Care is needed of underwater ballasting in places.

*Áy Irini* Anchor and take a long line ashore to the NE side. There are a number of rings set into the rock for lines. The quay is too shallow to berth stern or bows-to. Reasonable shelter from the *meltemi* although some swell is pushed into here making it uncomfortable.

### Facilities

*Services* Water and electricity points on the quay at Loutra. Showers ashore.

*Fuel* May be able to get a mini-tanker down to the harbour.

*Provisions* Some provisions.
*Eating out* Several tavernas and cafés. Taverna at Áy Irini.
*Other* PO. Telephone.

### General

The hot mineral springs have been esteemed throughout history except for the present age when spa resorts have become unfashionable. The ancient Greeks and Romans used them and King Otto, Greece's first king, built the institute now standing. The hot springs still run and you can take a bath at the institute although it is pretty run-down these days. Alternatively, hot springs bubble up at the S end of the beach and you can take your own spa bath there.

Near Ák Kéfalos (about two hours' walk) are the ruins of a medieval citadel and town, though few buildings remain intact.

### ÁYIOS STEFANOS AND ÁYIOS ÍOANNIS

BA 1538

Two bays on the E coast of Kíthnos affording good shelter from the *meltemi*. There are gusts off the high land at the entrance. Care should be taken of the reef lying 100m SE of the headland separating the two bays.

Anchor near the head of either bay and take a line ashore to a tree or a rock. The bottom is sand and weed – bad holding in places. Good shelter from the *meltemi* despite the gusts once you are securely anchored.

Limited water ashore. A taverna opens at Áy Stefanos in the summer.

A number of modest villas and one palatial villa have been built here in these beautiful bays. The slopes behind drop precipitously down to the sea which is the clearest blue. It is an enchanting spot once you have got used to the wind whistling down into it and well worth a visit.

**Ó. AYIOS STEFANOS AND Ó. AYIOS IOANNIS**
⊕37°23'·6N 24°27'·6E

### LEFKES

37°22'·4N 24°27'·0E

A tiny cove approximately 1M S of Órmos Lousa. It would probably not pay to be here with the *meltemi*, but in calm weather the cove at the foot of a ravine is a spectacular spot. Taverna ashore.

### ÓRMOS KANALA AND ÓRMOS ÁY NIKOLAOS (Skillou)

Ó Kanala 37°20'·7N 24°26'·2E
Ó Áy Nikolaos 37°19'·8N 24°25'·3E

Lie respectively 4½ and 6¼ miles SW of Ák Áy Ioannou, the easternmost tip of Kíthnos. They offer indifferent shelter from the *meltemi*, but can be visited in calm weather. Both are open to the S and E. Care is needed of an isolated reef off the entrance to Órmos Kanala. No facilities.

Near Kanala is the monastery of the Panayía Kanala, the Virgin of the Canal, because reputedly the icon of the virgin in the monastery was discovered in a canal, though exactly where is uncertain. Her feast days are 15 August and 8 September when large numbers of pilgrims are said to come here.

## Nísos Síros

### (Syros, Syra)

A hilly, mostly barren island. The north is rugged and mostly uninhabited while the south has gentler slopes and is cultivated near the coast. Most of the population live in Ermoúpolis, the port and also the nominal capital of all the Cyclades.

Nothing much remains of ancient Síros which was sited where Ermoúpolis now stands. In the Middle Ages the inhabitants moved inland until the Venetians, ever mindful of the potential of the harbour and the strategic position of Síros along the Aegean trade route, occupied the island and restored its prosperity. In the 17th century the island came under the protection of the French and so escaped Turkish occupation. Síros took no part in the Greek War of Independence, but did take refugees from Psará and Khíos.

In the steam age Síros became the principal port in the Aegean and a major coal-bunkering station for ships on passage through the Cyclades. Its importance declined when oil replaced coal and ships could do longer passages without the need to refuel.

The twin villages on the two hills behind the harbour reflect the island's history. Old Síros became the Venetian and Genoese Roman Catholic village and the descendants remain predominantly Roman Catholic. The Psariote and Khiot refugees established Ermoúpolis (Hermoupolis: named after Hermes, the god of traders) which is the Greek Orthodox quarter. Ermoúpolis has spilled over from its original site and now spreads around the waterfront. The port is still a mercantile centre and a major ferry port. The island is also famous for the production of *loukoumi* or Turkish Delight which

**NÍSOS SÍROS**

⊕**5** ½M N of Ák Trímeson (Síros)
37°31'·4N 24°53'·0E
⊕**6** 0·2M S of Ák Velostási (Síros)
37°21'·58N 24°52'·53E WGS84
⊕**7** 0·2M S of Ák Khondra (Síros)
37°22'·75N 24°56'·60E WGS84

**ERMOÚPOLIS**
⊕37°26'·15N 24°56'·9E

here is excellent and not to be confused with some of the sickly-sweet imitations made elsewhere.

## ERMOÚPOLIS (Limín Sirou)

BA 1538
Imray-Tetra G31

### Approach

*Conspicuous* The twin villages on the hill above the harbour are easily seen from the distance. The most conspicuous object is the lighthouse on Nisís Gáïdharos which is easily identified from a considerable distance off. Closer in a large cathedral on the slopes behind the town and the breakwaters are conspicuous.

*By night* Use the light on Nisís Aspronisi Fl(2)12s7M and Nisís Gáïdharos Fl.6s12M. The entrance to the harbour is lit: Ák Kondoyiánnis Fl.3s5M; the N breakwater head Fl.G.3s6M and S breakwater Fl.R.3s6M and F.Y. Ifalos Karfomeni is marked by a light buoy Q.R though it is not to be relied upon.

*Danger*

1. Care is needed of Ifalos Karfomeni, a reef and shoal water on the SW side of the harbour. It is marked by a light buoy Q.R(occas).

    If a yacht keeps close to the end of the N breakwater where there are good depths, the bunkering station and reef are easily avoided.

2. Care is needed of the large ferries constantly churning in and out of the harbour.

### Mooring

Go stern or bows-to the quay on the N side of the harbour. The bottom is mud – good holding.

Approaches to Ermoúpolis looking NNW

*Shelter* Good shelter from the *meltemi* although there are gusts and a surge develops making it uncomfortable, as does the wash from ferries. With SE winds a swell rolls in making the harbour very uncomfortable and possibly dangerous for small yachts.

*Note* The harbour is very smelly in places from sewage emptying into it.

*Authorities* A port of entry: customs, port police and immigration authorities.

*Note* For Marina Sirou and the fishing harbour on the W side of the harbour see below.

### Facilities

*Services* Water and electricity points on the quay.

*Fuel* Near the W quay. ☎ 0281 23784 or call on VHF Ch 8 for a minitanker.

*Repairs* There are several yards here which can haul yachts.

*Lefteris Akilas* 65-ton hydraulic lift. 4m depths at slipway.

☎ 0281 23682 *Fax* 0281 23445.

*Vangelis Tzortis* Sledge and slipway. Used to hauling yachts.

☎ 0281 87086 *Fax* 0281 86000.

The commercial dry-dock is now open again and can take very large craft. Mechanical and engineering repairs. Chandlers near the yacht yards. Sail repairs can be carried out – go to the cheese shop at Chiou 28!

*Shopping* Good shopping for all provisions nearby. Near the W end of the town quay there is a market street leading up into town with all manner of butchers, fruit and veg shops, cheese shops and mini-markets. Sirou sausages are excellent.

*Eating out* Good tavernas around the waterfront and others in the town.

*Other* PO (open until 2400). OTE. Banks. Greek gas and *Camping Gaz*. Hospital. Hire cars and motorbikes. Buses to the principal villages. Ferries to Piraeus, nearby Cyclades, Crete, and Sámos.

### General

Ermoúpolis is still the capital of the Cyclades and although it may not have the commercial power it once did, it still bustles and buzzes with the self importance and assurance of a cultural and commercial hub. It is still the largest town and it feels like it.

The buildings around the harbour reflect the past power and glory. An 18th-century square paved with marble and shaded by trees and complete with bandstand. Impressive public buildings, including an opera house modelled on La Scala. Elegant 19th-century mansions with wrought iron balconies, and an extra-large Catholic cathedral. Ermoúpolis repays a wander around the back streets where neo-classical buildings and ship-owners mansions are impressive although crumbling here and there.

The quay is alive all day and night with a wide choice of bars and cafés to while away the day and night watching the ferries churn in and out of the harbour. In the back streets and around the west quay are some old-fashioned *ouzeries* and cafés while on the east quay and the east side of the old town are some traditional tavernas. It all comes as a bit of a shock after the quieter places, but the hustle and bustle is genuine and Ermoúpolis grows on you as something more essential and Greek than other tourist-orientated places.

### MARINA SIROU

The marina under construction on the S side of the harbour is not in any way ready for yachts at the time of writing. Work is going on but there is much left to do. The plan shows the work already completed and the intended final form of the marina. When complete it will offer all facilities, but will sadly be some distance away from the charms of Ermoúpolis on the other side of the harbour. Estimated completion date is 2002–2003.

MARINA SIROU

### ERMOÚPOLIS FISHING HARBOUR

The fishing harbour is complete and also full. Yachts can berth alongside the outer wall where shown and shelter here is good although there is some wash from craft entering and leaving Ermoúpolis. You are not too far away from town although you do need to dodge the traffic speeding in and out of town along the waterfront road. It is a convenient place to stop at if enquiring about hauling in the yards mentioned above.

### PROHIBITED ANCHORAGE

It is prohibited to anchor in an area ½ a mile N and S of Nisís Asproi and between Aspro and Síros. It is permitted to sail in this area.

*Caution* A reef (Tripita Reef) with 1·6m least depth over it lies one mile W of Nisís Aspro. N. Aspro is also fringed by reefs.

### NISÍS GAÏDHAROS

The island lying close off the coast opposite Ák Kondoyiánnis at the entrance to Ermoúpolis.

**ERMOÚPOLIS FISHING HARBOUR**

**NISÍS GAÏDHAROS ANCHORAGE**
⊕37°25′·6N 24°58′·7E

On the SE corner of the island there is a small cove that provides good shelter from the *meltemi*. Approximately halfway into the cove there is a bar with 2·5m depths over it. On the W side of the bar near the coast there is a sunken obstruction. Once over the bar anchor in 3m on a sand and weed bottom. No facilities.

## ÓRMOS VARIS

A deeply indented bay on the SE side of Síros immediately W of Ák Khondra. Anchor near the head of the bay in 2–4m or in the cove on the W side in 3–5m. The bottom is sand and good holding. Good shelter from the *meltemi* although there are gusts and a swell can be reflected into the anchorage.

Several tavernas around the waterfront and a hotel at the head of the bay. Fuel about 800m away on the road to Ermoúpolis.

**ÓRMOS VARIS**
⊕7  0·2M S of Ák Khondra (Síros) 37°22′·75N 24°56′·60E WGS84

## FINIKAS (Foinikas, Foinikou)

BA 1538
A sheltered bay on the SW coast of Síros.

### Approach

*Conspicuous* The villas around the slopes of Órmos Finikou will be seen and closer in the light structure on Psathonisi can be identified. Psathonisi is low-lying and difficult to make out from the distance. The rough stone breakwater built out from the point to Vrak Dhimitra on the W side of Órmos Foinikou will also be seen.

*By night* Use the light on Psathonísi Fl.2s5M and the light on Vrak Dhímitra Fl.R.1·5s4M vis only over 198°-085°. The end of the mole at Posidhonía is lit F.G.

**FINIKAS APPROACHES**
⊕1 37°23′·23N 24°52′·17E WGS84
⊕2 37°23′·51N 24°52′·48E WGS84

Finikas (Órmos Finikou) on Síros looking NNW across Ák Velostási into the bay of Órmos Finikou. The yacht pier and anchorage can just be discerned on the NW side of the bay
*Peter Kleinoth/MareTeam*

Finikas harbour looking NE

*Dangers* There are strong gusts into the bay with the *meltemi*. With southerlies a confused sea builds up in the approaches to the bay.

## Mooring

Go stern or bows-to the S side of the outer mole at Finikas. There are laid moorings tailed to a small buoy that you need to pick up on the outer dogleg end of the mole. On the inner section you will need to use your own anchor although there are plans to lay moorings here as well. Yachts can also berth

**FINIKAS**
⊕37°23'·83N 24°52'·62E WGS84

inside the basin if there is room. Go stern or bows-to the mole or alongside the inner mole.

*Shelter* With the *meltemi* blowing the best place to be is on the outside of the mole where the *meltemi* is blowing you off the quay. In unsettled weather and with southerlies berth in the basin. With strong southerlies the outside berths are untenable and you need to be inside the basin where there is a surge, but it is tenable.

*Authorities* Harbour attendant. Charge band 2.

*Anchorage* With the *meltemi* you can anchor off in the bay. The beach area has a line of small buoys marking out the swimming area, but there is plenty of room left to anchor. The bottom is sand and weed with some rocks, good holding once the anchor is in.

*Note* The area S of the basin has a number of laid moorings. Care is needed when navigating in the area and also if you intend to anchor here.

## Facilities

*Services* Water on the quay. You may be able to get electricity connected. A shower and toilet block although it is not always the most sanitary.

*Fuel* Can be delivered by mini-tanker (☎ 81858).

*Repairs* A number of yacht service companies can be called out for repairs. There is a notice board at the harbour with telephone numbers. Small chandlers around the waterfront.

*Provisions* Most provisions can be found.

*Eating out* Taverna at the harbour and others around the waterfront.

*Other* PO. Hire cars and motorbikes. Taxi and buses to Ermoúpolis.

## General

The bay and the beach are most attractive so it is not surprising that a number of hotels and villas have been built around the bay. Nearly everyone who visits here likes the place and it is well worth stopping here with the bonus in the *meltemi* season of excellent shelter.

## POSIDHONÍA

The military harbour in the SE corner of Órmos Finikou. Yachts are not permitted to berth inside the harbour which in any case is usually occupied by naval craft. Yachts can anchor off in the SE corner just clear of the prohibited area. The anchorage is not well sheltered from the *meltemi*, but is useful if it blows from the S. Taverna ashore.

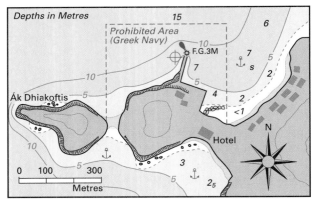

**POSIDHONÍA**
⊕37°23′·3N 24°52′·9E

## ÓRMOS GALISSAS

A small bay lying immediately S of Ák Katakefalos. Anchor in 4–5m at the head of the bay. There are 3m depths about 50m off the beach. The bottom is sand and good holding. Reasonable shelter from the *meltemi* although some swell penetrates into the bay. On the S side of the bay a short mole has been built and several yachts can squeeze in behind it getting better shelter from the *meltemi*. Care is needed of

**ÓRMOS GALISSAS**
⊕37°26′·88N 24°53′·86E WGS84

underwater ballasting off the mole so take a long line to it.

Mini-market and tavernas ashore as well as a disco producing industrial sound levels.

## ÓRMOS KINI

A small bay on the W coast of Síros immediately opposite Ermoúpolis on the E coast. Care must be taken of the reef lying just over half a mile off the coast WNW of the bay. Care must also be taken of a sand bar just under the water that extends from the S side of the bay to halfway across it. Anchor in 3–5m in the NE corner. There are numerous laid moorings here so care is needed not to foul your anchor. The mole on the N side of the bay has 2–3·5m depths off the quayed area, but is always full of tripper and local boats. Reasonable shelter from the *meltemi* although some swell is pushed into the bay. Open W.

Tavernas ashore and limited provisions can be obtained.

**ÓRMOS KINI**
⊕37°26′·52N 24°54′·68E WGS84

Órmos Kini looking W

## ÓRMOS DELFINO

A small bay approximately one mile N of Kini. It can be recognised when close in by the small islet in the middle. Care is needed of Ifalos Delfini with a least depth of 3·7 metres over it lying just under one mile W of the anchorage. Anchor in 3–4m behind the islet. Reasonable shelter from the *meltemi* although there are gusts off the high land. Taverna opens in the summer.

**ÓRMOS DELFINO**
⊕37°27'·5N 24°53'·8E

## ÓRMOS AETOU

A bay approximately 1M N of Delfino. The best anchorage is in the cove on the N side with a long line ashore. Anchor in 4–5m. Alternatively anchor at the head of the bay in 3–5m on sand. Adequate shelter from the *meltemi* although some swell rolls into the bay. Taverna opens in the summer.

**ÓRMOS AETOU**
⊕37°28'·6N 24°53'·8E

## ÓRMOS GRAMMATA (Megas Lakkos)

Lies at the N end of Órmos Megas on the NW of Síros. Ák Grammata, a bell-shaped light yellow rocky bluff conspicuous from seaward, forms the western side of the bay. Anchor on the W or E side of the bay in 4–5m. Although the bottom is sandy it does not appear to be good holding. With the *meltemi* there are severe gusts off the high land and it is prudent to take a long line ashore. No facilities.

Ák Grammata is covered with the names and dates of seafarers who have sheltered here over the centuries waiting for the infernal *meltemi* to die down, and no doubt many readers of this book will likewise add their names to the list.

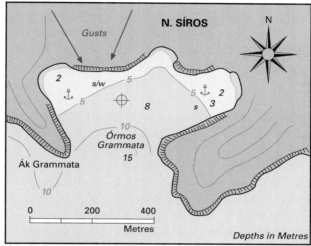

**ÓRMOS GRAMMATA**
⊕37°30'N 24°53'·3E

## NÍSOS YIAROS (Yioura) (Prohibited Area)

The island nearly midway between Kéa and Tínos about 8 miles NW of Síros. It is a barren uninhabited lump of rock with no anchorages. It is in any case prohibited to anchor off or land on the island. When the *meltemi* is blowing there are strong gusts off the south coast and a yacht should keep a prudent distance off.

## DORO STRAIT (Stenón Kafirevs/Kafireos)

⊕**8** Mid-channel Stenón Kafirevs 37°58'·4N 24°37'·7E

This strait lies between the N end of Andros and the S end of Evia. The strait is 6 miles across at its narrowest part. A current runs through the strait in a SW direction at 2–4 knots but the Admiralty Pilot reports that a southerly current of 7 knots was recorded with a strong northerly gale. The *meltemi* is funnelled through the strait and accompanying it are steep confused seas.

With gales from the N small yachts should exercise considerable caution in the vicinity of the strait. I have seen large ships anchor in the roadstead off Karistos rather than proceed through the strait and during a Force 10 gale which lasted several days I counted over twenty ships anchored off waiting for the gale to abate. Even after the *meltemi* dies down a confused sea will remain for some time. In the event of strong northerly winds a yacht can shelter at Karistos on Evia or the bays to the E of it (see Chapter VI).

# Nísos Andros

The northernmost and second largest of the Cyclades. It is mountainous throughout with the summit in the middle of the island, Mt Kouvarion, rising to 1,134m (3,721ft), and another peak, Mt Petalon, about a mile to the NE, rising to 944m (3,097ft). These peaks are snowcapped in the winter and in early spring. It is well wooded and cultivated in places.

The island is named after Andreus, a general from Crete. During the Persian invasions Andros sided with the invaders, which cost it dearly after the Athenian sea victory off Salamí. During the Peloponnesian War it sided with Sparta – it must have had some longstanding grudge against Athens. The ancient capital was at Palaioupolis on the west coast, but few ruins remain. It passed in turn to the Romans and to Byzantium and eventually to the Venetians in 1207 who built many of the fortified towers and the distinctive dovecotes dotted around it. It was occupied by the Turks in 1556 and became Greek after the War of Independence.

Today Andros is popular with Greek holidaymakers, although a few foreign tourists are discovering it. The *chora* at Kástro is well worth a visit by land if you decide not to take on the *meltemi* and sail around to it in the summer. In recent years the island has become something of a 'weekend cottage' suburb of Athens and the new bland villas of the Athenians have appeared around the coast, giving the island a case of villa-pox. It is still enchanting in places though you need to try harder to get away from it all.

**ANDROS AND TÍNOS**

# GAVRION

BA 1538
Imray-Tetra G31

### Approach

*Conspicuous* The entrance to Órmos Gavrion is difficult to see from the distance. The group of islands to the S of the entrance (Platí, Gáïdharos, Akamatis, Prasso, and Megálo) are easily identified and closer in the light structure on the W entrance point and the buildings of the village will be seen. Once at the entrance to the bay things are straightforward.

*By night* Use the lights on either side of the entrance to the bay: Ák Kastrí Fl.6s8M and Ák Mármara Fl.RG.2s3M, (the red sector covers If Vouvi and the islands described above over 248°-005°). The breakwater is lit on the extremity Q.G.3M. The reefs and the unlit islands lying to the S of the entrance make a night approach from the S difficult and possibly dangerous. (See Dangers below.)

*Dangers*
1. Care must be taken of Ifalos Vouvi, a reef and shoal water approximately half a mile SE of the entrance.
2. Shoal water extends some distance off the islets in the approach from the S, especially Nisís Akamatis and Nisís Platí.
3. If coasting towards Gavrion from Batsí care is needed of Vrak Rosa, an above-water rock and reef approximately 200m ESE of Ák Marmara.

**APPROACHES TO GAVRION AND BATSÍ**
⊕37°52´·55N 24°43´·6E

Gavrion looking ENE                    *Nigel Patten*

**GAVRION**
⊕37°52´·55N 24°43´·6E

4. With the *meltemi* there are strong gusts down into Gavrion. Although there is good shelter inside, the gusts can make manoeuvring difficult off the quay.

*Note* The ferries using Gavrion enter and leave at speed. A good lookout should be kept for them in the vicinity of the bay.

### Mooring

Anchor at the head of the bay or go stern or bows-to or alongside the quay between the ferry piers. It is also possible to tuck into the E corner of the ferry pier, though one of the ferries often spends the night here and will take a line across to the quay, effectively blocking yachts in until it leaves. When anchoring tuck as far into the NW corner as you can to ensure you leave sufficient room for the large ferries to manoeuvre. The sight of one of these maritime juggernauts steaming towards you before dropping its anchor and going hard astern towards the ferry quay takes a bit of getting used to. The bottom is mud and weed, mostly good holding once through the weed.

*Shelter* Good shelter from the *meltemi* although there are strong gusts off the land.

*Authorities* Port police.

**Facilities**

*Services* Water on the quay. Electricity can be connected.

*Fuel* Near the quay.

*Provisions* Good shopping for most provisions. Ice near the quay.

*Eating out* Tavernas in the village and around the beach.

*Other* PO. OTE. Bank. Hire cars and motorbikes. Bus to Kástro. Ferry to Rafina and Piraeus.

**General**

The natural harbour of Gavrion offers the best shelter on Andros. The village is a modest uninspired little place, but not unpleasant. It is the ferry port for Andros and the ferries come and go frequently in the summer, bringing Athenians getting away from the smog of Athens to the clear air of the islands and tourists getting away from more crowded islands. Gavrion is a safe enough place to leave your boat (put out a second anchor for security) and explore inland.

## ÓRMOS PETROS

37°52'·9N 24°44'·5E

The large bay immediately E of Gavrion. Poor shelter from the *meltemi* as a swell inevitably rolls into here.

Anchor in 3–5m in the NW corner on sand and weed. Tavernas and bars on the beach.

## ÓRMOS FOURNOS

37°52'·6N 24°45'·6E

The large bay after Petros on the E side of Ák Kourouni. Some shelter from the *meltemi* tucked into the NW corner although there is still some swell pushed into the bay. Anchor in 3–5m on sand and weed. Above the anchorage is a Hellenistic tower (Áy Petros). Tavernas and bars on the beach.

## BATSÍ

**Approach**

A small harbour 2¾ miles SE of Gavrion. Batsí village is conspicuous from seaward.

*By night* Use the light on Ák Kolóna Fl.3s5M and the light on the extremity of the mole Fl.G.2s3M.

*Dangers* With the *meltemi* there are strong gusts down into the bay and approaches.

**Mooring**

Go stern or bows-to the quay near the root of the mole if there is room. The mole itself is reserved for the hydrofoil and fishing boats. There are 2–3m depths for most of the quay. Alternatively anchor off in the N or W of the bay.

*Shelter* Good shelter from the *meltemi*, although the gusts off the land from the E can make it uncomfortable. With strong southerlies a surge develops and the harbour may become untenable.

**Facilities**

*Services* Water and electricity on the quay.

**ÓRMOS BATSÍ**
⊕37°51'·0N 24°46'·3E

**BATSÍ**
⊕37°51'·2N 24°46'·7E

*Fuel* In the village. A mini-tanker can deliver to the quay.

*Provisions* Most provisions can be found.

*Eating out* Tavernas on the beach and in the village and bars around the waterfront.

*Other* PO. OTE. Banks. Hire cars and motorbikes. Taxis. Bus to Gavrion and Kástro.

**General**

Batsí is a pleasant enough little place, if somewhat overwhelmed by tourists. The locals who aren't cashing in on the tourism with bars and boutiques seem mesmerized by the parade of foreigners through their village, who apparently come here to do little else than lie in the sun and drink in the bars.

## ÓRMOS PALAIOUPOLIS

37°54'·2N 24°48'·2E

An open bay 4 miles SE of Gavrion. Anchor at the N end of the bay under Ák Thiakion where there is reasonable shelter from the *meltemi* although some swell penetrates. There have been reports that the holding is suspect. Clear water and delightful surroundings. In calm weather it is possible to anchor off the small fishing hamlet built near the ruins of ancient Palaioupolis.

There are few ruins remaining (part of an ancient breakwater can be seen on the sea bottom), but the site is enchanting and a good lunch stop in calm weather.

## ÓRMOS PLAKA

37°46'·0N 24°52'·7E

A small bay under Ák Zagora. Anchor in 2–4m on a sandy bottom. The bay is subject to strong gusts off the high land with the *meltemi*.

Ashore on a plateau at Ák Zagora are the ruins of ancient Zagora, a fortified Geometric town excavated in the 1970s.

## NE COAST OF ANDROS

Along the NE coast are a number of bays that can be used in calm weather or in light southerlies. When the *meltemi* is blowing a heavy sea is set onto this coast and it can be hard work getting along it.

## KÁSTRO (Kástron, Port Andros)

BA 1538

### Approach

The harbour faces directly into the *meltemi* and the approach is difficult. The reef running out from the headland can be identified by the seas breaking on it and the spume over it. Stick close to the N side where there are good depths off the end of the mole.

*By night* During the *meltemi* season a night approach is not recommended for first time visitors to the harbour. Use the light Nisís Tourlitis on the reef running out from Kástro Fl(2)15s6M and the light on the end of the mole Fl.G.2s3M.

*Dangers* The *meltemi* gusts down the coast into here pushing considerable seas onto the coast. Care needed in the approach to the harbour.

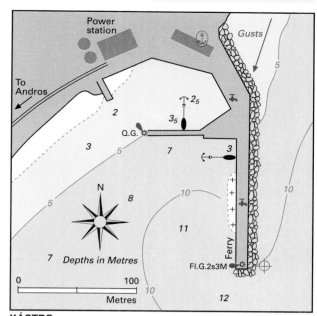

**KÁSTRO**
⊕37°50'·8N 24°56'·4E

### Mooring

Go stern or bows-to behind the mole. The bottom is rock and weed, poor holding, but there may be a laid mooring free behind the mole. Care must be taken of ballasting along the quay in places.

*Shelter* With the *meltemi* there is a surge in the harbour – more uncomfortable than dangerous in the inner basin.

### Facilities

*Water* On the quay.
*Fuel* On the outskirts of the village. You may be able to get a mini-tanker to deliver.
*Provisions* Good shopping in the village.
*Eating out* A taverna and bar near the harbour and others around the waterfront and in the village.
*Other* PO. OTE. Banks. Irregular bus to Batsí and Gavrion.

### General

Kástro, or more properly Andros, is the capital of the island. It is a long hot walk around the bay to the

**APPROACHES TO KÁSTRO**
⊕37°50'·6N 24°56'·2E

Kástro looking NW into the inner basin          *Nigel Patten*

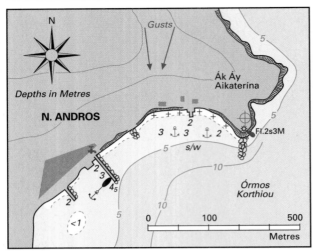

**KORTHION**
⊕37°46'·8N 24°57'·6E

village which straggles out along the rocky tongue forming the S side of the harbour, but it is well worth the effort to visit it. The town sits hunched over its rocky headland with the houses looking out over brown rock and the wind-tossed waters of the bay. On the end of the headland there is a small maritime museum and in the central square an archaeological museum and a museum of modern art.

Unfortunately a noisy power station has been built in the N corner of the port, which adds noise and visual pollution to this otherwise savage coast.

### KORTHION
**Approach**
The large bay and harbour lies approximately 6M S of Kástro. The houses of Korthion will be seen on the NW of the bay.

*By night* Use the light on Ák Áy Aikaterína Fl.2s3M and the light on the extremity of the mole F.R.3M.

*Dangers* As at Kástro the *meltemi* gusts down the coast and pushes a big sea into the bay.

**Mooring**
If there is room go stern or bows-to behind the mole. In calm weather you can anchor off, but with the *meltemi* the only place to be is under the mole.

*Shelter* Adequate if uncomfortable shelter from the *meltemi* under the mole. Southerlies are reported to make it untenable here.

### Facilities
Water near the root of the mole. Limited provisions. Several tavernas and cafés.

### STENÓN DHISVATON
⊕9  Mid-channel Stenón Dhisvaton (Andros/Tínos)
37°40'·6N 24°58'·0E

This strait separates the S end of Andros and the N end of Tínos. Two islands, Nisís Dhisvaton and Nisís Kaloyeri, lie off the NW tip of Tínos. The strait is a little over half a mile across at its narrowest part. A current setting towards the SW runs through the strait, but not with the strength of the current in

the Doro Strait. With the *meltemi* there are strong gusts through the channel.

## Nísos Tínos

A mountainous rugged island lying immediately south of Andros across a narrow strait. The summit, Korifi Tsiknias (713m/2,340ft), lies at the SE end of the island and Polemos Kambos in the centre of the island rises to 637m (2,090ft). The island is wooded and the slopes are extensively terraced and cultivated. There are a large number of villages (there are said to be 64) peppered around the island and many Venetian dovecotes and towers. The main port and capital is Tínos.

The ancient name of the island was Ophiousa, referring to the large number of snakes to be found here in ancient times. The name Tenos, corrupted to Tínos, may be derived from the Phoenician word, *tenok*, for snake. Poseidon was credited with ridding Tínos of snakes by sending storks to devour them. The Venetians occupied the island and held it for 500 years until the Turks took it in 1714.

The long Venetian occupation established Catholicism on Tínos and today Catholic convents, schools and churches are scattered around the island. In 1822 the discovery of the miracle-working icon of the Virgin ironically transformed this very Catholic island to a place of pilgrimage for those of the Orthodox faith.

### TÍNOS
BA 1538

**Approach**
*Conspicuous* The large town of Tínos is clearly visible from the distance. Above the town the church of the *Panayía* is conspicuous. Closer in the harbour breakwater and the entrance are easily identified.

*By night* Use the lights on the extremities of the breakwaters Fl.R.3s7M/Fl.G.2s3M and the light on the inner mole Fl.R.2s3M.

*Dangers*
1. With the *meltemi* there are strong gusts off the high land in the vicinity of the harbour.
2. Care is needed of the reef and shoal water extending S from Ák Akrotíri, the cape in the S approaches to Tínos.

**Mooring**
Proceed into the inner harbour and go stern or bows-to the N quay between the cargo mole and the ferry quay or immediately E of the ferry quay. Care should be taken of the ledge protruding a short distance underwater from the quay. Care is also needed of a large ship's anchor chain fouling the bottom approximately where the pecked line is on the plan. In calm weather it is reported there is a usable quay in the SE corner although care is needed of underwater ballasting. The bottom is mud, good holding.

*Note* Do not anchor in the harbour as the ferries need the whole area to manoeuvre in when berthing.

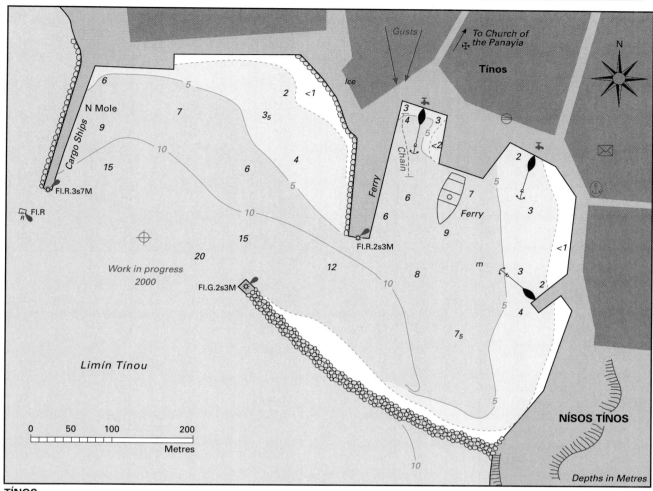

**TÍNOS**
⊕37°32′·25N 25°09′·4E

*Shelter* Good all-round shelter although strong southerlies are said to cause a surge. Wash from the ferries can also be uncomfortable.

*Authorities* Port police and customs.

### Facilities
*Water* On the quay (reputed to be the purest in Greece!).

*Fuel* In the town. A mini-tanker can deliver to the quay.

*Repairs* Some mechanical repairs and light engineering. Hardware shops.

*Provisions* Good shopping for all provisions close by. Ice available near the quay.

*Eating out* Tavernas nearby.

*Other* PO. OTE. Banks. Greek gas and *Camping Gaz*. Hire motorbikes. Buses to the principal villages. Ferries to Piraeus.

### General
Despite a sizeable Catholic population, Tínos is a centre of the Orthodox faith and the Church of the *Panayía* (the Virgin Mary/Our Lady – also called *Tiniotissa* and *Evangelistria*) is the focus of this faith. The modern church is sited above the town and is devoted to the miracle-working icon of *Our Lady of Good Tidings* discovered in 1822. Twice a year, on

Tínos harbour looking WNW across Ak Akrotíri in the foreground                    *Peter Kleinoth/MareTeam*

25 March and 15 August, thousands of sick and crippled pilgrims come to Tínos seeking a cure. This Greek Orthodox 'Lourdes' has apparently cured many, if the innumerable gold and silver votive offerings adorning the already ornate interior are anything to go by.

The church also contains a shrine commemorating the sinking of the Greek cruiser *Helle (Elli)*. On 15 August 1940 the cruiser was anchored outside the port attending the celebrations. An unknown submarine, probably Italian, torpedoed the ship, sinking her and killing many of the crew. Greece was not at war at this stage and the atrocity caused an uproar all over the country. Just below the church a museum contains some interesting finds including a sundial from the first century BC.

## ANCHORAGES ON THE EAST COAST OF TÍNOS

Most of these anchorages afford limited or poor shelter from the *meltemi* as a swell tends to be pushed down the coast and curve into any bays. They can be used in calm weather or when the *meltemi* is not blowing strongly.

*Órmos Isternia* 37°36'·9N 25°02'·4E The bay under Ák Isternia. Keep to seaward of the islet off the cape. Anchor in 6–10m off the hamlet. There is a quayed area off the hamlet with 3–4m depths off it, but you are better off at anchor because of the swell in here. The holding is reported to be mediocre only. Strong gusts with the *meltemi* and a swell curves around into the anchorage. Tavernas ashore.

*Órmos Kardiani* The small bay 2½M SE of Ák Isternia. Tuck up into the N cove in the bay. Poor shelter from the *meltemi*.

*Órmos Romanou* 37°34'·2N 25°06'·5E A bay affording some shelter from the *meltemi*. Anchor in 3–6m off the beach. A swell is pushed into the anchorage with a fresh to strong *meltemi*.

*Órmos Stavrós* 37°33'·0N 25°07'·9E The large bay immediately NW of Tinos harbour. With the *meltemi* there are strong gusts into the bay. Anchor in 5–10m at the NW end of the bay. Care is needed of the reef and shoal water extending off the beach. Tavernas on the beach.

## ÓRMOS PANORMOU

### Approach

A bay on the NE side of Tínos providing some protection from the *meltemi*. Nisís Planitís, with a light structure (Fl(2)14s10M) on it and connected by a narrow isthmus to Tínos, forms the N side of the bay and is easily identified. A beacon on the N side of the bay marks a reef.

### Mooring

The only place to be with the *meltemi* is in the cove (Áy Thalassa) on the N side of the bay. Anchor where possible in the cove. Care is needed as there are a number of permanent moorings here. In calm weather or with westerlies you can go on the quay at

ÓRMOS PANORMOU
⊕37°39'·2N 25°04'·1E

the head of the bay. The easternmost quay jutting out has 4–5m depths off it while the longer inner quay has 1·5–2m depths off it.

### Facilities

Water on the quay. Some provisions. Tavernas around the waterfront.

### General

Panormos used to be used for shipping marble from the hinterland and may still be used by small coasters at times. It has now become a modest tourist spot with much of the building of the 'pour-and-fill' variety.

## ÓRMOS KOLOMBITHRA

37°38'·5N 25°08'·5E

A large bay approximately halfway along the N coast of Tinos. It is of no use when the *meltemi* is blowing, being completely open to that direction, but would provide useful shelter from southerlies and westerlies. The approach is straightforward leaving the islet (Drakonissi) off the W entrance point to starboard. Anchor in either of the two coves at the head of the bay in 3–5m.

## STENON MIKONOU

⊕10 Mid-channel Stenón Mikonou 37°30'·9N 25°16'·4E

The channel between Tinos and Míkonos. With the *meltemi* the wind is channelled through here and can blow substantially stronger than over open water. A considerable confused sea occurs in the channel and care is needed when sailing in this area. There have been a number of masts lost and more blown sails than in the Americas Cup when skippers have underestimated the strength of wind from the gusts down through this channel.

# Nísos Míkonos

## (Mykonos)

A rocky barren island which is mostly low-lying. Mt Áy Ilías rises to 364m (1,194ft) in the NW and Mt Anomeritis rises to 351m (1,152ft) in the SE. The population mostly lives in Port Míkonos or in Tourliani in the middle of the island. The town of Míkonos, the tourist Mecca of Greece, is the real attraction because, apart from fine sandy beaches, the island has scenically little else.

**Note** Between Naxos and Míkonos a strong southerly current has been reported after a prolonged *meltemi*.

## MÍKONOS MARINA (Toúrlos)

### Note

All boats must now berth in the marina and not in Míkonos old harbour. You will be turned away from the old harbour if you try to enter.

### Approach

The harbour lies just over a mile N of the old harbour. From the W a large hotel looking a bit like the radiator grille of an American car is conspicuous. Normally the most conspicuous objects will be the cruise ships tied alongside the outside quay of the marina. Yachts should make for the E basin.

*By night* The W basin is lit at the entrance Fl.G.3s3M. The E basin is lit on the end of the mole Fl.R.3s3M. The central quay area is spot-lit.

**APPROACHES TO MÍKONOS**
⊕37°27'·74N 25°19'·54E WGS84

**MÍKONOS, DELOS AND RINIA**

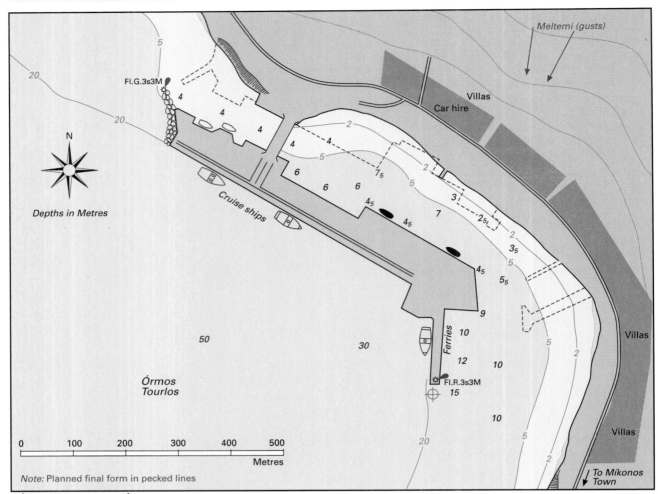

**MÍKONOS MARINA (MÍKONOS NEW HARBOUR)**
⊕37°27′·74N 25°19′·54E WGS84

*Dangers* The *meltemi* gusts down into the bay making manoeuvring difficult although, unlike the old harbour, there is plenty of room here.

Míkonos Marina looking W

**Mooring**
At the time of writing, yachts go alongside the quay on the S side of the basin. As work progresses pontoons and laid moorings will be installed.

*Shelter* Good all-round shelter although the *meltemi* gusting into the harbour can pin you against the quay.

*Authorities* Port police.

*Note* At the moment no charge is made for using the harbour, but this will change when work is more advanced and services are installed.

**Facilities**
*Services* None at the time of writing. It is planned to install water and electricity points and a shower and toilet block. You may be able to get a water tanker to deliver.
*Fuel* Can be delivered by mini-tanker to the quay.
*Repairs* Limited mechanical repairs only. Limited chandlers in Míkonos town.
*Provisions* Good shopping for all provisions in Mikonos town.
*Eating out* Wide choice of tavernas and restaurants in Míkonos town.
*Other* PO. OTE. Banks. Hospital. Greek Gas and *Camping Gaz*. Hire cars and motorbikes on the N

side of the marina. Ferries to Piraeus, Siros, Paros and Rhodes. Internal and European flights.

### General

*Mikonos Marina* The marina is a dusty deserted place at present, a sort of boon-docks miles away from the glitz of Míkonos town. That said, I think I speak for many, especially a lot of charter skippers pressured by clients to come here, when I say that the shelter in the marina is wonderful compared to the perils the old harbour used to present. At Míkonos old harbour you gritted your teeth as you came into it to berth between ferries, the howling *meltemi*, whistling port police and other boatowners swearing at you as anchors became crossed and topsides were gashed. It was a nightmare. The best thing to do at the marina is hire a motorbike from the agency on the N side and use that to zip in and out of town.

*Mikonos town* Mikonos has almost passed into the English language to describe a certain type of touristy island in the way that Benidorm describes the most down-market of resorts. To 'mikonos' means to take the most wonderful place and completely change the values and worth of the community so that while physically little appears to have changed, the place is soulless and possesses little that was valuable in the old community. So it is that in the summer the locals rub shoulders with the yacht set, the jet set, backpackers, artists – real and pseudo, nudists and recently the gay set as well as plain ordinary holidaymakers. Míkonos is bright and breezy by day and by night the hum of the bars and throb of discos into the wee hours is all part of the scene.

The town is a dazzling white cluster of cubes stacked around a natural amphitheatre above the harbour. Míkonos epitomizes the Greek flair for choosing a superb site and tailoring a natural architecture to it. The houses, the churches (there are said to be 365 of them, a bit of an exaggeration), and the narrow winding alleys appear to be a naturally evolved form sculpted from the rocks of the island itself. There may be hordes of tourists from all over the world, and more photographs of Míkonos than of any other town in Greece, films and documentaries may have featured it, yet Míkonos retains that wonderful appearance and certain architectural something that so many flock to see. For the yachtsman the cosmopolitan flavour of Míkonos may be a refreshing contrast to the simpler pleasures of the other islands.

### ÓRMOS MÍKONOU

In light southerlies or easterlies it is possible to anchor off Míkonos town. Anchor off in either of the two coves S of the old harbour. The bottom comes up fairly quickly in both bays so you will need to anchor in 7–10m.

In southerlies you can anchor in Órmos Korfos. Anchor in 4–6m on mud and weed.

### ÓRMOS ORNOS

The bay on the S side of Míkonos immediately E of Ák Alogomandra. Anchor in 5–10m at the head of the bay. The bottom is sand and weed – poor holding in places. Good shelter from the *meltemi* although there are strong gusts into the bay. Open to the S.

There is a hotel on the beach and several tavernas. Supermarket nearby. It is two miles to Míkinos town, buses every hour. Just to the E of Ornos there are a number of small bays sheltered from the *meltemi*. They have sandy beaches and tavernas nearby.

**ÓRMOS ORNOS**
⊕37°25'·3N 25°19'·5E

### ÓRMOS ÁYIOS ANNAS (Baraga)

Lies immediately E of Ák Makrokefalos. Anchor in 3–6m. The bottom is sand and weed. Good shelter

**ÓRMOS ÁY ANNAS**
⊕37°24'·8N 25°24'·0E

from the *meltemi*. Open S. Immediately W and E of Órmos Áy Annas are two other bays which afford similar shelter from the *meltemi*. In Órmos Kalafitis to the E of Órmos Áy Annas care is needed of a reef off the W headland and a number of mooring buoys in the bay for the gravel loading facility here.

Some of these beaches are unofficially 'no clothes' beaches and some are the preserve of men only who may take exception to being invaded from the sea. Mikonos after all is an island where reputedly anything goes, and outside of town you are on the fringe of 'anything goes'. Close your eyes and have another drink.

### KALAFITIS

A bight offering reasonable protection from the *meltemi* although completely open to the S and E. It lies immediately E of Órmos Áy Annas and Ák Tarsanas. Care must be taken of a reef on the W side of the bight. Anchor off the N end of the beach in 3–4m off the hotel complex. Taverna and café ashore.

### PANORMOS

37°30'·0N 25°17'·3E

The large bay on the N side of Míkonos. The *meltemi* blows straight down into the bay so most of it is a lee shore during the summer. On the W side of the bay at Áy Sostis there is a bight where you can get some shelter from the *meltemi*. Care is needed of Vrak. Moles, a group of rocks and a reef which

should be left to starboard before turning up into Áy Sostis.

With southerlies the bay affords good shelter and you can anchor at Áy Sostis or at the head of the bay.

Tavernas at Áy Sostis and Ftelia at the head of the bay. The bay is popular with windsurfers who come here for the wind and sea pushed into the bay by the *meltemi*.

## Nísos Delos

### (Dhilos, Mikró Delos)

A small low barren island with the extensive ruins of ancient Delos on the west coast. Every day in the summer tripper boats ferry sightseers over from Míkonos to see these ruins. It used to be prohibited for a yacht to berth or anchor at Delos. A large notice at the small harbour says simply 'No Yachts' and in Órmos Foúrnoi a notice prohibits landing and anchoring overnight. Recently it was reported that yachts could anchor off, but must depart before 1500 hours. Other yachts have reported staying overnight.

### DELOS CHANNEL (Stenón Dhilos)

A yacht transiting the channel must exercise caution when the *meltemi* is blowing. The channel between Delos and Rinia and the Nisídhes Remmatia is fringed by reefs. When the *meltemi* is blowing it is funnelled into the channel and may blow at Force 7

---

### Ancient Delos

Delos was once the political and religious centre of the ancient world. Legend has it that Apollo was born here and Artemis on nearby Rinia. The Delos oracle was consulted before major decisions and its fame was second only to that of Delphi. How did Delos become the centre of the ancient world? The most succinct answer is provided by Ernle Bradford:

`Delos, the hub around which the Cyclades (Kukloi – rings) radiate, was formed by nature to be the focal point of a seaman's world. If one is tempted to ask why so small an island, without any natural resources, ever became what it did, then the answer can be given by any sailor. Delos is the last, and best, anchorage between Europe and Asia. To the east it is shielded by Mykonos, to the north by Tínos, and to the west by Rheneia. Looking at a chart, it is easy to see how the direct sea route between the Gulf of Nauplia (with Argos at its head) flows straight across the latitude of 37°10' north of Pátmos and Sámos. Exactly in the centre of this trading route lies Delos. At the same time, it is almost in the centre of the trading route between the Dardanelles and Crete. Religious centres may sometimes, as at Rome or Lourdes, attract trade and commerce. But more often one will find that where the trade is, there are also temples. Merchants, then as now, are eager to purchase security in both worlds.'

Ernle Bradford *The Greek Islands*

In those days the ancient harbour was larger and better protected than it is today. The breakwater was some 165m long and the harbour extended south for half a mile and was divided by moles into five basins. Yet despite Ernle Bradford's praise for the natural attributes of Delos, I cannot help thinking there are other better natural harbours nearby. Órmos Náoussa on Páros or Órmos Dhespotico, for instance, are better protected and more accessible than Delos. In any case, for whatever reasons, the ancients settled on Delos and transformed this rocky little island into the centre of the world.

In 700 BC the island was under the protection of Naxos and the centre of the Ionian League of islands. Athens soon entered the league and before long was commanding Delian affairs. It was purified in 543 BC by Peristratos and thereafter the island was not to be defiled by human birth or death. The dying and any women nearing childbirth were taken across to nearby Rinia. The island was subsequently purified on several other occasions, presumably because someone had a heart attack or some similar fairly instant demise and died before they could be whisked off to Rinia.

After the defeat of the Persians, the first great period of prosperity for Delos began. In Macedonian times it enjoyed privileges akin to those of a 'free port' and its wealth and power were immense. By 200 BC the first Romans came to Delos and although the Athenians remained, the power soon shifted to Rome. Around 80 BC it was sacked and although it was rebuilt, its power was on the wane. A wall was built around it, but by AD 3 the island was finished. In that year it was put up for sale, but there were no takers.

The remaining ruins and the site should not be missed. The site has been likened to Pompeii, not for any architectural similarity, but for the completeness of the picture of ancient life that can be gleaned from it. Many of the ruins have been vandalised by past invaders and collectors of antiquities and of course by the Greeks themselves who have carted off the conveniently-hewn stone to build their houses on Míkonos, but much remains: the five lean lions guarding the sacred lake; the temple of Apollo in the great square of Apollo; the theatre; the bright mosaics of dolphins, panthers, birds, fruit and flowers; and the remains of what was the busiest harbour in antiquity.

**DELOS CHANNEL (STENÓN DHILOS)**
(⚓) until 1500 hours
⊕37°24'·2N 25°15'·5E

or more on occasions. The combination of a narrow shallow channel fringed by reefs and strong winds and short seas can make navigation a tricky business – care is needed.

# Nísos Rinia

### (Rhenea, Megálo Delos)

The barren rocky island separated from Delos by the narrow Delos Strait. The island is nearly divided into two by a narrow isthmus. The northern half is the higher of the two (149m/490ft). There are several sizeable farms on the island and even a herd of cows as well as sheep and goats.

## ÓRMOS SKHINOU

The bay has numerous above and below-water rocks fringing it and care is needed in the bay itself. There are two possible anchorages.

1. In the N. Care is needed of the rocks off the E side which are marked by a small pillar on one of them. Care is also needed of an underwater rock in the middle of the entrance which may be marked by a small buoy. Anchor in 4–5m on sand, good holding. Good shelter from the *meltemi*.
2. In the S. Care is needed of the reef on the E side fringing the coast. Anchor in 3–5m. The anchorage is not sheltered from the *meltemi* but is protected from the S.

## CHAPEL BAY

To the N of Órmos Skhinou is an islet with a chapel on it. It is possible to anchor under the SW end of the islet in 6–8m on sand, good holding. Some shelter from moderate northerlies.

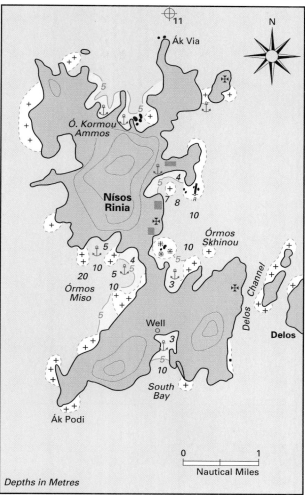

**NÍSOS RINIA**

⊕**11** ¾M N of Ák Via (Rinia)
37°27'·12N 25°13'·58E WGS84

## SOUTH BAY

On the S side of Rinia, affords good shelter from the *meltemi*. Anchor near the head of the bay in 3–5m on a sandy bottom. No facilities. Water from a well in the field nearby.

## ÓRMOS MISO

A large bay on the W side sheltered from the *meltemi*. Anchor in one of the two coves at the northern end where shown on a sandy bottom. No facilities.

## ÓRMOS KORMOU AMMOS

The bay on the N end of Rinia. It is open to the *meltemi*, but would be useful with southerlies. Anchor in 3–5m near the head of the bay.

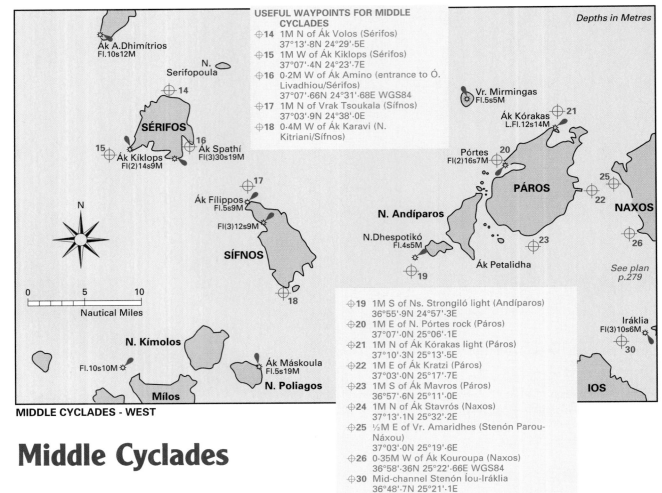

USEFUL WAYPOINTS FOR MIDDLE CYCLADES

⊕14 1M N of Ák Volos (Sérifos)
37°13'·8N 24°29'·5E
⊕15 1M W of Ák Kiklops (Sérifos)
37°07'·4N 24°23'·7E
⊕16 0·2M W of Ák Amino (entrance to Ó. Livadhiou/Sérifos)
37°07'·66N 24°31'·68E WGS84
⊕17 1M N of Vrak Tsoukala (Sífnos)
37°03'·9N 24°38'·0E
⊕18 0·4M W of Ák Karavi (N. Kitriani/Sífnos)

⊕19 1M S of Ns. Strongiló light (Andíparos)
36°55'·9N 24°57'·3E
⊕20 1M E of N. Pórtes rock (Páros)
37°07'·0N 25°06'·1E
⊕21 1M N of Ák Kórakas light (Páros)
37°10'·3N 25°13'·5E
⊕22 1M E of Ák Kratzi (Páros)
37°03'·0N 25°17'·7E
⊕23 1M S of Ák Mavros (Páros)
36°57'·6N 25°11'·0E
⊕24 1M N of Ák Stavrós (Naxos)
37°13'·1N 25°32'·2E
⊕25 ½M E of Vr. Amaridhes (Stenón Parou-Náxou)
37°03'·0N 25°19'·6E
⊕26 0·35M W of Ák Kouroupa (Naxos)
36°58'·36N 25°22'·66E WGS84
⊕30 Mid-channel Stenón Íou-Iráklia
36°48'·7N 25°21'·1E

MIDDLE CYCLADES - WEST

# Middle Cyclades

## Nísos Sérifos

### (Seriphos)

A dome-like island with the white houses of the *chora* on a conical hill SE of the summit of Mt Troullos (585m/1,919ft). The island appears barren from seaward but at Livádhi it is green and wooded around the shore, and inland from the *chora* there are several green valleys in startling contrast to the burnt brown mountain sides. There are a number of iron ore mines at Megálo Khorio on the west coast of the island and at Koutala on the south, but there is little active mining today. Livádhi has a modest tourist trade in the summer, but for the most part the island is populated by the old (particularly noticeable in the *chora*) as the young have deserted the island for Athens.

### LIVÁDHI (Livadhiou)

BA 1538
Imray-Tetra G33

### Approach

*Conspicuous* Coasting around the S coast the lighthouse on Ák Spathí is conspicuous. From the N and E Nisís Vous can be recognised and closer in the white houses of the *chora* on the hill above the harbour are easily seen. Once at the entrance to Órmos Livadhiou the approach is straightforward.

NÍSOS SÉRIFOS

⊕14 1M N of Ák Volos (Sérifos)37°13'·8N 24°29'·5E
⊕15 1M W of Ák Kiklops (Sérifos)37°07'·4N 24°23'·7E
⊕16 0·2M W of Ák Amino (entrance to Ó. Livadhiou/Sérifos)
37°07'·66N 24°31'·68E WGS84

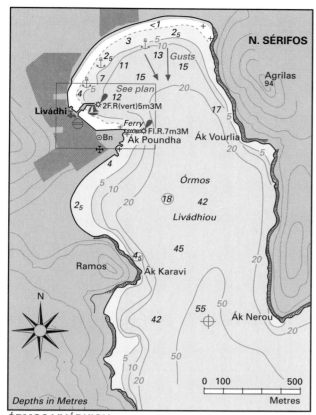

**ÓRMOS LIVÁDHIOU**
⊕37°07'·97N 24°31'·34E WGS84

**LIVÁDHI**
⊕37°08'·49N 24°31'·19E WGS84

*By night* From the S use the light on Ák Kíklops Fl(2)14s9M and Ák Spathí Fl(3)30s19M. The extremity of the breakwater is lit Fl.R.2s3M. The end of the yacht jetty is lit 2F.R(vert), but should not be relied on. From the N a night approach can be difficult, especially if visibility is not good. There are no useful lights and Nisís Vous is not lit – if coming from the Saronic a S approach is safer if slightly longer.

*Dangers* With the *meltemi* there can be strong gusts off the lee side of the island and in the immediate approaches to Livádhi.

Livádhi on Sérifos looking W into the harbour
*Peter Kleinoth/MareTeam*

### Mooring
Anchor in the bay or go stern or bows-to the jetty off the village on the SE side of the bay. In the summer when the *meltemi* is blowing the S side of the jetty is preferable. Yachts can go stern or bows-to the outer part of the jetty, but closer in it is too shallow off the shore to drop anchor so it is best to go alongside. On the N side you will need a good anchor and all your chain as well as a bit of nerve when the *meltemi* gusts down into the bay. The bottom is sand and weed – mostly good holding although there have been reports of bad holding in places. When the ferry is not due yachts also go alongside or stern-to the ferry quay.

*Shelter* Good shelter from the *meltemi* although there are gusts into the bay. With strong SE winds a swell works around into the bay although it is still tenable. In the summer the harbour is often crowded with yachts.

*Authorities* Port police.

### Facilities
*Water* On the jetty.
*Fuel* A mini-tanker can deliver to the quay ☎ 0281 51512.
*Provisions* Most provisions can be obtained at Livádhi. Ice from a mini-market nearby.
*Eating out* Good tavernas in the village and around the beach.
*Other* PO and OTE at the *chora*. Exchange facilities. Greek gas. Bus to the *chora*. Hire motorbikes. Ferry to Mílos and Piraeus.

### General
The nearly landlocked bay is fringed by trees providing welcome shade from the sun, and the white houses of the *chora* on the hill above, like icing on a bun, are like a cliché of received ideas of the Cyclades. The view from the *chora* down onto the bay and over the sea and islands beyond is worth the trip, even if you miss the infrequent bus to the *chora*

and have to walk up for the view. The *chora* remains much as it always was, but the settlement around the bay has acquired the usual trappings for the summer tourist trade including highly amplified disco music which, in this otherwise tranquil spot, pierces the night-time air with an unnatural cacophony.

## ÓRMOS KOUTALA

An open bay on the S side of Sérifos offering good shelter from the *meltemi*. Anchor in either of the two coves at the head of the bay. In the NE cove anchor in 3–5m on a sandy bottom. In the NW cove care must be taken of a foul area where large mooring chains have been laid. Anchor where shown in 6–10m on a sandy bottom. Good shelter from the *meltemi* although there are strong gusts into the bay.

On either side of the bay are the remains of iron ore mines and jetties and the concentration of ore is reported to cause local magnetic anomalies. A number of villas have been built around the shores.

**ÓRMOS KOUTALA**
⊕37°07'·8N 24°27'·3E

## MEGA LIVÁDHI

37°08'·5N 24°25'·8E

An inlet NE of Ák Kíklops. It is reported to offer good shelter from the *meltemi*.

## NISÍS SERIFOPOULA

A barren uninhabited island lying 4½ miles NE of Sérifos.

# Nísos Sífnos

## (Siphnos)

The high bold island lying 7 miles SE of Sérifos across the often windy Sífnos Channel. The island is hilly throughout, rising near the centre to Mt Áyios Ilías (694m/2,277ft). The west coast is barren and burnt rock, but on the east side of the island, where

**NÍSOS SÍFNOS**

⊕**17** 1M N of Vrak Tsoukala (Sífnos) 37°03'·9N 24°38'·0E
⊕**18** 0·4M W of Ák Karavi (N. Kitriani/Sífnos)
　　 36°53'·50N 24°42'·91E WGS84

most of the population live, it is greener and cultivated in places. Most people live in the capital, Apollonia, on a hill inland.

In ancient times the inhabitants were vilified for their greed and deceit. On one occasion the Sifniotes offered a gilt egg at Delphi instead of the customary gold one and Apollo in revenge destroyed the gold mines which had formerly earned a great deal of revenue for the island. On the east coast the decaying medieval village of Kástro is a delightful place surrounded by a wall into which two and three-storey houses have been built. The village and former capital looks down onto Órmos Kástro and across to Andíparos and Páros.

Today the beaches on the SE coast of the island are popular and a number of small hotels have been built around the coast.

## ÁYIOS YEÓRYIOS

A narrow inlet on the NW tip of the island. It provides good shelter from the *meltemi*, and indeed from all but W winds. There is room for one or two small yachts at the head of the bay. Anchor fore and aft as there is no swinging room, or moor bows-to the outer end of the S quay taking care of the underwater rocks projecting some distance out. A local tripper boat also uses the quay. There are 8–10m depths at the dogleg and 3–4m in the middle of the inlet with 2m depths until quite close to the edges. The head of the inlet is shallow.

Two tavernas and two ceramic workshops ashore. At one time the last hand-formed giant amphora-like pots were made here.

**ÓRMOS ÁY YEÓRYIOS**
⊕37°02′·2N 24°38′·8E

## VOURLITHA

Lies between North Bay and Áyios Yeóryios. It has been recommended as an anchorage, but I find it a bleak desolate spot affording little shelter, certainly not as good as that offered by nearby anchorages.

## NORTH BAY

Just N of Kamáres there is a small bay affording some shelter from the *meltemi*. Cliffs surround the bay except where two deep gullies descend into the bay. Anchor in 4–5m between the gullies. The bottom is sand and weed, not everywhere good holding. No facilities.

## KAMÁRES

BA 1538

### Approach

*Conspicuous* It is difficult to see where the entrance is to the bay – vessels appear to pop out of a slit in the cliffs. The light structure on the N side of the entrance is conspicuous. Once near the entrance the buildings of the town and the outer mole can be seen.

*By night* Use the light on Ák Kokkála Fl(3)12s9M and on the S side of the entrance Fl.3s7M. The breakwater is lit on its extremity: Fl.G.1·5s3M.

*Dangers* It is advisable to take down your sails before entering the bay as with the *meltemi* there are strong gusts from all directions at the entrance and inside the bay.

### Mooring

Berth stern or bows-to the quay between the two moles or anchor at the head of the bay. The bottom is hard sand and weed with some rocks – fair holding only.

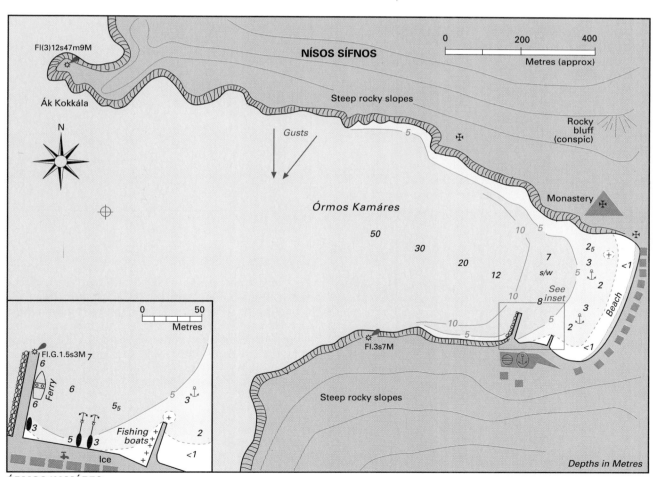

**ÓRMOS KAMÁRES**
⊕36°59′·50N 24°39′·21E WGS84

Sífnos. Kamáres looking WNW from the slopes behind the bay
*Nigel Patten*

*Shelter* Good shelter from the *meltemi* although there are gusts. With W winds a swell rolls into the bay.

*Authorities* Port police and customs.

### Facilities
*Water* On the quay.
*Fuel* Can be delivered by mini-tanker to the quay.
*Provisions* Most provisions although supplies are much dependent on the ferries.
*Eating out* Good tavernas on the waterfront and around the beach.
*Other* A regular bus runs to Apollonia, the island capital, where there are a PO and OTE and better shopping for provisions. Ferries to Mílos and Piraeus.

### General
Kamáres is the ferry port for Sífnos and while the setting between the high cliffs and hills is spectacular, the village lacks that certain something.

Vathi on Sífnos looking SE          *Nigel Patten*

However I recommend a trip to Apollonia and Kástro from here.

## ÓRMOS VATHI
A landlocked bay affording the best all-round shelter on Sífnos. The entrance is somewhat difficult to identify until you get there, when the cliffs on either side open up to an amphitheatre of a bay. There is a light structure on the S side of the entrance Fl.2s7M. Anchor in the N of the bay in 3–4m on the gently shelving bottom – sand and weed, good holding. Off the chapel there is a section of quay with 2–2·5m depths off it where a few boats can go stern or bows-to with care. There are a also number of coves on the S side where a yacht can anchor. There are strong gusts from the *meltemi* into the bay, but the holding is good and no sea enters.

Water near the church. Tavernas ashore. The surroundings here are wonderful, the water a translucent turquoise, and there are several tavernas on the beach for a run ashore.

ÓRMOS VATHI
⊕36°55'·62N 24°41'·01E WGS84

## FIKIADHA
A deserted inlet immediately S of Vathi which offers reasonable shelter from winds N through E to S. Open to the W only. Anchor in the inlet with a long line ashore or go bows-to the short pier below the chapel (1·5m depths at the extremity). The bottom is sand and mud with some rock, not everywhere good holding. Apart from the chapel the inlet is quite deserted, magnificently so.

## PLATÍ YIALOS
A U-shaped bay on the SE coast. Good shelter from the *meltemi* although there are strong gusts into the bay. Anchor off the NE corner in 5–7m. There are 2m depths approximately 80m off the beach. The bottom is sand and rock, not everywhere good holding. Tavernas and hotels on the beach.

**ÓRMOS FIKIADHA**
⊕36°54'·4N 24°41'·6E

**ÓRMOS PLATÍ YIALOS**
⊕36°55'·6N 24°44'·0E

Faros looking NE towards the head of the bay    *Nigel Patten*

**ÓRMOS FAROS**
⊕36°56'·3N 24°45·2E

## FAROS (Pharos)

BA 1538

An inlet near the SE tip of Sífnos providing good shelter from the *meltemi*. Open only to the S. The church on Ák Petalos, on the W side of the entrance, and the light structure on Ák Stavrós, on the E side of the entrance, are conspicuous. Anchor off the village in 3–12m. There is a short quay with 2–3m depths on the E side of the bay where a few yachts may be able to go stern or bows-to. Often it is occupied by local and tripper boats. Alternatively anchor in one of the coves on the W and E side of the entrance. The bottom is sand and weed – good holding once through the weed. Good shelter from the *meltemi* although there are strong gusts into the bay.

Tavernas at the head of the bay and limited provisions. A number of villas and small hotels have been built around the adjacent coastline – mostly frequented by the young. The bay, hemmed in by high land, is a wonderful place with good swimming in the clear water and good snorkelling around the adjacent coast.

## KÁSTRO

An open cove under the medieval village on the slopes above. The cove lying immediately N of Ák Miti is suitable only in calm weather, being entirely open to the prevailing summer northerlies. Anchor in 3–4m off the tiny beach and take a long line

**ÓRMOS KÁSTRO**
⊕36°58'·3N 24°45'·1E

**ÓRMOS DHESPOTICO**
⊕36°58'·2N 25°02'·0E

ashore. The bottom is sand and weed, mostly adequate holding.

There is a hamlet by the beach and a track leading up to the fascinating huddle of medieval houses perched on the steep slopes. If the weather does not permit a visit by yacht then take a bus or taxi from Kamáres to Apollonia and from there to Kástro.

# Andíparos

## (Anti-Páros)

The island of Andíparos lies close off the SW side of Páros, separated by a narrow shallow channel. It is low-lying (299m/981ft at the summit in the middle) and barren. The village of Andíparos lies on the east coast near the narrowest part of the channel. Near the south end of the channel there is a deep cave containing a small chapel and spectacular stalactites and stalagmites. Excursions from Andíparos village and Paroikia by tripper boat.

The two islands to the south of Andíparos, Nisís Dhespotico and Nisís Strongiló, are barren and uninhabited.

### NISÍS DHESPOTICO

36°57'·4N 25°00'·6E

On the S side of this island there is a deserted bay offering good shelter from the *meltemi*. Open only to the S.

### ÓRMOS DHESPOTICO

The large bay between Nisís Dhespotico and Andíparos. It is protected on the N and E by Andíparos and on the S and W by Nisís Dhespotico and the islet of Tsimindri in the NW. The channel on the N side of Nisís Tsimindri has less than one metre depths. The channel on the S side of Tsimindri has 2m depths in the fairway. It should be attempted in calm weather only with someone up front conning you through, and is not one for the faint-hearted.

Anchor in 2–4m where convenient on the N side. The bottom is sand and weed – good holding. In the 16th and 17th centuries the bay was a laying-up port for pirate galleys. The recent construction of a number of roads has opened up the area to development. Several tavernas on the Andíparos side open in the summer.

### STENÓN ANDÍPAROU (Anti-Páros Channel)

BA 1539
Imray-Tetra G33

The narrow channel should only be attempted by day with due care and attention. Remmatonisi and the coast of Páros are fringed with above and below-water rocks and with the *meltemi* there are strong gusts down the channel raising a short disturbed sea. A deep-draught yacht should not attempt the channel and small to medium-sized yachts should do so with someone up front conning you through and one eye on the depth-sounder. A yacht attempting the passage for the first time should do so in calm weather if possible when the reefs fringing the passage are easily seen. With the *meltemi*, identifying the green of the safe passage and the brown of rocks in the underwater mosaic becomes more difficult.

The channel on the W side of Remmatonisi can also be used by shallow-draught yachts with due care and attention although there are less depths than on the E side.

*Note* Recent charts show the deeper passage to be on the W side of Remmatonisi, but in my experience the passage on the E side is better. Recently least depths of 3·8m were reported in the W Channel. If anyone out there wants to survey either passage again in calm weather, please let me know the results.

## ANDÍPAROS

In the cove off the village on the W side of Andíparos channel a yacht can find some shelter from the *meltemi*. There is only a limited amount of space here. Try for a berth at the N pier. Spaces here are normally reserved for local boats and you should not occupy the ferry berth as ferries run frequently from Pountas on the other side of the channel. You can try anchoring off on the N side of the bay keeping clear of the piers although most of the bay is shallow. Anchor in 2–2·5m on sand and weed, good holding once the anchor is in. Reasonable shelter from the *meltemi* although gusts blow in from the channel.

Several tavernas on the waterfront and limited provisions can be found in the village.

**STENÓN ANDÍPAROU**
**(ANDÍPAROS CHANNEL – 14 FOOT PASSAGE)**
⊕37°03'·15N 25°05'·3E (N. Salango light)

**ANDÍPAROS**
⊕37°02'·4N 25°05'·2E

Andiparos has been much developed in recent years and there are now numerous hotels and the accompanying bars and tavernas. Once you penetrate the concrete overcoat around the old village it reveals itself to be a wonderful fortified little town. The fortified wall that surrounds the village was built by Loredano in the mid-15th century to protect the population from pirate raids.

Around the southern end of the channel there are numerous enchanting coves to be explored in calm weather. The shallow water and sandy bottom produce those wonderful blues and greens so often reproduced on postcards.

## POUNDHA

37°02'·3N 25°06'·0E
A small port on the Paros side of the channel for the ferries to Andiparos. There are 1·5–2m depths off the pier but there is really no room here for a yacht.

# Páros

A large oval island which is essentially one mountain with two peaks: Mt Áyios Ilías (771m/2,530ft) to the NW and Mt Karamboli (747m/2,450ft) to the SE. The land slopes down evenly from the two peaks to the sea. The land is mostly barren and burnt rock with few trees. The port and capital is Paroikia on the NW coast.

The island was colonised early on by the Ionians from Asia Minor. In the 7th century BC the new Parians sent a party to colonise Thásos. Archilochus, the lyric satirist credited with inventing Iambic verse, was born on Páros and accompanied the colonizing party to Thásos. Ernle Bradford relates some amusing details about the poet: he was thrown out of Sparta for his 'cowardice and licentious character' and when fighting the Thracians admitted on one occasion to throwing away his shield and running away. Unfortunately this likeable muse was killed whilst fighting the neighbouring Naxians. During the Persian invasions Páros sided with the Persians and with their defeat was consequently subdued and became subject to Athens. In the Middle Ages the island was colonised by the Venetians until falling to the Turks in 1537.

In ancient times Parian marble was famous. The marble was called *Lychnites* – won by lamplight – as it was mined underground in tunnels. Because the marble was difficult to mine, the mines were abandoned after classical times and were last used in 1844 when marble was required for Napoleon's tomb. The mines and tunnels can still be seen today. Parian wine was also famous in antiquity and today the red wine made on the island is passably palatable. Páros is a popular tourist island, Paroikiá fairly bulges at the seams in summer, and consequently facilities are well developed.

**ANDÍPAROS, PÁROS AND NAXOS**

## PAROIKIÁ

BA 1539

### Approach

*Conspicuous* In the approaches to Paroikiá there are a number of islands and reefs encircling the bay. From the N these are: Pórtes, two in number and looking like a pair of bookends; Petrokáravo, an almost submerged rock difficult to identify in rough

seas; Vouves, low with a reef off the NE end and a reef with 3m over it 0·2 miles to the SW; Nisídhes Áy Spirídhonos, high and jagged (with a white chapel on one) except for the easternmost islet which is low; and Mavro Toúrlos off the N end of Nisís Kavoúras, high and jagged. Further into the bay, Kakí Skála and Peponas are low-lying. The white houses of Paroikiá are easily seen once into the bay. A white church with a blue cupola is conspicuous on Ák Áy Fokas. The harbour off Paroikiá is easily identified when close in.

*By night* Use the light on Pórtes Fl(2)16s7M and on Ák Áy Fokas Fl.3s6M. Two pillar buoys Q.G/Q.R mark the deep water channel into Limín Paroikiá. Street lights illuminate the ferry quay.

*Dangers*

1. Care is needed of the reef and above-water rock just N of Nisídhes Áy Spiridhonos and of the shoal water just N of Vouves in the approaches to Órmos Paroikiás.
2. Care must be taken of the reef and shoal water extending out from Ák Áy Fokas. There are depths of 3m or less some 300m S of the cape.
3. Care is needed of a reef running out from the coast on the S side of the entrance to Órmos Paroikiás.
4. There is an extensive shallow rock shelf on the E side of Ák Krios. An old mole now underwater runs out from the N side of the bay for 250m between the more easterly of the two houses with white arches (conspic.) in a roughly SE direction. Depths over the submerged mole are less than 2m and in places only just 1m over.
5. The light structure on Ifalos Paroikiá has been removed and the reef levelled. Two pillar buoys now show the deep water channel into the harbour.

Ák Áy Fokas (light structure and church conspicuous), the N entrance point to Órmos Paroikiás looking NW

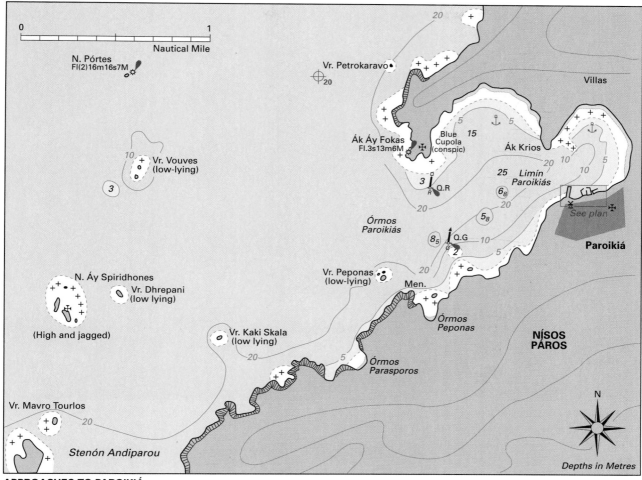

**APPROACHES TO PAROIKIÁ**

⊕20 1M E of N. Pórtes rock (Páros) 37°07'·0N 25°06'·1E

*Note* On 26 September 2000 the ferry *Samina Express* hit the Pórtes rocks in the approaches to Paroikiá. The ship sank in 40 metres in the vicinity of the rocks at 37°05'N 25°07'E. Over 80 people drowned in the worst maritime disaster in Greece for 35 years. Rob and Di Brown who have lived on Paros for 31 years make the following observations:

'It is a matter of observation that a sustained *meltemi* gale sets up a current that can exceed 2 knots going south around the Pórtes rocks and down the Antiparos channel. This was almost certainly the direct cause of the sinking of the *Samina*. (It is commonly believed on Paros that the ship was on a compass autopilot course, which would normally have carried it nearly 1/3 of a mile further north. My brother-in-law was swept close to the Pórtes himself three hours before the accident.) The rescue at night from the sea in a F8 gale in the no-go area itself of 400 of the 500 or so on board is little short of miraculous to those who know the area.

Except for a few fishermen, almost all local boats treat the sea between the Pórtes rocks and the Áy Spiridhones islets as a 'no-go' area. It is simply too easy to go wrong even in half-metre waves. The unmarked Vouves reef is awash in calm weather, and lost in white horses in any sea. The outliers from the Áy Spiridhones islets are underwater and run a long way north and also east towards Kaki Skala. There are two safe routes in and out of Paroikiá, used by the ferries: firstly passing N of Pórtes and keeping at least ¼ mile offshore and S of Áy Fokas headland; secondly passing about 300m N of Peponas and Kaki Skala (both easily visible by day), then keeping to the channel S of the Áy Spiridhones islets and N of the Mavros and Kókkinos Toúrlos pillars.'

**Mooring**
Berth stern or bows-to in the inner harbour or in calm weather off the outside of the mole. The bottom is mud and weed, mostly good holding.

*Shelter* Excellent shelter inside the harbour. If the inner harbour is crowded and the *meltemi* makes berthing on the outside of the moles impossible, it is best to anchor in one of the bays to the N of the harbour.

*Note* Works are in progress to the W of the ferry quay.

*Authorities* Port police and customs.

*Anchorage* A yacht can anchor in either of the two bays on the N side of Órmos Paroikiás. The bay in the NE affords the best shelter from the *meltemi* but you need to be careful of the rock shelf off the shore and the sunken mole running for 250 metres out from the shore mentioned in 'Dangers' above. Anchor in 4–6m on sand, mud and weed, good holding once through the weed. This anchorage is untenable in southerlies.

Paroikiá on Páros looking NW across Órmos Paroikiás

*Peter Kleinoth/MareTeam*

**PAROIKIÁ**
⊕37°05'·3N 25°09'·1E

## Facilities
*Water* On the quay once the 'water man' is located.
*Fuel* On the outskirts of town. A mini-tanker can deliver to the harbour.
*Repairs* Yacht service agency. Call *Afros Yacht Service* on VHF Ch 73 or ☎ 0284 23625. Mechanical repairs. Sailmaker. Chandlers. General hardware.

*Provisions* Good shopping for all provisions in the town. Ice available.
*Eating out* Good tavernas of all types. I favour some of the local tavernas in the streets behind the harbour, but there are all sorts of other tavernas in town.
*Other* PO. OTE. Banks. Greek gas and *Camping Gaz*. Hire cars, motorbikes and bicycles. Buses to the other villages on the island. Ferries to Piraeus, Rhodes, Iraklion and nearby Cyclades islands.

## General
Built on a gentle slope beside the sea with steep slopes behind, Paroikiá is typically Cycladic – houses, shops, churches are dazzling white cubes

Ák Kórakas and lighthouse on the W side of the entrance to Órmos Naoúsis looking SW with bougainvillea and wisteria providing splashes of natural colour. The old quarter around the 13th-century *Kástro* is an intriguing place full of narrow winding alleys and archways, stone houses and shops with wooden balconies.

Paroikiá possesses the finest church in the Aegean, the Katapoliani (Ekatontepiliani). The name is said to mean 'the church of the 100 doors', but more probably means simply 'below the town'. The church is in fact three churches under one roof and it is well worth a visit for the beautiful interior – a mixture of the original and some recent renovation in neo-Byzantine style. On 15 August pilgrims converge on the church although the celebrations cannot compete with the Tiniot festival. Near the church the archaeological museum houses some interesting finds including a slab of the Parian Chronicle recording Greek history from pre-Homeric times and some sculptures in Parian marble.

The harbour is busy in the summer with ferries constantly coming and going bringing throngs of holidaymakers to the main port. The town resounds to the babble of different languages, the entreaties of waiters wanting your custom, and the click of camera shutters, and no wonder – some of the streets ending literally at the sea on the W of the town rival those in Míkonos for wonderful Cycladic architecture.

## NÁOUSA

BA 1539

### Approach

This large much-indented bay lies on the N end of Páros between Ák Kórakas and the islet of Gaïdhouronísi.

*Conspicuous* The white lighthouse on Ák Kórakas is conspicuous and from the entrance to the bay the power station buildings on the S side of Órmos Langeri, the white houses of Náousa, and a large church with a red cupola behind the village, are conspicuous.

*By night* A night approach is not recommended. In good visibility use the light on Ák Korakas LFl.12s14M and the lights at the entrance to Náousa harbour Fl.R.1·5s3M/Fl.G.1·5s3M.

*Dangers* Care is needed of the above and below water rocks fringing the islets and shores of the large bay.

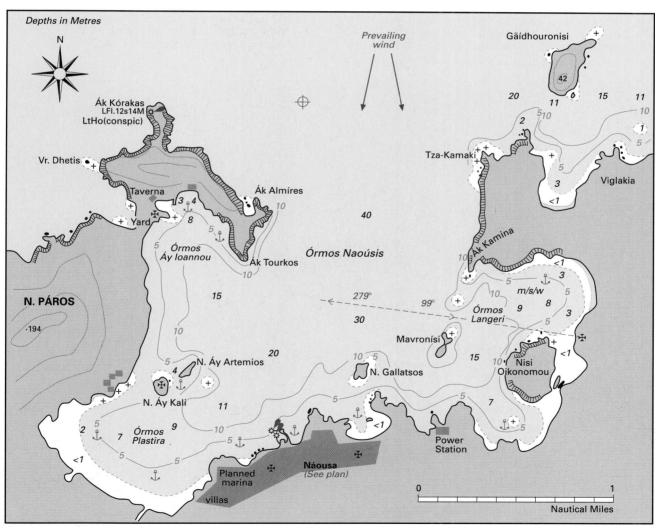

**ÓRMOS NAOÚSIS** ⊕37°09'·44N 25°14'·35E WGS84

**NÁOUSA**
⊕37°07′·6N 25°14′·2E

## Mooring

There are numerous anchorages around the bay.

1. **Órmos Langeri** Care is needed of the reef in the W entrance to the bay midway between Mavronísi and Ák Kamína. A bearing of 99° on the chapel on the shore leads safely into here and conversely, a back-bearing of 279° leads safely out. Anchor at the N end where convenient in 4–10m on mud, sand, and weed, good holding. Good shelter from the *meltemi* tucked into the N end. Yachts can also anchor at the S end of the bay in calm weather or southerlies. The S end is somewhat spoiled by the large power station there.

2. **Órmos Áy Ioannou** Care is needed of the reef running out from the chapel on the W. Anchor where convenient at the N end in 3–10m. The bottom is mud, sand and weed, good holding. Good shelter from the *meltemi*. A small chapel in the NW corner of the bay is conspicuous and nearby there is a small boatyard. This anchorage is idyllic: sun-baked rock eroded into wonderful shapes, clear turquoise water, a small white chapel perched on the rock near the water, even the boatyard with bright *caïques* hauled out fits into the scene, so consequently it is popular in the summer. Taverna ashore. A local tripper boat operates a service on the half hour to Náousa until 1800 in the summer.

*Note* The beaches around here are popular for nude swimming and sun-bathing. That so, it should always be remembered that in the vicinity of a church or chapel it is frowned upon. As the sign at the chapel here puts it: 'These grounds are holly – plese do not swim in the nude' *(sic)*.

3. **Órmos Plastira** In calm weather anchor where convenient. With the *meltemi* some shelter can be found anchored in 3–4m under Nisís Áy Kali.

4. **Náousa** Most of the space in the harbour is

Órmos Naoúsis looking NW across to Órmos Áy Ioannou and Ák Almíres on the W side of the entrance. Náousa harbour is middle left
*Peter Kleinoth/MareTeam*

taken up with local boats and tripper boats. Yachts now go on the outside of the W mole leaving the striped area in the middle free for the ferry. There are mostly 1·5–3m depths off the quay although care is needed of underwater ballasting in places. Good holding and reasonable shelter from the *meltemi*.

In calm weather you can use the bay on the E side of the fort, although care is needed of a mooring chain lying approximately W–E in the bay. Yachts also anchor off just W of the harbour in 4–10m on sand and weed, good holding. The *meltemi* doesn't normally blow home here although it can at times.

*Authorities* Port police at Náousa.

### Facilities
*Water* On the quay.
*Fuel* Can be delivered by mini-tanker to the harbour.
*Repairs* Minor repairs at Náousa. Yachts are hauled at the yard in Órmos Áy Ioannou using a cradle and slipway. It is a bit isolated but has the advantage that you can wander down to the water and have a swim.
*Provisions* Most provisions can be found at Náousa.
*Eating out* Good tavernas at Náousa.
*Other* PO. OTE. Bank. Greek gas. Hire motorbikes and bicycles. Bus to Paroikiá.

### General
The bay is a much indented amoeboid shape of sun-baked rock enclosing clear blue and turquoise water. Much of the rock has been sculpted into weird and wonderful shapes that give the bay a desolate feel. Although popular in the summer, there is nearly always somewhere to tuck yourself into away from the others. Out of season it is positively lonely.

**GAÏDHOURONISI TO NISÍS FILIZI**
⊕37°09'·45N 25°15'·35E

Náousa was a small fishing village that has grown into a large straggling tourist resort. The tavernas and bars clustered around the edge of the inner basin provide a pleasant spot to while away an evening. A windsurfing school operates from a hotel on the E side of the bay.

**Note** There are plans to build a marina immediately W of Náousa harbour utilising the bight in the coast here. At the time of writing work had not started and there was some uncertainty over when or if work would begin.

### VIGLAKIA
This is the knobbly NE tip of Páros with a number of off-lying islets (Gaïdhouronisi, Tourlites, Ovriokastro and Fonisses). Local boats take a shortcut between the islands and Paros to get to the Parou-Naxou Channel and in calm weather with someone up front keeping an eye on things, navigating between the islands and Paros is straightforward. When the *meltemi* is blowing it is prudent to go around the outside of the islets. In calm weather there are a number of delightful anchorages, but with any hint of northerlies you should leave.

### ÓRMOS FILIZI
37°08'·0N 25°17'·2E
The bay directly under Ák Gria. In calm weather or light westerlies it is an attractive anchorage. Care is needed of a wreck on the bottom on the N side of the bay. Anchor in 4–6m on sand and weed.

There is also a delightful anchorage tucked under Nisís Filizi which lies close off the S side of the bay.

### ÓRMOS MARMARA
37°03'·4N 25°16'·1E
A large bay on the E coast. Although it looks as if there should be good shelter here, the *meltemi* blowing down the strait between Páros and Naxos sends a swell in. Anchor in the NW corner in light N winds or calm weather.

### PISO LIVÁDHI (Marpissa, Tsipidho Bay)
#### Approach
A small harbour approximately 1½ miles SSW of Órmos Marmara.

*Conspicuous* A peak with a conspicuous white building on the summit immediately N of Piso Livádhi is easily identified. Closer in a cluster of villas and small hotels around the coast will be seen. The breakwater is easily identified once up to the bay.

*By night* There are no lights and a night approach is not recommended (see Dangers below).

*Dangers* A reef and shoal water extends E from the breakwater for about 250m. Keep well off and approach the bay from the SE.

*Note* Works are in progress inside the harbour repairing the breakwater and dredging parts of the basin. It is planned to extend the quayed area

**PISO LIVÁDHI**
⊕37°01'·9N 25°15'·5E

*Provisions* Some provisions available in the village.
*Eating out* Several tavernas around the waterfront with wonderful views over the harbour and the strait.
*Other* Ferry to Naxos and Amorgós.

### General
The small village has a modest amount of tourism in the summer and is a convivial place much removed from the hustle and bustle of Paroikiá. The setting is wonderful under the slopes of Páros on the edge of Stenón Parou-Náxou. The anchorage in the S part of the bay makes a good lunch stop in calm weather.

### FARANGA
A double-headed bay on the S side of Paros. Care is needed of the reef off the SW entrance point. Anchor in either of the two heads of the bay with the more easterly considered the best. In the E bay anchor off the beach in 4–7m on sand and weed. Reasonable shelter from the *meltemi* although some swell swings around from the Parou-Naxou Channel into the bay – uncomfortable rather than dangerous.

**ÓRMOS FARANGA**
⊕36°58'·8N 25°09'·2E

around the breakwater which will considerably increase the number of berths available. Care needed of works in progress at the time of writing.

### Mooring
Go stern or bows-to the breakwater with a long line to it. Some care is needed of permanent moorings fouling the bottom and of a wreck on the bottom. With care you can also go bows-to the short W breakwater with a long line to it. Care is needed of underwater ballasting extending out in places. The bottom is sand and weed, good holding. When the ferry is not due in (it normally arrives in the morning and early evening, but does not stay for long) small yachts can go bows-to the short pier where there are 1·5–2m depths.

*Shelter* Reasonable shelter from the *meltemi* although with a prolonged blow there can be a surge in here. Open to the SE when it is uncomfortable and can become untenable.

*Anchorage* In calm weather a yacht can anchor in the S part of the bay.

*Note* Yachts should not anchor in the vicinity of the entrance where the ferry needs room to manoeuvre.

### Facilities
*Water* At the root of the mole.

**ÓRMOS ALIKI**
⊕36°59'·7N 25°08'·0E

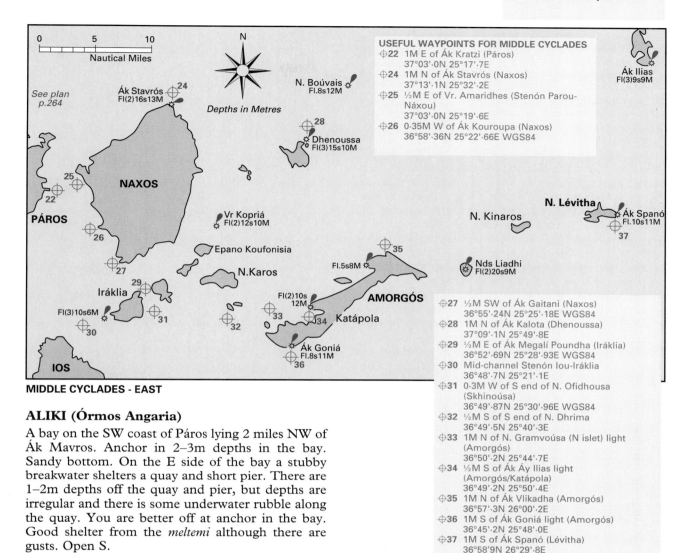

Ák Ilias
Fl(3)9s9M

N. Boúvais
Fl.8s12M

Ák Stavrós
Fl(2)16s13M

See plan
p.264

*Depths in Metres*

28

Dhenoussa
Fl(3)15s10M

25

22

**NAXOS**

**PÁROS**

26

Vr Kopriá
Fl(2)12s10M

N. Lévitha

Ák Spanó
Fl.10s11M

37

N. Kinaros

27

Epano Koufonisia

35

Nds Liadhi
Fl(2)20s9M

N.Karos

Fl.5s8M

29

Iráklia

31

Fl(2)10s
12M

**AMORGÓS**

Fl(3)10s6M

30

32

33

34

Katápola

Ák Goniá
Fl.8s11M

36

**IOS**

**MIDDLE CYCLADES - EAST**

### ALIKI (Órmos Angaria)

A bay on the SW coast of Páros lying 2 miles NW of Ák Mavros. Anchor in 2–3m depths in the bay. Sandy bottom. On the E side of the bay a stubby breakwater shelters a quay and short pier. There are 1–2m depths off the quay and pier, but depths are irregular and there is some underwater rubble along the quay. You are better off at anchor in the bay. Good shelter from the *meltemi* although there are gusts. Open S.

A hotel and tavernas ashore.

### STENÓN PAROU-NAXOU (Páros-Naxou Strait)

This strait separating Páros and Naxos is fringed by rocks and reefs. There are also two reefs in the fairway: Ifalos Kalipso (Vrákhoi Tsamban), and Vrákhoi Amarídhes, which has a conspicuous light structure on it (Fl.WR.4s5/3M red sector covers 185°-015°) and a wreck at its S extremity, though the latter has now all but disappeared underwater. With the *meltemi* a current sets to the S at about ½–1½ knots, although with southerlies there is a N-going current. These currents also affect the group of islands to the S of Naxos, but are much modified by the channels between the islands and it is difficult to determine precise directions and rates.

## Nísos Naxos

The largest and most fertile of the Cyclades. From seaward the west coast appears rocky and bare but inland the island is wooded and cultivated. The island is mountainous throughout with two high peaks: the summit Mt Zeus lies just to the south of the middle of the island and is 1,084m (3,308ft) high, and 6 miles to the north Mt Korna is 1,065m (3,250ft) high. In the interior valleys the slopes are terraced and olives, citrus orchards and cypresses grow. The lower plains are cultivated with figs, vines and market gardens.

Naxos is the island where Theseus abandoned Ariadne on his way back to Athens from Crete. It was with Ariadne's help that Theseus penetrated the labyrinth and slew Ariadne's half-brother the Minotaur. Ariadne, in love with Theseus and he apparently in love with her, sailed away from Crete and the first place they landed at was Naxos. Just why Theseus abandoned her has always puzzled classical scholars, but it at least provided the material for one of Catullus' best long poems:

'...Here are the never silent sands of Naxos
here Theseus vanishes towards the north,
a woman watches from the empty beach
unflagging grief in her heart
Ariadne doesn't yet believe, quite,
she is witnessing what her eyes see –
she's only just woken from a trap
(of sleep)
found herself alone on the island...'

Catullus transl. by Peter Whigham

Luckily Dionysus landed on the island and they fell in love at first sight. They appear to have been happy together and Ariadne bore the god many children. Dionysus, the god of the vine, appears to have been a gentler, less raucous god than his Roman namesake, Bacchus, and he blessed Naxos with great fertility and good wine. Today Naxian white wine is still quite palatable, though perhaps not good enough for Dionysus if he is around.

Naxos was sacked by the Persians in 490 BC and thereafter the island steadfastly aided the Athenians. In 1207 the Venetian adventurer Marco Sanudo occupied the island and it remained a Venetian duchy for 300 years. The succeeding dynasty of Sanudo, the Crispi, ruled over most the Cyclades until Naxos fell to the Turks in 1566. It became Greek in 1832.

If you decide to leave your yacht at Naxos town, the only really safe harbour on the island, then the magnificent interior is well worth visiting. The young Byron on visiting Naxos wanted to buy the island and return here to retire. In Apollonia a large unfinished marble statue some 10·5m high lies in the marble bed it was carved from. It was intended for Delos, but probably it was decided that the marble was of poor quality. There are also a number of Byzantine churches with good frescoes.

## NAXOS

BA 1539
Imray-Tetra G33

**Approach**

*Conspicuous* Ák Moungri to the SW of the town has a conspicuous conical peak on it. Closer in the hump of white buildings of Naxos town and a marble arch on Nisís Apollonas (joined by a causeway to Naxos) will be seen. The breakwater and harbour are easily identified and there is usually a ferry or two in the harbour or coming or going to aid identification.

*By night* The extremity of the breakwater is lit: Fl.R.4s7M.

*Dangers*

1. Care must be taken of Vrakhos Frouros, the reef lying approximately 1¼ miles WSW of the harbour and 0·3 miles N of Ák Moungri, the S extremity of Órmos Náxou. By day the reef, two rocks just above water surrounded by underwater rocks and shoal water, is easily identified in calm weather and there are no problems in passing between it and the cape. With any sea running the above-water rocks are more difficult to locate and it is prudent to go well outside them.

APPROACHES TO NAXOS AND ÓRMOS ÁY PROKOPIOU
⊕37°04'·4N 25°20'·2E

In 2000 a small ferry hit the rocks and sank between Vrak. Frouros and the coast. The top of a mast on the superstructure is just above water and a buoy (conical Y with two balls vertical) has been laid just N of the wreck in the channel between Frouros and the coast. Navigation warnings give position for the wreck as 37°06'N 25°21'E.

2. With the *meltemi* there are gusts and some swell at the entrance to the harbour.

3. A good lookout must be kept in the approaches to the harbour for the numerous ferries coming and going, often at considerable speed, until right up to the harbour.

**Mooring**

There are several places a yacht can go depending on the wind direction and strength.

1. Anchor under the breakwater in the NE corner. There are convenient depths of 4–7m. Take care to avoid the 2m shoal shown on the plan. The bottom is sand, rock, and weed, good holding once the anchor bites properly. Care is needed of a number of permanent moorings in the anchorage. Good shelter from the *meltemi*. Southerlies send a swell in.

2. ***Naxos Marina*** Work on the marina is well in hand and although not yet complete, it is in partial use by yachts. Whether there is a berth here really depends on what work is going on at the time. At present yachts go alongside where possible, but when work is finished yachts will berth stern or bows-to with laid moorings. Good shelter now the outer mole has been extended.

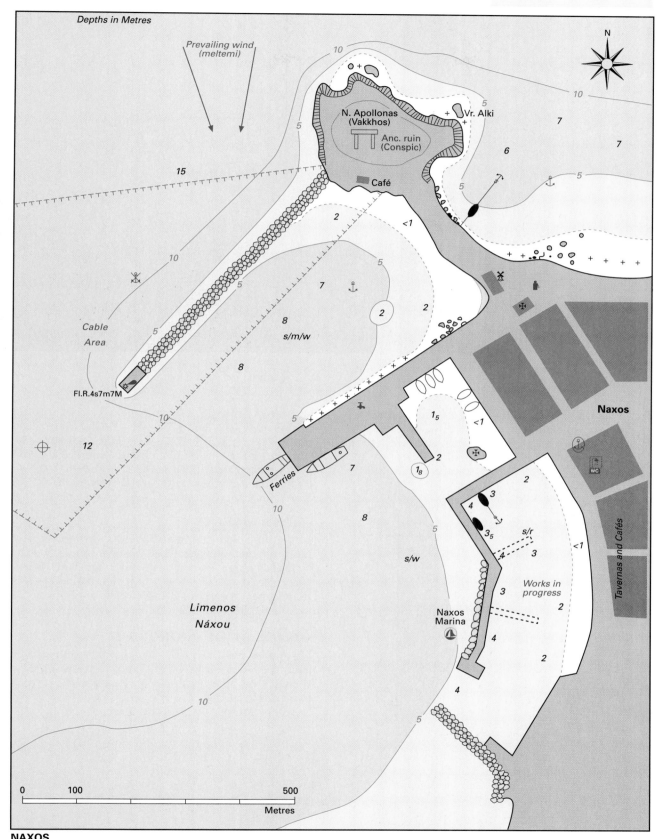

Depths in Metres

Prevailing wind
(meltemi)

N

10

10

N. Apollonas
(Vakkhos)

Vr. Alki

Anc. ruin
(Conspic)

7

7

6

15

5

Café

5

2

<1

10

5

5

5

Cable
Area

7

2

2

8

s/m/w

8

Naxos

Fl.R.4s7m7M

5

1₅

<1

10

2

1₈

7

2

Ferries

12

⊕

2

3

4

10

3₅

s/r

3

<1

8

s/w

4

3

Works in
progress

3

2

Limenos
Náxou

Naxos
Marina

4

2

4

10

2

5

10

0        100                          500

Metres

**NAXOS**
⊕37°06'·36N 25°21'·98E WGS84

Tavernas and Cafés

wc

281

Naxos harbour looking NE with Nisís Apollonas middle left
*Peter Kleinoth/MareTeam*

3. Anchor and take a long line ashore on the NE side of the isthmus joining Nisís Vakkhos to Naxos. The bottom is sand, rock, and weed, good holding once the anchor is in. Open to the *meltemi* but sheltered from southerlies.

*Authorities* Port police and customs.

### Facilities

*Water* On the main ferry mole. and near the café/bar on Apollonas. Showers and WC near the new basin.

*Fuel* Close to the root of the mole. A mini-tanker can deliver to the harbour.

*Repairs* Some mechanical repairs can be carried out. Hardware shops.

*Provisions* Good shopping for provisions in the town behind the 'marina'. Wine from the barrel. Ice available.

*Eating out* Good tavernas in the town.

*Other* PO. OTE. Banks. Greek gas and *Camping Gaz*. Hire cars, motorbikes and bicycles. Buses to the main villages on the island. Ferries to Piraeus, Rhodes, Iraklion and nearby Cyclades islands.

### General

The town, built on a low hummock by the water, is a typically whitewashed Cycladic place with a smattering of Venetian here and there. I have been reprimanded for calling it 'somewhat scruffy' in earlier editions, but it has been cleaned up since then. The warren of alleys, arches and tunnels around the Venetian castle on the summit of the hill is the most fascinating part of the town. It was the up-market end of town and many of the entrances sport coats of arms from the time when Naxos ruled over the surrounding islands.

The marble arch on Nisís Apollon Vakkhos (or Bacchus) is part of a temple begun about 530 BC

and never finished. The archaeological museum in the town houses early Cycladic finds, Mycenaean pottery and gold jewellery and classical finds. The museum was once a schoolhouse where the writer Nikos Kazantzakis (best known for *Zorba the Greek*) taught for 12 years before returning to his native Crete.

### NAXOS MARINA

At the time of writing work is underway to complete the mole and quayed areas. Two pontoons will be installed where shown and moorings laid. When complete it will afford good all round shelter. It is intended to install water and electricity points and a toilet and shower block. A charge will be made.

### ÓRMOS ÁYIOS PROKOPIOU

Lies under the lee of Ák Prokopis about 3 miles S of Naxos. Anchor off in 4–6m. Sandy bottom. There is shelter from the *meltemi* but nearly always some swell in the bay.

Beach tavernas open in the summer.

Ák Katomeri looking SE

## ÁY ANNAS

A small resort at the southern end of Órmos Áy Prokopiou. Anchor off the resort in 4–6m on sand. Alternatively go stern or bows-to the outer end of the pier. Reasonable shelter from the *meltemi*.

Water and electricity on the pier. Limited provisions and tavernas ashore.

## DANGERS IN PAROU-NÁXOU CHANNEL

1. Care must be taken of Ifalos Kalipso (Vrákhoi Tsamban) lying approximately 0·8 miles SW of Ák Prokopis.
2. Care must be taken of the reef lying 0·4 miles off Áy Nikólaos in the S of Órmos Prokopis.
3. Care must be taken of Vrákhoi Amarídhes already mentioned on page 279.
4. From a position roughly parallel to Vrákhoi Amarídhes and extending down to Ák Parthenos, above and below-water rocks fringe the coast of Naxos up to just over a mile off.

## ÓRMOS KOUROUPA (Áy Ioánnis)

An open bay under Ák Kouroupa. A large unfinished hotel complex on Ák Kouroupa is conspicuous from seaward. Anchor off in 4–6m. There is a short pier, but it is rock-bound. The bottom is sand with some rocks – good holding. The *meltemi* is funnelled down the Páros-Naxos Strait and pushes a swell around the cape, making it uncomfortable in here.

**ÓRMOS KOUROUPA**
⊕26 0·35M W of Ák Kouroupa (Naxos)
36°58'·36N 25°22'·66E WGS84

## ÓRMOS KALANDO

A bay on the SE coast about 1½ miles NE of Ák Katomeri. Anchor near the head of the bay in 3–6m. Sandy bottom. Good shelter from the *meltemi* although there are gusts into the bay. No facilities.

## ÓRMOS PANORMOU

A bay under Ák Panormos on the SE tip of Naxos. Care is needed in the approaches of Ifalos Dhilos, an isolated reef lying off the coast. The approach is best made from the E towards Ák Panormos. Anchor in 3–5m at the head of the inlet. The bottom is sand and weed, good holding once dug in. There are severe gusts down into the bay with the *meltemi* and it is advisable to lay a second anchor.

**ÓRMOS KALANDO**
⊕36°56'·2N 25°28'·4E

**ÓRMOS PANORMOU**
⊕36°57'·3N 25°32'·6E

## ÓRMOS MOUTSOUNA

37°04'·7N 25°35'·25E
An anchorage under Ák Moutsouna on the E side of Naxos. A large ore loading pier is conspicuous in the bay. Indifferent shelter from the *meltemi*. Care is needed of a reef on the N side of the bay. Anchor S of the pier in 3–5m on sand and shingle, poor holding. Tavernas ashore on the beach.

## APOLLONIA

A bight near the NE tip of Naxos. A short breakwater provides some protection from the *meltemi* although some swell is pushed around the end of it. Go stern or bows-to the outside of the short mole that protects the fishing harbour. Care is needed as depths are uneven off the mole. The small basin is shallow. Indifferent shelter from the *meltemi* and really only tenable in calm weather.

A small village ashore with several tavernas and a hotel. The unfinished statue of Apollo lies a short distance directly inland from the village.

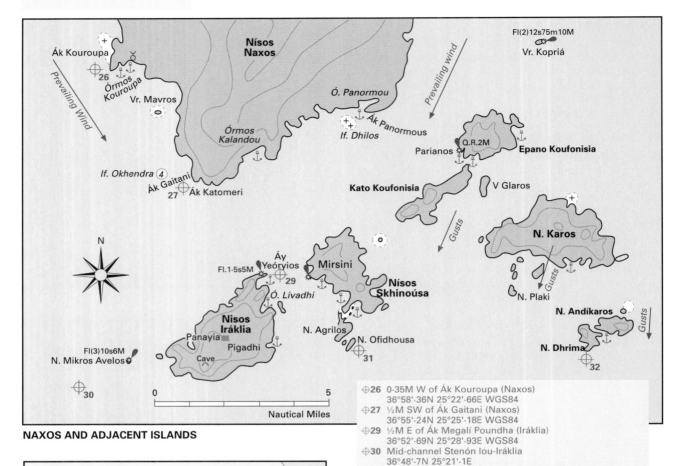

**NAXOS AND ADJACENT ISLANDS**

⊕26  0·35M W of Ák Kouroupa (Naxos)
      36°58'·36N 25°22'·66E WGS84
⊕27  ½M SW of Ák Gaitani (Naxos)
      36°55'·24N 25°25'·18E WGS84
⊕29  ½M E of Ák Megalí Poundha (Iráklia)
      36°52'·69N 25°28'·93E WGS84
⊕30  Mid-channel Stenón lou-Iráklia
      36°48'·7N 25°21'·1E
⊕31  0·3M W of S end of N. Ofidhousa (Skhinoúsa)
      36°49'·87N 25°30'·96E WGS84
⊕32  ½M S of S end of N. Dhrima
      36°49'·5N 25°40'·3E

**APOLLONIA**
⊕37°11'·0N 25°33'·2E

**NÍSOS DHENOUSSA**

⊕28  1M N of Ák Kalota (Dhenoussa) 37°09'·1N 25°49'·8E

# Nísos Dhenoussa

## (Dhonoussa)

A small high island (489m/1,064ft) lying nine miles off the east coast of Naxos. There are three anchorages: Órmos Roússa on the NE corner, Órmos Dhendro on the south, and in calm weather off the village of Stavrós.

The island has been settled since the Bronze Age period and was latterly used by the Romans as a prison island. Today it is still out on a limb off the tourist track, although sadly EU money has been used to score rude roads across the island and scar its natural if barren visage.

## ÓRMOS ROUSSA

A bay on the E coast of Dhenoussa partially sheltered by Nisís Skilonisi (Trigono). Although there is a narrow channel between Skilonisi and Dhenoussa with good depths, the prudent course is to enter the bay from the SE. The cove in the NW corner (5–6m) affords the best shelter from the *meltemi*, but the holding on a rocky bottom is not the best. It may be better to anchor on the W side of the bay in 3–5m where the holding is better. The anchorage is safe enough when the *meltemi* is blowing but gets very uncomfortable with the swell that rolls in.

**ÓRMOS ROUSSA**
⊕ 37°07′·4N 25°49·8E

Meagre provisions can sometimes be obtained from a 'shop' in a house near the shore. Simple taverna.

## ÓRMOS DHENDRO (Khendro)

A bay on the S coast of Dhenoussa lying immediately E of Ák Dhendro. A chapel is conspicuous on the cape. Care must be taken of the reef lying off the cape. Anchor near the head of the bay in 5–6m. Further into the bay (in 3–4m) lies a wreck. Good shelter from the *meltemi* although there are gusts into the bay.

## STAVRÓS

A small village on the western side of Ák Dhendro. Anchor off the village in 4–5m. If there is room you can go bows-to the quay where there are 1·5–2·5m depths in the middle. Shelter here is not as good as in Órmos Dhendro, but is useful in calm weather or light northerlies.

Tavernas ashore. Limited provisions can be found, but the islanders are much dependent upon the ferry from Naxos for most things.

# Nísos Iráklia

A small barren island lying 3 miles SSE of Ák Katomeri. There is a small hamlet at Áyios Yeóryios.

Like the other islands, civilisation in the form of anonymous pour-and-fill concrete buildings has changed the face of the island in places, though it still remains a wild and mostly inaccessible island.

On the S side of the island is a cave which you will have to walk to from the *chora* Panayia – about an hour.

**ÓRMOS DHENDRO AND STAVROU**
⊕ 37°05′·2N 25°48′·0E

**ÁYIOS YEÓRYIOS**
⊕ 36°52′·3N 25°28′·6E

Áy Yeóryios on Iráklia looking NNE          *Nigel Patten*

### ÁYIOS YEÓRYIOS (Iráklia)

A deep inlet on the NE tip of Iráklia. The entrance is somewhat difficult to see from the N. The houses at the head of the bay can be seen from the entrance. Although open to the NE the *meltemi* does not always blow home although on other occasions it will do so. Anchor in 3–6m. There is just room for a few yachts to go bows-to inside the short mole. Care is needed of old mooring chains on the bottom so use a trip-line on the anchor. Good shelter from the *meltemi* tucked in behind the mole. The bottom is sand with some rocks – good holding.

Tavernas ashore. The small hamlet in the rocky bay is most attractive despite the new houses that have been built around it.

### ÓRMOS LIVÁDHI (Mourto)

Immediately S of Áy Yeoryios is Livádhi, not really tenable with the *meltemi*, but a suitable anchorage in calm weather. Anchor in 4–5m on sand with some rocks, good holding once dug in.

A taverna sometimes opens on the beach. Ashore on the hill is the village of Livádhi which was abandoned in 1940 and not re-inhabited after the war. The ruins of the houses built of and into Hellenistic and later Venetian ruins is a melancholy spot.

### PIGADHI (Pegadi)

36°50'·0N 25°28'·8E

A deep inlet near the SE tip of Iráklia. Open to the ENE and consequently a swell rolls in with the *meltemi*. In calm weather it is an attractive fjord to visit. Anchor in 6–10m near the head of the bay. The bottom is sand with some rocks – reasonable holding.

## Nísos Skhinoúsa

A small island one mile to the NE of Iráklia. There are a few houses at Mirsini and a small *chora* on the hill above. There are a number of attractive deserted coves around the island, their shelter depending on the wind direction. Nisís Agrilos lies off the SW side of Skhinoúsa, but the passage between Agrilos and Skhinoúsa is shallow and rock-bound.

**NÍSOS SKHINOÚSA**
⊕36°51'·97N 25°30'·47E WGS84

**ÓRMOS MIRSINI**
⊕36°51'·97N 25°30'·47E WGS84

### MIRSINI (Myrseni)

#### Approach

A narrow inlet on the W side of Skhinoúsa, almost directly opposite Áyios Yeóryios on Iráklia. The entrance is difficult to locate until the small white chapel immediately due W of the entrance and the light structure are spotted. The entrance is lit Fl.4s6M, but a night approach needs care.

Skhinoúsa. Mirsini looking ESE          *Nigel Patten*

## Mooring

Anchor in the bay in 5–8m. The bottom is sand and weed, not everywhere good holding. Small yachts can squeeze in bows-to just N of the ferry quay or go on the ferry quay when it is not in use. Good shelter from the *meltemi*, although there are gusts into the bay.

## Facilities

Several tavernas on the shore. Ferry to Naxos and Amorgós.

## General

A few tourists arrive here in the summer on the ferry, but most visitors arrive by yacht. The *chora* on the hill above is quite untouched and a delight to visit. You will also find a few provisions there and a good old fashioned *caféneion* where the loudest noise is the clack of counters from the old men playing backgammon.

## ANCHORAGES S OF MIRSINI

To the SE of Mirsini are two bays offering some shelter from the *meltemi* although they are better visited in calm weather. The southernmost of the two bays affords the best shelter from the *meltemi*.

## NISÍS AGRILOS

The skinny islet running S from Skhinoúsa approximately a mile SSE of Mirsini. There is not a passage around the N end of the islet as stated in the Admiralty *Pilot*. The bay under the headland opposite the islet affords reasonable shelter from the *meltemi* in rugged but attractive surroundings.

# Nísoi Koufonisia

Two islands about one mile NE of Skhinoúsa: Lower (Kato) Koufonisia is the southwestern island while Upper (Epano) Koufonisia lies to the NE.

There are three anchorages on Upper Koufonisia:

1. A bay on the NE tip of the island provides some shelter from the *meltemi* although a swell rolls in. Open to the E. Anchor in 3–5m. Sandy bottom. Deserted.

**EPANO KOUFONISIA ANCHORAGES**
⊕36°55'·8N 25°35'·9E

2. *Koufonisia village*. Anchor in the bay in 3–5m on a sandy bottom. Reasonable shelter from the *meltemi* but there is always a residual swell with the *meltemi* which causes yachts at anchor to roll horribly. A breakwater and quay have been built on the W side of the bay for the ferry. When the ferry is not in here a yacht can go stern or bows-to, but the swell causes awful snatching at the shore lines and it is not a comfortable place to be. Open S and E. Some provisions and tavernas ashore. A quaint OTE in the bottom of a village house.

3. *Parianós* A small harbour on the SW side of Epano Koufonisia. A mole closes off part of the inlet with 5–6m depths in the entrance and 3m depths in the middle. The end of the mole is lit Fl.R.3s3M. A number of fishing boats are kept

**PARIANÓS**
⊕36°56'·1N 25°35'·6E

Parianós looking W                    *Nigel Patten*

**NISOI DHRIMA AND ANDÍKAROS**

⊕32  ½M S of S end of N. Dhrima 36°49'·5N 25°40'·3E

here on permanent moorings and the bottom is littered with permanent moorings. Anchor with a trip-line and you may also be able to pick up a mooring if one is free. It is possible to go bows-to the quay in a few places, but care is needed of rock ballasting along the quay and permanent moorings off it. Good shelter from the *meltemi* although there are gusts. The bay is a pleasant 20 minute stroll from the village. The fishing harbour has a bleak but beautiful aspect to it – and the water is clean enough to swim in.

# Nísoi Karos and Andíkaros
## (Keros)

The southeasternmost of this group of islands off the south coast of Naxos. The SW tip of Amorgós lies 3 miles to the SE of Andíkaros. On the S side of Karos there is a tiny cove about halfway along

(36°52'·7N 35°39'·3E), but there are severe gusts into here with the *meltemi*. Anchor in 4–5m near the head. The bottom is sand and rock and not everywhere good holding. The surroundings are bleak and inhospitable on this sun-baked barren island.

Andíkaros consists of two islands: Nisís Dhrima to the SW and Andíkaros to the NE. The narrow channel between them has 4m least depth. In calm weather a yacht can anchor at the SE end of the channel where there is reasonable shelter from the *meltemi* although there are severe gusts.

*Note* There is an above-water rock approximately ¼ mile N of the E end of Andíkaros. The rock sits on a shelf with least depths of 10m which extends approximately ½ mile N of the E end of Andíkaros. The above-water rock is normally easily spotted, but with the *meltemi* it can be difficult to see until close to. Sailing around here I spotted what I thought was a shallow area at the extremity of the shelf, but a Force 7 *meltemi* made investigation a little difficult.

*Caution* In the vicinity of Koufonisia, Karos and Andíkaros there can be severe gusts off the lee side of the islands with the *meltemi*. Care is needed with a strong *meltemi* when there can be extremely fierce gusts when on passage from Stenón Parou-Náxou to Amorgós.

# Nísos Amorgós

The easternmost of the Cyclades apart from the small islands of Kinaros and Levithia. It is mountainous throughout, dropping sheer into the sea in many places. Mt Krikelos is 821m (2,693ft) high at the NE end; Mt Áyios Ilías is 698m (2,290ft) high in the middle; and Mt Korax (Raven) is 607m (1,991ft) high at the SW end. The cliffs are spectacular, especially at the NE end and on the south coast where they drop straight down into the sea for 300m or so, giving you the impression that the island was simply sliced off here like a wedge of cheese. Most of the island is burnt barren rock though inland the valleys are cultivated in places.

In the past the islanders had a reputation as wreckers and pirates. The island was colonised in classical times but appears to have been of minor importance. The poet Simonedes settled here and became known as Simonedes of Amorgós. The island is off the main tourist route and mostly visited by backpackers. There is excellent fishing around the coast and a school of dolphins will often be seen in the vicinity of the island.

For film buffs the island is known as the setting for Luc Besson's film *The Big Blue* (*Le Grand Bleu*) and numerous locations around the coast were used during filming. In the rocky cove E of Órmos Kalotaritissa at the SW end of the island is the wrecked coaster *Olympia* which figures prominently in the film.

*Note* When the *meltemi* is blowing there are severe gusts off the S side of Amorgós and big seas on both the NW and SE sides.

⊕**33** 1M N of N. Gramvoúsa (N islet) light (Amorgós)
36°50'·2N 25°44'·7E
⊕**34** ½M S of Ák Áy Ilias light (Amorgós/Katápola)
36°49'·2N 25°50'·4E
⊕**35** 1M N of Ák Vlikardha (Amorgós)
36°57'·3N 26°00'·2E
⊕**36** 1M S of Ák Goniá light (Amorgós)
36°45'·2N 25°48'·0E

**NÍSOS AMORGÓS**

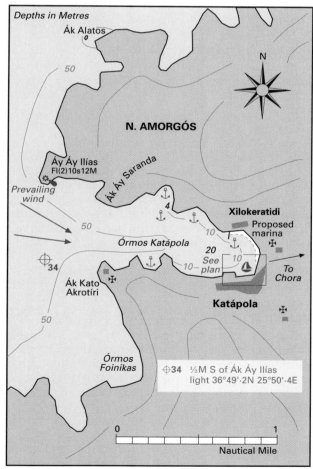

⊕**34** ½M S of Ák Áy Ilías
light 36°49'·2N 25°50'·4E

**APPROACHES TO ÓRMOS KATÁPOLA**

**KATÁPOLA**
⊕36°49'·62N 25°51'·80E WGS84

## KATÁPOLA (Vathi)

### Approach

*Conspicuous* The *chora* and a line of windmills on the hill above the harbour are conspicuous from seaward. Houses straggle around the head of the bay with a monastery and church with a blue cupola conspicuous in the middle. Katápola lies in the SE corner of the bay.

*By night* Use the light on Ák Áyios Ilías: Fl(2)10s12M. Apart from this light there are no others, but with good visibility it is possible to make a night entrance.

*Dangers* With the *meltemi* there are strong gusts into the bay though these lift at Katápola.

### Mooring

Go stern or bows-to the quay under the lee of the ferry quay. The bottom is mostly sand and weed with some rocks – good holding once the anchor bites.

Katápola on Amorgós looking N. Ák Áy Ilias is top left and the village and harbour middle right          *Peter Kleinoth/MareTeam*

*Shelter* The shelter under the lee of the ferry quay is better than it appears even with the *meltemi* funnelling in.

*Note* Sewage emptying into the harbour makes it smelly in the summer heat.

*Authorities* Port police.

*Anchorage* A yacht can anchor in several places in the bay.

1. In the cove immediately W of Katápola. Shelter in here is better than it looks as there is something of a lee from W–NW winds.
2. In calm weather anchor off the hamlet in the NE corner of the bay. Care needs to be taken of laid moorings on the bottom. Good tavernas ashore.

3. In the cove W of the NE hamlet. Shelter from the *meltemi* is not the best here.

*Note* There are plans to build a marina at Xilokeratidi opposite Katápola itself. At the time of writing no plans were available and work has yet to begin.

**Facilities**

*Services* Water and electricity on the quay.

*Fuel* Can be delivered by mini-tanker to the quay. Alternatively the nearest petrol station is a few kilometres away on the road to the *chora*.

*Provisions* Most provisions can be obtained.

*Eating out* Pleasant tavernas and bars on the waterfront. *The Corner* taverna has excellent Greek cuisine that I couldn't fault during an enforced stay with a Force 9 gale here.

*Other* PO. OTE. Bank. Greek gas. Hire motorbikes. Ferries to Naxos, Piraeus and Rhodes.

**General**

Órmos Katápola is a magnificent deep bay with steep cliffs dropping sheer into the sea. The small village of Katápola is a pleasant relaxed spot and the harbour quite secure. Few tourists come here although recently there has been an influx of backpackers who have not helped the foreigner's image in Amorgós.

The *chora* above is typically Cycladic. It is on the way to the monastery of the Panayía of the Presentation which occupies a spectacular site on a cliff suspended between the sky and the sea below. The best way to get there is either to hire a motorbike or alternatively to get the local bus to the *chora* and then on to a stop nearby – the driver is

Nikouria Passage (Stenón Kakoperator) looking N from Amorgós

290

used to dropping people off at the nearest stop to the monastery. It is then a hot steep climb (remember to take a bottle of water) to the monastery itself which, even in this secular age, manages to instill a feeling of reverence and monastic quiet into the most hardened of sceptics.

**KALOTARITISSA AND APPROACHES**

⊕**33** 1M N of N. Gramvoúsa (N islet) light (Amorgós)
36°50'·2N 25°44'·7E

Órmos Kalotaritissa looking N towards the bay and Nisís Gramvoúsa

## ÓRMOS KALOTARITISSA

An enclosed bay at the SW end of Amorgós lying under Nisís Gramvoúsa. Care is needed in the approaches of the reefs and low-lying islets in the approaches. Anchor in the bay in 3–5m or go stern-to the stubby quay on the N side. There are numerous moorings in the bay for the local fishing boats. Reasonable shelter from the *meltemi* although a surge is generated with a prolonged blow from the N.

A beach taverna opens in the summer. In a rocky bight to the E of here is the wrecked coaster *Olympia* which was used during the filming of *The Big Blue*.

## ÓRMOS AKROTÍRI

36°48'·8N 25°47'·4E

A long narrow inlet lying under Nisís Petalidhia. It is only useful during calm weather as the *meltemi* sends a swell in. Taverna opens in the summer. There is a pier in the bay with 2m depths at the extremity.

## ÓRMOS KALOTÍRI

Lies on the SE side of Nisís Nikouria. Anchor on the NW side of the bay in 4–5m. Sandy bottom. Reasonable shelter from the *meltemi* although there are gusts into the bay which can be severe with a strong blow from the N.

Nisís Nikouria is connected to Amorgós by shoal water. The narrow passage, Stenón Kakoperator, has 5m depths close off Nisís Nikouria. Keep closer to the N side than the S side where a reef and shoal water extend out into the channel.

On the Amorgós side at Áy Pavlos several tavernas open, in the summer.

**ÓRMOS KALOTÍRI**
⊕36°52'·6N 25°55'·2E

## ÓRMOS ÁYIOS ANNAS (Aghios Ioanna, Yialis, Aigiali)

### Approach

The small harbour lies off the village of Yialis in the SE of Órmos Áy Annas. From the W the houses of

Áy Annas looking NW

**APPROACHES TO ÁYIOS ANNAS**
⊕36°54'·15N 25°58'·51E WGS84

the village are easily identified. From the E the houses will not be seen until into the bay, but the small islet N of Ák Langadhia is easily identified. Closer in the mole off the village is easily identified.

*By night* Use the light on Ák Langadhia Fl.5s8M and on the mole head Fl.G.3s3M.

*Dangers* With the *meltemi* there are strong gusts into the bay and big seas in the vicinity.

### Mooring

Go stern or bows-to the mole or the quay clear of the ferry berth. The bottom is mostly rock and not good holding – make sure your anchor is well in.

Care is needed of permanent moorings chains on the bottom in the approximate locations shown so it may be wise to use a trip-line on the anchor.

*Shelter* The bay is open to the W–NW and with the *meltemi* some swell rolls into the bay, but the harbour is tenable if not always comfortable. There are also strong gusts into the bay.

*Anchorage* In calm weather you can anchor in the bay in 3–6m on sand and weed. Some swell invariably rolls into the bay even when there is no wind and it can be very rolly at anchor.

### Facilities
*Water* On the quay in front of the village.
*Provisions* Mini-market.
*Eating out* Tavernas on the waterfront.

### General
The small bay has a modest tourist income, but is relatively untouched. The hinterland supports a few small villages, though how they survive is difficult to know in this barren baked landscape. For the visitor the steep-sided bay with small villages around the slopes is a wonderful spot well worth a visit despite the *meltemi*.

### ÓRMOS VILAKARDHA
36°56'·2N 26°00'·0E
On the NE tip of Amorgós there is a magnificent fjord-like inlet which can be used in calm weather. With the *meltemi* a swell is pushed straight into it. Anchor near the head of the inlet where convenient – though depths are considerable. At the head of the inlet a ravine cuts through the high cliffs. Around Ák Vilakardha on the NE end of Amorgós are spectacular cliffs rising sheer to some 700m (2,275ft) in places.

## Nísoi Kinaros and Lévitha
Kinaros is a barren jagged island 11 miles ENE of Amorgós. It is inhabited only occasionally by a solitary shepherd and his flock. Lévitha, lower in aspect than Kinaros, lies 5 miles to the east. The deep bay on the south coast affords good shelter and two families live at the head of the bay. A tale, probably anecdotal, relates that a member of one of the families here was suddenly taken ill while a large yacht belonging to a Greek minister was anchored off. He ordered up a helicopter to take the patient to hospital and, concerned by the lonely situation of the island, had a radio installed so that if help was needed again the inhabitants needed only to call for it and it would come – on his special authorisation.

*Note* A strong SE current is reported to flow in the vicinity of the islands and between the islands and Amorgós.

### ÓRMOS LÉVITHA
A landlocked bay on the S coast. The entrance to the bay is located in the saddle between the higher ends of the island. There is a large conspicuous rock immediately W of the entrance.

Lévitha. The anchorage in the creek on the E side of Órmos
Lévitha                                                              *Nigel Patten*

The E arm of the bay offers the best shelter.
Anchor in 10–5m near the head with a long line to
bollards ashore on the N side. The bottom is mud
with some rocks, good holding. Good all-round
shelter.

Recently mooring buoys have been laid in the
eastern arm and one of the locals makes a charge
(3000Dx at the time of writing) for using the
moorings. Presumably if you use your own anchor
no charge can be made.

Only a lighthouse keeper and a few fishermen
inhabit the island. There is a small taverna in a
farmhouse about 15 minutes' walk up the hill from
the quay. Good fresh fish is served in pleasant
surroundings. Remember to take a torch for the
return trip.

You can also anchor in the W creek on Lévitha in
4–5m depths with a long line ashore.

KINAROS AND LÉVITHA

Depths in Metres

ÓRMOS LÉVITHA
⊕37  1M S of Ák Spanó (Lévitha) 36°58'9N 26°29'·8E

## ÓRMOS VATHI 36°59'·9N 26°25'·5E

On the W side of Lévitha there is a deep bay offering
some shelter from the *meltemi* although some swell
penetrates into here. Anchor in 4–5m near the head
of the bay. The bottom is sand and rock, not
everywhere good holding.

## ORMISKOS PNINGO (Kinaros)
36°58'·4N 26°17'·6E

On the S side of Kinaros there is a long narrow inlet
affording nearly all-round shelter. Anchor near the
head of the inlet in 4–5m. The bottom is rock and
not the best holding – it is prudent to get a line
ashore if possible. Good shelter from the *meltemi*.
Closed in by the inlet you feel closed off from the
world in here. It is a lonely spot – wonderfully so.

# Southern Cyclades
## Nísos Mílos
### (Melos)

The southwesternmost of the Cyclades, Mílos is an
ancient volcano which, like Thíra, long ago erupted
and scooped out the giant bay. The circular
mountain ridge enclosing the bay is mostly barren
and sterile. The summit at the SW end is Mt Profitis
Ilías, rising to 751m (2,464ft). Alum, sulphur (hot
sulphur springs still exist), barium and kaolin are
mined and the open-cast mines around the slopes of
the island are easily identified from seaward.

Mílos was the centre of a pre-Minoan Bronze Age
civilization and finds on the island of the distinctive
'harpy' sculptures have added much to our
knowledge of this early Cycladic civilization. No
doubt these early settlers used the island as a
stepping stone during their island by island
colonization of the Aegean. Later it came under the
Minoans and later still passed to the Mycenaeans.

Mílos opted for the Spartan side during the
Peloponnesian War, thereby angering the Athenians
to such an extent that they carried out the infamous
massacre recorded by Thucydides. The Athenians
besieged Mílos which, after some months,
surrendered unconditionally, whereupon all able
males were slaughtered and the women and children
enslaved.

The Franks and later the Turks colonized the
island, but it enjoyed considerable freedom and
prospered. A large part of the income of the island
during this time was derived from pirate fleets who
used the remote anchorages around the islands and
sold their booty at Mílos from where it was resold to
merchants. In the First World War the large natural
harbour was a British naval base.

It was during the Hellenistic period that the Venus
de Milo, properly, the Aphrodite of Mílos, was
sculpted, and though it is probably one of the best-
known pieces of ancient Greek sculpture,
reproduced thousands of times in history and art
history books, its source and the island it comes

*293*

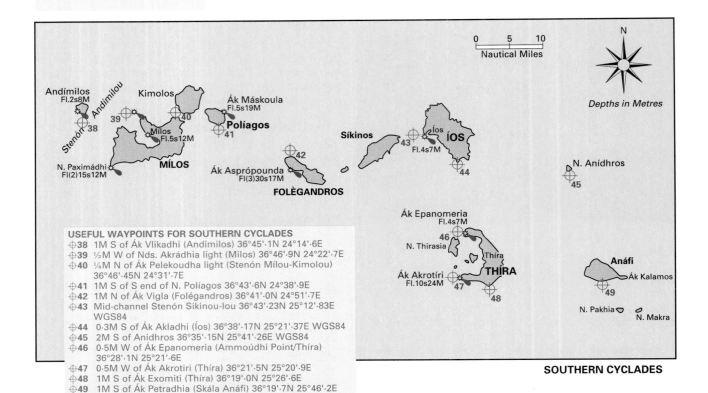

USEFUL WAYPOINTS FOR SOUTHERN CYCLADES
⊕38 1M S of Ák Vlikadhi (Andímilos) 36°45'·1N 24°14'·6E
⊕39 ½M W of Nds. Akrádhia light (Milos) 36°46'·9N 24°22'·7E
⊕40 ¼M N of Ák Pelekoudha light (Stenón Mílou-Kimolou) 36°46'·45N 24°31'·7E
⊕41 1M S of S end of N. Políagos 36°43'·6N 24°38'·9E
⊕42 1M N of Ák Vigla (Folégandros) 36°41'·0N 24°51'·7E
⊕43 Mid-channel Stenón Sikinou-Iou 36°43'·23N 25°12'·83E WGS84
⊕44 0·3M S of Ák Akladhi (Íos) 36°38'·17N 25°21'·37E WGS84
⊕45 2M S of Anidhros 36°35'·15N 25°41'·26E WGS84
⊕46 0·5M W of Ák Epanomeria (Ammoúdhi Point/Thíra) 36°28'·1N 25°21'·6E
⊕47 0·5M W of Ák Akrotiri (Thíra) 36°21'·5N 25°20'·9E
⊕48 1M S of Ák Exomiti (Thíra) 36°19'·0N 25°26'·6E
⊕49 1M S of Ák Petradhia (Skála Anáfi) 36°19'·7N 25°46'·2E

**SOUTHERN CYCLADES**

from are little known. The statue was found in the late 19th century by a farmer collecting old Greek stones for fieldwalls. He removed the top half (the statue is carved from two pieces of marble) and negotiated to sell it to the French consul who took it to his house for safekeeping. The French ship sent to collect it arrived to find that the Sultan's governor had forcibly taken the statue and put it aboard a ship bound for Istanbul. Captain de Marcellus decided to retake the statue and landed an armed party which, after a brief skirmish, got it back and aboard the French ship. It is said that it was during this skirmish that the Venus de Milo lost her arms which were spirited away by a local. Despite reports of the arms being rediscovered at various times, the Venus still hasn't acquired them and probably shouldn't lest it change our accepted perception of the armless beauty art historians are so familiar with.

## ADHAMAS (Port Mílos)

BA 1539

### Approach

*Conspicuous* Approaching the entrance to Órmos Mílos the lighthouse on Nisídhes Akrádhia and the village of Mílos (the *chora*) on the peak on the E side of the entrance are conspicuous. Rounding Ák Bombárdha the village of Adhamas will be seen.

**NISOI ANDÍMILOS, MÍLOS, KÍMOLOS AND POLIAGOS**

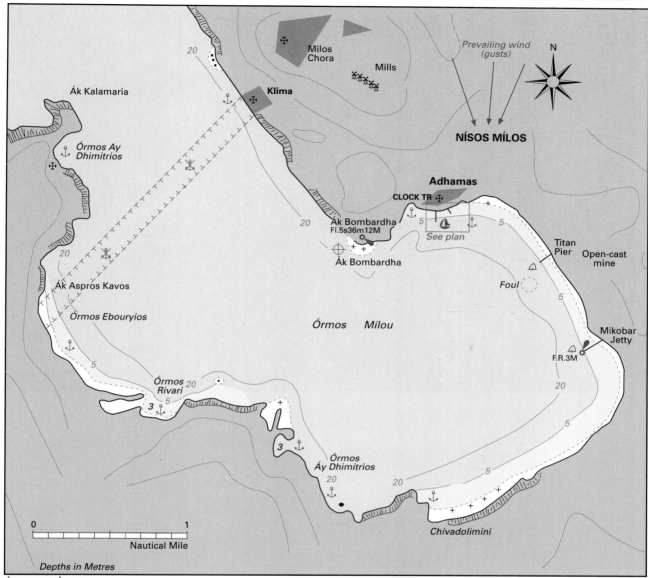

**ÓRMOS MÍLOU**
⊕36°43´·3N 24°26´·0E (Fl.5s12M)

*By night* Use the light on Nisídhes Akrádhia Fl.10s10M and Ák Bombárdha Fl.5s12M. The jetties off the opencast mine on the E side of Órmos Mílou are lit: 2F.R.3M and F.R.3M.

*Dangers*

1. With the *meltemi* there are heavy confused seas off the entrance to Órmos Mílou. Special care must be taken between Voi Kounidhi and Nisídhes Akrádhia where the waves rebound off the N side of Mílos and cause a heavy sea up to a mile off.

2. Care must be taken of rocks and reefs bordering the E side of the entrance to Órmos Mílou. Vos Monopodhro is a square rock easily identified. Off Ák Fourkovouni there are several detached above-water rocks eroded into fantastic wind-sculpted shapes.

3. At times the *meltemi* can gust down off the high land in the vicinity of Ák Bombárdha.

**Mooring**

Go stern or bows-to the E side of the ferry pier or bows-to the short pier to the E of it. Alternatively anchor off the village E of the short pier. The bottom is mud, rocks and weed – poor holding in places.

*Shelter* Good shelter from the *meltemi* although there is some residual swell. With strong S winds Adhamas is dangerous from the long fetch across the bay.

*Authorities* Port police and customs.

**Facilities**

*Water* On the ferry pier. Apply to the tourist office nearby.

*Fuel* On the outskirts of town. A mini-tanker can deliver.

*Repairs* Limited mechanical repairs. Hardware shop.

*Provisions* Good shopping for most provisions. Ice available.

Adhamas on Órmos Mílou looking NE. Yachts go on the E side of the ferry quay or on the W side of the pier further E

*Peter Kleinoth/MareTeam*

**ADHAMAS**
⊕36°43′·5N 24°26′·7E

*Eating out* Tavernas at Adhamas. Others along the waterfront.

*Other* PO. OTE. Bank. Greek gas and *Camping Gaz*. Hire cars, motorbikes and bicycles. Ferries to Piraeus, Thíra and Soúdha. Internal flights to Athens.

### General

The huge natural harbour is impressive to look at but the yachtsman is liable to curse this very size for the sea that can be raised inside in strong winds. I have always found Adhamas an indifferent sort of place – perhaps a few too many reinforced concrete buildings to be classified as attractive and a few too many tourists for the size of the place. Others disagree and find it has its own charm.

The *chora* (Mílos) on the hill above is attractive and the view over the bay superb. As at Thíra, the eye sees the volcanic crater that is now the bay, but the mind finds it difficult to compute the size of the explosion that produced it.

### OTHER ANCHORAGES IN ÓRMOS MÍLOU

1. ***Órmos Áy Dhimitrios*** A bay on the S side of Órmos Mílou approximately SSW of Ák Bombárdha. It looks to offer reasonable shelter from the *meltemi* and small yachts could creep in under the headland. Open to the E.

Nisís Akrádhia and lighthouse in the approaches to Órmos Mílou looking N

2. **Chivadolimini** An open bay to the E of Áy Dhimitrios. Anchor off the beach in calm weather or with southerlies. There are strong gusts off the slopes with southerlies.
3. **Órmos Rivari** An enclosed by on the SW side of Omos Mílou. Anchor in 3–4m. Poor shelter from the *meltemi* but good shelter from southerlies.
4. **Órmos Ebouryios** A large bay on the W side of Órmos Mílou. Anchor in the NW corner. Open to the NE–E and not really a good place to be in the *meltemi*.

## NÍSOS ANDÍMILOS (Anti-Milos)

⊕**39** ½M W of Nds. Akrádhia light (Milos) 36°46'·9N 24°22'·7E

A high steep-to island lying 5 miles WNW of Mílos. It rises to 686m (2250ft). With the *meltemi* there are severe gusts off the SW side of it, such that small whirlwinds are created. Keep well off! On the W side there is a light on Ák Kokhlídi: Fl.2s8M.

## NÍSOS KIMOLOS

A low barren island lying immediately NE of Mílos from which it is separated by a narrow channel. The small population lives in the *chora* or at Psathi. Formerly it was called Echinousa on account of the sea urchins found here (Pliny) and Argentiera on account of its silver mines. In the Middle Ages it was an infamous pirate haunt.

## STENÓN MÍLOU-KIMOLOU (Kímolos Channel)

BA 1539
Imray-Tetra G33

The area enclosed by Mílos, Kímolos and Políagos islands is an attractive mini-cruising area with a number of well-sheltered anchorages. In one or other of the anchorages shelter can be found from winds from any direction. Care must be taken of the reefs and shoals which fringe the islands and islets. In the plan these cannot be shown in great detail.

*Caution* With the *meltemi* there are severe gusts off the SW side of Nísos Políagos, down through Stenón Kimolou-Políagos (the channel between Kímolos and Políagos) and off the S side of Nísos Kímolos. Although there is not a big sea in the lee of the islands, the wind can be very strong indeed.

1. **Órmos Sikia** On the SW side of Kímolos. Open to the W–NW and unsuitable when the *meltemi* is blowing. With light northerlies and easterlies there is adequate protection in here. Anchor in 3–4m on the S side of the islet (Áy Andreas) in

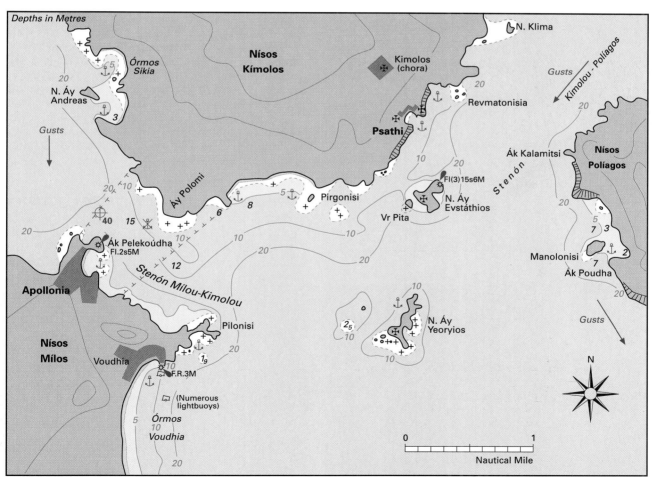

**STENÓN MÍLOU-KIMOLOU**

⊕**40** ¼M N of Ák Pelekoudha light (Stenón Mílou-Kimolou) 36°46'·45N 24°31'·7E the middle of the bay. Care must be taken of the reef connecting Áy Andreas to Kímolos. A yacht can also anchor on the N of the islet in 3–5m.

2. *Apollonia* A bay on the S side of Stenón Mílou-Kimolou directly under Ák Pelekoúdha. Care is needed of the reefs running out from the N and S entrance points. Anchor in 2–4m on the E side of the bay off the beach or off the hamlet on the S side. A line of small buoys marks off a swimming area inside of which anchoring is not allowed. Alternatively in calm weather go stern or bows-to the pier which has 3m depths at the extremity. Good holding on a sandy bottom. The shelter from the *meltemi* is better than it might appear on the plan although there are still strong gusts into the bay. It is completely open to the E.

Tavernas and a mini-market ashore.

3. *Órmos Voudhia* A bay lying about one mile SE of Apollonia. A 1·9m patch lies 0·2 miles S of Pilonisi (connected to Mílos by a causeway). Anchor in 5–8m in the N corner of the bay. You can also anchor under the bight further SW of the

Pilonisi anchorage. There are a number of mooring buoys in the bay (Q.Y(occas)) for the ships that load here. Good shelter from the *meltemi*. There are open-cast mines ashore and a wharf and ore-carrier on the waterfront, so the bay is not really the most attractive place to bring up for the night.

4. *Pirgonisi anchorage* A long sandy beach extends nearly right around the S side of Kímolos. A yacht can anchor anywhere off the beach and obtain excellent shelter from the *meltemi*. Care is needed of a rocky shelf running W–E approximately 1m underwater some way off the shore. At the E end of the beach a low rocky islet, Pirgonisi, is connected to the shore by a reef. A yacht can tuck under Pirgonisi off the beach in attractive surroundings. The bottom is sand and weed, good holding. A few villas have been built around the shoreline.

*Note* An underwater rock (1·5m over) was reported approximately ¼M offshore in the middle of the bay. As no-one else has been able to locate it I suggest you disregard notices of its apparent location.

5. *Psathi* A cathedral in the *chora* above and 4 windmills on a ridge are conspicuous. Closer in, the houses around Psathi Bay are conspicuous. A ferry uses the quay on the N side. Anchor in the bay in 2–3m on sand, weed and rock, not everywhere good holding so make sure your anchor is well in. Alternatively go stern or bows-to the stubby quay on the N side (W of the ferry quay) or bows-to the extremity of the S mole. Care is needed on the latter as rocks extend underwater from the quay. The bay is not well sheltered from the *meltemi* and should only really be used in calm weather. Open to the S–SE. Limited provisions and taverna/cafés ashore. *Caïque* ferry to Mílos.

**APOLLONIA**
⊕36°45′·9N 24°31′·6E

Apollonia · *Nigel Patten*

**PSATHI**
⊕37°47′·1N 24°35′·0E

Psathi on Kímolos looking SW — *Nigel Patten*

**MANOLONISI**
⊕36°46'N 24°36·5E

6. ***Sémina Creek*** 36°48'·4N 24°35'·4E A fjord-like bay approximately 1¼ miles N of Psathi. The N side of the entrance is lit Fl.G.5s5M although the operation of the light is reported to be intermittent. There is a short mole which the fishing boats use. Anchor in the bay in 4–6m. Poor shelter from the *meltemi* which is funnelled straight down Stenón Kimolou-Políagos.

7. ***Prasonisi anchorage*** Under the NE tip of the island (Ák Anatoli) is a small cove with an islet in the middle. Anchor in 3–4m on either side of the islet and take a line ashore. Care should be taken of the reef connecting the islet to Kímolos. Poor shelter from the *meltemi*.

## NÍSOS POLÍAGOS (Poliagaios, Polino)

A barren island close SE of Kímolos.

## MANOLONISI

On the W side of Políagos a yacht can anchor behind Manolonisi Island in 2–3m. Sandy bottom.

Shelter from the *meltemi*. The islet is connected to Políagos by a sand bar with 1·5m depths over it. A delightful, utterly secluded spot.

## POLÍAGOS S SIDE

On the S side of Políagos there are several anchorages which can be used in calm weather. With the *meltemi* there are strong gusts off the land and a swell is pushed around to here making the anchorages uncomfortable.

# Nísos Folégandros
## (Pholegandhros, Polikandros)

A barren rocky island lying 14 miles east of Mílos. It is steep-to with some impressive cliffs on the south side. At the NW end the island is 311m (1,020ft) high and at the SE end Mt Elevtherios is 415m

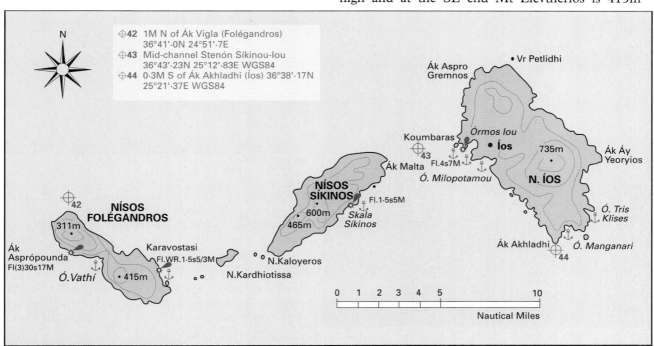

**FOLÉGANDROS, SÍKINOS AND ÍOS**

(1,361ft) high. The small *chora* sits on the edge of the cliff on the NE side and is a delightful oasis of green trees and shrubs in the otherwise barren island.

## KARAVOSTÁSI
BA 1541

### Approach
*Conspicuous* Nisídhes Adhelfia, the jagged islets lying E of Karavostási and SW of Nisís Kardhiotissa, are easily recognised. Closer in Dhio Adhelfia, the small islet in the middle of the entrance to Karavostási, will be seen. The white houses around the bay and a church on a low hill behind are also conspicuous.

*By night* A night approach is not recommended. Use the light on the N side of the entrance (Fl.WR.1·5s5/3M red sector covers 202°-248° and 322°-344° over Ifalos Poulioxeres) and the light on the end of the new mole Q.G.3M.

*Dangers*
1. Care is needed of Ifalos Poulioxeresi to the NNE of the entrance and the reef running NE from the N entrance point to Karavostási.
2. With the *meltemi* there are strong gusts and a disturbed swell at the entrance to the bay.

### Mooring
Go stern or bows-to the mole where shown. When the W side of the ferry mole is not in use a yacht can go alongside here overnight. When the harbour is packed you may be able to squeeze in somewhere in the fishing boat area though berths here are jealously guarded. The bottom is sand and rock – poor holding in places.

*Shelter* Reasonable shelter from the *meltemi* although a prolonged blow sets up a surge in the bay which makes things uncomfortable though still tenable. Open SE–E.

**KARAVOSTÁSI APPROACHES**
⊕36°37'.0N 24°57'.2E

**KARAVOSTÁSI**
⊕36°36'.9N 24°57'E

*Anchorage* In calm weather you can anchor off in Órmos Karávostasi. It is uncomfortable and can be untenable in here with the *meltemi*. Likewise in calm weather Órmos Vintsentsos and Órmos Livádhi have suitable depths for anchoring.

### Facilities
Limited. Some provisions can be obtained although supplies are much dependent on the ferry. Tavernas and bars. Bus to the *chora*. Ferry to Íos and Mílos.

### General
The bay with its jagged headland and small islets in

Karavostási on Folégandros looking NW. Nisís Áy Íoannis is bottom right                    *Peter Kleinoth/MareTeam*

the approaches is attractive in a parched sun-baked way. A few backpackers come here in the summer. It is about an hour's walk (or much shorter bus ride) to the *chora* sited on the edge of a cliff and something of an oasis with trees and greenery contrasting with the otherwise barren island. There are a few tavernas and limited supplies here.

Karavostási literally means a 'ship-stop'. Before the new ferry mole was built the ferry would anchor in the bay and passengers and cargo were brought ashore in small boats. Even a strong *meltemi* could not stop the ferry and it literally roared into the bay, unloading and loading again as quickly as possible, before steaming off to some more secure port.

## ÓRMOS VATHI

A large bay on the W side of Folégandros to the E of Ák Aspropounda. With the *meltemi* there are very strong gusts into the bay and a swell works its way in. In calm weather anchor off in 4–5m. The bottom is sand and weed, poor holding in places.

**ÓRMOS VATHI**
⊕36°37′·6N 24°53′·3E

# Nísos Síkinos

A barren dry island to the E of Folégandros. It was once called the wine island because of the excellence of its wine, but I cannot attest to this fact today. The small *chora* lies inland under a ruined fortified monastery.

**SKÁLA SÍKINOS**
⊕36°40′·7N 25°09′·0E

## ÓRMOS SKÁLA

The only harbour on Síkinos, situated 3 miles SW of Ák Malta. The buildings around the bay are conspicuous from the S, but not from the E. There is a light on the E side of the bay Fl.1·5s5M and the short mole is lit Fl.R.2s3M.

The mole and quayed area on the W side of the bay have been extended and there is room under the stubby mole to go alongside with an anchor out to hold the yacht off the quay. Local boats use the quayed area N of the stub mole. Alternatively anchor off in 3–5m. Good shelter from the *meltemi* although there are strong gusts. Open to the S.

Some provisions available and tavernas ashore. The small village around the bay is most attractive and popular with Greek tourists.

# Nísos Íos

Lies to the east of Síkinos across a narrow (3½ miles) strait. The island is mountainous and barren but in the words of the Admiralty *Pilot* '. . .it has a softer and more genial aspect than either Folégandros or Síkinos.' Mt Pirgos in the middle of the island rises to 790m (2,410ft).

Íos is claimed to be the burial place of Homer. On a voyage from Sámos to Athens the old blind bard died. His body was thrown overboard and washed up on Íos where the sea buried him on the beach. His body is now said to be buried on the northern slopes of Mt Pirgos. An apocryphal story, but then you never know.

Today the island is extremely popular with young sun-lovers. Nude bathing is tolerated here (although it is still technically illegal in Greece) and the beaches around the island are packed with lobster-red bodies.

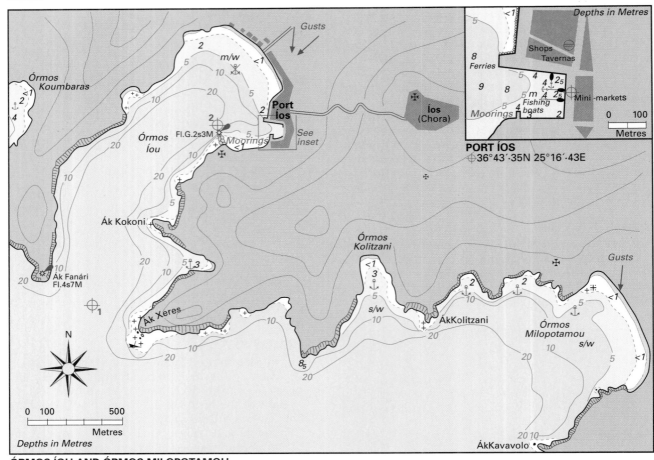

**ÓRMOS ÍOU AND ÓRMOS MILOPOTAMOU**
⊕₁ 36°42'·73N 25°15'·72E WGS84
⊕₂ 36°43'·36N 25°16'·21E WGS84

## PORT ÍOS

BA 1541

### Approach

*Conspicuous* The *chora* of Íos on the hill above the harbour and two windmills on the hill below the village are conspicuous from seaward. Nisís Dhiakofto NW of the entrance to Órmos Íou stands out clearly. Once up to the entrance the light structure on Ák Fanári can be distinguished and a few buildings around the beach will be seen. The buildings around the harbour cannot be seen until you are into the bay.

*By night* Use the light on Ák Fanári Fl.4s7M and the light on the end of the rough stone breakwater Fl.G.2s3M.

*Dangers*
1. Care should be taken of the reef that runs S for about 100m from Ák Xeres.
2. With the *meltemi* there are strong gusts into the bay.

### Mooring

Go stern or bows-to in the basin. Some suggest it is better to go alongside on the N side of the basin although you will need plenty of fenders because of the surge from the ferries. The bottom is mud – excellent holding.

*Shelter* All-round shelter out of the gusts from the *meltemi*. Ferries entering the harbour do so at speed and create a big surge in the basin. Yachts should keep pulled well-off the quay or the surge will smash you onto the quay.

*Authorities* Port police and customs.

*Note* It is now prohibited to anchor in Órmos Íou as it obstructs the ferry turning area. All yachts must use the yacht harbour.

Órmos Íou looking SW from the *chora*          *Nigel Patten*

302

Ios harbour looking N

## Facilities

*Water* A mini-tanker can deliver good drinking water.

*Fuel* A mini-tanker can deliver to the basin.

*Provisions* Most provisions can be found near the harbour. Ice from the NE corner of the harbour.

*Eating out* Tavernas and bars around the harbour.

*Other* PO. OTE. Bank. Greek gas. *Camping Gaz* in the *chora*. Hire motorbikes. Bus to the *chora*. Ferries to Piraeus, Thíra and Iraklion.

## General

By night the waterfront throbs to the sound of music from bars and discos as young bodies weave their way from bar to bar to disco. Íos is the centre for the young backpackers sleeping rough on the nearby beaches. By day nudism rules (a sign painted on a cliff proclaims: 'Clothes are prohibited') and the nearby beaches are packed with the young of all nationalities complying with this sign. The *chora* above is a maze of streets packed with bars, boutiques and backpackers, although to be fair it is a more convivial place outside of high season.

## ÓRMOS KOUMBARAS

The bay immediately N of Port Íos. Anchor in 3–4m. Indifferent shelter from the *meltemi*.

## ÓRMOS MILOPOTAMOU

The large bay immediately S of Port Íos. On the N side of the bay there are four coves where a yacht can anchor. The two easternmost coves are the better sheltered. Anchor where convenient. The bottom is sand – good holding. Good shelter from the *meltemi* although there are strong gusts into the bay and some swell may enter with a prolonged blow. Open to the W and S. There are a number of hotels and tavernas on the beach. Much frequented by nudists.

## ÓRMOS MANGANARI

A large bay on the S coast of Íos. In the NE corner of the bay there is a rocky islet. Anchor near the head of the bay in 3–8m or in the W or E of the bay.

The bottom is sand, excellent holding. You can tuck into the cove on the W with a long line ashore to the N side. Open only to the S. Good shelter from the *meltemi* although there are gusts into the bay. A small hotel and tavernas ashore. A *caïque* brings the nature-lovers (topless and bottomless) daily from Íos.

**ÓRMOS MANGANARI**
⊕36°39′·05N 25°22′·23E WGS84

## ÓRMOS TRIS KLISES

A bay on the S coast about 1½ miles NE of Manganari. Anchor in either of the two coves in 3–5m. The bottom is rocky and not reliable holding. Good shelter from the *meltemi* although there are strong gusts into the bay. No facilities.

Care must be taken of a reef on the W side of the bay and of a shallow patch near the head of the E cove.

**ÓRMOS TRIS KLISES**
⊕36°40′·0N 25°23′·3E

# Nísos Thíra

## (Thera, Psira, Santorini)

Like Mílos, Thíra is a giant volcano. The principal island is Thíra, shaped like a new moon encircling the rim of the crater now filled with water. To the NW Thirasia forms another part of the rim and in the middle a black mass of cinder and lava (Kamméni and Néa Kamméni) is the volcanic plug. Thíra is steep-to on the west coast: variegated pumice cliffs in pastel shades of red, brown, grey, green and slate blue drop sheer into the sea from 150–300m and keep going down for another 300m. The east coast is low-lying, sloping evenly up to a hilly ridge running along the island. The summit of Thíra, Mt Áyios Ilías, is a conical peak in the SE of the island with a white monastery and a cluster of communication towers on top which are conspicuous from seaward. The white domed houses of the capital, Thíra (Fira), extend along the cliff top on the west coast about 213m (700ft) above the tiny harbour and present a remarkable (and much photographed) sight from seaward.

Legend has it that Thíra originated from a lump of earth presented to Jason and the Argonauts by Triton (a local African god) which was later dropped into the sea where Thíra (or *Kalliste* – the most beautiful – as it was called then) is now. The island was an important Minoan settlement until it blew itself to pieces in c.1440–1450 BC and destroyed the Minoan civilization as well (see 'Thíra and the Atlantis Legend'). It was later subject to Athens and the Egyptian Ptolemys made it into a naval base. In the Middle Ages it was part of the duchy of Naxos. In the early 20th century it was a place of exile for political prisoners.

Thíra is unlike anywhere else in the world. The volcanic crater is some six miles long by four miles wide and viewing it from Thíra town, the mind cannot comprehend the sort of massive explosion that moved so much solid material to scoop out this deep bay. It may give you pause for thought to remember that the volcano is still active and that your yacht is moored in the crater.

The strange landscape breeds strange tales. Vampires are said to exist on the island and the inhabitants report that ghostly apparitions haunt the countryside at night. The volcanic soil is especially fertile and like the land around Mt Etna and Vesuvius the soil produces fine grapes for wine. Of the bottled wines Atlantis white or red and Nikteri white are good. Local wine can also be obtained from the barrel.

Thíra is unique and consequently it is one of the places in the Aegean that must be visited. In the summer as many as four cruise ships may be anchored in the bay beneath Thíra town disembarking thousands of sightseers. Yachtsmen are lucky in so far as they can visit Thíra town and then retire to the peace of another anchorage around the crater.

**NÍSOS THÍRA**

⊕46 ½M W of Ák Epanomeria (Ammoúdhi Point/Thíra) 36°28'·1N 25°21'·6E

⊕47 ½M W of Ák Akrotíri (Thíra) 36°21'·5N 25°20'·9E

⊕48 1M S of Ák Exomiti (Thíra) 36°19'·0N 25°26'·6E

## NISÍS THIRASIA

The westernmost island. The only anchorage is in Órmos Áyios Nikólaou (36°25'·3N 25°21'·2E). Anchor off the small hamlet at the foot of the cliffs. The short pier has 3m depths at its extremity but it is used by *caïque*-ferries from Thíra and Finikia. Good shelter from the *meltemi* although there is invariably some swell in the bay. Open to the S and E. Tavernas ashore. A zig-zag track leads up the cliffs to the village above where some provisions can be obtained.

## NISÍS NÉA KAMMÉNI

The once hot lump of ash and cinders in the middle of the crater. There are a number of very small inlets around the island where a yacht can anchor. The anchor must have a trip line as the bottom consists of very large rocks which easily snag an anchor.

The best anchorage on Néa Kamméni is in a cove on the SE corner. There is a light structure on the S side of the entrance (Fl.3s5M). Unfortunately most of the quayed area here is used by the local tripper boats and there is little room for even small yachts. Squeeze in where you can. Care must be taken of a foul area off the W side of the cove where a sunken coaster lies on the bottom. There is a small chapel ashore. Open only to the E.

A yacht can also anchor immediately N of the entrance to the cove with a long line ashore. There is reasonable shelter from the *meltemi* here. Several

## Thíra and the Atlantis legend

Plato first recorded the Atlantis legend that has baffled historians to the present. His description of an ancient island civilization which vanished as the result of a great natural catastrophe has been variously fixed in the Antilles, America, an island somewhere on the continental shelf off the Mediterranean, Malta – and most often in Plato's imagination. In the last forty years the location of Atlantis has moved to Greece and many eminent authorities now believe that Thíra was in fact the fabled island.

We know that Thíra was populated before 2000 BC and that in the period before the catastrophic eruption an advanced and inventive Minoan civilization existed on Thíra and Crete. Although the excavations at Akrotíri on Thíra are interesting, the range of technological and artistic achievements of the Minoans is best seen at Iraklion and the Palace of Knossos. This civilization ended abruptly around 1400 BC and for some time it was hypothesized that a Mycenaean invasion had simply swept it away. Yet Thíra erupted at about the same time and the hypothesis of Professor Marinatos and others is that this mega-explosion not only destroyed Thíra but also caused a *tsunami* or seismic sea wave which destroyed the Cretan-based Minoans.

Thíra is the largest known active caldera in the Mediterranean and one of the largest in the world. It is about five times the size of Krakatoa near Java and the eruption of Thíra is estimated have been about three times greater than that of Krakatoa in 1883. Here is a description of that recent eruption:

`In the course of two days, 26-27 August 1883, 23 sq. km of Krakatoa disappeared as a result of a series of violent explosions. The biggest explosion at 10 a.m. on the 27th, was heard from Alice Springs in Australia to Martinique, and from Ceylon to Northern Malaya. Atmospheric shock waves from it travelled three and a half times round the globe. The blast caused serious damage to houses up to 160 km away. Tidal waves were associated with the explosions and that associated with the biggest explosion was reliably reported as 17m high at Vlakke Hoek lighthouse 88 km away from Krakatoa. The waves destroyed nearly 300 towns and villages on the surrounding coasts of Java and Sumatra, and a large proportion of the coast population, amounting to over 36,000 people, was drowned.'

J. V. Luce *The End of Atlantis*

From this it may be inferred that the earlier Thíra explosion could effectively destroy life on Crete only 60 miles away. The blast would destroy buildings and tidal waves perhaps 60–100m high moving at 160 km per hour would swamp nearby islands. Crete would have been covered in a layer of acidic ash between 10–75cm thick (10cm effectively destroys the soil for 2 years or more). And so in the end we come back to Plato's words: `But afterwards there occurred violent earthquakes and floods; and in a single day and night of misfortune the island of Atlantis disappeared in the depths of the sea.'

The excavation of Akrotíri on the south of Thíra has revealed a prosperous city with three-storey mansions and wall paintings of quite exquisite beauty. However the excavations have added to the puzzle of Thíra as not a single inhabitant has been found buried in the ash and pumice. Excavations on Crete and other islands in the vicinity reveal previous eruptions and it is likely that Thíra was abandoned before the final catastrophic eruption that engulfed Akrotíri.

Since the great eruption of about 1400 BC the volcano of Thíra has remained active. In 236 BC it erupted again and separated Thirasia from the NW end of Thíra. In 196 BC Old Kameni (Hiera) appeared. In AD 1570 the south coast of Thíra collapsed into the sea. Three years later Small (Mikra) Kamméni appeared and in 1711–12 Néa Kamméni appeared. In 1866 a violent eruption began and lasted two years. At the end of 1868 an islet, Afotessa, appeared and then disappeared again. In 1925–26 another eruption joined Small Kamméni to Néa Kamméni. In July 1956 a massive earthquake caused much damage destroying many of the buildings at Finikia and Thíra. The epicentre of this earthquake was off the north coast of Amorgós and it produced *tsunamis* up to 17m high.

**NÉA KAMMÉNI (SOUTHEAST COVE)**
⊕36°24'·1N 25°24'·3E

coves N of this anchorage can also be used with care.

*Caution* Néa Kamméni is infested with very big and bold rats who will not hesitate to come aboard.

## Thíra

BA 1541

The principal island. There are a number of anchorages around the island:

1. **Finikia (Epanomeria)** Lies on the N end of Thíra under Ák Epanomeria. There is a short pier with 6m depths at the extremity, but it is usually crowded with fishing boats and *caïque*-ferries. Anchor to the W of the mole in 10–20m. The bottom is rocky and the anchor should have a trip line. Some shelter from the *meltemi* although there is always some ground swell here. Completely open to the S.

   Tavernas on the waterfront. A track leads up the cliff to the village of Finikia above.

2. **Skála Thíra** The harbour for the capital of Thíra (Fira) on the steep slopes above. The harbour here, really just a quay cut into the base of the cliff, is very open and you should not leave a yacht unattended. Go stern or bows-to the quay using your anchor or a long line to the buoy. (See *Note*). If you are using the buoy there is invariably considerable confusion when a yacht on the inside wants to leave. All the yachts on one side or the other must drop their lines or pass them around the yacht leaving, an exercise which leaves ample scope for confusion. Getting out

from the spider's web of lines is further complicated by the wash from tripper boats, ferries, and boats carrying passengers to and fro from the cruise ships anchored off. It is recommended you do not leave a yacht unattended on the quay.

Berths on the quay have a lee from the *meltemi* although there is a slop onto the quay. However the wash from other craft passing nearby, especially ferries and cruise ships, is significantly worse than any slop generated by the wind. The small harbour is for local craft.

Water on the quay. There are several taverna/cafés by the harbour. A donkey can be hired for the climb up to the town above or you can take the recently installed funicular. At Thíra town there is good shopping for provisions and excellent restaurants and bars. The view from the *chora* is simply stupendous.

*Note* The buoy is not always in place and not always in the best condition. Winter storms or more likely galvanic corrosion in the sulphurous waters corrodes the mooring chain and it can take some time before the authorities replace it. If it is not in place there are few alternatives. You can drop an anchor and go stern or bows-to, but it shelves very steeply off the quay to 20 plus metres. In addition the bottom is foul with large boulders and a trip-line on the anchor is essential. If you take a long line to the buoy it is at your own risk. Americans should take note that a libel action against the port authorities is doomed to failure in the Byzantine intricacies of the Greek legal system.

3. **Athinios** A small harbour 4 miles ENE of Ák Akrotíri used for loading pumice from nearby quarries. It is usually crowded with coasters loading or waiting to be loaded. The village of Megálo Khorion stands atop the cliff behind. If you are going to berth here care must be taken of a submerged mole and debris immediately E of the short pier. There are mostly 6m depths off the quay. Go and reconnoitre by dinghy before

**SKALA THÍRA**
⊕36°25´.1N 25°25´.7E

attempting to berth. Shelter is not the greatest here as the prevailing wind pushes a swell straight onto the quay.

4. **Ák Akrotíri** On the S side of Ák Akrotíri there are a number of anchorages sheltered from the *meltemi*.

Directly under the cape there is a deserted bay used by a few local fishing boats on permanent moorings. Anchor in 4–6m on a boulder-strewn bottom – use a trip line. A light breeze blows around the W point of the bay and holds you into the ground swell making for a comfortable night's sleep.

Approximately 1½ miles to the E there is a bight with a few houses and a taverna on the shore. Anchor in 4–5m. A further 1½ miles to the ESE there is another bight used by local fishing

Skála Thíra looking E          *Peter Kleinoth/MareTeam*

Thíra looking down to the caldera from the *chora*   *Nigel Patten*

boats. The bottom off the S coast is coarse sand – good holding. These latter anchorages get some ground swell which causes yachts here to roll awfully.

5. *Monolithos* A small harbour approximately halfway along the E coast. A rough breakwater extends for 150m in an easterly direction with 2–3m depths inside the outer end. The western half of the harbour is shallow. Go bows-to with a long line ashore to the breakwater near its extremity. With the *meltemi* some swell works its way into the harbour. Ashore there is a taverna and showers.

**MONOLITHOS**
⊕36°24'·8N 25°29'·3E

## VLIKADHA

### Approach
Care is needed in the approach because of the old breakwaters now underwater and the associated rocks and reefs in the vicinity. From approximately ¾M off the coast head on a course of 45° for the chimneys on the shore. Approximately 400 metres off the harbour head for the end of the outer breakwater.

*Conspicuous* The chimneys and hotel immediately E of the harbour are easily identified. Closer in the outer breakwater and boats in the harbour will be seen.

*By night* The entrance is not lit at present and an approach by night would be dangerous because of the reefs in the approaches.

### Dangers
1. Care is needed of the reefs which border both the E and W approaches to the harbour. At the time of writing the dangers are marked in a haphazard fashion with a red flag marking the end of the reef that must be left to starboard.
2. Unless you get exactly the right line into the harbour, depths are variable with some shallow patches. You should have someone up front conning you in.
3. In the entrance to the marina there is an underwater rock just off the inner breakwater and

you should keep close to the end of the outer breakwater.

### Mooring
At present yachts are berthing alongside one of the piers under the breakwater. In the future yachts should go stern or bows-to so that there is more space for everyone

*Shelter* Good all-round shelter.

### Facilities
*Services* Water and electricity points to be installed.
*Fuel* Fuel jetty to be established on the E pier.
*Eating out* Taverna ashore.
*Other* Bus to *chora*. A taxi can be arranged from the hotel.

### General
Vlikadha affords the best shelter on Thíra and for that it is worth making for. The entrance is tricky, although once you have piloted your way in it does

**VLIKADHA APPROACHES**
⊕48   1M S of Ák Exomiti (Thíra) 36°19'·0N 25°26'·6E

**VLIKADHA**
⊕36°20'·2N 25°26'·0E

not present the same adrenalin rush as the first time. You can get to *chora* from here and at least take your time over a visit without worrying about your boat down on the exposed quay at Skála.

## NISÍDHES KHRISTIANA

Khristiana light 36°13'·3N 25°13'·7E

A group of jagged rocks lying about 9 miles SW of Ák Akrotíri on Thíra. There are no anchorages and they are uninhabited.

# Nísos Anáfi

## (Anaphe)

The southeasternmost of the Cyclades. A barren burnt lump of an island with a small *chora* and an exposed anchorage on the south coast. Legend has it that Apollo raised the island from the sea to provide refuge for Jason and the Argonauts during a storm – a myth probably connected to the Thíra eruption. A few backpackers are attracted to the island's long sandy beaches.

## SKÁLA ANÁFI

A bight on the S coast. The *chora* on the hill and the hamlet around the landing place are conspicuous. There is a light at Skála: Fl.R.2s3M. The eastern end of the island is a high precipitous peak separated by flat land from the rest of the island and looks like a separate island from the distance. A white chapel on the summit of the peak is conspicuous. Care must be taken of the low-lying Voi Rokana, a rock lying 1¼ miles E of the hamlet and approximately ¼ of a mile offshore.

Immediately W of the hamlet a broken-down breakwater running S provides some shelter from westerlies. Anchor in 3–6m and with the *meltemi* try to tuck yourself under the breakwater with a long line to it. There is a small pier, but it is always crowded with *caïques*. The bottom is sand – good holding. Although I have experienced a swell working its way around the island into here, others recommend the shelter at Anáfi and have had a comfortable time despite the *meltemi* screaming outside. Open to the SW–S–E. Limited provisions and tavernas in the hamlet. The *Seashore (Poppy)* taverna has been recommended.

About 3 miles to the E an open bay with a long sandy beach can be used in calm weather.

NÍSOS ANÁFI

⊕49  1M S of Ák Petradhia (Skála Anáfi) 36°19'·7N 25°46'·2E

SKÁLA ANÁFI
⊕36°20'·6N 25°46'·2E

The eastern end of Anáfi looking NW. Note the conspicuous chapel perched on the summit

Skala Anáfi                                              *Nigel Patten*

# VI. Evia and the Northern Sporades

This chapter covers the island of Evia lying parallel to mainland Greece, the mainland coast itself from Ák Sounion to the Tríkeri peninsula, (Locris, Boeotia, Attica) and the northern Sporades. The inner route up the narrow gulf between Evia and the mainland is the more often travelled, there being sheltered waters and many safe harbours and anchorages. Along the east coast of Evia there are few safe anchorages sheltered from the prevailing wind. Nonetheless in the days of sail, *caïques* bound for the north would take the open water route making for Skiros and then slanting NW to Thessaloniki. The return trip was generally down the inner route.

In classical and Venetian times Evia and Skiros were important intermediate ports along the northern Aegean trade route between Athens and what is now northern Turkey. The trip from west to east was a gruelling slog (with a lot of rowing) against the prevailing winds.

The agricultural and mineral wealth of Evia ensured its own early development into a powerful state with a large fleet of its own, but it was later subdued by Athens. When the Venetians occupied it they considered it important enough to rank it as a kingdom and the standard of Negroponte (as Evia was called under the Venetians) was one of the three flown in St Mark's Square in Venice. Today, despite its proximity to Athens, Evia remains for the most part a wild and unspoiled island.

In ancient times an enemy of Athens wishing to invade the city-state would follow a fairly standard route from the north down through Evia and the adjacent mainland to southern Greece. The Pass of Thermopylae and the Plain of Marathon are probably the two best-known classical battle sites. The land force would be landed or supported from the sea and consequently this stretch of sea resounded to sea battles of which the Athenian harassment of Xerxes' fleet in the Tríkeri Channel is possibly best known. Not only the Persian invaders under Xerxes, but also the Macedonians, the Romans (under Glabrio and Cato), and the Turks, used this passage to get to southern and western Greece. In 1941 the British force (with the Australians and New Zealanders), retreating from the Germans in Macedonia, came down through here and were evacuated from beaches in Evia and the Saronic Gulf.

Kólpos Petalíon and the southern part of Evia are regularly cruised by Athens-based yachts, but further N there are fewer yachts to be seen except around the northern Sporades where a number of flotillas are based.

## Weather patterns in Evia and the Northern Sporades

The prevailing wind in the summer is the *meltemi* blowing from the NE. As in the Cyclades the *meltemi* begins fitfully in June, blows strongest in July and August, and dies at the end of October. In July and August it blows at Force 4–6 and may reach Force 7 on occasion. In the spring and autumn the wind is again predominantly from the N (NE–NW) but there are regular winds from the S as well.

There are a number of local variations to the overall weather pattern. In the Tríkeri and Orei Channels (Stenón Tríkeri and Stenón Oréon) the wind is funnelled into the channel so that it blows from the E–ENE. In the gulf of Volos (Pagasitikós Kólpos), a NW wind, Force 2–5, often blows down the valley at the head of the gulf in the spring and autumn. There may also be southerlies which can also blow in the summer months.

In the winter, gales are more often than not from the NE and can be exceptionally harsh. In early December 1980 a gale from the NE reached Force 10 and snow covered most parts of Evia down to sea level. In the mountains, up to a metre of snow fell and transport, telecommunications and electricity facilities were knocked out for three days. Snow on the decks is not what most people associate with Greece.

As in the Cyclades care must be taken of gusts off high land when the *meltemi* is blowing. Places noted for these squalls are the Evia coast in Kólpos Petalíon, the Evia coast N of Khalkís, and the E coast of Skiros.

In the summer the temperatures are high averaging 25°–26°C. Thessaly has the reputation of being the hottest place in Europe and certainly Volos is very hot in the summer (average temperature 27°C). In the spring and autumn there may be rain showers and thunderstorms. The latter may be accompanied by squalls, but they are normally short-lived affairs, usually over in 2 hours or so. The winters are harsher than those in more southern climes with colder temperatures and substantial snowfalls.

▲ Ports of entry

**Pilio (Volos)**
*Frequency*
VHF Ch 60
(announce Ch 16) | *Weather forecast* 0600, 1000, 1600, 2200 UTC | *Nav warnings* 0500, 1100, 1730, 2330 UTC

0    10    20
Nautical Miles

**Pilio Coastguard**
VHF Ch 16, 03, 60
MF 2182kHz

18 Psathoura
Fl.10s17M

**Northern Sporades**

Yioura

**VOLOS** ▲

13

*Pagasitikos Kólpos
(Gulf of Volos)*

Tríkeri
Pen
LFl.10s10M

Pelagos

17

Pilio Coastguard

Skiathos

**Alonnisos**

Aegean
Sea

14

Fl(3)30s20M

**Skópelos**

Piperi

LFl(3)20s
20M

15

Peristeri

12

Stenón
Trikeri

Pondikonisi
Fl(2)WR.15s15/12M

16

Skantzoura

19
N Pódhi
Fl.3s6M

Fl.5s16M

11

**Orei**

39°N

Stilidhos

Orei Channel

Loutro

Levkonisia

**Skíros Coastguard**
VHF Ch 16
MF 2182kHz
DSC VHF (Ch 70)

**Skíros**

Linaria

10
Fl(2)WR.10s12/9M

Kimassi

Ák. Sarakiniko

N. Skiropoula

N. Valaxa

Fl(3)30s
16M

Fl(2)5s19M

*Vorios Evvoikos Kólpos
(North Gulf of Evia)*

20

21

**EVIA
(Nísos Evvoia)**

22 Prasoúdha
Fl.5s16M

**Kimi**

**Piraeus Coastguard**
VHF Ch 16
MF 2182kHz
DSC MF 2187·5kHz
DSC HF ☎ (0)1 411 2500
Fax (0)1 411 5798

Fl(2)8s7M

Larimna

Fl.3·5s6M

9

Ák. Oktonia

8

Fl(2)R.18s12M

**Khalkis**

**Petries**

Ák. Pounda

Fl(2)12s6M

7

**Pérama**
*Frequency*
VHF Ch 86
(announce Ch 16) | *Weather forecast* 0600, 1000, 1600, 2200 UTC | *Nav warnings* 0500, 1100, 1730, 2330 UTC

Fl.4s7M

6

*Notios Evvoikos Kólpos
(South Gulf of Evia)*

Ák. Kafirevs

23

5

Fl(2)16s
6M

Fl(2)15s
10M

**Saronic**
*Frequency*
VHF Ch 25
(announce Ch 16) | *Weather forecast* 0600, 1000, 1600, 2200 UTC | *Nav warnings* 0500, 1100, 1730, 2330 UTC

3

Fl.4s6M

**Karistos**

**ATHENS**

38°N

*Corinth
Canal*

**Rafina** Fl.1·5s4M

Ó. Kastri

4

Fl(3)20s
15M

**Andros**

Porto
Rafti

*Kólpos
Petalion*

*Saronikos
Kólpos*

**Likhada Coastguard**
VHF Ch 16,01
MF 2182kHz

**Peloponnisos**

**Lavrion** ▲ Fl.5s16M

2

N Makronisi

N Aigina

Gaidouronissos

1

LFl.10s6M

**Kea**

Ák. Sounion

23°E    24°E

**EVIA AND NORTHERN SPORADES**

## Routes

Routes going N via Evia are basically up or down the outside of the island or the inside channel. The prevailing wind in the summer is the *meltemi* blowing from the NE and outside of the *meltemi* season most winds are still from the northerly quadrant. Yachts going N will usually take the inside channel which although still windy, offers more flat water and importantly more safe harbours and anchorages. Yachts coming S will often take the outside route and roar down to the Cyclades and Stenón Kafirevs with the wind behind. Some also take the inside channel and still have the wind behind.

Yachts heading N should, if they have time, leave in the spring or early summer before the *meltemi* begins or is not as strong as in mid to late summer. Often you will have days of calm and even some southerlies in the spring and early summer making going N a relaxed affair. If any depressions threaten there are more than enough safe harbours to take refuge in until the depression passes.

Yachts heading S in the summer or autumn will usually find that they have more than enough wind for a quick passage. There are several harbours along the E coast of Evia that can be used, although care is needed along what is in effect a lee shore most of the time. The seas can build up substantially, and as you get towards Stenón Kafirevs you will find some wicked steep cross-seas. In gales from any direction Stenón Kafirevs is a place to steer clear of – even big ships seek shelter in northerly gales rather than tackling the strait.

## Data

### PORTS OF ENTRY
Lavrion
Volos

### PROHIBITED AREAS
1. Anchoring is prohibited in the northern part of Órmos Marathon and at Órmos Áyios Marina.
2. Landing is prohibited in the vicinity of Órmos Áyios Marina and on the nearby islands of Stíra, Verdhouyi and Kavaliani.
3. Landing is prohibited on Nísos Yiouri in the Northern Sporades.

### MAJOR LIGHTS
**Nisís Patróklou** (Gaïdhouronissos) LFl.10s6M
**Ák Vrisáki** Fl.5s16M
**Nisís Mandhíli** (Doro Channel) Fl(3)20s15M
**Ák Veláni** Fl.1·5s4M
**Vrakhinisis Dhípsa** Fl.4s6M
**Nisídhes Verdhouyi** (Nisís Ligia) Fl(2)16s6M

**Órmos Oropoú** (SE point) Fl.4s7M
**Ák Avlís** (Dhíavlos Avlidhos) Fl(2)12s6M
**Ák Kakokefalí** Fl(2)R.18s12M
**Ák Mníma** Fl.3·5s6M
**Ák Stalamáta** Fl(2)8s7M
**Ák Arkítsa** Fl(2)5s19M
**Nisís Strongilí** (S islet) Fl(2)WR.10s12/9M
**Ák Vasilína** Oc.WG.5s14/11M
**Ifalos Panagitsa** (Orei Reef) Fl(2)12s9M
**Aryiorónisos** (E end) Fl.5s16M
**Ák Tríkeri** LFl(3)20s20M
**Volos – Cement Factory** W jetty Fl(2)10s12M
**Pondikonisi** Fl(2)WR.15s15/12M
**Ifalos Levthéris** Fl(2)8s9M
**Ák Sépia** LFl.10s10M
**Nisís Répi** (Skíathos) Fl(2)WR.10s12/8M
**Ák Gouroúni** (Skópelos) Fl(3)30s20M
**Ák Télion** (Alonissos) Fl(3)12s12M
**Nisís Psathoúra** Fl.10s17M
**Ák Lithári** (Skíros) Fl(3)30s16M
**Nisís Arápis** (Ák Kafirevs) Fl(2)15s10M
**Nisís Prasoúdha** (Kími) Fl.5s16M
**Levkonísia** (NE Evia) Fl(3)15s10M

### USEFUL WAYPOINTS
⊕1 0·15M S of Ák Angálistros (Makronisí S end) 37°38'·56N 24°01'·31E WGS84
⊕2 1M E of Ák Vrisáki 37°44'·7N 24°05'·9E
⊕3 1½M E of Ák Marathonas 38°07'·4N 24°05'·4E
⊕4 1M S of Nisís Paximádhi (Órmos Karistou) 37°56'·6N 24°23'·3E
⊕5 Mid-channel between Vrak Levkasia and Áy Marina 38°11'·5N 24°04'·8E
⊕6 2M N of Áy Apóstoliou 38°19'·8N 23°53'·9E
⊕7 Mid-channel Stenón Avlídhou-Boúrtzi (Ák Avlís) 38°24'·65N 23°38'·1E
⊕8 Entrance to Vorios Limani/Khalkís 38°28'·4N 23°35'·7E
⊕9 1M S of Ák Mníma 38°33'·6N 23°31'·9E
⊕10 ½M S of Nisís Strongilí 38°47'·9N 22°49'·2E
⊕11 ½M S of E end of Nisís Ayironisos 39°00'·0N 23°04'·4E
⊕12 Mid-channel Stenón Vólou (1.6M W of Ák Kavoulia) 39°05'·8N 23°00'·8E
⊕13 Ák Seskoulo (approaches to Limín Vólou) 39°20'·62N 22°56'·60E WGS84
⊕14 Mid-channel Stenón Skiathou 39°09'·9N 23°21'·8E
⊕15 Mid-channel Stenón Skopelou 39°09'·9N 23°34'·0E
⊕16 Stenón Alonissou (mid-channel between N. Mikró and Ák Telioni) 39°08'·5N 23°49'·3E
⊕17 Mid-channel Stenón Pelagonisou 39°17'·9N 23°59'·6E
⊕18 2M N of Nísos Psathoúra light 39°32'·3N 24°10'·8E
⊕19 2M N of Nisís Vorios Pódhi (Skíros N end) 39°03'·2N 24°28'·1E
⊕20 1M S of Ák Valáxa light 38°47'·0N 24°29'·5E
⊕21 2M S of Nisís Sarakino light (Skíros S end) 38°43'·5N 24°37'·6E
⊕22 1M E of Ák Kími 38°38'·9N 24°10'·7E
⊕23 1M E of Nisís Arápis/Ák Kafirevs 38°09'·6N 24°37'·1E

# Quick reference guide

| | Shelter | Mooring | Fuel | Water | Provisioning | Tavernas | Plan |
|---|---|---|---|---|---|---|---|
| **Evia and adjacent mainland coast** | | | | | | | |
| Gaïdhouromandra (Olympic Marina) | A | A | A | A | C | C | • |
| Lavrion | B | A | A | A | B | B | • |
| Órmos Thoriko | B | C | O | O | O | O | • |
| Frangolimani | B | C | O | O | O | O | |
| Tourkolimani | C | C | O | O | O | O | |
| Porto Rafti | B | AC | B | B | B | B | • |
| Órmos Vravronas | C | C | O | O | O | C | |
| Loutsa | A | A | O | A | C | C | |
| Rafina | C | A | B | B | B | B | • |
| Naoma | C | A | O | O | O | O | |
| Néa Mákri | C | A | B | B | B | C | |
| Órmos Marathonas | O | C | O | O | O | O | |
| Áy Apóstoliou | B | A | O | B | C | C | |
| Órmos Oropos | O | C | B | B | B | C | |
| Órmos Kastrí | B | C | O | O | O | O | • |
| Órmos Angistri | C | C | O | B | C | C | |
| Karistos | A | A | B | A | A | A | • |
| Nisídhes Petaloi | C | C | O | O | O | O | • |
| Néa Marmari | C | AC | B | A | B | B | • |
| Órmos Vlikho | B | C | O | O | O | O | |
| Órmos Animvoriou | B | C | O | O | O | O | |
| Néa Stíra | C | C | O | B | C | C | • |
| Nísos Stíra | B | C | O | O | O | O | • |
| Órmos Tigani | C | C | O | O | O | O | |
| Almiropotamos | B | C | O | B | C | C | • |
| Voufalo | A | C | O | O | O | C | • |
| Aliverion | A | A | O | A | B | B | • |
| Amarinthos | O | BC | B | B | B | B | |
| Erétria | B | C | B | B | A | B | • |
| Khalkís | B | AB | A | A | A | A | • |
| **Northern Evia Channel and the Gulf of Volos** | | | | | | | |
| Órmos Skorponeriou | B | C | O | B | O | O | |
| Lárimna | C | C | B | A | B | C | • |
| Kólpos Atalántis | B | C | O | O | C | C | • |
| Skála Atalantis | B | AB | O | A | C | C | • |
| Áyios Konstandinos | O | AB | O | B | B | B | |
| Néa Artaki | B | AC | B | B | A | B | • |
| Órmos Politika | A | AB | O | B | O | O | |
| Limni | A | AB | B | B | B | C | |
| Loutra Adhipsou | A | AB | B | B | A | B | |
| Órmos Yiali | C | C | O | O | O | O | |
| Ay Yeoryios | C | A | B | A | C | B | • |
| N. Likhades | C | C | O | O | O | O | • |
| Stilidhos | B | AB | B | B | A | C | • |
| Karavomilos | C | C | O | B | A | C | |
| Rahes | C | C | O | B | C | B | |
| Akladhi | AC | ABC | B | A | C | B | • |
| Órmos Vathikelon | A | C | O | O | O | O | • |
| Órmos Glifa | C | C | B | A | B | B | |
| Aryronísos | C | C | O | B | O | O | |
| Pirgos | B | AB | B | A | C | B | • |
| Orei | B | A | B | A | B | B | • |
| Órmos Ptelou | B | C | O | B | C | B | • |
| Órmos Nies | B | C | O | O | O | C | |
| Áy Kiriakí | C | C | O | B | C | C | • |
| Nisís Palaio Tríkeri | C | C | O | O | C | C | |
| Palaio Tríkeri | B | C | O | B | C | C | • |
| Tríkeri | C | C | O | O | O | O | |
| Limín Vathoudhi | A | C | O | B | C | C | • |
| Petraki | B | C | O | O | O | C | |
| Amalioupolis | C | AC | B | A | B | B | • |
| Fearless Cove | B | C | O | O | O | O | |
| Néa Ankhialos | B | B | B | B | C | B | |
| Áy Yeóryios | B | AC | O | B | C | C | |
| Volos | A | A | A | A | A | A | • |
| Órmos Agria | C | C | O | B | C | C | |
| Kato Gatsia | C | C | O | O | C | C | |
| Órmos Andriami | C | C | O | O | O | O | • |
| Platania | B | BC | B | B | B | B | • |
| Pefki | B | A | O | A | B | B | • |
| Pondikonisi | C | C | O | O | O | O | |
| **Skíathos** | | | | | | | |
| Koukounaries | A | A | O | B | O | C | • |
| Órmos Platania | C | C | O | B | O | C | • |
| Skíathos | B | ABC | B | A | A | A | • |
| **Skópelos** | | | | | | | |
| Loutráki | B | AC | O | A | C | B | • |
| Néa Klima | B | AB | O | O | O | O | |
| Órmos Panormou | B | C | O | O | O | C | • |
| Limonari | C | C | O | O | O | C | |
| Órmos Agnóndas | B | AC | O | O | O | C | • |
| Órmos Stafilos | C | C | O | O | O | C | |
| Limín Skopelou | B | A | B | A | A | A | • |
| **Alonissos** | | | | | | | |
| Órmos Mourtia | C | C | O | O | O | C | • |
| Patitíri | B | A | A | A | B | B | • |
| Votsi | B | C | O | B | O | C | • |
| Órmos Tzorti | B | C | O | O | O | C | |
| Steni Vala | B | C | O | B | C | C | • |
| Órmos Firaki | O | C | O | O | O | O | |
| **Peristeri** | | | | | | | |
| Órmos Peristera | B | C | O | O | O | O | |
| Órmos Xero | B | C | O | O | O | O | |
| Órmos Vasiliko | A | C | O | O | O | O | • |
| **Pelagos** | | | | | | | |
| Órmos Kira Panayía | C | C | O | O | O | O | |
| Planitís | A | C | O | O | O | O | • |
| **Skantzoura** | | | | | | | |
| Órmos Prasso | C | C | O | O | O | O | • |
| Órmos Skantzoura | B | C | O | O | O | O | |
| **Skíros** | | | | | | | |
| Áy Fokas | C | C | O | O | O | O | |
| Linaria Cove | B | C | O | O | O | C | |
| Limín Linaria | B | A | B | A | B | C | |
| Órmos Akladhi | B | C | O | O | O | O | • |
| Órmos Tribuki | O | C | O | O | O | O | |
| Órmos Renes | C | C | O | O | O | O | |
| Órmos Glifadha | B | C | O | O | O | O | |
| **East Coast of Evia** | | | | | | | |
| Órmos Petriés | B | AC | O | B | C | C | • |
| Kími | B | A | A | A | C | C | • |
| Órmos Loutro | B | C | O | B | C | C | • |
| Áy Vasilikos anchorage | B | C | O | B | C | C | |

# West coast of Evia and adjacent mainland coast

This section covers the stretch of water hemmed in between the island of Evia and the adjacent mainland coast. The section is split into a further two sub-sections covering the sea area S of Khalkís (Kólpos Petalíon and Notios Evvoïkós Kólpos/the S Gulf of Evia) and N of Khalkís (Vórios Evvoïkós Kólpos/the N Gulf of Evia).

Evia (also Evoia, Euboea, or Euripos after the narrow channel at Khalkís) or Negroponte, the Venetian name, is the long mountainous island lying parallel in a NW–SE direction to the mainland coast. After Crete it is the largest Greek island. The irregular mountain range is geographically the continuation of the Pilion range running down the east side of the Gulf of Volos. Mt Dhirfis (Dhelfi), 45 miles NW of Ák Kafirevs, is the summit of the island at 1,874m (5,718ft). Ten miles further NW, Mt Pixaria is 1,445m (4,406ft) high, and at the southern end of the island Mt Okhi (*Okhi* = no, and here means the mountain defies all), is 1,398m (4,586ft) high. Between these considerable peaks the island is rugged and steep-to with little flat land except on the W coast. The peaks are covered in snow in the winter and often far into the spring. On the lower slopes the mountains are densely wooded in pine, plane, holm oak and olive trees. The coastal plains on the west are fertile and intensively cultivated in corn, vines, figs and market gardens. Lignite and magnesite are mined and marble quarried – Evian *cipollino* was prized above all others by the Romans.

The mainland coast opposite is also mountainous, although it is not in the league of the Evian mountains. Mt Knimis, standing inland from the cape of the same name in the N, is 946m (3,077ft) high, a peak opposite Khalkís with a conspicuous white patch near the summit rises to 1,030m (3,350ft), and Mt Pendelikon near Athens rises to 1,119m (3,638ft). For the most part the mainland mountains are barren or covered in *maquis*, but the coastal plain is wooded or cultivated. From a point opposite Khalkís the motorway north mostly follows the coastline.

In antiquity Evia was divided between seven city-states of which Khalkís and Eretria were the two most important. These two cities were rivals for the fertile Lelantine Plain lying between them with Khalkís finally winning by default when Eretria was razed by the invading Persians. After the Persian wars Evia came under the sway of Athens. It passed on to Rome and to Byzantium without too many hiccups.

When the Venetians took Evia they renamed the island, calling it Negroponte, meaning 'black bridge' – a corruption of the name of the bridge spanning the Euripos Channel. Under the Venetians it ranked as a kingdom. In 1470 the island was occupied by the Turks and remained under Turkish rule until it became Greek in 1830.

The proximity of the mainland coast to Athens (Rafina is only 18½ miles away) has raised this area to the dubious status of a summer commuter belt. Large villas line much of the coast between Lavrion and Khalkís and land development is beginning north of Khalkís. The opening of the new airport for Athens at Sparta near this coast will no doubt bring further development. Athenians have also started to go to Evia, but the poor roads and sheer size of the island ensure that large parts of it remain virtually untouched.

# Coasts south of Khalkís

## Mainland coast

### GAÏDHOUROMANDRA and OLYMPIC MARINA

#### Approach

From the S the marina and yard will not be seen until you are up to Ák Foniás. Once you have opened the bay the outer breakwater, yard buildings and the masts of yachts will be seen. From the N the buildings and harbour at Lavrion will be seen and closer in the breakwater and shoreside buildings at the Olympic yard.

*By night* Use the light on Ák Foniás Fl.2·5s6M. The marina entrance is lit Fl.R.3M.

*VHF* Ch 09 for Olympic Marine.

#### Mooring

*Data* 680 berths. Visitors' berths. Max LOA 30m+. Depths 2–10m.

*Berth* Where directed. Laid moorings.

*Shelter* Excellent all-round shelter.

*Authorities* Port police and customs. Harbourmaster and marina staff. Charge band 3.

#### Facilities

*Services* Water and electricity at every berth. Shower and toilet block. Laundry service.

*Fuel* On the quay near the travel-hoist bay.

*Repairs* Olympic Marine 1,000 dry berths. 300 covered berths. 200/65/40-ton travel-hoists. Covered workshops. All mechanical and engineering repairs. GRP repairs including osmosis treatment and spray-painting facilities. Wood repairs. Electrical work. Liferaft certification. Sail repairs arranged. Chandlers.

Olympic Marine S.A., GR 19500 Lavrion, Attica, Greece. ☎ 0292 27701-5 *Fax* 0292 22569.

*Provisions* Mini-market. Better shopping in Lavrion (market on Thursdays).

*Eating out* A restaurant cum yacht club and a snack bar are planned in the marina. Fotis, previously within the yard, has built a new restaurant outside just up the hill and those who have visited say he still cooks good food (☎ 60875). Otherwise tavernas in Lavrion.

*Other* Bank planned in the marina. Telephone and fax facilities. Hire cars and taxis. Bus to Athens.

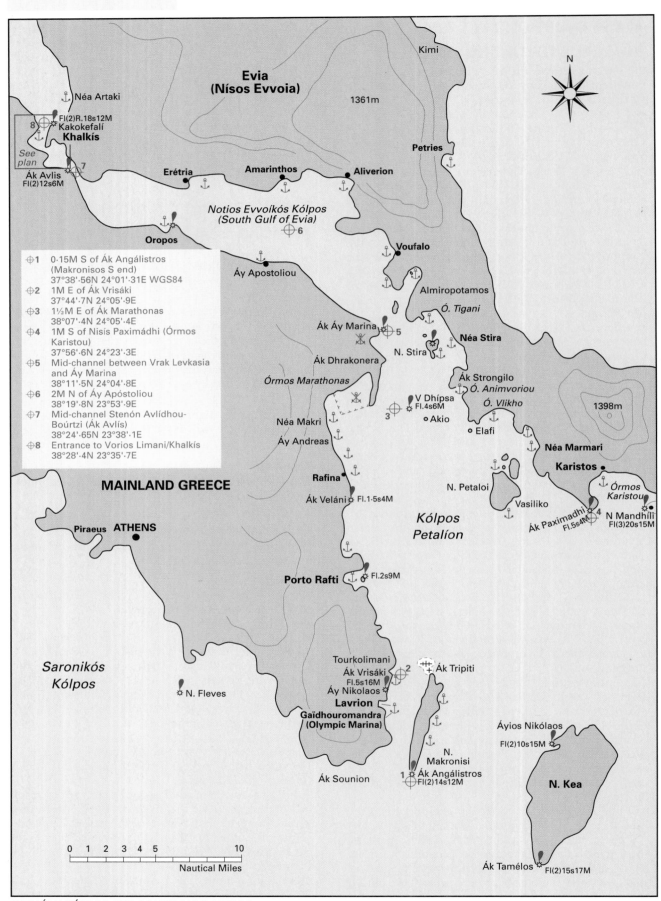

**Evia (Nísos Evvoia)**

Kimi

1361m

Néa Artaki

Fl(2)R.18s12M
Kakokefalí
**Khalkís**

8

See plan

7

Ák Avlis
Fl(2)12s6M

Erétria

Amarinthos

Aliverion

Petries

*Notios Evvoíkós Kólpos (South Gulf of Evia)*

6

**Voufalo**

Oropos

Áy Apostoliou

Almiropotamos

*Ó. Tigani*

Ák Áy Marina

5

**Néa Stira**

N. Stira

Ák Dhrakonera

Ák Strongilo
*Ó. Animvoriou*

*Órmos Marathonas*

*Ó. Vlikho*

1398m

V Dhípsa
Fl.4s6M

3

Akio

Néa Makri

Elafi

**Néa Marmari**

Áy Andreas

**Karistos**

N. Petaloi

*Órmos Karistou*

Rafina

Vasiliko

N Mandhíli
Fl(3)20s15M

Ák Veláni  Fl.1·5s4M

*Kólpos Petalíon*

Ák Paximadhi
Fl.5s4M  4

**Piraeus  ATHENS**

**MAINLAND GREECE**

- ⊕1 0·15M S of Ák Angálistros (Makronisos S end) 37°38'·56N 24°01'·31E WGS84
- ⊕2 1M E of Ák Vrisáki 37°44'·7N 24°05'·9E
- ⊕3 1½M E of Ák Marathonas 38°07'·4N 24°05'·4E
- ⊕4 1M S of Nisís Paximádhi (Órmos Karistou) 37°56'·6N 24°23'·3E
- ⊕5 Mid-channel between Vrak Levkasia and Áy Marina 38°11'·5N 24°04'·8E
- ⊕6 2M N of Áy Apóstoliou 38°19'·8N 23°53'·9E
- ⊕7 Mid-channel Stenón Avlídhou-Boúrtzi (Ák Avlís) 38°24'·65N 23°38'·1E
- ⊕8 Entrance to Vorios Limani/Khalkís 38°28'·4N 23°35'·7E

**Porto Rafti**  Fl.2s9M

*Saronikós Kólpos*

N. Fleves

Tourkolimani
Ák Vrisáki
Fl.5s16M
Áy Nikolaos

Ák Tripiti

2

**Lavrion**
**Gaïdhouromandra
(Olympic Marina)**

*Áyios Nikólaos*
Fl(2)10s15M

N. Makronisi

Ák Sounion

1  Ák Angálistros
Fl(2)14s12M

**N. Kea**

0  1  2  3  4  5        10

**Nautical Miles**

Ák Tamélos  Fl(2)15s17M

**PETALÍON KÓLPOS AND SOUTH GULF OF EVIA**

**Depths in Metres**

Covered storage workshops

N

Olympic Marine Yard

Restaurant/bar

Minimarket

Office

Villas

FI.R.3M

| 0 | 100 | 200 | 300 |

Metres

**OLYMPIC MARINA**
⊕37°41´·8N 24°03´·7E

### General

A marina has been planned off the Olympic Marine Yard for a good number of years and it has finally been built. The marina is now up and running and fairly full with Athens-based yachts, but there is still room for visiting yachts here. Some infrastructure still needs completion, but it is likely with the opening of the new airport at Sparta that this will soon be accomplished.

Olympic Marine is a long-established yard and at one time Carter 33s, 37s and 39s were built here as well as the Olympic 45. There were even some ferrocement Endurance 45s built here in the '70s. With the demise of yacht-building Olympic Marine turned to laying up yachts and has an impressive infrastructure including large covered workshops. It is now a competent and well-run yard with just about all facilities for the care and repair of yachts ashore and afloat.

If it has a drawback it is that it is some distance from Athens and Piraeus where you may need to have specialist work carried out. The bus in and out can occupy the best part of a day by the time you have organised things in Athens, but with the much improved roads it is now fairly quick to get in and out by car, except, that is, when you arrive at the traffic snarl-ups in Athens itself.

Olympic marina looking N

**LIMÍN LAVRIOU**
⊕37°42′·7N 24°04′·0E

## LAVRION (Limín Lavriou)

BA 1571

### Approach

*Conspicuous* The harbour lies immediately N of Gaïdhouromandra and from the S the buildings of the town are easily identified. From the N the two tall chimneys at Áy Nikólaos in the bay N of Lavrion (Órmos Thorikou) will be seen.

*By night* Use the lights on Ák Foniás Fl.2·5s6M and Ák Ergastíria Fl.1·5s4M. The entrance is lit Fl.G.3s3M/Fl.R.3s3M. The two chimneys at Áy Nikólaos are lit by fixed red lights with a good range.

*Note* At the time of writing work was still in progress on the new breakwaters although they are basically in place.

### Mooring

Go stern or bows-to the town quay or the inside of the L-shaped mole. A number of charter companies use Lavrion as a base and it can get crowded on turn-around days. Laid moorings tailed to the quay in places.

*Shelter* Good shelter. A bit of slop is pushed across the harbour onto the town quay, more uncomfortable than dangerous.

*Authorities* A port of entry: port police, customs and immigration.

Lavrion town quay

## Facilities

*Services* Water and electricity on the town quay. Water on the mole.

*Fuel* Near the quay on the W. A mini-tanker supplies yachts on the quay or go to the fuel quay at Olympic Marina nearby.

*Repairs* Most mechanical repairs. The extensive repair facilities of the Olympic Yard are nearby.

*Provisions* Good shopping for provisions nearby.

*Eating out* Tavernas in the town.

*Other* PO. OTE. Bank. Greek gas and *Camping Gaz*. Infrequent bus to Athens. Ferry to Kéa and Kíthnos.

## General

Lavrion was once an important port shipping cadmium and manganese and small amounts of lead from the reworking of the ancient mine tailings. The mines were probably worked as early as 1000 BC and in classical times large amounts of silver were extracted from the Lavrion mines whose wealth boosted Athens' commercial power.

Today Lavrion is a grubby 'has-been' port with piles of slag and ore littered around the coast. Yet it has its own charm, a sort of faded dignity and glimpses of old-world wealth in the villas around town. The waterfront has now been cleaned up and there are new cafés and bars along it. Most of those who spend some time here while working on a boat in the Olympic yard have a certain fondness for the place that is not readily apparent on a first visit.

## ÓRMOS THORIKO

The large bay just over 1 mile N of Lavrion. Anchor in the NW of the bay taking care of the above water rocks off the shore. The bottom is sand and weed, good holding. Good shelter from the *meltemi* tucked under the N entrance point.

To the N of Órmos Thoriko is Frangolimani (Órmos Áyios Nikolaos), the site of a large power station and several other factories. Two very tall chimneys (red and white bands) are conspicuous from a considerable distance off. There is a substantial pier and quayed sections, but these are for cargo ships only. Anchor in the bay. Good shelter from the *meltemi*. Open only to the E.

## TOURKOLIMANI

Half a mile N of Ák Vrisáki this bay offers reasonable shelter from the *meltemi*. Anchor in the N cove. Open to the SE.

## NÍSOS MAKRONISI (Nísos Eleni)

The long thin island lying parallel to the Attica coast between Ák Sounion and Nísos Kéa. It is a rugged hilly island rising to 274m (899ft) at the N end. The E coast of the island has numerous bays and coves along it that can be used according to the wind direction. Most of them are open to the *meltemi* blowing down from the NE although Órmos Angálistros at the S end and Órmos Yerolimonias about a third of the way up on the E side look as if they would give some shelter from the *meltemi*. Care is needed of Ifalos Angálistros, the reef lying 0·15 miles S of the entrance to Órmos Angálistros.

*Note* When passing through Stenón Makronisou, the channel between Makronisi and the mainland coast, care must be taken of Ifalos Tripiti, a reef just awash, lying half a mile NW of Ák Tripiti, the N extremity of Makronisi. The remains of a wrecked coaster that formerly marked the reef have all but disappeared.

## PORTO RAFTI (Órmos Markopoulo, Raptis, Mesoyaias)

### Approach

*Conspicuous* Nisís Raftis with a large statue atop is conspicuous from seaward. Closer in the cluster of villas and apartment blocks skirting the shore will be seen.

*By night* Use the light on Nisís Raftis: Fl.2s9M. A night approach should be made with caution.

ÓRMOS THORIKO
⊕37°44'·7N 24°04'·9E

PORTO RAFTI
⊕37°53'·2N 24°02'·7E

*Dangers*
1. Caution must be exercised in the vicinity of the anchorage on account of the permanent mooring floats on the surface.
2. Care must be taken of the remains of a mole now underwater on the N side of Limín Mesoyaias.

## Mooring

Anchor in the NW corner in 4–10m. Care is needed of uneven depths in the NW part of the bay with some shallow patches. Proceed with care. Alternatively go stern or bows-to the quay in the cove on the N side of Ák Pounda if there is room. The bottom is mud or sand – good holding.

*Shelter* Good shelter from the *meltemi*. Although the bay is open to the E and SE these winds do not blow home and the islands in the entrance break up the swell. A number of yachts are wintered afloat here.

*Authorities* Port police.

## Facilities

*Water* On the quay at Rafti.
*Fuel* Near the quay at Rafti.
*Provisions* Most provisions can be found at Rafti. A supermarket, although it is a fair distance from the harbour.
*Eating out* Tavernas at Rafti and others around the shore.
*Other* PO. OTE. Infrequent bus to Athens.

## General

Around the shores of this fine natural harbour the Athenians have built their summer villas and apartments, transforming what was a simple fishing community into a prospering summer commuter belt. Incredibly the inhabitants have taken the worst of instant reinforced concrete non-architecture found around Athens and transplanted it here – the result is simply awful and were it not for the remarkable beauty of the bay, it would look like Athens itself.

The statue on Rafti Island probably dates from the Roman occupation and is known locally as the tailor – whence the modern name of the harbour (*rafti* = tailor).

## ÓRMOS VRAVRONAS

37°55'·8N 24°01'·4E

A large bay just over 2 miles N of Porto Rafti. Local boats are kept on permanent moorings and in calm weather a yacht can anchor here. It is partially sheltered from the NE by a small islet on the N side.

## LOUTSA

Along the coast between Órmos Vravronas and Rafina, the coast is lined by villas and apartment blocks which stretch in an almost unbroken line along the coast. The effect is not attractive. At Loutsa (37°58'·5N 24°00'·8E) there is a small private yacht harbour, the Artimedos Yacht Club, where small yachts may find a berth. Good shelter inside the harbour. Provisions and tavernas nearby.

## RAFINA

Imray-Tetra G26

## Approach

A ferry harbour 7 miles N of Porto Rafti. The cluster of buildings on a knoll above the harbour and the slopes behind is easily identified. Closer in the new mole and breakwater will be seen.

*By night* Use the light on Ák Veláni Fl.1·5s4M and the light on the outer mole Fl.G.1·5s3M and inner mole F.G.3M.

*Note* There is now so little safe berthing for yachts here that it is best to bypass the port if possible.

## Mooring

In calm weather try the basins on the S side or anchor off under the lee of the northernmost breakwater.

*Shelter* Poor in any moderate winds and untenable with strong N or S winds.

*Authorities* Port police and customs.

## Facilities

Water on the quay. Fuel nearby. Provisions and tavernas in the town. PO. OTE. Ferries to Evia and the northern Cyclades. Bus to Athens.

## General

The town is a pleasant enough place, but the uncomfortable harbour means that most yachtsmen's memories of it are less than favourable. Unless it is flat calm outside, the surge in the harbour is simply awful.

**RAFINA**
⊕38°01'·4N 24°00'·6E

## The Battle of Marathon

The Battle of Marathon in which the Athenians defeated the Persians has come down through history as the battle *par excellence* where the valiant few triumphed over superior forces. Of it Dr Johnson said: 'That man is little to be envied whose patriotism would not gain force upon the Plain of Marathon.' For the layman there is little to see but the site of the battle and the grave mounds.

The Persian invasion of Greece reached the Plain of Marathon without hindrance. The Athenians commanding the only road to Athens numbered 10,000 while the Persian force numbered at least 24,000. (Estimates of the Persian force vary between an impossible 5¼ million and 24,000). The Persians delayed attacking the strong Greek position and eventually decided to take Athens from the sea. Some time around mid-August 490 BC the Persians began to embark for the sea invasion whereupon the Greeks launched a surprise attack. The Persians were not properly drawn up for battle and the surprise attack confused their forces. In the rush to put to sea 6,400 Persians were killed while the Athenians lost 192.

This battle proved that the Persians, once thought to be invincible, could be defeated. During the battle the ghostly figures of Pan and Theseus are said to have appeared to assist the Athenians and to this day the plain is said to resound to the cries of battle and the clash of arms. Contrary to normal practice the bodies of the dead were buried where they fell in honour of their valour. Excavations of the grave mounds confirmed this ancient tradition associated with battle.

### NAOMA (Áyios Andreas)

Ák Áy Andreas light (Fl.3s3M) 38°04'·1N 24°00'·2E

About ¾ of a mile N of Rafina there is a small boat harbour affording protection from the *meltemi*. There are 2m depths reported close inside. Open to the S. There are a number of large hotels nearby.

### NÉA MAKRI

38°03'·5N 24°00'·0E

About 3¾ miles N of Rafina an 'L' shaped mole forms a small harbour offering shelter from the *meltemi*. The entrance is lit F.G/F.R. There are 1·5m depths in the entrance and 1–2m depths inside. With onshore winds a swell heaps up at the entrance and you should try elsewhere. The harbour is very small (approximately 50m x 50m in the basin) and only small yachts under 8 metres LOA should attempt to enter.

Water and electricity on the quay. Tavernas along the beach.

### ÓRMOS MARATHONAS

Ák Marathonas 38°07'·3N 24°03'·5E

In calm weather a yacht can anchor on the W side of the bay tucked as far up under Ák Marathonas as possible. Technically it is prohibited to anchor here, but either the prohibited area is not often enforced or you will be told when target practice is taking place, as a number of yachts have used the anchorage. (See Prohibited Anchorage notes that follow.) If the *meltemi* is blowing a considerable swell sets into the bay and it is unwise to anchor off this lee shore.

### PROHIBITED ANCHORAGE AND LANDING

1. Anchoring is prohibited in the area enclosed by an imaginary line running 2¼ miles SW of Ák Marathonas and then 1½ miles NW (the N half of the bay). A floating target lies in this area.
2. Landing is prohibited between Ák Dhrakonera and a point 2 miles NW of Ák Áy Marina.
3. It is prohibited to enter the harbour enclosed by a mole under Ák Áy Marina.

These areas and the harbour at Áy Marina belong to the Greek army and are mostly used for recreational purposes.

### ÁYIOS APOSTOLIOU

38°17'·6N 23°54'·0E

A small harbour on the mainland coast opposite Ák Aliveri. The harbour is very small and usually full of local craft so do not count on finding shelter here. There are 3m depths in the entrance and 2–3m depths on the outer dogleg of the mole. Care is needed of underwater ballasting off parts of the quay. Good shelter from the prevailing NE wind under the mole.

Water on the quay. Fuel nearby. Provisions and tavernas ashore.

### ÓRMOS OROPOS

38°19'·0N 23°47'·7E

An open bay directly S of Erétria, it is the mainland ferry terminal for Erétria. Local craft are kept here in the summer on permanent moorings. Although open to the prevailing NE winds the anchorage can be used in light northerlies which are reported not to blow home. With any sort of fresh breeze it is best to seek shelter elsewhere. Anchor in 4–5m on mud keeping clear of the ferry quay. Provisions and tavernas in Néa Palatea.

### ÓRMOS ANGISTRI

38°20'·0N 23°44'·0E

This bay affords poor shelter from the prevailing winds but does have a boatyard that has been recommended. Evia Sea Centre can haul yachts up to 55ft on a hydraulic trailer. Hardstanding ashore. ☎ 0295 71963.

## Evia coast south of Khalkís

### ÓRMOS KASTRÍ

Lying 2 miles NE of Nisís Mandhíli on the SE coast of Evia, this bay affords good shelter to a yacht waiting for the wind and sea to moderate in the Doro Strait. Anchor at the head of the bay in 4–6m. There are strong gusts into the bay with the *meltemi* and it may be advisable to lay a second anchor for a sound nights sleep. The bottom is sand – good holding. Órmos Livádhi 1¼ miles NE of Kastrí also provides good shelter from the *meltemi*. No facilities.

**ORMOS KASTRI**
⊕37°58'·4N 34°32'·7E

## DORO STRAIT (Stenón Kafirevs/Kafireos)

See Andros in Chapter V.

## KARISTOS (Karysto)

### Approach

*Conspicuous* The town of Karistos at the foot of the high mountain range is easily seen from seaward. Nisís Áy Pelayia with a chapel on it lies a mile SW of the harbour and a fort immediately E of the harbour is conspicuous.

*By night* Use the lights on Nisís Paximádhi Fl.5s4M and Nisís Mandhíli Fl(3)20s15M and once into Órmos Karístou the lights at the entrance to the harbour: Fl.G.1·5s4M/2F.R(vert)3M.

*Dangers* With strong N winds there are violent gusts into Órmos Karístou off the surrounding mountains. Care must be taken if sailing into the bay.

*Note* The Admiralty *Pilot* states that light cloud around the summit of Oros Okhi, the peak inland of Karistos, heralds N winds.

### Mooring

Berth stern or bows-to the town quay in the inner basin. It is often very crowded in here with fishing boats – if you can't find a berth go stern or bows-to

**KARISTOS**
⊕38°00'·5N 24°25'·E

the quay W of the ferry pier. The bottom is mud – good holding.

*Shelter* Good all-round shelter.

*Authorities* Port police and customs.

*Anchorage* Just to the E of the fort it is possible to anchor off the beach off the Hotel Apollon. Sheltered from the *meltemi* although there are strong gusts.

### Facilities

*Water* On the town quay or in the square.

*Fuel* In the town. A mini-tanker can deliver to the quay.

*Repairs* Minor mechanical repairs.

*Provisions* Good shopping for provisions nearby in the town.

*Eating out* Good tavernas and bars around the waterfront.

*Other* PO. OTE. Bank. Greek gas and *Camping Gaz*. Infrequent bus to Khalkís. Ferry and hydrofoil to Rafina.

### General

Karistos is a growing tourist resort situated on a narrow strip of land at the foot of a magnificent mountain range. In places the range drops sheer to the sea for 500m or more and if the seafarer is daring or foolhardy he can take a bus trip along the road cut into the mountainside. The rugged interior is well worth an excursion and there is good trekking in the hills behind.

## Nisídhes Petaloi

This group of islands lies off the SW coast of Evia a short distance to the NW of Nisís Paximádhi. The two largest islands are Megálo Petali and Xero. There are numerous anchorages between them and it is possible to find shelter from just about all winds:

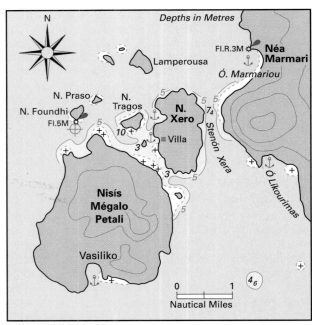

**NISIDHES PETALOI**
⊕38°01'·8N 24°15'·0E

1. *Vasiliko* On the S side of Nisís Megálo Petali, this bay offers reasonable shelter from the *meltemi*. Anchor in 4–6m at the head of the bay. Sandy bottom. Open only to the S.
2. *Nisís Xero* A cove on the SW corner of the island off a large villa affords some shelter from the *meltemi*. Care needs to be taken in the approach of a reef off the SE corner of Nisís Tragos which is sometimes marked by a stake. There are now fish farms in here though it is still possible to get in. Between Nisís Xero and Nisís Mégalo Petali there are mostly 3m minimum depths.
3. *Nisís Tragos* On the S side there is a large villa with a small harbour, but this is strictly private.

*Caution* In Órmos Marmari between Evia and Nisídhes Petaloi there are strong gusts off the high land on Evia with the *meltemi*.

## NÉA MARMARI

### Approach
Órmos Marmariou is the bay opposite the northernmost of Nisídhes Petaloi. Néa Marmari is in the SE corner of the bay. The village is easily identified from seaward.

*By night* The end of the ferry pier is lit Fl.R.1·5s3M.

*Dangers* With the *meltemi* there are strong gusts down into the bay off the high land around it.

### Mooring
Go stern or bows-to the E end of the ferry quay. Alternatively anchor off clear of the area with

**NÉA MARMARI**
⊕38°03'·0N 24°19'·0E

permanent moorings. The bottom is mud and weed with some rocks.

*Shelter* Good shelter from the *meltemi* although there are fierce gusts into the bay. Open to the W when a swell is pushed onto the quay.

*Authorities* Port police.

### Facilities
*Water* On the quay.
*Fuel* In the town. It may be possible to arrange a mini-tanker to deliver.
*Provisions* Good shopping for provisions nearby.
*Eating out* Tavernas on the waterfront.
*Other* PO. Bank. Ferry to Rafina.

Néa Marmari on Evia looking WNW into Petalion Kólpos
*Peter Kleinoth/MareTeam*

## General

Néa Marmari has changed from small fishing village to reinforced concrete tourist resort, though it still retains some charm and its situation under the steep-to mountains behind is spectacular. It is a handy stop on the way up the coast to stock up on provisions before the simpler places to come.

## ÓRMOS VLIKHO

### 38°05'·8N 24°14'·8E

In the NW corner of Órmos Marmariou you can also obtain shelter from the *meltemi*. Care is needed of the shoal patch off the E side of the entrance. Anchor off the beach in 3–6m on sand and weedy patches, good holding. Good shelter from the *meltemi* although there are gusts off the high land. Taverna ashore.

## ÓRMOS ANIMVORIOU

### 38°07'·7N 24°12'·0E

The large bay under Ák Strongiló. On the N side of the bay some shelter from the *meltemi* can be found in several coves (Animvoriou = North wind bay). Care is needed of a reef running out from the point between the two N coves. Anchor in 4–5m on sand in the coves or off the long beach running around the NE side. Reasonable shelter from the *meltemi* although there are gusts and some swell tends to be pushed around Ák Strongiló.

ÓRMOS ANIMVORIOU
⊕38°07'·7N 24°12'·0E

## NÉA STÍRA

Three miles NE of Ák Strongiló lies the village of Néa Stíra. The natural camber of the coast provides some protection from the *meltemi* although there are strong gusts into the bay. The end of the pier is lit Fl.G.3M. There are 2–3m depths off the outer end and yachts can go alongside if there is room. The miniature fishing harbour S of the pier is shallow and in any case too small and crowded for yachts. Alternatively anchor off in 4–5m. Mediocre shelter with gusts off the high land when the *meltemi* is blowing.

Provisions and tavernas ashore. Like Néa Marmari the fishing village has become something of a small resort.

## NÍSOS STIRA

The island of Stira which sits in the entrance of Órmos Stira has a number of useful anchorages around it. In the approach from the NW care is needed of the reef running SE from the S end of Vrak Fonias.

NÍSOS STÍRA AND NÉA STÍRA
⊕1 38°11'·3N 24°10'·3E
⊕2 38°10'·8N 24°12'·4E

1. ***Nisís Petousi anchorage*** On the NE side of Nisís Petousi there is a slight camber in the coast of the islet that affords some shelter from the prevailing wind. Anchor in 5–10m on sand.
2. ***Stíra E coast*** About halfway up the E coast there is a bay which affords some shelter from the *meltemi*. Anchor in 5–10m tucked as far into the bay as depths allow.
3. ***Marina Stíra*** There are plans to build a marina on the W coast of Stira tucked under the islet of Nisís Áy Andreas. The plans are for a 400-berth marina with all facilities including travel-hoist and workshops ashore. There will be an associated hotel and apartment complex around the marina. To get to and from the marina and apartments there will be a ferry service from Áy Marina on the mainland coast opposite. Work has yet to begin on the marina and apartment complex which hopes to capitalise on the new airport at Sparta. It remains to be seen whether the project gets off the ground.
4. ***Stíra N coast*** On the N coast there is a cove sheltered by an islet in the entrance which can be used in calm weather. Anchor in 4–6m on sand and weed.

## ÓRMOS TIGANI

### 38°13'·6N 24°09'·5E

Under Ák Tigani ('the frying pan') some shelter from the *meltemi* can be found anchored off on the N side. Anchor in 5–10m. There are strong gusts with the *meltemi*.

## ALMIROPOTAMOS (Almyro Potamo)

A long attractive bay with steep-to mountains above. There are strong gusts into the bay with the *meltemi*. The bottom is mostly sand and weed, good holding once you find a patch of sand. There are a number of anchorages:

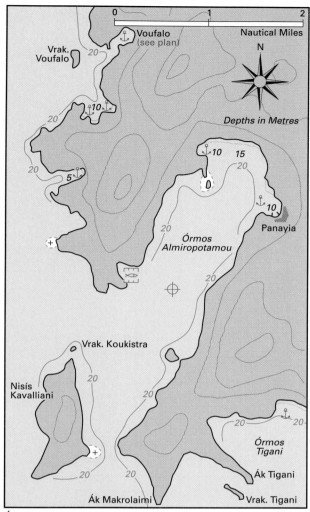

**ÓRMOS TIGANI TO VOUFALO**
⊕38°15'·0N 24°07'·8E

**VOUFALO**
⊕38°17'·8N 24°06'·8E

1. At the entrance there is a cove on the W side though it is reported to be blocked by a fish farm.
2. In the cove NW of the islet. Anchor in 5–7m on mud and weed. Good shelter.
3. In the cove on the NE side. Several concrete piers and a ferry ramp have been constructed and it may be possible to berth stern or bows-to on one of the piers. Alternatively anchor off although it is quite deep in here and you will be anchoring in 10–12m. Good shelter.

   Provisions and tavernas ashore. Ferry to Áy Marina. Irregular bus to Khalkis from the village above.

## VOUFALO (Bouphalo)

An almost landlocked bay lying approximately 4 miles N of Nisís Kavaliani. The houses of the tiny hamlet in the inlet can be seen from seaward. On the W of the N entrance there is an islet with a fish farm on the E side.

A sand spit with concrete blocks along it extends from the E side and partially protects the anchorage. Anchor in 5–6m behind the sand spit. A very small yacht can go bows-to the short pier (1m depths). The holding has been reported to be poor although others have reported no problems anchoring. Virtually all-round shelter tucked behind the sand spit.

Simple tavernas ashore.

*Note* Between Voufalo and Almiropotamos there are several bays which provide shelter from the *meltemi*. When coasting these can be investigated. Most have a bottom of sand and weed and sufficient depths to anchor in. The surroundings here are wild and you are much removed from the resort areas around other parts of the coast. Simple tavernas ashore.

## ALIVERION (Karastos)

BA 1571
Imray-Tetra G26

### Approach

*Conspicuous* The two tall chimneys of Pirgos power station are visible from a considerable distance off. Closer in a small chimney and the harbour breakwaters are conspicuous.

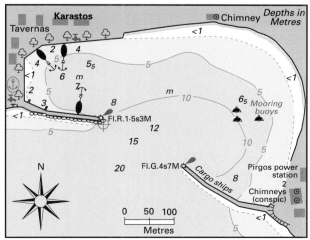

**ALIVERION**
⊕38°23·5N 24°02'·4E

*By night* Use the lights at the entrance to the harbour: Fl.G.4s7M/Fl.R.1·5s3M. The power station is lit up with bright lights at night.

*Note* In the bay SE of Aliverion is Milaki industrial harbour and cement factory. There are no facilities for yachts even if you did want to park next to a cement factory. The S pier is lit 2F.R(vert)5M.

## Mooring

Go stern or bows-to behind the mole or on the town quay. A small cargo ship occasionally uses the long section of the town quay. The bottom is mud – excellent holding.

*Shelter* Good all-round shelter although strong S winds produce some surge and spray comes over the mole. Strong N winds do not blow home.

*Authorities* Port police.

## Facilities

*Water* On the town quay and N side of harbour.
*Fuel* None available locally.
*Provisions* Limited provisions locally.
*Eating out* Several tavernas around the harbour with good local fare.
*Other* PO, OTE and bank in Aliverion town about 30 minutes away.

## General

The harbour is properly called Karastos and the town a short distance away is Aliverion. It is a captivating and friendly place that has mostly been bypassed by tourism. The giant power station of Pirgos on the opposite side of the bay is soon accepted as a part of the scenery and not the blot on the landscape it might first appear to be.

## AMARINTHOS

38°23'·2N 23°53'·8E

A small resort and fishing village lying approximately 7 miles W of Aliverion. A yacht can anchor off here for provisions and a bite in settled weather, but although the *meltemi* does not blow strongly here, it is still a very exposed anchorage.

There is a small fishing harbour here with 3m depths in the entrance and 2–3m depths off the outer dogleg of the mole, but it is usually so crowded with fishing boats that it is all but impossible to find a berth. Water on the mole. Fuel in town. Provisions and tavernas ashore.

## ERÉTRIA (Néa Psará)

BA 1571
Imray-Tetra G26

## Approach

The bay lying approximately 5 miles W of Amarinthos. The approaches are surrounded by above and below-water rocks and a yacht should make the approach to the bay from the S. The light structure on the W side of the entrance (Fl.WR.1·5s5/3M red sector covers 061°-342°) is at the extremity of a sunken ancient mole running out from the coast.

**ERÉTRIA**
⊕38°22'·9N 23°47'·4E

## Mooring

Anchor in the NE corner in 3–10m. There is a small *caïque* harbour on 'Dream' Island, but it is too small and mostly too shallow for even a small yacht. At the quay in the NW corner where the car ferries berth the depths are insufficient for a yacht. Good shelter from the *meltemi*. Open to the W and S.

## Facilities

Port police and customs. Fuel in the town. Good shopping for provisions and good tavernas on the waterfront. Bus to Khalkís and ferry to Oropos.

**APPROACHES TO KHALKIS (SOUTH HARBOUR)**
⊕7  Mid-channel Stenón Avlidhou-Boúrtzi (Ák Avlís) 38°24'·65N 23°38'·1E
⊕8  Entrance to Vorios Limani/Khalkís 38°28'·4N 23°35'·7E

## General

Erétria is also called Néa Psará. In 1822 the Turks massacred the population of Khíos and nearby Psará after a rebellion and the survivors of Psará fled to Evia where they were given land at Erétria/Néa Psará. It is a growing tourist resort, hence the inevitable renaming of the island on the E side of the bay as 'Dream' Island.

## DHIAVLOS EVIRIPOU (Approaches to Khalkís)

BA 1554
Imray-Tetra G2, G26

### S approach

*Conspicuous* The huge cement factory complex on the W side of the entrance to the S harbour and the new road bridge (air height 36m) are conspicuous from a considerable distance off. There are always a number of ships anchored off the entrance to Órmos Mikró Vathi. The narrow buoyed entrance to the S harbour is easily negotiated.

*By night* Use the light on Ák Avlís Fl(2)12s6M and the light buoys: Q.G and Fl.G.2s. Further in use the light on Vrak Passándassi Fl.3s5M and in the approaches to the bridge the lights on the S side Fl.R.2s4M/2F.R.3M and the light buoys Q.G/Q.R.

*Note*
1. Overhead electric cables cross the strait 130m W of the new bridge with an air height of 37·3m.
2. Anchoring is prohibited in Dhíavlos Stenón.

### N approach

*Conspicuous* The large modern buildings of Khalkís are visible from the distance. Ák Kakokefalí is conspicuous as a rocky promontory without buildings on it.

*By night* Use the light on Ák Kakokefalí Fl(2)R.18s12M, on the W bank Fl.G.2s3M, and the light buoys marking the channel: Q.G/Q.R.

### Mooring

*S harbour* In the S harbour anchor on the N side of the basin or go stern or bows-to or alongside on the E quay in Voukari. Care is needed of metal

KHALKIS
⊕38°27'·9N 23°35'·4E

## KHALKÍS BRIDGE

The bridge spans the narrow gap between Evia and the mainland. The gap is 39·3m (129ft) wide and the bridge slides back into a recess under the road. The bridge is opened at slack water for a very short time only, usually at night. As it is impossible to predict the times of slack water with any accuracy the skipper of a yacht should go to the port police as soon as possible to find at what time the bridge is going to open and to pay the bridge fees. The bridge is rarely opened during the day because of the disruption to road traffic. Yachts have been kept waiting for up to 30 hours so it is wise to anticipate long delays here.

The bridge officials use VHF channel 12, though this should not be relied upon for getting the word to proceed through the channel. A charge is made (4500 Dx) with a 75% surcharge on weekends. The bridge is closed on Fridays.

*Signals* These signals are displayed on the signal mast on the W side of the bridge platform.

| By day | By night | Meaning |
|---|---|---|
| Three vertical black balls | Green, white, red vertical lights | Bridge closed |
| | White fixed light in the middle of the bridge | Bridge closed at night |
| Two black cones points together above a cone point down | Green, white, green vertical lights | Bridge open to S-bound vessels |
| Two black balls separated by a black cone point up | Red, white, red vertical lights | Bridge open to N-bound vessels. |

A siren sounds and a flashing light warns boat traffic that the bridge is opening.

The new road bridge at Khalkís looking SE          *Nigel Patten*

protrusions on the quay wall. In both places a yacht is completely out of the current.

***Note*** In the NW corner of Órmos Vourkari is Khalkís Yacht Club. It may be possible to find a berth here. Yachts normally berth bows-to because ballasting extends a short distance out from the quay. Depths are variable with 1–2m off the quay. Water and electricity. Showers and toilets. Yachts are craned onto the hard.

***N harbour*** Go stern or bows-to or alongside the town quay where indicated on the E side of the harbour or stern or bows-to the short mole extending from the W side where a few local yachts are kept. Care is needed of an obstruction reported off the E quay. On the town quay a yacht is completely out of the current but on the W mole the weak current could make manoeuvring difficult. There is no good shelter from the *meltemi* in the N harbour. A very large yacht should anchor off in the bay to the E of Ák Kakokefalí.

***Tidal streams*** In the N harbour the spring range is about 0·8m (2·5ft) and the neap range about 0·2m (0·5ft). This must be borne in mind when mooring up or you may take the ground and miss the bridge. In the S harbour the spring and neap ranges are small. All depths given in the harbour plans are at mean low water springs. High water occurs in the N harbour approximately 1 hour 12 minutes after high water in the S harbour. The difference in time and range produces strong tidal streams which may reach 6–7 knots at springs. However this is only in the very narrow section spanned by the bridge and a short distance N and S of the bridge the stream is considerably less. When the bridge is opened the current may still be running at 2–3 knots but there is no difficulty negotiating the narrows. Sailing through is prohibited.

***Buoyage*** The direction of the buoyage system changes at Khalkis Bridge. S of the bridge the direction is for northbound traffic. N of the bridge the direction is for southbound traffic. This bizarre little system could cause confusion so it worth remembering when transiting from N–S or S–N.

### Facilities

*Services* Water and fuel on the quay in the N harbour (☎ 22609/22280 for fuel; ☎ 22213/29770 for water). Also fuel on S side of the bridge.
*Repairs* Some mechanical repairs. Yachts are hauled out in the boatyards in Voukari. Hardware shops.
*Provisions* Good shopping for all provisions. Ice at the fish market.
*Eating out* Numerous good tavernas nearby.
*Other* PO. OTE. Banks. Greek gas and *Camping Gaz*. Hire cars, motorbikes and bicycles. Buses and trains to Athens.

### General

Khalkís is the modern capital of Evia and the centre of communications for the island. Ancient Khalkís was similarly a prosperous city-state controlling the passage of commerce in the Evia channel.

The dangerous currents in the channel are mentioned by ancient sources: Livy, Cicero, Pliny and Strabo commented on them and tradition has it that Aristotle flung himself into the channel because of his inability to explain the phenomenon. The channel was first spanned as early as 411 BC. Under Justinian the fixed bridge was replaced by a movable wooden bridge. Under the Venetians the island took its name of Negroponte, the 'black bridge', from the bridge across to the mainland from Khalkís. In 1896 a Belgian company built an iron swing bridge that remained until 1962 when the existing bridge was built.

# Coasts north of Khalkís
## Mainland side of the channel

### ÓRMOS SKORPONERIOU
38°31'·1N 23°22'·7E
The large bay under Ák Gatza with the islet of Gatza on the N side of the entrance. In the NW corner there is a cove which affords good shelter from the *meltemi*. Anchor in 7–10m on mud, good holding. In calm weather or with southerlies there is a useful anchorage on the W side of the headland on the S side of the bay. Anchor in 7–10m on mud, sand and weed. Camping ground ashore.

### LÁRIMNA (Larmes)

The very tall chimney belching smoke at the cupronickel refinery is conspicuous from a considerable distance off. The chimney is painted in red and white bands and lit at night with red lights. Anchor off or go bows-to the short pier. The bottom is mud and shells – excellent holding. Fuel in town. Water near the pier. Most provisions available. Poor tavernas.

LARIMNA
⊕38°34'·3N 23°17'·3E

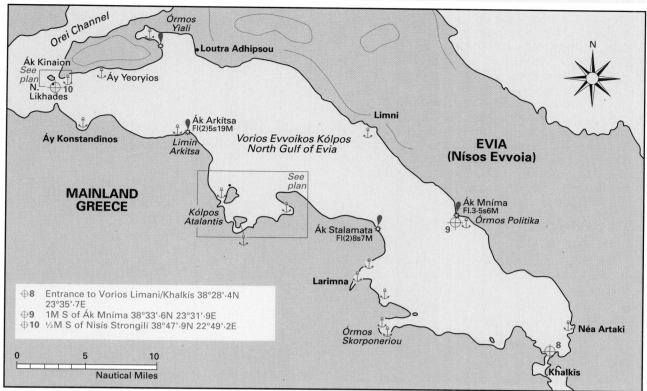

**NORTH GULF OF EVIA** (Vorios Evvoikos Kólpos)

The village is grimy and blackened from the fumes of the refinery. These fumes deposit an oily unpleasant grime over a yacht. The only reason for a visit here is to see the ancient harbour which is in good condition although parts of it have been wantonly destroyed in recent years.

### UNNAMED BAY

38°35'·1N 23°18'·7E

About 2 miles SE of Ák Larmes there is a bay offering good shelter from the *meltemi*. The SW side of the bay is a low-lying islet connected to the land by a reef just below water. Some of the bay is now obstructed with fish farms, but there is still room to anchor in here. Anchor in 10m on sticky red clay, excellent holding.

### KÓLPOS ATALÁNTIS (Atlandi, Atalante, Opuntius)

In this large bay on the W side of the gulf there are a number of anchorages affording shelter from the *meltemi*.

1. ***Órmos Áy Ioánnis Theológos*** Anchor at the head of the bay. A short mole has been built out from the E end of the bay, but is usually full of local boats. Open to the W. Provisions and tavernas ashore.
2. ***Órmos Amirou (Almyro)*** In the S corner of Órmos Atalántis under the lee of Nisís Gáïdharos. In the middle of the entrance care must be taken of a below-water rock. There is now a fish farm and a mussel farm in the bay, but yachts can anchor to the W of them. All-round shelter can be found in this bay although there

**KÓLPOS ATALÁNTIS**
⊕38°41'·1N 23°05'·5E

**SKÁLA ATALÁNTIS**
⊕38°40'·4N 23°04'·6E

are strong gusts into it with W winds. The motorway N runs past the head of the bay.

3. *Nisís Atalántis* Anchor in a cove on the SW side of the island. There are now fish farms here. The island has a guardian on it who gets upset if you go ashore.

4. *Skála Atalántis* (see harbour plan). A small fishing harbour opposite the cove on Nisís Atalántis. Moor stern or bows-to the outer end of the mole. Care must be taken entering the harbour as the entrance silts. Taverna and café at the root of the mole. Good shopping for provisions in Atalántis village on the low hill to the NNW of the harbour.

## LIMÍN ARKÍTSA

38°45'·1N 23°01'·9E

A small harbour on the W side of Ák Arkítsa. Ák Arkítsa is lit Fl(2)5s19M and off the harbour there is a light buoy Q. There are 2–3m depths in the entrance to the harbour and 1–2·5m depths inside. Good shelter inside the harbour.

## ÁYIOS KONSTANDINOS

38°45'·4N 22°51'·4E

The mainland ferry terminal for Skíathos. Two jetties project from the shore which are used by the ferries. A 3F.G.3M is exhibited on the quay and a F.G.7M on the end of the mole. The roadstead and quays are completely open to the prevailing wind and it is untenable here if the *meltemi* is blowing. In calm weather it may be useful to provision up, but you should be prepared to move out if the wind picks up. There is a small fishing harbour (50m by 15m!) but this is always crowded with fishing boats. Inside the fishing harbour there are 3–5m metre depths off the mole.

Ashore most provisions can be obtained and there are good tavernas.

# Evia side of the channel

## NÉA ARTAKI (Vatondas)

### Approach

The harbour and anchorage lies approximately 3M NNE of Khalkis in a bight on the Evia coast. The buildings of Néa Artaki on the stubby headland are easily identified.

*By night* The headland is lit Fl.1·5s5M and the entrance to the harbour 2F.R(vert)2M. Care is needed in a night approach because of the shoal water in the approaches.

### Mooring

You may be able to anchor under the W breakwater with a line ashore, but most of the space is taken up with local boats. Alternatively anchor off the beach in 3–5m.

*Shelter* Reasonable shelter from the *meltemi* although there are gusts off the high land and some swell curves around the headland into the anchorage.

**NÉA ARTAKI**
⊕38°30'·8N 23°37'·7E

### Facilities

Water on the quay. Provisions and tavernas ashore. PO.

## ÓRMOS POLITIKA

38°34'·7N 23°32'·5E

The large bay under Ák Mníma. Ák Mníma is lit Fl.3·5s6M. You can anchor off the beach under the cape where there is reasonably good shelter from the *meltemi*. Anchor in 5–8m on sand and weed. There is a small pier here with 2–3m depths off the end.

Water tap ashore. Tavernas open in the summer. The village of Politika lies a few kilometres inland.

## LIMNI

### Approach

The buildings at Limni will be seen in a bight on the coast SE of Ák Yianitsa.

*By night* The stubby headland is lit on the end Fl.1·5s5M. The end of the mole is lit F.R(occas).

### Mooring

Anchor off the village in 10–12m. It is everywhere fairly deep for anchoring. Alternatively you can try the harbour off the village. The entrance is a bit tricky as you need to make a sharp turn to port to enter. Go alongside or stern or bows-to the outer end of the mole if there is room.

*Shelter* Adequate shelter in settled weather at anchor although there are strong gusts off the high land with the *meltemi*. Good shelter in the harbour.

**LIMNI**
⊕38°46'·0N 23°19'·3E

### Facilities

Water near the harbour. Provisions and tavernas in town. PO.

### LOUTRA ADHIPSOU

38°51'·3N 23°02'·3E

The ferry terminal on Evia for the ferries from Áy Konstandinos. It is exposed off the ferry quay. The ferry quay is lit 3F.Y.3M. The fishing harbour here is usually crowded, but you may be able to find a berth inside. There are 4–5m depths in the entrance and mostly 2–4m depths inside. Go alongside or stern or bows-to where possible. Good shelter in the harbour.

Water on the quay. Provisions and tavernas ashore.

### ÓRMOS YIALI

38°53'·0N 22°58'·0E

This large bay looks as if it should afford good shelter, but it is very deep for anchoring in most places. The W entrance is lit Fl.3s5M. There are a number of fish farms around the sides of the bay.

In the NW corner there is a bight where you can anchor off in 4–8m. Gusts with the *meltemi*. No facilities.

### ÁY YEORYIOS

38°50'·3N 22°53'·0E

A village lying approximately 3½ miles E of the Likhades Islands. A short jetty approximately 60m long projects out from the village. The ferries and local boats use the W side of the jetty. Yachts can go stern or bows-to the E side where there are 8m depths reported at the end. Alternatively anchor off in 6–10m and sand and weed. The prevailing wind tends to blow off the land. Useful in settled conditions.

Water at the root of the jetty. Provisions and tavernas ashore.

### NISOI LIKHADES (Likada)

BA 1571

Lying close off Ák Lithada (Kinaion), the westernmost point of Evia, there is a narrow but easily navigable channel between the islands and the cape. A current of up to 2 knots may run through the channel in either direction depending on the wind direction. With the *meltemi* there is a S-going current, generally less than 2 knots. Keeping close to Ák Lithada there are good depths in the channel except for a 4m patch extending 500m in a NNE direction from the SE tip of Nisís Monolia.

A yacht can anchor on the S side of Ák Lithada where there is a good lee from N winds. Fishing boats anchor on the S side of Nisís Monolia (open only to the E), but care must be taken of the above and below-water rocks surrounding this anchorage.

## Northern Evia channels and the Gulf of Volos

**(Maliakós Kólpos, Dhíavlos Oréon, Dhíavlos Tríkeri, Gulf of Volos or Pagasitikós Kólpos)**

## Mainland coast

### MALIAKOS KÓLPOS

A shallow gulf bulging westwards from the W extremity of Evia. The coast is predominantly low-lying. The northbound motorway skirts the head of the gulf. The Pass of Thermopylae lies near the corner of the gulf.

### STILIDHOS (Stilis, Stylis)

BA 1571

Situated on the N side of Maliakós Kólpos, Stilidhos is the port for the town of Lamia. It is surrounded

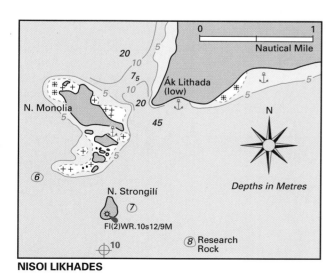

**NISOI LIKHADES**

⊕10 0·5M S of Nisís Strongilí 38°47'·9N 22°49'·2E

**STILIDHOS**
⊕38°54'·2N 22°37'·3E

**NORTHERN EVIA CHANNELS AND THE GULF OF VOLOS**

by shoal water and a dredged channel leads into it. The channel is marked at the outer end by a pair of light buoys Q.G/Q.R and the beacon Fl.R.2s3M on Nisís Kaloyiros, a low sandy islet, and a beacon Fl.G.2s3M off the low shore on the other side.

Moor stern or bows-to or alongside the quay. The bottom is mud – good holding. Good shelter from the *meltemi*. Open to the S.

Fuel in the town. Small yachts can be craned onto the quay. Good shopping for provisions. Tavernas in the town. Buses to Athens and Volos.

The harbour is right on the edge of the main road northwards and is consequently not the quietest place around.

## KARAVOMILOS

38°53'·0N 22°42'·2E

Karavomilos is at the head of Órmos Ekinou about 4½ miles SE of Stilidhos and opposite Ák Khiliomili. Local fishing boats are kept on moorings in the summer. Good holding in mud is reported on the E side of the bay near the military college. Protection from the *meltemi* appears to be good. Provisions and tavernas ashore.

## RAHES

38°52'·6N 22°46'·3E

Immediately E of Ák Dhrépanon is Rahes where local fishing boats and a few yachts are kept on moorings through the summer. A large cement factory and quayed area are conspicuous just E of

Rahes. The shelter in the bight is better than it looks on the chart although a swell is reported to enter the bay with NE–E winds. Provisions and tavernas ashore.

## AKLADHI

A small fishing harbour in the bay E of Ák Gounari. The end of the mole is lit F.G.3M. If there is room go alongside or stern or bows-to the mole. Good shelter from the prevailing E–ENE winds. Alternatively anchor off the village where the camber of the coast gives some shelter although a swell still runs into the bay.

Water on the foreshore. Provisions and tavernas in Akladhi.

*Note* Approximately 1M E of Akladhi is a quay for the Agroinvest factory. The quay is lit at either end 3F.G.3M/3F.R.3M.

**AKLADHI**
⊕38°53'·1N 22°48'·8E

# Stenón Oréon

## (Orei Channel)

This channel separates Evia from the Thessaly coast. The channel is very narrow – in places it is little more than a mile across and there can be currents of up to 2½ knots in places. The tidal range at springs is 0·8m (2·5ft) at Orei, the highest tidal range in the eastern Mediterranean. The coast is mostly mountainous and wooded although there is a narrow low-lying strip of land bordering the mountains along the Evia coast.

## ÓRMOS VATHIKELON (Vathykelos)

Lying 1½ miles W of Glifa, this almost landlocked bay offers good all-round shelter. An islet off the W entrance point with a white church on it is easily identified. Care is needed of the dangerous rock lying approximately 20m off the E side of the entrance.

The bay is very deep for anchoring – mostly 10–20m around the NE side. The E side of the bay, where there are better depths for anchoring, is used to leave the car ferries from Glifa for the night. The bottom is mud and weed – good holding once through the weed. There are no facilities, just a few villas around the olive-clad slopes.

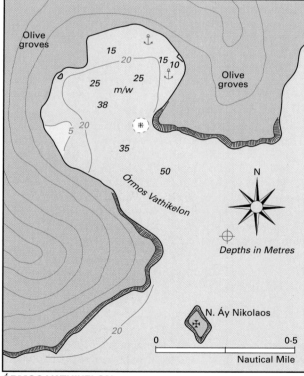

**ÓRMOS VATHIKELON**
⊕38°55'·8N 22°56'·7E

## GLIFA (Glypha)

38°57'·0N 22°57'·8E

The ferry terminal for the car ferry running to Nisiotissa on Evia. The short pier is used by the car ferry. With the *meltemi* some swell works its way into the bay. Anchor off the village or in the cove to the E.

Fuel in the village and water on the quay. Most provisions available and several tavernas.

## ARYRONÍSOS ANCHORAGES

Aryronisos is the flat island lying off the SW entrance to Pagasitikos Kólpos (Gulf of Volos). Care is needed of the reef running out from the N side of the islet to an above water rock.

1. A good lee from the prevailing E winds can be found under the SW side of the islet. Anchor in 8–15m on sand. The depths drop off quickly here so you will have to anchor fairly close in. The islet is private and while you can anchor, you cannot land.

2. On the mainland coast opposite you can anchor off the beach under a stubby headland in 5–8m on mud, sand and weed. There is a reasonable lee from the prevailing E wind although some swell enters. Camping ground ashore.

**ARYRONÍSOS ANCHORAGES**
⊕39°00'·5N 23°04'·4E

# Evia side of Stenón Oréon

## PIRGOS

A small fishing harbour off the resort of Pirgos. The end of the mole is lit Fl.G.3s3M. Berth stern or bows-to on the end of the mole where possible. Reasonable shelter from the prevailing wind although some swell is pushed into the harbour making it uncomfortable at times.

Water on the quay. Provisions and tavernas ashore.

**PIRGOS**
⊕38°56'·4N 23°04'·1E

## OREI (Oréon, Oreios)

### Approach

*Conspicuous* This part of the coast is low-lying and wooded and it can be difficult to identify features. The hut and metal tower on Ifalos Oréon (Panagitsa) lying ½ a mile off the coast is easily identified – there are good depths in the fairway between the reef and the coast. Just N of the harbour a factory is conspicuous. Closer in the buildings of Orei and the mole and the light structure will be seen.

*By night* Use the light on Ifalos Oréon (Panagitsa) Fl(2)12s9M and at Orei Fl.R.1·5s3M.

*Note* Works are in progress extending the mole and building another mole out from the coast. At the time of writing work is in progress and care is needed of underwater obstructions around the works. The end of the works on the outer mole is marked by a lightbuoy Q.R(occas) and the works on the S mole by small flag buoys.

### Mooring

Go stern or bows-to the mole at the N end. The hydrofoil uses the outer part of the mole. The bottom is sand and weed – good holding.

**OREI**
⊕38°56'·9N 23°05'·0E

*Shelter* Good shelter from the prevailing winds. The *meltemi* does not blow home here. Strong E winds are reported to cause a surge.

*Authorities* Police.

*Danger* The old iron wharf used for berthing in the past is in disrepair and is now dangerous. A gate closes it off from the promenade so you cannot get ashore anyway.

*Note* It should be remembered that the tidal range at Orei is 0·8m (2·5ft) at springs and allowance should be made for this. Some, like myself, lulled into a false sense of security in the virtually tideless Mediterranean, have found themselves stuck on the bottom here.

### Facilities

*Water* At the root of the mole.
*Fuel* In town nearby.
*Provisions* Good shopping for provisions.
*Eating out* Pleasant tavernas on the waterfront.
*Other* PO. OTE. Irregular bus to Khalkís. Hydrofoil to the Volos and the Northern Sporades.

### General

In ancient times Orei was an important maritime city. Above the harbour the remains of the Acropolis which guarded the harbour can be seen. In 1965 a Hellenistic marble bull was dredged from the sea by fishermen and placed in the town square. Today it remains a pleasant place with a modest summer tourist trade and the few yachts which venture into Stenón Oréou.

## Gulf of Volos

### (Pagasitikós Kólpos)

This gulf opens up to the north from Stenón Vólou. The coast is mountainous except for the west coast which is low and marshy between Amalioupolis and Volos. The Tríkeri peninsula beginning at Mt Pilion (1,548m) is rugged and densely wooded. Mt Pilion is covered with snow in the winter and much of the spring – a ski lift operates in the winter. The gulf has a number of attractive anchorages and it is well worthwhile detouring from the northern channels to explore it.

**Note** The prevailing winds in the summer are from the NE or SE.

### ÓRMOS PTELOU

The large bay on the W side of the entrance to Stenón Vólou entered between Ák Pigadhi and Ák Khondhros. The bay has now been much developed on the N side with clusters of villas around the slopes. There are several anchorages around the bay.

1. ***Ahilio (Akhileion)*** 39°00'·5N 22°57'·5E
   Although the anchorage off the village is exposed to the *meltemi*, it does not normally blow home. Tuck into the bight off the village as close as you can in 3–4m and there is reasonable shelter. Good shelter with SE winds. The small fishing

*Orei looking NW*        *Nigel Patten*

**STENÓN VOLOU (Volos Channel)**

⊕11   0·5M S of E end of Nisís Ayironisos 39°00'·0N 23°04'·4E
⊕12   Mid-channel Stenón Vólou (1·6M W of Ák Kavoulia)
        39°05'·8N 23°00'·8E

**ÓRMOS PTELOU**
⊕39°01'·8N 23°00'·0E

harbour is too shallow for yachts. Provisions and tavernas ashore.

2. ***Ormiskos Loutró*** 39°01'·8N 22°57'·6E The large bay in the NW corner bordered by low

Ahilio in the SW of Órmos Ptelou

marshland. A ruined tower, called Achilles Tower, sits on the headland E of the bay. Anchor in the N where there is something of a lee from the meltemi. Open SE across the bay.

3. ***Ormiskos Pigadhi*** 39°02'·0N 22°58'·7E The bay immediately E of Loutró. Anchor in the cove on the E side of the bay in 6m. On the W side of the bay there is a small projecting quay to which you can go stern or bows-to with care. Good shelter from the *meltemi*. Open SE across the bay. The tower on the W side of the bay is locally called Achilles' Tower and Pigadhi is said to be the bay from which Achilles set sail for Troy.

4. Immediately N of Ák Pigadhi (Alkini) there is a cove with a settlement around it. There is a quayed area used by local fishing boats and there appears to be something of a lee from the *meltemi* here. Provisions and tavernas ashore.

### ÓRMOS NIES

39°06'·8N 22°56'·0E

The bay running back S opposite the Tríkeri peninsula. On the E side near the entrance there is a cove affording reasonable shelter from the *meltemi*. Anchor in 4–6m on mud and weed. Alternatively anchor in the SE corner in 3–6m on mud, good holding. Good shelter although the *meltemi* tends to gust from the E–SE over the ridge into the anchorage. A camping ground in the SW corner and a number of villa developments along the W side of the bay.

## Tríkeri Peninsula

### ÁYIA KIRIAKÍ (Skála Tríkeri)

An open bay on the E side of the entrance to the Gulf of Volos. The village of Áyia Kiriakí on the hill above is conspicuous from seaward.

The bay is very deep. Anchor off the boatyard or in the SE corner of the bay, though the latter is crowded with fishing boats. Just to the E of the boatyard a new quay has been built. There are 2–3m depths off the quay but the bottom drops away quickly. Some 20m off the quay there are 20m depths and 25m off there are 30m depths. The bay is sheltered from the *meltemi*, but open to the W and

**ÁYIA KIRIAKÍ**
⊕39°05'·4N 23°03'·9E

S. There is another cove immediately W of the fishing hamlet where a yacht can anchor.

A large fleet of fishing boats is based at Áyia Kiriakí. Limited provisions and taverna/cafés ashore. The boatyard in the bay hauls out yachts. The village of Tríkeri (Áy Kiraki) above the bay used to be dependent on the ferry from Volos until the rough road from Milina was built.

## NISÍS PALAIO TRÍKERI (Palaeo Trikiri)

On the S side of this island there is the small village of Palaio Tríkeri which is conspicuous from the S. Anchor off the village in 3–10m although there is limited space to swing. Good shelter from the *meltemi*. Taverna ashore. Drinking water from a public tap. Daily hydrofoil service to Volos.

## ÓRMOS TRÍKERI

Entrance 39°07'·8N 23°08'·0E

The deep bay running SW into the Tríkeri peninsula. In calm weather anchor off the small fishing village of Kotte (open to the NE–E). Spectacular scenery under the steep slopes above. Taverna ashore.

The bay in the SW corner now has a marble quarry at the head and is unsuitable for anchoring. There are several other anchorages suitable for lunch-stops on the W side of the bay.

## ZASTENI ANCHORAGE (Avra)

39°07'·6N 23°09'·5E

¾ mile ESE of Ák Marathea there is an idyllic anchorage for a small yacht in a cove with a white house at the head. Open from N–W so really only suitable in calm weather. Anchor in 6–8m, mediocre holding on sand and weed.

## ÓRMOS VATHOUDHI (Vathudi)

Situated in the SE corner of the Gulf of Volos (Pagasitikós Kólpos), this anchorage is protected by Nisís Alatas on the W and the Tríkeri peninsula on the E. The anchorage is normally entered from the N and there are good depths right into the bay. There are a number of places to anchor:

1. Anchor in 10–15m in the NE corner of the bay. A short jetty extends from the shore with 1–2m depths off the end. The bottom is mud and sand – good holding. Good all-round shelter.

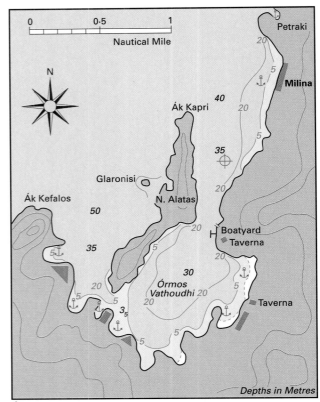

**ÓRMOS VATHOUDHI AND APPROACHES**
⊕39°10'·0N 23°12'·8E

A number of yachts are wintered afloat here and it can be difficult to find space to swing in the NE corner on account of the numerous permanently moored yachts there. Yachts are hauled out at the boatyard on the E side of the entrance.

Tavernas ashore. Water tap at the root of the jetty. Provisions and tavernas at Milina, the village about 3 kilometres N.

2. Anchor in either of the two coves opposite the S end of Nisís Alatas. Care is needed to stay in the fairway of the channel to avoid the rocks and shoal water on either side of the channel before turning into the coves. There are 3·5m least depths in the fairway of the channel.

3. In the cove to the W of the S end of Nisís Alatas. Anchor in 3–5m on mud and weed, good holding.

## PETRAKI

39°10'·8N 23°13'·0E

Half a mile N of Milina, Petrakia cove offers good shelter from the *meltemi*. Anchor in 5–10m on mud and weed, good holding. Open to the NW.

## KHORTOS

39°11'·2N 23°12'·7E

In settled weather when the *meltemi* is not blowing hard you can anchor off the resort of Khortos. Anchor in 5–8m on mud. There is a jetty off the beach with 2–3m depths at the end. Provisions and tavernas ashore.

## W side of the Gulf of Volos

### AMALIOUPOLIS AND NEARBY ANCHORAGES (Órmos Mitzellas, Órmos Soupis)

On the W side of the entrance to the Gulf of Volos a steep-to headland juts out from the coast ending in Ák Periklis and Ák Almiros. The headland is indented with a number of bays and on the E side is the village of Amalioupolis at the head of Órmos Mitzellas.

*Note* Navigation is prohibited within a 5 mile radius of the military area at 39°13'·3N 22°48'·5E. However, in practice local yachts do not observe the prohibition and anchor at Amalioupolis and nearby anchorages.

**AMALIOUPOLIS**
⊕39°10'·0N 22°53'·4E

1. *Amalioupolis* 39°10'·0N 22°53'·5E The village is conspicuous from seaward. Anchor off the town or go stern-to one of the two piers off the village (2·5m depths at the extremity). The bottom is sand – good holding. The small fishing harbour here is usually full of local boats. With the *meltemi* some swell rolls into the anchorage. Good shelter from SE winds. Port police. Water near the pier. Good shopping for provisions. Tavernas and cafés.

2. Half a mile N of Amalioupolis there is an unnamed cove providing some shelter from the *meltemi*. Anchor near the head of the bay in 2–4m.

3. *Loutráki Amalioupolis (Fearless Cove)* 39°10'·2N A sheltered cove in Órmos Sourpis on the W side of the headland. Anchor near the head of the cove in 3–6m. The bottom is mud, excellent holding. Good all-round shelter. Although the cove is open to the W for 1½ miles the wind does not blow home from that direction. A boatyard on the N side of the bay hauls yachts.

4. *Órmos Áy Ioánnis* Lies just to the S of Loutráki Amalioupolis. Anchor in 2–5m. Much of the bay is shallow towards the head. Good shelter from the *meltemi* and the SE.

*Note* On the W side of Órmos Soupis there is a large factory complex with storage tanks, gantries and several long jetties.

### NÉA ANKHIALOS (Néa Aghialos)

39°16'·53N 22°49'·29E WGS84

About 7 miles N of the factory complex in Órmos Soupis and tucked into the W corner of the gulf is Néa Ankhialos. The entrance is difficult to make out until very close-to when a few boulders extending from the beach and a half submerged breakwater to port become visible. Here there is a small circular fishing harbour entered by a narrow channel. There is room for a couple of yachts alongside the outer end of the quay where there are 2–2·5m depths. Here there is enough of a lee from the *meltemi* for it

Amalioupolis looking S across the N pier

The small harbour at Néa Ankhialos looking out to the entrance

Áy Yeóryios looking SSW

to be comfortable. The channel and basin are shallow with 1–<1m depths.

Provisions and tavernas nearby. The little harbour is a pleasant enough stop despite the busy road along the shore. Just across the road from the harbour are the ruins of ancient Pyrasos.

## ÁYIOS YEÓRYIOS

39°18'·00N 22°53'·93E WGS84

A bay lying under Ák Spilla. The inner part of the bay is mostly shallow, but you can tuck under the SW side as far as possible and find reasonable shelter from the *meltemi*.

There are also several other bays to the W that afford some shelter from the *meltemi*.

## VOLOS

BA 1571

### Approach

*Conspicuous* The large city and a cement factory one mile to the E of the city are easily seen from the distance. The commercial docks, a large grey silo behind the docks and the church of Áyios Konstandinos (especially the clock tower) immediately behind the small yacht harbour are conspicuous. The harbour is generally full of cargo ships.

*By night* Use the light on Ák Seskoulo Fl.1·5s7M and at the cement factory Fl(2)10s12M. The NE

**APPROACHES TO VOLOS**

⊕13 Ák Seskoulo (approaches to Limín Vólou)
39°20'·62N 22°56'·60E WGS84

end of the detached breakwater is lit Fl.R.3s. The end of the breakwater is lit Fl.G.3s4M, as is the extremity of the commercial pier F.G/F.R.

*Note* The new detached breakwater sits very low in the water and can be difficult to pick out from the distance, but the light structure on the NE end of the detached breakwater stands out well.

### Mooring

Go stern or bows-to the town quay or the N end of the E mole where shown. There are laid moorings tailed to small buoys, although these have been reported as suspect so it may be best to use your own anchor. The bottom is mud and good holding although in parts of the harbour the bottom is very soft mud through which most anchors just plough furrows.

*Note* Pontoons are to be installed in the near future.

*Shelter* Good shelter although there is a fetch across the bay with SW winds.

*Authorities* A port of entry: port police, customs and immigration. Charge band 2.

*Note* To the E of the commercial harbour a small yacht harbour has been constructed. Local boats are kept here.

### Facilities

*Services* Water and electricity points on the quay. Water points on the breakwater.

*Fuel* Near the quay. A mini-tanker can deliver.

*Repairs* Most mechanical repairs. General light engineering including stainless steel welding and machining work can be carried out. General electrical work. Yachts are hauled out in the bay S of the commercial harbour. Good chandlers. Excellent hardware and tool shops.

*Provisions* Excellent shopping for all provisions. Good SPAR supermarket in the W of the town. Wine from the barrel. Ice from the fish market.

*Eating out* The tavernas and bars fronting the quay are fairly flashy and of varying quality. Towards the fishing harbour and further along to the SE are more convivial tavernas and there are a number of good *ouzeries* with good *mezedes*.

*Other* PO. OTE. Hospital. Banks. Hire cars, motorbikes and bicycles. Buses and trains to

Volos looking N from Ák Sesoulo with the detached breakwater in the foreground

**VOLOS**
⊕39°21′·58N 22°56′·77E WGS84

Thessaloniki and Athens. Ferries to the northern Sporades and Syria. Internal flights to Athens.

*Note* Volos is a good base from which to visit the spectacular monasteries at Meteori – buses and trains run regularly.

### General

Volos is one of the most important commercial harbours in Greece, handling most of the Thessalian exports: cereals, silk, cotton, olive oil, sugar and soap. Until the disastrous earthquakes of 1954 and 1955 Volos rivalled Piraeus in commercial power. After the earthquakes, which flattened a large part of the city, it was rapidly rebuilt and once again it is prospering.

The present harbour was built in 1912, but Volos has always been an important maritime town. Jason and the Argonauts set sail from Volos (then Iolkos) – a fact commemorated by a bronze model of the *Argo* in a square by the harbour. The local wine is also called, appropriately enough, Argo.

The museum (towards the SE end of the city) contains an excellent collection of artifacts from Iolkos and Pagasai-Demetrias (across the bay S of Volos). Its collection of painted *stelai* is one of the best in the world and I recommend a visit. The faded paintings on the *stelai* show touching scenes from everyday life in ancient Greece – Protos, a muscular-looking man walking his dog, Metrophanes holding out his hands to his child, Hediste lying wan in bed – scenes far removed from the friezes of warriors and chariots and wounded lions we commonly think of as ancient funereal art.

### ÓRMOS AGRIA

39°20′·4N 23°00′·7E

A large bay lying just over 3M ESE of Volos. The bay itself is fairly exposed but there is a small fishing harbour here where you may be able to find a berth. There are 2–3m depths in the entrance and 2–3·5m depths under the breakwater. Go alongside or stern or bows-to near the dogleg if there is a space. Good shelter.

Tavernas and cafés ashore.

### KATO GATSIA

39°18′·5N 23°06′·0E

A very small fishing harbour. It is crowded with local boats. In calm weather you can anchor off in 3–5m on sand. Limited provisions and tavernas ashore.

## Tríkeri Channel
### (Stenón Tríkeri)

This channel separates Evia from the Tríkeri peninsula (Khersónisos Tríkeri). Although it is wider than Stenón Oreou, there can still be appreciable currents of up to 1½ knots, usually setting towards the SW. The coast is mountainous on both sides. The mountains of the Tríkeri peninsula drop sheer into the sea – they are scarred and scoured and mostly devoid of vegetation and habitation.

Off the mouth of the gulf, Athenian *triremes* had their first brush with the invading Persians under

337

Xerxes. This was a delaying tactic by the Athenians rather than an attempt to hold the invaders. The tactic had an unforeseen success as soon afterwards a NE gale wrecked many of the Persian craft. Herodotus relates the story:

'The Persian fleet...made the Magnesian coast between Casthanea and Cape Sépias and on its arrival the leading ships made fast to the land, while the remainder, as there was not much room on the short stretch of beach, came to anchor and lay off-shore in lines, eight deep. In this position they remained during the night; but at dawn next day the weather, which was clear and calm, suddenly changed, and the fleet was caught in a heavy blow from the east – a 'Hellespontian' as the people there call it – which raised a confused sea like a pot on the boil. Those who realised in time that the blow was coming, and all who happened to be lying in a convenient position, managed to beach their vessels and to get them clear of the water before they were damaged, and thus saved their own lives as well; but the ships which were caught well off-shore were all lost...'

Trans. Aubrey de Selincourt (quoted in Ernle Bradford *The Greek Islands*)

The modern yachtsman can only wonder why the Persian fleet did not choose the nearby natural harbour of Skíathos.

## ÓRMOS ANDRIAMI (Khondhri Ammos)
39°07'·0N 23°13'·0E

A large bay on the N side of the channel. Anchor in a cove on the N side in 5–8m on mud, good holding. Reasonable shelter from the *meltemi* although some swell works around into the cove. Open S. No facilities.

## PLATANIA

An open bay 2½ miles E of Andriami affording some shelter from the *meltemi*. The village of Platania at the bottom of a valley is conspicuous from seaward. A mole has been built out near the old short jetty at the E end of the bay. The end of the mole is lit Fl.G.3s3M. The mole much improves the shelter here if you can get on it or behind it. Go alongside or stern or bows-to if there is room. The hydrofoil berths at the outer end of the mole. The bay shelves gently to the shore with a mud and sand bottom so you can anchor off behind the mole near the permanent moorings if there is no space on it. Reasonable shelter from the *meltemi*.

Water tap near the bridge on the waterfront. Provisions and tavernas ashore. The bay is an attractive place with a wooded valley rising up from the bay with numerous plane trees dotted about – hence the name Platania.

## PEFKI
39°00'·5N 23°12'·4E

A new fishing harbour on the N coast of Evia approximately 4 miles E of Ák Kefala. The mole head is lit: Fl.R.2s3M.

The harbour is full of fishing boats but it may be possible to find a berth. Alternatively anchor off clear of the permanent moorings. Good shelter from the *meltemi* under the mole.

**PLATANIA**
⊕39°08'·4N 23°16'·5E

**PEFKI**
⊕39°00'·5N 23°12'·4E

Water tap ashore. Provisions and tavernas. Hydrofoil service. The area is a popular holiday destination for Greeks, with long sandy beaches along the adjacent coast.

## PONDIKONISI

Pondokonisi light Fl(2)WR.15s15/12M 39°02'·9N 23°20'·2E

Lies on the S side of Stenón Tríkeri NE of Ák Artemision on Evia. A cove on the SW corner of the island gives good shelter from the *meltemi*. On the N side of the island is a landing leading up to the lighthouse.

# Northern Sporades

The Sporades ('Sporades' means scattered or sown) are divided into two groups: the northern Sporades described here and the southern or eastern Sporades lying along the coast of Asia Minor. The latter group is today commonly known as the Dodecanese (the islands stretching from Kárpathos to Pátmos) and the eastern Sporades (those islands north of Pátmos to Limnos). The eastern Sporades are less visited than the northern Sporades and consequently the name 'the Sporades' invariably refers to the northern group described here.

The main group of islands curves in a sickle shape from the southern corner of the Tríkeri peninsula northwards to the tiny sea-washed rock of Psathoúra. Forty miles north of here Mt Athos rises out of the sea at the bottom of the Khalkidhiki. Skíros lies to the SE of the main group and although it belongs geographically and politically to these islands, it has tended to develop independently.

Lying out of the mainstream of history, the islands have few archaeological remains. Recently indications of Minoan occupation have been unearthed at Stafilos on Skópelos. The islands were subject-allies of Athens and later of Macedonia and Rome. Skíros has always been of more importance than the other islands, situated as it is on the trade route between Athens and Asia Minor.

During the Middle Ages the islands were easy prey for pirates. The inhabitants moved inland to fortified villages and not until the late 19th century did they begin to return to coastal villages.

Consequently, most of the towns around the coast are of comparatively recent origin.

The popular architecture of the group is distinctive – the houses are washed in white, blue and pink and have gabled roofs with grey or red slates. Today the beautiful scenery and fine sandy beaches have been attracting growing numbers of tourists to the more accessible islands of the group.

**Note** The islands are not blessed with very much in the way of natural water supplies, nor when it is available is it always potable. The rapidly expanding tourism infrastructure ashore has cut supplies even further. Consequently water is in short supply and in harbours where it is available it is charged out at a high, not to say extortionate, rate.

## Weather patterns in the northern Sporades

The *meltemi* does not blow as strongly down through the northern Sporades as it does further S. It blows from the NNE, but the direction is much altered by the islands and channels between them. The islands stop most of the sea on the S side except around Pelagos which gets the whole fetch of the sea from northern Greece. The combination of the *meltemi* and the flat seas on the lee side of the islands makes for some exhilarating sailing and not surprisingly the area is popular for flotilla holidays.

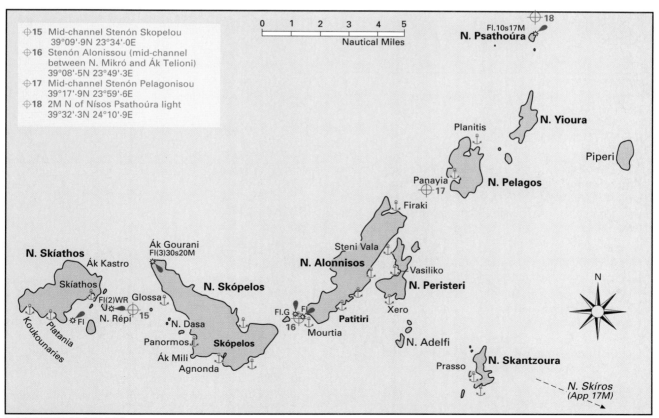

⊕15 Mid-channel Stenón Skopelou
       39°09'.9N 23°34'.0E
⊕16 Stenón Alonissou (mid-channel
       between N. Mikró and Ák Telioni)
       39°08'.5N 23°49'.3E
⊕17 Mid-channel Stenón Pelagonisou
       39°17'.9N 23°59'.6E
⊕18 2M N of Nísos Psathoúra light
       39°32'.3N 24°10'.9E

**NORTHERN SPORADES**

# Nísos Skíathos

The nearest of the islands to the mainland coast. With good ferry services and an airport it attracts more visitors than the other islands. From 1538 until 1830 the inhabitants moved to an almost inaccessible rocky spur on the northern end of the island. The Kástro, as it was called, was connected to the island by a drawbridge which could be raised in times of siege. Today most of the population lives in Skíathos town.

## STENÓN SKÍATHOU (Skíathos Channel)

This narrow channel separates Skíathos from the mainland. Ifalos Levthéris (Lephtari Rock) lies in the channel 1¾ miles E of Ák Arápis. It is marked by a light structure (conspic): char. Fl(2)8s8M. A variable current sets either N or S through the channel at ½–1½ knots.

**STENÓN SKÍATHOU**

⊕14 Mid-channel Stenón Skiathou 39°09'·9N 23°21'·8E

## KOUKOUNARIES

### Approach
A small harbour in the NE corner of Órmos Koukounaries on the SW corner of Skíathos. The large Skíathos Palace Hotel at the E end of the bay is conspicuous and the small harbour is immediately below it.

### Mooring
Go stern or bows-to either mole. The tiny harbour is usually crowded and you will probably have to anchor off.

*Shelter* Excellent shelter. A number of boats are wintered afloat here.

*Anchorage* Anchor off the beach clear of the ski channel in 4–6m on sand, good holding. Good shelter from the *meltemi* anchored off here.

### Facilities
Several tavernas nearby.

**ÓRMOS KOUKOUNARIES**
⊕39°08'·3N 23°24'·2E

### General
Koukounaries is often said to be the best beach in the Aegean. It is a fine beach with the pines providing a wonderful aspect, but is not the best beach in the region in my opinion (see Khalkidhiki section).

## ÓRMOS PLATANIA

A large bay to the E of Koukounaries with several hotels on the beach. Anchor off the beach in 4–8m on sand, good holding. Good shelter although there are strong gusts off the land with the *meltemi*.

Tavernas ashore.

**ÓRMOS PLATANIA**
⊕39°07'·8N 23°26'·2E

## SKÍATHOS

BA 1571
Imray-Tetra G25

### Approach
*Conspicuous* The cluster of islands surrounding Skíathos harbour is easily identified. The lighthouse on Nisís Répi is conspicuous from the S and E. The buildings of Skíathos around the harbour, particularly a large building on the headland forming the E side of the old harbour and a church with a conspicuous clock tower on high ground to the N of the old harbour, are conspicuous.

*By night* Use the lights on Nisís Prassou Fl.6s6M, Nisís Répi Fl(2)WR.10s12/8M (red sector covers

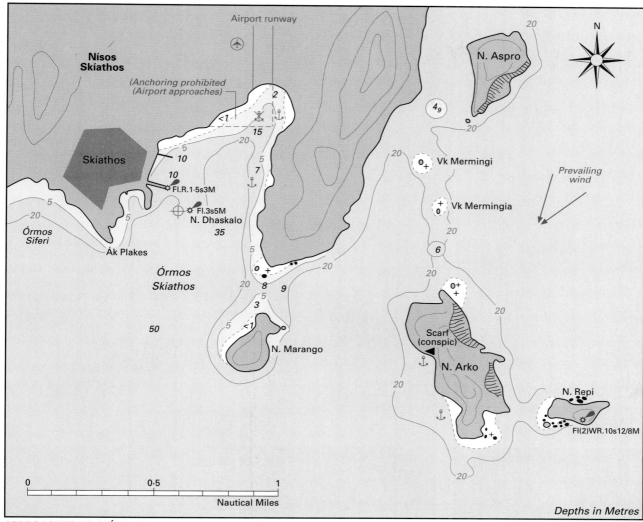

Nísos
Skíathos

Airport runway

(Anchoring prohibited
(Airport approaches)

N. Aspro

N

4₉
20

Skíathos

20

Vk Mermingi

Prevailing
wind

10
10 ✪ Fl.R.1·5s3M
⊕ ✪ Fl.3s5M
N. Dhaskalo
35

Vk Mermingia

Órmos
Siferi

Ák Plakes

Órmos
Skiathos

6

50

N. Marango

Scarf
(conspic)
N. Arko

N. Repi
Fl(2)WR.10s12/8M

0                    0.5                    1

**Nautical Miles**

*Depths in Metres*

**APPROACHES TO SKÍATHOS**
⊕39°09'·7N 23°29'·7E (N. Dhaskalo)

261°-313°), and Dhaskalonísi in the immediate approaches Fl.3s5M. The end of the mole is lit: Fl.R.1·5s3M.

### Mooring

Go stern or bows-to the quay N of the ferry berths or on the new pontoon off the quay. The harbour is often full with local and charter boats. The bottom is mud and weed, good holding. The old harbour on the S side is reserved for excursion boats though there may be a few berths here for small yachts.

*Shelter* Good shelter from the *meltemi* in the new E harbour, but the wind does blow beam on if you are on the N–S quay, so make sure your anchor is well in. With southerlies a swell rolls in and unless you are tucked right under the mole, it is very uncomfortable and may become untenable.

*Authorities* Port police and customs.

*Anchorage* It is also possible to anchor at the head of the bay and a number of yachts are wintered afloat here. Keep well clear of the area where anchoring is prohibited under the flight path of the airport. The bottom is mud, sand and weed – good holding.

### Facilities

*Water* On the quay, though you need to find the 'waterman' to unlock the tap. Showers.

*Fuel* Can be delivered to the harbour by mini-tanker – contact the port police or ☎ 42921.

*Repairs* Some mechanical repairs. Yachts are hauled out at the yard at the head of the bay. Chandlers. Hardware shops.

*Provisions* Good shopping for all provisions. Ice can be ordered.

*Eating out* Good tavernas in the town.

*Other* PO. OTE. Banks. Greek gas and *Camping Gaz*. Hire cars, motorbikes and bicycles. Ferries and hydrofoils to Volos, Áyios Konstandinos and Skópelos. European charter flights. Internal flights to Athens and Thessaloniki.

### General

The small town of Skíathos has grown in recent years to become a sort of junior league Míkonos with discos, bars and good restaurants livening up the night. In the summer the town is packed with tourists attracted to the sandy beaches, yet it remains a pleasant easy-going town and most of the locals are still friendly enough. But a quiet place it is

**SKÍATHOS**
⊕39°09′·8N 23°29′·6E

not and those seeking less noise and fewer people
are advised to head east.

# Nísos Skópelos

Skópelos (ancient Peparethos), like Skíathos, is
densely wooded in pine over its slopes. It is also very
fertile – vines, olives, almonds, pears, citrus fruit and
plums, for which the island is famous, are grown. It
is more intensively cultivated than Skíathos and the
inhabitants (perhaps because they are farmers and
not seafarers risking their lives at sea) are said to be
more conservative.

The capital is Skópelos (*chora*-Skopélou) on the
east side of the island. The island has long been
considered a remote place – dissident Byzantines
were exiled here far from the pleasures of
Constantinople. In 1538 Barbarossa slaughtered the
entire population of the island so presumably all the
present inhabitants are immigrants who arrived in
the 16th century. The island still has a remote feel
to it in places and in the winter you can feel
positively isolated on it. Today the islanders are an
industrious and prosperous lot who seem quite
happy to see tourists coming to their island, yet
make few concessions to them outside Skópelos and
Glóssa.

Skíathos harbour looking W with Skíathos town top middle
*Peter Kleinoth/MareTeam*

## LOUTRÁKI (Glóssa)

### Approach

*Conspicuous* The village on the hill above the harbour is easily seen from a considerable distance off. A large brown church in the middle of the village is conspicuous. Closer in the small settlement behind the harbour will be seen.

*By night* The entrance is lit: Fl.G.3s3M/Fl.R.3s5M.

### Mooring

Go stern or bows-to the new pontoon in the NE corner. The bottom is sand and weed – good holding.

*Shelter* Good shelter from the *meltemi*. Strong southerlies may be bothersome.

### Facilities

Good shopping for provisions. Good tavernas on the waterfront. Bus to Skópelos. Ferry to Skíathos.

### General

Loutráki has grown into a modest tourist resort and the once sleepy village is now invaded every day by visitors from Skíathos who come for its splendid beaches to the SE of the harbour. It is an arduous walk in the hot sun to the village of Glóssa above, but worth it for the magnificent views over to Skíathos and Evia.

**LOUTRÁKI**
⊕39°09′·8N 23°37′·0E

**NISOI SKÓPELOS AND ALONNISOS**

Loutráki looking SW across the yacht pontoon    *Hans van Rijn*

### NÉA KLIMA

39°08'·4N 23°38'·5E

A small harbour with a narrow entrance channel into a basin. The entrance is lit Fl.G.3s5M/Fl.R.3s3M. Care is needed in the channel and inside the harbour as depths are irregular. Depths in the channel are mostly 2m and in the basin 1·5–2m. The harbour is mostly crowded with local boats and you would be lucky to find a berth.

### ÓRMOS PANORMOU

#### Approach

The bay lies half a mile SE of Nisís Dhasia which is easily identified. From the S it is difficult to see the bay until close to. The apartment complex on the N side with red roofs is conspicuous.

#### Mooring

The large bay is very deep even close to the beach. A swimming area cordoned off by small buoys blocks off the NE side of the bay. Anchor in the E side outside the buoyed area. The inlet running S from the bay has better shelter. Anchor in the S corner in 4–8m and take a line ashore. There can be strong gusts from the N and NW into the bay so make sure your anchor is well in. The bay is popular in the summer and often packed with yachts and other craft.

#### Facilities

Limited provisions and tavernas ashore.

#### General

The secluded inlet on the S features in Michael Carroll's *Gates of the Wind*. Anyone who has read this book will immediately recognise his house on the E side of the inlet. Those who have not read it should obtain a copy (it is published in paperback by a Greek publisher and available locally) for the descriptions of the islands and particularly of Skópelos and Panormos just before the outside world learnt of these enchanted places.

ÓRMOS PANORMOU
⊕39°06'·5N 23°40'·0E

### LIMONARI

39°05'·4N 23°41'·3E

A large bay ½ mile W of Agnondas with a popular beach at the head. Anchor where convenient in 5–7m on sand. All the day-trippers have left by the evening returning tranquillity to the place.

### ÓRMOS AGNÓNDAS

An enclosed bay 2½ miles E of Ák Miti. When strong N winds make the approach to Limín Skópelos dangerous the ferry calls here and a bus connects to Skópelos. The entrance to the bay is not obvious until close-to when the light structures on either side of the entrance will be seen. (Char Fl.R.2s3M and Fl.G.2s3M.)

Limited room to anchor in the bay. If possible go alongside or stern or bows-to the quay. Good shelter from the *meltemi*, but with southerlies a swell rolls in.

AGNÓNDA
⊕39°05'·4N 23°42'·1E (Fl.R.3M)

Taverna/bars ashore. The pine-clad inlet is a popular spot with Skopelites in the summer.

## ÓRMOS STAFILOS (Staphylos)

An open bay on the S coast W of a craggy headland joined by a low isthmus to Skópelos. Care needs to be taken of the reef immediately S of an islet on the W side of the bay although it is not in the obvious approach to the bay.

The large bay offers good protection from the *meltemi* although a swell often curves around into the bay. Anchor in 3–4m off the beach in the NE corner. Open to the S.

A few summer villas have been built around the slopes and the beach is popular in the summer. Taverna ashore.

The bay is named after a Minoan prince (Staphylos), and recently archaeologists discovered evidence of a Cretan settlement, including a gold-plated sword handle and a gold diadem. This makes Stafilos the most northerly Minoan settlement so far unearthed.

**ÓRMOS STAFILOS**
⊕39°04'·8N 23°44'·8E

## LIMÍN SKOPÉLOU (SKÓPELOS)

BA 1571

### Approach

*Conspicuous* From the E the town of Skópelos will not be seen until you enter Órmos Skopélou. Once you are in the bay the cluster of houses above the harbour stand out in dazzling white. The harbour moles are easily identified.

*By night* Use the light on Nisís Mikró Fl.4s6M and the lights at the entrance Fl.G.2s6M and Fl.R (on the light buoy off the works or on the new E breakwater).

*Dangers* With strong NE winds (including a prolonged *meltemi*) a steep and dangerous sea builds up over the shoal water in the approaches to the harbour. In these conditions it is difficult and sometimes dangerous to enter or leave the harbour. In this weather the ferry goes to Agnonda on the W coast of Skópelos.

*Note* At the time of writing harbour works are in progress so care is needed in the final approach and in the entrance.

### Mooring

Go stern or bows-to the N quay. A large mooring chain lying 30m out from the quay and parallel to it has been reported. Care is needed not to snag it with your anchor. The bottom is mud – excellent holding.

*Shelter* With a strong *meltemi* it can get very uncomfortable in the harbour. Ease off the warps and keep the yacht some distance off the quay. The wash from the numerous ferries and hydrofoils using the harbour is also bothersome. Otherwise shelter is good.

*Authorities* Port police and customs.

### Facilities

*Water* Tap in the SE corner or a mini-tanker can deliver.

*Fuel* Can be delivered by mini-tanker from the FINA agent.

*Repairs* Limited mechanical repairs. Hardware shops.

*Provisions* Good shopping for all provisions. Ice available.

*Eating out* Good tavernas on the waterfront and in the town.

*Other* PO. OTE. Bank. Hire motorbikes and bicycles. Bus to Glóssa. Ferries and hydrofoils to Patitíri and Volos.

### General

The houses and churches (there are said to be 120) of the town are piled one upon another around a rock amphitheatre above the harbour. The houses are jammed together along narrow curving alleys that restrict access to pedestrians, donkeys and the occasional suicidal motorcyclist. An altogether delightful and relaxing place that has altered little (apart from acquiring some more tavernas and bars)

**APPROACHES TO SKÓPELOS**
⊕39°08'·0N 23°44'·5E

**SKÓPELOS**
⊕39°07'·5N 23°44'·1E

despite the growing numbers of tourists discovering it.

# Nísos Alonnisos

## (Khelidromi)

In ancient times called Ilkos, this hilly wooded island relies on the donkey and the *caïque* as much as on motor vehicles. The old capital of Alonnisos, on a hill in the south of the island, was largely deserted after a severe earthquake in 1965. The islanders moved to Patitíri and Votsi, but eventually returned and most of the houses in the hill village have been restored. At Órmos Tzorti evidence of Neolithic and other ancient habitation has been discovered. Whether this was also the site of ancient Halonessos, a city that ancient commentators say disappeared into the sea during a catastrophic earthquake, is uncertain, as some authorities believe Psathoúra, the northernmost island, to be the site.

## ÓRMOS MOURTIA (Mourtias)

An open bay on the SW of Alonnisos offering some shelter from the *meltemi*. Open to the S and prone to swell entering. Anchor in 4–6m around the bay

**ÓRMOS MOURTIA**
⊕39°08'·5N 23°50'·0E

taking care to avoid the prohibited area where there are underwater cables. Taverna ashore.

The village of Alonnisos on the hill above is 30 minutes' steep climb up an unpaved road. In unsettled weather Patitíri is a safer harbour to leave a yacht in if you want to visit the hill village.

## PATITÍRI

### Approach

*Conspicuous* The old village of Alonnisos on the hill behind is visible from seaward. The village and harbour of Patitíri are not easily seen from the N or S until you are close to.

*By night* The entrance is lit: Fl.R.1·5s3M/ Fl.G.1·5s3M.

*Dangers* Care is needed of ferries entering and leaving the narrow entrance to the harbour.

### Mooring

Go stern or bows-to the NE quay or anchor fore and aft off the beach on the W side where shown. The bottom is sand and weed – good holding.

*Shelter* Good shelter from the *meltemi*, although some swell tends to creep around into the harbour making it a bit rolly at times. Partially open to the E and SE.

*Authorities* Port police.

### Facilities

*Water* Tap on the quay or a mini-tanker will deliver.
*Fuel* Near the quay.
*Provisions* Good shopping for provisions. Ice available.
*Eating out* Tavernas and bars on the waterfront.
*Other* PO. Exchange facilities. Ferries and hydrofoils to Skíathos and Volos.

**PATITÍRI**
⊕39°08'·7N 23°52'·0E

### General

As has recently happened on the other islands in the group, the capital of the island has moved from the hill village down to the harbour. Patitíri is a lovely spot surrounded by the cliffs on the S and pine-clad slopes behind, so inevitably it has attracted a growing number of tourists, but remains a pleasant spot still.

### VOTSI

A cove immediately N of Patitíri which a number of fishing boats use in preference to Patitíri. A short breakwater extends from the E side of the cove and a 'snoot' of a breakwater on the W. Room is very limited but it may be possible to anchor in 2·5–4m in the NE corner with a line ashore taking care of the numerous permanent moorings. Alternatively try the inside of the E breakwater. One or two yachts may find room to go bows-to the quay on the W side amongst the local fishing boats. Good shelter from the *meltemi* and open only to the S. The bottom shelves gradually towards the beach at the head of the bay.

Tavernas ashore. It is a short walk over the saddle to Patitíri.

An alternative anchorage to Votsi is the bay between Patitíri and Votsi. Anchor off in 4–7m in sand. Several tavernas near the beach.

**VOTSI**
⊕39°08·9N 23°52'·4E

### ÁK KOKKINOKASTRO

Kokkinokastro is the red cliffy cape 2½ miles N of Patitíri (*kokkino* means 'red'). Kokkinokastro is thought to be the site of ancient Ilkos (about the fifth century BC).

### ÓRMOS TZORTI

The bay immediately N of Ák Kokkinokastro. Care is needed of the above and below-water rocks extending out from Kokkinokastro. Anchor in 4–8m

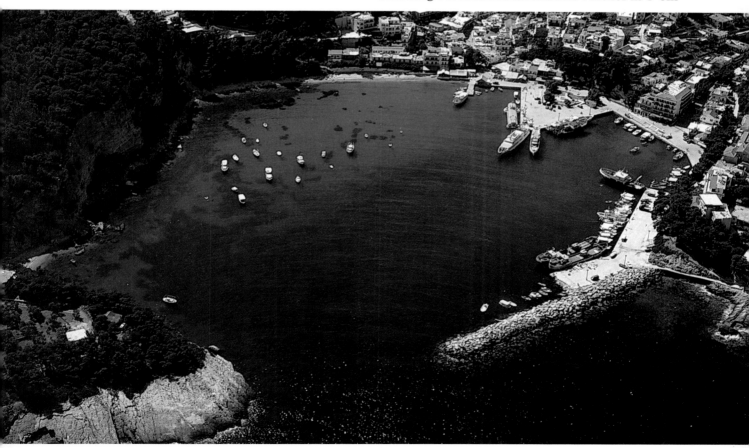

Patitíri on Alonnísos looking W from the entrance
*Peter Kleinoth/MareTeam*

**ÓRMOS TZORTI**
⊕39°09′·9N 23°54′·5E

off the beach on sand and weed, good holding once the anchor is in. Good shelter from the *meltemi*.

A number of villas have been built around the bay. The beach is popular in the summer, but is usually deserted at night.

Immediately NE of Tzorti is another bay, Órmos Leptos Yialos, which also gives reasonable shelter from the *meltemi*. Anchor in 4–6m off the beach.

### STENI VALA

A small cove on Alonnisos opposite the S end of Nísos Peristeri. Sheltered from the *meltemi* and only open SW. On the N side of the cove there is a quay with 1–2m depths off it where it is possible to go stern or bows-to. Several tavernas ashore. The spot is popular with charter yachts.

Alternatively a yacht can anchor in a cove lined with pine trees and bamboo immediately S of the 'taverna' cove. Care is needed of the islet on the port side of the entrance. Good shelter.

**STENI VALA**
⊕39°11′·3N 23°55′·6E

### ÓRMOS FIRAKI (Port Eiraka)

39°16′·2N 23°57′·0E

A bay on the N end of the island. The bay is very exposed and is untenable with the *meltemi*, but in calm weather makes a good lunch stop. At the head of the bay there is a small quay used by the tripper boats with 2–2·5m depths reported off it.

# Nísos Peristeri

## (Xero)

The island lying roughly parallel to and just to the E of Alonnisos.

## ÓRMOS PERISTÉRA AND XERO

Two bays on the S end of Nísos Peristéra.

***Órmos Peristéra*** Anchor off the beach at the head of the bay in 3–6m on mud and weed, good holding. Good shelter from the *meltemi*. A number of houses have now been built around the slopes.

***Órmos Xero*** The bay immediately E of Órmos Peristéra. Anchor in 5–10m at the head of the bay. Adequate shelter from the *meltemi*.

**ORMOS PERISTÉRA AND XERO**
⊕39°09′·7N 23°59′·0E

## ÓRMOS VASILIKO

The bay at the N end of the large bay on the W coast. Care must be taken of the reef on the W side of the entrance. Anchor in 4–8m in the bay. Nearly all-round shelter. At the time of writing the bay is partially occupied by a decommissioned ferry, but there is still room for yachts to anchor. Recent visitors have remarked that the bay and beaches nearby are knee-deep in rubbish, principally plastic and old tyres.

Órmos Vasiliko on Peristéri *Nigel Patten*

**VASILIKO**
⊕39°11'·8N 23°58'·4E

## ÓRMOS KLIMA

39°11'·4N 23°58'·7E

The large bay on the W side of Nísos Peristéri. In calm weather it is a spectacular spot to visit with a gorge running down to the head of the bay. The *meltemi* pushes a swell into the bay and although tenable in a light *meltemi*, if the wind pipes up it is not a good spot to be.

## NOTE

The 3 fathom patch shown on the old Admiralty charts Nos. 1085 and 1087 extending across the northern passage between Alonnisos and Peristeri is in fact a smallish patch off the end of Peristeri. There are considerable depths in the fairway.

# Nísos Pelagos

## (Nísos Kira Panayía)

Lies 4 miles to the NE of Alonnisos. It is deserted except for large herds of goats, a herd of cows, some horses, a big black bull and a guardian. A number of sunken Byzantine ships have been discovered off the coast and in 1970 a quantity of pottery was recovered.

*Note* Pelagos Island is now a nature reserve. Along with Yioura and Piperi which are also nature reserves, this is one of the few remaining habitats of the Mediterranean Monk seal (*Monarchus monarchus*). Other habitats are around Cephalonia in the Ionian and the Atlantic coast of Morocco. At one time there was talk of banning yachts from the island, but this does not seem to have happened and yachts continue to visit the island. Yachtsmen should take care not to disturb wildlife around the island or they may find they are banned from here.

## MONASTERY COVE

39°19'·3N 24°05'·6E

A small cove on the E side of the island where a yacht can moor in settled weather to visit the monastery. On BA 1062 it is the bay immediately S of the bay showing 8 and 2 fathoms. On Imray-Tetra G25 it is marked as Monastery Bay. The monastery itself is on a small headland at the S end

of the bay. Anchor in 5m and take a line ashore. The cove is protected only from W winds and should be visited in calm weather only.

Steps are cut in the rock to climb to the monastery several hundred feet above. About a 40-minute walk. It is a lonely and haunted place inhabited by one old monk and caretaker keeping a last vigil here. Visitors should take care not to desecrate the spot whether believers or not.

## KIRA PANAYIA (Áyios Petros)

A large bay on the SW corner of Pelagos. Nisís Pelérissa and the high plateau on the SE side of the bay are easily distinguished. There is deep water N and S of Nisís Pelérissa.

Good shelter from the *meltemi* can be found in Órmos Paigniou, although with northerlies there are vicious gusts into the bay. Anchor in the cove on the NW side or behind the islet in the middle of the bay and take a line ashore. The bottom is sand – good holding.

A yacht can also anchor in the cove on the E side in 2–4m. The bottom is sand and thick weed – poor holding.

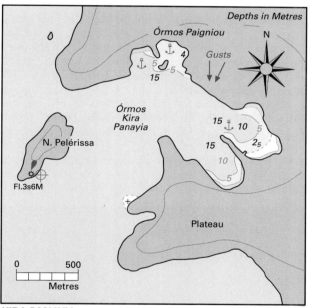

**KIRA PANAYIA**
⊕39°18'·8N 24°02'·3E

## ÓRMOS PAIGNIOU

39°19'·8N 24°02'·8E

In calm weather or with a light *meltemi* shelter can be found in the bay on the W side of Nísos Pelagos. Anchor in 5–10m on sand and rock, poor holding in places. In unsettled weather you should leave here and go to a more secure anchorage such as Vasiliko on Peristeri.

## ÓRMOS PLANITIS (Planidhi)

A large landlocked bay on the N side of Nísos Pelagos. Nisís Sfika lies close to the W side of the

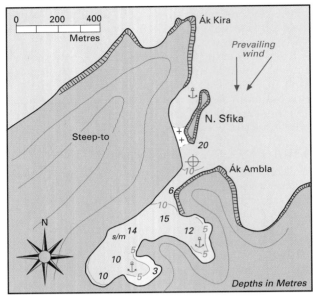

**PLANITIS**
⊕39°21'·2N 24°04'·5E

narrow entrance which is difficult to see until you are close in. With strong N winds a considerable sea piles up at the entrance to Planitís and it is a frightening experience being pushed by the wind and sea towards the entrance which is only 82m (270ft) wide. Conversely with strong N winds it can be difficult to leave the bay. There is a least depth of 6m over the bar at the entrance. Inside the bay the water is always smooth.

Anchor in either of the two forks of the bay. A favourite place is in 3m in the NE corner of the southernmost part of the bay. Excellent all-round shelter. The bottom is sand and mud with some weed – good holding. It is deserted apart from a large herd of goats, and the crackle of several million cicadas.

Planitís on Pelagos looking NE with Nísos Yioura at the very top of the photo         *Peter Kleinoth/MareTeam*

There is a shallow passage between the N end of Nisís Sfika and Pelagos which in settled weather makes an attractive lunch stop. Explore with caution.

## NISÍS YIOURA

A precipitous jagged island with no sheltered anchorages. A herd of the European wild goat, the now rare ibex, lives on the island and every year an armada of *caïques* sets out to cull the herd under the supervision of an official. Michael Carroll gives a lively description of the cullers and the culling in his *Gates of the Wind*.

## NISÍS PIPERI

The Pepperpot. There are no anchorages around it.

## NISÍS PSATHOÚRA

N. Psathoúra light (Fl.10s17M) 39°30'·3N 24°10'·9E

The northernmost of the northern Sporades, it is very low (0·6m/2ft), but the lighthouse (40m/131ft) is conspicuous. An extensive submerged city, possibly ancient Halonnesos, is reported to lie off the N end of the island.

*Currents* Around Psathoúra Island and also to the N of it the current sets strongly towards the SW. On passage between Porto Koufó and Pelagos in November, I estimated the current to be about 1½ knots to the SW. Quite possibly it is stronger at other times of the year. With strong winds from the N and S the seas in the vicinity of Psathoúra can be exceptionally disturbed and steep.

## NÍSOS SKANTZOURA

Lies about 15 miles E of the S end of Skópelos. A number of small islands and shoals lie off the coast. A yacht can anchor in a number of places:

1. **Órmos Prasso** (opposite Nisís Prasso) which is made up of two small coves. Anchor in 4–6m sand.
2. **Nisís Prasso S side** On the S side of the islet there is a cove which you can tuck into. Anchor in 4–6m on sand and weed and take a long line to the shore.
3. **Órmos Skantzoura** A deep narrow bay on the S side of Skantzoura. Anchor in 3–5m and take a long line ashore.

The bays here afford adequate if not always comfortable shelter from the *meltemi*. A swell usually works its way into the bays after the wind dies and the waves are not 'blown' past the anchorages. Open to the W–SW. The bottom is sand and weed. Excellent underwater fishing in the vicinity of the island.

*Caution* Nísos Skantzoura and the islets surrounding it are comparatively low-lying and are unlit. Care must be taken in the vicinity of the islands, especially at night.

**NÍSIS SKANTZOURA ANCHORAGES**
⊕39°03'·0N 24°05'·9E

# Skíros

## (Skyros)

The most easterly and the largest of the northern Sporades. It is nearly divided into two by a narrow isthmus in the middle. The summit of the island lies in the rugged southern half where Mt Kokhilas rises to 792m (2,600ft). The lower slopes of the high ground are wooded in pine and *maquis*. The northern half of the island is fertile and cultivated in parts.

The capital, Skiro or Khorio, is more like a Cycladic village than the villages on Skíathos or Skópelos. The white cubist houses with flat roofs are built on a steep slope with a Venetian castle on the summit. In the village there is an unusual amount of carved wood – doors, shutters, chairs and stools. Skíros embroidery is also much in evidence. Some

of the best island folk art is contained in the Faltaitz Museum near the castle – one of the best of its kind in Greece.

Ancient Skíros was ruled by King Lykomedes. It was he who treacherously killed Theseus, king of Athens, by hurling him over a cliff into the sea. His body was recovered and forty years later taken to Athens for a burial befitting his rank. Later Achilles was sent here by his mother to keep him away from the Trojan Wars in which it had been prophesied he would die. The wily Odysseus, en route to the wars, discovered his identity and lured him away to his prophesied death.

The island has always been important because of its position on the trade route across the northern Aegean. The Athenians colonised it and the Venetians held it for some considerable time. The Venetian castle overlooking Khorio has ancient masonry incorporated in its construction and was the likely site of the ancient acropolis.

The inhabitants of the island have been little touched by tourism although the 'younger set' are beginning to discover it. Some of the old men wear linen blouses and black pantaloons and boots and most sport big bushy moustaches. A herd of wild ponies, descendants of the ancient breed called Pikermic and akin to Shetland ponies, roam the island. Despite the rough seas and strong winds around the island it is well worth a visit; the islanders are friendly and the scenery is grand and wild.

## SKÍROS (Skyros)

On this island battered by both wind and sea, (its ancient name was Anemosa meaning 'windy'), the anchorages are mostly on the SW coast. From the N these are:

*Órmos Áy Fokas* Offers good shelter from the *meltemi* in attractive wooded surroundings. Anchor and take a long line to the shore to hold the bows into the slight swell that enters when the wind dies down in the evening. The bay is used by a few

**NÍSOS SKÍROS**

⊕19  2M N of Nisís Vorios Pódhi
     (Skiros N end) 39°03'·2N 24°28'·1E
⊕20  1M S of Ák Valáxa light
     38°47'·0N 24°29'·5E
⊕21  2M S of Nisís Sarakino light (Skíros S end) 38°43'·5N
     24°37'·6E

**SKIROS – SOUTHWEST COAST**
⊕38°48'N 24°29'·5E

holiday-makers who come for the surroundings rather than the pebble beach. A taverna opens in the summer.

***Órmos Pevki*** A large bay due N of the passage between Skíros and Nisís Valáxa. Good shelter from the *meltemi* and plenty of room to swing to anchor. There is a quay and slipway for small craft on the S side of the bay. The long beach is popular in the summer and a couple of tavernas open for the season.

***Dhíavlos Valaxou*** There are depths of 2–5m in this passage. Keep to the centre of the passage or closer to the Skíros side. Usually you will encounter least depths of no less than 3·5–4m. It is scary but the ferry between Linaria and Kimi often uses this passage.

***Ormiskos Linaria*** Lies further to the N from the ferry port of Linaria. Good shelter from the *meltemi*. The bottom is mud – good holding. Taverna on the beach.

## LIMÍN LINARIA

BA 1571
Imray-Tetra G18

### Approach

Once past Nisís Valáxa some of the buildings around the harbour will be seen. The harbour proper will not be seen until you are right up to it when approaching from the S.

*By night* Use the light on the S end of Nisís Valáxa (Ák Valáxa) Fl.3·3s5M and the light on the end of the mole at Linaria Fl.WRG.2·5s6-4M (353°-R-021°-W-120°-G-300°).

*Dangers* With the *meltemi* there are strong gusts off the high land and confused seas in the approaches to the harbour.

### Mooring

Go alongside where shown. It is reported that the E side of the quay has been dredged and it may be possible to moor on the quay there.

**LINARIA**
⊕38°50'·6N 24°32'·2E

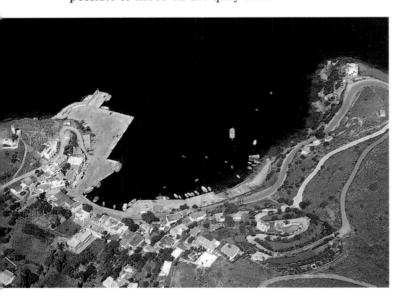

Linaria on Skíros looking WNW

*Shelter* Good shelter from the *meltemi*. Open to the NW–W.

*Authorities* Port police.

### Facilities

*Water* On the quay.
*Fuel* On the quay.
*Provisions* Good shopping for provisions in Linaria. Better shopping in the *chora*.
*Eating out* Several tavernas nearby and others in the *chora*.
*Other* PO and OTE in the *chora*. Irregular bus to the *chora*. Ferries to Kimi and Volos and a hydrofoil to Skíathos.

### General

Linaria is the place most yachts make for and the small amount of quay space can be cluttered in the high season. It is more of a staging post for passengers on the ferry to get to the *chora* than a village as such, but is a pleasant enough place and really the only place from which to visit the *chora*.

## Anchorages S of Linaria

***Órmos Akladhi*** 38°46'·8N 24°34'·1E Lying on the W side of Órmos Tristomou, this bay offers good shelter from the *meltemi*. Anchor in 3–5m near the

Linaria on Skíros looking SW  *Hans van Rijn*

head of the bay and take a long line ashore. The bottom is sand and weed.

***Órmos Tristomou*** (Trebuki, Tris Boukes) If you want to visit the grave of Rupert Brooke anchor off the river mouth on the E side of Órmos Tristomou in 4–8m. The E side of the bay is now a military area and you should report to the shore station for permission to go ashore and visit Rupert Brooke's grave. The naval guards ashore have been helpful to visiting yachties once they have understood the purpose of the visit. The bottom is sand and weed. To get to the grave follow the river bed for about 20 minutes and the grave will be found in an olive grove on the W side. I am not much of a fan of Rupert Brooke's poetry, more a fan of the man, but there are few of us who do not know the last lines of *The Old Vicarage*:

'And after, ere the night is born,
Do hares come out about the corn?
Oh, is the water sweet and cool,
Gentle and brown above the pool?
And laughs the immortal river still
Under the mill, under the mill?

Órmos Akladhi on the SW coast of Skíros          *Nigel Patten*

Say, is there Beauty yet to find?
And Certainty? and Quiet kind?
Deep meadows yet, for to forget
The lies, and truths, and pain?...oh! yet
Stands the Church clock at ten to three?
And is there honey still for tea?'

***Órmos Renes*** Anchor in a cove in the NW or NE corner. There are mostly 5–8m depths to anchor in. The bottom is sand and weed. Good shelter from the *meltemi* although there are fierce gusts down into the bay.

***Ormiskos Glifadha*** 38°45'·0N 24°36'·8E Lies on the S side of Nisís Sarakino. Anchor at the head of the creek in 4–6m. The bottom is sand and weed. Good shelter from the *meltemi*. Open only to the S.

***Caution*** With a strong *meltemi* blowing there are violent gusts down onto the SW coast off the high mountains. These are especially fierce in Órmos Tristomou. Caution must be exercised on the lee side of the island on account both of the gusts and of the considerable seas raised by the *meltemi*.

**ÓRMOS RENES**
⊕38°46'·4N 24°38'·0E

## ACHILLES BAY 'MARINA'

38°52'·3N 24°34'·5E

On the exposed NE coast of Skíros a large new 'marina' has been built in Achilles Bay. This is on the N side of the low isthmus connecting the N and S parts of Skíros. The port is practically finished, complete with several dredging barges left half sunk inside the harbour. The entrance is lit Fl.G.3s3M/Fl.R.3s3M.

The entrance is fringed with rocks and reefs and with the entire NE Aegean as fetch for the *meltemi* there will likely be horrendous seas at the entrance when any northerlies are blowing. It is reported that there is a surge in the harbour with northerlies and it would seem that the project is another of those awful EU-funded white elephants where some bureaucrat who had nothing to do with yachts and sailing just decided this was a 'good' place to build a marina.

353

## SKIROPOULA

The island lying approximately 8M W of Linaria on Skíros. On the SE of the island there is a bay affording some shelter from the *meltemi* (38°50'·0N 24°22'·0E). Care is needed in the approaches of the rocks and reefs running out from the SE side of the island and the approach to the anchorage should be made on a NE course. Anchor in either of the two coves at the head of the bay in 4–5m on sand. With the *meltemi* there are gusts into the anchorage.

# East coast of Evia

For the most part this coast is rugged and precipitous with little shelter for yachts. The prevailing NE winds push considerable seas across the northern Aegean until they crash onto this coast. The coast is only sparsely populated and the scenery spectacular and wild. The only harbour of any size is Kimi approximately halfway along the coast, but there are a number of other anchorages offering some shelter from the prevailing winds.

## ÓRMOS PETRIÉS (Áy Apostoli)

Lies 23½ miles NW of Ák Kafirevs tucked into the corner under Ák Pounda.

### Approach

The entrance is difficult to identify from the N or S. Closer in the light structure at the entrance to the bay will be seen and once into the bay the village and breakwater are easily located. With the *meltemi* there is some swell at the entrance, but once into the bay the water is flat.

*By night* Use the light at the entrance to the bay Fl.5s4M and the lights at the entrance to the harbour: Fl.G.2s3M/Fl.R.2s3M.

*Caution* In the middle of the entrance to the harbour lies a sunken wreck of a small coaster about 35m long. The bow of the wreck faces N and the anchor

**PETRIES**
⊕38°24'·7N 24°11'·8E

winch here is just under 2m underwater. Otherwise it is covered with at least 3m. In calm weather it can be seen underwater. It is prudent to enter either close N or S of the entrance.

### Mooring

Anchor in 4–5m in the bay or go stern-to the breakwater with a long line ashore. The bottom is sand and weed and not the best holding everywhere. There are numerous laid moorings and anchors on the bottom so a trip-line is advised. There are numerous permanent moorings around the bay so beware of floating lines. Good shelter from the *meltemi*.

### Facilities

Several tavernas and mini-markets in the village. Public water tap.

### General

The setting in the large bay is spectacular, but the village is a sorry collection of reinforced concrete houses mostly thrown up in the last few years. Nonetheless it is well worth a visit and the harbour is conveniently placed to break a voyage on the outside of Evia.

## KÍMI (Kímis, Kymi, Paralia)

BA 1571
Imray-Tetra G26

### Approach

*Conspicuous* From the S and E the village of Kími above the harbour is visible from seaward. From the north Nisís Prasoúdha and the lighthouse on it are easily identified and closer in a communication tower and dish on the ridge above the harbour are conspicuous. The harbour breakwater and entrance are easily identified.

*By night* Use the lights on Nisís Prasoúdha

Petries looking WSW       *Hans van Rijn*

**KÍMI**
⊕38°37′·6N 24°07′·6E

(properly Paralia Kímis, Kími being the village on the hill above) are unprepossessing, but the setting is magnificent; the high mountains severed by deep gorges are densely wooded and drop down to long sandy beaches battered by the angry seas that crash onto this coast. It is a pleasant if steep walk up to Kími along the wooded road and the view from the village across the sea to Skíros is spectacular.

## ÁK ÁY VASILIOS ANCHORAGES
38°52′·8N 23°26′·3E

Under Ák Áy Vasilios there are several coves which afford reasonable shelter from the *meltemi*. The best shelter is in the cove directly under the cape itself. Anchor in 4–5m on sand and weed, good holding once in. Alternatively anchor in the adjacent SW cove or off the beach fronting the small resort. The latter two anchorages are more exposed than the cove directly under the cape.

Some provisions and tavernas ashore.

## ÓRMOS LOUTRO

Lies 9 miles SE of Ák Artemision. A reef runs from the NE side of the entrance in a SE direction for approximately 150m. Enter the bay from the S. Anchor in 3–4m in the bay. Sheltered from the *meltemi*. Open to the E and S. Some provisions and tavernas ashore.

**ÓRMOS LOUTRO**
⊕38°56′·0N 23°25′·6E

Fl.5s16M and at the harbour entrance Fl.R.3s3M/Fl.G.3s6M and Fl.R.1·5s3M/Fl.G.1·5s2M.

*Dangers* With the *meltemi* blowing a heavy sea rolls onto the Evia coast. There is invariably a confused swell around Ák Kími and at the entrance to the harbour.

## Mooring
Go stern or bows-to the N mole or the N end of the W quay taking care to avoid the shallow patch. The harbour is often crowded with fishing boats and it can be difficult to find a berth. Care is needed of permanent moorings fouling the bottom. The bottom is mud – excellent holding.

*Shelter* Good shelter from the *meltemi*.

*Authorities* Port police and customs.

## Facilities
*Water* On the quay or in the town.
*Fuel* Near the quay.
*Provisions* Some provisions available. Better shopping in Kími 30 minutes' walk up the hill. Ice available.
*Eating out* Several tavernas near the harbour.
*Other* Bus to Khalkís. Ferry to Skíros.

## General
The grubby harbour and the hamlet around it

# VII. Northern Greece

This section covers the sea area from Thermaïkos Kólpos eastwards to Alexandroupolis in the northeast corner of Greece. It is a sea seldom cruised by yachtsmen, yet it offers some of the grandest scenery and without doubt the finest sandy beaches in Greece. Describe northern Greece to a yachtsman who has cruised solely in southern Greece, in the Saronic, Cyclades, Crete or the Dodecanese, and he will be inclined to think you are describing a country geographically removed from the Mediterranean.

The climate is Balkan rather than Mediterranean, with extreme differences between the summer and winter. The winters are harsh and cold with a high average rainfall and occasionally snow even at sea-level – no place for a yacht to spend the winter. The summers are hot and often described as languid. The terrain is mountainous and densely wooded. Pine, chestnut, plane, oak and poplar are common down to the water's edge. The coastal plains, deposited by the large rivers flowing through the

region, are fertile and cultivated in maize, tobacco, rice, beans, sugar-beet, sunflowers and of course the vine. The fauna is prolific and said to include the jackal, wild cat, boar, roe deer and, in the remote areas, wolves. By the lakes and marshes bird life abounds: vultures, sea eagles, storks, herons, cormorants, pelicans, waders and ducks can be seen in large numbers. Flatfish, mussels and scallops are found in the shallows off the large rivers.

Just as the climate is Balkan rather than Mediterranean, so the peoples of this area are partly of Balkan origin. In ancient times the mountain-dwelling folk were regarded as wild and barbaric by the civilization centred around Athens. Around the coast the Greeks intermarried with the indigenous population and have always been regarded with suspicion by Greeks from the south. The objection by Greece to the adoption of the name Macedonia by the (now) FYRO Macedonia is ironic in that most of Greece used the term as an insult for those who came from northern Greece. Worried that

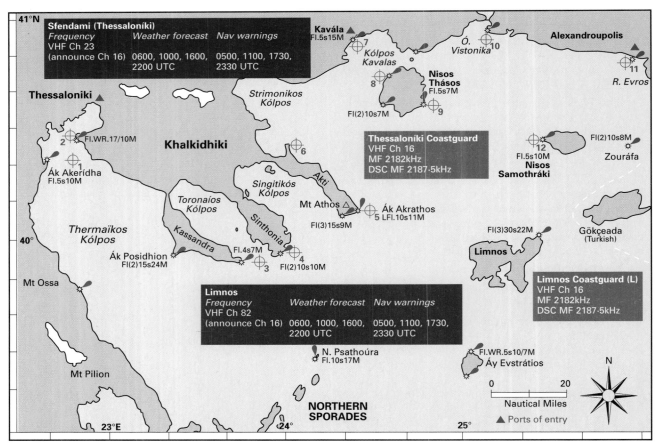

**NORTHERN GREECE**

# Routes

Like other parts of the Aegean, the *meltemi* is the prevailing wind in the summer blowing from the NE–E, but because it is not as consistent nor as strong as further S, it is not such a big component in determining routes in northern Greece. The matter is further complicated because a southerly sea breeze usually blows when the *meltemi* is not developed. This means that getting to northern Greece before the *meltemi* is established further S is the real problem and most people aiming to cruise around northern Greece will try to get up here in the late spring or early summer.

Once in the area yachts really can cruise only along a W–E axis from Thessaloniki to Samothrace. Going S after cruising here is comparatively easy whether you are headed back down to the Saronic or down through the eastern Sporades as you will have the *meltemi* behind you. It is worth remembering that the weather closes down quicker here and winter arrives earlier than further S with depressions winging through in the autumn and temperatures dropping at night to mid-European lows.

## USEFUL WAYPOINTS

⊕1  5M W of Ák Epanomí
(northern end of Thermaïkos
Kólpos)
40°22'·5N 22°48'·5E

⊕2  1M W of Ák Mégalo Émvolon
(Kólpos Thessalonikis)
40°30'·2N 22°48'·0E

⊕3  Southern entrance to
Toronaiós Kólpos
39°55'·2N 23°49'·0E

⊕4  1M E of Ák Psevdhókavos
(Singitikós Kólpos)
39°57'·0N 24°00'·6E

⊕5  1M E of Ák Ákrathos (S end
Ayion Oros)
40°08'·6N 24°25'·0E

⊕6  1M E of Ák Arápis (Kólpos
Ierissou)
40°27'·4N 24°01'·6E

⊕7  Kavála
40°55'·9N 24°24'·3E

⊕8  1M W of Ák Prinos (NW
Thásos)
40°45'·9N 24°32'·9E

⊕9  1M E of Ák Boumbaras (SE
Thásos)
40°36'·4N 24°47'·5E

⊕10 1M S of Ák Fanari (Órmos
Vistonias)
40°56'·5N 25°07'·8E

⊕11 Alexandroupolis
40°50'·2N 25°53'·6E

⊕12 1M W of Ák Akrotíri
(Kamariótissa/Samothrace)
40°28'·6N 25°25'·7E

northern Greece might join the FYRO Macedonia, politicians and others fell over backwards to adopt Macedonian as intrinsically Greek in culture and history when for years they had kept things Macedonian on the fringes.

The region reached its zenith when Alexander the Great toppled the Athenians and made Macedonia the centre of his empire. Not that things changed very much as the young Alexander was a great admirer of the Greeks and their civilization. After his death the power slipped away in the internecine struggles which went on for nearly two centuries. The usual succession of invaders followed the collapse of power, taking a harsher toll than in other regions since this was the first part of Greece they encountered after a long and hungry march over the mountains. The Goths, Huns, Ostrogoths, Bulgars, Slavs and Saracens laid waste to the region. By 1444 the Turks had secured the region and it remained under Turkish rule until 1913. At the beginning of the Second World War a combined Greek, English, Australian and New Zealand force was smashed by the German army and what had been an attempt to hold the German invasion turned into a frantic retreat to the southern beaches. The allied troops were evacuated from beaches on Evia and in the Saronic.

Until recently these northern provinces were little known to outsiders and indeed even Greeks from the southern regions viewed northerners with some suspicion. Today, tourism has opened up the area, especially around Kavala and on Thásos. Yet much of the coast has a solitude and beauty outside high season and most yachtsmen who visit northern Greece come back enchanted by the place.

## Weather patterns

Because there is no outstanding weather pattern for the whole region the weather patterns are described in each section.

# Data

## PORTS OF ENTRY
Thessaloniki
Kavála
Alexandroupolis

## PROHIBITED AREAS
Off the mouth of the Evros river near the Greek/Turkey border. (Yet the local fishing boats frequent the area and sometimes anchor off here whilst fishing.)

## MAJOR LIGHTS
**Ák Sépia** LFl.10s10M
**Ák Dhermatás** Fl(2)10s11M
**Ák Atherídha** Fl.5s10M
**Thessaloniki** (Nisís Kavoúra. Axios)
Fl(2)WRG.12s10-8M
**Thessaloniki** (Yacht Club)
Dirlso.WRG.10s19M
**Thessaloniki** Airport Aero
Al.WG.6s13M

**Ák Mikró Émvolon** Fl(3)G.15s5M
**Ák Megálo Émvolon**
Fl.WR.10s17/10M
**Ák Epanomí** Fl(3)18s6M
**Ák Posidhion** Fl(2)15s24M
**Ák Psevdhókavos** Fl(2)10s10M
**Ák Pínnes** Fl(3)15s9M
**Ák Ákrathos** LFl.10s11M
**Nisídhes Stiliária** N islet Fl.2·5s6M
**Nisís Kavkanás** Fl(3)18s7M
**Ák Kará Ormán** Fl.5s15M
**Ák Ammódhis** Fl(2)10s7M
**Ák Keramotís** Fl.WR.4s6/4M
**Ák Prínos** (Thásos) Fl.5s7M
**Ák Atspas** (Thásos) Fl(2)10s7M
**Ák Boumbouras** (Thásos) Fl.3s7M
**Ák Fanári** Fl.8s6M
**Alexandroupolis** Fl(3)15s24M
**Ák Akrotíri** (Samothráki) Fl.5s10M
**Nisís Zouráfa** (Samothráki)
Fl(2)10s8M

## Quick reference guide

| | Shelter | Mooring | Fuel | Water | Provisioning | Tavernas | Plan |
|---|---|---|---|---|---|---|---|
| Áy Íoannis | B | AB | O | B | C | C | |
| Kamari | B | B | O | B | O | C | |
| Stómion | B | AB | B | A | B | B | • |
| Platamonas | B | AB | B | A | B | B | • |
| Litokhorou | B | AB | B | B | O | C | |
| Áy Katerini | A | AB | A | A | C | B | |
| Limeniskos Pierias | B | C | O | O | O | O | |
| Methóni | C | C | O | B | C | C | |
| N. C. Thessaloníki | A | A | B | A | B | B | |
| Mikró Émvolon | A | A | B | A | B | B | • |
| Thessaloniki Marina (Aretsou) | A | A | B | A | A | A | • |
| Néa Mikhaniona | B | AB | B | A | C | C | • |
| Ák Epanomí | O | C | O | O | O | O | |
| Néa Kallikrátia | B | AB | B | A | B | B | • |
| Néa Moudhania | A | AB | B | A | A | A | • |
| Potidhaias (Portas) | C | C | B | B | B | B | • |
| Porto Sani | A | A | B | A | C | C | |
| Néa Skioni | B | AB | B | A | C | B | • |
| Néa Fokaia | C | C | B | B | B | B | |
| Port Marina | A | AC | O | B | O | C | |
| Paliourion | O | C | O | B | O | C | |
| Nikitas | B | AB | O | B | C | C | |
| Néa Marmarás | B | A | B | A | A | A | • |
| Porto Carras | A | A | B | A | C | A | • |
| L. Toronis | B | C | O | O | O | C | |
| Porto Koufó | A | ABC | B | A | B | B | • |
| Órmos Kalamitsi | C | C | O | O | C | C | |
| Órmos Sikias | B | AC | O | B | C | C | • |
| Órmos Sarti | C | A | B | B | C | C | • |
| Akladhi | B | A | O | O | O | O | • |
| Nisís Dhiaporos | A | C | B | B | C | C | • |
| Panayía | B | AC | B | B | B | B | • |
| Pirgadhíkia | C | C | B | B | C | C | |
| Ammouliani | B | AC | B | B | C | C | • |
| Ammouliani caïque harbour | B | AC | B | B | C | C | • |
| Ouranopolis | O | C | B | B | B | B | |
| Órmos Platí | B | C | O | O | O | O | |
| Néa Rodha | B | AC | B | B | C | C | |
| Ierissós | B | AC | B | B | B | C | • |
| Stratonion | C | C | B | B | C | C | |
| Ó. Olimbiadhos | C | C | B | B | B | C | |
| N Kavkanás | C | C | O | O | O | O | |
| Stavrós | B | AC | B | A | B | B | • |
| Amphipoleos | C | C | O | O | O | O | |
| Órmos Elevtherón | A | ABC | B | B | B | B | • |
| Néa Iraklitsa | B | AB | B | A | B | B | • |
| Kavála | B | A | A | A | A | A | • |
| Keramotís | B | AB | B | B | B | B | • |
| **Thásos** | | | | | | | |
| Port Thasos | A | A | B | A | A | A | • |
| Skála Sotiros | B | AB | O | B | C | C | |
| Kallirakhis | B | A | B | A | B | C | • |
| Limenária | B | C | B | B | A | B | |
| Aliki | B | C | O | B | C | C | • |
| **Mainland coast** | | | | | | | |
| Port Lágos | A | AB | B | A | B | C | • |
| Fanarion | A | AB | B | B | C | C | • |
| Áy Kharalambos | A | AB | O | B | O | C | |
| Mákri | A | AB | O | B | O | C | |
| Alexandroupolis | A | AB | B | A | A | B | • |
| **Samothráki** | | | | | | | |
| Kamariótissa | A | AB | B | A | B | B | • |

# Thermaïkos Kólpos and Thessaloníki

Thermaïkos Kólpos, the Gulf of Thermai, is enclosed by the northern Sporades in the south, by the high mountain range beginning at the Pilion range and extending north to towering Mt Olympus on the west, and by the relatively low-lying Kassandra Peninsula on the east. The gulf terminates in the small Kólpos Thessaloníkis in the north.

The dominating feature of the gulf is without doubt the massive mountain range on the west side stretching from Thessaly to Macedonia. In the south Mt Pilion at 1,545m (5,079ft) is the highest of the Pilion range. Thirty miles further north the first peak of the Olympus range, Mt Ossa (Kissavos), climbs to 1,978m (6,489ft). To the northwest of Mt Ossa the towering peaks of the Olympus Range proper begin: Mt Kato Olimbos (Low Olympus) at 1,587m (5,205ft) stands to the south of Pano Olimbos (High Olympus), the massif being topped by Mítikas (the needle) at 2,911m (9,550ft) and Stefani (the Throne of Zeus) at 2,909m (9,545ft). Surrounding the highest peak are nine other peaks standing over 2,680m (8,800ft). The range is the highest in Greece and peaks are covered in snow from autumn through to late spring.

Although there are other mountain ranges in Greece, also called Olympus, this is the one famous for its association with the gods. Here Zeus ruled and the gods dined, played, drank and argued in what the mortals down below believed was the ultimate in the good life. The first recorded ascent of Mítikas by mortals was as late as 1910 and the range was not properly mapped until 1921. Today the ascent is described as arduous rather than difficult and in fact the major part can be made by four-wheel drive and donkeys.

## Weather patterns in Thermaïkos Kólpos

In the summer months the *meltemi* blows in the gulf from the NE, but not with any consistency. In the S of the gulf it is more regular, normally blowing Force 3–5 although it may blow Force 6–7 on occasions, raising a short steep sea. Although the *meltemi* is not a regular occurrence in the N of the gulf, when it does blow it can be with considerable strength and it has on occasions reached Force 8.

The regular wind in the N half of the gulf, and in the S if the *meltemi* is not blowing, is from the W–SW. This sea breeze gets up about mid-morning, blows Force 2–4, and dies down at night. A light northerly may blow at night.

In the spring and autumn the wind is predominantly from the N although S winds may also occur. In the winter, spring and the autumn a NW wind, locally called the *vardaris* and similar to the *mistral* that blows down the Rhône, may blow down the Axios river at Force 6–8 and may last from a day to a week.

**THERMAÏKOS KÓLPOS**

⊕1  5M W of Ák Epanomí (northern end of Thermaïkos Kólpos)
40°22'·5N 22°48'·5E
⊕2  1M W of Ák Mégalo Émvolon (Kólpos Thessalonikis)
40°30'·2N 22°48'·0E

## Current
In March and April a strong current is reported to set out of the gulf, owing to the melting of snow in the mountains increasing the flow of fresh water into the sea.

## ÁYIOS ÍOANNIS
39°25'·3N 23°09'·7E

A small harbour set into a bight on the coast. A dogleg mole shelters the harbour with the entrance on the S side. The entrance is lit Fl.G.3s3M. There are 3–4m depths in the entrance and 2–3m depths on the outer end of the quay along the mole. The harbour is very small and usually full of local boats, so do not rely on finding a berth here.

Provisions and tavernas ashore.

## KAMARI
39°35'·0N 22°56'·3E

A small harbour with two breakwaters extending out from the steep-to coast. The N longer breakwater is approximately 80m long. There are reported to be 5–6m depths in the entrance and 2–3m depths along the quay on the N breakwater. Go alongside where possible. The inner part of the harbour off the coast is shallow. Adequate protection although strong NE–E winds cause a surge.

Taverna ashore.

## STÓMION
A small harbour lying approximately 7M NW of Ák Dhermatás. The outer breakwater is easily identified. The entrance is lit Fl.G.2s3M/ Fl.R.2s3M. There is also a light a little further NW at Stómion Fl.3s5M.

Go alongside or stern or bows-to under the breakwater. Good shelter. The harbour is a busy fishing port but small yachts can usually find a berth.

Water nearby. Provisions and tavernas ashore.

**STÓMION**
⊕ 39°51'·1N 22°44'·1E

## PLATAMONAS
A small harbour off the town of Platamonas. The buildings on the town are easily identified. The entrance is lit Fl.R.3s3M/Fl.G.3s3M. Go alongside or stern or bows-to the outer end of the inner mole. Good shelter.

Water nearby. Provisions and tavernas ashore.

## LITOKHOROU
40°09'·4N 22°33'·1E

A small fishing harbour with a narrow and tricky entrance. Shoal water extends from the W side of the entrance and with fresh to strong onshore winds the entrance could be dangerous. The entrance is lit Fl.R.3s3M/Fl.G.3s3M. The shoals on the W side of the entrance may occasionally have a small buoy marking them. Stay close to the outer breakwater in the entrance before turning into the mole which forms one side of the retaining wall for the canalised creek that runs into the sea at the entrance.

Go stern or bows-to the mole or anchor and take a long line to the breakwater. Most berths are

**PLATAMONAS**
⊕39°59'·6N 22°37'·6E

Órmos Methóni

occupied by small local craft. Good shelter.

Fuel on the main coast road running past the harbour. Taverna and café nearby.

## ÁYIOS KATERINI

40°15'·7N 22°35'·9E

A small fishing harbour. Care is needed in the entrance of the shoal water off the outer end of the N breakwater. The entrance is lit Fl.R.3s3M/Fl.G.3s3M. Anchor and take a line to the E breakwater. Reasonable shelter although northerlies look as though they would blow straight in. The inner basin is very small and full of local boats.

Water on the quay. Fuel on the quay. Provisions and tavernas ashore.

## LIMENISKOS PIERIAS

40°22'·8N 22°38'E

Lying 1¾ NW of Ák Atherídha, this small-craft basin affords good shelter from all winds. The approach channel is reported to be dredged to 1·8m and the inner basin reported to have depths of 5m. The harbour entrance is lit Fl.R.3s3M/Fl.G.3s3M. Approach from the NE and anchor in convenient depths.

## ÓRMOS METHONI

Lying 6½ miles NW of Ák Atherídha is the open bay of Methóni which is used by fishing boats. Anchor in the SW corner. Care is needed as shallows run a considerable distance out from the coast. Tavernas ashore.

## THESSALONÍKI (Salonika)

BA 2070

The large built-up city is visible from a considerable distance off. Large cargo ships anchored in the bay and the commercial docks are conspicuous. A yacht should head for the yacht marina at Aretsou on the S side of Ák Mikró Emvolon.

**THESSALONIKI**
⊕40°35'·2N 22°55'·2E

## NAUTICAL CLUB OF THESSALONÍKI

40°35'·4N 22°56'·5E

*Note* The club should be contacted in advance for a berth.

A private club harbour on the N side of Ák Mikró Émvolon. Care is needed in the approaches because of shoal water and rocks off the coast. Make the approach from the NW and then through the narrow entrance channel between the end of the breakwater and a beacon. There are 1–2·5m depths inside. Berth where directed.

The yacht club has a wonderful and quite exclusive clubhouse and restaurant overlooking the bay. There is also a small yard here where some yacht repairs can be arranged.

Nautical Club of Thessaloníki ☎ 429 945.

## MIKRÓ ÉMVOLON YACHT HARBOUR

### Approach

Directly under Ák Mikró Émvolon is a yacht harbour (formerly a fishing harbour) that appears to offer good shelter. The harbour is difficult to spot from the distance as the outer breakwater is covered in grass and blends in with the slopes behind. A small white chapel on the end of the inner breakwater will be seen when closer in.

*By night* The end of the outer breakwater is lit F.R.

### Mooring

*Note* The harbour is private and it is best to enquire for a berth in advance.

*Berth* Where directed. Catwalks run out from around the outer breakwater. Two pontoons extend out from the shore. Some laid moorings.

*Shelter* Excellent shelter.

*Authorities* Harbourmaster ☎ 414 493/454 111.

### Facilities

*Services* Water and electricity at or near most berths.
*Fuel* Can be delivered by mini-tanker.
*Repairs* Some yacht repairs can be arranged.
*Provisions* Good shopping in Aretsou suburb above.
*Eating out* Tavernas ashore and above in Aretsou.

### General

You get the feeling that this harbour has an ancient pedigree somewhere under those grassy banks, but there seems little consensus on what it is amongst the locals, apart from: 'it is very old'.

**MIKRÓ ÉMVOLON YACHT HARBOUR**
⊕40°34′·86N 22°56′·29E WGS84

## THESSALONÍKI MARINA (Aretsou)

### Approach

A church on the hill and a radio mast behind the marina are conspicuous. Closer in, the outer breakwater and the yachts in the marina can be easily seen.

*By night* Use the lights on Ák Megálo Émvolon Fl.WR.10s17/10M (red sector covers 335°–025°), Ák Mikró Émvolon Fl(3)G.15s5M and at the

Yacht harbour under Ák Mikró Émvolon and just W of Aretsou marina

entrance to the marina Fl.G.2s5M/Fl.R.2s5M. The radio mast behind the marina is lit with F.R lights.

*VHF* Ch 09 for marina office.

*Dangers* With the *meltemi* blowing there are strong gusts into Órmos Thessaloníkis.

### Mooring

*Data* 300 berths. Visitors' berths. Max LOA 30m. Depths 3–5m.

A marina attendant will direct you to a berth. Moorings are laid and you pick up one of the small plastic buoys floating on the surface.

*Shelter* Excellent all-round shelter although W–SW winds cause an uncomfortable slop at some berths. Yachts are wintered afloat in the marina.

*Authorities* Port police and marina staff at the marina. Charge band 2.

### Facilities

*Services* Water and electricity on the quay. Showers and toilets.
*Fuel* On the quay.
*Repairs* A crane can be arranged to haul yachts out onto the hard by the marina. Most mechanical repairs. Electrical repairs. Chandlers and hardware shops in the city.
*Provisions* Most provisions can be found in the vicinity of the marina. Better shopping in the nearby suburbs. Ice can be ordered.

**THESSALONIKI MARINA (ARETSOU)**
⊕40°34′·6N 22°56′·5E

Thessaloníki Marina looking SE towards the W entrance

*Eating out* Taverna in the marina and others up on the main road above.

*Other* PO and OTE in the city. Banks. Greek gas and *Camping Gaz*. A gas filling station on the outskirts of the city. Hire cars and motorbikes. A regular bus runs every 15 minutes from just above the marina into the city. Buses to Kavala and Athens. Ferries to Limnos, Lésvos and Khíos. Internal flights to Ioannina, Limnos and Athens. International flights to some European countries.

### General

Thessaloníki, or Salonika as it is still known to many, is the second largest city in Greece. Although it has an ancient pedigree, the modern office buildings and apartment blocks radiating from the centre effectively shroud this past. I must confess to an instant dislike of Thessaloníki – it is a noisy industrial city where the industry has covered the waters of the bay in a black oily scum and poisoned the fish. As in Athens it is wise in any fish restaurant to enquire as to whether the fish is local. If it is don't touch it.

The marina is sited outside the badly polluted bay in the green and wooded suburb of Aretsou. In the city the Archaeological Museum houses important finds from Neolithic to Byzantine times from all over northern Greece.

### NÉA MIKHANIÓNA (Kerasia)

#### Approach
A fishing harbour in the large bay under Ák Megálo Émvolon.

*By night* The entrance is lit F.G.3M/F.R.3M.

#### Mooring
Go stern or bows-to the quay in the S corner. Alternatively you may have to find a berth alongside a fishing boat.

*Shelter* Reasonable shelter although northerlies would probably cause some slop.

#### Facilities
Water on the quay. Fuel on the outskirts of the village. Provisions and tavernas.

**NÉA MIKHANIONA**
⊕40°28'·3N 22°50'·8E

*Note* A short distance S of the harbour is a yard which hauls yachts.

### ÁKRA EPANOMÍ
Ák Epanomí light 40°22'·5N 22°53'·5E

The termination of a low-lying neck of land approximately 8½ miles SE of Ák Megálo Émvolon. The cape is marked by a light structure Fl(3)18s6M and a light buoy Fl.G at the outer end of the shoals extending from the cape. Anchor on either side of the cape according to the wind direction. Open to the W.

### NÉA KALLIKRÁTIA
#### Approach
The small resort town of Néa Kallikrátia lies approximately 10M SE of Ák Epanomí. The harbour sits under a cliff close NW of the village. The apartment blocks on top of the cliff are conspicuous.

**NÉA KALLIKRÁTIA**
⊕40°18′·55N 23°03′·49E WGS84

Néa Kallikratia looking S

*By night* The end of the mole is lit Fl.G.3s3M.

*Dangers* Although the immediate approaches are free of dangers, the inner half of the harbour is shallow and also has the remains of an old mole underwater. Care needed.

### Mooring

The harbour is usually full of fishing boats. Try in the SE corner or see if you can go alongside a fishing boat.

*Shelter* Reasonable shelter although strong westerlies could make it uncomfortable and possibly untenable.

### Facilities

Water on the quay. Fuel on the road running out of town. Provisions and tavernas in the village.

### General

Néa Kallikrátia is something of a Greek resort which for some reason has also attracted the Russians looking for some sun. It is something of a pour-and-fill sort of place, but the fishing harbour is tucked away from the beach and the bodies.

## NÉA MOUDHANIA

### Approach

A village lying approximately 5M NW of the Portas Canal. The buildings of the town are easily identified and the harbour is situated in front of it. A church and cupola are conspicuous in the town. There is often a cargo ship or two unloading here which helps to identify where the harbour is.

*By night* The outer entrance is lit Fl.R.3s5M/Fl.G.3s3M and the entrance to the inner basin Fl.R.3s3M/Fl.G.3s3M. Although the characteristics are the same for the entrance and inner basin, a little care in the approach should sort out what is where.

### Mooring

The quay in the outer port is for commercial ships. Proceed into the basin and try to find a berth in the NW corner or in the SE corner.

*Shelter* Good all-round shelter.

*Authorities* Port police and customs.

### Facilities

Water on the quay. Good shopping for provisions in town. Tavernas and cafés including a good internet café near the waterfront. PO. OTE. Banks. Bus to Thessaloníki.

**NÉA MOUDHANIA**
⊕40°14′·30N 23°16′·63E WGS84

Néa Moudhania looking SW into the inner basin

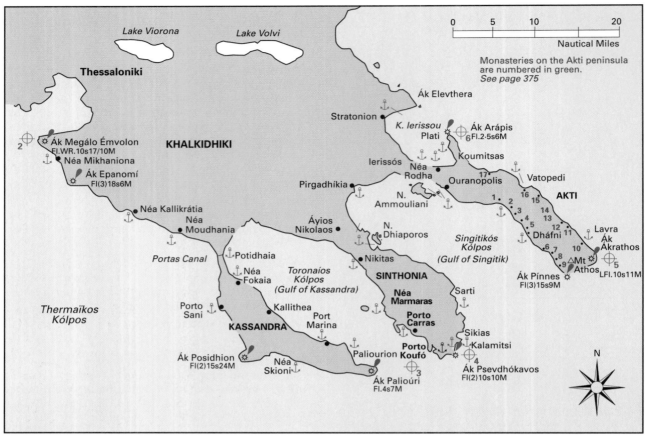

**KHALKIDHIKI**

⊕2 1M W of Ák Megálo Émvolon (Kólpos Thessaloniki)
40°30'·2N 22°48'·0E

⊕3 Southern entrance to Toronaíos Kólpos 39°55'·2N 23°49'·0E

⊕4 1M E of Ák Psevdhókavos (Singitikós Kólpos) 39°57'·0N
24°00'·6E

⊕5 1M E of Ák Ákrathos (S end Ayion Oros) 40°08'·6N 24°25'·0E

⊕6 1M E of Ák Arápis (Kólpos Ierissou) 40°27'·4N 24°01'·6E

## General

Néa Moudhania is more of a working town than a resort and all the more pleasing for that. It serves as a hub for the Kassandra Peninsula and the agricultural interior. The waterfront is a busy place, busy with commerce that is, rather than tourism, and in the harbour you are pretty well in the middle of town.

# Khalkidhiki

### (Halkidiki, Chalcidice)

The Khalkidhiki peninsula (Khalkidhiki Khersónisos) is the most prominent geographical feature of Macedonia. It is like a hand reaching down into the northern Aegean with three small peninsulas forming the fingers: Kassandra, Sinthonia, and Akti or Mt Athos. On the west side the Khalkidhiki is low-lying, with the highest point on the Kassandra peninsula rising to a miserly 353m (1,158ft). The rest of the Khalkidhiki is mountainous, with Mt Athos rising sheer from the sea to 2,033m (6,670ft) at the southern end of the Akti peninsula. The countryside is densely wooded – mostly with pine, but also with olive, hazel, oak

and poplar. In many places the pine and poplar grow down to the water's edge and shade what are, in my opinion, the finest sandy beaches in Greece.

The Khalkidhiki received its name from the colonies established there from Khalkís in Evia around 800 BC. The most important city to emerge from the colonisation was Olynthos, situated at the head of Toronaíos Kólpos (also called Kólpos Kassandras and the Gulf of Sinthonia). It reached its zenith in the fifth and fourth centuries BC. In 480 BC Xerxes gathered his troops and ships here for the assault on Thessaly and Attica. Prior to this he had a canal cut across the narrow neck of land connecting the Akti peninsula to the rest of the Khalkidhiki to avoid the terrible storms encountered around Mt Athos. A few earth scars are all that remain of the canal-cut today.

## The Akti Peninsula
### (Khersónisos Akti, Áyios Oros)

This rugged peninsula has for over 10 centuries existed as a world unto itself. Divorced from the modern world, the holy community has no roads or electricity and few telephones. The medieval monasteries occupy spectacular sites on rocky bluffs and precipitous cliff-sides and have been likened to Tibetan monasteries such as the Potala of Lhasa. Time is still reckoned by the Julian calendar (13 days behind the Roman calendar) and the day is ruled by the Byzantine clock with hours of variable length.

Females are not allowed to set foot in the monasteries and a yacht with women on board is not allowed to approach closer than 500m from the shores of the peninsula. In former times the rule was stricter, formulated by Constantine Monomachus in 1060: access was denied to `every woman, every female animal, every child, and smooth-faced person'. Although officially the rule is still in force, female animals can now be found in the community and visitors do not have to be bearded.

The monasteries are divided into coenobite and idiorrhythmic communities. Coenobite monasteries are communal and the members are clothed alike and live from a common pool of resources. In the idiorrhythmic monasteries the members live apart and provide the clothes and food from their own resources. As well as 20 monasteries there are hermits (Anchorites) who live by themselves in what often seem to be inaccessible cells (particularly on the southern slopes of Mt Athos), the hermitage of two or three hermits (Sarabaites) and vagabond monks (Gyrovakes).

Although the peninsula is geographically and politically a part of Greece, it has administrative autonomy which includes financial and judicial authority. Monks of any race are accepted (apart from Greeks, the community includes Russians, Bulgarians, Serbs and Romanians) and on entering the holy community they become Greek subjects.

Without doubt the best way to see the Akti peninsula is from the sea. The medieval monasteries clinging to the cliffs at the edge of the wild interior (jackals are reported to be common) belong to a world that was bypassed by our modern age a long time ago. To visit the interior it is easiest to go on a conducted tour, although a more sedate visit to a single monastery captures more of the spirit of the place and is more convenient for a yacht on this desolate shore.

Permits are issued by the Grafio Proskyniton Ayiou Orous, the Pilgrims Office for Mount Athos, at the First Floor on Konstandinou Karamanli 14, Thessaloníki. ☎ 031 833 733 Fax (031) 861 811. You must take your passport although you can fax for a permit if you fax the relevant pages of your passport to them. Given the small number of permits (10 per day in 2000) issued to heterodox foreigners, you are unlikely to get a permit around the time of the application and will probably just have to wait for a date to come up. Once you have your permit go to the Grafio Proskyniton (Pilgrims Bureau) at Ouranopolis for the Dhiamonitirion (a fee, typically 10,000Dx, is charged) which entitles you to stay for four days on the Akti Peninsula. Many of the monasteries are often booked in advance so do not depend on staying in your chosen monastery, especially in high season. It is important to remember at all times that you are a guest here and for Greek Orthodox believers, this is the Holy Mountain.

A permit is not necessary to sail around the peninsula, but of course you cannot land. Ierissos is the safest place to leave a yacht if taking the local ferry to the community.

## Weather patterns around the Khalkidhiki

In the summer the *meltemi* blows with considerably less force than it does further south. Normally it will blow from the NE–E at Force 2–4, but often it does not blow for days and even weeks on end. In spring and early summer there will often be SE winds but these rarely blow more than Force 3–4.

With strong winds from any direction, caution must be exercised in the vicinity of the Akti peninsula where there will be strong gusts off the high mountains. Around Mt Athos particular care must be taken as the gusts can be violent and the seas disturbed around Ák Pínnes and Ák Akrathos, although Xerxes was being over-cautious digging a canal to get his ships safely into Singitikos Kólpos.

### PORTAS CANAL (Dhiórix Neas Potidhaias)

This shallow canal cuts the Kassandra peninsula off from the mainland. It is over ½ mile long and has a minimum width of 36m. A bridge spans the canal with a vertical clearance of 18m. The canal is dredged to 2·5m minimum depth, but is subject to silting particularly at the W entrance and at the edges. The W entrance is lit: Fl.R.2s3M and Fl.G.2s3M. The E entrance is lit: Fl.G.2s3M and Fl.R.2s3M.

At the W end there is a short quay usually occupied by local fishing boats and a small basin too shallow for most craft. At the E end there is a small basin in the canal where a small yacht might find a berth. It is shallow around the edges. The village of Portas or Potidhaia is on the S side of the canal. You can anchor off the E end of the canal where there are convenient depths and, at least in the morning, it is usually calm. Fuel station nearby. Provisions and tavernas.

### PORTO SANI

40°05'·5N 23°18'·4E

At the Hotel Porto Sani on the W side of the Kassandra Peninsula, a small basin has been

Portas Canal looking W from the bridge

**PORTAS CANAL**
⊕₁ 40°11'·77N 23°19'·30E WGS84
⊕₂ 40°11'·81N 23°20'·08E WGS84

excavated with a dredged channel to it. The channel is reported to have 1·5m depths and the basin 1–1·5m depths. Good shelter inside. With any sort of onshore wind it would be unwise to enter and even small yachts are advised to reconnoitre beforehand.

Water on the docks. Provisions and tavernas ashore.

## NÉA SKIONI

A fishing harbour lying approximately halfway between Ák Posidhion and Ák Paliouri on the SW coast of the Kassandra Peninsula. The approach is clear of dangers. Go stern or bows-to the stubby pier running out from the mole wherever there is a berth. The harbour is usually full of fishing boats and you may have to negotiate a berth alongside a fishing boat. Reasonable shelter although westerlies would make it uncomfortable and possibly untenable at some berths.

Water on the quay. Fuel nearby in town. Provisions and tavernas ashore.

Néa Skioni is a modest resort with the fishing fleet to back it up when the tourists go home. The setting is wonderful although you can't help feeling that you walk into a different, less fishy, world when you leave the end of the harbour mole to go into town.

**NÉA SKIONI**
⊕39°56'·79N 23°31'·62E WGS84

# Toronaiós Kólpos

## NÉA FOKAIA

A small resort about 8 miles SE of Portas Canal. A square stone tower on the bluff above the bight is conspicuous. Local fishing boats are kept on moorings in the bight on the N side of the bluff with the tower. There is a short jetty off the village. Provisions and tavernas ashore.

The setting is attractive although it is a pity about some of the new non-architecture ashore.

## KALLITHEA

A small resort. You can anchor off in calm weather. PO. Bank. Provisions and tavernas.

## PORT MARINA

Entrance channel 39°59'·02N 23°39'·96E WGS84

A lagoon with a narrow and treacherous approach channel. The channel has 1·5–1·8m depths although the channel and the depths change with winter storms. There are rocks extending seawards either side of the channel. The best thing to do here is take a dinghy to reconnoitre the channel. In any sort of onshore breeze the channel should not be attempted. Once into the lagoon there are 1·5–3m depths between the entrance channel and the catwalks around the eastern side. Anchor and take a long line ashore or see if you can use one of the catwalks around the lagoon. A number of yachts are kept here permanently. All-round shelter.

Hotel, taverna and bar on the main road behind the lagoon. The large lagoon is wonderful, with sandy beaches along the coastal flat and mature pines all around. There are usually only a few local tourists and they all depart at night. I assume the place is called Port Marina because it will eventually become so.

## PALIOURION (Kannavitsa Bay)

N corner 39°57'·85N 23°40'·50E WGS84

An open anchorage SE of Port Marina. Anchor in the N corner off the camping ground where there is a beach bar or off the hotel. There is a pier in the S corner with 2·5m depths reported off the end. You should be ready to move out with any sort of onshore breeze. The large hotel on the beach has an abandoned look to it. Open to all sectors E. Anchor at the head of the bay or off a pier which is reported to have 2·5m depths at its extremity. Fuel in the town and some provisions available.

## NIKITAS

40°13'·1N 23°39'·9E

A small resort under steep slopes on the E side of the gulf. There is a small fishing harbour here with 2–4m depths reported under the mole, but it is usually crowded with local boats. See if you can get a berth in the harbour or anchor off.

Provisions and tavernas ashore.

## NÉA MARMARÁS

### Approach

The harbour lies under the S side of Ák Néa Marmarás. The buildings of the town 3 miles NE of Nisís Kelifos (Khelona Island) are easily identified. A church on the waterfront is conspicuous.

*By night* The entrance is lit: by a Fl.R.1·5s3M and a Q.R on the end of the wave-breaker pontoon.

*Dangers* The wave-breaker pontoon is very low in the water and difficult to distinguish until close to.

### Mooring

Go stern or bows-to where directed or on a convenient berth on one of the pontoons. There are laid moorings tailed to a buoy to pick up. It is very tight for manoeuvring around and between the pontoons and you will need to take care to avoid the other yachts and moorings.

*Shelter* Good shelter although the sea breeze that often blows up the gulf can make it a bit rolly in here despite the wave-breaker pontoon. The breeze dies down at night so you get a good night's sleep.

*Authorities* Port police. Harbour attendant. Charge band 2.

### Facilities

*Services* Water and electricity on the pontoons.
*Fuel* A mini-tanker can deliver to the quay.
*Repairs* Limited repairs only.
*Provisions* Good shopping for all provisions.
*Eating out* Good tavernas including good fish restaurants around the waterfront.

Néa Marmaras looking SE from above the yacht pontoons

*Other* PO. OTE. Bank. Greek gas and *Camping Gaz*. Hire cars and motorbikes. Bus to Thessaloníki. Hydrofoil to the Northern Sporades.

### General

There was probably a settlement here in ancient times pre-dating the Byzantine settlement that no doubt made use of the natural harbour. Greeks from Turkey were resettled here in 1922 in one of the exchanges of populations and the new village was christened Néa Marmarás. It has developed into a large resort town and the original village around the

**NÉA MARMARÁS**
⊕40°05'·46N 23°47'·08E WGS84

natural harbour now climbs up and over the steep-to hummock behind the harbour. It is a pleasing spot, the sort of place where you take an evening promenade along the waterfront to view the bar or restaurant for the night, nod politely to the locals and ponder whether you will or won't leave on the morrow.

## PORTO CARRAS MARINA (Porto Karra)

### Approach

*Conspicuous* From the N and W the two hyper-hotels and the buildings of the marina complex can be easily distinguished from the town of Néa Marmara. From the S only the town of Néa Marmara will be seen until you are into the bay.

*By night* The entrance is lit: F.R.3M and F.G.3M. There are leading lights through the entrance on 095°: front F.Y.3M and rear F.Y.3M.

*VHF* Ch 09 for marina office.

*Dangers* With strong NW–W–SW winds there is a disturbed swell at the entrance but it is quiet inside.

*Note* The entrance channel is usually marked by 4 pairs of small red plastic buoys which are not lit.

Porto Carras Marina looking SE     *Photo Porto Carras*

### Mooring

*Data* 200 berths. Visitors' berths. Max LOA 45m. Depths 4–5m.

Go stern or bows-to where directed. There are laid moorings tailed to the quay or a buoy. Do not use your own anchor.

**PORTO CARRAS**
⊕40°04′·08N 23°47′·05E

Portas Canal looking W from the bridge

*Shelter* Good all-round shelter.

*Authorities* Harbourmaster and marina staff. Charge band 3.

*Note*
1. The harbour is mostly dredged to a least depth of 5m.
2. In the near future it is planned to build a mini-breakwater on the N side and install pontoons where shown to increase the capacity of the marina.

## Facilities

*Services* Water. Electricity (220V). Showers and toilets. Laundry service.

*Fuel* A mini-tanker can deliver.

*Repairs* It is planned to install a 50-ton travel-hoist. There will be hardstanding for around 35 yachts. Covered workshops. Some yacht repairs can be carried out including mechanical and engineering repairs.

*Provisions* Limited. Go to Néa Marmara.

*Eating out* Several restaurants and tavernas around the harbour.

*Other* PO. Exchange at the hotel. Bank in Néa Marmara. Medical centre. Golf course. Tennis. Horse riding centre. Telephone and fax service. Hire cars and bikes. Taxis. *Caïque* ferry to Néa Marmara.

Contact Porto Carras, Sithonia, 63081 Khalkidhiki
☎ 0375 71381 *Fax* 0375 72126

## General

Porto Carras marina was developed along the lines of the Languedoc–Roussillon marinas in the S of France by the Greek shipping magnate John Carras – hence the name. As well as two hyper-hotels, the marina complex houses squash and tennis courts, a swimming pool, theatre, conference centre, casino, restaurants, bars and an array of boutiques and other shops.

When Porto Carras was built, a model farm was developed nearby and improved wine-making facilities were imported. The wines produced here with improved techniques are now excellent and the reds and whites bottled under the appellation *Porto Carras Domaine* are well worth sampling.

## UNNAMED COVES S OF PORTO CARRAS

Less than a mile S of Porto Carras are two small coves with sandy beaches at the head. Open only to the W, they offer sufficient protection for an overnight stay in the summer. The more southerly of the two has a short quay where a small yacht can moor stern-to.

## LIMÍN TORONIS

Limín Toronis is an inlet at the head of Órmos Toronis, the bay on the S side of Ák Papadhia. Good shelter from northerlies in the bay which is open only S.

## PÓRTO KOUFÓ

### Approach

*Conspicuous* From the distance the entrance to the landlocked bay is difficult to make out. A white hut on Ák Laimos (½ mile S of Ák Pagona) and Peristeronisi are conspicuous and closer in the

Pórto Koufó looking SSW towards the entrance    *Nigel Patten*

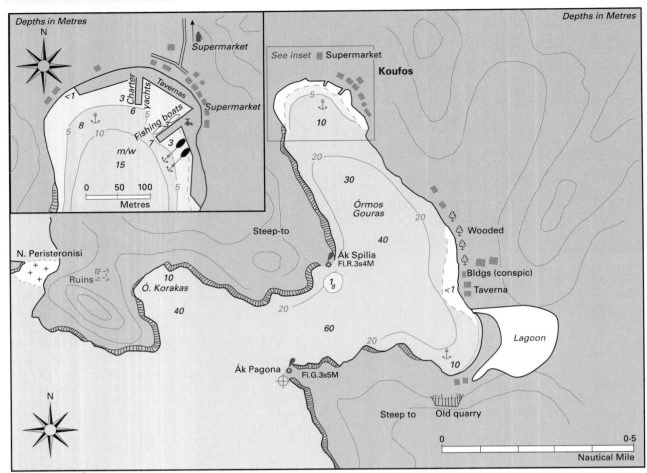

**PÓRTO KOUFÓ**
⊕39°57′·6N 23°55′E

wooded plain and the houses on the E side of the bay can be seen.

*By night* Use the lights on Ák Pagona Fl.G.3s5M and Ák Siliá Fl.R.3s4M.

*Dangers* With strong offshore winds there are severe gusts off the high land in the approaches to Porto Koufó.

### Mooring

Anchor in the bay in 7–10m. The N and NW of the bay have laid moorings making it difficult to find a place to anchor. Alternatively go bows-to the quay just S of the E pier where there are 2·5m about 10m off and 1–2m about 2m off the quay. Care is needed of ballasting extending out from the quay. Care is also needed in selecting a spot – reconnoitre first. Larger yachts may be able to negotiate a berth on the N pier which is used by a charter company. The bottom is mud and weed – good holding once the anchor is through the weed.

*Shelter* Good shelter although there can be violent gusts with strong S winds.

### Facilities

*Water* On the pier, though it is reported not to be potable.

*Fuel* On the road out to Néa Marmara. A mini-tanker can deliver.

*Provisions* Supermarket near the quay and another on the road out of town. Ice available.

*Eating out* Tavernas ashore, several with good fresh fish.

*Other* Metered telephone. Greek gas and *Camping Gaz*. Bus to Néa Marmarás and Thessaloníki.

### General

Porto Koufó must be one of the most magnificent natural harbours in the Mediterranean. Sheer red cliffs at the entrance open up to the large landlocked bay bordered by poplars and cultivated fields. What was a small fishing hamlet now caters for a few tourists in the summer. In the winter the harbour is a base for tunny fishing boats working around the Khalkidhikí.

## Singitikós Kólpos

### ÓRMOS KALAMITSI (Porto)

39°59′·0N 24°00′·0E

Two miles N of Ák Psevdhókavos is a bay with a number of above-water rocks in the entrance. In the southernmost cove a number of boats are kept on laid moorings in the summer. Anchor just clear of the moorings in 5–6m on sand. Some shelter from northerlies if you are tucked far enough up into the corner.

Limited provisions and tavernas ashore. A camping ground around the wonderful beach tucked in under the rocky coast.

## ÓRMOS SIKIAS

### Approach

Six miles N of Ák Psevdhókavos lies the large bay of Órmos Sikias. The rocks of Ifaloi Kepes (Kepes Reef) lying off the S entrance point can be identified and closer in the windmills and the buildings at the head of the bay are conspicuous. A new building is reported to obscure the windmills but should in itself be easy to identify.

*By night* The S entrance point, Ák Ádholo, is lit Fl.1·5s4M, as is the end of the breakwater at Skála Sikias Fl.R.3s3M, but a night entrance is not really recommended.

*Dangers*
1. Ifaloi Kepes. An above-water islet and reef borders the coast off the S entrance point for up to 700m off the coast.
2. Ifalos Sikias. A reef with 2·8m over it lying about 600m SE of Ák Sikias, the N entrance point. There is also an islet with a reef extending SSE for 250m from it closer to the N coast and a reef off Ák Sikias itself.

### Mooring

1. Anchor in either of the two coves on the N side of the bay. The bottom is sand and weed, mostly good holding. Reasonable shelter from northerlies but open to the E–SE.
2. Anchor at the head of the bay off the wonderful sandy beach around the head of the bay. Open NE–E.
3. *Skála Sikias* Anchor in the cove off the village in 3–5m or go bows-to the short mole if there is room. There are 3m depths at the extremity of the mole. Good shelter behind the mole from most winds.

Sikias looking NE to the stubby mole

*Shelter* The bay suffers from an uncomfortable swell rolling in after NE winds except if you are tucked in behind the mole at Skála Sikias.

### Facilities

Water and several tavernas at Skála Sikias. Other tavernas around the beach at the head of the bay. A mini-market and fuel on the main road back from the beach.

### General

The beaches around the bay are composed of wonderful fine golden sand shaded by pine and poplar, the stuff tour operators' dreams are made of. Unfortunately much of the beach-front has been turned into a dusty camp site and caravan park. Skála Sikias remains a wonderful little cove away from the beach.

## ÓRMOS SARTI

An open bay that affords some protection from N winds in the NW corner off the village. Care is needed of above water rocks and a reef just NW of the bay. Provisions and tavernas ashore. Fuel on the main road to the N.

ÓRMOS SIKIAS
⊕1 40°02'·5N 24°00'·8E
⊕2 40°02'·07N 23°59'·75E WGS84

AKLADHI
⊕ 40°06'·18N 23°59'·04E WGS84

## AKLADHI

A cove immediately N of Sarti. There is a small fishing harbour here and small yachts may find room to go bows-to behind the mole. Care is needed of the underwater rocks off the end of the mole and on the coast side of the entrance. Go alongside or stern or bows-to wherever you can squeeze in. Good shelter tucked under the mole.

Water on the mole. Taverna near the camping site on the coast.

Akladhi N of Sarti

## PORTO ZOGRAFU

A tiny inlet at the bottom of precipitous slopes between Ák Rigas and the Nisís Dhiaporos. It could be useful as a lunch stop in calm weather only. Taverna ashore and also, unfortunately, a caravan park.

## NISÍS DHIAPOROS AND ADJACENT ANCHORAGES (Dhimítri Island)

### Approach

*S Passage* This leads into Órmos Mesopanayia between Ák Xifaras and Ák Pláka, the SE extremity of Nisís Dhiaporos on about 240°. A reef extends N from Ák Xifaras with Petronisi and Kalamonisia islets marking the extremity of the reef. A stubby beacon on the reef should be left to port. A reef extends S and E from Ák Pláka with an above-water rock near the outer end. The S Passage lies between the last-mentioned rock and the Kalamonisia islets, all of which are clearly visible by day. There is 4m least depth in the fairway.

*N Passage* Leads into Órmos Dhimítri between Nisís Ambelitsi and Nisís Peristeri. A reef extends E and S from Peristeri with the SE edge of the reef marked by an above-water rock. A narrow rocky reef fringes Ák Zavos, the NW extremity of Nisís

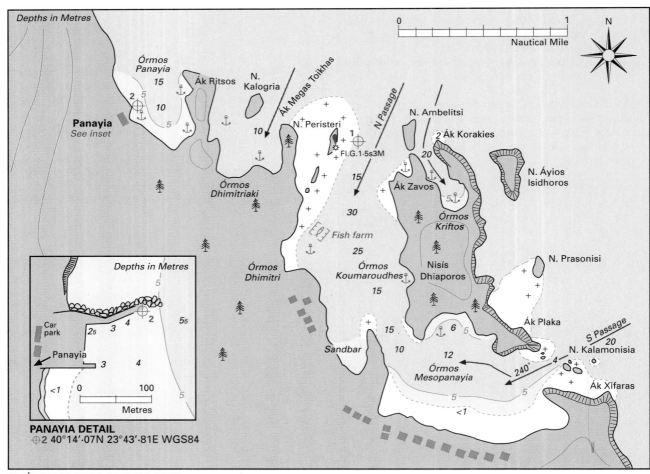

**NISÍS DHIAPOROS ANCHORAGES**
⊕₁ 40°13'·7N 23°46'·0E
⊕₂ 40°14'·07N 23°43'·81E WGS84

Dhiaporos, and the N Passage is between this reef and the reef surrounding Peristeri.

*Caution* On the accompanying plan it is impossible to show the reefs and above-water rocks in great detail. A yacht should proceed with caution and not attempt an approach by night. By day the reefs and above-water rocks are clearly visible and the approaches are in practice more straightforward than the accompanying notes might appear to indicate.

### Mooring
There are numerous anchorages around Nisís Dhiaporos and the adjacent coast. The bottom is mostly mud or sand – good holding.

1. *Órmos Mesopanayia* Anchor on the N side under Nisís Dhiaporos in 5–6m on mud. The S side of the bay is mostly shallow and a yacht should keep close to Nisís Dhiaporos when passing through Órmos Mesopanayia.
2. *Órmos Koumaroudhes* Anchor off the bight on Nisís Dhiaporos.
3. *Órmos Kriftos* The bay on the N side of Nisís Dhiaporos. Enter the bay on the E side of Nisís Ambelitsi. Anchor in 5–6m near the head of the bay or 8–10m in the bight on the E side about halfway down.
4. *Órmos Dhimitri* Anchor in the bight on the E side of the headland which encloses Órmos Kriftos in 5–6m. Alternatively anchor off the W side further down in 5–8m on mud. There is a fish farm here but still room to anchor.
5. *Órmos Dhimitriaki* Enter the bay between Nisís Kalogria and Ák Megas Toikhas. Anchor where convenient. Shelter is better than it looks in here with the normal summer settled weather.
6. *Panayía* Straightforward with good depths throughout. The best shelter is in the NE corner of the bay, but some care must be exercised as the bottom is foul with laid moorings. Anchor in 4–6m clear of the moorings. Good shelter.

On the W of the bay there is a pier used by a ferry that makes daily trips to the Akti peninsula. It can be used when the ferry is not in.

Anchorage in Órmos Dhimítriaki looking E to Nisís Kalogria

Panayía mole looking N

### Facilities
*Dhimítri* Water from a camp site and a mini-market.
*Panayía* Water on the pier. Fuel in the village. Most provisions can be obtained – mini-market near the pier. Ice available. Several tavernas and cafés. The village of Áyios Nikólaos about 2½km inland has additional facilities.

### General
Behind the island the water is a little murky from the river draining into it, but everywhere else the water is clear, a wonderful turquoise over sand and rock. Numerous villas and a few small hotels have been built around the coastal flat at Mesopanayia, but apart from that the coast is little built up. Because Panayía is used as the mainland port for the ferry to the Athos Peninsula and also by tripper boats, the little hamlet is overpowered by coaches waiting to drop off or pick up tour groups. Fortunately they all disappear off to Thessaloníki by the evening and the hamlet is once again a quiet little place. Around the various anchorages you are, thankfully, miles away from all this hubbub.

### PIRGADHÍKIA
40°20'·2N 23°43'E (Q.R.3M)
A small village at the head of the gulf in the NW corner. There is a small pier off the village with a light on the extremity (Q.R.3M). Fishing boats and a few small pleasure craft are kept on permanent moorings in the cove on the W side of the hummock the village is built on. Shelter is better than it looks although the anchorage should not be used in unsettled weather. Provisions and tavernas ashore. The little village is a gem of a place and well worth the effort to get up to.

### NISÍS AMMOULIANI
Lying in the NE corner of Singitikós Kólpos, this island offers a number of good anchorages according to the wind direction. Off the NW extremity of the island lie the islets Nisídhes Xiropotamina and off the SE extremity the islets Nisídhes Dhrénia. In the channel between the

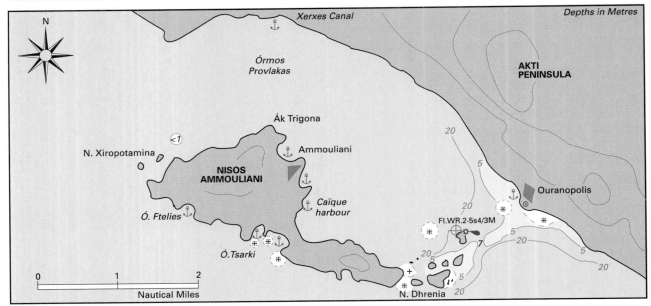

**NISÍS AMMOULIANI**
⊕40°19'.2N 23°57'.9E

easternmost of the Nisídhes Dhrénia and the Akti peninsula there are least depths of 4–7m in the fairway. Anchorages around the island are as follows:

1. ***W side*** On the W side of Nisís Ammouliani anchor in Órmos Ftelies (open to the W) or in Órmos Tsarki (open to the S). In both bays the holding is uncertain so make sure the anchor is well dug in and holding. Care is needed of the reefs on either side of Órmos Tsarki.

2. ***Ammouliani village*** On the NE corner of the island. A Fl.R.3s3M on the end of the mole. Go stern or bows-to the outer half of the mole. The central quay on the W is used by ferries. Alternatively anchor off N of the ferry quay in 3m. Provisions and tavernas ashore. Fuel from the supermarket near the root of the mole or on the outskirts of the village.

3. The bay immediately S of Ammouliani village. Anchor in 4–6m off the short mole. Indifferent shelter.

4. ***Caïque harbour.*** On the N of the large bay below Ammouliani village a small *caïque* harbour

**NISÍS AMMOULIANI - NEW CAIQUE HARBOUR**

has been constructed. Small yachts may find a berth inside. There are 4m depths in the entrance and 2m depths off the quay. Alternatively anchor off to the SW of the harbour.

## OURANOPOLIS

In fine weather a yacht can anchor off Ouranopolis in Órmos Provlakas. The square Prosforion Tower (24m high) is conspicuous on Ák Pirgos. Care must be taken of shoal water sometimes marked by a pole about 100m SW of the mole at Ouranopolis. The anchorage of Ouranopolis is not a secure one and in unsettled weather it is wise to return to one of the anchorages on Ammouliani Island.

Provisions and tavernas ashore. Fuel in the village.

## DHAFNI

The control port for the Akti peninsula. A yacht must clear in here before landing anywhere on the Akti peninsula. You will need the necessary

**AMMOULIANI VILLAGE** ⊕40°20'.2N 23°55'.3E

# THE MONASTERIES

(see plan on page 364)

1. *Moní Konstamonitou.* Coenobite. Founded in the 11th century. Most of the buildings in the deep defile are of the 19th century. A yacht can anchor off in the bay in calm weather.
2. *Dhoheiariou (Dohiariou).* Idiorrhythmic. Founded in the 10th century. The central church, the Katholikon, is said to be one of the finest on Mt Athos.
3. *Xenofondos.* Coenobite. Founded in the 10th century by the monk Xenofon.
4. *Moní Ayíou Panteleimonos.* Coenobite. Founded in 1169, it once supported 1,500 Russian monks. It was badly damaged by fire in 1968 but it is still spectacular. There is a very small harbour nearby.
5. *Xiropotamou.* Idiorrhythmic. First mentioned in the 10th century, most of the buildings date from the 18th century.
6. *Simonopetra.* Coenobite. Founded in 1257 by St Simon, this is one of the most spectacular of the monasteries. The monastery is built on a rocky bluff connected to the cliff by a bridge. Heavy beams overhang the rock sides so that the parts of the monastery built on the beams literally hang in space above the sea and rocks below.
7. *Gregoriou.* Coenobite. Founded c. 1395.
8. *Dionysiou.* Coenobite. Founded in 1375, it stands on a spectacular precipitous rock.
9. *Ayíou Pavlou.* Coenobite. Founded in the 11th century, it occupies a spectacular site on a cliff overlooking a gorge below.
10. *Grand Lavra.* Idiorrhythmic. Situated under the massive height of Mt Athos, this is the largest of the monasteries. Apparently it alone has never suffered from the fires which have badly damaged the other monasteries.
11. *Karakallou.* Coenobite. Founded in the 15th century.
12. *Filotheou.* Idiorrhythmic First mentioned in the 12th century. The monks employ themselves woodcarving.
13. *Iviron.* Idiorrhythmic. Founded in 979. There is a pier here with 2m depths at its extremity. In calm weather it is possible to anchor off in 4–9m.
14. *Stavronikita.* Idiorrhythmic. Founded in 1542.
15. *Pantokrator.* Idiorrhythmic. Built in the 14th century on a sea-washed rock in a small cove. It appears to be possible to anchor off the monastery in calm weather.
16. *Vatopedi.* Idiorrhythmic. Founded in the 10th century, this is the most modern monastery with electricity, telephone and regular communication by ferry with Ierissós. Anchor off the monastery in 5–8m. Open to all sectors N.
17. *Esphigmenou.* Coenobite. First mentioned in 1034. The most northerly of the monasteries. A yacht can anchor off in calm weather.

Around the southern end of the Akti peninsula live scattered colonies of monks and hermits in almost inaccessible (or so it seems, looking up at them) huts clinging to the mountainside. The important colonies are one at St Anne's on the SW corner and a colony of painters and woodcarvers at Kerassia on the SE corner. A yacht can anchor close under Ák Dhiapori at Voulevtiria or at a small cove one mile ENE of Ák Pínnes in calm weather only. A yacht should not be left unattended and must be prepared to leave with the slightest hint of a change in the weather.

Monastery on Athos                    *Nigel Patten*

paperwork from Thessaloníki to do this (see section on the Akti Peninsula).

Dháfni is situated about ½ mile N of Ák Kastanias in an open bay. There is limited shelter from N–NE winds from the natural camber of the coast but it is open from NW through W to S. The seabed rises abruptly making anchoring difficult. A short stone pier has 2m depths at its extremity and a yacht can go stern-to the pier. The bay is not safe in unsettled weather when the prevailing summer wind is funnelled in from the NW–W setting up an uncomfortable slop. A large mooring buoy in the bay is for ships.

## CAUTION

Violent gusts blow off Mt Athos with strong winds from any direction. In calm weather it is interesting to stand inshore to see the monasteries. With strong winds the violent gusts and the considerable seas raised around the bottom of the Akti peninsula make it prudent for a yacht to keep some distance off.

## LAVRA HARBOUR (Mandráki)

A minuscule harbour carved out of rock lying 2 miles N of Ák Ákrathos. The fort by the harbour and the monastery above are conspicuous. The entrance to the harbour is immediately S of the fort. There are reported to be 1·8m depths inside, but with any sort of swell running it would be dangerous for even a very small yacht to attempt to enter.

## ÓRMOS PLATÍ

Stiliária N islet light 40°27'·4N 24°00'·6E

Lying on the W side of Ák Arápis, this bay offers good shelter from the prevailing winds. It is open only to the SW. Anchor in 5–8m depths in either of the two coves in Órmos Platí or in Órmos Frangou immediately N of Órmos Platí. The bottom is sand and weed – good holding.

Both bays are deserted although fishing boats

from Ierissos and Koumitas occasionally shelter here.

*Note* This area is a part of the Akti peninsula and as such it is off-limits to yachts. In 1989 a yacht was requested to leave by a police patrol boat.

*Caution* The passage between Nisídhes Stiliária and Ák Arápis has less depth than that shown on the old BA 1679 and also appears more rock-bound than shown. Pass to seaward of the outermost of Nisídhes Stiliária.

## NÉA RODHA
40°23'·0N 23°56'·0E

A village between Koumitsas and Ierissos. There is a short mole on the W side of the bay. A chapel on the bluff above the miniature harbour is conspicuous. A light is exhibited at the end of the mole: Fl.R.2s3M. A small yacht may be able to go bows-to the end of the mole where there are 2–3m depths although it is usually crowded with fishing boats. The inner half of the mole is shallow (less than a metre).

Provisions and tavernas in the village a dusty 20-minute walk away.

## IERISSÓS

### Approach
A small fishing harbour lying about ½ mile to the SE of Ierissós village. The large hotel behind it is conspicuous.

*By night* The entrance is lit Fl.R.3s3M/Fl.G.3s3M but a night entry is not advised.

### Mooring
Go stern or bows-to with a long line to the breakwater in the outer half of the harbour or in the inner basin. Alternatively anchor inside the inner or

**KÓLPOS IERISSOU AND NISÍS AMMOULIANI**
⊕6 40°27'·4N 24°01'·6E

**IERISSÓS**
⊕40°23'·8N 23°53'·7E

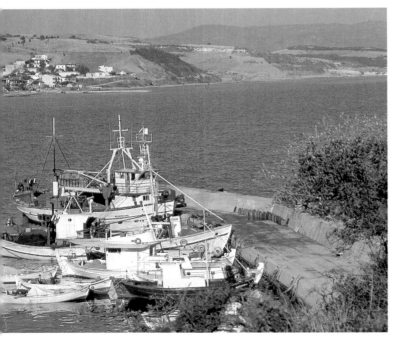

The miniature harbour at Néa Rodha

Ierissós looking NE

outer parts of the harbour. The inner harbour is crowded with local fishing boats. Care must be taken of the very large mooring chains on the bottom and of the numerous mooring buoys and lines on the surface.

*Shelter* With strong N winds a swell rolls into the harbour – more uncomfortable than dangerous. The local fishing boats and a small ferry are moored here all year round.

### Facilities

Tavernas at the harbour. Ierissós village is about one mile away from the harbour and here there is fuel and most provisions can be obtained. Also PO and OTE and several tavernas and cafés. A bus runs to Kavala. There are several yards building wooden fishing *caïques* along the beach from the harbour.

### General

There are good beaches of coarse sand on either side of the harbour and the hinterland is pleasantly wooded with poplar, pine and olive trees. Ierissós has developed into a dusty ramshackle resort on the strength of the sandy beach nearby. The harbour is the nearest safe harbour to the site of Xerxes Canal 2 miles to the SE, although you are likely to be disappointed – there is little to see of the famous canal today.

### STRATONION

40°30'·8N 23°49'·7E

Lies at the head of Órmos Stratonion in the NW corner of Kólpos Ierissou. Anchor off the village. To the N of the village there are two piers extending from the shore for loading ore from the nearby manganese mines. The bay is open to the E and S.

Provisions and tavernas ashore. Fuel in the village.

Between Stratonion and Ák Elevthera there are a number of coves offering good shelter from N winds, but open to the S. The cove nearest to Ák Elevthera offers the best shelter in beautiful surroundings. Open to the S and W.

# The mainland coast

This section covers the mainland coast of Northern Greece from Strimonikos Kólpos to Alexandroupolis, including the nearby island of Thásos. The region is mountainous although not spectacularly so, and much of the high land is bordered by low-lying plains and marshes deposited by the four large rivers emptying into the sea along the coast: the Strimon, the Nestos, the Akmar and the Evros. The river Nestor is the boundary between Macedonia and Thrace and the river Evros is the border between Greece and Turkey. The countryside is for the most part densely wooded in pine and olive. The coastal plains are well-watered and fertile, producing large crops of grain and tobacco.

## Weather patterns in Northern Greece

(These weather patterns also apply to Samothráki.)

In the summer months the *meltemi* blows only fitfully in this area. Normally the *meltemi* blows from the NE at Force 2–5, but on many days there will be little or no wind at all. If the *meltemi* does not blow a SW sea breeze will often set in about midday and blow at Force 2–4. In the winter, spring and autumn the wind is again from the NE or the S, but severe gales are most often from the NE.

In the comparatively shallow waters off this coast, particularly in Stenón Thasou, Órmos Vistonikos, Órmos Anoiko and the shallows off Alexandroupolis, a very short steep sea is kicked up with strong winds from the S. These seas can be aggravated by the W-going current setting along the coast which can vary from ½ to 1½ knots.

With S winds the sea level can increase by as much as 0·5m and conversely with N winds the sea level can decrease.

### ÓRMOS OLIMBIADHOS

40°35'·6N 23°47'·4E

Lies 6½ miles to the NW of Ák Elevthera. Anchor off the village in 2–4m tucked as far under the stubby mole as possible. Adequate shelter although some swell usually penetrates. The outer end of the mole has 2–3m depths but is usually occupied by fishing boats. The mole is lit Fl.R.3s3M.

In the village there are provisions and tavernas. The setting on a coastal plain with mixed deciduous and pine all hemmed in by steep-to mountains is spectacular. The village is a sleepy little place that sees some tourism, but not a lot.

### NISÍS KAVKANÁS

40°37'·0N 23°48'·5E

On the S side of the islet there is a bight that provides some shelter from the N and E. Care is needed of the reef off the W end of the islet. Anchor in 3–5m on sand and shingle.

The islet is lit on the SE corner Fl(3)18s7M.

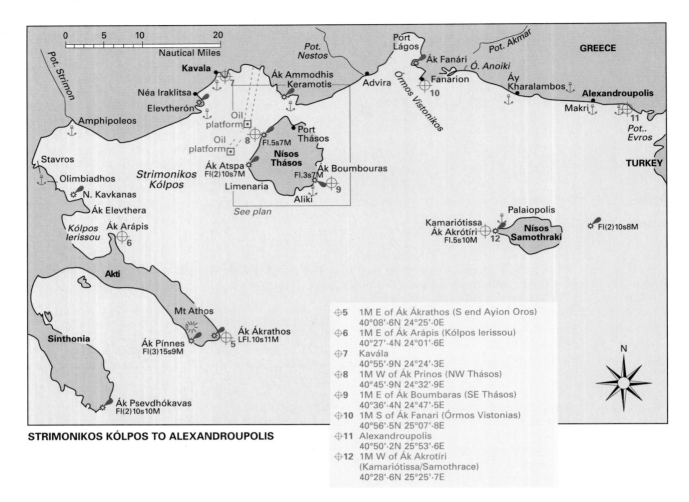

**STRIMONIKOS KÓLPOS TO ALEXANDROUPOLIS**

⊕5 1M E of Ák Ákrathos (S end Ayion Oros)
40°08'·6N 24°25'·0E

⊕6 1M E of Ák Arápis (Kólpos Ierissou)
40°27'·4N 24°01'·6E

⊕7 Kavála
40°55'·9N 24°24'·3E

⊕8 1M W of Ák Prinos (NW Thásos)
40°45'·9N 24°32'·9E

⊕9 1M E of Ák Boumbaras (SE Thásos)
40°36'·4N 24°47'·5E

⊕10 1M S of Ák Fanari (Órmos Vistonias)
40°56'·5N 25°07'·8E

⊕11 Alexandroupolis
40°50'·2N 25°53'·6E

⊕12 1M W of Ák Akrotíri
(Kamariótissa/Samothrace)
40°28'·6N 25°25'·7E

## STAVRÓS

A large bay in the SW corner of Strimonikos Kólpos. There is a short pier off the village and at the time of writing works were underway in the vicinity. As far as could be determined an additional mole was being built to form a small harbour enclosed by an L-shaped mole. A light is exhibited on the end of the pier (Fl.R.3s3M).

Fishing boats use the pier and are kept on permanent moorings off the village so shelter is probably better than it appears. Water on the quay. Fuel by mini-tanker.

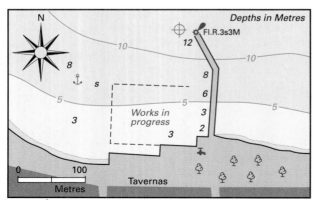

**STAVRÓS**
⊕40°40'·1N 23°42'·1E

The village has developed into a thriving resort with hotels, bars and cafés dotted around the shore. PO. Bank. Provisions and tavernas.

## AMPHIPOLEOS

40°47'·0N 23°51'·5E

In the N corner of Strimonikos Kólpos at the mouth of the river Strimon there is a shallow basin which was formerly Amfipoleos harbour. However the entrance has silted to depths of less than 1m.

It is possible to anchor off the entrance to the basin in 3–4m, but there is little shelter to be gained here.

*Caution* At the mouth of the river Strimon the shoals are reported to extend further than indicated on the chart. A current of about 2 knots is also said to set to the S because of the considerable flow of fresh water from the river.

## ELEVTHERÓN (Dhevtro)

BA 1687

### Approach

This large bay lies 6 miles to the S of Kavála. A number of large hotels around the beach on the W side of the bay and a large silo at the root of the oil wharf are conspicuous.

**ÓRMOS ELEVTHERÓN**
⊕40°50'·6N 24 19'·7E

*By night* Use the light on the N entrance point Fl.3s5M.

## Mooring
In settled weather anchor off Néa Peramos or in the SW corner of the bay. In unsettled weather go stern or bows-to or alongside the N side of the large cargo pier in the NE corner of the bay. There are 7m depths along the outer end of the pier. The surroundings are not attractive but the shelter is nearly all-round. In strong S winds many of the fishing boats normally based in Kavála shelter here.

## Facilities
In Néa Peramos most provisions can be obtained and there are tavernas and cafés.

## General
In settled weather the large bay has attractive anchorages on the S and W sides off long sandy beaches. The fort on the S side begs to be explored.

## NÉA IRAKLITSA
A small fishing harbour in the SE corner of Kólpos Kavalas. The entrance is lit Fl.R.3s3M/Fl.G.3s3M. Go alongside the end of the pier or go stern or bows-to the quay on the S. Good shelter.

Water on the quay. Fuel in the village. Provisions and tavernas ashore.

**NÉA IRAKLITSA**
⊕40°52'·1N 24°19'·1E

## KAVÁLA
BA 1687

### Approach
*Conspicuous* The large city on the rocky bluff and sprawled over the hills behind is conspicuous from the distance. Closer in, a fort and a church with a red cupola on the rocky bluff are conspicuous. The harbour moles are easily identified.

*By night* Use the light on Ák Kará Ormán Fl.5s15M and the lights at the entrance Fl.G.2s4M/Fl.R.2s4M.

### Mooring
Moor stern-to the N quay in the outer harbour if you can find room. The yacht club is strictly private

Elevtherón looking NE, across Órmos Elevtherón

Kavála looking WNW from the root of the outer mole
*Nigel Patten*

Kavála *Nigel Patten*

KAVÁLA
⊕40°55′·9N 24°24′·3E

*Provisions* Excellent shopping for all provisions. The best shopping area is immediately behind the fish market. Ice from the fish market.

*Eating out* Excellent tavernas including several fish tavernas near the fish market with delicacies such as sole, scallops and some of the best prawns in Greece.

*Other* PO. OTE. Banks. Greek gas and *Camping Gaz*. A gas filling station some distance out of the city. Hire cars and motorbikes. Buses to Thessaloníki and Alexandroupolis. Ferries to Thásos. Internal flights to Athens.

### General

Kavála is an important commercial port and first impressions of the city from a harbour churned up by ferries, tugs and workboats commuting to the oil rig are not likely to be favourable. Yet stay a day here and you begin to like this busy friendly city.

In the city an aqueduct (based on Roman design but built by the Turks in the 16th century) is prominent. On the rocky bluff the house of Mehmet Ali, a rich merchant of Kavála in the 18th century, who effectively ruled the city, has been preserved and is now a folklore museum. The archaeological museum near the harbour houses classical finds from the area.

### KAVÁLA FISHING HARBOUR

On the E side of Ák Kará Ormán there is a fishing harbour where a small yacht may find a berth. Fuel nearby. A small boatyard close by hauls yachts. Provisions and tavernas ashore.

### KAVÁLA WEST HARBOUR

On the W side of Órmos Kavála there is a dogleg breakwater extending NE for approximately 300m which protects a quayed area. This is a commercial port and not for yachts. The end of the breakwater is lit Fl(2)R.8s7M.

### KAVÁLA COMMERCIAL HARBOUR

40°57′·0N 24°28′·9E

Approximately 2 miles E of Kavála a large commercial harbour is under construction. Grandly titled the 'Phillip II of Macedonia' harbour, it is unlikely to offer much in the way of facilities for yachts. The entrance is lit Fl.R.2s/Fl.G.4s7M.

### KERAMOTÍS

BA 1687

### Approach

Keramotís is the principal ferry port connecting Thásos to the mainland. On the low-lying sand spit terminating in Ák Keramotís a few houses and the light structure will be seen before the sand spit itself. Once into the lagoon behind the sand spit, the village of Keramotís and the harbour are easily identified.

*By night* Use the lights on Ák Keramotís Fl.WR.4s6/4M and on the pier head Q.RG.2M.

with no facilities for visitors and, it is reported, few manners. The quay in the outer harbour is very high and you will have difficulty getting ashore unless you are near a ladder. The inner basin is usually crowded with fishing boats. You may be able to find a berth in the inner basin, but do enquire if it is OK to berth there – yachts which muscle into fishing boat berths should not be surprised to be unceremoniously evicted when boats return. The bottom is mud – excellent holding.

*Shelter* With strong S winds an uncomfortable surge develops and many of the fishing boats shelter at Elevtherón. However a number of yachts are moored all year round off the N mole and quay. Strong S winds are rare in the summer.

*Authorities* Port police, customs and immigration authorities.

### Facilities

*Water* On the N quay and in the inner basin.

*Fuel* Can be delivered to the N quay and near the quay in the inner basin.

*Repairs* Most mechanical and general engineering repairs. Chandlers. Excellent hardware and tool shops.

**KERAMOTÍS**
⊕40°51'·6N 24 42'·2E

### Mooring

Go stern or bows-to or alongside the quay. The wharf is usually crowded with coasters and fishing boats.

*Shelter* Is better than it looks. W winds cause a limited swell.

*Authorities* Port police and customs.

### Facilities

Water on the quay. Fuel near the quay. Good shopping for provisions. PO. OTE. A number of tavernas and cafés. Buses to Alexandroupolis and Kavála. Car ferry to Thásos.

*Note* On the N side of the lagoon a number of mooring buoys (red and white vertical stripes) probably belong to the Greek navy. It would be prudent not to anchor in this area.

### OIL RIG PLATFORM

Lying 3½ miles NW of Ák Prínos on Thásos and 9½ miles SSE of Kavála is an oil rig platform which is conspicuous by day and night. Recently another platform was erected approximately 6·3 miles SSW of the original platform and approx. 4 miles from the coast of Thásos. Workboats regularly ply between the platform and Kavála. At night the platforms are lit by a battery of white lights (they could be mistaken for large ocean liners) and a Mo(U)15s10m.

### ÁK AMMODHIS

A rock just under the water (0·9m) is reported to lie ½ mile SSW of Ák Ammódhis.

### RIVER NESTOS

Shoaling is reported to extend as much as ½ mile further than indicated around the mouth of this river. I have noticed discoloured water as far as 1

mile off the coast, but a check on the depth showed no disparity with charted depths. Nonetheless it would be prudent to keep some distance off the river mouth. The land in the vicinity of the river mouth is very low-lying and it is often difficult to establish the limits of the coastal plain around it. A cluster of communication towers approximately ½ mile inland on the coastal plain (Pedhias Khrisoupoleos) is conspicuous.

### STENÓN THASOU (Thásos Strait)

In the comparatively shallow water in the strait and in Órmos Vistonikos a short steep sea is quickly raised with strong winds. In Stenón Thasou a current sometimes sets to the E at a rate of ½–1½ knots.

# Nísos Thásos

This round lump of marble separated from the mainland by a shallow sea strait enjoyed some power and prosperity in ancient times. Its position allowed it to be easily defended and it was and still is an enchanting and beautiful island.

The early colonists were the Parians who soon prospered from the Thasian gold mines. Despite being a well defended and powerful city-state, Thásos meekly submitted to the invading Persians. After Xerxes was defeated at Salamís the island had its ups and downs with Athens, but its merchants

**NÍSOS THÁSOS**

⊕8  1M W of Ák Prinos (NW Thásos)
    40°45'·9N 24°32'·9E
⊕9  1M E of Ák Boumbaras (SE Thásos)
    40°36'·4N 24°47'·5E

prospered on its mineral wealth (including Thasian marble which was renowned throughout the ancient world) and its famous black wine. In medieval times it suffered from pirate attacks until the Genoese Gattelusis and later the Turks occupied the island and restored order.

Today its prosperity is based on the natural beauty of the island: its sandy beaches, pine-clad hills, running streams (even in summer) and ancient monuments attract a growing number of tourists each year.

## THÁSOS NÉA LIMANI

BA 1687

### Approach
The harbour is situated immediately W of the old harbour. In the closer approaches the outer breakwater will be seen and the light structures at the entrance can be identified.

*By night* The entrance is lit: Fl.R.3s3M/Fl.G.3s3M.

### Mooring
Go stern or bows-to the outer breakwater or stern or bows-to the middle part of the town quay. The hydrofoil is reported to use the SE corner.

*Shelter* Good all-round shelter.

*Authorities* Port police and customs.

### Facilities
See Port Thásos.

## PORT THÁSOS (Limín Panayía)

BA 1687

### Approach
*Conspicuous* The buildings of the town in the natural amphitheatre at the foot of the hills can be seen from the distance, but the harbour moles are very low and difficult to see. The two white light structures on the extremities of the moles will be seen before the moles.

Thásos. The old harbour (foreground) and Thásos Néa Limani (behind) looking W *Nigel Patten*

*By night* Use the light on the SE of Nisís Thasopoúla Fl.WR.4·5s6/4M and the lights at the entrance Fl.G.2s4M/Fl.R.2s4M.

*Dangers* Care should be taken of the remains of an ancient mole, mostly submerged, approximately 300m to the NE of the harbour. Approach the harbour from the N or NW.

### Mooring
Go stern or bows-to the quay in the SE corner of the harbour. If it is crowded here go bows-to the E mole although you will not be able to get close to the mole and you will have to use a dinghy to get ashore. The bottom of the harbour was said to be originally constructed of marble, but I found only mud and shingle – good holding.

*Shelter* Excellent all-round shelter.

*Authorities* Port police and customs (by the ferry quay).

### Facilities
*Water* On the quay in the new and the old harbour.
*Fuel* On the waterfront. A mini-tanker can be arranged to deliver to the harbour.
*Repairs* Limited mechanical repairs. *Caïques* are hauled out and built to the E of the old harbour.
*Provisions* Excellent shopping for all provisions. Wine from the barrel.
*Eating out* Excellent tavernas on the waterfront.
*Other* PO. OTE. Bank. Greek gas and *Camping Gaz*. Hire cars and motorbikes. Buses around the perimeter of the island. Ferries to Keramotís and Kavála.

### General
The town of Thásos is built on the same site as the ancient capital and wandering around the town you experience an architectural *pot-pourri* of the old and the new. Most of the new town is within the 2½ miles of walls and towers that surrounded the ancient city. Thásos possessed two fine harbours. The surviving oval harbour was the ancient naval harbour. The ancient commercial harbour to the E is now mostly destroyed.

Close by this latter harbour is one of the most charming spots in the town – shaded by trees and close to the ruins of the *agora*, it is a short but steep walk up the hill behind to the ancient theatre and the *acropolis* that look out over Thásos. More than many of the other classic sites I have visited in Greece, Thásos conveys in both its substance and its atmosphere what an ancient Greek city was like. The museum houses most of the valuable finds from the site.

Thásos black wine, for which it was famed in ancient times, is widely available, but in my experience the modern brew is of mediocre quality, though I have been told that much of it is now produced not on Thásos but on the mainland opposite.

*Depths in Metres*

N

12

11

Órmos
Panayias

10

10

10

8

9

7₅

7

6

8

6

5

Ferry

Fl.R.3s3M

Fl.G.3s3M

4₅

4

4

4

2

3

3

3

3

4

4

3₅

3

<1

5

5

Néa Limani

Ák Evraiokastro

<1

Ancient mole

<1

5

Fl.R.2s4M

Fl.G.2s4M

2₅

3

4

4

3

3

2

2

2

Old
harbour

<1

Ancient
theatre

Thásos

0          100                                        500

Metres

**THÁSOS**
⊕ 40°46′·9N 24°42′·3E

## Anchorages around Thásos

(Going anti-clockwise around the island)

### ÓRMOS PRINOS

Ák Prinos light 40°45′·9N 24°33′·9E

On the N side of Ák Prínos, this open bay affords some shelter from the prevailing NE winds by means of the natural camber of the bay. Off the village of Prínos there is a wharf and a short pier, but the latter is used by the car ferry to Kavála. Anchor in the bay. Some provisions available ashore and a number of good tavernas.

### SKÁLA SOTIROS

40°43′·9N 24°32′·8E

A small fishing harbour approximately 2M S of Ák Prinos. A dogleg breakwater with the entrance N protects a small harbour. The entrance is lit Fl.G.3s3M/Fl.R.3s3M. There are reported to be 3–4m depths in the entrance and mostly 2–3·5m

depths in the outer part of the harbour. Depths are irregular off the quay on the E side so investigate before going stern or bows-to. Good shelter.

Some provisions and tavernas ashore.

### KALLIRAKHIS

A fishing harbour lying approximately 3·5M S of Ák Prinos. Depths are irregular off the E quay so, if possible, go stern or bows-to the short section of quay near the base of the outer breakwater. Alternatively anchor and take a long line to the W breakwater. Good shelter.

Water in the village. Fuel near the harbour. Provisions and tavernas.

### ÓRMOS LIMENARIA

40°37′·5N 24°34′·5E

On the SW corner of Thásos, Órmos Limenária offers good shelter from N winds. Open to the S. Anchor in the bay in 3–5m on sand and weed. The small harbour is crowded with local boats and the

**KALLIRAKHIS**
⊕40°42′·7N 24°31′·9E

Aliki on the SE side of Nísos Thásos          *Nigel Patten*

ferry uses the S quay under the breakwater. There are 3–4m depths in the entrance and 1–2·5m depths in the tiny basin. It may be possible for a small yacht to find a berth in here where there is good shelter. Although shelter from northerlies is reasonable in the bay, there is usually some ground swell which can at times be uncomfortable.

Fuel and water on the waterfront. Good shopping for all provisions. Excellent tavernas and bars on the waterfront. Limenária was originally built to house workers from the nearby mines. In recent years it has developed into a large tourist resort.

### PEFKARI (Rosongremou) and POTOS (Astris)

Along the coast to the SE of Limenária are Pefkari and Potos where a yacht can anchor off in settled weather. Open to the S.

### ALIKI

On the SE corner of Thásos 2 miles to the W of Ák Babouras (Stravros) there are a number of small coves offering good shelter from N winds. Open only to the S, Aliki is the easternmost of the coves. Care is needed of the above and below-water rocks off the entrance. Anchor in 3–6m on sand and weed,

good holding once the anchor is in. The prevailing wind tends to blow in over the head of the bay so it may be prudent to lay two anchors.

Some provisions and tavernas ashore.

### ÓRMOS POTAMIAS

A large bay on the E coast of Thásos on the S side of Ák Pirgos. Anchor at the N end of the bay where there is reasonable shelter from NE winds. The bottom is sand and shelves gently to the shore. At the S end of the bay at Skála Potamias there is a rough stone breakwater, but the depths around it are insufficient even for a small yacht.

### MAKRIAMMOS

On the NE corner of Thásos there is the open bay of Makriammos. In the N corner of the bay there is a short mole which provides some protection from NE winds. Moor bows-to near the extremity where there are 2m depths.

# The Mainland coast

### ADVIRA

40°55′·8N 24°58′·2E
A rockbound harbour with a buoyed channel into it. The entrance is lit Fl.G.3s3M/Fl.R.3s3M. It could be worth investigating but reconnoitre in the dinghy first.

### PORT LÁGOS (Órmos Vistonikos)

BA 1636

#### Approach

Órmos Lágos lies in the NE corner of Órmos Vistonikos. It is a natural lagoon connected to the sea by a dredged channel. A hotel on Ák Fanári and a large factory and silo on the E side of the entrance to the harbour are conspicuous. The black conical buoy with a ⊥ cardinal topmark marking the outer edge of the shallows off Ák Fanári is difficult to see from seaward. Once inside Órmos Vistonikos, the

**ALIKI**
⊕40°36′·05N 24°44′·2E

**APPROACHES TO LÁGOS AND FANARION**
⊕40°57'·0N 25°07'·8E

buoys and beacons marking the dredged channel are easily identified and entry into the harbour is straightforward. The channel and the harbour are kept dredged to 6m.

**LÁGOS**
⊕41°00'·4N 25°07'·6E

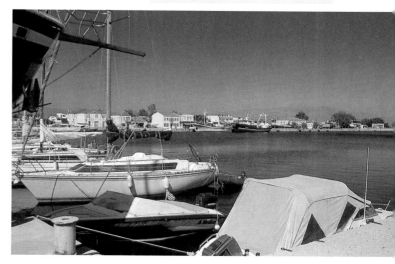

The basin at Lágos looking NE

*By night* Use the light on Ák Fanári Fl.8s6M, the light buoy off the cape Q(9)15s, the light buoys marking the channel Fl.G.1·5s and Fl.R.1·5s, and the lights at the entrance Q.R.3M and Q.G.3M. There are leading lights: on 023°30' F.Y.3M and F.Y.3M.

## Mooring

Go alongside or stern or bows-to on the W quay.

*Shelter* Excellent all-round shelter.

*Authorities* Port police and customs.

## Facilities

*Water* On the quay.
*Fuel* About 500m away.
*Repairs* Yachts are craned onto the hard in the SW corner.
*Provisions* Some provisions can be obtained. Ice available.
*Eating out* Tavernas.
*Other* Small Yacht Club.

## General

Lágos is an important port for the shipment of grain from the hinterland. Although it is a commercial port, the approach to and setting of Port Lágos are attractive. The surrounding marshes are a haven for all types of water birds rarely seen in other parts of Greece. The surrounding area is now a protected bird reserve and a walk through the lagoons is recommended. Just E of Lágos on the main road there is a delightful monastery built on an islet in the middle of one of the lagoons.

## FANARION

A fishing harbour tucked into the W side of Ák Fanari. Care is needed in the approaches as the harbour is fringed by shoal water on the W side right out to the buoy (✗ topmark) marking the shallows in the approaches to Lágos. Make the approach from a WSW direction where the least depth should be 2·2m close off the entrance. The entrance is lit Fl.G.2s3M.

Care is needed in the harbour where there are irregular depths in the entrance channel of 1·8–2·5m

**FANARION**
⊕40°57'·9N 25°07'·5E

**ALEXANDROUPOLIS**
⊕40°50'·2N 25°53'·6E

depths. Go alongside or stern or bows-to the S quay. Good shelter.

Water near the quay. Fuel near the quay. Provisions and tavernas.

## ÁYIOS KHARALAMBOS

40°52'·6N 25°30'·4E

One mile to the W of Ák Maronias at Áyios Kharalambos a rough stone L-shaped breakwater extends W and then N from the coast. There are reported to be 4–5m depths in the entrance and 2–3m depths off the quay on the E side. Good shelter.

Tavernas ashore.

## MAKRI

40°50'·9N 25°44'·9E

Seven miles to the W of Alexandroupolis lies a very small *caïque* harbour serving the village of Mákri on the hill above. At the entrance there are less than 2m depths and it is rock-bound. Inside there would be excellent shelter. The entrance is lit F.G/F.R.3M. It deserves further exploration in settled weather.

## ALEXANDROUPOLIS

BA 1636

### Approach

*Conspicuous* The buildings of the large town are visible from the distance. The white lighthouse on the promenade and three red storage tanks behind the harbour are conspicuous. The outer mole of the harbour and the entrance are easily identified.

*By night* Use the main light Fl(3)15s24M and the lights at the entrance Fl.R.3s6M/Fl.G.3s3M.

*Note* Harbour works are in progress at the time of writing. Some of the lights listed may be in different positions and other lights may mark works being carried out. Care needed.

*Dangers* With strong S winds there is usually a lumpy sea over the shallow bank extending some miles off the coast in the approaches to the harbour.

### Mooring

Go stern or bows-to or alongside the N quay near the entrance to the inner harbour or in the inner harbour itself. The bottom is sticky mud – excellent holding.

*Shelter* Good shelter, although strong S winds send in some swell – uncomfortable but not dangerous.

*Authorities* A port of entry: port police, customs and immigration authorities.

### Facilities

*Water* On the quay in the inner harbour.
*Fuel* Near the quay.
*Repairs* Most mechanical and light engineering repairs. Excellent hardware shops.
*Provisions* Excellent shopping for all provisions. Ice from a fish shop near the waterfront.
*Eating out* Good tavernas in the town.
*Other* PO. OTE. Banks. Greek gas and *Camping Gaz*. Hire cars and motorbikes. Buses to Kavála and İstanbul. Train to Thessaloníki and İstanbul. Ferry to Samothráki. Internal flights to Athens.

### General

Alexandroupolis, named after King Alexander (born 1893) and not Alexander the Great, is a modern bustling city and port. It is important as the major road and rail link with Turkey and also for the shipment of grain and tobacco from the hinterland. In the shallows 8 miles to the SE of the harbour where the Evros river flows into the sea, the local fishing boats net flatfish, mostly sole, and though most of it finds its way to Thessaloníki and Athens, some can be found in the tavernas at Alexandroupolis.

# Samothráki

## (Samothrace)

Until recently Samothráki has not had a secure harbour and for this reason has remained a solitary island shrouded in mystery. It is a forbidding-looking place, a gigantic lump of marble rising up to 1,600m (5,200ft) at the summit of Mt Fengari. On the west, Ák Akrotíri forms a shallow bay in which the harbour of Kamariótissa nestles.

The mysterious ancient inhabitants of the island, the Kabeiri (Cabeiri), were of pre-Greek origin, possibly of Phoenician or Phrygian stock, and worshipped the Great Earth Mother rather than the male gods which dominated classical times. The strength of the Kabeiri was such that Samothráki was regarded as a sacred island and a sanctuary for initiates of the cult, although this may have been a spin-off from the inaccessibility of the island.

They had a soft spot for seafarers, and initiation into their rites was deemed to be good luck and a safeguard against shipwreck. The power of the Kabeiri throughout the ancient world ensured Samothráki an independent existence throughout the Greek struggles until late into the Roman period.

The ruins of the ancient temple-city lie on a rocky ridge amongst wild olives and *maquis*. The American school of archaeologists have mainly been responsible for clearing the site and organising the small museum housing most of the finds that were not spirited away by early explorers. Of these the best known is the *Winged Victory of Samothrace* removed by the French in 1863 and now in the Louvre in Paris. The splendid site looking across to the mainland is well worth a visit. Above, in a craggy pocket, is the principal village (*chora*) of Samothráki.

## KAMARIÓTISSA

### Approach

*Conspicuous* From the N and W a tower on the NW corner of the island and the small village of Kamariótissa are conspicuous. From the S the low-lying sand spit terminating in Ák Akrotíri is not visible until you are very near it, but the light structure on the extremity is visible from some distance off. Four white wind generators are conspicuous from the N and W. Closer in the cluster of buildings at Kamariótissa and the harbour mole are easily identified.

*By night* Use the light on Ák Akrotíri Fl.5s10M and the lights at the entrance: Fl.R.3s3M/Fl.G.3s3M.

*Dangers* By day or night caution must be exercised whilst navigating in the vicinity of the low-lying Ák Akrotíri when relative distances between the cape and the high mountains behind can be confused.

### Mooring

Go stern or bows-to or alongside the mole or the quay wherever there is room. The bottom is sand and shingle – good holding. The harbour is usually crowded with fishing boats and it can be difficult to find a berth. You may have to go alongside a fishing boat and then move when it leaves.

*Shelter* Good all-round shelter although a strong SW wind might make the harbour uncomfortable.

*Authorities* Port police.

**KAMARIÓTISSA**
⊕40°28'·6N 25°28'·2E

### Facilities

*Water* At the root of the mole.
*Fuel* On the waterfront. A mini-tanker can deliver.
*Provisions* Most provisions can be obtained.
*Eating out* Good tavernas on the waterfront.
*Other* PO. OTE. Bus to the *chora*. Ferry to Alexandroupolis.

### General

Kamariótissa is essentially a small fishing hamlet and the ferry port for Samothráki. The inhabitants are very friendly towards visiting yachtsmen as they rarely see a great number of yachts here. It is a safe place to leave a yacht when visiting the archaeological site on the N side of the island.

To get there take a taxi inland to Palaeopolis and then enquire at the hotel for admittance. It is a short walk to the site itself where there are remains of several of the initiation buildings including the Arsinion which was the largest circular building in ancient Greece. A small museum nearby houses finds from the site. While you are there it is worth going on to the *chora* which is not far away.

# VIII. The Eastern Sporades

The eastern Sporades stretch down the coast of Asia Minor, linking northern Greece to the Dodecanese. Like the other islands in the Aegean, they are the peaks of mountains that once stood on the plain of the Aegean. Geographically Samothráki belongs to this group of islands, but politically it is administered from Alexandroupolis and its communications are with the north. Limnos, the most northerly of the group described here, hovers in its own limbo in the middle of the northern Aegean. Generally the islands are more fertile and greener than the Cyclades and the Dodecanese. Lésvos and Sámos in particular will surprise the visiting yachtsman with their well-watered, cultivated plains and extensive pine forests.

The history of the group of islands is patchy and difficult to summarise as a whole – the historical detail for each island can be found in the introduction to each one. Very early on Limnos was an important link between Europe and the islands to the south. It had a highly developed Bronze Age culture of a Minoan-Mycenaean type and metalworking probably filtered into the Cyclades and Crete from there. With the decline of Limnos, the Dorians and Ionians moved in. The Ionic Confederacy was centred around Khíos and Sámos and the adjacent mainland coast. The confederacy prospered and for some time rivalled Athens in its high life and appreciation of the arts. The chief cities of the group – Khíos, Ephesus, Smyrna and Miletus – endured as important centres long after the decline of the confederacy.

Lésvos existed outside the confederacy in a somewhat chaotic state until the beginning of the 6th century BC when Pittacus calmed the island and earned for himself a place as one of the Seven Sages of Greece. Soon afterwards, around 540 BC, Polykrates of Sámos achieved his meteoric rise to fame and fortune and control of the group revolved around this tyrannical genius and the Persians pushing up from Asia Minor.

The decisive Battle of Salamís ousted the Persians and ushered in the usual succession of invaders: the Romans, the Saracens, Byzantine rulers, the Venetians and the Genoese, and the Turks. Looking at the islands today (with the exception of Psará), it is hard to believe that they were often entirely abandoned by the native inhabitants as successive waves of invaders swept down on them and corsairs mopped up whatever was left. Indeed it is unlikely that the present populations of the islands are descended from the original inhabitants at all. The group became part of Greece in 1912 after the Balkan Wars.

Today the eastern Sporades are considered to be important military outposts and soldiers are stationed on all of the islands. Photographs of many of the harbours, much of the coastline and some of the interior are forbidden. A sign in Greek and English or of the pictorial type (a camera with a cross through it) will usually be found prohibiting photographs. It should be observed, or all your film may be confiscated and exposed!

With the exception of Sámos, the islands are to a large extent off the tourist track. Consequently many facilities are underdeveloped. Yacht equipment and servicing beyond the basic fisherman's needs is limited. Tavernas are mostly of the local type and the comparatively sophisticated (such as it is) fare of Corfu, Míkonos or Rhodes will rarely be found. However the friendliness of the locals more than makes up for these small deficiencies and prices on the whole are cheaper than elsewhere. The basics are there – good harbours, good centres for provisions and communications – but not the gloss. For many including myself that is a blessing.

## Weather patterns in the eastern Sporades

The prevailing wind in the summer is the *meltemi*. It blows fitfully at first in June, getting up to full strength in July, August and September and dies in October. In July and August it blows strongly, about Force 4–6, and may reach Force 7 on occasions. In the more southerly islands of the group it blows from the N–NNW but in Limnos it blows from the NE. Around much of the group the *meltemi* is funnelled by the land including the adjacent Turkish coast so in places it can be blowing from the N, W or E. In the spring and autumn there are often S winds, but they rarely exceed Force 4–5.

In the winter strong winds may be from the SE or the NE. In the more northerly islands strong winds are most often from the NE and strong S winds can be expected to become strong NE winds which may blow for several days. In the winter exceptionally severe storms can strike the group. (In December 1980 Force 10 was reported in Lésvos.)

In common with the other islands in the Aegean there are gusts off the high land on the lee side of an island. With the *meltemi* these gusts are especially severe off Sámos and Ikaría and parts of Lésvos. With prolonged strong winds from the N the seas surrounding Limnos can become especially confused and it is prudent to wait a day after the wind has died to let the sea subside.

# Routes

The geography of the Eastern Sporades lying approximately north to south means that routes north in the summer are directly into the *meltemi* while routes south are off the wind.

With the *meltemi* blowing down the Turkish coast from the N–NNE some yachts use the coastal route up the Turkish coast, where the wind direction is modified by the coast and there is more possibility of getting some wind that is not directly on the nose. The wind is usually channelled into the gulfs along the Turkish coast and this can give some useful slants, enabling yachts to sail up the coast. Yachts heading N through the Eastern Sporades in the summer when the *meltemi* is blowing are in for a bash to windward and the going can be tough at times. If a yacht leaves in early summer or late autumn the northerlies are less frequent and less strong. You may even get a few southerlies to help you on your way.

Coming S down through the Eastern Sporades is a sleigh ride in the summer with the *meltemi* behind giving you good sailing all the way down and on through the Dodecanese. The wind direction will change somewhat as it is funnelled through the channels, but generally is aft of the beam.

If you are heading across to the Eastern Sporades from the Cyclades then it pays to stay high and head for somewhere like Andros or Tínos before setting off across to Lesvos, Khíos or Ikaria. Initially you will be close reaching, but the wind will free off the further you get across and it is a rollicking if wet ride with the *meltemi* across to the Eastern Sporades.

# Data

## PORTS OF ENTRY
Mirina (Limnos)
Mitilíni (Lésvos)
Limín Khíos
Pithagorion (Sámos)

## PROHIBITED AREAS
*Khíos* It is prohibited to enter or anchor in the N cove at Laghana.

Photographs of many of the harbours and parts of the coastline of Limnos, Lésvos, Khíos and Sámos are prohibited.

## MAJOR LIGHTS
**Áy Evstrátios**
**Ák Tripití** Fl(2)10s8M
**Nisís Áy Apóstoloi** Fl.WR.5s10/7M

**Limnos**
**Ák Pláka** Fl(3)30s22M
**Ák Moúrtzeflos** Fl(2)14s13M
**Ák Kástron** Fl.6s11M
**Vrak Kómbi** (Ák Lena) Q(2)6s10M
**Ák Kávos** (Sagradha) Fl.3s5M

**Lésvos**
**Ák Kórakas** Fl.WR.5s11/8M
**Ák Mólivos** LFl.WG.10s12/8M
**Nisís Sígri** Fl(2)15s21M
**Nisís Kelloni** Fl.3s6M
**Ák Agriliós** Fl(2)12s9M
**Mitilíni** Fl(3)14s6M
**Nisídha Panayía** Fl.10s7M

# Quick reference guide

| | Shelter | Mooring | Fuel | Water | Provisioning | Tavernas | Plan |
|---|---|---|---|---|---|---|---|
| **Limnos** | | | | | | | |
| Mirina | A | ABC | B | A | A | B | • |
| Órmos Platí | B | C | O | O | O | C | • |
| Órmos Thanos | B | C | O | O | O | C | |
| Órmos Áy Pavlou | C | C | O | O | O | O | |
| Órmos Kondiá | B | C | O | O | O | C | |
| Órmos Moúdhrou | A | AC | B | A | B | C | • |
| Órmos Plakas | C | A | O | O | O | O | |
| Órmos Hefaistia | C | C | O | O | O | O | |
| Órmos Kotsinas | C | C | O | O | O | O | |
| Órmos Moúrtzeflos | B | C | O | O | O | O | |
| Áyios Evstrátios | B | AB | O | A | C | C | • |
| **Lésvos** | | | | | | | |
| Mitilíni | A | AB | B | A | A | A | • |
| Panayioudha | B | A | O | B | C | B | • |
| Pamfilla | C | C | O | B | O | C | |
| Skála Thermis | A | AB | B | B | C | B | • |
| Skála Mistegna | B | AC | O | B | O | C | • |
| Órmos Mákris Yialos | O | C | O | O | O | O | |
| Skála Sikaminéas | O | A | O | B | C | C | |
| Mithimna | A | A | B | A | A | A | • |
| Pétra | B | AC | B | B | C | C | • |
| Ghavadholos | B | AB | O | B | C | C | • |
| Sígri | B | ABC | B | A | B | C | • |
| Erresos | B | AC | O | B | B | B | • |
| Kólpos Kalloni | C | C | O | B | C | C | • |
| Skála Polikhnitos | BC | AC | B | B | C | B | • |
| Plomárion | B | AC | B | A | A | B | • |
| Órmos Mersinia | B | C | O | O | O | C | |
| Kólpos Yéras | BC | C | O | C | C | C | • |
| Psará | B | A | O | B | C | C | • |
| **Oinoussa** | | | | | | | |
| Mandráki | A | AC | O | A | C | C | • |
| Nisís Pasas | B | C | O | O | O | O | • |
| **Khíos** | | | | | | | |
| Limín Khíou | A | AB | B | A | A | B | • |
| Khíos Marina | A | A | B | A | C | C | • |
| Vrondados | B | A | O | A | C | C | |
| Órmos Kolokithias | C | C | O | B | C | C | |
| Marmaro (Kardhamila) | B | AC | B | A | B | B | • |
| Limnia (Volissos) | B | A | B | B | C | C | |
| Lithi | B | AB | O | B | O | C | • |
| Ó. Mestá | C | C | O | O | O | O | • |
| SW corner | B | C | O | O | C | C | • |
| Ó. Kamari | B | C | O | B | C | C | |
| Kataraktis | B | AB | 0 | B | C | C | |
| **Ikaría** | | | | | | | |
| Evdhilos | C | A | O | B | B | C | • |
| Áyios Kirikos | B | AC | B | A | A | B | • |
| Órmos Loutró | C | C | O | B | O | C | |
| **Sámos** | | | | | | | |
| Karlóvasi | B | A | B | A | B | B | • |
| Kokkari | C | C | O | B | O | C | |
| Vathi | C | AB | B | A | A | A | • |
| Órmos Mourtia | C | C | O | O | O | O | |
| Órmos Possidonion | B | C | O | O | O | O | |
| Pithagorion | A | A | A | A | A | A | • |
| Pithagorion Marina | A | A | B | A | A | A | • |
| Ireon | B | C | O | O | C | C | |
| Samopoula | O | C | O | O | O | C | |
| Marathakambos | B | AC | B | B | C | C | • |
| Órmos Limnionas | C | C | O | O | O | C | |
| **Foúrnoi** | | | | | | | |
| Órmos Korseon | B | A | B | B | C | B | • |
| Foúrnoi anchorages | B | C | O | O | O | O | • |

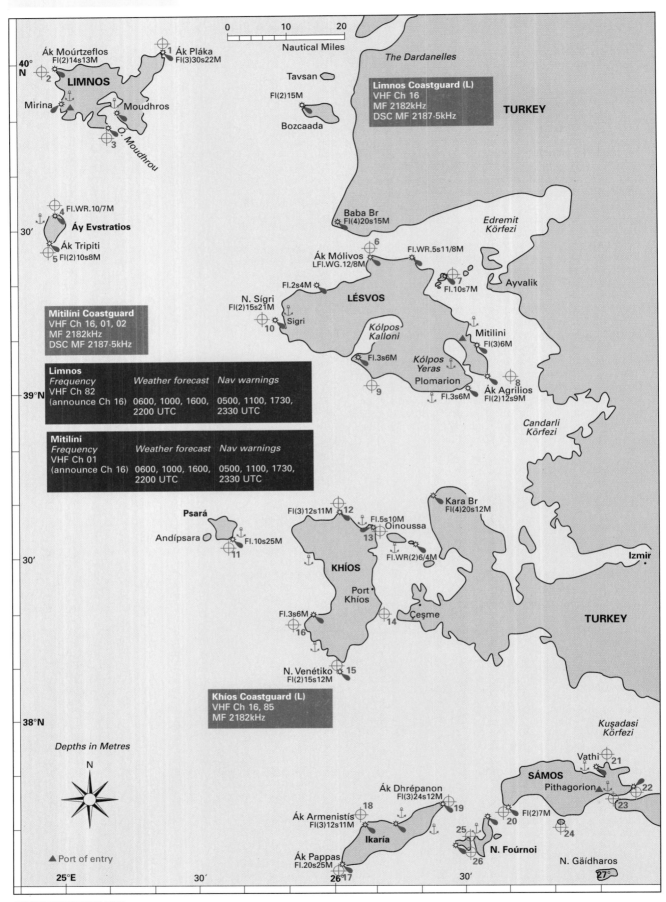

0    10    20
Nautical Miles

Ák Moúrtzeflos
Fl(2)14s13M
1 Ák Pláka
Fl(3)30s22M
40°
N
2
LIMNOS
Mirina
Moudhros
3   O. Moudhrou

The Dardanelles

Tavsan

Fl(2)15M

Bozcaada

**Limnos Coastguard (L)**
VHF Ch 16
MF 2182kHz
DSC MF 2187·5kHz

**TURKEY**

Fl.WR.10/7M
4
30'
Áy Evstratios
Ák Tripiti
5 Fl(2)10s8M

Baba Br
Fl(4)20s15M

Edremit
Körfezi

6
Ák Mólivos
LFl.WG.12/8M

Fl.WR.5s11/8M

7
Fl.10s7M

Ayvalik

**Mitilíni Coastguard**
VHF Ch 16, 01, 02
MF 2182kHz
DSC MF 2187·5kHz

Fl.2s4M

N. Sígri
Fl(2)15s21M
10   Sigri

**LÉSVOS**

Kólpos
Kalloni

Fl.3s6M

Kólpos
Yeras
Plomarion

Mitilini
Fl(3)6M

8
Ák Agrilios
Fl(2)12s9M

Candarli
Körfezi

| | Limnos | | |
|---|---|---|---|
| | *Frequency* | *Weather forecast* | *Nav warnings* |
| 39°N | VHF Ch 82 | 0600, 1000, 1600, | 0500, 1100, 1730, |
| | (announce Ch 16) | 2200 UTC | 2330 UTC |

| | Mitilíni | | |
|---|---|---|---|
| | *Frequency* | *Weather forecast* | *Nav warnings* |
| | VHF Ch 01 | 0600, 1000, 1600, | 0500, 1100, 1730, |
| | (announce Ch 16) | 2200 UTC | 2330 UTC |

9

Fl.3s6M

**Psará**
Andípsara
11   Fl.10s25M

Fl(3)12s11M   12

Fl.5s10M
13   Oinoussa

Kara Br
Fl(4)20s12M

Fl.WR(2)6/4M

30'

**KHÍOS**

Port
Khíos

Fl.3s6M
16

Çeşme
14

Izmir

**TURKEY**

N. Venétiko   15
Fl(2)15s12M

**Khíos Coastguard (L)**
VHF Ch 16, 85
MF 2182kHz

38°N

Kuşadasi
Körfezi

*Depths in Metres*

N

Vathi   21

**SÁMOS**
Pithagorion   22

23

Ák Dhrépanon
Fl(3)24s12M
18           19

Fl(2)7M
20

24

Ák Armenistís
Fl(3)12s11M

25

Ikaría

N. Foúrnoi

26

▲ Port of entry

Ák Pappas
Fl.20s25M

N. Gäidharos

27

25°E        30'        26°17        30'        27°

**Megalonisi** Fl(2)15s21M

**Psará**
**Ák Áyios Yeóryios** Fl.10s25M

**Khíos**
**Ák Anapómera** Fl(3)12s11M
**Vrak Stróvilo** Fl.5s10M
**Ormiskos Mestá** Fl.3s7M
**Nisídha Venétiko** Fl(2)15s12M
**Nisís Pasas** Fl(2)20s11M

**Ikaría**
**Ák Páppas** Fl.20s25M
**Ák Armenistís** Fl(3)12s11M
**Vrak Evdhilos** (Kofinás) Fl.7·5s11M
**Ák Dhrépanon** Fl(3)24s12M

**Sámos**
**Ák Kótsikas** Fl(2)7·2s7M
**Ák Gátos** Fl(3)14s7M
**Ák Áyios Dhoménikos** Fl.3·6s5M
**Ák Pangózi** (Karlóvasi) Fl.5s11M

**Foúrnoi**
**Ák Trakhíli** Fl(2)15s7M
**Ák Saíta** (Malaki) Fl(2)12s8M

**USEFUL WAYPOINTS**
⊕1   1M N of Ák Pláka (Limnos)
      40°03'·1N 25°26'·8E
⊕2   1M W of Ák Moúrtzeflos
      (Limnos)
      39°59'·2N 25°01.0E
⊕3   1M S of Ák Kómbi (Limnos)
      39°46'·9N 25°14'·2E
⊕4   1M N of Ák Áy Apóstoliou (Áy
      Evstrátios)
      39°35'·0N 25°00'·2E
⊕5   1M S of Ák Tripití (Áy
      Evstrátios)
      39°26'·9N 24°59'·2E
⊕6   1M N of Ák Mólivos (Lésvos)
      39°23'·8N 26°11'·1E
⊕7   Mid-channel between N.
      Panayía and Yumurta Ad
      (Lésvos)
      39°19'·2N 26°29'·2E
⊕8   Mid-channel S end of Stenón
      Mitilinis
      39°00'·6N 26°41'·6E
⊕9   2M S of Ák Áy Fokas (Lésvos)
      38°58'·6N 26°10'·5E
⊕10  1M W of Vrak Sedhousa
      (Sígri/Lésvos)
      39°11'·9N 25°47'·8E
⊕11  2M S of Ák Áy Yeóryios (Psará)
      38°30'3N 25°36'·6E
⊕12  1M N of Vrak Gertis (Khíos)
      38°37'·4N 26°01'·6E
⊕13  Mid-channel N end of Stenón
      Oinoussa (Khíos)
      38°33'·0N 26°10'·4E

⊕14  Mid-channel S end of Stenón
      Khíou
      38°18'·0N 26°10'·5E
⊕15  ½M N of Nisídha Venétiko
      38°08'·1N 26°00'·9E
⊕16  1M W of Ák Mestá (Khíos)
      38°14'·6N 25°50'·7E
⊕17  1M S of Ák Páppas (Ikaría)
      37°29'·8N 25°58'·8E
⊕18  1M N of Ák Armenistís (Ikaría)
      37°39'·2N 26°05'·1E
⊕19  1M E of Ák Dhrépanon (Ikaría)
      37°41'·3N 26°22'·9E
⊕20  1M S of Ák Dhoménikos
      (Sámos)
      37°39'·7N 26°35'·5E
⊕21  1M N of Makronisi (Sámos)
      37°49'·0N 27°00'0E
⊕22  E end of Stenón Sámou
      (Sámos Strait)
      37°42'·1N 27°04'·0E
⊕23  ½M W of Bayrak Adasi light
      37°41'·6N 27°00'·6E
⊕24  1M S of Samioupoula
      37°36'·4N 26°48'·4E
⊕25  Mid-channel N end of Póros
      Fournon
      37°36'·0N 26°27'·8E
⊕26  Mid-channel S end of Póros
      Fournon
      37°33'·7N 26°27'·5E

# Limnos

(Lemnos)

Although it geographically belongs to the eastern Sporades, Limnos, situated as it is in the middle of the northern Aegean, is isolated from the other islands of the group. Few tourists go there and ships no longer call on the way to the Dardanelles – even the soldiers stationed there act as if the strategic significance of the island has been somehow overrated by the top brass and really they should be somewhere else. In ancient times none of this was true, when Limnos was an important island with one of the most advanced Bronze Age civilizations in Greece.

There were two main reasons for its importance. Lying halfway across the wind-tossed Aegean, it was the logical stepping stone between Europe and Asia Minor. It is likely that Troy was founded from Limnos and there was contact with Lésvos and northern Greece. As a stepping stone, Limnos possessed an abundance of well-sheltered natural harbours including the great Bay of Moudhros. Today, although the island is only partially wooded and cultivated on the east coast, it is easy to see how once, when the soft contours (there are no very high peaks) were covered in green woods, this was one of the finest islands in the northern Aegean.

The name Limnos is possibly derived from a cult of the Minoan mother-goddess, but the principal gods of the island were Hephaestus and the Kabeiri based on Samothráki. Hephaestus is supposed to have berated Zeus one day about his treatment of Hera whereupon he was thrown out of Olympus and fell onto Limnos – breaking both legs. Not until he had fashioned special leg-braces of gold could he walk. The myth probably derives from the volcanic nature of the island and also the tradition of metalworking that existed from early times when these skills spread from the north down to the Greek archipelago.

In classical times the island acquired ill repute from the so-called 'Limnian deeds'. The women of the island refused to serve Aphrodite who was making poor old Hephaestus miserable with her numerous affairs with other gods and mortals. Aphrodite responded by afflicting the unfortunate women with evil smells (Ernle Bradford suggests 'body odour and halitosis' in the euphemistic jargon of advertising) causing their husbands to ignore them. The incensed women of Limnos went on the rampage and murdered all males on the island. Jason and the Argonauts on their adventures discovered the island full of frustrated women and not surprisingly dallied two years repopulating it.

The site of the principal Bronze Age city is at Hephaestia on the east of the island. The Italians have excavated the site and also conducted underwater exploration of Charos Reef (Ifalos Keros) lying 7 miles off the east coast. The discovery of marble blocks gives some substance to the

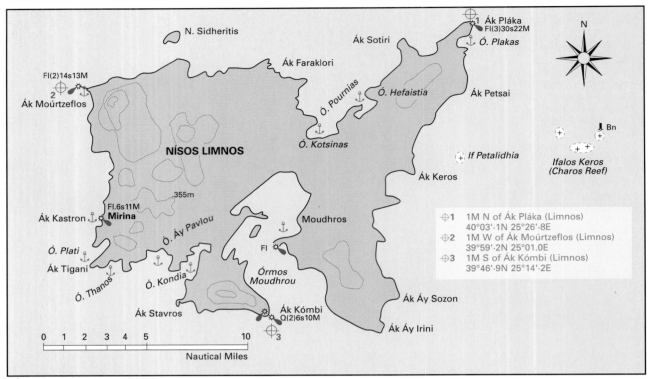

**NÍSOS LIMNOS**

identification of the reef with ancient Chryseis. It is thought this was the site of the ancient city until, as Herodotus recorded, it was engulfed by the sea after an earthquake.

Limnos achieved some prominence again when Moudhros Bay was the base for the Gallipoli campaign. Almost as if the failure of that campaign affected the island, ever since its importance has declined and even the tourist boom has only just touched the island. A local asked me when I was there: 'We have fine beaches, clear water, good harbours, friendly people, but no tourists – why?' I couldn't really tell him that I liked Limnos as it is, in its splendid isolation.

### MIRINA (Myrinas, Merini, Kástro)

BA 1636

### Approach

*Conspicuous* The castle on the rocky bluff on the N side of the entrance and a white church on a rocky bluff at the root of the outer breakwater are conspicuous. The buildings of the town can be seen from the N and W, but not from the S until you are into the bay. The S breakwater is easily identified.

*By night* Use the light on the castle Fl.6s11M and the lights at the entrance Q.R.3M/Q.G.3M. The inner basin is lit: F.R.2M.

### Mooring

Go stern or bows-to or alongside the N mole or the quay. The bottom is mud – good holding.

*Note* Care is needed of ferries which sometimes berth on the inside dock area. Usually the port police will come along and ask you to move off when this is going to happen.

*Shelter* Good shelter from the prevailing NE winds. Southerlies may cause a surge.

*Authorities* A port of entry: port police, customs and immigration. The most convenient port for clearing out to the Dardanelles.

*Note* The inner harbour is normally crowded with fishing boats. Because the inner harbour is so narrow anchor lines are weighted – a yacht wishing to moor here should enquire for a place and also ensure its anchor line is weighted. Under normal conditions the outer harbour affords good shelter so there is little to be gained by going into the inner harbour.

*Anchorage* It is possible to anchor off just inside the 5m line where convenient. The *meltemi* gusts down

Quay at Mirina looking across to the small inner basin

**MIRINA**
⊕39°52´·3N 25°03´·2E

into the bay but the holding is good on sand and weed.

*Note* Works are in progress on the S side of the bay constructing a large quay area for commercial ships.

### Facilities
*Water* On the quay.
*Fuel* Can be delivered by mini-tanker.

Mirina looking SE                    *Nigel Patten*

*Repairs* Some mechanical repairs and light engineering work. Good hardware and tool shops.
*Provisions* Good shopping for all provisions. Ice available nearby.
*Eating out* Several good tavernas near the inner harbour and on the beach.
*Other* PO. OTE. Banks. Greek gas. Helpful tourist office. Buses to the principal villages. Ferries to Lésvos, Piraeus and Kavála. Internal flights to Thessaloníki and Athens.

### General
Built near the site of the ancient capital, Mirina has only recently readopted its ancient name. Formerly it was called Kástro after the Genoese castle dominating the town. The castle is worth a visit as much for the site as for the castle itself – photographs are prohibited.

Few yachts visit Mirina and those which do use it primarily as the most convenient port for clearing for the Dardanelles. Yet it is a friendly place and a convenient base for visiting other anchorages around the island.

### ÓRMOS PLATÍ
Lies N of Ák Tigani and provides good shelter from N winds. Open to the SW. Care should be taken of the reef extending SE from the N side of the entrance and a reef on the SE side of the bay.

**ÓRMOS PLATI**
⊕39°51′·1N 25°03′·3E

Anchor in 4–8m on sand.
Tavernas on the beach.

## ÓRMOS THANOS

The double-headed bay lying just E of Ák Tigani. Care is needed of the reef and shoal water extending for half a mile SSW of Ák Tigani. Ifalos Tigani, a rock which occasionally dries, lies approximately 0·2 of a mile SSW of Nisís Tigani. There is reported to be a passage between Ifalos Tigani and Nisís Tigani with 7m depths, but this is not recommended. A yacht must keep well off the cape before making the approach to the bay. There are several places a yacht can anchor.

1. *Órmos Stiri* Immediately under Ák Tigani there is a cove where a yacht can anchor with a long line to the shore. Anchor in 4–8m.
2. On the W side of the islet in Órmos Thanos a yacht can anchor in 4–8m on sand. The head of this cove is rock-bound.
3. On the E side of the bay and the islet. This is the best anchorage. Anchor off the beach in 4–8m on sand. Good shelter from the *meltemi*. Taverna ashore.

**ÓRMOS THANOS**
⊕39°49′·2N 25°02′·9E

## ÓRMOS ÁY PAVLOU

The large bay lying E of Órmos Thanos. Care is needed of the reef and above-water rock in the middle of the bay. It is easily identified in calm weather. There are a number of places a yacht can anchor around the large bay.

1. In the SW corner. The head and sides of the cove are obstructed by reefs and shoal water. Anchor in 4–5m in the middle of the cove. Mediocre shelter from the *meltemi*.
2. In the NW corner. The N side of the cove is obstructed by reefs and shoal water. Anchor in the SW of the cove in 4–5m on sand and weed. Mediocre shelter from the *meltemi*.
3. At the head of the bay off the long beach. Anchor in 4–6m on sand and shingle. Reasonable shelter from the *meltemi*.
4. In the cove on the E side. Anchor in 3–6m on sand. Good shelter from the *meltemi*.

**ÓRMOS ÁY PAVLOU**
⊕39°50′·7N 25°07′·6E

**ÓRMOS KONDÍA**
⊕39 50′·8N 25 09′·8E

## ÓRMOS KONDÍA

The large bay E of Órmos Áy Pavlou and N of Ák Stavrós. There are several places a yacht can anchor around the large bay.

1. On the W side of the bay there are several coves where a yacht can anchor. Mostly 3–8m on sand. Reasonable shelter can be found from the *meltemi*.
2. *Dhiapori* At the NE head of the bay is Dhiapori. Anchor in 4–7m off the hamlet on mud. Good shelter from the *meltemi*.
   Tavernas ashore.

## ÓRMOS MOUDHROU (Moudra)

BA 1636

### Approach

*Conspicuous* The entrance to the large bay is easily identified. Nisís Kómbi and the light tower on it are conspicuous. Once through the channel between Ák Áspro Kávos and Pondikonisia, the village of Moudhros and a cathedral in it are easily identified.

*By night* Use the lights on Nisís Kómbi Q(2)6s10M and Ák Áspro Kávos Fl.3s5M, the light buoys marking the channel Q.G/Q.R, and the lightbuoys at Moudhros (Q.G and Q.R, but not to be relied upon).

*Dangers*
1. Care must be taken of the reef extending for half a mile SW from Ák Velanidhia, the E entrance point.
2. Once up to Ák Áspro Kávos care is needed of the extensive reefs and shoal water bordering the coast and islets in the bay. The plan can only show these approximately and it is recommended you use BA 1636 if you intend to explore the bay in detail.

### Mooring

Once into the bay there is a choice of anchorages or a yacht can proceed to the town of Moudhros on the E side of the bay.

*Moudhros* At Moudhros there are 3–4m depths off the outer half of the pier. Go alongside or stern or bows-to as far towards the root of the pier as possible to leave room for local coasters to berth. The S side is recommended as giving better shelter from the *meltemi*. A small harbour with the entrance

**MOUDHROS - HARBOUR AND ANCHORAGES**
⊕₁ 39°47′·9N 25°14′·2E (Kombi light)
⊕₂ 39°51′·1N 25°14′·33E

**MOUDHROS HARBOUR**
⊕39°52′·3N 25°15′·8E

on the S side is mostly shallow, but with care a small yacht can use it.

*Shelter* Good shelter from the *meltemi*.

*Authorities* Port police at Moudhros.

*Anchorages* There are numerous anchorages around the large bay.

Freshwater Bay in Órmos Moudhrou       *Nigel Patten*

1. **Blenheim Cove (Ó. Pedhinou)** Open NE–E.
2. N of Nisís Alogo under the headland ending in Ák Kaloyeraki.
3. **Órmos Vourlidhia** Open NE. Care is needed of the shoal in the bay. 3–4m depths on the E and SE of the shoal reported.
4. **Fuller Cove** Open NE.
5. **Tarrant Cove** Open NE.
6. **Órmos Kávos** Under Ák Áspro Kávos. Open S.
7. **Freshwater Cove** Good shelter from N winds reported here.

### Facilities
(At Moudhros village)
*Water* On the quay.
*Fuel* In the town.
*Provisions* Most provisions can be obtained in the village.
*Eating out* Several tavernas.
*Other* PO. OTE. Bus to Mirina. The airport is near the head of the bay.

### General
Órmos Moúdhrou is one of the finest fleet anchorages in the northern Aegean and it was from here the ill-fated Gallipoli campaign was launched. North of Moudhros village lies Australian pier and the remains of Egyptian pier. I find it difficult to conjure up what it must have been like when the bay was packed full of battleships, cruisers, destroyers and transport ships when looking at the forgotten and deserted bay today.

In the plan of Moudhros Bay I have identified Yam, Yrroc, Eb and Denmad Hills which when read from right to left, as H. M. Denham points out, tells us what the British surveyors thought of their captain who was alleged to have worked them too hard and stopped their leave. Photographs are prohibited of some sites around the bay.

## East and north coast
On the E coast there are several large bays that can be used in calm weather. Care must be taken of Ifalos Petalidhia and Ifalos Keros (Charos Reef) lying off the E coast.

### ÓRMOS PLAKAS
40°01'·25N 25°27'·0E
On the SE side of Ák Pláka there is a large bay with a short breakwater at the N end. There are 2–4m depths on the outer end of the quay where a yacht can go bows-to with care. Alternatively anchor in 3–5m in the lee of the breakwater.

### ÓRMOS HEFAISTIA (Ekato Kefales)
39°58'·3N 25°20'·3E
The large bay of Órmos Pournias lies on the N coast between Ák Sotini and Ák Faraklon. On the E side of this bay is Órmos Hefaistia where some shelter can be found from the *meltemi*. Anchor in 5–8m on mud or sand.

### ÓRMOS KOTSINAS
39°57'·0N 25°17'·5E
The bay on the SW side of Órmos Pournias. Some shelter from the *meltemi* tucked under the N side of the bay. Anchor in 5–8m. Military post ashore. Taverna on the S side of the bay.

### ÓRMOS MOÚRTZEFLOS
39°58'·9N 25°02'·8E
On the S side of Ák Moúrtzeflos there is a small cove under the sand bar that affords good shelter from the *meltemi*. Open S. Anchor in 5–7m on sand and shingle.

# Nísos Áyios Evstrátios

### ÁYIOS EVSTRÁTIOS
#### Approach
*Conspicuous* The harbour lies 1½ miles SSW of Ák Kalamáki, beneath a small hill with a conspicuous whitewashed cemetery on the top.
*By night* The end of the mole is lit: Fl.R.2s3M.

#### Mooring
There are 3m depths along most of the length of the new quay and yachts can berth alongside or stern or bows-to. A sandy bottom with scattered rocks gives fair holding although there is some weed causing difficulty in places.
*Shelter* Reasonable shelter from the *meltemi* although a surge develops with prolonged NE winds. Open SW.

#### Facilities
*Water* On the quay although a long hose is needed.
*Provisions* Most provisions can be found in the village.
*Eating out* One taverna.
*Other* PO. Metered telephone at the taverna. Infrequent ferries in summer to Evia and Limnos.

ÁYIOS EVSTRÁTIOS
⊕39°32'·4N 24°59'·2E

Áyios Evstrátios looking NW                    *Nigel Patten*

of room for visitors and no commercialism, but very little of interest to see either.

The harbour is a useful stopover between the northern Sporades and Lésvos. The rest of the island is rocky and barren, but there are some pleasant beaches and caves under the cliffs. Until recently political offenders were deported to the island.

# Nísos Lésvos
## (Lesbos, Mitilíni, Mytilene)

One of the largest islands in the Aegean after Crete and Evia and the largest of the eastern Sporades, Lésvos is the jewel of the group. It is grander, greener and more fertile than any of the other islands. A prosperity founded on agriculture and local industry provides an economic balance rarely seen in the Greek islands and tourism simply provides the icing on the cake.

The island is roughly oval in shape with two deep landlocked gulfs on the southern side. It is mountainous throughout, rising from Mt Ordhimos (512m, 1,680ft) in the west to the twin peaks of Mt Olympus in the southeast and Mt Lebetimnos in the northeast (by coincidence they are both 958m or 3,176ft). In the west the island is mostly barren and

## General

Since the 1968 earthquake which destroyed many of the buildings the population has dwindled to about 300, almost all of whom live in the one fishing village. The new breakwater and quay were only finished at the end of 1986 and as yet there is plenty

**NISOS LÉSVOS**

⊕6  1M N of Ák Mólivos (Lésvos)
    39°23'·8N 26°11'·1E
⊕7  Mid-channel between N. Panayía and Yumurta Ad (Lésvos)
    39°19'·2N 26°29'·2E
⊕8  Mid-channel S end of Stenón Mitilinis
    39°00'·6N 26°41'·6E
⊕9  2M S of Ák Áy Fokas (Lésvos)
    38°58'·6N 26°10'·5E
⊕10 1M W of Vrak Sedhousa (Sígri/Lésvos)
    39°11'·9N 25°47'·8E

rocky, but the interior and the east are forested with olives, chestnuts, oak, pine and poplar, though sadly in 1992 a forest fire razed a large area. The flat land is cultivated with market gardens and fields of tobacco. The olives of Lésvos have long been celebrated and today the plump olives and Lésvos olive oil are among the best in Greece.

Just as the spacious and wooded island is pleasing to the eye, so the ancient associations are memorable ones of the gentle arts of music and philosophy. Greatest of all is the poetess Sappho who was born on Lésvos about 612 BC, although it is uncertain exactly where she was born – perhaps Eressos or Mitilíni. Allegations that Sappho was a lover of her own sex gave the word Lesbian to the world, although this is based on just a few lines of her poetry (to Atthis – 'I was in love with you once Atthis, long ago . . .') and appears to have been contrived to cast a slur on her character and poetry after the 7th century AD. Today allegations of homosexuality matter less and we are only just beginning to uncover fragments of her poetry. For nearly 1,000 years Sappho was regarded almost as a goddess, Plato called her the tenth muse and later only Catullus and Horace came close to her flowing and sensual poetry. These lines are from a translation of Catullus:

'Godlike the man who
sits at her side, who
watches and catches
that laughter
which (softly) tears me
to tatters: nothing is
left of me, each time
I see her,
. . .tongue numbed; arms, legs
melting, on fire; drum
drumming in ears; head–
lights gone black.'

Sappho is said to have died in true poetic style, jumping off the cliffs on the southwest corner of Levkas when rejected by her lover Phaon – though in fact there is no real evidence that she ever visited Levkas. Still, it's an appropriately tragic story.

Sappho did not emerge from a cultural vacuum. The names associated with Lésvos are a rollcall of gentle artists and wise sages: Terpander the father of Greek music; Arion the dolphin-loving poet; Alcaeus, a contemporary of Sappho; Pitticus, who united the cities of the island and whose wise rule won him a place among the Seven Sages of Greece; Epicurus, whose benign humanitarian philosophy was forgotten after Christianity and only later rediscovered; Aristotle, who resided for some time here; and Aesop who wrote many of his fables on Lésvos. Indeed it is difficult to find anybody who was nasty living on Lésvos in ancient times, though I'm sure they were lurking in the background.

The geographical position of Lésvos and its sheltered natural harbours meant that from ancient times the island was an important trade link between Asia and Greece. Mitilíni is still reminiscent of the Levant and the old trading days, but the division between Greece and Turkey severed communications and destroyed the island's role as a commercial intermediary. After prosperity in ancient Greek and Roman times the island suffered from Saracen invasions and Byzantine expulsions of the invaders and, not surprisingly, the local inhabitants moved away from the sea to the hills. Not until the 14th century, when Lésvos was given to that remarkable Genoese adventurer Francesco Gattelusio, did the island again enjoy some measure of calm and prosperity. For a century the island was once more a trading centre. In 1462 the Turks occupied Lésvos and it effectively remained under Turkish occupation until 1912.

The heritage of the island is largely literary and cultural and its archaeological remains are few and undistinguished. It was Sappho who said that poets attain immortality and long after hewn stones have gone, her poetry and her loves will be remembered.

## MITILINI (Mytilene)

BA 1675
Imray-Tetra G27

### Approach

*Conspicuous* The buildings of the town and the castle on the headland are conspicuous from some distance off. Closer in, a large circular building and a monument in front of it are conspicuous. The outer breakwater and harbour entrance are easily identified.

*Note*
1. Work is in progress on a new breakwater enclosing Vórios Limineas Mitilinis on the N side of Ák Kástro and the castle. This is expected to be the new commercial port.
2. A detached breakwater has been built across the entrance to Mitilíni harbour. Entrance is between the E end of the detached breakwater and the old E harbour breakwater. The ends of the detached breakwater are marked by a green buoy at the W end and a red buoy at the E end.
3. Work is in progress improving the outer harbour. Care needed.

*By night* Use the lights on Ák Kástro (the castle headland) Fl(3)14s6M, on the outer breakwater Fl.G.3s7M, and at the entrance to the inner basin Fl.G.1·5s3M/Fl.R.1·5s3M. The Fl.G at the entrance to the inner basin is weak and cannot be confused with the Fl.G on the outer breakwater. The detached breakwater is lit Q.G and Fl.R.3s5M, and the yacht club pier Q.R.4M.

### Mooring

Proceed into the inner harbour and moor alongside or stern or bows-to on the N or E side. The bottom is soft mud and some plough-type anchors will drag through it. The harbour can be smelly at times from sewage emptying into it.

*Shelter* Good all-round shelter, although the harbour can be uncomfortable with strong S winds. Moor in the SW corner of the inner harbour during these winds.

*Authorities* A port of entry: port police, customs and immigration authorities.

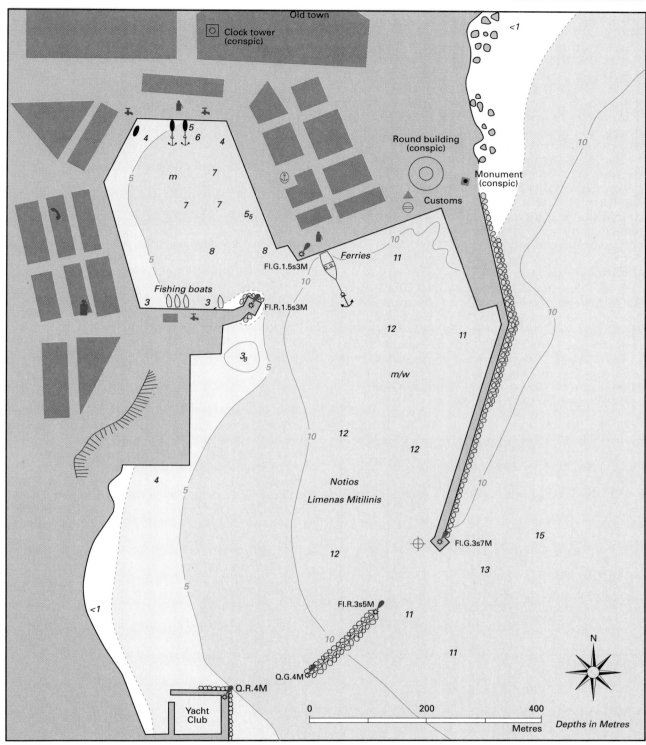

**MITILINI**
⊕39°06′.0N 26°33′·8E

## Facilities

*Water* On the quay by arrangement with the resident 'water man'.

*Fuel* Near the quay. A mini-tanker can deliver.

*Repairs* General mechanical repairs and light engineering work. A yard on the N side of the castle can haul yachts. Good hardware and tool shops. Limited chandlery.

*Provisions* Excellent shopping for all provisions. Ice available out of town.

*Eating out* Good tavernas including some good fish tavernas on the S mole.

*Other* PO. OTE. Banks. Greek gas and *Camping Gaz*. Hire cars and motorbikes. Buses to the principal towns and villages. Ferries to Piraeus and Ayvalik in Turkey. Internal flights and some European flights in the summer.

## General

Mitilíni is the commercial heart of the island. Coasters, trading *caïques* and large fishing craft clutter the harbour. The town hums with local industry. In the old town the narrow winding streets are lined with market stalls and local craft shops – the atmosphere is redolent of an Oriental bazaar. The whole combines into a likeable Levantine mixture and the city, at first noisy and grubby, in the end charms the visitor.

On the waterfront and scattered around the outskirts of Mitilíni are some grand old baronial houses dating from the prosperous mercantile era of the harbour. The archaeological museum houses finds from the classical period and some wonderful mosaics from a Roman villa showing figures from Menander's comedies.

## PANAYIOUDHA

The small harbour of Panayioudhia lies close NW of Ák Asfali, the prominent cape 1¾ miles N of Mitilíni. The entrance is lit F.G/F.R, though the lights should not be relied on. There is little room for yachts, but with care a small yacht can go bows-to the W quay. Care is needed of the shoal water extending from the N quay across to the end of the N breakwater. Good shelter from the *meltemi*.

Provisions and tavernas ashore.

**PANAYIOUDHA**
⊕39°08'·4N 26°31'·5E

## PAMFILLA

39°09'·7N 26°32'·4E

Lying close under Ák Makhaira there is an attractive bay sheltered from the *meltemi*. Anchor at the head of the bay N of the islet in 4–6m. Taverna ashore.

## SKÁLA THERMÍS

A small harbour for Thermís village above. Care is needed at the entrance which is narrow and close to the coast. Make the approach from the E and then turn hard to starboard to enter. The entrance is lit F.G/F.R, though the lights should not be relied on. Go stern or bows-to or alongside the quay on the W side near the entrance. There is shoal water off the

**SKÁLA THERMÍS**
⊕39°10'·9N 26°30'·0E

quay along the breakwater. Good shelter.

Water near the quay. Fuel nearby. Taverna.

Ancient Thermís is inland. The hot mineral springs still exist and a hotel has been built nearby. The springs were famous in the ancient world and a temple to Artemis and a complex of baths were excavated by the British School of Archaeology in the early 1930s.

## SKÁLA MISTEGNA

Lying 7 miles NW of Mitilíni, this is the small harbour for the village of Mistegna on the hill above. The harbour is open to the SE–E. Moor bows-to the outer end of the mole taking care of the ballasting which extends underwater. The mole is usually crowded with local fishing boats so you will probably have to anchor in the more exposed S half of the bay. The bottom is mostly sand and weed with some rock patches. With strong winds from any sector this is not he best place to be.

Tavernas ashore and most supplies can be obtained in the village above.

**SKÁLA MISTEGNA**
⊕39°13'·0N 26°28'·9E

## ÓRMOS MAKRIS YIALOS

Nisídha Panayia light 39°18'·9N 26°26'·8E

In the large bay of Makris Yialos SW of Ák Tomari there are a number of coves on the N side providing some shelter from the *meltemi*.

*Caution* Órmos Makris Yialos and Nisídhes Tomaria in the bay are fringed by above and below-water rocks. Caution must be exercised in this area. Approximately one mile S of Ák Tomari a reef extends for some 400m in a NE direction from the shore. In the S part of Órmos Makris Yialos there is an islet known as Praselogos or Erimonisi which is fringed by underwater rocks. Special care must be taken of these as they are not well marked on earlier charts.

## SKÁLA SIKAMINEAS

39°22'·5N 26°18'·3E

One and a half miles SW of Ák Skamnia (Kórakas) lies the miniature fishing harbour of Skála Sikaminéas in which there is room for 1 or 2 small yachts drawing no more than 1·5m. A Fl.G.3s3M is exhibited at the end of the mole. Moor bows-to the extremity of the mole. Good shelter with N winds but in strong NE winds the harbour could be dangerous. A taverna and limited provisions available in the fishing hamlet.

*Note* There are plans to extend the mole in a NE direction for approximately 50 metres.

## MITHIMNA (Methymna, Mólivos)

### Approach

*Conspicuous* The castle on the hill above the town is conspicuous from some distance off. Closer in, the town and the huddle of buildings around the small harbour at the foot of the hill can be seen.

*By night* Care needed. Use the light on Ák Mólivos LFl.WG.10s12/8M (green sector covers 219°-239° only) and the light at Mithimna F.R.3M. A Fl.R.3s3M is exhibited at the end of the mole.

*Dangers*

1. Above and below-water rocks fringe Ák Mólivos and the harbour mole for some distance. The harbour should be entered from the SE.
2. The entrance to the inner basin is very narrow (about 10m wide but free of obstructions) and small yachts only will be able to enter the harbour which is crowded with fishing boats.

### Mooring

Go stern or bows-to or alongside the outer mole where convenient. The bottom is mud, sand and weed, good holding. In the inner basin there is little room amongst the fishing boats. The bottom in the inner basin is thin mud over rock, bad holding.

*Shelter* Good shelter in the outer part of the harbour and excellent shelter in the inner basin.

*Authorities* Port police and customs.

*Anchorage* In calm weather a yacht can anchor in the bay, but a swell sets in with the *meltemi* and the holding is uncertain.

**MITHIMNA**
⊕39°22'·1N 26°10'·2E

Mithimna looking up to the castle

## Facilities
*Water* On the quay.
*Provisions* Good shopping for all provisions in the town. Ice on the quay.
*Eating out* Good tavernas in the town and around the harbour.
*Other* PO. OTE. Bank. Hire bikes. Bus to Mitilíni.

## General
Arion, the lyric poet (625 BC), who was saved from drowning by a music-loving dolphin, was born here. Presumably his spirit survives as the town has developed into something of an artists' resort as well as a tourist resort.

The town is a maze of cobbled streets and passages winding in and out of medieval fortifications, and a historical preservation order will hopefully keep it that way. The stone and timber houses, many with small timber balconies, look over the cliffs to the bay beneath. A growing number of tourists come to Mithimna as not only is the town pleasant and near to good bathing beaches, but the locals are welcoming – the clink of glasses will often be heard late into the night.

## PÉTRA (Kavaki)
A small village off a sandy beach under Ák Kavaki. There is a small harbour N of Pétra village on the S side of Ák Kavaki. Anchor off the village in 5–10m on sand and weed. Poor shelter from the *meltemi* here. Under the mole on the N side of the bay there

is reasonable shelter from the *meltemi*. A Fl.R.3s3M is exhibited on the end of the mole. Go stern or bows-to the outer end of the mole. A few fishing boats are kept here but otherwise it is deserted.

The village of Pétra is a sleepy place with some modest tourism in the summer. Some provisions can be obtained and there are tavernas. The bay and the village are a delight, being wooded and well-watered. In the village the church of Panayía Glykofiloussa built on a rocky bluff near the beach stands out from seaward.

*Caution* Care is needed of the reef in the bay off the village. A stick sometimes marks the reef but is not to be relied upon. In calm weather it is possible to anchor under the islet to the W – care is needed in the vicinity of the islet of the above and below-water rocks around it.

**PÉTRA**
⊕39°20´.3N 26°10´.7E

## GHAVDHOLOS (Gavatha)

### Approach
The islet to the E of the harbour (Vrakhos Megálo Gavatha) and the church and bell-tower on the headland are conspicuous. Once around the island the mole and harbour entrance are easily identified.

### Mooring
Go stern or bows-to or alongside the mole where there is room. The bottom is mud and weed, good holding. Good shelter from the *meltemi*.

*Dangers* You will have to turn sharply to starboard to avoid the shallows on the W side of the harbour.

### Facilities
Water near the quay. Some provisions in the village and a taverna.

### General
The little village is a friendly place where the locals

**GHAVADHOLOS**
⊕ Nisis Ghavadas light Fl.2s4M 39°18′·1N 26°01′·4E

eke out a living fishing or cultivating the fertile land around the head of the bay. There are reported to be hot springs here, but although I got whiffs of sulphuretted hydrogen from the shore by the village, I couldn't find them.

## LIMÍN SIGRIOU (Sígri)

BA 1675
Imray-Tetra G27

### Approach

From the N the narrow N channel between Megalonísi (Nísos Sígri) and Lésvos can be used by day. There are least depths of 4·5m in the fairway of the N channel. The reef extending NE from Megalonísi is marked by breakers. In the S channel between Vrak Sedhousa and Lésvos there are considerable depths.

**APPROACHES TO SÍGRI**
⊕ 39°11′·4N 25°50′·0E

*Conspicuous* From the S, Vrak Sedhousa, the lighthouse on Megalonísi and Sígri village are conspicuous.

*By night* Use the light on Megalonísi Fl(2)15s21M and the light on Ák Saratsina Fl.WR.3s5/3M (red

Ghavadholos looking SE from the hamlet

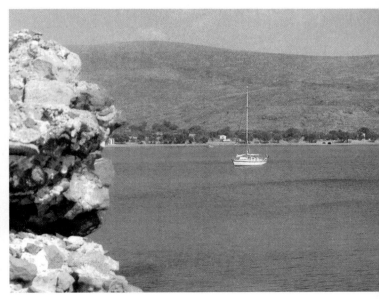

Sígri. The anchorage on the S side of the headland

**PORT SIGRI**
⊕39°12'·8N 25°50'·8E

sector covers 122°–160° and 219°–270°). Care is needed in a night approach from the S. The N channel should not be attempted at night under any circumstances. The NW corner of the quay is lit Fl.2s5M.

*Dangers* Care is needed in the N channel when a heavy sea is running and breakers heap up over the shoal water in the vicinity and the channel itself.

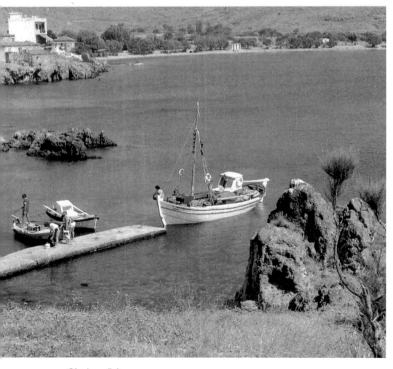

Sígri on Lésvos

### Mooring

Anchor in the cove on the S side of Sígri village or go alongside the quay tucked as far as possible into the NE corner. The bottom is sand, weed and rock and is poor holding in patches.

*Shelter* It can get a little bumpy on the quay, but not dangerous unless the wind turns to the W or S in which case anchor N of the promontory.

*Note* The fishing harbour on the N side of Sígri has been enlarged and there may be room inside for yachts. Shelter in here would appear to be good.

### Facilities

*Water* On the W quay and near the *caïque* harbour.
*Fuel* Near the quay.
*Provisions* Most provisions in the village.
*Eating out* Several tavernas and cafés.
*Other* PO. Bus to Mitilini.

### General

A few tourists visit this fishing village for the nearby sandy beaches, but for the most part life carries on much as it has always done. Sígri is noted in most guide books for its petrified forest on the W coast, but most visitors are not impressed by the sight. For the yachtsman the petrified remains near the lighthouse on Megalonísi (Nisís Sígri) are more accessible.

### ERRESOS (Skála Erresos)

A small fishing harbour approximately midway between Sígri and Kólpos Kalloni. Care is needed in the approaches of a rock just awash between Vrak Niraki and the end of the breakwater. A yacht should leave Niraki to starboard in the approaches to the harbour.

In calm weather a yacht can anchor off the beach in 2–4m or go stern or bows-to the end of the breakwater if there is room. Small yachts may find a berth inside the small basin with local boats. Adequate shelter from the prevailing winds on the breakwater. Open S and W.

The village ashore is a small and amicable resort. PO. OTE. Exchange office. Provisions and tavernas. Taxis.

It is a pleasant walk to the main village of Erresos about 2km inland.

### KÓLPOS KALLONI

BA 1675
Imray-Tetra G27

#### Approach and entrance

The narrow mountainous entrance to this large landlocked gulf is easily negotiated by day. Proceed on the N side of Vrak Kalloni taking care of the reef extending 0·15 miles NE of it. The channel is on the S side of the shoal and reef obstructing most of the channel close to the land on the S side. It is well marked by buoys.

*By night* Not recommended despite the lights available. Use the light on Vrak Kalloni Fl.3s6M and the light buoys marking the channel Q.R and Q.G.

**ERRESOS**
⊕39°07′·8N 25°55′·8E

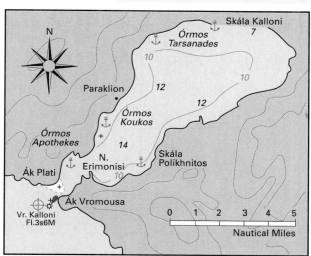

**KÓLPOS KALLONI**
⊕39°04′·7N 26°04′·7E

Erimonisi and the isolated reef 250m off Ák Apothekes on the W entrance to the bay. Anchor in the bay in 5–10m or go bows-to the short pier where there are 3m depths off the end, though care must be taken of rock ballasting. A number of fishermen and their families inhabit the hamlet and in a simple taverna at the root of the pier simple fare is served.

2. **Órmos Koukos** A bay approximately 2½ miles N of the entrance to the gulf. Anchor in 8–10m. Some shelter from the *meltemi*.

3. **Paraklion** A bight just above Koukos. Anchor in 4–6m off a small breakwater. Poor shelter from the *meltemi*.

4. **Órmos Tarsanades** A bight in the NW corner of the gulf. Poor shelter from the *meltemi*.

5. **Skála Kalloni** An L-shaped mole protects a small harbour at the head of the gulf. There are 1·5–2m depths along the outer end of the mole. Go alongside if possible. Further inside it gets shallow. Alternatively anchor off the beach. Provisions and tavernas ashore. PO.

6. **Skála Polikhnitos** A small harbour just E of the entrance to the gulf. Go bows-to (there is some underwater ballasting) the outer mole. Good protection from the *meltemi*.

**ENTRANCE TO KOLPOS KALLONI**
⊕39°04′·7N 26°04′·7E

## Anchorages in the gulf

1. **Órmos Apothekes** This bay on the N side of the entrance affords the best shelter in the gulf. Care must be taken of the reefs and shoal water around

Órmos Apothekes looking SE

**SKÁLA POLIKHNITOS**
⊕39°06′·1N 26°10′·1E

Plomárion harbour looking SE from the town

Water on the quay and fuel nearby. Some provisions and tavernas ashore.

**Note** With the *meltemi* there are fierce gusts into Kólpos Kalloni and a considerable sea can be raised despite the limited fetch.

## PLOMÁRION (Plomari)

### Approach

*Conspicuous* The town is conspicuous from some distance off. A cathedral with belfry behind the harbour is conspicuous. The harbour moles and light structures are easily identified.

*By night* Use the lights at the entrance: Fl.G.3s3M/Fl.R.3s3M.

### Mooring

Go stern or bows-to or alongside the projecting quay or on the W mole with a long line ashore. Care is needed as underwater ballasting extends out from the quay in places. The bottom is sand with some rocks.

*Shelter* Good shelter from the *meltemi*, although somehow a surge can develop making it uncomfortable. With S winds a swell enters the harbour. Nonetheless the fishing boats are kept here in the winter in the SW corner of the harbour.

*Authorities* Port police and customs.

### Facilities

*Water* On the quay.

*Fuel* In the town and can be delivered by mini-tanker.

*Repairs* Some mechanical repairs possible. General hardware shops.

*Provisions* Excellent shopping for provisions.

*Eating out* Good local tavernas in the town.

*Other* PO. OTE. Bank. Hire bikes. Bus to Mitilíni.

### General

Plomárion was established in the 19th century (as Bilmar) when the islanders moved down to the shores after piracy had been suppressed. Narrow cobbled streets and passages wind in and out of the stone and timber houses built in a Turkish style with wooden balconies. Behind the town the countryside is covered in olive groves and thick chestnut and pine forest so that the town, sandwiched between the sea and the mountains, is a wonderful place. Plomárion is also famous for its *ouzo*, marketed as *Barbajanis Ouzo*, which is praised by connoisseurs of the aniseed-flavoured brew all over the northern Aegean.

## ÓRMOS MERSINIA AND ÓRMOS TARTI

A large bay lying 3 miles SW of the entrance to Kólpos Yéras behind Ák Petras. It is a double-headed bay. Anchor at the head of the W cove in 4–10m. The bottom is sand and weed – bad holding. It is difficult getting the anchor through the thick weed on the bottom. Good shelter from the *meltemi*, although there are gusts so make sure the anchor is properly dug in. Alternatively anchor in the E cove in 5–10m.

The bay sits under heavily wooded slopes and is a

**PLOMÁRION**
⊕38°58′·4N 26°22′·2E

**ORMOS MERSINIA**
⊕38°58´·0N 26°30´·8E

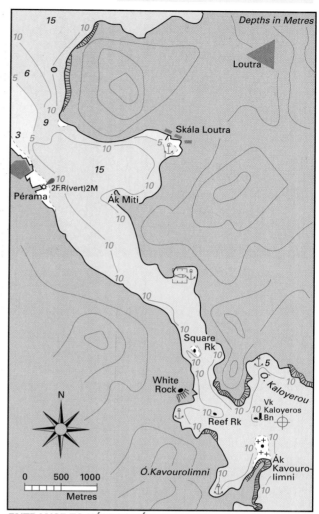

**ENTRANCE TO KÓLPOS YÉRAS**
⊕39°00´·5N 26°32´·7E

**KÓLPOS YÉRAS**
⊕39°00´·5N 26°32´·7E

delightful place. There is also a good anchorage in Órmos Tarti immediately W. Taverna at Órmos Tarti.

## KÓLPOS YÉRAS

BA 1675
Imray-Tetra G27

### Approach and entrance

This second landlocked gulf lies about 25 miles E of Kólpos Kalloni. The approach is straightforward by day but should not be attempted at night. Keeping well clear of Ák Kavourolimni which has a reef running N of it, pass between the cape and Vrak Kalóyeros, a reef marked by a beacon. Leave the beacon about 150m to starboard and proceed up the channel leaving Reef Rock (Vromonisi) and Square Rock (Áy Vasilios) to port.

### Anchorages in Kólpos Yéras

1. *Skála Loutra* The bay on the E side of the entrance channel. Anchor in 5–10m on mud. There are 2–4m depths off most of the short pier. Water ashore. Several café/tavernas. A yard on the E side of the bay.
2. *Angali Palaioloutrou* In the cove in the entrance channel S of Loutra. There is now a fish farm here, but there is still room to anchor.
3. *Diption* (Dipti, Nipti) In the NW corner of the gulf. There are 5m depths off the extremity of the mole and a taverna ashore.
4. SE corner. In settled weather there is a delightful cove in the SE corner of the gulf.
5. *Pérama* On the W side of the entrance channel. In calm weather a yacht can go bows-to the end of the pier where there are reported to be 2·5m depths. It is a shabby place and the water is polluted by the nearby tannery. Port police.
6. *Órmos Kavourolimni* The bay tucked under the W entrance point to the gulf. Also just N of

Skála Loutra in Kólpos Yéras on Lésvos looking NW
*Peter Kleinoth/MareTeam*

Kavourolimni on the W side there is an attractive bay.

7. ***Órmos Kaloyerou*** The bay tucked under the E entrance point looks to offer good shelter from the *meltemi*.

*Note* With the *meltemi* blowing gusts into the gulf are not as fierce as those blowing into Kólpos Kalloni.

# Nísos Khíos and adjacent islands

## Nísos Psará

Psará is a small barren island lying 10 miles west of the north of Khíos. Together with Spétsai and Hydra, Psará was one of the first islands to revolt against the Turks. Its ships harried Turkish shipping along the coast, scoring some notable successes. On a number of occasions the Turks mounted expeditions to squash the small island community, but were unable to land because of bad weather until June 1824. In that year Hosref Pasha landed a large force and massacred the population. A few survivors established Néa Psará (Erétria) on Evia. The island has never recovered.

### PSARÁ

BA 1058
Imray-Tetra G28

### Approach

*Conspicuous* The small village on the low ridge of Ák Trifilli is easily seen from the distance. Two large churches in the village are conspicuous from the E and S. The mole will not be seen until close to. A green conical buoy is reported to be in place approximately 150m due E of the N entrance point.

*By night* Use the light on Ák Áy Yeóryios Fl.10s25M

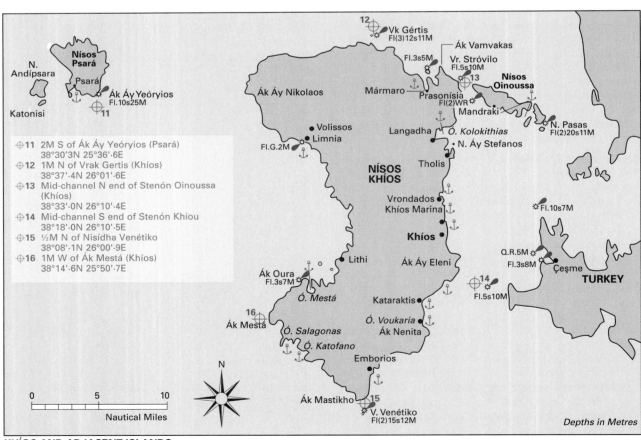

11   2M S of Ák Áy Yeóryios (Psará)
    38°30′3N 25°36′·6E
12   1M N of Vrak Gertis (Khíos)
    38°37′·4N 26°01′·6E
13   Mid-channel N end of Stenón Oinoussa
    (Khíos)
    38°33′·0N 26°10′·4E
14   Mid-channel S end of Stenón Khíou
    38°18′·0N 26°10′·5E
15   ½M N of Nisídha Venétiko
    38°08′·1N 26°00′·9E
16   1M W of Ák Mestá (Khíos)
    38°14′·6N 25°50′·7E

**KHÍOS AND ADJACENT ISLANDS**

Psará harbour looking W          *Peter Kleinoth/MareTeam*

**PSARA**
⊕38°32′·4N 25°34′·1E

and the light at the entrance Fl.R.1·5s3M. The green buoy is lit Fl.G but should not be relied upon. The inner mole is lit: F.R.3M. The harbour lights are not always to be relied on.

*Dangers* When approaching from the W care should be taken of the reefs fringing Nisís Andípsara and Katonisi. These islands and rocks are not lit at night making a night approach from the W difficult.

### Mooring
Go stern or bows-to where convenient. The bottom is mud and weed with some rocks – good holding.

*Shelter* Good all-round shelter although strong NE winds may make it uncomfortable.

*Authorities* Port police.

### Facilities
*Water* Limited supplies on the island.
*Provisions* Limited provisions available but the villagers are dependent on the ferry from Khíos for many things.
*Eating out* Several tavernas.
*Other* PO. Local ferry to Khíos.

### General
There is little left of what was a prosperous town: a few crumbling houses and warehouses, windmills on the ridges and the large natural harbour. In recent years some of the houses have been restored and a little life is creeping back into the village.

Inland amongst the scorched rock of the island (there is little good earth for cultivation) is a Mycenaean necropolis, though it has not been systematically excavated to date. Homer mentioned the island, (he called it Psyrie), but said nothing about it, and apart from the brief age when it possessed a fine merchant fleet and lost it all against the Turks, to most people including Greeks the name Psará means little or nothing to this day.

## Nísos Oinoussa

This barren island lies just over a mile to the east of the north of Khíos. At one time it supported a prosperous seafaring community, but today the population is much diminished.

### MANDRÁKI (Oinoussa)
### Approach
*Conspicuous* From the S the village is conspicuous from the distance. From the N Vrak Prasonísia and

**MANDRÁKI (Oinoussa)**
⊕38°30′·7N 26°13′·2E

the light structure on it are easily identified. Closer in the church and light structure on Nisís Mandráki (Áy Pantelimonios) are easily seen and rounding Mandráki the harbour mole will be seen.

*By night* Use the light on Prasonísia Fl(2)WR.10s6/4M (red sector 301°-323°), on Nisís Mandráki Fl.2s4M, and the lights at the entrance Q.G.3M/Q.R.3M. The pier inside is lit: F.G.3M.

*Caution* The island of Oinoussa is fringed by reefs. Care should be taken of the reef lying approximately

Mandráki harbour on Oinoussa looking W from close to the short N mole

0·7M SE of Prasonísia – it usually has breaking water over it. There are 10m depths in the fairway between this reef and Nísos Oinoussa. The three islets protecting Mandráki harbour are joined to one another by shallow rock-bound bars and there is no entrance between them.

**Mooring**
Go stern or bows-to where convenient or anchor off. The bottom is mud and weed – good holding.

*Shelter* Good all-round shelter: a yacht can always find somewhere secure to moor in the harbour, even with strong SE winds which do not blow home.

*Authorities* Port police and customs.

**Facilities**
*Water* A tap near the quay.
*Provisions* Some provisions can be obtained but the villagers are largely dependent on the local ferry from Khíos.
*Eating out* A few tavernas – fresh fish is sometimes available.
*Other* PO. OTE. Bank. Local ferry to Khíos.

**General**
Closing the harbour, one gains the impression that Oinoussa is a large and prosperous village, but on closer inspection many of the large and once elegant houses are shuttered and in need of a lick of paint. That is because the island's ship owners no longer live here, but in New York, London, Paris, Athens, or wherever the high life and big business come together. This apparently insignificant little island has produced the richest ship-owning families of Greece including the richest of them all, Costa Lemos. Contrary to popular belief the biggest Greek shipping magnate is not Niarchos or the late Onassis, but this private man whose name means nothing to most people. Apparently Greek ship owners control some 70 million tons of shipping, the same tonnage as all the other EU countries put together.

## NISÍS PASAS AND CHANNEL (Pashá)

BA 1625

*Note* The bay on the NW end of Nisís Pasha is now a military area and yachts are prohibited from entering the bay and immediate area.

Nisís Pasas lies off the E end of Nísos Oinoussa separated by a narrow channel with 3·5m least depth in the fairway. The W coast of Nisís Pasas is indented with several bays and coves which offer good shelter from the *meltemi*. A bay on the E coast of Nísos Oinoussa also offers good shelter. The bottom is mostly sand with some weed – reported to be indifferent holding.

Recently a number of fish farms have sprung up in several of the bays and coves restricting the amount of space available around the island, though there is still room enough to find shelter here.

*Caution* The coasts of Oinoussa, Nisís Pasas and the islets in this area are fringed by reefs. By day these are readily picked out but care must be taken as the sketch plan can only show these reefs crudely.

**NISIS PASAS**
⊕38°30′·1N 26°17′·7E (Pasas light)

# Nísos Khíos

## (Chios, Hios)

Many islands claim to be the birthplace of Homer, but Khíos seems to be the most likely. Homer called the island 'craggy' and the epithet is deserved. Much of Khíos, especially the high mountain ridge running from Mt Profitis Ilías (1,297m, 4,255ft) in the north and terminating in low-lying Ák Mastikho in the south, is a lunar landscape of parched and pitted rock. Only on the northwest coast where thick pine forest covers the lower slopes and on the fertile plains in the south does the island bear any resemblance to ancient descriptions praising its fertility. In fact both the geography and history of Khíos are like a pattern that has been broken so many times that the original concept has been forgotten. Fertile plains rise up to barren rock, a severe plateau descends to a wooded valley, and the valley ends in a rocky bay scarred and broken by the sea.

The ancient history of Khíos was illustrious enough, but it has been somewhat overwhelmed by the tragedy of contemporary history. The name of the island was possibly derived from a word of Phoenician origin meaning 'mastic'. Along with Sámos and Smyrna (Izmir), Khíos became part of the Ionic Confederacy and enjoyed a considerable measure of affluence in which the arts prospered. Homer, that 'blind old man of rocky Khíos', Thales of Miletus, and later the tragic poet Ion were of the era. The Romans sacked it and thereafter the island sank into obscurity, being invaded by the Saracens and later becoming a pirate stronghold. With the Gattelusio family in control of Lésvos, the Genoese Giustianni family established control of Khíos in the early 14th century and it again became prosperous.

The Turks took it in 1566 and occupied the island until 1912. The Greek war of independence began in 1821 and in 1822 the Khians joined the revolt. The Turks took a terrible revenge that reverberated around the world. The towns of Khíos were razed, 25,000 Khians were massacred and 47,000 enslaved (in Néa Moni there is a bizarre chamber full of the bones of a few of those massacred). Delacroix commemorated the event in his famous picture and Victor Hugo was inspired to write his *The Child of Khíos*. The Greek Admiral Kanaris achieved a small revenge in the same year when he destroyed the Turkish flagship and its commander, but the real effect of the massacre was to awaken the world to the Greek struggle.

Those Khians who managed to escape were scattered all over Europe. Many later became prosperous merchants and ship owners (the Rallis brothers of London were from Khíos). Khíos had barely recovered when the great earthquake of 1881 shattered the island and killed 3,500. Yet the island has recovered and modern Khíos bustles and chatters still with the sounds of the Levant.

If there is one pattern to Khíos it is the cultivation of the mastic tree (*Pistacia lentiscus*) for its resin. Polunin and Huxley in their *Flowers of the Mediterranean* have this to say about the shrub:

'A resin is obtained from the punctured stems which is the mastic used in medicine and varnish-making; it is cultivated in the island of Chios for this purpose. Mastic has been used since classical times as a chewing-gum for preserving the gums and sweetening the breath. The Arabs produce an oil from the berries which is edible and used for illumination; it makes a popular sweet meat called *masticha*, and a liqueur known as 'mastiche'. Probably the balm of Genesis and the mastic tree of Susannah.'

I might add that Sultans' ladies also believed it to be an aphrodisiac, ensuring its cultivation under Turkish occupation and today it is used mainly to make *mastika*, which is a potent liqueur, and in that strange concoction, the 'Submarine'. The latter is a spoonful of sickly sweet mastic jam in a glass of water, and just how you properly consume this treat without getting it all over yourself and the table I have yet to discover.

### LIMÍN KHÍOU (Khíos, Hios)

BA 1625
Imray-Tetra G28

### Approach

*Conspicuous* The tall buildings of the city are visible from some distance off. A communications tower festooned with discs is conspicuous to the S of the city. A cathedral with a blue cupola is conspicuous in the city. The harbour moles and harbour entrance are readily identified.

*By night* Use the lights at the entrance: Fl.G.3s12M/ Fl.R.3s12M. The N mole exhibits a F.R.17m, 209m from the head. The jetty off the S breakwater has a 2F.R(vert)3M on the end. The harbour lights are difficult to see against the lights of the city.

**LIMIN KHÍOU**
⊕38°22′.3N 26°08′.7E

*Dangers* With the *meltemi* there is a disproportionately lumpy sea in the Khíos Channel and the approaches to Khíos harbour with the prevailing northerlies blowing against the north-going current. This can make the passage up the channel from the S an uncomfortable and prolonged affair.

**Mooring**
Go stern or bows-to under the mole in the SE corner. Local craft are berthed here but you can usually find somewhere to squeeze in. In calm weather go alongside the W quay S of the ferry quay.

*Shelter* Good shelter from the *meltemi* tucked under the mole in the SE corner. Elsewhere in the harbour a slop is set up by the *meltemi* blowing across the large harbour (nearly half a mile long).

*Authorities* A port of entry: port police, customs and immigration authorities.

*Note* Sewers emptying into the harbour make it smelly in the summer when the sewage has stewed a bit.

**Facilities**
*Water* On the stub jetty in the SE corner.
*Fuel* In the town. A mini-tanker can deliver to the quay.
*Repairs* Most mechanical repairs. Light engineering work possible. Excellent hardware and tool shops.
*Provisions* Excellent shopping for provisions. A sort of permanent market will be found in the area behind the W quay. Ice available.
*Eating out* Tavernas in the town.
*Other* PO. OTE. Banks. Greek gas and *Camping Gaz*. Hospital. Hire cars and motorbikes. Buses to the major villages. Ferries to Piraeus and Volos. Local ferries to Sámos, Oinoussa, Psará and Ceşme in Turkey. Internal flights.

**General**
Khíos is a noisy bustling harbour with an atmosphere closer to the Levant than to the islands to the W. Two-stroke three-wheelers buzz about, local ferries charge in and out, cranes creak

Khíos harbour looking W. Yachts berth on the pier centre left
*Peter Kleinoth/MareTeam*

unloading coasters – the only noise which penetrates the hubbub is the toot of the inter-island ferry.

The city largely dates from the 1881 earthquake which devastated the island and although a few of the old buildings survive they are overshadowed by the newer buildings. Even being generous, the city cannot be described as architecturally distinguished.

The town makes few concessions to tourism although an optimistically large hotel has been built near the SE corner of the harbour. A small museum in a converted mosque houses a few ancient finds. The dull white lumps of mastic are for sale everywhere.

## KHÍOS MARINA

### Approach

The marina has been built approximately 1M N of Khíos harbour.

*By night* The entrance is lit Fl.G.3s3M/Fl.R.3s3M.

*VHF* Ch 09 will be used.

*Note* Work is still in progress completing the marina so keep a good lookout for ongoing works when entering the marina.

### Mooring

*Data* 275 berths. Visitors' berths. Max LOA 30m. Depths 2–3m.

Go stern or bows-to one of the piers. Laid moorings are to be installed.

*Shelter* Good all-round shelter.

*Authorities* Harbourmaster to be appointed.

### Facilities

All services including water, electricity and a toilet and shower block to be installed. It is planned to install a travel-hoist and workshops. No doubt tavernas and cafés will spring up around the development.

## VRONDADOS

A miniature fishing harbour lying 2½ miles N of Limín Khíou. It offers some shelter for a small yacht, but is normally very crowded and you will have problems finding a berth. Care must be taken entering and berthing as the bottom is uneven and there is very little room for manoeuvring.

Water near the quay. Cafés and tavernas. The area now has mushrooming hotels and not inconsiderable numbers of tourists.

**VRONDADOS**
⊕38°24′·8N 26°08′·3E

## ÁYIOS ÍOANNIS THOLIS

This narrow inlet lies immediately W of Ák Pakhis. At the head of the inlet there is a large yard which hauls out very big *caïques* and yachts. The owner states he can haul vessels out up to 1,000 tons – this figure should be taken with the proverbial grain of salt, but 200–300-ton *caïques* and a 25-ton displacement motorboat have been hauled. Apart from the yard the inlet is deserted.

## ÓRMOS KOLOKITHIÁS

This large bay lies just N of Nisís Áyios Stefanos with the hamlet of Langadha in the SW corner. The

**KHÍOS MARINA**
⊕38°23′·2N 26°08′·4E

bay in the SW corner is very deep for anchoring with 20–25m depths a short distance off the quay on the N side. On the S side there are 10–20m depths where a yacht can anchor and take a line ashore. Provisions and tavernas in the village.

*Note* The cove in the NW corner is a naval establishment and it is prohibited to enter it or navigate in the vicinity.

**ÓRMOS KOLOKITHIÁS**
⊕38°28'·9N 26°07'·6E

Approach to Mármaro on Khíos looking S. Note conspicuous windmill on rocky spur

## ÓRMOS PARAPANTA

The long inlet on the E side of Nisís Margaríti. Anchor near the head of the bay in 5–10m on sand. The *meltemi* pushes a swell down into here, but with light northerlies or any other wind the bay is tenable.

### MÁRMARO (Kardhamila)

#### Approach

*Conspicuous* The village cannot be seen until you are into the bay. A windmill on a rocky spur and the village and a cemetery above it are easily identified once you are in the entrance.

*By night* Use the lights on Nisís Margaríti at the entrance to the bay Fl.3s5M and on the end of the mole Fl.G.2s3M.

*Dangers* Depths of just 2m have been reported between Nisís Margaríti and the coast although 10m depths are shown on the chart. The prudent course is to stay outside Margaríti.

#### Mooring

Go stern or bows-to or alongside the inside of the mole. The bottom is mud and weed, patchy holding, so it is better to go alongside if possible.

*Shelter* Good shelter from the *meltemi*.

*Authorities* Port police and customs.

#### Facilities

*Water* At the root of the mole.
*Fuel* In the town.
*Provisions* Most provisions can be found. Ice available.
*Eating out* Tavernas on the waterfront.

**ÓRMOS MÁRMARO AND ÓRMOS PARAPANTA**
⊕38°33'·7N 26°06'·9E

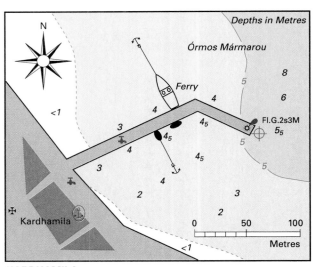

**KARDHAMILA**
⊕38°32'·7N 26°06'·6E

*Other* PO. OTE. Bank. Buses and a ferry to Psará and Khíos.

## General

The village of Kardhamila is a delightful spot at the foot of a rough gorge cutting down through the mountains. A stream keeps everything watered and green through the summer in contrast to the parched and almost lunar mountains above the village.

## LIMNIA (Volissos)

### Approach

*Conspicuous* The village of Volissos and the castle above are visible from some distance off. Closer in the light structure on the SE side of the entrance can be seen.

*By night* Not recommended. The entrance is lit Fl.G.3s3M/Fl.R.3s3M. The inner mole is lit Fl.R.1·5s3M.

*Dangers* Care should be taken of the above and below-water rocks fringing the coast in the approaches to the harbour.

### Mooring

Go stern or bows-to the quay in the NW corner. The bottom is sand and weed, good holding.

*Shelter* Good all-round shelter although SW winds make it a bit uncomfortable.

### Facilities

*Water* From the taverna.
*Fuel* In Volissos village up the hill.
*Provisions* Most provisions can be obtained in Volissos about 1½ miles up the hill.
*Eating out* Tavernas by the harbour and several others in Volissos.
*Other* Bus to Khíos from Volissos village.

### General

The harbour is a quiet little place occupied only by a few fishermen. The village above is crumbling and ruinous but engaging. There is a little tourism here but nothing overwhelming, and the village and harbour are well worth a detour up the W coast of Khíos.

Limnia (Volissos) looking SW          *Peter Kleinoth/MareTeam*

## LITHI

A small fishing harbour built on the W coast of Khíos above Mestá. Care is needed in the approach when the *meltemi* is blowing as heavy seas are set onto the W coast of Khíos. Go alongside the outer end of the N mole if there is room. The pier looks inviting but it is mostly shallow off it. Good shelter from the *meltemi* despite its location.

Taverna ashore.

**LIMNIA (Volissos)**
⊕38°28′N 25°55′·5E (Fl.G.2M)

**LITHI**
⊕38°20′·6N 25°59′·5E

## MESTÁ

A long inlet on the W coast below Lithi. A light Fl.3s7M is exhibited on Ák Ourá on the W side of the entrance to the bay and further in the entrance to the inner part of the bay is lit Q.G.2M and Q.R.2M on the N quay end. The inner lights should not be relied on.

On the SE side of the inlet near the head there are several long quays with good depths off them and recently two pontoons have been built out from the shore. Berth stern or bows-to or alongside where convenient. Shelter from the *meltemi* is reported to be better than it looks in here. Good shelter from southerlies, but there may be a surge with strong westerlies.

Water from a tap near the root of the pier. Limited provisions and several tavernas ashore.

# Southwest Khíos

## ÁY LORRIAS, SALAGONA AND KATOFANO

On the S side of the SW corner of Khíos under Ák Venétiko there are several bays affording good shelter from the *meltemi*. They are all open to the S and in the event of southerlies a yacht should make for Órmos Mestá or proceed up the Khíos Channel to Khíos.

Anchor where shown in any of the bays on the plan. The bottom is mostly sand with some weed and is good holding.

Camping ground in Katofano. Small development at Salagona. Apart from a few olive groves and dwellings ashore nothing else disturbs this peaceful and quite enchanting corner of the island.

**ÁY LORRIAS, SALAGONA & KATOFANO**
⊕38°13′·0N 25°54′·0E

## ÓRMOS KAMARI (Emborios)

Lying 3 miles NNE of Ák Mastikho this small cove provides good shelter from the *meltemi*. A ruined monastery on a hilltop immediately N is conspicuous. It is open to the SE. Anchor where convenient. The bottom is sand – good holding.

Tavernas and hotels ashore.

**MESTÁ**
⊕38°18′·0N 25°55′·7E

**ÓRMOS KAMARI (Emborios)**
⊕38°11′·3N 26°01′·8E

## VOUKARIA

38°14'·5N 26°06'·5E

A small and shallow (1–<1m) harbour. Only very shallow-draught craft should attempt to enter and even then should do so with caution.

## KATARAKTIS

38°16'·0N 26°06'·3E

A small fishing harbour. There are reported to be 2–3m depths in the entrance and 1–3m depths inside. It may be possible for small craft to find a berth.

Provisions and tavernas ashore.

# Ikaría

## (Nicaria)

Ikaría is a huge precipitous slab of rock wedged into the sea to the west of Sámos. The island has green wooded and cultivated valleys in the north, but the high slopes and the south coast are mostly barren. The name probably derived from the Phoenician word *ikor* referring to an abundance of fish, and there are still considerable fleets working the waters here and around the nearby Nisídhes Foúrnoi. The alternative and mythological origin of the name is derived from the legend of Daedalus and Icarus who contrived to escape from Crete by fabricating wings from feathers and wax. Icarus flew too high and the sun melted the wax so that he fell into the sea near Ikaría.

⊕17  1M S of Ák Páppas (Ikaría)
       37°29'·8N 25°58'·8E
⊕18  1M N of Ák Armenistís (Ikaría)
       37°39'·2N 26°05'·1E
⊕19  1M E of Ák Dhrepanon (Ikaría)
       37°41'·3N 26°22'·9E
⊕20  1M S of Ák Dhoménikos (Sámos)
       37°39'·7N 26°35'·5E
⊕21  1M N of Makronisi (Sámos)
       37°49'·0N 27°00'0E
⊕22  E end of Stenón Sámou (Sámos Strait)
       37°42'·1N 27°04'·0E
⊕23  ½M W of Bayrak Adasi light
       37°41'·6N 27°00'·6E
⊕24  1M S of Samioupoula
       37°36'·4N 26°48'·4E

## EVDHILOS

BA 1526

### Approach

*Conspicuous* Vrakhonisís Kofinás with the light structure on it is conspicuous. From the E the village and the harbour mole are easily seen.

*By night* Use the light on Vrak Kofinás Fl.7·5s11M and the light on the end of the mole Fl.G.2s3M.

### Mooring

Go stern or bows-to the mole or the pier in the S or

**EVDHILOS**
⊕37°38'·1N 26°11'·0E

**NISOI IKARIA AND SAMOS**

Evdhilos on Ikaría looking NW from the S side of the bay
*Neville Bulpitt*

Áy Kirikos looking SW          *Nigel Patten*

**ÁYIOS KIRIKOS**
⊕37°36'·8N 26°17'·9E

anchor off. Much of the quay and parts of the mole have underwater ballasting extending out from them so it is best to go bows-to. The mole quay is also quite high and there are few places to secure warps to.

*Shelter* With a strong *meltemi* some swell creeps around the end of the mole. With strong NE winds the harbour is untenable.

*Authorities* Port police and customs.

### Facilities
*Water* A tap near the quay.
*Provisions* Some provisions in the village.
*Eating out* Several tavernas and a number of cafés.
*Other* PO. Bus to Áyios Kirikos. Ferries to Sámos and Piraeus.

### General
The tiny village sandwiched between a rocky bluff and high mountains is attractive and friendly. Ikaría doesn't get a lot of tourism compared to nearby Sámos although the new ferry service is changing that. Good fishing along the precipitous coast that drops sheer into the sea in the vicinity.

### CAUTION
Along the S coast of Ikaría severe gusts sweep down off the high mountains.

### ÁYIOS KIRIKOS (Agios Kirykos)
BA 1526
Imray-Tetra G32

### Approach
The capital and ferry port of Ikaría lies on the SE side of the island.

*Conspicuous* The town and the harbour mole are easily identified from the distance.

*By night* Use the light on the end of the mole: Fl.R.3s4M.

*Dangers* With N winds there are severe gusts into the

harbour and off the high land in the approaches – some caution is advised with the *meltemi*.

### Mooring
Go alongside or stern or bows-to one of the piers inside the new inner breakwater. Care is needed towards the root of the piers where it shallows.

*Shelter* Adequate shelter from the *meltemi*. With moderate S winds the harbour should now be tenable with the construction of the new inner breakwater, but with strong southerlies it may become untenable.

*Authorities* Port police and customs.

### Facilities
*Water* Near the mole.
*Fuel* In the town (about ¼ of a mile). A mini-tanker will deliver.
*Provisions* Good shopping for provisions.
*Eating out* Good tavernas.
*Other* PO. OTE. Bank. Hire motorbikes. Ferry to Piraeus.

### General

The town is an attractive straggle of buildings up the steep slopes from the harbour and the locals are friendly. The only problem in this part of the world is the *meltemi* which howls down off the slopes and makes getting around the island a nightmare at times. Personally I think Icarus had his feathers blown off around here by the *meltemi* and didn't get anywhere near the sun.

*Note* It is reported a marina is to be built approximately 6 miles W of Áy Kirikos. No details are available.

### KARKINAGRI

A small harbour situated W of Áy Kirikos has been reported. It has a difficult entrance and is crowded with local boats. No details are available.

### ÓRMOS LOUTRÓ (Thermia)

37°37'·3N 26°18'·2E

Just over half a mile NE of Áy Kirikos is the bay of Loutró which affords reasonable shelter from the *meltemi*. Anchor in the bay, or small yachts can go on the quay off the old hydropathic institute. The former name of the place was Thermia, describing the hot springs now utilised by the hydropathic institute.

Loutro (Thermia) on Ikaría looking NE          *Nigel Patten*

### ÁKRA DHREPANON

37°41'·3N 26°21'·8E

Immediately S of the cape there is an open bay partially protected from the *meltemi* which in calm weather could be used for visiting the ancient ruins of Drakanon. The ancient circular tower is conspicuous from seaward.

# Nísos Sámos

While Lésvos is the jewel of the eastern Sporades, Sámos is the rough-cut diamond. The high mountain ridge running the length of the island is an extension of Mt Mykale in Turkey – from the southeast corner of the island it is a single sea mile across to Cape Mykale, making Sámos the closest of the Greek islands to Turkey. In the west the range rises sheer from the sea to Mt Kertetevs (1,437m, nearly 5,000ft) and runs to the east to the Ambelos range (1,041m, 3,730ft). Deep gullies score the mountainsides and peaks and bluffs assume shapes which even the restrained language of the Admiralty *Pilot* describes as 'fantastic'. Thick pine forest covers most of the lower slopes and villages perch precariously on small plateaus. There is a grandeur and grace to Sámos unequalled elsewhere.

In ancient times Sámos was lavishly praised: it was known as Parthenoarroussa for its beauty: Dryoussa for its oaks, Anthemis for its flowers, and Hydrele for its abundant springs. The name Sámos is probably derived from a Phoenician word meaning 'high'. As part of the Ionic Confederacy it prospered, but it was under the ambitious Polykrates that the island rose to the height of its prosperity in the 6th century BC.

Polykrates was equal parts tyrant and aesthete – a sort of latter-day Odysseus. He rose swiftly to power, conquering nearby islands and assembling a large fleet and army. To Sámos he invited poets and artists and under his patronage three of the greatest engineering feats in the ancient Greek world were achieved: the harbour at Pithagorion, the underground conduit and tunnel behind Pithagorion, and the temple to Hera on Ák Kolonna. The temple has gone, but the remains of the harbour and the tunnel are still there. Polykrates was finally lured to the mainland coast and crucified by the Persians.

Sámos then passed from Sparta to Athens and thence to the Romans. Anthony sacked it before the Battle of Actium. Aided by Cleopatra, he gave a mammoth feast on the island to which all the civilized world was invited and which went on for months. This was his way of starting a war and the only question men had was what the victory feast would be like. As we know there was no victory feast, only defeat and hopeless suicide.

After the Roman occupation the island fell into obscurity and was the lair of pirates, apart from a brief period of Byzantine rule. The inhabitants fled to Khíos and Lésvos leaving the island open for the Turks to occupy in 1566. It became part of Greece in 1912.

You might expect an island ravaged and pillaged by corsairs for so long to be run down and poor in spirit. Not a bit of it. Sámos leaves you with the feeling of a happy island populated by friendly people. The scenery is superb from the extensive pine forests on the mountain slopes (Samian pine is considered to be the best for *caïque* building) to the cultivated plains. Sadly, forest fires have destroyed much of the pine forest on the S coast. Apart from the sweet white Sámos muscat wine, the excellent *Saimaina* dry white is available in Vathi, Karlóvasi and Pithagorion. A sweet red *moschata* is also produced.

## KARLÓVASI

BA 1526
Imray-Tetra G32

### Approach

*Conspicuous* From the distance the buildings of the town are easily identified. A church with a blue cupola on a precipitous rock bluff and two large churches with blue cupolas in the town are conspicuous. The harbour is to the W of the town and the harbour moles are easily identified.

*By night* Use the light on Ák Pangózi Fl.5s11M and the lights at the entrance Fl.G.4·5s5M/ Fl.R.4·5s4M.

*Note* Work is in progress extending the outer breakwater. The light on the extremity is moved as work progresses but may not mark the end of underwater obstructions off the breakwater. Care needed in the immediate approaches.

*Dangers* With the *meltemi* there can be a confused sea off the coast around the harbour and at the entrance.

### Mooring

Go stern or bows-to in the SE corner. The bottom is sand, mud and weed, good holding.

*Shelter* Good shelter, but with the *meltemi* some swell creeps around the end of the outer mole – uncomfortable but not dangerous. With strong S winds there are gusts off the high mountains behind.

*Authorities* Port police and customs.

*Note* Photographs of the coast to the W are prohibited.

### Facilities

*Water* On the quay.
*Fuel* In the town about 2 miles away. A mini-tanker may be able to deliver.

**KARLÓVASI**
⊕37°47'·9N 26°40'·9E

*Repairs* Limited mechanical repairs. The yard in the SW corner of the harbour hauls out yachts.

*Provisions* Some provisions at the harbour. Good shopping for provisions in Karlóvasi village.

*Eating out* Tavernas on the waterfront.

*Other* PO and OTE in Karlóvasi village. Bus to Vathi.

### General

The harbour is a sleepy little spot that seems to have seen more prosperous times. In recent years a little tourism has arrived to brighten up the harbour front. Inland, Karlóvasi proper is a straggling market village serving the agricultural needs of the hinterland. The centre is most attractive – all stone houses and cobbled streets.

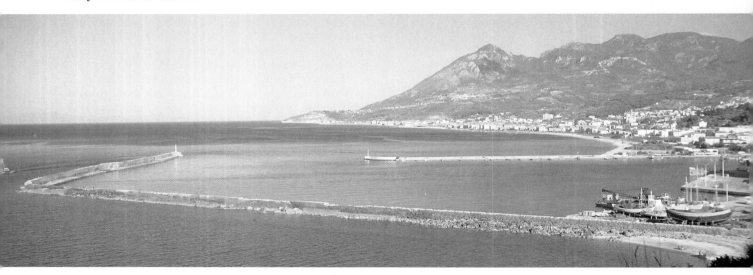

Karlóvasi harbour looking ENE

## KOKKARI

37°46'·9N 26°53'·8E

The bay on the E side of Ák Kokkari. Care is needed of the reef off the end of the cape. In calm weather or light westerlies anchor off the village in 7–10m on sand and weed. Taverna ashore.

*Note* It is reported a small harbour has been built here. The entrance is reported to be marked by a Fl.G.3s3M.

## VATHI (Sámos)

### Approach

The capital and principal ferry port of Sámos lies in a large bay on the NE corner of the island.

*Conspicuous* The buildings of the town straggling around the bay and up the slopes behind are easily identified.

*By night* Use the light on Ák Kótsikas Fl(2)7·2s7M and the light on the end of the mole Fl.R.3s4M. The small yacht harbour is lit F.R.3M/F.G.3M.

*Dangers* Órmos Vathi is completely open to the N–NW and consequently the *meltemi* sends a heavy confused swell into the bay. There are also strong gusts off the high land in the vicinity.

### Mooring

Go stern or bows-to the quay where shown, keeping clear of the ferry quay.

In the SE corner a small yacht harbour has been built and you may be able to find a berth in here. There are mostly 3m depths inside. Berth stern or bows-to in a vacant spot or where directed. There are laid moorings tailed to small buoys.

*Shelter* Shelter on the town quay is just adequate with the *meltemi* and is certainly very uncomfortable. A considerable surge can be set up and you will need to keep pulled well off. The yacht basin is sheltered from the *meltemi* although a surge is set up – more uncomfortable than dangerous.

*Authorities* Port police and customs. A charge is made in the yacht basin.

### Facilities

*Water* On the quay in the yacht basin..

*Fuel* On the waterfront to the E. A mini-tanker can deliver to the quay.

*Provisions* Good shopping for all provisions nearby.

*Eating out* Good tavernas nearby.

*Other* PO. OTE. Banks. Greek gas and *Camping Gaz*. Hire cars and motorbikes. Buses to the principal villages. Ferry to Piraeus, Kavála, Khíos and Kuşadasi in Turkey.

### General

The waterfront is an ugly huddle of modern buildings on the dusty main street. The large bay is attractive towards the head and the old town (Sámos) on the hill behind is a more sympathetic place.

## Stenón Samou

### (Sámos Strait)

BA 1526

Imray-Tetra G32

The narrow strait between the E end of Sámos and mainland Turkey. (The Turks call the strait Dilek Boğazi.) At its narrowest the strait is less than a mile across. In the strait there is the small rocky islet of Bayrak Adasi (Turkish) with a light structure on it (Fl.5s8M). A yacht can pass either N or S of the islet. On the N side there is a rocky shoal with a least depth of 9m in the fairway. On the S side there are greater depths.

The narrow strait channels the fairly weak N-

### STENÓN SAMOU (SÁMOS STRAIT)

⊕**21** 1M N of Makronisi (Sámos) 37°49'·0N 27°00'·0E

⊕**22** E end of Stenón Sámou (Sámos Strait)
37°42'·1N 27°04'·0E

⊕**23** 0·5M W of Bayrak Adasi light 37°41'·6N 27°00'·6E

**VATHI**
⊕37°45'·4N 26°58'·2E

going current into a strong current with overfalls. The current sets to the E and may attain a rate of 3–4 knots in the narrow section of the strait although it is normally less at around 1–2 knots. The overfalls are usually worse on the N side than the S side. The overfalls combined with strong gusts off the high land of Sámos with the *meltemi* can make the passage very uncomfortable at times and care is needed.

## ÓRMOS MOURTIA

37°45'·5N 27°02'·3E

The large bay on the E end of Sámos. A monastery on the slopes is easily identified. Anchor in the cove at the head of the bay in 5m on a sandy bottom. Some shelter from the *meltemi* although a swell normally enters. Open to the S and E.

## ÓRMOS POSSIDONION

37°42'·5N 27°03'·4E

A small bay lying on the S side of Ák Gátos, the SE tip of Sámos. The light structure on the cape (Fl(3)14s7M) is easily identified from the N. Anchor in 5–10m on a sandy bottom. Good shelter from the *meltemi* although there are strong gusts down into the bay and channel. Ashore there are a few houses and several tavernas in attractive surroundings.

About 2 miles to the W at Psili Amos there is an anchorage behind an islet. A few houses and a simple taverna ashore.

## PITHAGORION (Pythagoreon, Tigani)

BA 1526
Imray-Tetra G32

Pithagorion on Sámos looking W from the entrance
*Peter Kleinoth/MareTeam*

### Approach

*Conspicuous* A line of 9 wind generators on the ridge E of Pithagorion are conspicuous and the buildings of the town are visible from some distance off. A large red-roofed hotel to the W of the town and Metamorfosis, a fortified stone monastery on the waterfront, are conspicuous. Closer in, the outer mole is easily identified.

*By night* Use the light on Ák Foniás Fl.4s5M and the lights at the entrance Fl.R.2s3M/Fl.G.2s2M. From the W the lights at the entrance cannot be seen until close in. Care is needed of the beacon at the entrance to the inner harbour which is unlit.

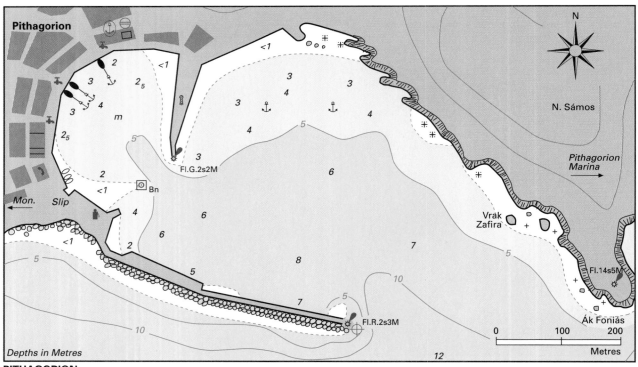

**PITHAGORION**
⊕37°41'·3N 26°56'·9E

*Dangers* With the *meltemi* there are strong gusts off the high land in the approaches to the harbour.

*Note* Once inside the outer mole the beacon marking the limit of the shallows on the S side of the entrance to the inner basin is easily identified. There are 4m least depths in the fairway between the beacon and the inner mole.

## Mooring
Go stern or bows-to the W quay. The bottom is mud – excellent holding.

*Authorities* A port of entry: port police, customs, and immigration. A small charge is sometimes made.

## Facilities
*Water* On the quay. Showers and toilets.

*Fuel* About 3km out of town. A mini-tanker can deliver to the quay. There is a fuel quay at the entrance to the harbour but hours are somewhat unpredictable.

*Repairs* Some mechanical repairs. Hardware shops and limited chandlery.

*Provisions* Good shopping for provisions nearby. Ice available.

*Eating out* Good tavernas on the waterfront and in town.

*Other* PO. OTE. Bank. Greek gas and *Camping Gaz*. Hire cars, motorbikes and bicycles. Regular bus to Vathi. Ferries to Pátmos and Kuşadasi in Turkey. Internal flights to Athens.

## General
Set at the foot of pine-covered hills and looking over to the Turkish mountains, the town of Pithagorion is becoming increasingly popular as a tourist resort, and justifiably so. It is a thoroughly agreeable place, set in magnificent surroundings with high wooded mountains behind and just big enough to have good facilities yet small enough to be intimate.

The town was named Pithagorion comparatively recently, in 1955, in honour of Pythagoras. Formerly it was called Tigani meaning 'frying pan' – a name which is self explanatory once you have seen the shape of the harbour. Pithagorion is situated on the site of the ancient city of Sámos which rose to prominence under Polykrates the tyrant. During Polykrates' swift rise to power, what Herodotus described as three of the greatest engineering feats in the Greek world were achieved.

The first was the mole which protected the harbour and which survives in part today as part of the quay and the root of the outer mole.

Approach to Pithagorion looking N. Note wind generators

Pithagorion inner harbour looking SW

The second was the temple of Hera built on Ák Kolonna. In its day bigger and better than any other, today only a single column remains standing amongst the ruins. A small museum in Pithagorion houses some of the finds from the temple site.

The third was the tunnel hewn through the mountain to bring water to the city and also probably as an escape route. It still exists today although the middle section has collapsed. The original was a mile long and 2·4m (8ft) square and for its day an extraordinary engineering feat. The entrance is immediately behind Pithagorion and a part of the tunnel can be explored by those who don't suffer from claustrophobia, though considerable care is needed. It is open six times a week on three days – enquire at the tourist office.

## PITHAGORION MARINA
Imray-Tetra G32

### Approach
The new marina lies immediately E of Pithagorion harbour on the E side of Ák Foniás.

*By night* Use the light on Ák Foniás Fl.4s5M and the lights at the entrance Fl.G.3s3M/Fl.R.3s3M.

*VHF* Ch 09 will be used.

*Note* Work is still in progress so care is needed in the entrance and the marina proper.

### Mooring
*Data* 250 berths. Visitors' berths. Max LOA 20m. Depths 3–5m.

Go stern or bows-to where directed. Laid moorings to be installed.

*Shelter* Good all-round shelter.

*Authorities* Harbourmaster to be appointed.

### Facilities
All services to be installed including water, electricity, toilets and showers. It is planned to install a travel-hoist and workshops.

**PITHAGORION MARINA**
⊕37°41'·5N 26°57'·5E

## IREON

37°40'·0N 26°53'·2E

At the W end of the large bay running around to Pithagorion is the village and small fishing harbour at Ireon. A short breakwater provides some shelter. Anchor off in 3–4m. The *meltemi* does not gust into this corner as strongly as elsewhere along this coast.

Provisions and tavernas ashore.

## NISÍS SAMOPOULA (Samioupoula)

A *caïque* from Pithagorion runs tourists out to the island in the summer and anchors in a cove on the E side of the island. Ashore there is a small hamlet with a taverna.

## MARATHAKAMBOS

A fishing harbour on the SW of Sámos. An outer breakwater runs E from a natural bight with a short inner breakwater extending S from the coast. There are 3-4m depths in the entrance and outer part of the harbour. Anchor in the outer part or go bows-to the short pier running out from the shore. There are 2m depths at the extremity of the pier. With the *meltemi* there are strong gusts off the land so ensure your anchor is holding well.

Provisions and tavernas ashore. The surroundings are spectacular with precipitous cliffs and hills rising abruptly from the shore. Sadly much of the pine has been burnt in recent forest fires.

*Note* This is a military area although now opened up for a little tourism. Photographs are prohibited.

## ÓRMOS LIMNIONAS

37°41'·2N 26°37'·6E

Lying close SW of Ák Khondhros Kávos, this bay offers shelter from N winds, but is subject to fierce gusts off the mountains above. It is open to the S.

Taverna opens in the summer.

## CAUTION

On the W and S sides of Sámos severe gusts sweep down off the high mountains with the *meltemi*. Unless a yacht is proceeding to Limnionas or Marathakambos it is a good policy to keep at least 2–3 miles off the S coast.

**MARATHAKAMBOS**
⊕37°42'·5N 26°42'·3E

# Nisídhes Foúrnoi
## (Phournoi)

### FOURNOI (Órmos Korseon, Kampos)
BA 1625

### Approach
The steep-to high islands (of Foúrnoi and Fimaina) are visible from many miles away (Nisís Foúrnoi is 515m, 1,686ft high at its northern point).

*Conspicuous* From the N the village of Foúrnoi (Korseon) and 2 windmills on the ridge to the SW of the village are conspicuous. From the S the village cannot be seen but the windmills are conspicuous.

*By night* Not recommended. There is only the light on Ák Svistokáminos (S side of Órmos Korseon): Fl.WR.3·5s4/3M (red sector covers 034°-138° and 172°-243°).

### Mooring
Go stern or bows-to the new N quay or better still find a fishing boat to go alongside because of the bad holding. The bottom here is a thin layer of mud over rock and it is difficult to find a patch where the anchor will hold.

*Shelter* Reasonable shelter from the *meltemi* although the poor holding means it is not a secure place to be.

*Authorities* Port police and customs.

### Facilities
*Water* Tap near the quay.
*Fuel* Small quantities may be available.
*Provisions* Some provisions can be obtained but the

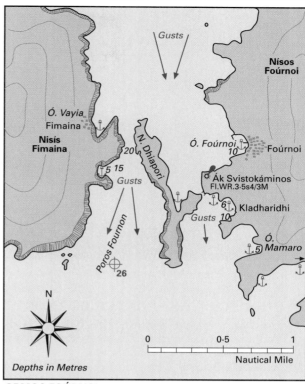

**ORMOS FOÚRNOI**

⊕26  Mid-channel S end of Póros Fournon
37°33'·7N 26°27'·5E

**ORMOS FOURNOI**
⊕37°34'·5N 26°29'E

villagers are largely dependent on the ferry from Samos for supplies. Ice available.
*Eating out* Several tavernas – fresh fish is often available.
*Other* PO. Ferry to Sámos.

### General
Foúrnoi (Korseon, Kambos) is the only major village on the island and the population and facilities are concentrated here. A large fishing fleet is based here and the locals are generally friendly to visiting yachts. The coves S of the village are mostly deserted and the surrounding jagged coastline offers good fishing.

**NISIDHES FOÚRNOI**

⊕25  Mid-channel N end of Póros Fournon
37°36'·0N 26°27'·8E
⊕26  Mid-channel S end of Póros Fournon
37°33'·7N 26°27'·5E

Anchorage on the bottom of Nísos Foúrnoi    *Nigel Patten*

## ANCHORAGES AROUND THE ISLANDS

1. *Fimaina (Órmos Vayia)* The bay on Nisís Fimaina opposite Órmos Korseon. Poor shelter from the *meltemi*. Taverna ashore.
2. *Nisís Dhiapori* The bay on the E side immediately SW of Ák Svistokáminos.
3. *Cliff Bay* The cove on Nisís Fimaina on the W side of the narrow channel between Fimaina and Dhiapori. Some shelter from the *meltemi*.
4. *Kladharidhi* Anchor in the bay sheltered on the W by Nisís Dhiaporoi. Reasonable protection from the *meltemi*.
5. *Órmos Mármaro* Anchor at the N end of the bay with a long line ashore. Depths are considerable. Good protection from the *meltemi*.
6. *Quarry Bay* In the large bay immediately S of Mármaro there is reported to be good shelter from the *meltemi*. Anchor at the head of the bay in 5–8m, good holding once the anchor is in. Ashore

there is an ancient marble quarry with unfinished columns and other bits and pieces lying around.

7. At the S end of Nisís Foúrnoi there is a large bay immediately W of Ák Agridhio that looks as though it would offer good shelter from the *meltemi*. There is also another inlet NW of it.
8. *Órmos Khrisomilia* On the N end of Foúrnoi on the W side there is the large bay of Khrisomilia. A yacht can anchor off here in calm weather though depths are considerable. To the E there is the small cove of Vali which is said to afford some shelter from the *meltemi*, though again depths are considerable.

## CAUTION

With the *meltemi* there are severe gusts off the high land of the islands and in the strait between Fimaina and Foúrnoi (Póros Fournon) considerable confused seas are pushed down. Care is needed when navigating in the vicinity of the islands which in the *meltemi* season are very windy places indeed.

**ÓRMOS KLADHARIDHI AND MÁRMARO**
⊕37°33′·3N 26°28′·7E

# IX. The Dodecanese

The Dodecanese, the Twelve Islands, lie in a crescent chain down the Asiatic Turkish coast curving west towards Crete. The name 'Dodecanese' is of comparatively recent origin. It came into use in 1908 when twelve islands of this group excluding Lipso, Kós and Rhodes but including an outsider, Ikaría, protested about their deprivation of the special privileges and tax exemptions they had been granted in the 16th century by the Turks. Since then the name has come to include Lipso, Kós and Rhodes, but to exclude Ikaría. The group is also known as the Southern Sporades.

Like most of the Greek Islands, the Dodecanese are the tops of mountains that stood on the plain of the Aegean long since flooded. The islands are for the most part bare of vegetation, although not to such an extent as the Cyclades. Several of the islands with abundant natural springs, notably Kós and Rhodes, are relatively green and wooded.

The history of the Dodecanese has largely revolved around the fortunes of Rhodes, which dominated trade in this corner of the Aegean from ancient times until the 19th century. Today Rhodes dominates the new trade in tourists in the Dodecanese. In the early Middle Ages the Knights of St John, based in their fortress in Rhodes, stamped the area with their military signatures. Most of the military architecture is not the ubiquitous Venetian and Genoese architecture so prevalent in other parts of Greece, but that of the Knights. The occupation of the Knights nonetheless ensured the Venetians access to the trade in this part of the world. After the Knights finally capitulated to the Turks in 1522, the Dodecanese were to remain under Turkish rule until 1912.

Despite such a long period of unbroken occupation the islands have remained intrinsically Greek, and there is as little here to remind you of the long years under Turkish rule as elsewhere in Greece. After the Italo-Turkish war (1911–12) the islands were awarded to Italy although they were to be passed on in due course to Greece. This promise was later conveniently forgotten and the Dodecanese remained under the Italians until the Second World War. Finally in 1947 they officially became part of Greece. For those not familiar with modern Greek history it comes as quite a shock to learn that these islands have been a part of Greece for such a short time, when visually and culturally they appear to be as much a part of Greece as any of the other islands.

## Weather patterns in the Dodecanese

In the summer the prevailing wind is the *meltemi* blowing from the NW–W. It starts fitfully in June, blows strongly in July through to September and again fitfully in October. In the summer months it regularly blows Force 4–6 and may on occasion reach Force 7. It does not blow every day, but may blow without a break for 5–10 days.

In the spring and autumn the wind frequently blows from the SE, about Force 2–4, although it may be stronger on occasion. In the winter the wind is predominantly from the SE although gales may come from the N or S.

When the *meltemi* is blowing at full strength in July and August the gusts off the lee side of an island can be considerably stronger than the wind strength in the open sea. Gusts are particularly strong off Pátmos, Kalimnos, Kós, Nísiros, Tílos, Kárpathos

---

## Routes

In the summer routes through the Dodecanese are basically off the wind or bashing into the wind. The *meltemi* blows from the N–NW around Pátmos, curving down through the islands to blow from the W around Rhodes. The problem here is really how to get N and E in the summer. There are not too many options. The *meltemi* does have something of a thermal component which means the wind is augmented in the afternoon by a sea breeze blowing onto Asia Minor. With any luck if you leave early in the morning there will be less wind than in the afternoon. We are really talking of relative amounts of wind here and at times the *meltemi* can blow all through the night with as much force as in the day.

If you are heading W through the Cyclades the usual plan is to head as far N as possible in the Dodecanese and then dive off through the Cyclades where the *meltemi* will blow from the N in the middle and the NE towards the westerly Cyclades. An alternative is to head W and SW around the bottom Cyclades to Serifos and then up to the Saronic. The *meltemi* tends not to be as strong around the southern edges of the Cyclades and towards the Peloponnese.

In the spring and autumn you will likely pick up southerlies and if you are planning to go N to the eastern Sporades or Northern Greece then spring and early summer is the time to do it before the *meltemi* is well established. Then you can come back S with the *meltemi* aft of the beam.

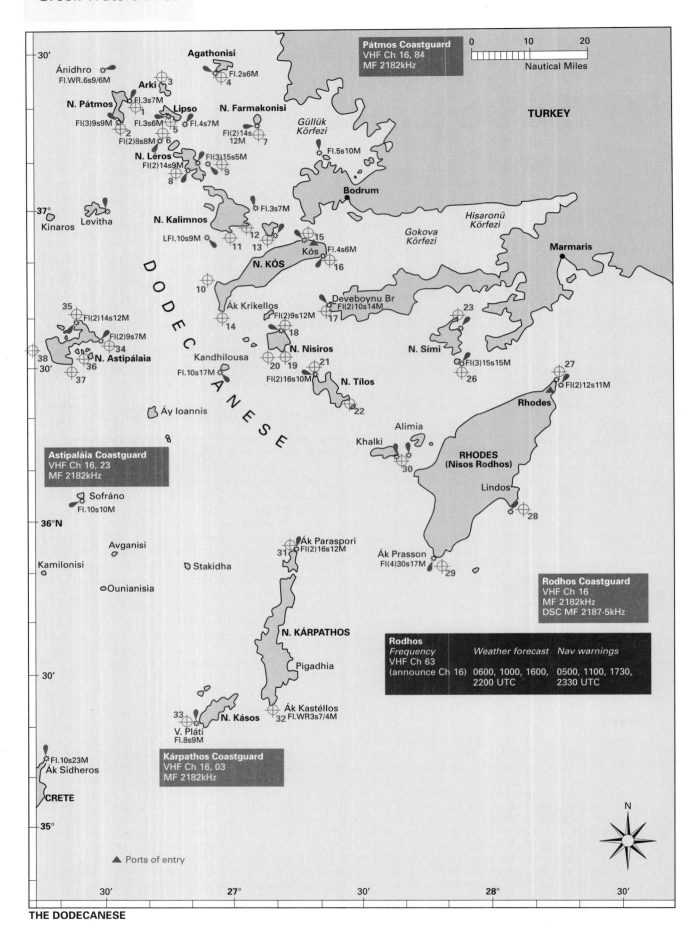

**Pátmos Coastguard**
VHF Ch 16, 84
MF 2182kHz

0   10   20
Nautical Miles

30'
Ánidhro ✹
Fl.WR.6s9/6M

**Agathonisi**
✹ Fl.2s6M
4

**Arki** ♠ 3
Fl.3s7M
**N. Pátmos** ♠ 1
Fl(3)9s9M **Lipso** **N. Farmakonisi**
2 Fl.3s6M ✹ Fl.4s7M
Fl(2)8s8M 6 5
Fl(2)14s
12M 7

*Güllük
Körfezi*

✹ Fl.5s10M

**N. Léros**
Fl(2)14s9M
8
Fl(3)15s5M
9

**Bodrum**

37°
Kinaros Levitha

*Hisaronü
Körfezi*

✹ Fl.3s7M
**N. Kalimnos**
LFl.10s9M 11 12
13
15
Kós ✹ Fl.4s6M
**N. KÓS** 16

*Gokova
Körfezi*

**Marmaris**

10

Ák Krikellos
14
Fl(2)9s12M
18
**N. Nisiros**
Deveboynu Br
Fl(2)10s14M
17

23

**N. Sími**

35
Fl(2)14s12M
Fl(2)9s7M
34
38
36
37
**N. Astipálaia**

Kandhilousa
Fl.10s17M
20 19 21
Fl(2)16s10M
**N. Tílos**
22

☿Fl(3)15s15M
26

27
✹Fl(2)12s11M

**Rhodes**

Áy Ioannis

Alimia
Khalki
30

**RHODES**
**(Nisos Rodhos)**

Lindos
28

**Astipáláia Coastguard**
VHF Ch 16, 23
MF 2182kHz

36°N

Sofráno
Fl.10s10M

Avganisi

Kamilonisi

Ounianisia

Stakidha

Ák Paraspori
31 Fl(2)16s12M

Ák Prasson
Fl(4)30s17M
29

**Rodhos Coastguard**
VHF Ch 16
MF 2182kHz
DSC MF 2187·5kHz

**N. KÁRPATHOS**

Pigadhia

**Rodhos**
*Frequency*          *Weather forecast*   *Nav warnings*
VHF Ch 63
(announce Ch 16)   0600, 1000, 1600,    0500, 1100, 1730,
                    2200 UTC              2330 UTC

30'

33
V. Pláti
Fl.8s9M
**N. Kásos**
32
Ák Kastéllos
Fl.WR3s7/4M

**Kárpathos Coastguard**
VHF Ch 16, 03
MF 2182kHz

✹Fl.10s23M
Ák Sidheros

**CRETE**

35°

N

▲ Ports of entry

30'          27°          30'          28°          30'

**THE DODECANESE**

and Astipálaia. In the comparatively open stretch of sea between Astipálaia and Kárpathos a large and disturbed sea is set up when the *meltemi* blows for days on end.

In the summer months it is very hot in the Dodecanese, although the *meltemi* provides some relief. Temperatures may reach 35°C although the average temperature is less. In the winter the climate is mild.

# Data

## PORTS OF ENTRY
Kós
Sími
Rhodes (Rodhos)

## PROHIBITED AREAS
*Léros* It is prohibited to navigate and land on the S side of Órmos Lakki in the vicinity of the naval buildings.

## MAJOR LIGHTS
Nisís Ànidhro Fl.WR.6s9/6M

**Pátmos**
Ák Yeranós Fl.3s7M
Ák Ilías Fl(3)9s9M

**Lipso**
Ák Gátos Fl.3s6M
Nisís Kalapódhia Fl.4s7M
Vrak Saráki Fl(2)8s8M
Nisís Gäïdharos Fl.2s6M
Nisís Farmakonisi (S summit) Fl(2)14s12M

**Léros**
Órmos Alíndas Fl.3s5M
Vrak Áy Kiriakí Fl(3)15s5M
Órmos Lakkí (Ák Lakkí) Fl(2)14s9M
Nisís Gláros Fl.2s4M

**Kalimnos**
Nisís Kalólimnos Fl.3s7M
Limín Kalímnou Fl.R.2s4M
Vrak Safonídhi LFl.10s9M

**Psérimos**
Ák Rousa Fl(2)WR.10s12/9M
Vrak Nekrothikes Fl.WR.5s6/4M

**Kós**
Ák Ammóglossa Fl.R.4s9M
Ák Loúros Fl(3)WR.15s6/4M
Ák Foúka Fl.4s6M
Nisís Yialí (Áy Andónios) Fl.2s5M
Nísiros (Ák Palos) Fl(2)9s12M
Nisís Kandheliousa Fl.10s17M
Tílos (Vrak Gäïdharos) Fl(2)16s10M

**Sími**
Nisís Marmarás Fl.3s6M
Nisís Khondrós Fl.3s5M
Ák Koutsoúmba Fl.3s5M
Vrak Kouloundrós (Troumbeta Rock) Fl(3)15s15M
Nisís Khálki (Skála) Fl.WR.6s8/6M

**Rhodes**
Nisís Tragusa Fl(2)WR.14s8/6M
Kámiros Skála Fl.3s8M
Ák Milon (Zonari) Fl.WR.4s6/4M
Rhodes Harbour (Áy Nikólaos) Fl(2)12s11M

Vrak Paximádha Fl.WR.4s9/6M
Ák Prasson Fl(4)30s17M

**Kárpathos**
Ák Kastéllos Fl.WR.3s7/4M
Nisídha Dhespotiko Fl.5s6M
Ák Paraspóri (Saria) Fl(2)16s12M
Nisís Stakidha Fl.3s8M
Ounianísia Fl(2)16s7M
Nisís Megálo Sofráno Fl.10s10M
Vrak Strongilí Fl(2)WR.10s7/5M

**Kásos**
Vrak Platí Fl.8s9M

**Astipálaia**
Ák Floúdha Fl(2)14s12M

## USEFUL WAYPOINTS
⊕1 1M E of Ák Yeranós (Pátmos)
37°20'·5N 26°37'·9E
⊕2 1M S of Ák Ilias (Pátmos)
37°15'·2N 26°34'·3E
⊕3 1M N of Ák Koumaro (Arki)
37°25'·8N 26°43'·2E
⊕4 1M S of Ák Stifí (Gäïdharos)
37°25'·8N 26°57'·6E
⊕5 ½M S of Ák Gátos (Lipso)
37°17'·35N 26°45'·9E
⊕6 ½M N of Vrak Saráki (Stenón Lipsou)
37°14'·3N 26°42'·0E
⊕7 1M S of Ák Petronkopis (Farmokonisi)
37°15'·5N 27°05'·3E
⊕8 1M W of Ák Lakki (Léros)
37°06'·8N 26°48'·2E
⊕9 1M E of Vrak Áy Kiriakí (Léros)
37°08'·8N 26°54'·4E
⊕10 3M S of Vrak Safonídhi (Kalimnos-Kós Channel)
36°50'·27N 26°54'·49E WGS84
⊕11 ½M S of Áy Yeóryios (Kalimnos)
36°54'·97N 26°59'·21E WGS84
⊕12 ¾M S of Ák Khali (Kalimnos)
36°55'·95N 27°02'·97E WGS84
⊕13 ¼M S of Vrak Krevvatio (Psérimos)
36°54'·82N 27°09'·39E WGS84
⊕14 1M S of Ák Krikellos (Kós)
36°39'·2N 26°58'·4E
⊕15 ¾M N of Ák Ammóglossa (Kós)
36°55'·70N 27°16'·42E WGS84
⊕16 ¼M E of Ák Áy Fokas (Kós)
36°51'·67N 27°21'·69E WGS84

⊕17 ¾M W of Deveboynu Bükü (Knidos/Turkey)
36°41'·45N 27°20'·90E WGS84
⊕18 1M N of Ák Katsouni (Nísiros)
36°38'·2N 27°11'·2E
⊕19 ½M S of Ák Loutros (Nísiros)
36°32'·92N 27°11'·66E WGS84
⊕20 1M S of Ák Levkhos (Nísiros)
36°32'·72N 27°08'·28E WGS84
⊕21 1M N of N. Gäïdharos (Tílos)
36°30'·2N 27°17'·2E
⊕22 Mid-channel between Tílos and Andítilos
36°22'·6N 27°26'·9E
⊕23 1M N of Ák Makria (Sími)
36°41'·1N 27°51'·5E
⊕24 W entrance of Nímos Passage (Sími)
36°38'·72N 27°49'·76E WGS84
⊕25 E entrance of Nímos Passage (Sími)
36°38'·66N 27°50'·30E WGS84
⊕26 1M S of Vrak Kouloundros (Sími)
36°30'·0N 27°52'·2E
⊕27 1M N of Ák Milon (Rhodes)
36°28'·5N 28°13'·3E
⊕28 1M E of Vrak Paximádha (Rhodes)
36°01'·4N 28°06'·8E
⊕29 1M S of Ák Prasso (Rhodes)
35°51'·8N 27°45'·1E
⊕30 1M S of Vrak Nisáki (Khálki)
36°12'·0N 27°38'·0E
⊕31 1M N of Ák Paraspóri (Karpathos)
35°55'·3N 27°13'·7E
⊕32 1M S of Ák Kastéllos (Karpathos)
35°22'·9N 27°08'·3E
⊕33 1M W of N. Platí (Kásos)
35°21'·7N 26°48'·2E
⊕34 0·3M S of Ák Exópetra (Astipálaia)
36°34'·44N 26°28'·55E WGS84
⊕35 1M N of Ák Floúdha (Astipálaia)
36°39'·6N 26°22'·8E
⊕36 0·2M S of Nisís Ligno (Astipálaia)
36°33'32N 26°23'·97E WGS84
⊕37 0·2M S of Ák Khilos (Astipálaia)
36°30'·16N 26°21'·94E WGS84
⊕38 1M S of Nisís Ofidhousa (Astipálaia)
36°30'·63N 26°08'·77E WGS84

## Quick reference guide

| Pátmos and adjacent islands | Shelter | Mooring | Fuel | Water | Provisioning | Tavernas | Plan |
|---|---|---|---|---|---|---|---|
| Skála Pátmos | B | AC | A | A | B | A | • |
| Anchorages near | | | | | | | |
| Skála Pátmos | BC | C | O | O | O | C | • |
| Nísos Arki | A | AC | O | B | C | C | • |
| Port Stretto | B | C | O | O | O | O | |
| N. Marathos | B | C | O | O | O | C | • |
| **Lipso** | | | | | | | |
| Órmos Lipso | B | AC | B | A | C | B | • |
| Lera Lipso | B | C | O | O | O | C | • |
| **Agathonisi** | | | | | | | |
| Áy Yeóryiou | B | ABC | O | B | C | C | • |
| East Bay | B | C | O | O | O | O | • |
| **Nisís Farmakonisi** | | | | | | | |
| O Tholou | C | C | O | O | O | O | • |
| **Léros** | | | | | | | |
| Port Lakkí | B | A | B | A | B | B | • |
| Partheni | A | C | B | B | C | C | • |
| N. Arkhangelos | C | C | O | O | O | O | |
| Órmos Plakoudi | C | C | O | O | O | O | • |
| Órmos Alindas | C | AC | B | A | B | B | • |
| Pandeli | B | AC | B | B | C | B | • |
| Xerocambos | B | C | O | B | C | C | • |
| **Kalimnos** | | | | | | | |
| Limín Kalímnos | A | A | B | A | A | A | • |
| Órmos Akti | C | C | O | O | O | C | |
| Vathi | B | A | O | B | C | C | • |
| Órmos Palionisou | O | C | O | O | O | O | |
| Emborios | B | C | O | B | C | C | • |
| Mirties | C | C | O | B | C | C | • |
| Telendhos | O | C | O | B | C | C | • |
| Órmos Linarias | O | C | O | O | C | C | |
| Vlikadia | B | C | O | B | C | C | |
| Psérimos | C | AC | O | O | C | B | • |
| N. Platí | C | C | O | O | O | O | |
| **Kós** | | | | | | | |
| Limín Kós | B | A | B | A | A | A | • |
| Kós Marina | A | A | (A) | (A) | B | B | • |
| Mastikhari | B | AB | O | A | C | B | • |
| Kardamena | B | AC | O | B | C | B | • |
| Órmos Kamáres | B | AC | O | A | C | C | • |
| **Nisís Yialí** | C | C | O | O | O | O | |
| **Nísiros** | | | | | | | |
| Mandráki | C | AB | B | A | B | B | • |
| Palon | B | A | O | B | C | B | • |

| Nísos Tílos | Shelter | Mooring | Fuel | Water | Provisioning | Tavernas | Plan |
|---|---|---|---|---|---|---|---|
| Livádhi | C | BC | B | A | B | C | • |
| Áy Andonis | C | C | O | B | O | C | |
| **Sími** | | | | | | | |
| Sími | B | A | B | A | A | A | • |
| Pethi | B | AC | O | B | C | C | • |
| Áy Marina | B | C | O | O | O | C | |
| Órmos Thessalona | C | C | O | O | O | O | |
| Órmos Nanou | C | C | O | O | O | O | |
| Panormittis | A | C | O | O | C | C | • |
| Órmos Marathouda | C | C | O | O | O | O | |
| Órmos Faneromeni | C | C | O | O | O | O | |
| Áy Emilianos | C | AC | O | O | O | O | • |
| Nisís Seskli | C | C | O | O | O | O | |
| **Rhodes** | | | | | | | |
| Mandráki | A | A | A | A | A | A | • |
| Rhodes Marina | A | AB | B | B | A | A | • |
| Ák Ladhiko | B | C | O | O | O | C | |
| Órmos Trianda | O | C | O | O | O | O | |
| Lindos | B | C | O | B | C | A | • |
| Áy Apostoli | C | C | O | O | O | O | |
| Órmos Lardhos | O | C | O | O | O | C | |
| Istros/Vigli | O | C | O | O | O | O | |
| Órmos Langonia | O | C | B | B | B | C | |
| Fanes | B | A | O | B | O | C | • |
| Khálki | B | ABC | O | B | C | C | • |
| Potamós | B | C | O | O | O | C | |
| Alimia | B | C | O | O | O | O | • |
| **Kárpathos** | | | | | | | |
| Port Karpathos | C | AB | B | A | B | B | • |
| Órmos Mákri Yialo | C | C | O | O | O | O | |
| Órmos Amorfos | C | C | O | O | O | O | |
| Finiki | C | A | O | A | C | C | • |
| Trístoma | B | C | O | O | O | O | • |
| Dhiafani | C | C | O | O | C | C | |
| **Kásos** | | | | | | | |
| Limín Kasou | C | A | B | B | C | C | • |
| Órmos Khelatronas | C | C | O | O | O | O | |
| Nisídhes Kaso | O | C | O | O | O | O | |
| **Astipálaia** | | | | | | | |
| Skála | B | ABC | B | A | B | B | • |
| Maltezana | B | BC | O | B | C | C | • |
| Órmos Agrilithi | B | C | O | O | O | O | • |
| Vathi | A | C | O | O | O | C | • |
| Panormos | B | C | O | O | O | O | • |
| Órmos Livádhi | C | C | O | O | O | C | |
| N. Áy Ioánnis | B | C | O | O | O | O | |

# Nísos Pátmos

The northernmost of the Dodecanese. The island is composed of three barren volcanic lumps joined to one another by narrow isthmuses. The natural harbour of Skála lies on the central isthmus and above it is the focal point of the island – the *chora* of Pátmos crowned by the monastery of St John the Divine. The *chora*, like that of Astipálaia, belongs more to the Cyclades than to the Dodecanese. The glaring white squat houses and courtyards contrast vividly with the grey stone monastery above.

Pátmos belongs to the Christian age rather than to antiquity. St John the Divine was banished to Pátmos by the Emperor Domitian. Here he dictated the wild poetry of the Apocalypse, found in the book of Revelations, to his disciple Prochorus. Halfway up the road between Skála and the *chora* is the Church of the Apocalypse and the Cave of St Anne where St John transmitted the fiery words of god to his disciple – at least so legend says, as we have no real proof that St John did actually write the Apocalypse whilst on Pátmos.

For centuries the island was the home of Saracen pirates until 1088 when St Christodoulos was granted permission to establish a monastery in honour of St John. The continued presence of the pirates dictated the fortified walls surrounding the monastery. The monastery prospered and its library became one of the largest in Greece outside Mt

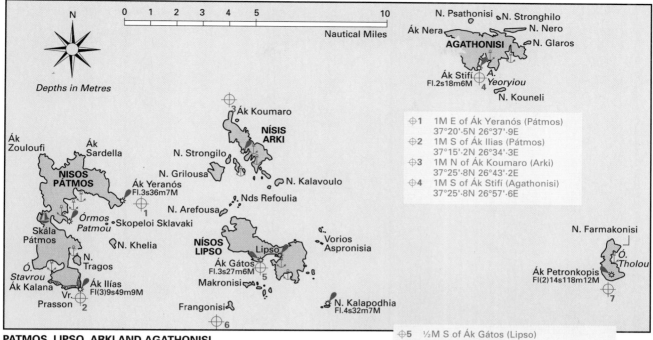

⊕1 1M E of Ák Yeranós (Pátmos)
37°20'·5N 26°37'·9E
⊕2 1M S of Ák Ilias (Pátmos)
37°15'·2N 26°34'·3E
⊕3 1M N of Ák Koumaro (Arki)
37°25'·8N 26°43'·2E
⊕4 1M S of Ák Stifi (Agathonisi)
37°25'·8N 26°57'·6E

**PATMOS, LIPSO, ARKI AND AGATHONISI**

⊕5 ½M S of Ák Gátos (Lipso)
37°17'·35N 26°45'·9E
⊕6 ½M N of Vrak Saráki (Stenón Lipsou)
37°14'·3N 26°42'·0E
⊕7 1M S of Ák Petronkopis (Farmokonisi)
37°15'·5N 27°05'·3E

Athos. Many of the manuscripts have since been dispersed (many of them to England), but the valuable *Codex Porphyrius* written on purple vellum in silver and gold, and some excellent Byzantine illuminations, remain. The Treasury has a number of valuable icons and stoles. Special arrangements have to be made to see items not on display.

Pátmos is the spiritual centre of the Greek Orthodox Church after Mt Athos. Near the Church of the Apocalypse stands the new theological college attended by students from all over Greece. At Easter celebrations are carried out with considerable pomp and later much gusto.

## SKÁLA PÁTMOS

BA 1531
Imray-Tetra G32

### Approach

*Conspicuous* In the approaches to Skála Pátmos there are a number of rocks and islets which are easily identified by day. Pátmos *chora* and the fortress-like monastery on the crown of the hill S of Skála Pátmos are conspicuous from some distance off. Skála Pátmos lies almost in the middle of the island at the lowest point. The white houses of Skála Pátmos are easy to see as you enter the bay.

*By night* Use the light on Ák Ilías Fl(3)9s9M, Vrak Kavouronísia (Tragos Rock) Fl(2)WR.12s5/3M (red sector covers 087°–232° over the reef N of the islet), Ák Áspri Fl.WR.2s5/3M (red sector covers 272°–320° over Ifalos Khelia, Nisís Khelia and Skopeloi Sklavaki), and the light at Skála Pátmos Fl.R.1·5s3M.

### Dangers

1. Care should be taken of the numerous reefs associated with the rocks and islets in the approaches. Skopeloi Tragos lies 0·1 mile N of

**APPROACHES TO SKÁLA PÁTMOS**
⊕37°19'·7N 26°33'·9E

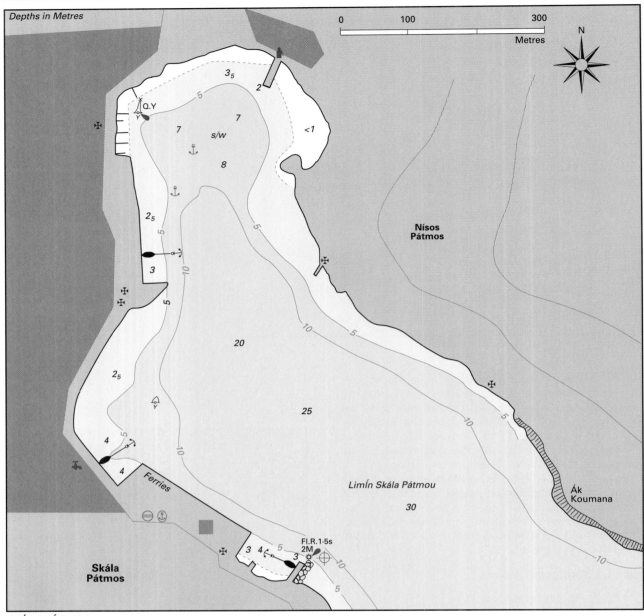

Depths in Metres

0    100    300
Metres

N

Nísos
Pátmos

Ák
Koumana

Limín Skála Pátmou

30

Ferries

Skála
Pátmos

Fl.R.1·5s
2M

**SKÁLA PÁTMOS**
⊕37°19′·2N 26°32′·8E

Vrak Kavouronísia (Tragos Rock). Ifalos Khelia lies 0·6 miles S of Nisís Khelia. Ifalos Sklavaki lies 0·2 miles SW of the more westerly of the two Sklavaki islets.

*Note* Ifalos Khelia is at the limit of the red sector of Ák Aspri light.

2. With the *meltemi*, strong gusts blow into the bay off the surrounding high land.

**Mooring**
Go stern or bows-to the quay N of the ferry quay or on the new quay a bit further N. It may also be possible to go on the stubby protecting mole in the S. The bottom is sand and weed, good holding.

*Shelter* Shelter from the *meltemi* is better than it looks on the plan. The bay is open SE and with moderate SE winds it is uncomfortable – with strong SE winds probably untenable.

*Authorities* Port police and customs.

*Anchorage* Yachts can anchor near the head of the bay in 6–10m. Good shelter from the *meltemi*.

**Facilities**
*Water* On the S quay. You need to find the waterman (try the *Skála Hotel*).

*Fuel* Can be obtained from a station at the head of the bay. There is a jetty near the fuel station with 2–3m depths at its extremity. A mini-tanker will deliver to the quay at Skála Pátmos.

*Repairs* A slip at the head of the bay hauls out local *caïques*. Some mechanical repairs can be carried out at Skála Pátmos. Good general hardware shops.

*Provisions* Good shopping for provisions at Skála.

*Eating out* Good tavernas on the waterfront.

*Other* PO. OTE. Bank. Greek gas and *Camping Gaz*. Hire motorbikes and bicycles. Bus to the monastery.

Approach to Pátmos looking W. The houses of the *chora* and the fortress-like monastery are easily identified

Daily ferry to Piraeus and Rhodes and local ferry to Kós and Sámos.

### General

Skála Pátmos has largely grown up to meet the needs of cruise ships and the daily ferry bringing people to see the monastery of St John. Most of the buildings around the harbour date from the Italian occupation and unlike many of the towns that grow up around a busy ferry port, Skála is a pleasant town in itself. Remember when visiting the monastery to dress appropriately – bikinis and even shorts are inappropriate.

### OTHER ANCHORAGES NEAR SKÁLA PÁTMOS

BA 1531
Imray-Tetra G32

These anchorages near to Skála are all protected from the *meltemi* although subject to gusts off the high land.

Skála Pátmos looking NNW across to Órmos Mérikha on the other side of Pátmos Island          *Peter Kleinoth/MareTeam*

1. **Órmos Meloyi** The first bay to the NE of Skála Pátmos. Anchor at the head of the bay in 5–7m. The bottom is sand and weed. Open to the SE. Taverna ashore.
2. **Órmos Livádhi** Immediately N of Órmos Meloyi. An islet, Nisís Panayía, in the entrance to the bay is easily recognised. Anchor at the head of the bay in 4–6m. With the *meltemi* there are gusts into the bay. Open SE.
3. **Órmos Kambos** Immediately NE of Livádhi. Anchor where convenient. Holding as for Meloyi, but open to the S as well as the SE. There are a number of villas around the bay, a taverna, and a shop where basic provisions can be obtained.
4. **Órmos Grikou** Lies 2 miles to the SE of Skála. Anchor in 8–10m off the hamlet at the head of the bay. A jetty on the N side is reported to have 2m depths alongside. The bottom is thick weed – difficult to get through so make sure your anchor is well dug in. Open to the SE although Nisís Tragos provides some protection from this direction. Taverna ashore. Bus to Skála in the summer.

### ÓRMOS STAVRÓS

37°17'·4N 26°33'·3E

On the W coast of Pátmos almost opposite Órmos Griko. The bay is quite deep. Anchor in 5–10m in the N part of the bay or in 5–10m in the N end of the E part of the bay. The bottom is sand and weed, reasonable holding. Reasonable shelter from the *meltemi* although some swell may work around into the bay – more uncomfortable than dangerous.

# Nísos Arki

A much indented island lying six miles ENE of Ák Yeranóa on Pátmos. About halfway along the W coast lie Port Augusta and Port Stretto, protected by a number of small off-lying islands.

### PORT AUGUSTA

**Approach**
The dogleg inlet on the W side of Arki. The islets in the approach are easily recognised. The light structure is conspicuous. A light (Fl.3s5M) is exhibited on the N side of the entrance but a night entrance is not advised. Care is needed of the reef running out for approximately 15m from the N entrance point.

**Mooring**
The inlet is very narrow once around the dogleg. In the middle of the inlet there are 4–5m depths shelving gradually to the sides. Go stern or bows-to the quay at the head of the inlet where there are mostly 2–4m depths. Alternatively anchor in the entrance and take a long line ashore to the E side. The bottom is mud and weed with a few rocks, good holding. Good all-round shelter in attractive surroundings.

**ARKI AND LIPSO**

⊕3  1M N of Ák Koumaro (Arki)
    37°25'·8N 26°43'·2E
⊕5  ½M S of Ák Gátos (Lipso)
    37°17'·35N 26°45'·9E
⊕6  ½M N of Vrak Saráki (Stenón Lipsou)
    37°14'·3N 26°42'·0E

### Facilities

Two tavernas on the waterfront.

### PORT STRETTO

37°22'·5N 26°44'·4E

Two inlets lying immediately S of Port Augusta.
Anchor in 4–5m in the W inlet and in 10–12m in the
E inlet. The head of the W inlet is shallow. The
bottom is sand and weed – good holding. Good
shelter from the *meltemi* but open S.

### NISÍS MARATHOS

The island lying in the approaches to Port Augusta
and Port Stretto. Between the S tip of Nisís
Marathos and the small islet of Spatala immediately
E there is a dangerous reef with less than 2m over it.
The reef is normally visible as a greenish patch.
Between the reef and Marathos there is a passage
with 5m depths. Enter the anchorage from the E
rather than between Marathos and Spalato.

Port Augusta looking NE inside the inlet

**PORT AUGUSTA**
⊕37°22'·9N 26°43'·8E (Fl.3s5M)

**NISÍS MARATHOS**
⊕37°22'·1N 26°43'·8E

In the cove on the SE side of Maratho two tavernas open in the summer. There are laid moorings which can be picked up. Good shelter from the *meltemi* but open S. The tavernas use VHF Ch 12 and are helpful to yachties.

# Nísos Lipso

## (Lipsa)

The island lying two miles S of Arki. It supports a small population in the village of Lipso (Sokora) on the S side of the island. There is a harbour here in a dogleg bay, and there are a number of small bays under the SW tip of the island.

### ÓRMOS LIPSO (Sokora)

A 1531

### Approach

*Conspicuous* Nisídhes Khalava, the islets off the SW corner of Lipso, are easily identified from the distance. Closer in, a white church on the S side of the entrance and the light structure on the N side of the entrance will not be seen until the bay opens up and the houses of Lipso become visible.

*By night* Use the light on Ák Gátos Fl.3s6M and on the quay in the bay F.R.3M/2F.R(vert)3M.

*Caution* With the *meltemi* there are fierce gusts into the bay.

### Mooring

Go stern or bows-to the quay on the W side. A short

**LIPSO**
⊕37°17'·8N 26°45'·8E

pontoon extends from the quay and yachts can go stern or bows-to the pontoon. Alternatively anchor off in the bay. The bottom is sand, mud and weed – bad holding.

*Shelter* Good shelter from the *meltemi* although there are strong gusts. In the event of strong southerlies anchor in 4–5m at the southern end of the bay.

Lipso harbour looking SW with Nisídhes Khalava at the top of the picture *Peter Kleinoth/MareTeam*

*Authorities* Customs and port police.

**Facilities**
*Water* On the quay and on the pontoon. Electricity can be connected.
*Fuel* On the SE side of the harbour.
*Provisions* Most provisions can be obtained in the village.
*Eating out* A number of good tavernas near the waterfront, some with good fresh fish.
*Other* PO. Exchange. Ferry to Pátmos.

**General**
The small village is attractive in a higgledy-piggledy sort of way. A few tourists come here but mostly the villagers derive a living from fishing and agriculture.

## LERA LIPSO

On the S side of Lipso in the bay situated between Ák Acerba and Ák Korakia there are several coves affording good shelter from the *meltemi*.

Care must be taken of a reef extending S from Ák Acerba. Proceed around either side of the islet (Lera) in the bay and anchor where convenient in any of the coves around the N side. Off the taverna there are stakes on the shore to which a long line can be taken. The bottom is sand and weed and good holding. Good shelter from the *meltemi* but completely open to the S. There is a small taverna on the beach in the centre cove but otherwise there are no facilities.

**LERA LIPSO**
⊕37°16'·5N 26°46'·5E

# Nísos Agathonisi

**(Gaïdharos)**

The much-indented island lying 10 miles NE of Arki and 8 miles W of the Turkish coast. It is easily identified from the distance. I am not sure whether the island is technically part of the Dodecanese or the eastern Sporades, but include it here for convenience.

**NISOS AGATHONISI**

⊕4    1M S of Ák Stifí (Agathonisi)
        37°25'·8N 26°57'·6E

**Note** On the E side of Agathonisi the passage between Agathonisi and Nisís Gláros is shown on BA and Greek charts as having least depths of 8m. In fact a sand bar obstructs most of the passage in the middle and you should not attempt to pass between Agathonisi and Nisís Gláros. There is a deeper passage reported close to Agathonisi, but the prudent course is to go to seawards of Nisís Gláros and spare yourself the trouble of finding the channel.

On the S coast there are two deep bays.

## ÁY YEORYIOU

**Approach**
This is the triple-headed bay near the SW end of the island. The entrance is lit on the W side (Ák Stifí) Fl.2s6M.

**Mooring**
At the head of the bay there is a quay where you can go stern or bows-to the N corner. Alternatively anchor near the head of the bay or in either the W or E coves. It is fairly deep for anchoring and you will generally be dropping anchor in 7–12m. The bottom is mud and weed, generally good holding.
*Shelter* Good shelter from the *meltemi*. Open S.

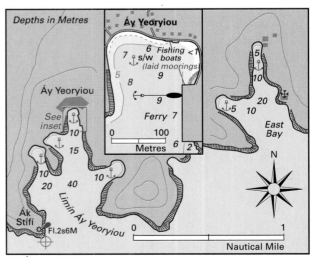

**LIMÍN AY YEORYIOU AND EAST ANCHORAGE**
⊕37°26'·8N 26°57'·6E

Áy Yeoryiou on Agathonisi looking E to the quay   *Nigel Patten*

**FARMAKONISI**
⊕37°16'·9N 27°05'·3E (light on S end)

### Facilities

Water, although it is reported to be non-potable. Some provisions and tavernas. Ferry to Pithagorion.

### General

Ashore there is the fishing village and the *chora* is a short distance inland. This has always been a fishing port and often the boats will stray across into Turkish waters to poach the richer fishing grounds there.

### AGATHONISI EAST BAY

37°27'·3N 26°59'·7E

Approximately 1½M E of Áy Yeoryiou is another deep indented bay. Anchor in either the W cove or at the head of the bay in 4–7m on sand and weed. Good shelter from the *meltemi*.

## Nisís Farmakonisi

### (Pharmako Island)

**Note** In recent years there has been a military presence on the island and yachts have been prohibited from anchoring in the bay on the E side. I include the details of the island here as the restrictions may be relaxed, as they have been in previous years.

This small island lies 14 miles E of Lipso just off the Turkish coast. On the E side of the island there is a small cove in Órmos Tholou offering some shelter from the *meltemi*, but completely open to the S and E. The cove can be recognised by four arches near the shore, the remains of a Roman villa.

Ashore there are a few ruins dating from the Romans and a small Byzantine church. It is here that Julius Caesar was captured by pirates and held to ransom for 38 days. H. M. Denham relates that he kept in good spirits and exercised and jested with his captors. Once released after the ransom was paid, he gathered an expedition together and in turn captured the pirates who were sentenced to death by crucifixion.

## Nísos Léros

Léros lies close north of Kalimnos and the two islands were referred to as one in antiquity – the Kalydnian Isles of Lero-Kalimno.

Léros is less harsh than its sister island Kalimnos. The hills are rounded and the countryside around Órmos Lakkí and Platanos is wooded and green. Platanos itself is a jumble of hibiscus, jasmine,

**LEROS AND KALIMNOS**

⊕8    M W of Ák Lakki (Léros) 37°06'·8N 26°48'·2E
⊕9    1M E of Vrak Áy Kiriaki (Léros) 37°08'·8N 26°54'·4E
⊕11   0·5M S of Ák Áy Yeóryios (Kalimnos)
         36°54'·97N 26°59'·21E WGS84
⊕12   0·75M S of Ák Khali (Kalimnos)
         36°55'·95N 27°02'·97E WGS84

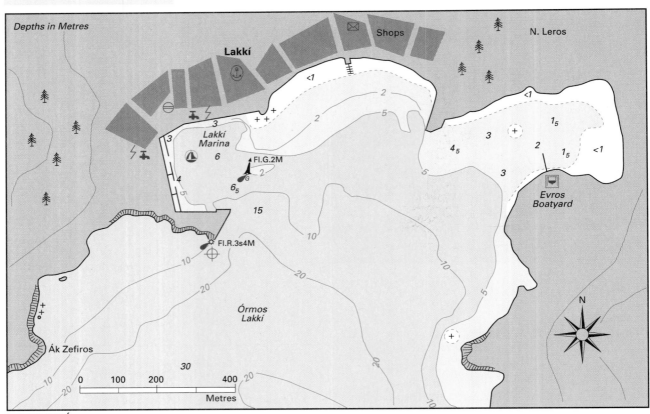

**PORT LAKKÍ**
⊕37°07'·7N 26°51'·0E

bougainvillea and oleander. It is a thoroughly likeable island capital with friendly inhabitants and a fine view over Órmos Alindas and Panali.

The island was associated in antiquity with the cult of Artemis. The worship of the mother-goddess when most of the civilized world had switched to the worship of the father-god left the islanders out of kilter with the rest of the islands and Leros had something of a reputation as a 'strange' island. During the carnival (in February or March) satirical verses are composed which the children recite at parties given in the houses of newly-weds. Stuart Rossiter in the *Blue Guide to Greece* considers these customs to derive from ceremonies associated with Dionysus of Eleusis. Whatever the mythopoeic origins everyone has a good time.

### PORT LAKKÍ (Porto Lago)

BA 1531

### Approach

*Conspicuous* From the W the Kalaboshi peninsula has a distinctive white appearance. The group of rocks NW of the entrance and the light structures on either side of the entrance can be seen closer in. At the entrance to the bay the fort and 4 windmills at Alinda will be seen, but they are obscured by a hill as you proceed further into the bay. The buildings of Lakkí and the mole are conspicuous once inside the bay.

*By night* Use the lights on either side of the entrance to Órmos Lakkí (Ák Lakkí Fl(2)14s9M and Ák Angistro Fl.2·5s5M) and the light on the end of the mole at Lakkí Fl.R.3s4M.

*VHF* Ch 11 for the marina at Lakkí and Ch 10 for Evros boatyard.

Port Lakki on Léros looking W to the yacht harbour
*Peter Kleinoth/MareTeam*

*Dangers*
1. With the *meltemi* there are strong gusts off the high land in the approaches and in the bay. There is also a confused sea at the entrance to the bay.
2. With strong southerlies there are gusts and a confused sea in the entrance to the bay and a considerable swell penetrates right into the bay itself.

*Note*
1. It is prohibited to approach within 200m of the naval establishment on the S side of Órmos Lakkí. The buildings of the naval establishment are clearly visible once inside the bay.
2. There are fish farms inside the N and S entrance points although the locations may vary as they are moved around.

### Mooring

*Data* c.50 berths. Visitors' berths. Max LOA 24m. Depths 3–5m.

*Berths* Go stern or bows-to in the new marina within Lakkí harbour. There are laid moorings to pick up.

*Shelter* Good shelter from the *meltemi* although there are gusts into the harbour. With S winds Lakkí is not as safe as it appears and a surge develops in the bay and harbour.

*Authorities* Harbourmaster. Port police and customs. Charge band 2.

### Facilities

*Services* Water and electricity at every berth. WC and showers. Laundry.

*Fuel* A mini-tanker can be arranged at the marina.

*Repairs Agmar Marine* The company which runs the marina also has a boatyard in Partheni. 70-ton travel-hoist. 350 berths on hardstanding. All yacht repairs including mechanical, engineering (including stainless steel work), wood and GRP repairs, sail repairs, and *gardiennage*. Chandlers. Contact details as for Agmar Marine.

*Evros Boatyard* At the head of Lakkí Bay. 50-ton travel-hoist. Mechanical and some engineering repairs. Showers and toilets. Make enquiries locally or amongst other cruisers regarding this yard as there have been a few accidents here.

Contact Evros Boatyard ☎ 0247 24733 *Fax* 0247 23947.

*Provisions* Good shopping for most provisions nearby. Ice can be delivered from a factory outside the village.

*Eating out* Taverna at the marina. Tavernas nearby.

*Other* PO. OTE. Hire motorbikes and bicycles. Bus to Platanos, the island's capital near Órmos Alindas. Taxis. Ferries to Piraeus and Rhodes.

*Lakkí Marina (and Partheni Boatyard)* Agmar Marine S.A., Leros Island, 854 00 Dodecanese, Greece
☎ 0247 26010, 26009, 24812, 22120, 25240
*Fax* 0247 26009, 22120 *E-mail* agmar@12net.gr

### General

The large buildings surrounding Órmos Lakkí all date from the Italian occupation when the bay was the Italian naval base. The large art deco buildings are arranged around wide boulevards and the place has the feel of a mock-up for a film about Mussolini or any Second World War movie set in Italy. Many of the building were used as mental hospitals and Leros acquired something of a reputation as a 'Devil's Island', something the present influx of tourists that arrive by ferry rarely see as they flee through Lakkí to the resorts at Alinda and Pandeli.

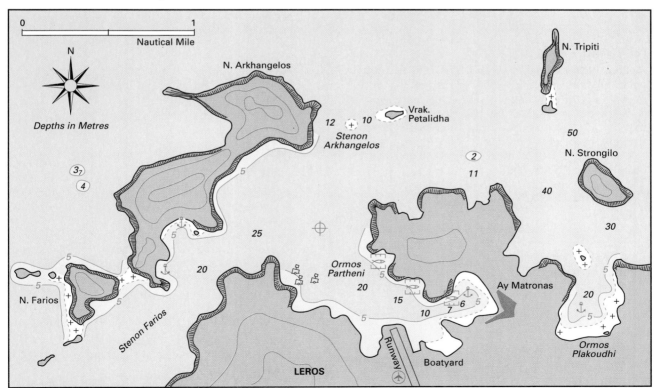

**ORMOS PARTHENI AND APPROACHES**
⊕37°12'·0N 26°47'·5E

Despite the overpowering architecture and the recent scandals over the mental institutions, I have always had a sneaking fondness for Lakki. It is a little out of kilter just like Leros used to be, and is the better for it.

## ÓRMOS PARTHENI

A large dogleg bay offering good all-round protection on the N side of Léros. It would seem that the military who once were here in force may have down-sized and instead there is now a boatyard ashore run by Agmar Marine who also run the marina at Lakkí. With the *meltemi* the best place to be is tucked into the E side of the bay. Taverna ashore.

Anchor in 3–8m at the head of the bay off Ayias Matronas. The bottom is mud and weed – good holding.

*Agmar Marine* 70-ton travel-hoist. 350 berths on hardstanding. 3-ton jib crane. 2-ton crane. All yacht repairs including mechanical, engineering (including stainless steel work), wood and GRP repairs, sail repairs, and *gardiennage*. Electricity and water points. Chandlers. Showers and WC. Canteen.

Contact Agmar Marine S.A., Leros Island, 854 00 Dodecanese, Greece
☎ 0247 26010, 26009, 24812, 22120, 25240
*Fax* 0247 26009, 22120 *E-mail* agmar@12net.gr

## NISÍS ARKHANGELOS

On the S side of the island just W of the entrance to Órmos Partheni is a bay with a sandy beach. Anchor in 4–5 m on sand, good holding. Reasonable shelter from the *meltemi*. On the W side it is reported there are stakes ashore to take a long line to. Good fishing around the nearby rocks.

## ÓRMOS PLAKOUDI

On the NE coast of Léros, Órmos Plakoudi offers good shelter in all except NE–E winds. In the middle of the entrance to the bay the group of above-water rocks can be left to either side (5m depths and over on both sides). Anchor off the small fishing hamlet in 4–7m.

It is around 1½km over to Áy Matronas on the other side of the headland.

## ÓRMOS ALINDAS

### Approach
This deep bay situated on the E coast of Léros is the alternative ferry port in strong W–SW winds.
*Conspicuous* The Venetian castle on the rocky summit of Ák Kastello and four windmills on the saddle of a hill above the town are conspicuous from some distance off.
*By night* Use the light W of Ák Kastello Fl.3s5M and the light on the pier in the bay F.R.3M.
*Dangers* With the *meltemi* there are strong gusts into the bay.

### Mooring
When northerlies are not blowing go stern or bows-

**ÓRMOS ALINDAS**
⊕37°09′·7N 26°51′·5E

to the short mole off Ák Kástro or stern or bows-to the central pier. Alternatively anchor off on the W side of the pier. The bottom is hard sand and rock – bad holding. When the *meltemi* is blowing strongly the best place to be is in the NW corner of the bay. Anchor in 3–8m.

*Shelter* The *meltemi* gusts into the bay from W–NW setting up an uncomfortable choppy sea. With a strong *meltemi* the anchorage off Áy Marina is untenable. Anchor in the NW corner or go to Pandeli.

### Facilities
*Water* Near the quay at Áy Marina.
*Fuel* In the village. A mini-tanker can deliver to the quay.

Ormos Alindas looking W from Platanos          *Nigel Patten*

*Provisions* Most provisions can be found nearby.
*Eating out* Tavernas on the waterfront.
*Other* PO. OTE. Bank.

## General

The village of Áyia Marina is the village near the water while on the saddle of the hill above the bay, about fifteen minutes' walk away, is Lero or Platanos, the main town of the island. Both Áyia Marina and Lero are thoroughly pleasant places with an abundance of bougainvillea and clematis adorning the houses.

## PANDELI (Panali)

### Approach

On the S side of Ák Kastello and Ák Pandelis lies a large bay and in the NW corner is Pandeli with a small harbour off the beach.

*By night* The end of the mole is lit Fl.G.3s3M.

**PANDELI**
⊕37°09′·1N 26°51′·8E

Pandeli harbour looking ENE

### Mooring

Go alongside or stern or bows-to the outer part of the mole or anchor off the beach in 4–8m depths. The bottom is sand and weed – good holding.

*Shelter* Good shelter from the *meltemi*. Strong southerlies could make it uncomfortable.

*Note* Immediately SW there is a small cove that can be used although shelter from the *meltemi* is not as good as the anchorage at Pandeli.

### Facilities

Water on the quay. Diesel can be delivered to the quay. Provisions ashore and better shopping in Platanos up the hill. Tavernas and cafés. Showers in some of the cafés.

### General

The setting is wonderful with a few houses around the beach and the local fishing boats drawn up close to the beach. Oleander, bougainvillea and tamarisk grow profusely in the village, with fishing nets strung up to dry along the beach. Platanos is about a fifteen minute walk up the hill.

## ÓRMOS XEROKAMBOS

On the S side of Léros this large bay offers good shelter from the *meltemi*, being open only to the S. Anchor off or pick up a laid mooring off one of the tavernas. There is a miniature fishing harbour in the SW corner.

Tavernas ashore. A number of houses and villas have been built around the slopes above the bay.

**XEROKAMBOS**
⊕37°05′·8N 26°52′·9E

# Nísos Kalimnos

The sister island of Léros, lying immediately S of it and separated by Stenón Lerou. This great craggy lump of rock is for the most part steep-to and bare of vegetation. Kalimnos imparts a feeling of prehistoric permanence – long after the human race has disappeared, you feel that Kalimnos will remain much as it is today. It is not so much the height of the mountain range (Mt Profitis Ilías or Parasivia is a scant 679m, 2240ft) but the sheer bulk of it which is impressive from seaward.

In ancient and medieval times the island followed the fortunes of Kós. The Italian occupation in 1912 was actively opposed by the Kalimniots who painted the Greek national colours everywhere to annoy their masters. During the Second World War many of the islanders, faced with starvation when their livelihood of sponge-fishing was denied them, emigrated all over the world. You will meet many American and Australian Greeks in the capital who have returned home to live here.

The grubby sprawling capital of Pothia (Port Kalimnos) is the centre of sponge-fishing in Greece. In ancient times the sponge was used much as we use artificial sponges today – for washing and cleaning up the after-dinner mess. It also had other uses:

'The servants in the 'Odyssey' swabbed tables with it, while it was in great demand with artisans, who used it to apply paint, and with soldiers who had no drinking vessels to hand. In the Middle Ages, burned sponge was reputed to cure various illnesses. Together with olive oil it has been used from time immemorial as a contraceptive pessary by the oldest professionals – who oblivious of the fact that they figure in the pages of Athenaeos, still flourish in Pláka today – using roughly the same sort of slang, in which the word 'sponge' finds many a picturesque use.'

Lawrence Durrell *The Greek Islands*

Artificial sponges have replaced many of the uses of this little animal and most of the natural sponges being washed out in Kalimnos harbour are sold to tourists.

## LIMÍN KALÍMNOS (Kalymnos, Pothia)

BA 1531
Imray-Tetra G34

### Approach

*Conspicuous* From the E the buildings of Kalimnos town around the bay and a number of white oil storage tanks to the E of the town are conspicuous. From the W the town will not be seen until you are up to the entrance of the bay. Closer in, the monastery on the hill above the town, the silver cupola of the cathedral on the waterfront and the outer mole are easily identified.

*By night* Use the lights at the entrance: Fl.R.2s4M/Fl.G.2s3M. The harbour lights are difficult to make out against the loom of the town lights. The church on the top of the ridge and a large cross lower down the slopes are floodlit at night.

*Note* At the time of writing the Fl.R had been removed and the buoy marking the end of the works was lit Q.R. The Fl.R will be repositioned at the end of the extended breakwater.

*Dangers*

1. With the *meltemi* blowing there are strong gusts off the high land down into the approaches and in Órmos Kalímnou itself.
2. At the time of writing the breakwater extension was still largely underwater. Its extremity is marked by a smallish red buoy (Q.R). Works are expected to be completed on the breakwater in the near future.

### Mooring

*Note* Kalimnos Marina is expected to be finished around the time of publication of this book. If the marina is not operational see the notes that follow.

Limín Kalimnos looking N from the coast. Note the works on the outer breakwater

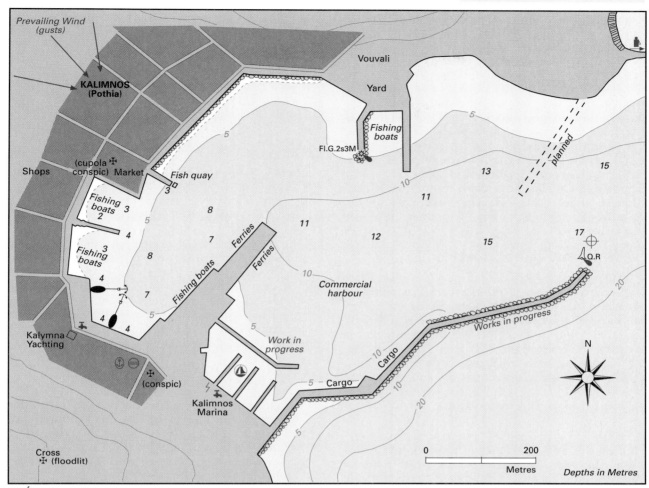

**LIMÍN KALIMNOS**
⊕36°56'·84N 26°59'·69E WGS84

*Data* 80 berths. Visitors' berths. Max LOA c.20m. Depths 2–5m.

Proceed into the marina and berth where directed. There are to be laid moorings tailed to the pontoons.

*Shelter* Good shelter.

*Authorities* Harbourmaster. Port police and customs on the main ferry pier. A charge will be made in the marina.

*Note* If the marina is not operational then go stern or bows-to the S quay on the W side of the ferry pier. It is very crowded here and it can be difficult to find a berth. The bottom is mud and weed and not everywhere good holding. Good shelter although the *meltemi* gusts down onto the quay so make sure your anchor is well in.

**Facilities**

*Services* (Kalimnos Marina) Water and electricity to be installed. A shower and toilet block to be built.
*Fuel* At the fuel quay on the N side of the bay outside the harbour.
*Repairs* Most mechanical repairs can be carried out. Some light engineering work. Kalimnos Yachting on the yacht quay can provide a haul-out service using a crane and slings for yachts up to 10 tons. They also arrange repairs and gardiennage. A boatyard to the E of the town hauls out large *caïques* and a few yachts. Good hardware and tool-shops. Basic chandlery can be obtained from a number of shops near the fish quay.

Kalymna Yachting, PO Box 47, 85200 Kalimnos
☎ 0243 24083/24084/23043 *Fax* 0243 29125
*E-mail* kalymna@europlanet.com
*Provisions* Good shopping for all provisions. Ice available.
*Eating out* Tavernas on the waterfront and in the town. Noisy bars on the waterfront.
*Other* PO. OTE. Banks. Greek gas and *Camping Gaz*. There is a gas filling factory just outside the town. Hire cars, motorbikes and bicycles. Intermittent bus service to the other villages on the island. Daily ferries to Piraeus and Rhodes.

**General**

Kalimnos is the home of the Kalimniot sponge-divers – the sponge-boats, most of the *trehandiri* type and about 10–12m in length, are built in the boatyard immediately E of the town. Originally the sponge-divers fished in shallow waters, jumping overboard with a heavy stone slab and scooping the sponges off the bottom into a net. Nowadays a compressor is used and deeper waters off Africa and

Cyprus are fished. An interesting book worth getting on the harrowing lives of the sponge fishermen has just been published by a resident Kalimniot: *Bitter Sea* by Faith Warn (available locally).

The town of Kalimnos is attractive from the distance. Many of the houses are washed in various shades of blue – a practice continued from the days of the Italian occupation when the blue houses reminded their Italian masters of the Greek colours. On closer inspection the town is rather dusty and grubby, with the hustle and bustle of tripper boats and fishing boats loading and unloading their cargoes, and trucks, cars, vans, motorbikes, three-wheeler mini-trucks and vans buzzing along the waterfront. Sponges are, of course, for sale everywhere.

## ÓRMOS AKTI (Ati, Katsouni)

36°57'·7N 27°02'·8E

Immediately NW of Ák Kahli, the SE extremity of Kalimnos, lies Órmos Akti. Much of the bay is now obstructed by fish farms, though there is still room to anchor. With a strong *meltemi* a swell enters the bay and there are gusts off the surrounding hills. Care is needed of an underwater rock near the head of the bay which is sometimes marked by a white buoy. Anchor in 10m on the S side of the submerged rock. Tavernas ashore.

## VATHI

One mile N of Órmos Akti lies the deep fjord of Vathi. From the E the deep slit in the hills can be seen from the distance. Go bows-to the pier or the quay after the pier, leaving the quay for the tripper boats clear. Care is needed as there is underwater ballasting extending out in places. It may also be possible to anchor fore and aft further in although it is reported there are now numerous local moorings here. The bottom is sand and weed – good holding. Good shelter from the *meltemi* although there are strong gusts off the surrounding hills.

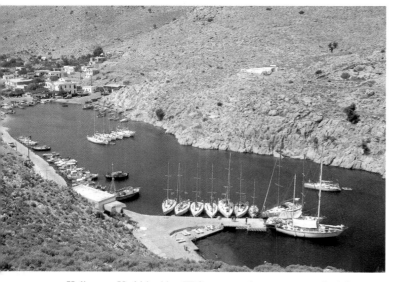

Kalimnos. Vathi looking W from near the entrance to the inlet
*Nigel Patten*

**VATHI**
⊕36°58'·5N 27°02'·2E

In the small hamlet at the shallow head of the inlet, limited provisions can be obtained and there are several tavernas. Water on the quay. A 'yacht club' near the quay.

The valley inland from Vathi is extremely attractive – orange and lemon groves and lush market gardens contrast with the steep red rock hills in this, one of the few lush parts of Kalimnos.

## ÓRMOS PALIONISOU (Baia Isolavecchia)

37°02'·0N 26°59'·5E

A bay on the S side of Ák Poundha. Although this bay appears suitable, the holding (rock covered by a thin layer of sand and weed) is bad. Near the shore there are several iron stakes to take a line ashore, but the bay should only really be used in calm weather. Taverna opens in the summer.

## EMBORIOS (Emporios, Vorio Bay)

A bay lying on the SE side of Ák Kefala. The islet of Kalavros lying in the entrance can be identified and closer in, the hamlet at the head of the bay will be seen. Pick up one of the laid moorings off the taverna. If you are anchoring here the holding is poor and it is useful to take a long line ashore if possible. The bottom of mud and sand has thick weed over it. A jetty in the N of the bay has 4m off the end but is usually occupied by fishing boats. Good shelter from the *meltemi*.

Mini-market and tavernas ashore. The bay is an attractive spot and usefully located on the W coast of Kalimnos.

## MIRTIES

36°59'·7N 26°55'·8E

A small village on the Kalimnos side of Stenón Telendhou. There is a small harbour here used by local *caïques* and tripper boats running to Nísos Telendhos. Although there are 2–3m depths off the outer part of the mole, most of the harbour from around the middle is shallow. As the harbour is very small anyway, this leaves little room for manoeuvring. In calm weather you can anchor off the village, but it is too exposed if there is any wind about.

Provisions and tavernas ashore.

**EMBORIOS**
⊕37°02′·3N 26°55′·6E

### NISÍS TELENDHOS

In calm weather anchor off the small hamlet on the E coast. Just adequate shelter from the *meltemi* with very strong gusts off the high land. Shallow draught boats may be able to get onto the quay but reconnoitre first.

The craggy lump of Telendhos conveys a prehistoric permanence – 'always has been there and always will be' – and indeed has been inhabited since prehistoric times as well as by the Greeks, Romans and later in the Middle Ages. The island was joined to Kalimnos up until the 15th century when an earthquake rearranged the topography and submerged the land-bridge.

**STENÓN TELENDHOU**
⊕36°59′·4N 26°55′·4E

### ÓRMOS LINARIAS

Is virtually untenable except in calm weather. It is open to all sectors westward and subject to strong gusts off the hills in southerly winds.

### ÓRMOS VLIKADIA (Vlikhadhia)

36°55′·5N 26°58′·0E

On the S coast of Kalimnos, one mile W of Ák Áyios Yeóryios, Vlikhadia is open only to the S. It provides good shelter from the *meltemi* although there are gusts off the surrounding hills. Anchor in 5–6m keeping clear of the swimming area at the head of the bay. The bottom is mostly rock so anchoring is difficult. Make sure your anchor is well in if going ashore.

Summer villas and tavernas ashore.

## Nísos Psérimos

### ÓRMOS PSÉRIMOU

Situated on the SW side of Nísos Psérimou, the entrance to Órmos Pserimou is difficult to see except from the SW. Once at the entrance the

**PSÉRIMOS**
⊕36°55′·8N 27°07′·8E

Approaches to Psérimos looking E

Órmos Psérimou on the W coast of Psérimos looking W.
*Peter Kleinoth/MareTeam*

houses of the hamlet and the rough stone mole are easily seen. In the summer the tripper boats take up all the sheltered quay space and there is little chance of finding a slot. After the tripper boats have returned to Kós in the evening you will be able to go on the quay until they return around mid-morning. The bottom is sand and weed with some rocky ledges – good holding on the sand. With a *meltemi* blowing a swell enters the bay but if a yacht can manage to tuck itself into the NW corner behind the mole it is not unduly uncomfortable.

Tavernas on the beach. The hamlet of gleaming whitewashed houses is a holiday place for the locals from Kós and Kalimnos and when the tripper boats arrive the beach is packed solid with sun-bathers.

*Caution* Care must be taken to avoid the reef just N of Ák Sphuri off the island. The outer rocks are awash and easily spotted.

### NISÍS PLATÍ

36°57'·2N 27°05'·7E (Vrak Nekrothikes light)
The long thin islet lying N to S off the W coast of

Pserimos. In settled weather tripper boats anchor off the bight about in the middle of the islet and also at the NE end. Here there is some protection from the *meltemi* which has mostly been funnelled to blow from the WNW. Anchor in 3–5m on sand.

## Nísos Kós

### (Stanko, Istankoy)

Kós lies tucked into the Gulf of Kós (the ancient Ceramic Gulf, Turkish Gökkova Körfezi) between the Myndus peninsula to the north and the Dorian promontory to the south. The fingers of Turkey reach out to touch the island, enclosing the ancient triangle of trading power that vied with Rhodes to dominate the southwestern Aegean. Kós was probably not an important partner in the power hexapolis, and not until the city of Kós was founded in 366 BC on the present site of the modern capital did it prosper and become an important maritime power. Today the harbour is probably much as it was when Kós was a powerful city.

The island has always been much praised for its fertility. A mountain ridge runs its length (the summit attains a height of 845m (2788ft) near the NE end) and on the eastern side it is precipitous and barren. It is the western side which is well-watered and fertile. Sandy beaches fringe the cultivated plain which produces fine vegetables, melons and grapes. The Kós variety of lettuce was introduced to England from here. Perhaps the mulberry trees on which the silkworm feeds also covered these slopes in antiquity. Kós was once famous for its silk and in particular the *Coae vestes*, the diaphanous flowing silk dresses prized by Roman women – sadly no longer made or worn.

Ancient Kós had many famous citizens but above them all stands Hippocrates, the great physician of antiquity and the father of modern medicine. We know little of the old healing methods but we do know that for the Hippocratic school the site of the sanatorium was as important as the methods. (The tranquillity of Epidavros, of mysteries earlier than Hippocrates, is proof enough.) The Aesculapion (Ascelepion) is just outside Kós town and should not be missed. The three terraces lie in a peaceful setting near to medicinal springs on a limestone hill overlooking the Gulf of Kós. The Italians rebuilt

Ák Ammóglossa on the NE corner of Kós looking E. The shoal water off the end is deceptive and care is needed

**KALIMNOS TO NÍSIROS**

⊕**10** 3M S of Vrak Safonídhi (Kalimnos-Kós Channel)
36°50'·27N 26°54'·49E WGS84

⊕**11** ½M S of Áy Yeóryios (Kalimnos)
36°54'·97N 26°59'·21E WGS84

⊕**12** ¾M S of Ák Khali (Kalimnos)
36°55'·95N 27°02'·97E WGS84

⊕**13** ¼M S of Vrak Krevvatio (Pserimos)
36°54'·82N 27°09'·39E WGS84

⊕**14** 1M S of Ák Krikellos (Kós)
36°39'·2N 26°58'·4E

⊕**15** ¾M N of Ák Ammóglossa (Kós)
36°55'·70N 27°16'·42E WGS84

⊕**16** ¼M E of Ák Áy Fokas (Kós)
36°51'·67N 27°21'·69E WGS84

⊕**17** ¾M W of Deveboynu Buku (Knidos/Turkey)
36°41'·45N 27°20'·90E WGS84

⊕**18** 1M N of Ák Katsouni (Nísiros)
36°38'·2N 27°11'·2E

⊕**19** ½M S of Ák Loutros (Nísiros)
36°32'·92N 27°11'·66E WGS84

⊕**20** 1M S of Ák Levkhos (Nísiros)
36°32'·72N 27°08'·28E WGS84

much of the Aesculapion to the original plan without destroying the calm of the place. It is the appropriate place to remember the Hippocratic Oath:

'I shall look upon him who shall have taught me this art even as one of my parents. I will share my substance with him and relieve his need should he be in want. His children shall be as my own kin, and I will teach them the art, if they so wish, without fee or covenant...The regimen I adopt shall be for the benefit of my patients according to my ability and judgement, and not for their hurt or for any wrong. I will give no deadly drug to any, though it be asked of me, nor will I counsel such, and especially I will not aid a woman to procure abortion. Whatsoever house I enter, there I will go for the benefit of the sick refraining from all wrong doing or corruption, and especially from any act of seduction, of male or female, of bond or free. Whatever things I may hear concerning the life of men during my attendance of the sick, or even apart from them, which should be kept secret, I will keep my own counsel upon, deeming such things as sacred secrets.'

Recently more tourists have been discovering Kós and several large hotels have been built around the sandy beaches. In many ways it resembles Rhodes – the green slopes, large hotels, the bustling harbour under the castle of the Knights – and like Rhodes it wants to have an ever larger slice of the tourist pie whatever the cost.

## KÓS (Ko, Stanko)

BA 1531
Imray-Tetra G35

### Approach

*Conspicuous* From the E the fort on the S side of the entrance, the palace, a chimney near the entrance and a minaret in the town are conspicuous. From the N and W a large brown hotel on the spit ending in Ák Ammóglossa is conspicuous from some distance off. Rounding the point the entrance to the harbour is easily seen.

*By night* Use the lights on Ák Ammóglossa Fl.R.4s9M, Ák Foúka Fl.4s6M, and Ák Loúros Fl(3)WR.15s6/4M. The entrance to the old harbour is lit Fl.G.3s3M/Fl.R.3s3M.

*Dangers* The shoals extending from Ák Ammóglossa

**KÓS**
⊕36°53′·88N 27°17·34E WGS84

**APPROACHES TO KÓS AND KÓS MARINA**
⊕₁ 36°53′·88N 27°17′·34E WGS84
⊕₂ 36°53′·84N 27°17′·97E WGS84

should be given a good offing. With a strong *meltemi* blowing there are often confused seas off Ammóglossa, but once around it the sea is comparatively flat.

### Mooring

Go stern or bows-to the quay on the E side. The bottom is mud – excellent holding.

*Note* The harbour is very crowded in the summer and it can be difficult to find a berth. Unless you specifically want to be here it is better to go to the marina.

*Shelter* With a strong *meltemi* there is often an uncomfortable surge in the harbour although shelter on the E side is good. With gales from the N–NE the harbour is close to untenable.

*Authorities* A port of entry: port police, customs, health and immigration authorities. For some reason Kós seems to get some of the most obnoxious port policemen in Greece.

*Anchorage* Large yachts can anchor off the beach S of the entrance in settled weather. Care is needed to keep clear of the approaches to the hydrofoil quay.

### Facilities

*Water* On the quay. The waterman usually does the rounds twice a day.

*Fuel* In the town. A mini-tanker can deliver to the quay.

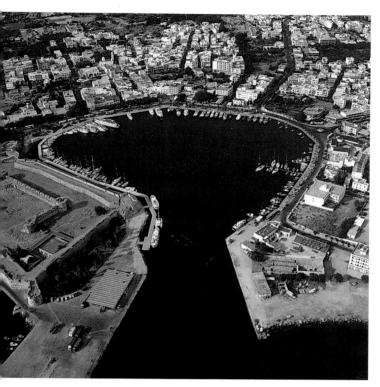

Kós harbour looking SSW in from the entrance
*Peter Kleinoth/MareTeam*

*Repairs* Some mechanical repairs. Hardware shops and some chandlery available. Sail repairs by Kavas Yachting ☎ 0937 213403.

*Provisions* Excellent shopping for provisions and a good market just up from the harbour. Ice from a factory on the outskirts of town.

*Eating out* Good tavernas in the town.

*Other* PO. OTE. Banks. Greek gas and *Camping Gaz*. Hire cars, motorbikes and bicycles. Intermittent bus service to the other villages on the islands. Daily ferries to Piraeus and Rhodes and to Bodrum in Turkey. International and internal flights to Kós airport.

## General

Kós is a likable mixture of medieval Frankish and Turkish architecture with a few contributions of Italian monumental. Oleander, bougainvillea, jasmine and hibiscus grow in profusion and classical remains from the era of Greek prosperity are used in novel ways – a sarcophagus forms the basin for a fountain, fragments of ancient marble prop up the branch of a tree, part of a marble column forms the base for a flower box, huge hewn blocks of stone line the path in a park. The fort and the adjacent park, shaded by old spreading plane trees (one of which is reputed to be that which Hippocrates taught under, although it is only 400–500 years old – a nice tradition anyway) and cooled by the *meltemi*, is quite one of the most pleasant places to be on a hot summer's day. A small museum in the town houses Greek and Roman finds from the excavations.

In recent years Kós has attracted growing numbers of tourists and it seems as if the city of Kós is set to revive ancient rivalries and challenge Rhodes for the valuable annual cargo of bodies craving sun and sand. The town has changed to accommodate this new trade and though I think it retains much of its character, you may, like some others, think it has become 'all fast food and discos'.

## KOS MARINA

### Approach

The marina lies approximately ¾M SE of the old harbour at Kós town. The approach and entrance are straightforward.

*By night* The entrance is lit Fl.G.4s3M/Fl.R.4s3M.

*VHF* The marina will operate on VHF Ch 09.

### Mooring

*Data* 250 berths. Visitors' berths. Max LOA c.25m. Depths 3–6m.

Berth where directed. There are laid moorings tailed to the quay.

*Shelter* Good shelter although northerlies including a strong *meltemi* cause a surge at the SE end of the marina. If possible try to berth on the first two piers in from the entrance.

*Authorities* Harbourmaster. A charge will be made.

### Facilities

*Services* Water and electricity at all berths. Shower and toilet block under construction.

*Fuel* Fuel quay to be installed at the entrance.

*Repairs* Travel-hoist to be installed.

*Provisions* Some shopping nearby. Better shopping on the outskirts of Kos.

**KÓS MARINA**
⊕36°53′·84N 27°17′·97E WGS84

*Eating out* Tavernas and restaurants nearby on the waterfront.

*Other* An ATM, boutiques and a restaurant and bar to be established within the marina.

## General

The marina is basically complete and in use by a number of charter companies. Services were being installed at the end of 2000 and it is expected the marina will be functional by 2001, though not with all facilities. It is a bit out of the way compared to the old harbour at Kos, but then for some that will be a blessing.

## MASTIKHARI

A harbour about halfway along the NW coast of Kós. An L-shaped breakwater provides good protection from the *meltemi*. The entrance is lit (Fl.G.3s6M) though the light is not to be relied upon. The harbour is used by inter-island ferries, local ferries, and coasters.

The harbour appears to have silted since it was built and care is needed over depths. Go stern or bows-to the N quay close to the 'square' quay in the corner. The bottom is soft mud and dead weed, poor holding. The W quay has mostly less than 1m depths off it.

Provisions and tavernas ashore. Ferry to Kalimnos.

**MASTIKHARI**
⊕36°51'·2N 27°04'·6E

## NOTE

Off the SE coast of Kós fierce gusts blow down off the surrounding hills when a strong *meltemi* is blowing. The worst spots seem to be off the three prominent capes, Krikellos, Khelona, and Foúka. Around Cape Krio on mainland Turkey there are also fierce gusts and disturbed seas.

## KARDAMENA

### Approach

The small harbour lies almost exactly halfway along the SE coast of Kós. The long sprawl of hotels and bars and tavernas along the coast is easily identified. Care needs to be taken of two swimming platforms lying off the harbour (lit: F.R).

*Caution* With the *meltemi* there are fierce gusts off the high land of Kós and care is needed.

### Mooring

Go stern or bows-to off the pier running out from the beach, checking first with the locals to see you are not taking a local's berth. The bottom is sand and weed, good holding.

*Shelter* Good shelter from the *meltemi* which gusts off the land. Open S.

### Facilities

*Water* At the root of the pier.
*Fuel* About 200m away in the village.
*Provisions* Good shopping for provisions.
*Eating out* Numerous tavernas and bars nearby.
*Other* PO. OTE. Exchange. Hire cars and motorbikes. Internal and international flights from the airport about 5 km away.

### General

Once a small fishing village, Kardamena is now a sprawl of a resort, catering for package holidaymakers who want little to do with things Greek and frequent any establishment that remotely resembles the 'local' at home. The resort is only 5 kilometres from the airport so getting the hordes to and from Kardamena is simplified. The prize of the resort is the wonderful long sandy beach often described as the best in the Dodecanese. At night

**KARDAMENA**
⊕36°46'·8N 27°09'E

the resort fairly pulsates to the sound of over-amplified music of all descriptions, so don't bank on getting a lot of sleep.

### ÓRMOS KAMARES (Kamara, Palaeokastro)

Situated on the S end of Kós, this bay and the small harbour offer good shelter from the *meltemi*. A large white hotel on the N side of the bay is conspicuous from some distance off and the small harbour is on the W side of the bay. Anchor in the bay in 4–6m or go stern or bows-to or alongside the outer end of the mole. There is also room in the small fishing harbour for a few yachts. The bottom is sand and weed – good holding. With the *meltemi* blowing the gusts into the bay are not strong or prolonged.

Water at the root of the mole. Also a taverna at the root of the mole and a disco further round the beach.

Kamáres is no longer a tranquil spot, being plagued with waterbikes and water-ski boats which make an irritating noise, and appear to be driven largely by irritating people.

**KAMARES**
⊕36°44′·2N 26°58′·3E

### NISÍS YIALÍ (Yalí)

BA 1531
36°39'·9N 27°07'·5E (Yialí S Bay)

Three miles NW of Nísiros an open bay on the S coast of Nisís Yialí offers some lee from the *meltemi*. The island is scarred by extensive quarries and in the bay a large loading chute extends into the sea. The sea is usually discoloured by dust from the quarry. A yacht seeking shelter here should anchor in 5–6m to the NE of the loading chute. The bottom is sand and good holding. Care must be taken of a reef 350m S of the islet (Áy Antonios) off the E end of Yialí and of numerous large mooring buoys in the vicinity of the quarry.

*Caution* About half a mile off the SW tip of Yialí lies a reef just under water which is not easily seen, especially when the *meltemi* is blowing.

# Nísos Nísiros

Almost square, Nísiros is an extinct volcanic crater poking out of the sea SW of Deveboynu Burun (Cape Krio) in Turkey. The rich soil on the slopes of the cone is terraced and cultivated with olives and citrus trees. Until recently the hot sulphurous springs were renowned for their medicinal properties, but the hydropathic institute looks abandoned today. If the weather allows, it is a thoroughly pleasant excursion to the crater (2½ miles across) where there is a spectacular view of the surrounding sea and islands. If Mandráki harbour is untenable, which it usually is with a strong *meltemi*, tuck into Palon where there is better shelter.

## LIMÍN MANDRAKI

### Approach

The buildings around the harbour and the harbour mole on the NW corner of the island are easily

**MANDRAKI**
⊕36°36'·9N 27°08'·5E

Nísiros. Mandráki looking WSW

identified from the N. The harbour actually lies a short distance E of Mandráki village.

*By night* A Q.G.3M is exhibited on the end of the mole.

### Mooring

Go alongside or stern-to the mole or the quay. With a strong *meltemi* a swell creeps around the end of the mole making the harbour uncomfortable and possibly dangerous. With a strong N–NE wind the harbour is untenable. Port police.

*Note* Care is needed of the ferry calling here, which does not normally anchor but holds itself off with its propeller against lines ashore, causing a lot of wash for yachts berthed nearby.

### Facilities

Good shopping in the nearby village. Good tavernas. PO. OTE. Daily ferry to Kós.

### General

The village on the terraced slopes is most attractive and in calm weather the harbour is well worth a visit. A bus runs from Mandráki (there is one at 1000 hours) to the crater and it is an excursion which shouldn't be missed.

### PALON (Palos)

#### Approach

This small *caïque* harbour lies 2 miles to the E of Mandráki harbour.

*Conspicuous* From the E the buildings of the abandoned hydropathic institute, a cluster of large stone buildings with red roofs immediately E of Palon, are conspicuous. From the W the harbour will not be seen until you are around the rocky headland sheltering it, but a gantry and a cluster of buildings on the coast immediately W of the headland will be seen. Closer in a church in the village and the harbour breakwaters are easily identified.

*By night* The entrance is lit: Fl.G.2s3M/Fl.R.2s3M.

Nísiros. Palon harbour looking E from the ridge above

**PALON**
⊕36°37′·3N 27°10′·7E

*Dangers*
1. Care needs to be taken of the reef running N for about 100m from Ák Ammodes. The final approaches to the harbour should be made on a course due S towards the entrance.
2. With the *meltemi* there are fierce gusts and a wicked short sea off the N side of Nísiros.

### Mooring

Go stern or bows-to the N mole. The bottom is mud, sand, and rocks, good holding.

*Shelter* Reasonable shelter from the *meltemi* although there may be a surge with a prolonged blow which can make entry difficult and possibly dangerous.

*Note* The harbour appears to be silting since my earlier surveys.

### Facilities

A mini-market and several tavernas in the village. Good fish sometimes available. Irregular bus to Mandráki.

### General

The little harbour and the village are wonderful. You can swim in the harbour. The hinterland is green and wooded. The tavernas sit on the edge of the harbour and you can spend most of the day in one sipping cold beer and watching the locals watching you. Around Palon there is good if steep walking, or you can wander along the coast to the old hydropathic institute.

## NISÍS PERIOUSA

Approximately 4½ miles WSW of Mandráki is Nisís
Perigousa. Local fishing boats sometimes shelter in
the bay on the E coast where there is some shelter
from the *meltemi*.

# Nísos Tílos

Situated between Nísiros and Khálki, this long thin
island is seldom visited by tourists or yachts. It was
known in medieval times as Episcopi, a name that
probably referred to its watchtowers from which it
could signal to Rhodes of an approaching enemy.
The Italians revived the name calling it Piscopi.
Today, as in many of the small islands off the tourist
track, many of the young leave for the big cities of
Rhodes or Athens.

Tílos. Órmos Livadhiou looking SW          *Nigel Patten*

**NISOS TILOS**

⊕21  1M N of N. Gáïdharos (Tílos)
      36°30'·2N 27°17'·2E
⊕22  Mid-channel between Tílos and Andítilos
      36°22'·6N 27°26'·9E

**ÓRMOS LIVÁDHIOU**
⊕36°25'·0N  27°23'·3E

## ÓRMOS LIVADHIOU (Livadia)

BA 1532

On the E coast of Tílos lies the large bay of Livádhia
with a small quay for the ferry. Go bows-to the quay
or alongside the left side of the quay amongst the
local *caïques*. With a strong *meltemi* blowing there are
gusts off the surrounding hills and a swell works its
way around into the bay, so it can become very
uncomfortable in here. Care is also needed when
fishing boats come in at speed creating a large wash
which can push yachts onto the quay. Keep yourself
pulled well off the quay or anchor off. The quay and
the anchorage are open from NE through to SE.
Port police.

Water near the quay. Contact the waterman via
the noticeboard on the quay. Most provisions can be
obtained and there are a number of tavernas. In
settled weather it is an attractive and friendly place
to visit.

*Note* There are plans to build a new mole out from
the existing quay at Tílos. No details are yet
available on when work will start.

## LIVÁDHIA FISHING HARBOUR

36°25'·0N 27°24'·2E

In the SE corner of the bay there is a very small
fishing harbour which has 2m depths in the entrance
and off the N breakwater. A small yacht may be able
to squeeze in here with care. The entrance is lit:
Fl.R.3s3M.

## ÁYIOS ANDONIS

36°27'·6N 27°20'·0E

A small fishing harbour in the SE corner of Órmos
Playiou on the N end of the island. A dogleg mole
extends for about 120m from the coast with another
shorter mole inside it. There are reported to be
3–4m depths at the entrance and 2–3m depths
inside. It is very small and yachts over 8–9m should
not even poke a nose inside.

Tavernas ashore.

**ÓRMOS ERISTOU** 36°25'·6N 27°21'·0E

A large bay on the S side of Tílos that provides some shelter from the *meltemi* although a swell usually works its way around into here. Anchor in 3–5m off the beach. Gusts into the bay with the *meltemi*.

You can work up to the *chora* N of the anchorage.

# Nísos Sími

Sími lies in the entrance to the Gulf of Doris (Turkish – Hisarönu Körfezi) looking like a giant Rorschach ink blob. From seaward it is a barren precipitous island, but inland there are patches of pine forest. The indentations in the coastline provide numerous anchorages and in fact the principal harbour is an entirely natural feature.

Sími was once famous for shipbuilding and sponge-diving. Simiot shipwrights built many of the fast galleys for the Knights of St John and later for their Turkish masters. Even today Simiot *caïques* seem to be better cared for than in many of the other islands. Simiot divers were once known as the best in the Aegean, although Kalimniot divers would contest that claim. Today few Simiots risk the dangers of sponge-fishing and Kalimnos is the undisputed centre.

### SÍMI (Limín Simis, Symi, Syme)

BA 1532
Imray-Tetra G35

### Approach

*Conspicuous* From the N the houses of Sími on the ridge above the town are conspicuous. From the S and E the harbour will not be seen until you are right into the bay. From the S it is easy to confuse the entrance to Pethi, the large bay immediately SE, with that of Sími. Entering Órmos Simis the houses of Sími town are immediately conspicuous. A clock tower and a white church on the N quay are also conspicuous.

Sími harbour looking W from the ridge above the town
*Nigel Patten*

**NÍSOS SÍMI**

⊕23 1M N of Ák Makria (Sími) 36°41'·1N 27°51'·5E
⊕24 W entrance of Nímos Passage (Sími) 36°38'·72N 27°49'·76E WGS84
⊕25 E entrance of Nímos Passage (Sími) 36°38'·66N 27°50'·30E WGS84
⊕26 1M S of Vrak Kouloundrós (Sími) 36°30'·0N 27°52'·2E

*By night* Use the light on Ák Koutsoúmba Fl.3s5M and the light on the quay Fl.G.3s3M.

### Mooring

Go stern or bows-to the quay on the N side of the harbour taking care to leave the part of the quay allotted to the ferries clear. Most of the western quay is reserved for local trip boats and the local ferry. The depths in the harbour drop off rapidly and you should be prepared to let go your anchor in 12–20m. The bottom is mud and rock – poor holding in places.

*Shelter* Good shelter from the *meltemi*. With strong S winds there is a considerable surge in the harbour which can become dangerous with prolonged southerlies. The ferries (five or more in the summer) create a considerable wash when they arrive about mid-morning.

*Authorities* Port police and customs. Charge band 2.

*Anchorage* In settled weather it is possible to anchor in Órmos Kharani and take a long line ashore. Reasonable shelter from the *meltemi* with the only problem being the wash from ferries as they charge into Port Sími. Keep pulled well off.

### Facilities

*Water* On the quay. The harbour attendant will open it up for you.
*Fuel* The harbour attendant can arrange for fuel to be delivered.

**SÍMI**
⊕36°37'·09N 27°50'·40E WGS84

*Repairs* Limited mechanical repairs. A boatyard hauls out large *caïques* and the occasional yacht in the cove N of the harbour.

*Provisions* Good shopping for provisions.

*Eating out* Excellent tavernas in some delightful locations in the town.

*Other* PO. OTE. Banks. Greek gas and *Camping Gaz*. Hire motorbikes. Daily ferries to Rhodes.

## General

Discovering Sími is like discovering an exotic plant in the desert. The muted blue, amber, cream and rose-hued houses have been built one upon the other up the steep sides of the inlet like a child's building block version of a town. On the S side of the harbour a staircase leads up the hill to the houses on the top and though this heart-thumping climb takes it out of you in the summer, it is worth the effort both for the views from the top and for the fine old houses built on rocky projections and inclines on the way. The people of Sími remain detached from the daily onslaught of tourists from Rhodes and you can almost hear the sigh when the ferry departs.

## PETHI (Pedhi)

Over the hill to the SE of Sími lies the deep inlet of Pethi. The S entrance is lit: Ák Filonika Fl.6s4M. Care needs to be taken of an above-water rock in the

**PETHI**
⊕36°37'·1N 27°52'·6E

455

middle of the entrance – it is easily seen by day.

Anchor in 6–10m N of the pier or in front of the hotel on the S side of the pier. Do not anchor in the approaches to the pier which is in constant use by the water tanker bringing water for Sími. There may be room clear of the tanker berth on the pier for a few yachts to find a berth. The bottom is sand and weed, poor holding in places. The holding off the hotel on the S side of the pier is reported to be better. Shelter from the *meltemi* is good but there are strong gusts into the bay so make sure your anchor is properly dug in or lay a second anchor to be on the safe side.

Tavernas on the waterfront. It is a long hike over the steep ridge to Sími town or take the bus from in front of the hotel.

## ÁY MARINA

Immediately N of the entrance to Pethi there is an attractive anchorage behind the islet of Áy Marina. A reef connects the islet to the coast on the N so the approach must be made from the S. Anchor in 4–5m on a sandy bottom. There is a lee from the *meltemi* here remarkable for its calm. A good bathing beach ashore under an elaborate stone wall and beautiful clear water. Taverna ashore.

## ÓRMOS THESSALONA

36°35'·6N 27°52'·8E

Lies just over half a mile S of Ák Filonika. Magnificent precipitous cliffs drop straight into the sea at the head of the bay. Anchor where convenient. Some protection from the *meltemi* although a swell will sometimes roll in depending on the strength of the *meltemi*.

## ÓRMOS NANOU

36°34'·6N 27°51'·5E

A large bay just S of Thessalona. A good lunch stop with wild steep-to scenery and clear water.

## ÓRMOS MARATHOUDA

36°33'·7N 27°52'·1E

Three miles S of Pethi lies Órmos Marathouda open only to the E. Anchor in 4–8m at the head of the bay. Subject to gusts off the hills.

## ÓRMOS FANEROMENI

36°33'·0N 27°52'·5E

One mile S of Marathouda lies the deep inlet of Órmos Faneromeni open only to the E. Anchor at the head of the bay. Also subject to gusts off the hills.

## NISÍS SESKLI ANCHORAGE

36°31'·0N 27°52'·2E (Vrak Kouloundrós light)

Nisís Seskli lies off the S end of Sími separated by a deep channel (Stenón Seskli). On the SE side of Nisís Seskli lies Órmos Skomisa, immediately N of Vrakhonisís Kouloundrós (Troumbeta). A small islet, Artikonisi, partially protects the cove from the W–SW. The cove should be approached from the E.

Anchor in the middle of the cove in 5–6m sand and rock, doubtful holding. On the W side there is a small quay you can take a line to. Good shelter from the *meltemi* in attractive deserted surroundings.

## PANORMITTIS

BA 1532

### Approach

An enclosed bay on the SW corner of Sími. A white windmill on the E side of the entrance and the large white buildings of the monastery are conspicuous.

*By night* Use the light on Nisís Marmarás Fl.3s6M and the light on the NE side of the entrance Fl.R.2s3M. Care is needed of yachts at anchor which may not be carrying anchor lights.

*Dangers* With the *meltemi* there can be gusts and confused seas off the entrance.

### Mooring

Anchor in 3–6m in the NE side of the bay. There is sometimes room on the pier in the S corner although most of the space is taken up by local ferries and tripper boats and by the water tanker which calls here. The bottom is sand and weed with some rocks – good holding once the anchor has cut through the weed.

*Shelter* Good all-round shelter.

### Facilities

Limited provisions and tavernas ashore. Bread available at the monastery.

### General

The bay is attractive in a sparse sort of way and the monastery on the SE side complements it, being a sparse sort of place itself. When the ferries and tripper boats arrive the bay is transformed into a noisy crowded place for a few hours, but outside that it is a peaceful spot.

PANORMITTIS
⊕36°33'·2N 27°50'·6E

## ÁY EMILIANOS

On the W coast of Sími some shelter from the *meltemi* can be found under a short headland on the E side of Ák Kefala. From the N the monastery of Áy Emilianos on the headland and another monastery on the slopes inland are easily identified. Anchor in 8–10m on the S side of the headland. There is only the monastery ashore.

## NISÍS NÍMOS (Nemos)

Nisís Nímos, immediately N of Nísos Sími, is separated from the latter by a narrow channel (Stenón Nimou). There is a least depth of 4m in the fairway of the channel and although it looks daunting the first time through, it is a convenient short cut that avoids circumnavigating Nímos. With a strong *meltemi* blowing into the channel the depth at the trough of any swell may reduce the

**ÁY EMILIANOS**
⊕36°36'·4N 27°46'·5E

**NIMOS PASSAGE (Stenón Nimou)**

⊕24  W entrance of Nímos Passage (Sími) 36°38'·72N 27°49'·76E
      WGS84
⊕25  E entrance of Nímos Passage (Sími)
      36°38'·66N 27°50'·30E WGS84

depth by about 1 metre at most. Just look straight ahead and not at the variegated sea bottom passing under the keel.

# Rhodes

### (Nísos Rodhos)

The largest island of the Dodecanese, Rhodes lies at the southern end of the chain of islands stretching down the west coast of Asiatic Turkey. Its name is of uncertain origin but possibly comes from the Greek word for the rock-rose which grows all over the island. In antiquity it had many names: Stadia, referring to its ellipsoid shape; Ophioussa, from the many snakes on the island; Poeissia, referring to its fertility; Olyessa, because it is earthquake prone; and Makaria, calling it simply the blessed isle.

As the ancient name, Stadia, states, the island is roughly ellipsoid or diamond-shaped. A mountain range runs from N to S with the highest peak, Mt Ataviros (1,215m, 4009ft), situated in the middle of the west coast. Unlike many of the other islands of the group, Rhodes is fertile not only in the valleys and on the plains but also on the high hills. Pine, olive, orange and lemon, fig and pear trees grow well. *Maquis* and wild flowers (including the rock-rose) grow in the countryside, while hibiscus, bougainvillea and jasmine run riot over village houses. Butterflies seem to be everywhere – so much so that Rhodes has been called the butterfly island. In addition to butterflies, the fauna is said to include deer, foxes, hares, badgers, partridges, vultures, jackdaws, jays and the Rhodes dragon – a lizard growing as long as 50cm (14in) – though you are unlikely to find any of these around the crowded north end of the island.

This garden island with its dry hot summers and mild winters (the climate resembles that of Sicily) has been popular throughout history: smiled upon by the sun-god Helios; extravagantly praised by Strabo; beloved by Tiberius who deserted Capri for a time, bringing his entire retinue with him; the Knights of St John were reluctant to leave their castle even when surrounded by hostile neighbours; and the Italians, who occupied Rhodes in 1912 intent on creating another Capri. Today Rhodes is without doubt the most popular tourist island in Greece. Hotels stretch along the east and west coasts from Rhodes city where sun and sandy beaches create an irresistible lure for sun-starved northerners.

The significant history of Rhodes is neatly compacted into two periods: the story-book times of ancient Greece and the violent period of the Knights of St John. Moreover, such has been the influence of Rhodes on the surrounding islands that its history can to a large extent be read as the history of most of the Dodecanese.

The island has always been important as a trading centre between Asia and Africa and Greece and Italy. Homer mentions three cities on Rhodes: Lindos, with its natural harbour on the east; Ialysos, in the northwest; and Kamiros, about 20 miles

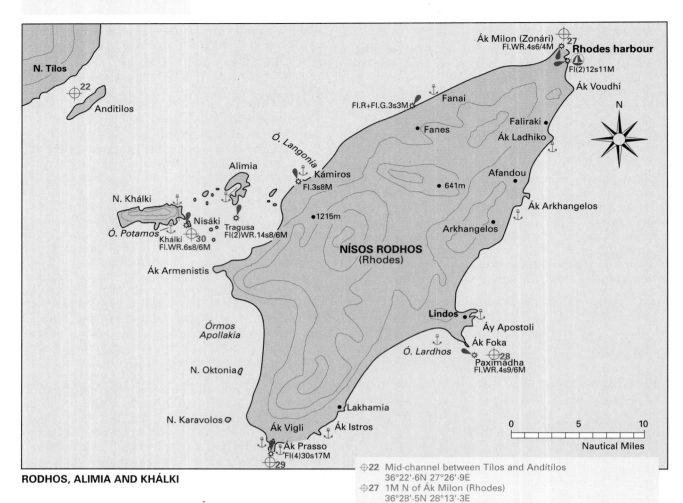

**RODHOS, ALIMIA AND KHÁLKI**

| | |
|---|---|
| ⊕22 | Mid-channel between Tílos and Andítílos 36°22'·6N 27°26'·9E |
| ⊕27 | 1M N of Ák Milon (Rhodes) 36°28'·5N 28°13'·3E |
| ⊕28 | 1M E of Vrak Paximádha (Rhodes) 36°01'·4N 28°06'·8E |
| ⊕29 | 1M S of Ák Prasso (Rhodes) 35°51'·8N 27°45'·1E |
| ⊕30 | 1M S of Vrak Nisáki (Khálki) 36°12'·0N 27°38'·0E |

down the west coast from Ák Milon (Zonari). Rhodes, along with Kós, Knidos and Halicarnassus, monopolised trade in this southwest corner of the Aegean.

In 408 BC the three cities mentioned by Homer decided to pool their resources and found the city of Rhodes on its present site. Hippodamus of Miletus designed the new city and built a series of harbours on the eastern side of the low-lying peninsula on which the city was built. The new city and its splendid harbour complex swiftly eclipsed the other three cities to become the most important city and trading centre in the southwestern Aegean. The Rhodians built up their own fleet of merchant vessels to become a major sea power. And they managed all this without upsetting the major warring powers around them – in effect a little Switzerland growing ever more prosperous.

The Rhodians managed successfully to evade being caught up in the international politics of the time until the death of Alexander the Great, when the Mediterranean was plunged into chaos. Rhodes refused to help Antigonus invade Egypt (which was, after all, its major trading partner). Demetrius Polioketes, a would-be Alexander, enters the history books at this point. To teach the Rhodians a sharp lesson he assembled a large force and also the gargantuan siege machine for which he is famous – the Helepolis. The contraption was estimated to be

nine storeys high, weighed perhaps 125 tons and rolled up to the city walls on giant oak wheels. It sprouted huge catapults, drawbridges which could be dropped down to release troops, a nest on top for archers, and was shielded against enemy arrows.

Around Rhodes today, piled in heaps or lying about the castle walls, you can see the heavy stone balls believed to be the missiles Demetrius flung at the city. He did a lot of damage, but at the end of a year he had still not beaten the stubborn Rhodians. He signed a treaty with them and ordered all his siege machinery to be sold and the money donated to the Rhodians for a statue to commemorate the great siege. Thus the statue of the sun-god Helios was born. Chares began the statue in 302 BC and twelve years later the Colossus of Rhodes was complete. Perhaps it did stand astride Mandráki harbour, as commentators say, and perhaps not. Wherever the precise site of the 35 metre high statue was, it became a landmark for all ships nearing the island until it was toppled by the earthquake of 227 BC.

Rhodes endured as an important economic and sea power until 43 BC when Cassius sacked the city and destroyed it. Rhodian marine law was universally admired, parts were absorbed into the Venetian sea code and its spirit is with us today. For centuries the city attracted artisans and artists. In Roman times Caesar, Brutus, Anthony, Cicero and Tiberius all studied in Rhodes. Pliny counted over 2,000 statues when he was there and yet today a mere handful remain, so complete was Cassius' sacking of the city.

Until 1309 Rhodes drifted with the mainstream of history: ruled by Byzantium; sacked by the Saracens; ruled by the Venetians and later by the Genoese who in 1306 gave shelter to the Knights of St John. In 1309 the refugees became the masters of Rhodes. They built the huge fortified castle that dominates the town today and acquired a fleet of fast galleys which harried Turkish merchant vessels up and down the coast. They expanded from Rhodes to Khálki and Alimia, Sími and Tílos, Kós and Kalimnos, and the adjacent coast of Asia Minor. In all of these places the castles or the remains of castles built by the Knights can be seen today.

The huge fortifications of Rhodes withstood two great sieges – in 1444 from Egypt and in 1480 from the Turks. In 1522 Suleiman I assembled a force reckoned to number over 100,000 men against 650 Knights and 1,200 supporters. The defence of the Knights against such a force is one of history's great battles. They held out for five months before the Grand Master, Villiers de l'Isle Adam, capitulated on honorable terms. It is said that Suleiman, watching the Grand Master leave, remarked, 'It is not without some regret that I oblige this old Christian to leave his home.'

Rhodes remained under Ottoman rule until the Italians occupied it in 1912. Intent on recreating the glory of Rhodes, they set about restoring and tidying up the castle and the town. They have been much criticized for their restoration work, but I do not think it is overdone, and most of it gives a good feeling of what medieval fortifications were like. For the student of military warfare, Rhodes has probably the best preserved medieval fortifications in Greece. During the Second World War the island was occupied by the Germans and in 1947 it became Greek along with the rest of the Dodecanese.

## RHODES HARBOUR – MANDRÁKI

BA 1532
Imray-Tetra G3, G35

### Approach

*Conspicuous* From the W and N the city of Rhodes on a low-lying spit of land can be identified from a long way off. Large hotels line the beach on the W. From the S and E a chimney S of the town and the E mole of Órmos Akandia are conspicuous. The large ferries in Limín Emborikós also show up well. Mandráki basin, where a yacht should make for, is easily identified by the small fort with the lighthouse (Áyios Nikólaos), a cupola, the belfry, the market and the three windmills on the mole forming the E side of Mandráki. On either side of the entrance to

Mandráki there is a tower with a bronze deer on top.

*By night* Use the light on Ák Milon Fl.WR.4s6/4M (red sector covers Ifalos Kolóna over 286°-314°), Áy Nikólaos Fl(2)12s11M, the W breakwater head Fl.G.2s4M, Limín Emborikós Fl.R.2s4M, and the lights at the entrance to Mandráki Q.RG.3M, F.R and F.G.2M. Some of the lights are difficult to identify against the loom of the city lights. Approaching from the W the light at Rhodes airport (AlFl.WG) some 10 miles S of the city is easily picked up.

*Dangers*

1. Keep well off Ák Milon (Zonári) and the shoal

**RHODES HARBOUR - MANDRÁKI**
⊕36°27'·0N 28°14'·3E

Mandráki looking into the entrance with Áy Nikólaos on the left of picture

Mandráki harbour looking SSW    *Peter Kleinoth/MareTeam*

water running N from it and the reef (Ifalos Kolóna) extending N from the outer mole protecting the entrance to Mandráki.

2. Care should be taken when strong southerlies and easterlies are blowing as there is a disturbed swell at the entrance to Mandráki, although once inside the basin there are no problems.

### Mooring

Berth where directed or where convenient. The harbour is hopelessly crowded in the summer with yachts often two or three out from the quay. Mandráki is now designated as a marina although as yet few additional facilities have been introduced. Hopefully moorings will be laid so that the crossed anchors and frayed tempers of the past are avoided. Yachts can also go on the pontoon on the W side just inside the entrance if there is room.

*Shelter* Good all-round shelter in the harbour. Numerous boats winter afloat here.

*Note* Fouled anchors are a common occurrence simply because there are so many yachts. A large mooring chain lying approximately 30m out from the quay is also easily fouled.

*Authorities* A port of entry: port police, customs and immigration authorities. Customs and immigration are at the root of the E mole in Mandráki and the port police are on the W side. Charge band 2.

***Limín Emborikós*** Very large yachts can go on the quay on the W side of Limín Emborikós. Call Yacht Agency Rhodes to arrange a berth here.

### Facilities

*Services* Water and electricity on the quay and on the W pontoon. Showers and toilets.

*Fuel* A mini-tanker delivers to the quay.

*Repairs* 60-ton travel-hoist. The channel to the hoist basin is normally dredged to 2–2·5m. Go first to the boatyard where the leading marks for the channel will be described. The telegraph poles in a street directly behind the hoist basin must be kept in line to show the channel.

*Nereus Boatyard*, Odos Australis 19, Rodhos, Dodecanese, Greece ☎/*Fax* 0241 22717.

Reservations advisable if you want to leave your boat here for the winter.

All mechanical repairs. Most engine spares can be obtained within a few days from Piraeus. Wood and GRP repairs. Light engineering work including stainless steel work carried out. Electrical and some electronic repairs. Sail repairs. Life raft service.

Depths in Metres

N

0    50    100    200
Metres

5

4

2

If. Kolona

Just submerged

Swimming platform

<1

High rise hotels

Cupola (conspic)

<1

Q.RG.3M     Ák Limokathartiríou

Y.C

2

2    4

10

Prevailing wind

<1

2

4

4₅

10

10

5

5

F.G.2M

<1

4

4₅

F.R.2M

Áy Nikólaos
LtHo (conspic)
Fl(2)12s11M

Hydrofoils

4

4

5

3

4₅

5₂

5

Hydrofoil

4₅

4

4₅

Local ferries

3

Mooring chain

Charter yachts

3

Windmills (conspic)

4

4

Kon Tiki Restaurant

2

Tripper boats

Immigration

Market

5

**MANDRÁKI**
36°26′·9N 28°14′·2E

461

Good hardware and tool shops. Several chandlers.

*Yacht Agency Rhodes* A long-established company in Rhodes who have a well-stocked chandlery, including many imported items and a good stock of books and charts. They are also brokers and charter agents. The staff are knowledgeable and helpful and can usually obtain most bits of gear. Mail can be sent to them and will be held for collection. Yacht Agency Rhodes, PO Box 393, Byronos 1 and Kanada St, GR85100, Rhodes (on the waterfront between Nereus boatyard and the commercial port). ☎ 0241 22927 *Fax* 0241 23393. VHF channel 73 is monitored. Call sign *Yacht Agency Rhodes*.

*Provisions* Good shopping in the new town around the harbour and in the white octagonal market. Ice available.

*Eating out* Good tavernas – ask around for recommendations. *Le Bistrot, Araliki* and *Cleo's*, all in the old town have been recommended.

*Other* PO. OTE. Banks. Greek gas and *Camping Gaz*. Turkish baths in the old town. Hire cars, motorbikes and bicycles. Bus service to the important villages. Organised excursions to Lindos, the Valley of the Butterflies, Kamiros etc. Daily ferries to Piraeus via Crete or the northern Cyclades. Daily ferries to Marmaris in Turkey in the summer. International and internal flights.

**General**

Rhodes city – you either love it or hate it. After the sleepy peace of many of the other islands in this area, Rhodes town fairly hums and bustles as only the most important tourist town in Greece can. But it is not overpowering, and once you are accustomed to the fact that you are back in a busy city the place does grow on you.

Rhodes city consists of two distinct parts: the old city surrounded by the walls built by the Knights and the new town largely built by the Italians during their occupation of the island. Much of the old city was restored by the Italians and although they have been criticized for producing 'Hollywood' castles and towers, with the passing of time the reconstruction has weathered and blended into the original medieval stonework. In the new town the buildings lining the waterfront were also largely built by the Italians in a monumental style to designs by Florestano di Fausto. The other notable buildings mostly date from the Turkish occupation.

Mandráki was probably the harbour used by the Knights to keep their swift galleys in, although some believe the basin now called Emborikós was the galley harbour and Mandráki was occupied only by small boatbuilders. The word Mandráki is the diminutive of *mandra* meaning 'a sheep fold' and is used in many other places to describe a small enclosed harbour.

Here in ancient times the Colossus of Rhodes may have stood – the bronze statue of Helios the sun-god, one of the seven wonders of the world (despite the postcards which show him looking more like a ridiculous jolly green giant). Although the popular opinion is that the statue did not stand astride the harbour entrance, I agree with Ernle Bradford that there is no reason why this should not have been so:

'My opinion is that, as is so often the case, the ancient story is true; the statue of the Sun God literally bestraddled the narrow entrance to the galley harbour. It is a small boat harbour, and one must bear in mind that the ships of the ancients were, by modern standards, only small boats. Most of them, no doubt, lowered their masts when entering harbour under oars – just as the galleys often did in the time of the knights. In any case, a statue with a total height of 105 feet would have given plenty of clearance between its legs even if their masts were raised.'
Ernle Bradford *The Greek Islands*

The statue was destroyed by an earthquake in 227 BC and 80 years later sold as scrap.

Beyond the old and new city stand the blank reinforced concrete hotels and suburbs of the holiday town relieved only by the abundance of oleander, bougainvillea and hibiscus. On Ák Zonari stands the Hydrobiological Institute, housing an interesting collection of preserved and live marine animals caught in local waters.

**RHODES MARINA**

Work is in progress on the new marina situated near the root of the breakwater protecting Limín Akandia where shown on the plan on page 459. The outer breakwater is complete and the pontoons have been installed. No facilities are available at the time of writing, but a number of yachts use the marina. When work progresses yachts may have to leave, but at this time work once again seems to have stopped. The completion date for the new marina is not known (even by those 'in the know' in Rhodes) and dates for completion are just extended into the future.

The plan is for the projected final form of the marina so details may (and probably will) differ when it is complete.

**RHODES MARINA**
Proposed/final form

**RHODES BOATYARD**

**Rhodes Marina** Projected 300-plus berths. All services including water and electricity, shower and toilet blocks, fuel quay, and yacht services.

## RHODES BOAT YARD

A separate project nearby for a huge yard with protected basin. 550 and 200-ton travel-hoists. Slipway. 100,000sq.m of hardstanding. This is a government project which will be put out to private tender when complete. A completion date in 2001–2002 is envisaged.

## NOTE

When on passage between Rhodes and Lindos there are fierce gusts off the high land when the *meltemi* is blowing strongly. If you are heading to Rhodes from Lindos it is best to leave very early in the morning when the *meltemi* sometimes dies off for a while.

Between Rhodes city and Lindos there are several bays and coves that can be used in settled weather.

## ÁK LADHIKO ANCHORAGE

36°19'·3N 28°12'·8E

A small bay under Ák Ladhiko. Care is needed of shoal water in the entrance (2m) and off the E entrance. The best policy is to stay closer to the W entrance point. Anchor in 4–5m on sand and rock, reasonable holding once you find a good sandy patch. Good shelter from the *meltemi*.

Tavernas ashore.

## LINDOS (Limín, Lindhou)

BA 1532

### Approach

The castle and the town are conspicuous. By night there are no lights although on a clear night entry is possible with care.

### Mooring

Anchor where convenient. The bottom is sand with some rock – good holding. The bay is open to the E and southerlies send in a swell. With the *meltemi* there are fierce gusts down into the bay so make sure your anchor is well in before leaving a yacht unattended.

### Facilities

*Water* Limited from local sources.

LINDOS
⊕36°05'·7N 28°05'·4E

Lindos looking NE                    *Nigel Patten*

Lindos on the E coast of Rhodes Island looking SSW
*Peter Kleinoth/MareTeam*

*Provisions* Most provisions can be found.
*Eating out* Numerous excellent if somewhat expensive tavernas.
*Other* PO. OTE. Banks. Hire cars, motorbikes and bicycles. Buses to Rhodes.

### General

Early in the morning or late in the afternoon, Lindos, with its small winding streets between medieval houses and the toy castle perched on a rock summit as if about to topple into the bay, is uniquely beautiful. In the heat of the day coaches and ferries transport hundreds of tourists from Rhodes – the narrow streets are packed tight and the beach resembles something from Cannes or Nice – but by dusk they have all departed..

Lindos, commanding the superb natural harbour, was the principal city of the island before the foundation of Rhodes in about 408 BC. The acropolis within the medieval castle affords an all-round view over land and sea – before 1000 hours or after 1600 hours there are few people about. In the village the old houses with black and white pebble mosaic courtyards and staircases are a legacy from the prosperous Middle Ages.

## ÁY APOSTOLI

Situated immediately S of Órmos Lindou. It is possible to anchor here – take a line ashore as there is limited swinging room. The enclosed inlet appears to offer good shelter, but any swell rebounds around the bay making it uncomfortable.

## ÓRMOS LARDHOS

36°04'·0N 28°01'·5E

To the S of Lindos under the rocky Ák Foka lies the wide bay of Lardhos. In settled weather anchor off the small hamlet at the E end of the bay. There is a friendly taverna ashore. The gusts off the hills here are often less bothersome than in Lindos.

## ÁK ISTROS

35°55'·8N 27°51'·9E

The cape 6 miles NE of Ák Prasso which is the southernmost tip of Rhodes. There is an anchorage off a small hamlet on the SW side of the cape.

## ÁK VIGLI

Lies 1 mile SW of Ák Istros. It can be easily distinguished by a tower on the extremity of the cape. There is an anchorage on the N side of the cape in 3–6m giving some shelter from the *meltemi*.

## ÁK PRASSO

35°52'·8N 27°45'·1E (Ák Prasso light)

The southernmost tip of Rhodes. It is connected to Rhodes by a low neck of land and from the distance looks like an island. The cape and the lighthouse on it are conspicuous from some distance off. On the N side of the cape there is good shelter from S winds in 2–4m depths. On the S side of the cape there is good shelter from the *meltemi* in a small cove in 2–4m depths. The bottom in both anchorages is sand and good holding.

### NOTE

When on passage along the E coast of Rhodes, the Khina Rocks lying 4 miles SE off Ák Vigli, are low-lying and difficult to pick out.

## ÓRMOS LANGONIA (Kámiros Skála)

36°16'·3N 27°49'·2E (Kamiros light)

On the W coast of Rhodes one mile to the E of Ák Kopriá lies Langonia. It offers only limited shelter from the W and some shelter from the S. A light is exhibited here Fl.3s8M. There is a quay where the *caïque* ferry from Khálki berths. Fuel and water ashore.

## FANAI (Mais)

A small harbour on the NE coast of Rhodes approximately midway between Ák Milon and Kamiros. The entrance is lit Fl.G.3s3M/Fl.R.3s3M. Care is needed in the entrance as silting is occurring and there is a 2m bar at the entrance which may build up over time. Go stern or bows-to wherever you can find a berth. Good shelter from the *meltemi*. NE winds may cause a problem.

Tavernas ashore. The village of Fanai (Fanes) is a short distance inland.

**FANAI**
⊕36°22'·0N 27°58'·6E

## ÓRMOS TRIANDA

36°25'·8N 28°11'·0E

Situated on the NE tip of Rhodes, this open bay offers shelter from the S and SE only. It is untenable with the *meltemi*. Anchor in 4–8m off the beach which is lined with large hotels. The bottom is sand and good holding.

# Nísoi Khálki and Alimia

Lying off the W coast of Rhodes, these two islands have always been dependent on their large neighbour. Khálki has a small dwindling population – nearly all of it living around the harbour. Alimia is deserted.

## Nísos Khalki

### KHALKI (Halkia, Skála, Emborios)

#### Approach
*Conspicuous* The three windmills on top of the ridge behind the village are conspicuous from a long way off. The harbour proper will not be seen until you are into the bay.

*By night* A night approach is not recommended because of the numerous unlit rocks and reefs in the approaches. Use the light on Nisáki Fl.WR.6s.8/6M (232°-R-244° and 280°-R-297°) and on the N entrance Fl.3s6M.

*Dangers* Care must be taken of the numerous above- and below-water rocks in the approaches and the strait between Khálki and Alimia. Xera rock although above water is difficult to see and the reef immediately due W of Nisáki is only just awash and difficult to spot. Most of the other rocks and islets can be identified by day even off a comparatively small scale chart, though care is needed.

#### Mooring
Go stern or bows-to or alongside the ferry berth or anchor off. If you are on the ferry berth on one of the days the ferry is due the port police will ask you to move off for the 30 minutes or so which it stays. The bottom is sand and rock – the holding uncertain in places.

*Shelter* Good shelter from the *meltemi* although there are gusts into the bay. With strong S winds a considerable swell enters the harbour.

*Authorities* Port police.

#### Facilities
*Water* Limited supplies locally.
*Provisions* Most provisions can be found although the island is dependent on the ferry for most things.
*Eating out* Several convivial tavernas. Fresh fish sometimes available.
*Other* PO. OTE. Ferry to Skála Kamiros on Rhodes.

#### General
Although many of the houses are in ruins the village on the slopes around the bay is attractive. In many ways it reminds me of Sími town on a smaller and poorer scale. The fort on the precipitous rock behind the village (cone-shaped and 670m high), like the fort on Alimia, was a watchtower for Rhodes. Inside is the small church of Áy Nikólaos.

### ÓRMOS POTAMOS

36°13'·2N 27°36'·3E

The bay on the S of Khálki immediately W of Khálki harbour. Good shelter from the *meltemi*. Care is needed of a reef and shoal patch before you get to the NW corner and of shoal water fringing the head

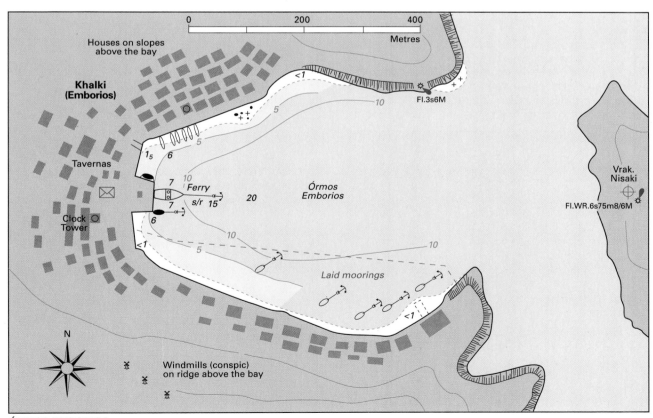

**ÓRMOS EMBORIOS**
⊕36°13'·2N 27°38'E (Nisaki light)

of the bay. Anchor at the head of the bay in 4–6m closer to the E side than to the W. The bottom is sand and rocks, reasonable holding.

Taverna ashore. It is a short walk over the headland into Khalki.

## Nisís Alimia

### ÓRMOS ALIMIA

#### Approach
The large bay on the S of Nisís Alimia. From the N and S the ruined fort above the bay is conspicuous. A few white houses and a small church are conspicuous once you are at the entrance to the bay.

*By night* Not recommended. There are no lights and the unlit rocks and reefs in the approaches make it dangerous.

*Dangers* Care must be taken of the numerous above- and below-water rocks in the approaches and the strait between Khálki and Alimia. See notes for Khálki.

#### Mooring
Anchor in either of the two bays. The S bay is mostly quite deep compared to the N bay. The bottom is sand and weed – good holding.

*Shelter* The S bay offers good shelter from the *meltemi* although there are gusts. The N bay may get some swell pushed in by a strong *meltemi* although there is some shelter tucked in behind the spit the church is built on.

#### Facilities
None.

#### General
Nobody lives on Alimia, although a few fishermen from Khálki have houses there. The fort above the E bay is a long hot walk up the rocky hill – from the summit there is a commanding view over Khálki and Rhodes. In the S bay there are a number of deserted buildings left over from the Second World War. In

one of these nostalgic German soldiers drew a series of cartoons depicting what life was like back home and what life might have been like on some distant tropical island if there had been no war.

# Nísoi Kárpathos and Kásos

These two sea-swept islands are the most southerly of the Dodecanese. Lying between Crete and Rhodes in a stretch of angry sea, the islands seem to have been bypassed by history. Today only a few tourists visit them and, of the islanders themselves, it is said that more Karpathiots live in Athens than in Kárpathos.

Kásos is ellipsoid in shape and steep-to on all sides. Very little vegetation is to be seen on the island even around the major village of Fri. In 1824 the Egyptians ravaged the island and from all appearances Kásos never recovered. (The Kasiots remember it as the Holocaust.) When I entered Órmos Khelatronas for the first time there appeared to be people lining the cliffs surrounding the bay – on closer inspection these were scarecrows. Yet nothing is grown in the vicinity of the bay and my imagination ran wild speculating that these

**KÁRPATHOS AND KÁSOS**

⊕31 1M N of Ák Paraspóri (Kárpathos)
35°55'·3N 27°13'·7E
⊕32 1M S of Ák Kastéllos (Kárpathos)
35°22'·9N 27°08'·3E
⊕33 1M W of N. Platí (Kásos)
35°21'·7N 26°48'·2E

**ÓRMOS ALIMIA**
⊕36°15'·8N 27°41'·5E

scarecrows were a device, perhaps an old custom, designed to let any invading Egyptians know the Kasiots were ready and waiting this time.

Kárpathos (also known by its medieval name of Scarpanto) is also mountainous and steep-to, but by comparison with Kásos is a green and fertile island. A mountain ridge runs from NE to SW with Mt Kalolimni (Lastra) at 1,200m (3960ft) the highest in the centre of the island. The W coast is mostly barren except in the valleys, but the E coast is covered in pine. On the S coast there are fertile valleys and plains planted in olives, citrus and fruit trees. Most of the population lives in the southern part of the island and there are many small and attractive villages in this region. It is well worth making an excursion inland from Pigadhia if the weather permits you to leave your yacht there safely.

## CAUTION

During the *meltemi* season strong gusts blow off the S and E sides of Kásos and Kárpathos. Large and disturbed seas will be encountered in Stenón Kasou (Kásos Strait) between Kásos and Crete and especially in Stenón Karpathou (Kárpathos Strait) near the southern tip of Rhodes. In the latter sea area the bottom comes up quickly from 600–700m to 100–200m causing a wicked cross-sea.

## PORT KARPATHOS (Pigadhia)

BA 1532

### Approach

*Conspicuous* The town, the mole and the small islands immediately S of the harbour are conspicuous.

*By night* Use the light on Nisídha Dhespotika in Órmos Pigadhia Fl.5s6M and the light on the end of the mole Q.R.1M. A fixed red light is also exhibited on a television repeater just W of the town.

*Dangers* With the *meltemi* there are fierce gusts in the approaches.

### Mooring

Go alongside or stern or bows-to the new mole in the SW corner. It may be possible for small yachts to squeeze in under the mole although most berths are occupied by local boats – care is needed of the depths under the mole and it would be best to reconnoitre first.

*Shelter* With the *meltemi* there are strong gusts into the harbour making it most uncomfortable. The harbour is open to the NE and there is a surge with strong S winds.

*Authorities* Port police and customs.

### Facilities

*Water* On the mole.
*Fuel* In the town. It may be possible to get deliveries to the quay.
*Provisions* Good shopping for provisions in the village.
*Eating out* Good tavernas in the town.
*Other* PO. OTE. Bank. Greek gas. Hire motorbikes. Ferry to Piraeus and Rhodes.

Port Kárpathos (Pighadia) looking SW         *Nigel Patten*

**PORT KÁRPATHOS (Pigadhia)**
⊕35°30'·7N 27°13'·5E

### General

The small town of Pigadhia more than makes up for the uncomfortable harbour – fringed by green trees and gardens, it is both attractive and friendly. In recent years travellers getting off the beaten track have come here and the place has acquired a modest tourist trade, though not an overpowering one. It is the best place to use as a base for exploring the island.

### ÓRMOS AMORFOS (Amorphi Bay)

35°27'·7N 27°12'·0E

The large bay under Ák Volokas. Anchor in the N corner of the bay. Care is needed of the reef off Ák Skrofa in the S of the bay and of rocks and shoal water fringing the shore. The bottom is sand with some rocks, good holding. This bay has been reported to be less subject to gusts off the hills than Mákri Yialo to the S. Open to the S and SE.

Hotel and tavernas ashore.

## ÓRMOS MAKRI YIALO (Makris Yialos)

A deserted bay lying near the S end of the island close northward of Ák Lingi. Anchor in 4–8m near the head of the bay. The bottom is sand – good holding. The bay offers good shelter from the *meltemi* although the bay is subject to strong gusts. Open to the E.

## FINIKI (Foiniki)

### Approach

The small harbour lies on the N side of the bay close N of Ák Palaiokastro. The houses around the bay will be seen closer in.

*By night* The end of the breakwater is lit: Fl.R.3s3M.

*Dangers* Care must be taken of a reef lying approximately 60m SE from the extremity of the

**FINIKI**
⊕35°29'·5N 27°06'·9E

breakwater. Keep close to the end of the rough stone breakwater.

### Mooring

Go stern or bows-to the quay where there are 2–2·5m depths off. The N and E sides of the bay are shallow.

*Shelter* Adequate shelter from the *meltemi* but open to the S. With southerly winds dangerous gusts are reported to blow off the high land and a swell enters the harbour.

### Facilities

Ashore in the small fishing hamlet there is a café/taverna but little else.

## TRISTOMA

This long sheltered inlet on the NW corner of Kárpathos appears on the chart to offer the best shelter on the island. However, with a strong *meltemi* heavy seas pile up at the entrance and there are fierce gusts off the hills. With strong southerlies

**TRÍSTOMA**
⊕35°49'·3N 27°12'·3E (Notia light)

there are also gusts off the surrounding hills. Entry is by the southernmost passage. Anchor at the head of the inlet or in the cove on the NE side.

## DHIAFANI

35°45'·2N 27°12'·9E (Dhiafani light Fl.3s4M)

On the NE coast of Karpathos you can anchor off under a bight where there is some protection from the *meltemi*. Anchor in 4–6m on sand and shingle, reasonable holding. There are strong gusts into the anchorage.

There are reports that a small harbour is under construction at Dhiafani, but no details of what it looks like or on depths is available.

## NISÍS SARIA (Saros)

Lies immediately N of Kárpathos separated only by a narrow channel. The channel has been reported to have 3–4m depths and to be easily navigated in calm weather. (I have not navigated the channel and cannot confirm these depths.) With strong winds gusts blow out of the channel according to the wind direction.

## IFALOS KÁRPATHOS (Kárpathos Rock)

A reef in the channel between Kásos and Kárpathos near the SW end of Kárpathos. The reef has less than 2m depths over it and can be difficult to spot with any swell running. Unless a yacht is proceeding along the W coast of Kárpathos it is no danger to yachts crossing between Kásos and Kárpathos.

# Nísos Kásos

## ÓRMOS FRI

A new harbour is under construction off the small harbour at Fri. At the time of writing the outer breakwater and inner E breakwater and quays are in place. It is uncertain when the harbour will be

**APPROACHES TO FRI AND LIMÍN KASOU**
⊕35°25′·3N 26°57′·4E

completed. Several yachts have berthed alongside the new quay, but with strong northerlies it may be better to anchor off under the new breakwater. At the moment exercise caution in the vicinity on account of the harbour works off Fri.

## LIMÍN KASOU (Port Kásos, Emborió, Ophris, Ofris, Fri)

### Approach

*Conspicuous* From the W the town of Fri to the W of the harbour and a pink-roofed church fronted by palms near the harbour are conspicuous. From the E a white church on the headland to the E of the harbour and the mole are also conspicuous.

*By night* The end of the mole is lit: Fl.G.1·5s3M. On Ák Áy Yeóryios a light is exhibited: Fl.WR.3s 5/3M (red sector covers 083°-175° and 241°-251°). Care must be taken not to head for the Q.R.2M exhibited in the shallow and rock-bound *caïque* harbour off the village of Fri.

*Dangers* With the *meltemi* there are gusts and a confused sea in the approaches to the harbour.

**LIMÍN KASOU (PORT KASOS)**
⊕35°25′·3N 26°57′·4E

### Mooring

Go stern or bows-to the mole. The bottom is rock and sand.

*Shelter* Reasonable shelter from the *meltemi* although there is a surge in the harbour with a prolonged blow. Open to the NE. With strong winds from the S there are gusts off the high hills behind. With

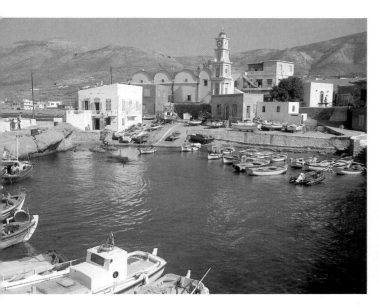

The miniature harbour at Fri (Ofris)          *Nigel Patten*

Limín Kasou looking N

southerlies the fishermen either move elsewhere or anchor on the S side of the harbour with a line ashore.

*Authorities* Port police and customs.

## Facilities
*Water* Tap on the beach.
*Fuel* Limited amounts in the town.
*Provisions* Most provisions can be found in Fri.
*Eating out* Several tavernas in Fri.
*Other* PO. OTE. Bank. Greek gas. Ferry to Piraeus and Rhodes.

## General
Fri, situated just W of the harbour, is a tatty town with a run-down charm. In many ways it seems like something out of North Africa. The small *caïque* harbour surrounded by houses is a pleasant spot and the friendly locals make up for its neglected appearance.

## KASONISIA (Kaso Islets)
Shelter from the *meltemi* can be obtained in a number of small coves on the S side of these islands – sponge-boats fishing the area often use the low-lying Makronisi or Armathia (the largest of the group) where some shelter from N winds can be obtained. The bottom is sand and reported to be good holding.

## IFALOS KASOU (Kásos Rock)
Lies in the channel between Kásos and Kasonisia. It is no real danger to most sailing yachts since the least depth over it is 4·5m. A transit of Ák Áy Yeóryios and Nisís Kolofonos clears it.

## ÓRMOS KHELATRONAS
35°20'·0N 26°52'·5E

At the S end of Kásos this deserted bay offers good shelter from the *meltemi*. Anchor in 4–8m at the head of the bay. The bottom is sand with not a patch of weed in sight – excellent holding. The *meltemi* gusts down off the hills and a swell invariably works its way around into the bay making it a little rolly, but you are safe enough. Idyllic and sometimes spooky surroundings.

# Nísos Astipálaia
## (Astypalaea, Stampalia)

Lying like an almost forgotten part of the Dodecanese, 35 miles west of Nísiros, Astipálaia (also called Stampalia in the Middle Ages and again during the Italian occupation) consists of two mountain ranges joined by a long slender isthmus. When approaching from the north or south it appears to be two islands. The coastline is much indented and offers a number of safe anchorages. Until the Romans and later the English suppressed

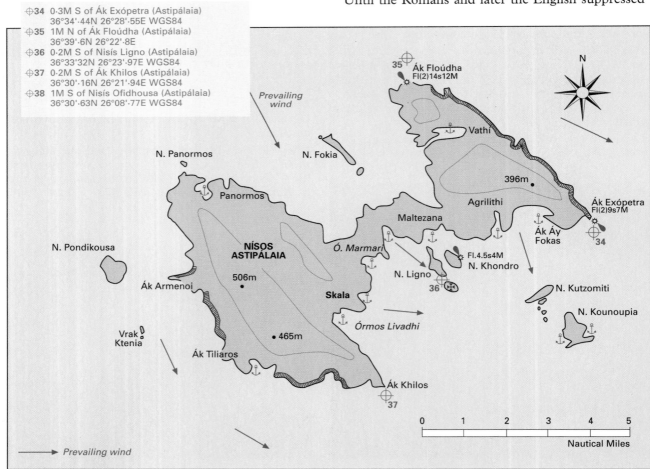

⊕34 0·3M S of Ák Exópetra (Astipálaia)
36°34'·44N 26°28'·55E WGS84
⊕35 1M N of Ák Floúdha (Astipálaia)
36°39'·6N 26°22'·8E
⊕36 0·2M S of Nisís Ligno (Astipálaia)
36°33'32N 26°23'·97E WGS84
⊕37 0·2M S of Ák Khilos (Astipálaia)
36°30'·16N 26°21'·94E WGS84
⊕38 1M S of Nisís Ofidhousa (Astipálaia)
36°30'·63N 26°08'·77E WGS84

ASTIPÁLAIA (Astypalaea, Stampalaia)

piracy in the Aegean, the island was a natural lair for pirates, with good shelter and a strategic position to pounce on merchant shipping.

In antiquity the island was famed for its seafood and its fertility. Pliny praised its mussels and the surrounding seabed was supposed to have the best sponges in the Aegean. Today little of this is evident – the land is mostly barren or scrubby, the mussels nonexistent, and the sponge-divers go to the African coast. However, crayfish often appear on taverna menus. In the Middle Ages the Venetian family Quirini ruled the island. In 1912 it was the first of the Dodecanese to be occupied by the Italians. These last occupants built little and the character of the island is more like that of the Cyclades than that of the Dodecanese.

## CAUTION

From Ák Exópetra (Poulari) across the S coast of Astipálaia to Ák Khilos there are strong gusts off the land when the *meltemi* is blowing.

## SKÁLA ASTIPÁLAIA (Periyialo)

### Approach

*Conspicuous* The castle with two white churches

Skála looking E to the bay                    *Nigel Patten*

inside is conspicuous from some distance off. The white houses of the *chora* and a line of 4 windmills on the hills are also conspicuous. Entering the bay, the houses along the waterfront and the quay are easily seen.

*By night* Use the light on the N side of the bay

**SKÁLA ASTIPÁLAIA**
⊕36°32'·83N 26°21'·53E WGS84

Skála Astipálaia looking NW across the quay and the chora on the hill on the S side of the entrance   *Peter Kleinoth/MareTeam*

Fl.WR.3s5/3M (red sector covers 261°-293°) and the two lights on the quay: 3F.R.3M and 3F.G.3M in an inverted triangle configuration.

*Dangers* With the *meltemi* there can be strong gusts off the high land in the approaches.

### Mooring

Moor alongside the ferry quay, although you may have to move off for a short time when the ferry is due. Alternatively anchor in the bay. With care a couple of yachts can go bows-to the short pier off the town. The bottom is sand and weed, reasonable holding.

*Shelter* With the *meltemi* there are gusts into the bay which can make a berth on the quay uncomfortable. The bay is completely open to the SE and in the event of such a wind the local fishermen go to Maltezana.

*Authorities* Port police and customs.

### Facilities

*Water* Near the quay.

*Fuel* On the N side of the bay. A mini-tanker can deliver to the quay.

*Provisions* Most provisions can be obtained in the village, but the island is largely dependent on the ferry for supplies and there may be a shortage of some items (particularly fruit and vegetables).

*Eating out* Good tavernas around the waterfront, several with superb views over the bay.

*Other* PO. OTE. Bank. Hire motorbikes. Ferry to Piraeus and Rhodes.

### General

The harbour and the *chora* above, which virtually form one town straggling from the bay to the summit, are most attractive from seaward although a little dilapidated on closer inspection. The castle dominating the *chora* (variously named Astipálaia or Stampalia or Kastello after the castle) was built in the 13th century by John Quirini. Legend has it that the castle was successfully defended on one occasion by the defenders throwing beehives onto the attackers. From the castle there is a magnificent view across to Maltezana to the NE and Órmos Livádhi to the SW.

### ÓRMOS MALTEZANA (Analipsis)

BA 1541
Imray-Tetra G34

### Approach

This bay is situated on the middle of the S coast where the island is almost divided into two by the isthmus. The normal entrance is on either side of Nisís Khondró.

*Conspicuous* Nisís Áy Kiriakí, the low islet just S of Ligno, has a conspicuous white chapel in the middle. Nisís Khondró and Nisís Ligno are easily identified from the distance and closer in the mole and the hamlet behind it are easily seen.

**APPROACHES TO MALTEZANA**
⊕1 36°34′·48N 26°23′·15E WGS84

⊕36 0·2M S of Nisís Ligno (Astipálaia)
36°33'32N 26°23'·97E WGS84

*By night* Not recommended. Use the light on Nisís Khondró Fl.4·5s4M and the light on the extremity of the mole Fl.G.2s4M. The fuel barges and buoys are marked by a F but this is not to be relied upon (not working 2000).

*Dangers* With the *meltemi* there are gusts in the approaches.

*Note*
1. It is possible to enter and leave Órmos Maltezana by the passage between the islet connected by a reef to Nisís Ligno and the islet N of it. There are 5·5m least depths in the fairway. The passage is easily negotiated by day though the clarity of the water makes it look shallower than it really is.
2. Care is needed of the fuel barges moored in the middle of the bay.

**Mooring**
Anchor in the bay or go alongside the pier if there is room. Do not take berths belonging to local fishing boats on the pier. The bottom is sand and weed, good holding.

*Shelter* Good shelter from the *meltemi* with few gusts. Although partially open to the SE the wind does not blow home and little swell enters the bay.

Maltezana looking towards the pier from the anchorage

**MALTEZANA**
⊕36°34′·6N 26°23′·3E

**Facilities**
Some provisions in the hamlet. Several tavernas and cafés ashore.

**General**
The bay is attractive with an anomalous (for Astipálaia) green foreshore under the barren burnt slopes behind and clear water in the bay. The good lee from the *meltemi* also comes as a blessed relief. On the slopes NW of the hamlet there is an airstrip.

## ÓRMOS AGRILITHI

A deserted inlet lying approximately 1 mile NE of Nisís Khondró. Good shelter from the *meltemi*

**ÓRMOS AGRILITHI**
⊕36°35′·0N 26°25′·4E

although there are gusts off the slopes. Anchor where convenient and take a long line ashore. The bottom is sand – good holding. The deserted bay is a wonderful wild spot which, with the *meltemi* howling outside, can feel like your own private paradise.

*Note* The shoal patch (Ifalos Baraka) (4·5m/2½ fathoms) lying approximately half a mile SE of the E entrance point to Agrilithi is visible in calm weather but is difficult to spot with the *meltemi* kicking up a chop.

## ÓRMOS VLIKADHA

The large bay tucked under Ák Áy Fokas. It is very deep for anchoring around the bay and really the only place is tucked into the E part of the bay. Here there are gusts off the land from the N when the *meltemi* is blowing so it is not a safe place to be.

## NISÍS KOUNOUPIA

36°32'·0N 26°28'·2E

The southernmost islet off Ák Áy Fokas. The S end of the island has two inlets with a sand bar between. In calm weather a yacht can anchor in either of the two inlets, but with the *meltemi* a swell is pushed into the W inlet. The E inlet offers more protection but is not the best place to be with the *meltemi*.

## VATHI

BA 1666

This landlocked inlet on the NE tip of the island offers good all-round shelter. The entrance is somewhat difficult to pick out from the cliffs. Anchor off the small hamlet in the W corner in 3–5m depths. There is thick weed on the bottom, but find a clear patch to drop the anchor in and the holding is good. Mild gusts with the *meltemi*. A few large trawlers are usually moored off the fishing hamlet. A café/taverna.

There are also suitable depths for anchoring in at the E end of the inlet.

**VATHÍ**
⊕36°36'·5N 26°23'·0E

**ÓRMOS PANORMOS**
⊕36°35'·8N 26°17'·0E

## PANORMOS

In the bay at the NW tip of Astipálaia shelter from the *meltemi* can be found in a cove on the W side of the bay. Anchor in 4–5m on a sandy bottom. No facilities but peaceful surroundings.

In calm weather there are several other places to anchor in nearby, although they do not offer shelter from the *meltemi*.

## ÓRMOS LIVÁDHI

36°32'·3N 26°21'·0E

On the S side of the *chora* (Skála Astipálaia) is the large bay of Livádhi with a pleasant anchorage at the head off the beach. Anchor in 5–10m tucked up into the NW corner. The bottom is sand and the gusts from the *meltemi* are not too bad here.

Tavernas ashore.

# Nisís Áy Íoannis (Nisís Sirina)

36°17'·0N 26°44'·5E (Nisís Plakhida light)

A high domed island lying approximately 19 miles SE of Astipálaia. Nisídhes Adelfia, a group of high jagged islands approximately 4 miles NW of Sirina, are conspicuous and the bold outline of Áy Íoannis is easily identified. A light is exhibited on Nisís Plakidha (Fl.WR.6s9/6M), the largest island of Nisídhes Trianísia to the SE of Áy Íoannis, but navigating in the vicinity of these islands and rocks at night should be avoided.

On the S of Áy Íoannis there is a large bay which local fishermen use. It is reported that most of the bay is quite deep with a rock-strewn bottom, but in the NE corner there is a patch of sand suitable for anchoring in. The fishermen have a permanent mooring here and don't seem to mind visitors using it when they leave at night to fish around Nisídhes Trianísia. Good shelter from the *meltemi*. The bay is only open S.

Ashore there is little except two chapels and a herd of goats.

# X. Crete
## (Kriti)

Crete is the largest and most important island in the Aegean. Lying across the mouth of the southern Aegean, it both commands the southern approaches to Greece and forms the link between the Peloponnisos and Asia Minor through Kásos, Kárpathos, and Rhodes. While it is politically and geographically a part of Greece, its inhabitants have always thought of themselves as being Cretans first and Greeks second.

Crete is dominated by the high mountain backbone which runs throughout its length. Approaching from seaward the peaks of the mountains, snow-capped in the winter and well into the spring, can be seen from a considerable distance off. On the western end of the island the Levka Ori (White Mountains) are a mountain range reaching 2,469m (8,100ft); in the middle of the island the Idhi Ori (Ida) are three conspicuous peaks with the highest peak (Oros Psiloriti or Mt Ida) reaching 2,456m (8,060ft); and at the eastern end the Oros Dhikti (Lasithi Mountains) attain 2,133m (7,000ft).

For the most part the island is rocky and barren except for the plains on the north coast which are cultivated and the high Lasithi Plateau, a fertile bowl in the mountains. On the south coast the land drops away abruptly to the sea except around Ierapetra. The favourable climate enables a wide variety of fruit and vegetables to be grown: olives, grapes, carob beans, bananas, peaches, oranges (said to be the best in Greece), melons, tomatoes (early season tomatoes for Greece are grown at Ierapetra), and a wide variety of other fruits and vegetables. The flora of Crete is varied, with some 140 indigenous species including many varieties of the orchid family.

The history of Crete, both ancient and modern, has often been turbulent. It was inhabited in Neolithic times and again during the Cycladic period, but to most people Crete is known as the centre of the Minoan civilization which ruled over the eastern Mediterranean from 2000–1450 BC (middle and late Minoan). Perhaps one of the more gentle civilizations to exist, it gave us the beautifully decorated pottery which can be seen in the museum at Iraklion and the graceful palaces that Sir Arthur Evans lovingly excavated and recreated. The palace of Knossos is the best known, but the palaces at Phaistos on the south coast and Kato Zakros on the east coast, though there is less to see, are worth visiting for both the superb sites and the peace away from the crowds at Knossos. The Minoan civilization disappeared almost overnight around 1450 BC, probably as a result of the eruption on Thíra when it is thought tidal waves, earthquakes and ash obliterated the palaces, the fleet, and the land.

By about 800 BC the Dorians had established themselves on Crete and in the classical period small city-states were scattered around the island. There was an orderly progression through the Roman occupation into the Byzantine period. Many beautiful frescoes still exist from the Byzantine era in churches on Crete and a Cretan school of fresco painting flourished – so much so that Cretan artists were in demand all over Greece. Towards the end of the Byzantine period the Saracens occupied Crete and remained for over a century. The island was retaken for Byzantium by the Emperor Nikephoros who employed the bizarre device of catapulting the heads of captured prisoners into the stronghold of Iraklion (then Kandak or Kandia), so demoralizing the defenders that they eventually capitulated.

After the Fourth Crusade the island was ruled by the Genoese until the 13th century when it was sold to Venice. The Venetians occupied the island until 1669 and most of the castles and forts still standing date from this era. The harbours on the northern coast were of vital importance in the Venetian trade route from the Peloponnisos to Asia Minor and they fought long and hard to stop the Turks taking Crete. The Turks won through in 1669 and were to hold Crete until 1898. For the Cretans it was a time of much hardship and poverty and there were many insurrections, bloodily put down by the Turks. The spirit and the independence of the Cretans in their battle against the Turks is immortalised in the prose of Nikos Kazantzakis. Crete became a part of Greece in 1913.

The Cretans, battered by the misfortune of history, but never beaten, have today recovered some degree of prosperity through tourism. However much you despise the reinforced concrete dormitories lining the beaches, you cannot at the same time deny the rise in living standards they have brought with them. Crete is a booming tourist island and the yachtsman is lucky enough to be able to explore its more remote parts and so sample something of the island that is denied to most. The Cretan has a certain reserve that can be mistaken for hostility, but once this has been overcome visitors will find they are welcome and will be treated as privileged guests.

## Weather patterns in Crete

In the summer the prevailing wind is the *meltemi* blowing from the NW–WNW. In common with the rest of the Aegean it blows strongest in July and August. It does not usually blow more than Force 5–6 off the northern coast and is more often Force 3–4. In the spring and autumn the wind is predominantly from the S, about Force 2–4.

The southern coast is notorious for the squalls that blow off the high mountains with the prevailing summer winds. The Admiralty Pilot tersely warns that: 'Strong squalls blow down from the mountains during northerly winds. These squalls often begin suddenly, and they may be violent close inshore.'

In the summer months Crete is very hot: the average temperatures often get to 35°–36°C in July and August and can reach 40° at times. In the winter the mountains are covered in snow down to the lower slopes, but the coastal plains have a mild winter climate and the coastal towns are agreeable places to winter afloat.

## Routes

Routes in the summer are fairly straightforward. Along the northern coast you can proceed quietly along from W to E with the prevailing wind, or with a little more effort proceed from E to W. Although the *meltemi* tends to come from a westerly direction, there are usually enough days when the wind is light or there is a morning calm to make reasonable progress from E to W.

On the S coast the ferocity of the gusts off the mountains mean that it can be difficult whichever way you go. The wind also tends to blow around either end of Crete so you will have a bit of a bash getting out from either end.

In the winter, southerlies set large seas onto the S coast and the preferred route has to be along the N coast.

## Data

### PORTS OF ENTRY
Khania
Iraklion
Áyios Nikólaos

### PROHIBITED AREAS
1. Navigation is prohibited in an area extending 500m N, NE and E of Ák Maléka.
2. Navigation and anchorage are prohibited in Órmos Soudhas except for the channel running up the middle of the bay (not marked) and at Limín Soudhas. It is prohibited to enter at night.
3. It is prohibited to anchor in an area extending ¾ mile E and SE of Ák Soúdha.
4. Navigation and anchorage are prohibited in the areas shown around Ák Sidheros.

### MAJOR LIGHTS
**Nisís Gramvoúsa** (NW point) Fl.WR.10s17/13M
**Ák Maléka** Fl(2)12s10M
**Ák Dhrépanon** Fl(3)30s20M
**Nisís Soúdha** Fl.G.4·8s6M
**Rethimon** Fl.G.3s12M
**Ák Khondrós Kávos** Fl.WR.6s12/8M
**Ák Stavrós** Fl(2)14s11M
**Iráklion** (N mole head) LFl.G.6s9M
**Iráklion** (Pier head) LFl.R.6s7M
**Nisís Dhía** (N point) LFl.12s9M
**Nisís Dhía** (Ák Stavrós) Fl.6s12M
**Ák Áy Ioánnis** Fl(2)12·8s11M

CRETE

**Órmos Áy Nikólaos** (Mikrónisos) Fl.3s26m4M
**Ák Vamvakiá** Fl(3)18s10M
**Nisís Paximádha** Fl.WR.6s12/8M
**Ák Sidheros** Fl.10s23M
**Nisídhes Kaválloi** Fl(3)12s6M
**Koufonísi** Fl(2)16s10M
**Gaïdhouronísi** Fl(2)12s10M
**Ák Theófilos** Fl(2)12s10M
**Megalonísi** Fl(3)24s11M
**Ák Lítinos** Fl.6s12M
**Gavdhopoúla** (NW point) Fl.8s12M
**Nísos Gávdhos** (S point) Fl(2)16s12M
**Nisís Loutró** LFl.10s6M
**Nisís Skhistó** Fl.8s8M
**Nisís Elafónisos** Fl(3)24s12M

## USEFUL WAYPOINTS

⊕1  1M N of Ák Spáthi
    35°42'·8N 23°44'·0E
⊕2  1M N of Ák Maléka light
    35°36'·3N 24°10'·5E
⊕3  1M N of Ák Stavrós
    35°27'·0N 24°58'·4E
⊕4  1M N of Ák Marmara (N. Dhía)
    35°29'·0N 25°13'·0E
⊕5  1☎M N of Ák Khersónisos
    35°21'·2N 25°23'·1E
⊕6  1M N of Ák Áy Ioánnis
    35°21'·5N 25°46'·4E
⊕7  1M N of Ák Vamvakia
    35°14'·5N 26°07'·0E
⊕8  1M N of Ák Sidheros
    35°20'·0N 26°18'·7E
⊕9  1M E of Ák Pláka
    35°11'·9N 26°20'·2E
⊕10 1M S of Nisís Kaválloi
    35°00'·7N 26°13'·7E
⊕11 1M S of Ák Iereptra
    34°59'·3N 25°44'·3E
⊕12 1M S of Ák Theofilos
    34°58'·0N 25°30'·3E
⊕13 1M S of Ák Lítinos
    34°54'·4N 24°44'·0E
⊕14 1M S of Ák Mouros
    35°10'·6N 24°04'·6E
⊕15 1M S of Nisís Skhistó
    35°12'·3N 23°40'·3E
⊕16 1¼M W of Nisís Elafónisos
    35°16'·2N 23°30'·0E
⊕17 1M E if Pondikonisi
    35°35'·2N 23°30'·0E

# Northern coast of Crete

## KISSAMOS (Kavonisi, Kastelli)

### Approach

The harbour lies in the SW corner of Kólpos Kissamos to the E of a rocky spur. The town of Kastelli and the harbour mole are easily identified.

*By night* The entrance is lit: Fl.G.2s3M/Fl.R.2s3M.

*Note* If there is a blow from the N you can get stuck in here for a while. The bay is around 14 miles deep before you can get out to turn the corner.

*Dangers* Care is needed of the shoal water extending NNE from the headland the harbour is built under. There is 4m shoal patch approximately 600m N of the headland and a 2m shoal patch approximately 400m N of the headland.

## Quick reference guide

| | Shelter | Mooring | Fuel | Water | Provisioning | Tavernas | Plan |
|---|---|---|---|---|---|---|---|
| **North Coast** | | | | | | | |
| Kissamos | B | ABC | O | O | O | C | • |
| Khania | A | A | B | A | A | A | • |
| Soúdha | A | ABC | B | B | B | B | • |
| Yioryioupolis | B | BC | B | B | B | B | |
| Rethimon | B | AB | B | A | A | A | • |
| Pánormos | B | AB | O | B | C | C | |
| Órmos Balí | B | C | O | O | O | C | |
| Iraklion | A | A | B | A | A | A | • |
| Khersónisos | B | AC | B | B | B | A | • |
| Sissi | C | AB | O | B | C | C | |
| Milatos | A | AB | B | B | C | C | • |
| Spinalonga | A | C | B | B | B | B | • |
| Áyios Nikólaos | B | AB | A | A | A | A | • |
| Áy Nikólaos Marina | A | A | O | A | B | B | • |
| Pahia Ammos | C | A | B | B | B | B | |
| Sitía | B | A | A | A | A | A | • |
| Ák Sidheros | B | C | O | O | O | O | • |
| **South Coast** | | | | | | | |
| Nisís Gramvoúsa | B | C | O | B | O | O | • |
| Koutris | O | C | O | O | O | O | |
| Palaiokhora | B | ABC | B | B | B | B | • |
| Loutró | B | C | O | B | C | C | • |
| Sfakion | OA | C | B | B | B | B | • |
| Plákia | O | C | B | B | B | B | |
| Limni | O | C | O | O | O | O | |
| Áy Galini | B | A | B | A | B | B | • |
| Pirgos | B | AB | B | A | C | C | |
| Matala | C | C | B | B | B | B | |
| Kali Limenes | B | C | B | B | C | C | |
| Ierepetra | B | A | B | B | B | B | • |
| Órmos Zakros | C | C | O | O | O | C | |
| Órmos Grandes | C | C | O | O | C | C | |
| Órmos Kouremenos | B | ABC | B | B | C | C | |
| Vai | B | C | O | O | C | C | |

**KISSAMOS**
⊕35°31'·0N 23°38'·4E

## Mooring

Berth alongside or anchor off inside the mole.

*Shelter* Good shelter from the W and NW although there is often some surge inside. Open to the E and SE.

*Authorities* Port police.

## Facilities

Water standpipe. A taverna/café and a telephone at the harbour. Bus to Kastelli. In Kastelli fuel and provisions can be obtained.

## General

Kissamos is the harbour for Kastelli town about one mile to the E. The harbour is used by a few fishing boats and coasters and the ferry.

## KHANIA (Khania, Hania)

BA 1707
Imray-Tetra G37

## Approach

*Conspicuous* The town is visible from some distance off. Closer in a white mosque on the waterfront, the lighthouse on the E side of the entrance, and a number of chimneys in the town are conspicuous.

*By night* Use the light on the E side of the entrance Fl.R.2·5s7M and the lights on either side of the entrance to the inner harbour: F.G.3M/F.R.3M. The buoy off the detached breakwater is lit Q(3)15s.

*Dangers* The approach is difficult with strong onshore winds. A dangerous sea heaps up on the shoal water at the entrance and care is needed in the immediate approaches. The new detached breakwater improves matters, but it is still difficult with onshore winds.

*Note* It is reported that the new detached breakwater has subsided somewhat and is now only 1m above water.

## Mooring

The E basin is now a marina. Berth stern or bows-to or alongside where directed or where convenient. Laid moorings at most berths.

*Shelter* Good all-round shelter, although strong northerlies cause a surge in the harbour and spray comes over the outer mole. A number of yachts have wintered afloat here, but in bad northerly gales additional lines are needed.

*Authorities* Port of entry: port police, customs, and immigration. Harbourmaster. Charge band 2.

## Facilities

*Services* Water and electricity at or near every berth. WC and shower block.

*Fuel* In the town. A mini-tanker can deliver to the quay.

*Repairs* Mechanical repairs. Some light engineering work. Good hardware and tool shops. Chandlers at Skrydlof 26 near 1866 Square.

*Provisions* Excellent shopping for all provisions. Ice available.

*Eating out* Good tavernas near the waterfront and in the town.

**KHANIA**
⊕35°31'·2N 24°01'·0E

Khania looking W from the yacht harbour towards the entrance
*Nigel Patten*

*Other* PO. OTE. Banks. Greek gas and *Camping Gaz* in 1866 Square. Hire cars, motorbikes and bicycles. Buses to Iraklion. Ferries from Soúdha. Internal flights to Athens.

### General

Khania was for centuries the capital of Crete and was only recently demoted in favour of Iraklion. The Venetian city around the harbour is a fascinating place – cobbled streets, imposing Venetian houses, mosques and minarets, and the market. The lighthouse on the mole is of Venetian-Turkish origin. None of this has been tarted up and turned into a toy town – the city exists with modern additions and crumbling edges and a bustling, busy life to it. In recent years it has become popular with tourists, but the harbour provides a sanctuary from the hurly-burly if you need it.

Everyone who has wintered here has recommended it, even though the harbour can be uncomfortable at times. The town has a buzz to it that is there even when the tourists have departed and, unlike many other tourist spots, doesn't die in the winter.

### ÓRMOS SOÚDHAS

BA 1706
Imray-Tetra G37

### Approach

*Conspicuous* The high plateau of Akrotíri peninsula is easily recognised from the distance. Atop the peninsula are a number of high towers with military scanners. Nisís Soúdhas, with a fort and naval buildings, is conspicuous. The narrow entrance to the channel free for navigation is marked by two light buoys (Fl.R/Fl.G) which are difficult to pick out. On either side of the light buoys and extending to the shore are large black mooring buoys holding the anti-submarine net. The channel free for navigation which runs down the middle of the bay is unmarked. A large flour mill near the harbour is conspicuous. Proceed to the harbour taking care to avoid the restricted area around the naval dockyard.

**AKROTIRI PENINSULA**

⊕2   1M N of Ák Maleka light 35°36'·3N 24°10'·5E

*By night* It is prohibited to enter Órmos Soúdhas at night.

*Caution* Órmos Soúdhas is the Greek navy's southern base and care must be taken to avoid the prohibited area to the N and E of the Akrotíri peninsula (extending out approximately 0·75 to 1 mile from the coast) and the prohibited area N and S of the channel free for navigation in Órmos Soúdhas (the channel runs 283° true from the buoys at the entrance and is 0·2 mile wide).

### Mooring

Go alongside or stern or bows-to on the S quay.

*Shelter* Good shelter – so much so that the wind in Órmos Soúdhas is generally no indication of conditions outside.

*Authorities* Port police, customs.

### Facilities

*Water* On the quay.
*Fuel* In the town. A fuel tanker can be arranged.

**SOÚDHA**
⊕35°29'·5N 24°04'·7E

*Provisions* Good shopping for provisions. Ice available.
*Eating out* Tavernas ashore.
*Other* PO. OTE. Bank. Greek gas. Ferry to Piraeus – this is the ferry port for Khania. Regular bus service (every ten minutes) to Khania.

## General

Soúdha is a naval base so it does not have any of the trappings of a tourist resort. For many this is a blessing and the simple homespun pleasures of Soudha are a relief from the touts outside tavernas in some of the large Cretan resorts. Khania is nearby if you need an injection of pace into your life.

## YIORYIOUPOLIS (Georgioupolis)

BA 1707
Imray-Tetra G37

A small harbour at the mouth of the Almiros river in the SW corner of Órmos Almirou. From seaward the church on the small island connected by a causeway to the land and a hotel on the beach are conspicuous. Care must be taken in the approach because of the shoal water and underwater rocks in the bay. The approach has depths of 1·5–2·5m, but it would be wise to reconnoitre in the dinghy before entering. Moor alongside. Good shelter except from strong N–NE winds.

Water in the town. Most provisions can be obtained and there are several tavernas in the village. Buses to Khania and Iraklion. An attractive friendly little place well worth visiting.

**YIORYIOUPOLIS**
⊕35°22'·1N 24°16'·0E

## RETHIMON (Rethymno)

BA 1707
Imray-Tetra G37

## Approach

*Conspicuous* From the W the fort on the headland and the buildings of the town are conspicuous. From the E a white church on a hill to the E of the

Rethimon. The old Venetian harbour

town and two minarets in the town stand out clearly. Closer in the breakwater is easily identified.
*By night* Use the lights at the entrance: Fl.G.3s12M/Fl.R.4s6M. The mole sheltering the inner harbour is lit on the extremity: F.G.3M.
*Dangers* There is often a rolling swell at the entrance.

## Mooring

Go stern or bows-to the inside of the jetty on the E side or alongside the quay on the N.

*Note* A marina is under construction in the SE corner of the main harbour at the time of writing and it may not be possible to berth here while works are in progress. When complete it is expected that there will berths for 400 yachts and all the usual facilities, including water and electricity at all berths and a shower and toilet block. A charge will be made. Completion is envisaged for 2001–2.
*Shelter* Good shelter from the *meltemi* tucked under the jetty on the E.
*Authorities* Port police and customs.

## Facilities

*Water* On the quay.
*Fuel* In the town, but a mini-tanker can be arranged.
*Repairs* Some mechanical repairs. Hardware shops.
*Provisions* Good shopping for all provisions. Ice available.
*Eating out* Excellent tavernas including several good fish restaurants around the Venetian harbour.
*Other* PO. OTE. Banks. Greek gas and *Camping Gaz*. Hire cars, motorbikes and bicycles. Buses to Khania and Iraklion.

## General

The old Venetian town and harbour is one of the most attractive spots on Crete. The town also shows signs of the Turkish occupation with wooden balconies on some of the houses and two well-preserved minarets. In the last week of July the Cretan wine festival is held here.

## PÁNORMOS

35°25'·3N 24°41'·6E

A small harbour approximately 2M E of Ák Lianos Kávos. The entrance is lit Fl.G.3s3M/Fl.R.3s3M. Go stern or bows-to or alongside the outer end of

**RETHIMON**
⊕35°22'·5N 24°29'·0E

**PÁNORMOS**
⊕35°25'·3N 24°41'·6E

the mole. Reasonable shelter although the harbour is open to N–NE and would likely be uncomfortable and probably untenable with strong winds from this direction.

Water ashore. Some provisions and tavernas.

## ÓRMOS BALI

35°24'·9N 24°47'·1E

A large bay approximately 16 miles E of Rethimon. Care is needed of the rocks extending out from the W entrance to the bay. The two coves on the W side of the bay are reported to afford good shelter from the prevailing winds. The more northerly of the coves has a short breakwater providing additional shelter. The end of the breakwater is lit Fl.G.3s3M.

Tavernas ashore.

## IRAKLION (Herakleion, Candia)

BA 1707
Imray-Tetra G38

### Approach

*Conspicuous* From the NW the town and the long N mole (over a mile long) are easily distinguished. The fort at the entrance to the inner harbour and the ferries in the outer harbour are conspicuous. From

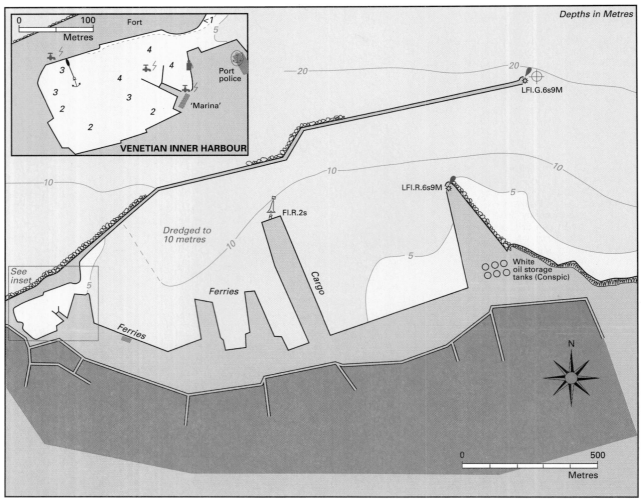

**IRAKLION**
⊕35°21′·N 25°09′·E

the E a large brown building at the airport to the E of the city and the white oil storage tanks in the SE corner of the harbour are also conspicuous. The gantries of cranes in the harbour are also conspicuous.

*By night* Use the lights at the entrance LFl.G.6s9M/LFl.R.6s7M and at the entrance to the inner harbour F.G.2M/F.R.2M. The commercial pier is

lit Fl.R.1·5s3M. There is also a light at the airport to the E of the harbour: Aero Al.WG.4s15M.

*Dangers*
1. With the *meltemi* there can be a confused swell at the entrance, but inside it is quiet.
2. Care is needed of the numerous ferries coming and going from the harbour.

**Mooring**

Proceed to the inner Venetian harbour and berth stern or bows-to at the so-called marina on the E or on the quay on the N where there are sufficient depths. Two pontoons have been installed off the 'marina'. Good holding in mud. The inner harbour is often full and it can be difficult to find a place to berth.

*Shelter* Excellent shelter although there is an uncomfortable surge with strong NE winds. The occasional boat winters here.

*Authorities* A port of entry: port police, customs and immigration.

**Facilities**

*Services* Water and electricity on the quay.
*Fuel* On the quay at the entrance to the inner basin.
*Repairs* Some mechanical repairs. Light engineering

Iraklion. The inner harbour looking E

## Knossos

Situated a short distance outside Iraklion (about a 2½ mile walk, or buses leave regularly from the town centre) are the remains of Knossos. In common with other well-known archaeological sites in Greece, Knossos is crowded in the summer and the bustling noisy tour parties detract somewhat from the architectural merits of the place. Nonetheless it is well worth a visit and in the early morning or late afternoon when most of the tourists have left, something of the atmosphere of Knossos can be felt.

Knossos was not the only Minoan palace in Crete, but it is considered to be the archetype of such palaces and reconstruction by Sir Arthur Evans makes it easier for the layman to visualize what Minoan architecture was like compared to, say, Phaistos or Zakros. The existing palace, lovingly excavated by Sir Arthur Evans from 1900 and later by the British School in Athens, was built around 1700BC. The heart of Knossos was the central court where business was conducted and the locals idled away the day discussing matters great and small. Around the central court were placed the archives, the storerooms, devotional areas and some living quarters – forming a whole unit that was light and airy and architecturally pleasing. The palace was not only a pleasant place to live in, but also boasted amenities such as running water and a proper drainage system. Some criticism has been levelled at Sir Arthur Evans' reconstruction of Knossos, but without his work there would be little for the layman to see.

The eruption of Thíra probably destroyed Knossos and the other Minoan palaces in Crete, indeed it effectively destroyed the Minoan civilization, and reduced to rubble a structure that outstripped much of the nearby contemporary architecture.

work possible. Small yachts can be hauled out in the 'marina'. Large *caïques* are hauled out at the slip in the SE corner of the harbour. Hardware shops.

*Provisions* Excellent shopping for provisions. Ice available. Fish is often for sale on the SW corner of the inner harbour.

*Eating out* Excellent tavernas including several good fish tavernas. Some good tavernas around the market in the centre of town.

*Other* PO. OTE. Banks. Greek gas and *Camping Gaz*. There is a factory to the W of the city where gas bottles can be filled. Laundromat nearby. Hire cars, motorbikes and bicycles. Buses to most parts of the island. Daily ferry service to Piraeus; less regularly to Rhodes. Regular air service to Athens and less regularly to Khania and Rhodes. International flights from many of the major European airports.

### General

Iraklion is the fifth largest city in Greece and appears to be a city composed almost entirely of travel agents and car-hire agencies:

'On the first day, one knows beyond contradiction that Iraklion is one of the least pleasant cities of the Mediterranean and nothing to do with that splendid imagined Crete of mountains and mountaineers, ancient palaces and tiny churches rich in paintings.'

Hopkins *Crete: Its past and people*

Adam Hopkins goes on to say that for some people...'It becomes possible to like Iraklion. . .only people born there actually love it' (*ibid*), but for

yachtsmen there is little attractive to find about the city in the short time they are likely to be there. The attraction lies outside the city at Knossos and later in the museum at Iraklion, where you can mull over the Minoan world that was.

### KHERSÓNISOS (Limín Khersonisou)

Imray-Tetra G38

### Approach

*Conspicuous* From the W a white church and a mill on Ák Khersónisos are conspicuous. Rounding the cape the headland behind which the harbour lies and a number of large white hotels to the E of the harbour are conspicuous. From the E the hotels lining the foreshore are conspicuous.

*By night* The end of the mole is lit Fl.G.2s5M but a night approach would be dangerous given the numerous underwater rocks and shoals in the approach and in the harbour.

*Dangers*

1. There are numerous reefs fringing the coast and harbour. Care should be taken of the reef off Ák Khersónisos, the reef around the square rock between the cape and the harbour, and the reef that projects N and E of the headland and the harbour.

2. On entering the harbour, care must be taken to avoid the submerged mole which has only a few rocks just above water, and to avoid the shoal patch immediately W of the head of the built-up mole (see plan).

### Mooring

Go bows-to the built-up mole or anchor off. Care must be taken in the harbour where the depths are uneven – reconnoitre first in a dinghy. The bottom is sand and rock, poor holding.

*Note* The harbour is reported to be so crowded with local boats that it is difficult to find a berth.

KHERSÓNISOS
⊕35°19'·3N 25°23'·6E

*Shelter* Good shelter from the *meltemi* and open only to the SE.

*Anchorage* It is possible to anchor off in the bay immediately S of Ák Khersónisos, although there is usually a swell in here.

## Facilities

*Water* In the town, though care is needed as it is not all potable. Enquire first.

*Fuel* In the town.

*Provisions* Good shopping for provisions in the town.

*Eating out* A wide choice of tavernas of all types.

*Other* PO. OTE. Bank. Hire cars, motorbikes and bicycles.

## General

Khersónisos is built on the ancient town of Chersonesos, though there is little left to see amid the concrete wilderness that has engulfed the site and spread out all along the coast. The resort has become something of a by-word for the sort of tasteless development akin to that in Benidorm where those who come on holiday are looking only for the proverbial sun, sand and sex. If you can find your way through the British thronging the streets there is a Venetian mosaic fountain in one of the hotels.

## ÁY PNEVMA

35°18'·0N 24°27'·2E

There are reports that a marina is to be built here. No details are available at the time of publication.

## SISSI

35°18'·6N 25°31'·1E

A small harbour has been built here with 2–3m depths reported. The basin is quite small and permanent moorings reduce the space in the harbour. Reconnoitre first in the dinghy.

## MILATOS

A small harbour approximately 2M E of Sissi and a better place to make for than Sissi. The entrance is lit Fl.G.3s3M/Fl.R.3s3M. Go stern or bows-to off the outer end of the mole. The bottom is sand and

**MILATOS**
⊕35°19'·3N 25°33'·8E

**KÓLPOS MERAMBÉLLOU**

weed. Good shelter.

Water on the quay. Some provisions and tavernas ashore.

Milatos is not a bad place for a visit to the Minoan Palace at Malia. The palace has not been reconstructed as at Knossos, but there is enough of the ground-plan intact to make it interesting and it has the advantage of being less crowded than Knossos. Also near Milatos is a cave that was used by Cretans to shelter from the Turks in 1823. In the end they were starved out and taken into slavery or slaughtered.

## NISÍS DHÍA (Standia)

⊕4  1M N of Ák Marmara (N. Dhía) 35°29'·0N 25°13'·0E

A barren rocky island lying 6 miles NNE of Iraklion. On the S coast Órmos Mesarios offers some shelter from northerly winds.

## SPINALONGA LAGOON

### Approach

*Conspicuous* From the W and E Nisís Spinalongas with a Venetian fort on top is conspicuous.

*Entrance* There are 3–4m depths over the sand bar between Nisís Spinalongas and the W shore of Crete. In the lagoon the depths vary between 3–6m.

*Dangers* There are usually strong gusts off the high land between Ák Áyios Ioánnis and Nisís Spinalongas with the *meltemi*. Once in the lagoon the gusts are less hard and not so frequent.

## Mooring

Anchor where convenient in the lagoon. A reasonable lee can be found under Nisís Spinalongas. There is some shelter with few gusts at Skhisma. Here there is a short pier with 1·5–2·5m depths off it, though it is invariably crowded with tripper boats.

## Facilities

At Skhisma: Most provisions can be obtained. Excellent tavernas including several good fish tavernas. PO. OTE. Hire cars, motorbikes and bicycles.

## General

It is fascinating to sail in the enclosed lagoon watching the sea bottom slip past a few metres under the keel. At one time the flat waters of the lagoon were a seaplane base.

Do not miss Nisís Spinalongas. Beneath the Venetian fort there is a small deserted settlement which was once a leper colony. The settlement and the fort surrounded by the shallow waters of the lagoon are most picturesque. Nisís Spinalongas makes a good lunch-stop before going on to Áyios Nikólaos.

## ÁYIOS NIKOLAOS (Limín Ayíou Nikoláou)

BA 1707
Imray-Tetra G38

### Approach

*Conspicuous* From the N and E, Nisís Áy Pantes with a white church on its summit is conspicuous. The buildings of the town including many large hotels along the foreshore are also conspicuous.

*By night* Use the light on Nisís Mikrónisos Fl.3s4M and the light on the extremity of the mole Fl.R.2s7M. The entrance to the marina is lit Fl.G.3s3M/Fl.R.3s3M.

*VHF* Ch 12 for Áyios Nikolaos Marina.

**ÁY NIKOLAOS**
⊕35°11′·2N 25°43′·0E

*Dangers* Ifalos Nikolos, the reef approximately in the middle of Órmos Áy Nikoláou, has 5m least depth over it.

## Mooring

*Note* There have been some complaints about port police procedure here. In a number of instances the boats papers have been impounded by the marina office and the skipper has had to report to the port police. This has been to do with both the Greek Cruising Permit (see the relevant section in the Introduction) and also on non-existent grounds for yachts which have the Permit. It is expected that this practice should cease once the Cruising Permit is outlawed by the EU, but for the time being there are some irate yachties out there, including one who has lived in Greece for some 25 years.

Yachts are now prohibited to berth in the old harbour and must proceed to the marina on the S side of the headland. Berth stern or bows-to where directed or convenient. There are laid moorings tailed to the quay.

*Shelter* Good all round shelter.

*Authorities* Harbourmaster. Charge band 2. Port police, customs and immigration in the old harbour.

*Data* 250 berths. Visitors' berths. Max LOA c.25m. Depths 3–9m.

Áy Nikolaos Marina ☎ 0841 82384 *Fax* 0841 82386 *E-mail* oanak@agn.forthnet.gr www.forthnet.gr/internetcity/yachting/marina

## Facilities

*Services* Water and electricity at or near every berth. WC and shower block.

*Fuel* Can be delivered by mini-tanker to the marina. A travel-hoist is to be installed. 50-berth hardstanding area.

*Repairs* Minor mechanical repairs. Hardware shops.

*Provisions* Good shopping for provisions. Ice available.

*Eating out* Numerous tavernas nearby.

*Other* PO. OTE. Banks. Greek gas and *Camping Gaz*. Hire cars, motorbikes and bicycles. Buses to Iraklion and Sitía.

## General

Áyios Nikólaos may once have been a small fishing village – now it is a booming tourist resort festooned with large hotels. Some people like the place, but personally I find the heart and soul of the town have been gutted to cater for the large numbers of tourists descending on it every summer. In the marina you are at least some distance away from the din of thousands of holiday-makers who are concentrated on the W side of Áy Nikólaos. A number of yachts have wintered here and recommend the place.

## PAHIA AMMOS (Pakhias Ammou)

35°06'·8N 25°48'·5E
BA 1707
Imray-Tetra G38

A small harbour in the SW corner of Kólpos Merambellou. Care must be taken of the reefs around the two small islets 100m and 400m NNW

of the harbour. Approach from the NE. There are 2–3m depths at the extremity of the mole. Sometimes a small coaster is moored stern-to the extremity of the mole and a warp is taken right across to the pier on the opposite side of the harbour effectively stopping any yacht entering. With the normal NW wind a swell works its way around the mole making the harbour uncomfortable. Open to the NE–E.

Some provisions can be obtained and there are several tavernas and cafés in the small village ashore.

## SITÍA

BA 1707
Imray-Tetra G38

### Approach

*Conspicuous* From the W the white light structure on Ák Vamvakiá is conspicuous. The buildings of Sitía and the outer (N) mole are conspicuous once the cape has been rounded. From the E the buildings of the town and the fort on the hill are conspicuous.

*By night* Use the light on Ák Vamvakiá Fl(3)18s10M, the light on the N mole Fl.G.2s5M and the lights at the entrance F.G.3M/F.R.3M.

### Mooring

Go stern or bows-to the inner N mole. The bottom is sand and weed with some rock.

*Shelter* With the *meltemi* there is a gentle surge of no consequence in the harbour. Open to the NE.

*Authorities* Port police and customs.

### Facilities

*Services* Water and electricity on the quay.

SITÍA
⊕35°12'·5N 26°06'·7E

*Fuel* On the outer N mole and in the town near the harbour.
*Repairs* Limited mechanical repairs. Hardware shops.
*Provisions* Good shopping for provisions. Ice available.
*Eating out* Excellent tavernas including several good fish restaurants, some in wonderful locations at the edge of the harbour.
*Other* PO. OTE. Bank. Greek gas and *Camping Gaz*. Hire cars, motorbikes and bicycles. Buses to Áyios Nikólaos, Iraklion and Ierapetra.

## General

Approaching from the sea, Sitía appears as a huddle of houses on a bare rocky hillside. Once in the inner harbour the tree-lined esplanade fronting the harbour comes as an unexpected surprise. Here you can sit in a friendly taverna over a good meal and watch dusk fall over the bay. Further inland is a green fertile plain mainly planted with vines. Sitía was formerly called La Sitía from whence the name of the province – Lasithi.

## ÁK SIDHEROS

⊕8  1M N of Ák Sídheros 35°20'·0N 26°18'·7E

### Approach

The lighthouse on the cape is easily identified. Approach the cape with caution because of the above and below-water rocks fringing it. A night approach would be dangerous because of these rocks and reefs.

*Dangers*
1. **Ifalos Spitfaiar** (*Spitfire*) A detached reef lying 3 miles W of Ák Sídheros. It is difficult to see with any swell running.
2. **Vrákhoi Pinakl (***Pinnacle***)** above and below-water rocks lying close off the coast just over a mile W of Ák Sídheros. The above-water rocks are easily identified.
3. **Nisís Sidhero** The islet half a mile W of Ák Sídheros. Approximately 200m N of the islet there is an isolated reef.
4. **Skopeloi Sídheros** The above and below-water rocks NNE of Ák Sidheros. The above-water rocks are easily identified.
5. **Vrákhoi Navayion** A reef just awash SE of Ák Sídheros.
6. Off the E side of Ák Sídheros a reef fringes the coast. It is just awash in places.

### Mooring

By day anchor in any of the bays and coves shown on the plan. In the small cove immediately S of Ák Sídheros it is necessary to anchor fore and aft or take a long line ashore. The bottom is mostly sand, rock and weed.

*Note* It is prohibited to use the anchorages on the W side of Ák Sídheros which are designated as a military zone.

### Facilities

None.

**ÁK SÍDHEROS**
⊕35°19'·0N 26°18'·7E (Ák Sidheros light)

## General

There are no inhabitants here, bar the lighthouse keeper and a few fishermen. The scenery is on a grand scale and the isolation, the utter quiet, the razor-back reefs surrounding the coast, can instill a sense of dread as the sun goes down.

# Southern coast of Crete

(Includes W and E coasts)

## NISÍS GRAMVOÚSA (Grambusa)

Imray-Tetra G37

On the SE side of this island there is a bay sheltered from northerly winds (NW–NE). Anchor in the bay on the S side of Nisís Gramvoúsa in 3–6m. In southerlies anchor under the isthmus formed by Khersónisos Tigani. On Gramvoúsa there is a quay with reasonable depths where a yacht can go bows-to with care.

Water from a well by the chapel. No facilities. At one time the island was a notorious pirate stronghold until an Anglo-French expedition flushed the pirates out in 1828.

## ÓRMOS KOUTRIS

35°29'·6N 23°34'·0E

The large bay under Ák Koutri. Shelter from N through to SE. Open NW to SW. Care is needed of the islet and reef running SSW for nearly 1M from the N entrance point. Anchor at the N end in 3–5m on sand.

No facilities.

Ashore at the N end is the ancient city and harbour of Phalasarna. The ancient harbour, hewn from the rock, now lies some 6m above the present sea level. The elevated harbour is dramatic evidence of the geological subsidence of Crete with the E and N 'tipping' downwards into the sea and elevating the S and W.

**ÓRMOS GRAMVOÚSA**
⊕35°35'·9N 23°34'·7E

## AKTI

35°28'·8N 23°34'·1E

A small and mostly shallow harbour tucked into the S corner of Órmos Koutris. The approaches are rock-bound and it is best to reconnoitre first by dinghy. The mole is lit Fl.G.3s3M.

## CAUTION

All along the S coast there are severe gusts off the high mountains with westerly and northerly winds. Care must be taken under these conditions as the

The quay and anchorage on the S side of Nisís Gramvoúsa looking SSE          *Nigel Patten*

squalls can be of exceptional violence. If a yacht is making a longish passage along the coast it is worthwhile standing off about 5 miles, as suggested by the Admiralty Pilot.

## PALAIOKHORA (Palaeohora)

BA 1707
Imray-Tetra G37

An anchorage lying near the SW tip of Crete. A prominent headland with a fort on it is easily recognised. Go alongside or stern or bows-to in the new harbour on the E side of the rocky headland. Alternatively anchor on either side of the headland according to the wind direction.

*Note* When entering the harbour do so from the E and keep close to the S mole in the entrance to avoid the underwater rocks off the end of the stubby N mole. Work is in progress on the harbour at an intermittent rate so keep an eye open for any changes to the harbour plan.

Palaiokhora. The new harbour looking S          *Nigel Patten*

**PALAIOKHORA**
⊕35°13'·3N 23°40'·3E (N. Skhistó light)

**PALAIOKHORA HARBOUR**
⊕35°13'·6N 23°40'·7E

Loutró looking SW          *Nigel Patten*

Water on the quay. Fuel in town, but a mini-tanker can deliver to the harbour. Good shopping for all provisions. Good tavernas. Bus to Khania.

### SOUGIA (Souyia)

35°14'·75N 23°48'·5E

There is a miniature harbour here about 500m W of the village. A small yacht could go on the outside of the W quay.

### ÓRMOS FOINIKIAS AND ÓRMOS LOUTRÓ

On either side of Ák Mouros shelter can be found depending on the wind direction. On the W side there is Órmos Foinikias sheltered from NE–E. On the E side there is Órmos Loutró offering better shelter from N–W–SW. In Órmos Loutró anchor in 4–10m off the village. The bottom is sand, good holding. Both bays are open to the S.

A few tavernas and limited provisions available ashore. Loutró is the ancient Phoenix described by St Luke in Acts (27:12) and was much used in those days by Alexandrian shipping.

### SFAKION

Imray-Tetra G37

In calm weather anchor off the village taking care of the above and below-water rocks in the vicinity. Just SE of the village a new yacht harbour is under construction. The outer breakwater is complete but there are no quayed areas at present. With care a yacht may be able to find a spot inside with a long line to the shore or the breakwater. It is reported there is a shoal patch in the entrance so it would be best to reconnoitre by dinghy first. The once small village has become a booming tourist resort in recent years. Good tavernas and good shopping for all provisions. Daily buses to Khania.

**ÓRMOS LOUTRÓ**
⊕35°11'·8N 24°05'E (N. Loutró light)

**SFAKION**
⊕35°11'·9N 24°08'·3E

## NÍSOS GAVDHOS (anc. Claudia)

34°48'·3N 24°07'·3E (Ák Tripití/SE end of Gavdhos)

The island lying about 20 miles S of Ák Mouros. There is a small quay inside the NW tip that the *caïque* ferry from Palaiokhora uses. Two tavernas.

The population has dwindled over the years from some 350 families in 1945 to around 70 individuals today. The island is the most southerly point of Europe if you allow islands into the geographical framework. It is about a 40-minute walk to the village on the summit.

## FRANGOKASTELLI

An open anchorage about 6 miles E of Sfakion. A Venetian castle (hence the name 'Frank's castle') stands on the cape.

## ÓRMOS PLAKIA

35°10'·3N 24°23'·8E

Lies 8 miles E of Kakomouri headland. Suitable only in settled weather. Anchor in 3–6m off the beach. There are severe gusts into the anchorage. There is a short mole here but it is rockbound and of no use to yachts.

## LIMNI

A cove at the foot of a ravine 5 miles E of Plakia. During the Second World War it was used to evacuate British, Australian and New Zealand troops from Crete to Egypt.

## ÁY GALINI (Erimoupolis)

BA 1707
Imray-Tetra G37

### Approach

From seaward the village and the mole are conspicuous. The end of the mole is lit: Fl.R.3s3M.

### Mooring

Go stern or bows-to or alongside the quay. The bottom is sand – good holding. Good shelter from the prevailing summer winds. In moderate southerlies the harbour should now be better protected with the extension to the mole although it is still likely strong southerlies would cause problems.

Port police and customs.

### Facilities

Water on the quay. Fuel on the quay. Good shopping for all provisions. Good tavernas. PO. OTE. Buses to Iraklion and Rethimon.

### General

At one time an important port for shipping produce from the hinterland, its importance declined when lorries began taking the produce to Iraklion for shipment. Recently it has become a popular tourist spot and a number of hotels have been built around the shore.

## PIRGOS

A fishing harbour lying nearly 3M ESE of Áy Galini. The entrance lit Fl.R.3s3M/Fl.G.3s3M. The entrance is prone to silting and you should keep close to the W breakwater at the entrance. Go stern or bows-to or alongside on the end of the quayed section of the W breakwater. Good shelter from northerlies. Strong southerlies would probably cause a problem in here.

Water at the root of the breakwater. Fuel ashore. Tavernas.

PIRGOS
⊕35°04'·8N 24°44'·2E

## MATALA

34°59'·7N 24°44'·8E
BA 1707

A horseshoe-shaped bay on the W side of Ák Lítinos. Suitable only in calm weather as the prevailing wind causes a swell to roll in. Good shopping for provisions and good tavernas ashore. Daily buses to Iraklion.

ÁY GALÍNIS
⊕36°05'·8N 24°41'·5E

Matala is mentioned in the Odyssey as the place where Menelaus' ships were wrecked when returning from Troy. It was known to be an important Roman port and was used at least up until Byzantine times.

## KALI LIMENES (Kalon Limenon)
BA 1707
Imray-Tetra G38

### Approach
A small bay on the E side of Ák Lítinos. A church on the S side of the bay and the oil storage tanks on Nisís Áy Pavlos are conspicuous. There is a light on Megalonísi: Fl(3)24s11M.

### Mooring
Anchor in the bay in 3–6m. Good shelter from the N and W, but open to the E and S. It is also possible to anchor under Nisís Trafos to the E where some shelter from easterlies can be found. Port police and customs.

### Facilities
Limited provisions and tavernas in the village.

### General
Nisís Áy Pavlos is a bunkering station and the 'T' piers on the island are used by large ships. Kali Limenes (Fair Haven or Good Harbour) was visited by St Paul in AD 59 when he was en route from Myra to Rome in a Roman corn ship. Bad weather had forced the ship to go south of Crete and it being late in the year, they considered wintering in Kali Limenes. Eventually a decision was made to leave and the ship was later wrecked in Malta.

## GAÏDHOURONISI (Donkey Island)
During strong southerlies a yacht can find a useful lee under the northern shores of the island. A *caïque* ferry from Ierepetra runs tourists to the island in the summer. A taverna on the island.

Kali Limenes looking NE — *Nigel Patten*

## IEREPETRA
BA 1707
Imray-Tetra G38

### Approach
*Conspicuous* The town at the foot of a plain is conspicuous from the distance. Closer in, a chimney in the town and the fort and a clock tower behind the harbour are conspicuous.

*By night* The entrance is lit Fl.R.3s4M, but a night approach is hazardous because of the reefs and shoal water in the immediate approach.

*Dangers*
1. Care must be taken of the reef lying close off the entrance. It is sometimes marked by two buoys, but these cannot be relied on to be in place. The entrance to the harbour is between the two buoys and the end of the breakwater. Care is needed as the violent winter storms in this area seem to rearrange the sea bottom.
2. With strong southerlies there is a confused swell off the entrance which makes the entry through the narrow entrance difficult.

### Mooring
Go stern or bows-to the N or W side. The bottom is mud and rocks.

*Shelter* Good shelter except in strong southerlies when seas may come over the breakwater. In past winters the harbour wall has been partially destroyed.

*Authorities* Port police and customs.

*Note* For a number of years there have been plans to extend the outer mole, but it seems likely that for the present further work will be confined to repairing storm damage to the existing harbour.

### Facilities
*Water* Near the quay.
*Fuel* In the town.
*Repairs* Some mechanical repairs. Hardware shops.

**KALI LIMENES**
⊕34°55'·7N 24°48'·3E

**IEREPETRA**
⊕35°00'·3N 25°44'·3E
Note: Entrance buoys not always in place

*Provisions* Good shopping for all provisions.
*Eating out* Good tavernas on the waterfront.
*Other* PO. OTE. Banks. Greek gas and *Camping Gaz*. Hire cars and motorbikes. Bus to Iraklion and Sitía. Ferry to Gáïdharos.

### General
Ierepetra (pronounced 'Erepetra') was an important town in Minoan and again in Roman times although few architectural remains are to be found today. Its importance now lies in its mild summer and winter climate: the nearby market gardens grow early produce for the European market and recently an increasing number of tourists have been attracted here. Several large hotels have been built around the shores of the bay to cater for the latter trade.

### MAKRI YIALOS
35°02'·2N 25°58'·5E

A small harbour off the resort. It is prone to silting and there are not adequate depths for yachts. In any case tripper boats servicing the resort take up much of the space.

### KOUFONISI (Kuphu Island)
34°56'·0N 26°08'·6E (Koufonisi light)

These islands lie off the SE tip of Crete. They are uninhabited today, but Minoan and Roman ruins on the largest island indicate they were inhabited in earlier times.

### KATO ZAKROS
35°05'·8N 26°16'·2E

A large sandy bay at the foot of a dramatic gorge. In settled weather anchor in the N of the bay. Care must be taken of a reef running out from the middle of the bay and of other rocks around the shore. Two tavernas on the shore.

At the foot of the gorge on an exquisite site are the ruins of a Minoan summer palace.

**KATO ZAKROS TO ÓRMOS ERIMOUPOLIS**

### ÓRMOS GRANDES
⊕9  1M E of Ák Pláka 35°11'·9N 26°20'·2E

The large bay on the N side of Ák Pláka. The best anchorage is at Kouremenos in the N of the bay where there is good shelter from the prevailing winds. At Kouremenos there is a short mole providing additional protection. It is usually crowded with fishing boats but a yacht may find a berth alongside the outer end where there are 2–3m depths. Water on the quay. Tavernas around the bay.

### VAI

Two miles to the N of Kouremenos is Vai, where a yacht can anchor off. The sandy beach is easily identified by the extensive groves of palm trees along the foreshore. A yacht reported being anchored off Vai for two weeks in June and experiencing only the normal summer winds blowing off the land.

A hotel and tavernas ashore. 'Vai' is probably an old word for palms and the place is named on modern Greek charts as Finikodassos (palm grove).

# Appendix

## I. USEFUL ADDRESSES

### National Tourism Organisation of Greece (NTOG)

**Australia – New Zealand**
*Greek National Tourism Organization*
   51, Pitt St, Sydney, NSW 2000 PO Box R203, Royal
   Exchange NSW 2000 Australia
   ☎ 00 61 2 92411663/4/5, 92521441 *Fax* 92352174

**Austria**
*Griechische Zentrale Für Fremdenverkehr*
   A-10105 Wien, Opernring 8
   ☎ 00 43 1 5125317 or 170 *Fax* 5139189

**Belgium**
*Office National Hellenique du Tourisme*
   172 Avenue Louise, Louizalaan, B-1050 Bruxelles
   ☎ 00 32 2 6475770, 6475944 *Fax* 6475142

**Canada**
*Toronto – Greek National Tourism Organisation*
   1300 Bay Street Main Level, Toronto, Ontario,
   Canada M5R 3K8
   ☎ 00 1 416 9682220 *Fax* 9686533
*Montreal – Greek National Tourism Organisation*
   1170 Place du Frère André, 3rd Floor, Montreal,
   Quebec, Canada H3B 3L6
   ☎ 00 1 514 8711535 *Fax* 8711498

**Denmark (information office)**
*Det Graeske Turistbureau*
   Vester Farimagsgade 6, 1606-København
   ☎ 00 45 33 325332, 325368 *Fax* 157376

**Finland (information office)**
*Kreikan Valtion Matkailutoimisto*
   Iso Roobertinkatu 10 A3, 00120 Helsinki 12
   ☎ 00 35 89 607113, 607552 *Fax* 601313

**France**
*Office National Héllenique du Tourisme*
   3 Avenue de l' Opera, Paris 75001
   ☎ 00 33 1 42 60 65 75 *Fax* 42 60 10 28

**Germany**
*Frankfurt – Griechische Zentrale Für Fremdenverkehr*
   Neue Mainzerstr. 22, 60311 Frankfurt - Main
   ☎ 00 49 69 236561/2/3 *Fax* 236576
*München – Griechische Zentrale Für Fremdenverkehr*
   Pacellistr. 5 W 80333 München
   ☎ 00 49 89 222035/6 *Fax* 297058
*Hamburg – Griechische Zentrale Für Fremdenverkehr*
   Abteistr. 33, 20149 Hamburg ☎ 00 49 40 454498
*Berlin – Griechische Zentrale Für Fremdenverkehr*
   Wittenbergplatz 3a, 10789 Berlin
   ☎ 00 49 30 2176262/3 *Fax* 00 49 30 2177965

**Israel**
*Greek National Tourism Organisation*
   5 Shalom Aleichem St, PO Box 2620, Tel Aviv
   61262
   ☎ 00 97 23 517 0501, 517 0351
   *Fax* 00 97 23/517 0487

**Italy**
*Rome – Ente Nazionale Ellenico Per Il Turismo*
   Via L. Bissolati 78-80, Roma 00187
   ☎ 00 39 06 4744249, 4744301 *Fax* 4883905
*Milan – Ente Nazionale Ellenico Per Il Turismo*
   Piazza Diaz 1, (Angolo Via Rastrelli) 20123 Milano
   ☎ 00 39 02 860470/860477 *Fax* 72022589

**Netherlands**
*Griekse Nationale Organizatie Voor Toerisme*
   Kerkstnaat 61, 1017GC Amsterdam
   ☎ 00 31 20 6254212/3/4 *Fax* 6207031

**Norway**
*Den Grekse Stats Turistbyrå* Ovre Slottsgate 15B, 0157
   Oslo 1
   ☎ 00 47 2 426501/2

**Spain**
*Oficina Nacional Hellenica de Turismo*
   C/Alberto Aguilera 17-1, Madrid 28015
   ☎ 00 34 91 5484889/90 *Fax* 5428138

**Sweden**
*Grekiska Statens Turistbyrå*
   Birger Jarlsgatan 30, Box 5298 Stockholm
   ☎ 00 46 86796480, 6796580 *Fax* 6118802

**United Kingdom and Ireland**
*Greek National Tourism Organisation*
   4 Conduit Street, London W1R ODJ
   ☎ 00 44 20 7734/5997 *Fax* 7287 1369
   www.tourist-offices.org.uk

**United States of America**
*Greek National Tourism Organisation*
   Olympic Tower, 645 Fifth Ave, New York, NY
   10022
   ☎ 00 1 212 4215777 *Fax* 8266940
*Greek National Tourism Organisation*
   168 North Michigan Avenue/Suite 600, Chicago,
   Illinois 60601 ☎ 00 1 312 782108 *Fax* 7821091
*Greek National Tourism Organisation*
   611 West Sixth Street/Suite 2198, Los Angeles,
   California 92668
   ☎ 00 1 213 6266696/9 *Fax* 4899744

### Consular offices in Greece
☎ prefix 00 30

**United Kingdom**
*Embassy* 1 Ploutarchou Street, 106 75 Athens, Greece
   ☎ 1 727 2600 *Fax* 727 2722 (Consular Section)
   www.british-embassy.gr *E-mail* britania@hol.gr
*Consulates*
*Corfu* 2 Alexandras Avenue, 491 00 Corfu
   ☎ 661 30 055 *Fax* 661 37 995
*Crete* 16 Papa-Alexandrou St, 71202 Heraklion
   ☎ 81 224 012 *Fax* 81 243 935
*Kos* 8 Annetas Laoumtzi St, 85300 Kos
   ☎ 242 215 49 *Fax* 242 259 48
*Patras* 2 Votsi Street, 262 21 Patras
   ☎ 61 277 329 *Fax* 61 225 344
*Thessaloniki* 8 Venizelou Street, Eleftheria Square, PO
   Box 10322, 541 10 Salonika
   ☎ 31 278 006 269 984

*Rhodes* 11 Amerikis St, 85100 Rhodes
☎ 241 272 47 *Fax* 241 226 15

**United States of America**
*Embassy* 91 Vasilissis Sophias Boulevard, Athens, Greece
☎ 1 721 2951 www.usisathens.gr
*E-mail* consul@ibm.net
*Consulate in Thessaloniki*
43 Tsimiski, 76th Floor, 54623, Thessaloniki, Greece
☎ 31 242 905

**Germany**
Odos Karoli Kai, Dimitriou 3, Athens
☎ 1 724 801

**Canada**
*Embassy* 4 Ioannou Gennadiou Street, Athens, Greece
115 21
☎ 1 727 3400/725 4011 *Fax* 727 3480
*Consulate in Thessaloniki* c/o Bank of Nova Scotia 17,
Tsimiski Street, 546 24 Thessaloniki, Greece
☎ 31 256 350 *Fax* 256 351

## II. USEFUL BOOKS AND CHARTS

### Admiralty publications
*Mediterranean Pilot Volume III (NP 47)*
Covers the Ionian Sea.
*Mediterranean Pilot Volume IV (NP 48)*
Covers the Aegean Sea.
*List of Lights Volume E (NP 78)*
Mediterranean, Black and Red Seas.

### Yachtsman's pilots
*Imray Mediterranean Almanac* editor Rod Heikell. Imray.
A biennial publication with light lists, radio, harbour
plans and other associated information.
*Mediterranean Cruising Handbook* Rod Heikell. Imray.
Companion volume to Mediterranean Almanac.
*The Ionian Islands to the Anatolian Coast: a sea-guide* H.
M. Denham. John Murray.
*The Aegean: a sea-guide to its coasts and islands* H. M.
Denham. John Murray. Classic yachtsman's guides,
although no longer revised and kept up-to-date.
Contain much interesting information, particularly on
naval history.
*Saronic* Rod Heikell. Imray. Covers the Saronic Gulf and
eastern Peloponnisos in detail.
*Ionian* Rod Heikell. Imray. Covers the Ionian, in detail.
*Häfen und Ankerplätze in Griechenland* Gerd Radspieler.
Covers the Ionian, Saronic Gulf and Eastern
Peloponnisos only. In German.
*Guide Pratique de Grèce et Turquie* Jacques Angles.
Editions du Pen Duick. Covers the Dodecanese. In
French.
*Turkish Waters and Cyprus Pilot* Rod Heikell. Imray

### Other guides
*Yacht Charter Handbook* Rod Heikell. Imray.
*The Blue Guide to Greece* Edited by Stuart Rossiter. A.
and C. Black. The usual excellent quality of this
series.
*The Greek Islands* Lawrence Durrell. Faber. Lots of
glossy photographs and Durrell's own inimitable
description of the islands.
*The Greek Islands* Ernle Bradford. Collins Companion
Guide. An excellent background guide from an
author who has sailed his own yacht around Greece.
*Dumont Guide to the Greek Islands* Edited by Evi Melas
and translated by Russell Stockman. Stewart Tabori
& Chang, NY; or Webb & Bower, UK. Good guide
with glossy photos.

*The Rough Guide to Greece* Ellingham, Jansz and Fisher.
Routledge and Kegan Paul. Down-to-earth guide.
*The Mediterranean Greenpeace.*
*Berlitz Guides* to Athens/Corfu/Crete/Greek Islands/
Peloponnese/Rhodes/Salonica and Northern Greece.
Good, compact and necessarily brief, guides.
*The Peloponnese* E. Karpodini-Dimitriadi. Ekdotike
Athenon.
*Prospero's Cell: a guide to the landscape and manners of the
island of Corcyra* Lawrence Durrell. Penguin. On
Corfu.
*Reflections on a Marine Venus: a companion to the landscape
of Rhodes* Lawrence Durrell. Penguin. On Rhodes.
*Bitter Lemons* Lawrence Durrell. Faber. On Cyprus.
*Crete: Its Past, Present and People* Adam Hopkins. Faber.
Excellent general introduction to Crete.
*Crete* John Freely. Weidenfeld & Nicolson. Good guide.
*Pausanias Guide to Greece Volumes I & II* Translated by
Peter Levi. Penguin. Pausanias was a doctor who
spent twenty years travelling around Greece in the
reign of Hadrian recording details of Greek cities,
customs and beliefs. Interesting and useful to this
day.
*Herodotus* The Histories (Historiai).
*Greek Society* Antony Andrewes. Pelican.
*The World of Odysseus* M. I. Finley. Penguin. Life in
Homeric times.
*The Penguin Atlas of Ancient History* Colin McEvedy.
*Fortresses and Castles of Greece Volumes I & II and
Fortresses and Castles of Greek Islands* Alexander
Paradissis. Translated by S. A. Paradissis, Efstathiadis
Brothers. The most detailed descriptive work on all
Greek forts and castles. Published and readily
available in Greece.
*The Venetian Empire* Jan Morris. Penguin. Very readable
account of the Venetian maritime empire that
touched so many Greek islands and coastal harbours,
leaving its forts and castles everywhere.
Recommended.
*The Greek Adventure* David Howarth. Collins. Excellent
and very readable account of the Greek War of
Independence.
*The End of Atlantis* J. V. Luce. Paladin. Good account of
the Thira eruptions.

### General
*The Colossus of Maroussi* Henry Miller. Penguin. A 'must'
to read even if you are not going to Greece.
*Zorba the Greek* Nikos Kazantzakis. Faber.
*Freedom and Death* Nikos Kazantzakis.
*Cavafy: a critical biography* Robert Liddell. Duckworth.
The biography of the forgotten poet of Alexandria.
*The Alexandrian Quartet* Lawrence Durrell.
*The Poems of Catullus* Translated by Peter Whigham.
University of California Press.
*Mani: travels in the Southern Peloponnese* and *Roumeli:
travels in Northern Greece* Patrick Leigh Fermor.
Penguin. Contain much interesting and esoteric
information on Greece and the Greeks in general as
well as on the areas covered.
*Eleni* Nicholas Gage. Fontana. Easy read on the Civil
War in Greece.
*Hellas – A Portrait of Greece* Nicholas Gage. Collins
Harvill. Contains some interesting information not
found in other 'portraits'.
*A Literary Companion to Travel in Greece* Edited by
Richard Stoneman. Penguin.
*Sappho to Shelley.* Greek Literature: An Anthology.
Edited by Michael Grant. Penguin.
*The Jason Voyage: the quest for the Golden Fleece* and *The*

*Ulysses Voyage: sea search for the Odyssey* Tim Severin. Arrow Books (Jason) and Hutchinson (Ulysses). The conventional and unconventional interpretations of two ancient voyages after retracing the routes in a replica galley.

*Gates of the Wind* Michael Carroll. John Murray. Interesting account of the Northern Sporades.

*Bitter Sea* Faith Warn. Guardian Angel Press.

## Flora

*Flowers of Greece and the Aegean* Anthony Huxley and William Taylor. Chatto & Windus.

*Flowers of the Mediterranean* Anthony Huxley and Oleg Polunin. Chatto & Windus.
Both the above have excellent colour photographs and line drawings for identification.

*Herbs of Greece* Alta Niebuhr.

*Trees and Bushes of Britain and Europe* Oleg Polunin. Paladin. Excellent guide with colour photographs for identification.

*Trees and Shrubs of Greece* George Sfikas.

## Marine life

*Hamlyn Guide to the Seashore and Flora and Fauna of the Mediterranean* A. C. Campbell. Comprehensive guide to Mediterranean marine life.

*The Yachtsman's Naturalist* M. Drummond and P. Rodhouse. Angus & Robertson. About Britain and northern Europe, but many species are common to the Mediterranean.

*British Whales, Dolphins and Porpoises* F. C. Fraser. As above.

*Mediterranean Wildlife. The Rough Guide.* Peter Raine. Harrap-Columbus. Patchy guide that includes a chapter on Greece.

*Fishes of Greece* Published by the Efstathidis Group and available in Greece. A poor guide.

*Dangerous Marine Animals* B. W. Halstead, P. S. Auerbach and D. R. Campbell. Wolfe Medical. The standard reference work.

## Food

*Greek Cooking* Robin Howe.

*Food of Greece* Vilma Chantiles.

*The Best of Greek Cooking* Chrissa Paradissis.

*Food in History* Reay Tannahill. Paladin. Contains some interesting details on Greek food as part of a general history.

## British Admiralty charts

| No | Chart | Scale |
|---|---|---|
| 176 | Cap Bon to Ra's A Tin | 1,175,000 |
| 180 | Aegean sea | 1,100,000 |
| 183 | Ra's At Tin to Iskenderum | 1,100,000 |
| 186 | Vlorë to Bar and Brindisi to Vieste | 300,000 |
| 187 | Punta Stilo to Brindisi | 300,000 |
| 188 | Entrance to the Adriatic Sea, including Nísos Kérkira | 300,000 |
| 189 | Nísos Sapiéntza to Nísos Paxoí | 300,000 |
| 196 | Bar to Split including Otok Palagruža | 300,000 |
| 202 | Kvarner, Kvarnerić and Velebitski kanal | 100,000 |
| 203 | Nísos Zakínthos to Nísos Paxoí | 150,000 |
| 206 | Nísos Kérkira and approaches | 150,000 |
| | Vórion Stenón Kérkiras | 25,000 |
| 224 | Marmara Denizi | 300,000 |
| | Izmit Körfezi | 300,000 |
| 236 | Nísos Ródhos to Taşlik Burnu, | 300,000 |
| | Finike | 12,500 |

| No | Chart | Scale |
|---|---|---|
| 1030 | Southwest entrance channels to the Aegean Sea | 150,000 |
| 1031 | Ákra Yérakas to Nísos Kéa | 150,000 |
| 1037 | Nisís Falconera to Nísos Íos | 150,000 |
| 1038 | Stenó Sífnou to Stenó Kafiréa | 150,000 |
| | Stenó Dhísvaton | 40,000 |
| 1040 | Nísos Íos to Vrakhonisída Kandhelioússa | 150,000 |
| 1041 | Nísos Náxos to Vrákhoi Kalóyeroi | 150,000 |
| 1055 | Rhodes Channel and Gökova Körfezi | 150,000 |
| 1057 | Kuşadasi Körfezí and approaches | 150,000 |
| | Kuşadasi | 15,000 |
| | Siğacik | 15,000 |
| 1058 | Nísos Khíos and Izmir Körfezi | 150,000 |
| 1062 | Nísoi Voríoi Sporádhes | 150,000 |
| 1085 | Stenó Kafiréa to Thessaloníki | 300,000 |
| 1086 | Strimonikös Kölpos to Edremit Körfezi | 300,000 |
| 1087 | Stenó Kafiréa to Edremit Körfezi | 300,000 |
| 1091 | Nísos Kríti | 300,000 |
| 1092 | Western approaches to the Aegean Sea | 300,000 |
| 1093 | Stenó Andikithíron to Edremit Körfezi | 3000,000 |
| 1095 | Stenó Kafiréa to Rhodes Channel | 300,000 |
| 1099 | Eastern approaches to the Aegean Sea | 300,000 |
| 1198 | Istanbul Boğazi (The Bosphorus) | 30,000 |
| | Haliç (The Golden Horn): Haydarpasa Limani | 12,500 |
| 1439 | Sicilia to Nísos Kriti | 1,100,000 |
| 1440 | Adriatic sea | 1,100,000 |
| 1513 | Kólpos Elevsínas | 25,000 |
| 1526 | Sámos Strait with harbours in the islands of Sámos, Ikaría and Foúrnoi | |
| | Marathokámbos | 5,000 |
| | Áyios Kírikos, Évidhilos, Liménas Karlóvasi and Pithagoríon | 7,500 |
| | Sámos | 10,000 |
| | Póros Fóurnon and Órmos KovSeón | 25,000 |
| | Sámos Strait | 50,000 |
| 1531 | Harbours in Northern Dhodhekánisos | |
| | Nísos Pátmos, Approaches to Skála | 30,000 |
| | Nísos Pátmos, Skála | 7,500 |
| | Nisídha Lipsoí, Lipsoí | 30,000 |
| | Nísos Kálimnos, Órmos Kalímnou | 7,500 |
| | N Yialí and N Nísiros, Órmos Yialí | 50,000 |
| | Nísos Kós, Órmos Kos | 10,000 |
| | Nísos Léros, Órmos Lakkí | 10,000 |
| 1532 | Harbours in Southern Dhodhekánisos | |
| | Nísos Tílos, Órmos Livádhia | 10,000 |
| | Nísos Ródhos, Ródhos | 7,500 |
| | Nísos Sími, Sími | 10,000 |
| | Nísos Sími, Panormítis | 5,000 |
| | Nísos Ródhos, Órmos Líndhou | 10,000 |
| | Nísos Kárpathos, Órmos Pigádhia | 10,000 |
| | Nísos Kásos, Órmos Frí and Limín Emborió | 5,000 |
| 1538 | Plans in the northern Kikládhes | |
| | Órmos Ày Nikólau | 10,000 |
| | Órmos Livádhi | 10,000 |
| | Órmos Mérikha | 10,000 |
| | Órmos Fáros | 10,000 |
| | Limín Tínou | 10,000 |
| | Órmos Kamáres | 10,000 |
| | Órmos Foínika | 15,000 |
| | Limín Sírou and approaches | 15,000 |
| | Órmos Kástro | 20,000 |
| | Órmos Gávrio | 25,000 |
| | Míkonos and approaches | 25,000 |
| 1539 | Plans in the Central Kikládhes | |
| | Órmos Mílou | 30,000 |
| | Stenái Kimólou with Órmos Voúdhia | 25,000 |

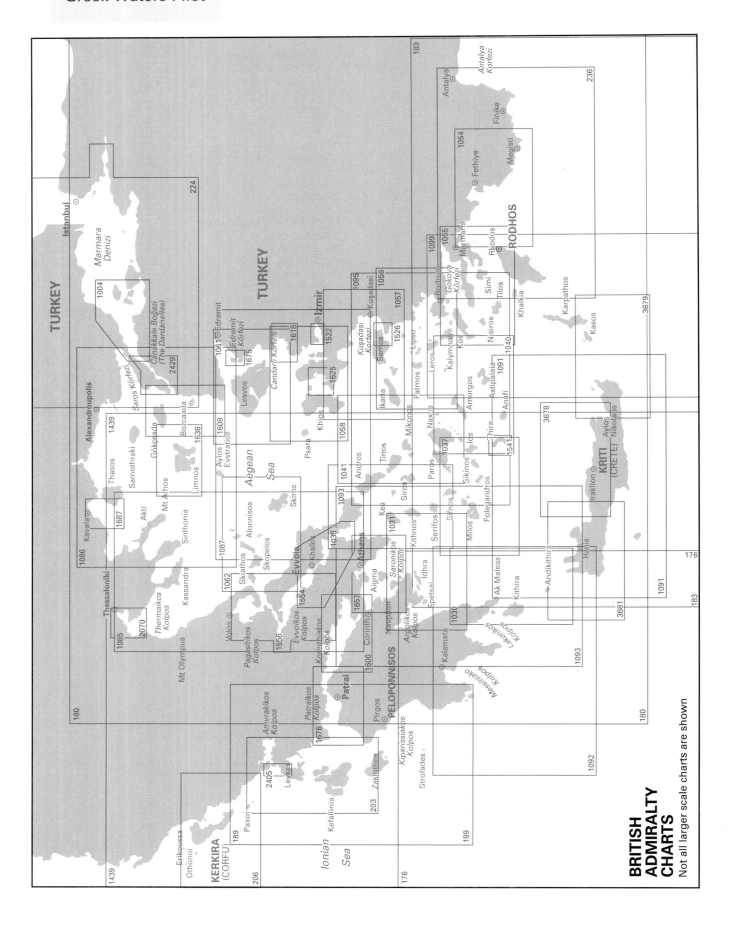

**BRITISH ADMIRALTY CHARTS**

Not all larger scale charts are shown

| No | Chart | Scale |
|---|---|---|
| | Stenó Andíparou with Órmos Paroikías | 25,000 |
| | Órmos Naoúsis | 25,000 |
| | Órmos Náxou | 15,000 |
| | Paroikía | 5,000 |
| 1541 | Plans in the Southern Kikládhes and Nísos Astipálaia | |
| | Órmos Athiniós | 5,000 |
| | Órmos Thíras | 5,000 |
| | Ormískos Skála | 7,500 |
| | Órmos Katápola | 10,000 |
| | Órmos Karavostási | 10,000 |
| | Órmos Manganári | 10,000 |
| | Órmos Análipsis | 15,000 |
| | Órmos Fou | 15,000 |
| | Órmos Vathi | 15,000 |
| | Nísos Thíra | 60,000 |
| 1554 | Nótios Evvoïkós Kólpos | 110,000 |
| | Approaches to Porthmós Evrípou | 27,500 |
| | Porthmós Evrípou | 7,500 |
| | Dhíavlos Stenó | 10,000 |
| 1556 | Vórias Evvoïkós Kólpos and approaches to Vólos | 110,000 |
| 1571 | Plans in the western Aegean sea | |
| | Liménas Linariás | 5,000 |
| | Stenó Valáxa | 7,500 |
| | Lávrion | 7,500 |
| | Skíathos | 7,500 |
| | Órmos Alivéri | 10,000 |
| | Stilís | 12,500 |
| | Kímis | 12,500 |
| | Skópelos | 15,000 |
| | Erétria | 20,000 |
| | Vólos and approaches | 20,000 |
| | Nisídhes Likhádhes | 25,000 |
| | Kólpos Kalamítsas | 30,000 |
| | Approaches to Liménas Skiáthou | 30,000 |
| 1596 | Piraiévs | 12,500 |
| 1598 | Póros Megáron Áyios Theódhoroi and Elevsís | |
| | Elevsís | 7,500 |
| | Ayois Theódhoroi (oil terminal) | 10,000 |
| | Póros Megáron | 12,500 |
| 1599 | Órmos Falírou and Liménas Pórou | |
| | Órmos Falírou | 12,500 |
| | Liménas Pórou and approaches | 15,000 |
| 1600 | Korinthiakós Kólpos | 100,000 |
| | Dhióriga Korínthou | 25,000 |
| 1625 | Khíos Strait and Ildir Körfezi | 50,000 |
| | Khíos | 10,000 |
| | Çeşme | 15,000 |
| 1636 | Plans in the northern Aegean Sea | |
| | Nísos Límnos | 150,000 |
| | Órmos Moúdhrou | 25,000 |
| | Lágos and approaches | 25,000 |
| | Alexandroúpoli | 20,000 |
| | Míruna | 12,500 |
| 1657 | Saronikós Kólpos | 100,000 |
| 1675 | Plans in the eastern Aegean Sea | |
| | Mitilíni | 7,500 |
| | Órmos Sígri | 20,000 |
| | Entrance to Kólpos Kallonís | 20,000 |
| | Entrance to Kólpos Yéras | 25,000 |
| | Approaches to Ayvalik | 50,000 |
| 1676 | Prokólpos Pátron to entrance of Korinthiakós Kólpos | 100,000 |
| 1683 | Plans on the south and east coasts of Pelopónnisos | |
| | Limín Monemvasías | 5,000 |

| No | Chart | Scale |
|---|---|---|
| | Návplion: Spétsai | 7,500 |
| | Koróni; Yíthion | 10,000 |
| | Órmos Methónis | 15,000 |
| | Kólpos Monemvasías Stenó Spetsó | 25,000 |
| 1687 | Port and anchorages in northern Greece | |
| | Kólpos Kaválas and approaches | 75,000 |
| | Keramotí | 20,000 |
| | Néa Kaváli | 20,000 |
| | Órmos Elevtherón | 20,000 |
| | Stratónion | 12,500 |
| | Kavála | 12,500 |
| | Thásos | 6,000 |
| 1706 | Órmos Soúdhas and approaches | 25,000 |
| | Limín Soúdhas | 7,500 |
| 1707 | Greece, harbours and anchorages in Nísos Kríti | |
| | Ormoi Palaiokhóras; Órmos Kaloí Liménas | 12,500 |
| | Iereptra; Áyios Nikólaos; Iráklion | 10,000 |
| | Réthimon; Órmos Mátala; Sitía | 7,500 |
| | Khaniá; Áy Galíni | 5,000 |

## IMRAY-TETRA CHARTS

**G1 Mainland Greece and the Peloponnísos Passage Chart**
*Plans* Approaches to Piraeus and Ormos Falírou
1:729,000

**G11 North Ionian Islands**
**Nísos Kérkira to Nísos Levkas**
*Plans* Ormos Gouvion (N. Kérkira), Vorion Steno Kérkiras,
Límin Kérkiras (N. Kérkira), Limin Alipa (N. Kérkira),
Ormos Lakka (N. Paxoi), Limin Paxon (N Paxoi)
*Insets* Amvrakikos Kólpos, Nísos Othonoi 1:182,400

**G12 South Ionian Islands**
**Nísos Levkas to Nísos Zákinthos**
*Plans* Kólpos Aetou (N. Ithaki), Dhioriga Levkadhos (Levkas Canal), Ormos Argostoliou (N. Kefallinia), Ormos Zákinthou
(N. Zákinthos) 1:188,200

**G121 The Inland Sea**
*Plans* Ormos Ayias Eufimas (N. Kefallina), Ormos Frikou
(N. Ithaki), Ormos Fiskardho (N. Kefallina), Ormos Vasilikas
(N. Levkas), Dhioriga Levkadhos (Levkas Canal)
1:93,400

**G13 Gulfs of Patras and Corinth**
*Plans* Mesolongiou, Ormos Loutrákiou, Kiaton, Patrai, Ormos Andíkiron, Ormos Aiyiou, Krissaios Kólpos, Dhiorix Korinthou (Corinth Canal) 1:218,800

**G14 Saronic and Argolic Gulfs**
*Plans* Marina Alimos, Ormos Falírou, Límin Porou (N. Póros), Steno Spétson (N. Spetsai), Límin Aiginis (N. Aigina) 1:189,000

**G141 Saronikos Kolpos**
**Corinth Canal to Akra Sounio and Nisos Poros**
1:109,000

**G15 Southern Peloponnísos**
**Ormos Navarinou to Nisos Kithíra and Akra Tourkovigla**
*Plans* Kalamata, Ormos Navarínou, Yíthion, Monemvasía (Yefira), Methóni, Koróni 1:189,700

**G16 Western Peloponnisos. Killini to Kalamata**
*Plans* Killini, Kiparissia, Steno Methonis, Pilos, Katakolon
1:189,000

**G2 Aegean Sea (North Part) Passage Chart**
*Plans* Canakkale Boğazi (The Dardanelles) 1:720,500

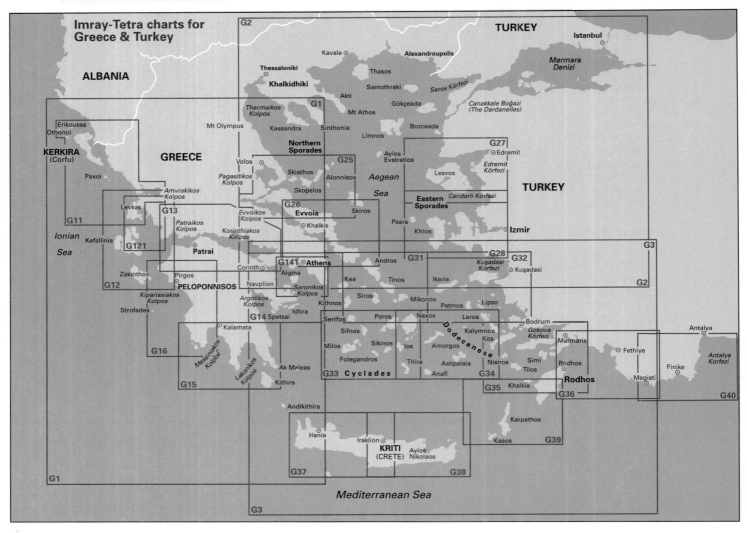

**Imray-Tetra charts for Greece & Turkey**

**G25 Northern Sporades and North Evvoia**
*Plans* Linaria (N. Skiros), Ormos Skiathou (N. Skiathos), Ormos Skopelou (N. Skopelos) 1:183,800

**G26 Nisos Evvoia**
*Plans* Approaches to Khalkis, Linaria (N. Skiros), Kimis (N. Evvoia), Eretria (N. Evvoia), Limenas Aliveriou (N. Evvoia), Rafina 1:184,600

**G27 Nísos Lésvos and the Coast of Turkey**
*Plans* Dikili (Turkey), Kólpos Yeras – N. Lésvos (Greece),
Kólpos Koloni – N. Lésvos (Greece), Sígri – N. Lésvos (Greece),
Mitilíni – N. Lésvos (Greece), Ayvalík (Turkey) 1:185,300

**G28 Nisos Khíos and the Coast of Turkey**
*Plans* Limin Khíou – N. Khíos (Greece), Ceşme Körfezi (Turkey),
Siğacik Limani (Turkey), Izmir (Turkey), Limin Psarou – N. Psará (Greece), Foça Limani (Turkey), Ormos Mandráki – N. Oinoússa (Greece) 1:187,500

**G3 Aegean Sea (South Part) Passage Chart**
*Plan* Limín Rodhou (N. Rodhos) 1:758,800

**G31 Northern Cyclades**
*Plans* Mikonos Marina (N. Mikonos), Ormos Gávriou (N. Andros), Límin A. Nikolaou (Nísos Kea), Limin Sirou (N. Siros), Ormos Naousis (N Paros) 1:189,700

**G32 Southern Sporades and Coast of Turkey**
*Plans* Kuşadasi Liman (Turkey), Límin Karlóvasi (N. Samos), Límin A. Kirikou (N. Ikaria), Steno Samou (N. Samos), Límin Pithagóriou (N. Samos), Ormos Patmou (N. Patmos) 1:189,700

**G33 Southern Cyclades (Sheet 1 – West)**
*Plans* Steno Kimolou (N. Kimolos), Ormos Livadhiou (N. Serifos), Steno Andíparou (N. Paros), Ormos Naxou (N. Naxos) 1:190,000

**G34 Southern Cyclades (Sheet 2 – East)**
*Plans* Ormos Kalímnou (N. Kalimnos), Ormos Analipsis (N. Astipálaia) 1:190,000

**G35 Dodecanese and Coast of Turkey**
*Plans* Bodrum (Turkey), Rodhos – N. Rodhos (Greece), Kós Marina – N. Kós (Greece), Marmaris (Turkey), Limin Simi – N. Simi (Greece) 1:190,000

**G36 South Coast of Turkey. Marmaris to Geyikova Adasi**
*Plans* Marmaris (Turkey), N. Rodhos (Greece), Meyisti (Greece), Approaches to Meyisti and Kaş (Greece/Turkey), Fethiye (Turkey), Göçek (Turkey) 1:193,000

**G37 Nisos Kriti (West)**
*Plans* O. Gramvousa, Hania, Rethimno, A. Galinis, Soudha, Palaiokhora, O. Sfakion 1:193,000

**G38 Nisos Kriti (East)**
*Plans* Iraklion, Sitia, A. Nikolaos, Ierapetra, Kaloi Limenes, Khersonisos 1:193,000

**G39 Nisos Karpathos to Nisos Rodhos**
*Plans* Ormos Tristoma, Ormos Fri & Limin Emborio, Ormos Pigadhia, Ormos Lindhou 1:194,000

**G40 Kaş to Antalya**
*Plans* Kekova Demiryeri (Turkey), Kemer Marina (Turkey), Finike (Turkey), Uçağiz Limani (Turkey), Antalya (Turkey), Setur Antalya Marina (Turkey), Approaches to Kaş & Megisti (Turkey/Greece) 1:193,000

## III. CONVERSION TABLES

1 inch = 2·54 centimetres (roughly 4in = 10cm)
1 centimetre = 0·394 inches
1 foot = 0·305 metres (roughly 3ft = 1m)
1 metre = 3·281 feet
1 pound = 0·454 kilograms (roughly 10lbs = 4·5kg)
1 kilogram = 2·205 pounds
1 mile = 1·609 kilometres (roughly 10  miles = 16km)
1 kilometre = 0·621 miles
1 nautical mile = 1·1515 miles
1 mile = 0·8684 nautical miles
1 acre = 0·405 hectares (roughly 10 acres = 4 hectares)
1 hectare = 2·471 acres
1 gallon = 4·546 litres (roughly 1 gallon = 4·5 litres)
1 litre = 0·220 gallons

### Temperature scale

t°F to t°C is 5/9 (t°F -32) = t°C
t°C to t°F is 9/5 (t°C +32) = t°F

So:

70°F = 21·1°C   20°C = 68°F
80°F = 26·7°C   30°C = 86°F
90°F = 32·2°C   40°C = 104°F

## IV. COMMUNICATIONS

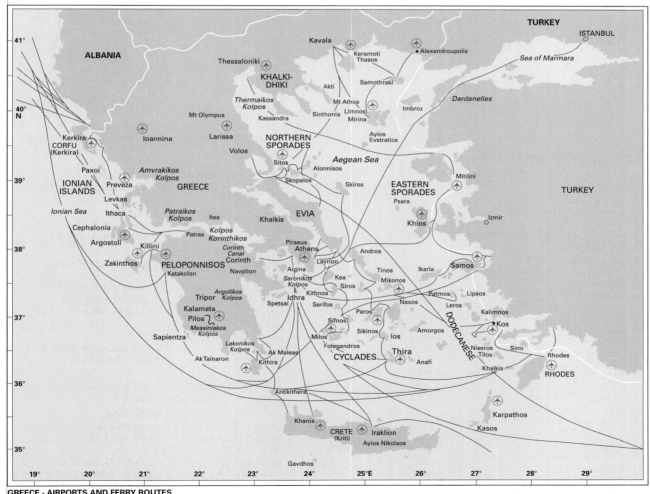

**GREECE - AIRPORTS AND FERRY ROUTES**

# Index